Crossing Cultures

To order additional copies, please contact us.
BookSurge, LLC
www.booksurge.com
1-866-308-6235
orders@booksurge.com

Crossing Cultures
Memoirs of a Travlin' Man

August 2006

Achimwene:
   Happy Reading! Here's
to the good ole days in Malawi
and to your steadfast
friendship,

   Galen

Galen Spencer Hull

2006

Crossing Cultures

Table of Contents

Dedication to Vera Mae Beighle Hull

 This book is dedicated to my mother, Vera Mae Beighle Hull, born on August 19, 1917, to Homer C. and Mabel Beighle on a farm in Kay County, Oklahoma. She graduated from Scott Community High School in 1935, four years after her husband-to-be, Norman Everette Hull. They were united in marriage on June 7, 1936, on her family's homestead east of Blackwell, Oklahoma. Vera Mae gave birth to four children: Galen, Judy, Everette and Kurt. She died of lymphoma cancer on March 20, 1965.

Vera Mae Beighle about 16, circa 1933

Introduction

A wise man is a travlin' man.

Robert Diggs, aka the RZA, popular American rapper,
interview on National Public Radio, April 11, 2005

When I reflect upon my life over the past half century, one of
the most salient observations to be made is that it has been a life
of travel. I have been enriched by extended residency in several
countries, short term professional work in others and travel as a
tourist in many others. In recent years I have persuaded myself that
it is worthwhile pulling together notes and reminiscences from these
experiences into one volume. Crossing Cultures is the result. The
very term seems to sum up much of what my life has been about.
These memoirs cover the years from 1956 to 2006, a recounting not
only of travel but life experiences conditioned and shaped by that
travel. I have been inspired by several figures who have reflected
upon their own lives and committed those reflections to writing
for posterity. Among them are Ibn Khaldun, Leonard Woolf and
Nelson Mandela.

Abd al Rahman ibn Khaldun (1332-1406 A.D.)—known to the
world simply as Ibn Khaldun—was a travlin' man, recognized as one
of the greatest historians of all time, certainly the most renowned of
all Arab scholars. While recording his astute observations of society
and the evolution of human history, he also took time to describe
his own life in his autobiography, telling us about the world in which
he belonged. It was a world full of reminders of the frailty of human
endeavor. His own checkered career illustrated how unstable the
alliances of interests were on which dynasties relied to maintain
their power. As it happened, the world in which Ibn Khaldun lived
reflected Arab culture at its zenith. The Arab language could open
the door to offices throughout the world in which he traveled, and
Islam was a unifying social force.

Leonard Woolf was a more recent world traveler and writer.
Brother of Virginia Woolf, he published his autobiography of the

years from 1880 to 1969 in five volumes. Writing about his experience as an "innocent imperialist" in Ceylon in the early part of the last century in Growing (1904-1911) Woolf observed that:

"We were all rather grand, a good deal grander than we would have been at home in London, Edinburgh or Brighton. We were grand because we were a ruling caste in a strange Asiatic country."

It was this element in the social atmosphere which Woolf said lent a touch of unreality and theatricality to their lives, as if he had observed himself out of the corner of his eye acting a part. By the time Woolf left Colombo in 1911 at the age of 31 after six and a half years in the British civil service he said he felt as though his youth ended. His life in Jaffna, Kandy and Hambantota seemed to vanish into unreality. Perhaps we modern-day development agents are not exactly a ruling caste, although we have been tagged the "Lords of Poverty". We have often tended to enjoy a certain status abroad that is not entirely warranted.

Not only will Nelson Mandela be regarded as one of the greatest figures of our era, he will remain a source of inspiration because of the prodigious efforts he invested in committing his memoirs to writing against insufferable odds. His Long Walk to Freedom is a kind of verbal museum of the events of the era of apartheid in South Africa, one of the most brutal periods in modern history. I was especially inspired by a recent trip to that country when I visited places where Mandela was kept prisoner for nearly three decades.

Like Ibn Khaldun and Leonard Woolf, I too, am a travlin' man. Whether travel has made me wiser, as Robert Diggs has suggested, is for others to judge. It would be nice to think of myself as a modern-day Ibn Khaldun or Woolf. My life has been one of crossing cultures, coming in contact with people and customs different from my own and attempting to understand them. I think it must have started as early as 1956 with my trip to Japan. Not until years later would I encounter the term "culture shock" but it surely applied to my visit to the Land of the Rising Sun. Coming as it did scarcely a decade after the end of World War II, this experience went a long way toward erasing vague notions I had grown up with of the Japanese as the "enemy". Rather, I was to come away from that brief cultural encounter with a thirst for experiencing other cultures first hand.

On the following pages I have included a chronology of my travels, as best I can recall them. From the list it appears that I have set foot in nearly 80 countries, if I am allowed to count places that no longer legally exist (e.g. East Germany and Hong Kong) or are actually territories such as Puerto Rico. Although I have only resided for extended periods of time in three foreign countries (Malawi, the Congo and Sri Lanka), my work has taken me on numerous short to mid-term assignments in some 30 odd countries. On a number of occasions I have managed to piggy-back tourist visits onto business assignments in neighboring countries.

I can only hope that the reader will gain some insight and/or inspiration from these memoirs. I must say that it has been a richly rewarding experience. So I invite you to come along with me on these travels and experiences, thereby reflecting upon your own life experiences.

References

Hourani, Albert, 1991, A History of the Arab Peoples, Cambridge, MA: Harvard University Press.

Ibn Khaldun, al-ta rif bi-ibn haldUn warihlatuhu. Garban wa-^sargan. (autobiography), published by Muhammad ibn Tawi al-Tanji, Cairo, 1951.

Mandela, Nelson (1994) Long Walk to Freedom: The Autobiography of Nelson Mandela, 1995 edition, London: Little, Brown & Company, published by Abacus.

Woolf, Leonard (1964) Growing: An Autobiography of the Years 1904 to 1911), New York: Harcourt Brace Jovanovich, Publishers.

Chronology of World Travel

Country Visited	Year/s	Tourist	Business
Canada	1953, 77, 91	x	
Japan	1956, 86	x	
Mexico	1960	x	
Iceland	1962	x	
Scotland	1962	x	
Netherlands	1962, 2002	x	
Belgium	1962, 69, 73	x	
Luxembourg	1962	x	
England	1962, 78, 85	x	
France	1962, 70, 74, 85, 03, 04, 05	x	
West Germany	1962	x	
East Germany	1962	x	
Switzerland	1962, 1996, 2003, 2004	x	
Italy	1962	x	
Greece	1962	x	
Malawi	1964-66, 74, 91, 95, 01, 03	x	x
Kenya	1965, 83, 95, 01, 03	x	x
Uganda	1965, 68, 69, 94	x	x
Tanzania	1965, 68, 83	x	x
Zambia	1966, 73	x	
Zimbabwe	1966, 95	x	
Mozambique	1966	x	
Swaziland	1966, 80	x	x
South Africa	1966, 93, 95, 2003, 2005	x	x
Congo Kinshasa (Zaire)	1966, 69-70, 72, 74, 76, 79	x	x
Liberia	1966, 1987	x	
Ghana	1966, 68, 87	x	x
Venezuela	1966	x	
Puerto Rico	1966, 2002	x	x
Bahamas	1967	x	
Ethiopia	1968	x	
Sierra Leone	1968		x
Cape Verde Islands	1968, 03	x	
Nigeria	1972, 87	x	x
Turkey	1972, 74	x	
Burundi	1973	x	
Bulgaria	1974, 96	x	x
Lesotho	1980, 92	x	x
Rwanda	1980		x

Country	Years		
Bourkina Faso	1981		x
Tunisia	1981, 2003, 04, 05	x	x
Cameroun	1974, 83, 86	x	x
Cote d'Ivoire	1982, 86, 94		x
Haiti	1983, 94, 97		x
Niger	1983		x
Indonesia	1984	x	x
Singapore	1984, 2002	x	
Sweden	1985	x	
Morocco	1985	x	
Spain	1985	x	
Philippines	1986		x
Taiwan	1986	x	
Hong Kong	1986	x	
China	1986, 2006	x	x
Brazil	1986	x	
Argentina	1986	x	
Jamaica	1987	x	
Colombia	1987	x	
Congo Brazzaville	1987		x
Guinea Conakry	1987, 88, 89, 90		x
Sudan	1988		x
South Korea	1988		x
Egypt	1988, 93, 94		x
Bangladesh	1991	x	
India	1991, 2003	x	
Pakistan	1991		x
Togo	1991		x
Benin	1991		x
Senegal	1991, 92, 94		x
Sri Lanka	1992, 2003, 2004	x	x
Thailand	1992, 2003	x	x
Vietnam	1992	x	
Maldive Islands	1992	x	
Guyana	1994		x
Malaysia	1993, 1997, 2003, 2004	x	x
Slovakia	1996, 97		x
Hungary	1996, 97		x
Czech Republic	1996, 97, 99		x
Poland	1996, 97		x
Romania	1996, 97		x
Albania	1997		x
Ukraine	2001, 2003		x
Botswana	2005		x

Chapter 1

Roots: Family and Cultural Origins

"Bud, you need to work on your stick-to-it-ive-ness."
- Vera Mae Hull to her young son Galen

There we were, the three sons of Norman and Vera Mae Hull, seated in an outdoor restaurant beside Oregon's scenic Rogue River. We had been joined by our respective male offspring on a once-in-a-lifetime rafting trip in the summer of 2004. Feasting on seafood and corn-on-the-cob, washed down with draft beer, we were having a grand time. It was your basic male-bonding experience, right out of the textbook. Then the youngest brother, Kurt, brought forth a casual request to the eldest: why don't you write up something about Mother? This was an understandable request since he was still a very young boy of seven when Vera Mae passed away in 1965. My first thought was of all the projects that I had going at work and the paucity of information available on the subject, other than scattered remnants of memories. But the challenge finally took hold, and this book is the result. How appropriate it is that the launching of this effort should be in Oregon, since I had made my first trip there in the womb in 1940!

Dinner at the Galice, Rogue River Oregon, 2004

Roots 1: What's a Beighle? And where did the Beighles come from?

Laura and Byron Beighle (latter-day Beighles pronounce the name BEATH/ly) spent a good portion of their senior years digging into family history, combing through genealogical records and visiting gravesites. The results of their efforts were bequeathed to their offspring. Thanks to my cousins Don Beighle and his daughter Monica and to Karolyn Beighle, these records found their way to me. It is hard to determine the source of many of these files, so the reader will have to account for a fair amount of literary license in the following narrative, which weaves together some historical facts with suppositions.

If we peer into the deep recesses of the history of the Beighle family it is possible to discern Scandinavian roots. How so? By the 13th century Viking invasions from the Scandinavian countries had become a major factor in the rise of cities in northern Europe. As the fearsome Vikings plundered more than they could carry, they established base camps for trading with the surrounding villages. For example, Dublin, Ireland, had its roots as a Viking camp. Walled cities grew up in response to these invasions, which became known as "bourgs" or "burghs" and later bouroughs, their inhabitants known as bourgeois.

So it was that Norwegians carrying the name of "Buehl" meaning farm dwellers, found their way into the Rhine Valley of Northern France in the early part of the 15th century. John Buehl, a descendent of those early Norwegians, was selected as the "gatherer of taxes" by his neighbors. According to parish records, one of his sons, Johan Buehl, was chosen as "game keeper." Here the plot thickens. When French king Louis XIV, a Catholic, seized the city of Strasbourg all the Protestant churches were closed. Protestants (known as Huguenots) who refused to submit to the Catholic authorities were subject to persecution. As it was the custom of Louis XIV to force the Catholic faith upon his subjects, he sent his representative to the home of Johan Buehl, who handed the officer a small Bible, saying to him, "I am guided by this book and I will flourish as yon evergreen tree." This story was recounted to Louis XIV, who so admired Buehl's courage that he knighted him and bestowed upon him a coat of arms, giving him the name of Buchli—meaning little book, referring to the Bible Johan had handed the soldier. (Why would a French King give a subject a German name? All we can say is that this makes an interesting story!) However, with the revocation of the Edict of Nantes in 1685, Johan Buchli and other French Huguenots fled across the border into Germany near Stuttgart.

Johan Buchli had five sons, among whom was Johannis Conrad Buchli, (1699 –?). He was married to Catherine Beighle (1698 – 1763)—possibly a cousin because of the similarity of names. They had five sons, among them Conrad Buchli (1737-1824)—listed in the U.S. genealogical records now as Beighley. Our story focuses on this Conrad Beighley because he was the first of the family to depart from Germany for America. He sailed from Stuttgart, landing in Philadelphia on October 22, 1754, at a time when the sun was about to set on British sovereignty over its colonies in the New World. Eventually the family name morphed into a variety of forms. Efforts to Anglicize the name resulted in several variations of the name Buchli, ranging from Buchle, Buechle, Beighley, Beithle and Beighlie to Beighle. In truth, few of these transmutations make much sense, given the meaning and pronunciation of the original name.

Conrad Beighley first settled in Frederick County, Maryland, where he was a member of the German Lutheran Reformed Church near Hagerstown, Maryland. Conrad was bound to the Wiles family as a blacksmith and married one of the daughters, Margaretta Wiles, in 1764 in Frederick, Maryland. Conrad and Margaretta had six sons: John, Henry, George, Jacob, Peter, and Johan William. According to the Pennsylvania archives, during the Revolutionary War Conrad Beighley served as a private 4th class soldier from Northampton County, Pennsylvania. For his military service, Conrad was allocated 150 acres in Westmoreland County, in western Pennsylvania where he lived until his death in 1824. All of the sons except William remained in nearby Butler County, north of Pittsburgh.

Butler County historical records state that the pioneers in the county were primarily of three groups—Scotch-Irish, German-American and German. The Scotch-Irish and German-Americans came into the area at about the same time but then moved on or died out. Germans (by now our Beighleys were defined as German, despite their French origin!) began settling the area in large numbers around 1835. The German-American families came from Maryland, Virginia and Eastern Pennsylvania. The records indicate that the Beighles were prominent in the development of Butler County.

Johan William Beighley (1780–1868) married Annie Magdalena Myers in 1854 in Butler County, Pennsylvania. William came from Westmoreland County to Muddy Creek Township in 1811 and settled on a farm in 1825. Eventually he moved from the farm to the village of Middle Lancaster where he served as Postmaster. William and Magdalena moved to Adams County, Ohio (just north of the Kentucky border). There the family belonged to St. John's German Lutheran Church, consonant with its German origins.

Among the ten children born to the union of William and Magdalena Beighley was Conrad Beighle (1820—1884), in the town of West Union, Adams County, Ohio. Conrad Beighle married Elizabeth Beighle (1824 –1903). (Possibly another coincidence of family names?) This union produced eight offspring, including Francis (Frank) G. Beighle (1853—1930). Frank would meet and marry Laura Mae Whinery, (1857-1941) born in Wilmington, Ohio.

The union of Frank and Laura Mae in 1880 would produce two sons. Homer Clinton Beighle (1881–1965) was born in Wilmington, Ohio. His brother Therl died when only six months old. Homer was still a young lad when Frank and Laura Mae headed west in 1883 to settle in Pleasanton, Kansas. Presumably they found slim pickins there since they moved on to Oklahoma in 1899, settling on a farm in the Prairie Chapel community in Kay County, while Homer was not yet out of his teens. This was only five years after the opening of the Cherokee Strip in 1893. In 1909 the Beighles moved to Ponca City where they resided until Frank's death in February 1930. Frank Beighle was a member of the United Brethren Church and a member of the Modern Woodmen Lodge of America.

Roots 2: The Emigrants: Norman Hull's Origins

Norman Everette Hull, born January 30, 1913, was the third child of Spencer Henry Hull (1880-1953) and Ada Luella Norman (1882-1987). Spencer Hull was born in Bloomfield, Iowa, the fifth of eight children of Arthur Duane and Louise Hull. Thanks to Dale W. Hull, a cousin of Norman's, we have a fairly detailed profile of Spencer's lineage. Both of Spencer's parents were born in upstate New York. His father, Arthur Duane Hull, was the son of Jesse Hull (1819-1907) and Sophia Randall. Jesse Hull was born on June 21, 1819, in Antwerp in upstate New York. The 1850 census listed Jesse as a farmer. He married Sophia Randall on November 29, 1840 and to this union were born five children, including Arthur Duane Hull (1850-1933). Jesse earned his living as a plasterer as well as a farmer before moving his family to Bloomfield, Iowa in 1873. Arthur Duane Hull married Louise Jane Pierson (1856-1939) in 1872 in New York. The following year they moved to Iowa where they lived for 11 years before moving once again in 1884. This time they settled in Scott County in Western Kansas, among the first families to do so. Arthur and Louise observed their 60th wedding anniversary together. They were life-long Baptists.

Despite the decidedly English surname of Hull, those roots on Norman's side of the family that have garnered the most interest and attention have been the Swedish ones. Ada Norman was only one generation removed from the old country since her own father, born Eric Hansson (1851-1937), was a Swedish immigrant who would later change his name upon arrival in the U.S. Although her mother, Mary Yelm, was born in the U.S., Ada's bloodline was distinctly Swedish, making her Swedish through and through. Eric Hansson was one of four sons and two daughters of Hans Johnson and Annie Olsen, daughter of Olof Olson. In Sweden Eric spent his youth on the farm during the summer he cultivated crops of oats, barley, rye, wheat and potatoes. In the winter months he worked with a timber contractor, measuring and cutting logs. His formal education was limited to a few months in secondary school. Eric's older brother had already visited America and had returned to Sweden telling of all the opportunities there.

We know that after his father died Eric Hansson packed his bags at the age of 21 and left Sweden with his mother and siblings, sailing on the S.S. Wyoming from Gothenberg to Hull (yes, Hull), England, and thence to America in 1872. There, like thousands of others passing through immigration in New York, Eric changed his name. He chose to call himself George Norman, a name he fancied to be more Anglo-sounding. Arriving in New York, George Norman pushed westward with his mother and siblings for Illinois. He first worked as a farmhand for local farmers, learning basic English on the job. George eventually saved enough money to buy his own farm implements and a team of horses, and the family took up residence on a farm 16 miles east of Galesburg, Illinois.

On June 8, 1881, George Norman was married to Mary Yelm, who was born in Elmore, Illinois. When Mary Yelm's grandfather, Anders Jonsson (born in Gundbo, Sweden in 1804), entered the Swedish military service he took the name of Anders Hjelm (Yelm), meaning helmet. Records indicate that Anders Yelm was on a ship that departed from Gavle, Sweden, on October 14, 1846, for America. He married Anna Nilsdotter and they were the parents of Anderson Yelm—Andrew C. Yelm (1833-1895). Andrew was born in Alfta Socken and married Priscilla Aby (1833-1919). Priscilla was born in Mifflin township, Richland Ohio. Andrew and Priscilla Yelm were the parents of 14 children, of whom Mary Evangeline Yelm (1859-1965) was the fifth born. Mary was first married in 1878, and again in 1881 to George Norman in Galesburg, Illinois.

We have fairly detailed information about the next period in family history, owing to an interview George Norman had with a granddaughter, Eunice Shull, in 1932. George and Mary would have their first three children—Ada, Charles and Allie—while living in Illinois. However, having grown dissatisfied with renting land, and fueled by the American dream of owning his own land, George left

Illinois in 1885 for western Kansas, thought to be the promised land. He left his family behind and traveled with another dissatisfied renter, each with a team of horses, a covered wagon and supplies (we're talkin' pioneers here!). Ada was only three years old at the time.

Both George and his companion had musical skills, violin and French harp respectively, and as they traveled the two entertained folks along the way. Arriving in western Kansas, near Dighton, they decided they had gone far enough, obtained a land agent and applied for a quarter of land. With the claim approved, they began to build on their property. First was a stable for the horses, then sod houses (12 ft. x 16 ft.), "shanties" they called them. There were hardly any other such shanties for miles around. Within a few weeks the houses were complete and the two pioneers began to communicate with their families in Illinois, telling them to come on down.

It was the dead of winter and a terrible blizzard had struck the region. Eventually the wives and children showed up at the Garden City train station (the closest western Kansas "metropolis" north of Dodge City). George and his companion stocked up on coal, flour and other supplies in order to make their families welcome. But the snow was piled high in all directions, and getting to the newly built shanties was a challenge. Despite the daunting elements, George managed to take the Norman family to his shanty, where they lived for another ten years. And here, another five children were born to George and Mary Norman. Meanwhile, George built a second sod house of four rooms near the original shanty to accommodate the rising tide. The Norman family lived here until 1903 when they moved into an eight-room frame house.

George Norman and family were thus settled in the flat, open plains of western Kansas, very unlike his native Sweden in many respects. Ada Norman and her brothers and sisters grew up on the farm. George continued farming in the area, watching the surrounding area become settled by newcomers. He pinned his faith on raising corn initially, but after a disastrous corn crop he began to sow wheat and his fortunes improved. Kansas became the breadbasket of the U.S. and farmers like George Norman prospered accordingly. He began converting his prosperity into land investments, adding to his homestead and school claim. In 1915 he sold his farm holdings and moved into a comfortable home in Scott City. On June 8, 1931, George and Mary Norman celebrated their 50th wedding anniversary, with all eight of their children and 23 grandchildren in attendance. Although George died six years later, Mary Norman would live on to the ripe old age of 106. The George Norman family and the Arthur Duane Hull family were pioneers in western Kansas, arriving in the area within a year of each other. And as will have been noted from this genealogical review, longevity was a common feature of the lives of both families!

Spencer and Ada Hull

Spencer Hull married Ada Norman on September 14, 1904 (the same year Homer Beighle married Mabel). Ada was born in Eugene, Illinois, the oldest of eight children of George and Mary Norman and eventually moved with them to western Kansas. Prior to her marriage, she taught school for five years in Scott County. Spencer and Ada homesteaded a quarter of land five miles southeast of Grigston, Kansas beginning in 1905. They farmed this and adjoining land until the fall of 1926 when Spencer was elected County Clerk, in which capacity he served for two four-year terms. He later served one term as County Commissioner. Although Spencer enjoyed farming, all done with horses, he found it difficult, due to suffering from hay fever. So when the Hull family moved from the homestead into Scott City, Norman finished the 8th grade there. My earliest recollections of visiting my grandparents on their farm are of milking the cows, gathering the eggs and riding the tractor. In typical grandmotherly fashion, Ada used her few Swedish expressions to try to butter up her grandchildren. She would say something like "gimme en puss" with an impish grin in her fractured Swedish, telling us it meant give me a kiss. I recall the gathering of the family clan to join her mother, Grandma Norman, in celebrating her 100th birthday. Longevity seemed to be a Norman family trait.

Homer and Mabel Beighle

Homer C. Beighle met and married Mabel Wright (1884–1973) of Prairie Chapel on December 4, 1904. Mabel was born to the union of Oliver Theodore Wright (??-1934) and Laura Linda Snow (1859-1947) in Arkansas City in southern Kansas, just across the Oklahoma border. Laura Snow, daughter of Mr. and Mrs. Joseph Snow, was born near Jackson, Michigan. She was married to Oliver Wright in 1880 and the Wrights established a home in Hackney, Kansas, later moving to Arkansas City. In 1893 the Wrights made the "Run" at the opening of the Cherokee Strip and homesteaded a claim six miles east of Blackwell, where they resided until Mr. Wright's death in 1934. Oliver and Laura celebrated their 50th wedding anniversary in May 1930. In 1943 Laura went to live with her daughter Mabel and husband Homer in Ponca City, where she died at the age of 88. The Wrights were life-long Baptists.

Mabel came to Kay County in Northern Oklahoma only a few miles from the place of her birth with her parents at the age of 10 in the spring of 1894. She attended Pleasant Valley School, although we have no record of how many years of study Mabel completed. Mabel and Homer were married at the home of her parents near Prairie Chapel, when Mabel had attained the ripe age of 20 and Homer was 23. They would celebrate their 50th wedding anniversary in 1954, and both would live into their golden years, he to the age of 83 and she to the age of 89.

Among his numerous skills, Homer was a blacksmith. We grandkids recall the story of how during the years of the Great Depression Homer went to Colorado where he sharpened drill bits that were used for drilling holes into the granite rock in the Royal Gorge. Steel cables were then attached to support the suspension bridge across the river. Like many other public projects of the period, his was a Works Progress Administration initiative.

As Aunt Laura's story (2001) tells it, Homer was "driven out of Oklahoma" by the combination of allergies which he referred to as hay fever, as did Spencer Hull. At the peak of the Depression, in 1930 at the age of 49, Homer held a Public Auction Sale in Kay County, Oklahoma. The poster announcing the event speaks volumes about his life and times:

Having Decided to Quit Farming On Account of Poor Health, I Will Sell at the M.V. Powers Farm Three miles East and One mile South of Blackwell on Thursday, June 5, 1930, Commencing at 10 AM.

The list of items to be sold and the proposed prices included 19 head of cattle, nine head of horses, 100 barred rock chickens, and a variety of farm implements, household goods and feed. This must surely have been a devastating experience for young Vera Mae at the tender age of 13. But then, it was hard times for the entire nation, and particularly the Great Plains region ravaged by dust storms.

Homer decided to try his luck in business in Scott City, Kansas, where he opened up a hatchery. The move to Scott City would be life-changing for Vera Mae, for it was there that she would become a young woman and meet the man she would marry. The Beighles arrived in time for her to graduate from Scott City Junior High School, in a class of 32 students, in which there were three Veras!

(A lock of Vera Mae's hair tucked away in the school program reveals that she was a distinct blond at the time!)

Homer was a hoot, a colorful figure by any measure, as seen through the eyes of a grandson. He had bright blue eyes (usually reflecting a twinkle), a ruddy complexion, a sanguine disposition and a lean (scrawny?) figure. But we have seen that he probably had some portion of Scandinavian blood, mixed with French, coursing through his veins. If he had been Irish, it would have been said of him that he was full of blarney since he loved telling stories. We have seen that the family was generally identified as German in America, having most recently immigrated from Germany. But on the plains of Kansas and Oklahoma, Homer carried no particular ethnic identity. Religious affiliation was a more important identifier than ethnicity in those parts. And the Beighles were Baptists, of sorts. We will have occasion to return to this theme.

Homer was a jack of all trades, dabbling in a wide variety of avocations and enterprises. He was a farmer, yes, like most of those who pioneered Kansas and Oklahoma in the early days. But he had an entrepreneurial itch that led him to undertake several money-making endeavors. Homer bought and maintained rental properties, which would eventually keep his son and grandsons busy evenings and weekends: painting, laying shingles, re-tiling and renovations of all sorts. These projects would be among my first income-generating activities, good for pocket change at least.

And Mabel, well she was different in every respect from her husband: quiet, unassuming, of placid demeanor, devoutly but unobtrusively religious, her warm brown eyes were always trained on the subject of her attention. She was always ready with a smile. Mabel was the Baptist in the family, a member of Sunset Baptist Church until her demise at the age of 89 in 1974. It was not unusual for the Beighles to house an itinerant Baptist evangelist, in town for a tent revival, at her urging. She spoke in the dialect of the region: e.g., "I've an "ay`- dee" (idea)".

Homesteaders: The Cherokee Strip

Let us look at the Oklahoma landscape at the turn of the century when Homer and Mabel came together. The opening of the Cherokee Strip in northern Oklahoma in 1893 was among the most remarkable events in United States history. The Strip, covering nearly 10,000 square miles in an area larger than the state of Vermont and stretching along the Kansas border to the north, was part of the Cherokee Nation in Indian Territory. It measured some 50 miles in width and 200 miles in length. The Cherokees had used the land as buffalo hunting grounds. A commission was appointed by President Benjamin Harrison to conduct negotiations with the Cherokees and other tribes to open up the area to settlement. In May 1983, the Cherokees consented to cede their claims to the Strip for the sum of $8,300,000, to be paid in five separate annual installments beginning March 4, 1895, with interest on deferred payments. In addition, the Cherokees received an immediate payment of $300,000. Thus the way was paved for the great "run" of 1893.

Although soldiers were sent throughout the Strip to drive out people who had drifted into the area ahead of time, there were inevitably those who managed to stake a claim before the gun was fired. These folks came to be known as "Sooners." And you thought that was just the name of the Oklahoma University football team! No, we are so proud of this sobriquet that we call ourselves the Sooner State. Sooner pride is summed up in the Sooner fight song that goes something like, "I'm Sooner born, and Sooner bred and when I die I'll be Sooner dead." Oklahoma would not become a state in the union until 1907—among the last states to be admitted—three years after Homer and Mabel were married.

Vera Mae as a Youth

Homer and Mabel were to have three children: Byron, born in 1910, Marvin in 1913 and Vera Mae in 1917, all reared in their early years on the farm. Vera Mae was born toward the end of World War I and came to full bloom as a young woman in western Kansas. Her brother Marvin took his own life while still a youth and Vera Mae rarely ever mentioned him to her family. The bond with older brother Byron, on the other hand, was strong and enduring throughout her life. Vera Mae's earliest years were spent on the Beighle family farm near Prairie Chapel, east of Blackwell, in northern Oklahoma. With little documentation from her early years, we must assume that Vera Mae's youth was devoted to a combination of chores on the farm and studies at school until 1930, when at the age of 13, the family moved to Scott City.

Vera Mae participated in an historic event as a young girl of 13 in Ponca City in 1930, shortly before the family moved to Kansas. It was the unveiling of the Pioneer Woman statue to commemorate the pioneering spirit of the settlers who only a few decades before had begun to homestead the northern Oklahoma area. E.W. Marland, founder of Marland Oil and later Governor of Oklahoma, commissioned the design of the Pioneer Woman sculpture in order to memorialize the strength and courage of the thousands of women who settled the American frontier. He called these women "America's Vanishing People". Marland could afford to be philanthropic, having made a lot of money in the oil business. In October of 1926, Marland arranged for artists to submit small models of a proposed work. He then began to have them exhibited around the country; more than 750,000 U.S. citizens cast their votes for the design of their choice.

The favorite piece was by Bryant Baker whose Pioneer Woman Statue was erected in 1930 at an overall cost to Marland of $300,000. At the unveiling ceremonies on April 22, 1930, President Herbert Hoover gave a radio address with forty thousand people in Ponca City for the unveiling. The most famous Oklahoman of all, humorist Will Rogers, addressed the crowd. The bronze statue stands 17 feet tall and depicts a woman in prairie garb—a simple long sleeved dress that reaches her ankles, a bonnet and well worn boots. In one hand she clutches a Bible, and over her arm carries a cloth bag. She is holding the hand of a young boy dressed in simple garments. His other arm is bent, his hand in a fist. They both wear determined expressions and are captured in mid-stride. By the time of the unveiling of the Pioneer Woman the folks of European stock had claimed the former Cherokee Strip area for their own. Blacks and Indians were eventually relegated to the fringes of northern Oklahoma society. Probably these distinctions escaped Vera Mae to a large extent since she spent her early youth on a farm outside of even the smallest urban areas.

Norman and Vera Mae: The Early Years (1930—1940)

To understand the lives of Norman and Vera Mae during their years of courtship and early marriage, we must look at the world in which they lived. On October 29, 1929, the crash of the U.S. stock market—known in history books as "Black Tuesday"—triggered a worldwide financial crisis. From 1929 to 1933, unemployment in the U.S. soared from 3% of the workforce to 25%, while manufacturing output collapsed by one-third. The Crash of '29 ushered in the bleakest period in American history since the Civil War. One can only begin to comprehend the lives of Americans during this period by looking at this catastrophic event, coupled with the effects of the Great Depression that followed in its wake. All Americans, whether rich or poor, were profoundly affected by these twin disasters. The Roaring Twenties, characterized by ostentatious lifestyles of the rich and super-rich, came to a screeching halt with the Crash of 1929 (http://www.livinghistoryfarm.org).

The most visible evidence of how dry the 1930s became were the dust storms. In 1932, 14 dust storms were recorded on the Plains. In 1933, there were 38 storms. By 1934, it was estimated that 100 million acres of farmland had lost all or most of the topsoil to the winds. By April 1935, there had been weeks of dust storms, but the cloud that appeared on the horizon that Sunday was the worst. Tons of topsoil were blown off barren fields and carried in storm clouds for hundreds of miles.

Technically, the driest region of the Plains—southeastern Colorado, southwest Kansas (including Scott City south to Dodge City) and the panhandles of Oklahoma and Texas—became known as the Dust Bowl, and many dust storms started there. But the entire region, and eventually the entire country, was affected. The Dust

Bowl got its name after Black Sunday, April 14, 1935. More and more dust storms had been blowing up in the years leading up to that day. Winds were clocked at 60 mph. Then it hit.

"The impact is like a shovelful of fine sand flung against the face," Avis D. Carlson wrote in a New Republic article. "People caught in their own yards grope for the doorstep. Cars come to a standstill, for no light in the world can penetrate that swirling murk... We live with the dust, eat it, sleep with it, watch it strip us of possessions and the hope of possessions. It is becoming Real." The day after Black Sunday, an Associated Press reporter used the term "Dust Bowl" for the first time. "Three little words achingly familiar on the western farmer's tongue, rule life in the dust bowl of the continent—if it rains." The term stuck and was used by radio reporters and writers, in private letters and public speeches. In the central and northern plains, dust was everywhere.

As we have seen, a scant seven months after the Crash of '29, Homer Beighle was obliged to quit farming in Oklahoma on account of poor health. He moved his family to Scott City, Kansas, and tried his hand at the hatchery business. Vera Mae had scarcely reached puberty at the time. Her bride book records that she first met Norman in 1931 at the tender age of 14. She had accompanied a friend to a party at the Baptist Church in Scott City. She then went with the friend to the dedication of Scott City's new High School building where she was to sing. It was there that Vera Mae met Norman, together with a group of friends. She records that on their first date they went with friends (always with friends) to a show in the nearby town of Leoti in a Model A Ford, which the driver managed to run into a fence! Afterwards their dating routine consisted of getting together with friends on Sunday and Wednesday evenings—church nights. By 1933 it is fair to say that they were going steady, in today's parlance.

Wilma Carson, Norman's cousin on his mother's side, fondly remembers those years in Scott City. Wilma and her husband Karl, now well into their nineties and living in Ft. Collins, Colorado, were high school friends of Vera Mae, although two years older than she was. Wilma recalls that Vera Mae, a soprano, sang the lead opposite Karl in their high school operetta, Pickles, In Old Vienna. Vera Mae played the piano as well. Wilma notes that even though Vera Mae was very popular around Scott City, it was Norman—four years older—who "won out" over other suitors. Karl and Wilma even double dated with Norman and Vera Mae.

Both Vera Mae and Norman were popular students in Scott Community High School where they were prominent in sports, academic and social affairs according to newspaper accounts. While in junior high and high school Norman participated in football and track at Scott Community High School. He played halfback on the first undefeated football team in the history of the Scott Community High School Beavers in 1930. The Beaver brochure had this to say about Norman, a two-year senior letterman:

> Nor was a hard fighter and great on the offense. He was a savage kicker and a stone wall on defense. Nor was a sure blocker and very efficient in running interference when it called for good hard driving. His former positions have always been in the line, but due to his speed and power he was able to break into the backfield and hold down a position in good shape.

His offspring would have a hard time reconciling this description of Norman with the father they knew as a gentle and unassuming soul, ill-equipped at dispensing punishment!

After his high school graduation in 1931 at the height of the Depression, Norman worked at a variety of jobs, including wheat harvests, Western Hardware and the county agent's office of the AAA program. Norman Hull was soon transitioning from high school graduate to an uncertain future in western Kansas. He would become a beneficiary of the programs of President Franklin Delano Roosevelt. In piecing together this period we find certificates from Norman's files that tell the tale of his employment. These were hard times, as the country struggled to dig out from under the Great Depression. Just out of high school, Norman completed a month-long basic course of instruction in infantry at the Citizens' Military Training Campus at Camp McHenry, Fort Des Moines, Iowa in 1931 and was recommended for further training. The following year he completed a second month of training at the same camp, receiving a Certificate of Corporal. This appears to have been the extent of Norman's military career.

For the next four years, from 1931 to 1935 Norman held a variety of jobs in Scott County, ranging from part time in the Office of the

Scott County Clerk, to Registrar of Deeds, to Western Hardware and Supply Company where he worked as sales clerk. Most of the work Norman found was with government agencies, both local and federal. Jobs were hard to come by, and Norman's employment applications often indicated that he left a previous job because of "insufficient work." One of his first jobs out of high school was as an office clerk for Scott County where his responsibilities consisted of general typing and selling hunting and fishing licenses. As clerk-typist in the Registrar of Deeds Norman recorded oil leases, mortgages and deeds to records. His annual salary during these years began at $360 and increased gradually to $720. It is clear from the neatly typed application forms that Norman had by this time developed exceptionally good typing skills as well as proficiency in the use of the adding machine and calculator. In 1935, Norman landed the first of several jobs in the newly created Works Progress Administration.

On June 7, 1936, Norman Hull and Vera Mae Beighle were married by a minister of the Christian Church of Blackwell in the home of Vera Mae's parents, who were now back in Oklahoma. It was a short, simple ceremony, with no more than 20 persons in attendance. Vera Mae's Bride's Book records the trip they made shortly afterward up to Hays, Kansas, where the newlyweds arrived exhausted and began making their first home. In the section under Honeymoon, there is the wistful plan to have it "whenever Norman gets his vacation." The couple lived in Hays until June of 1937, when Norman was transferred to Topeka. The "honeymoon" would not come until the second anniversary when the couple would spend a week in Missouri, including a stop at Branson.

In June 1940, they embarked on an extended trip that would eclipse the honeymoon. This time they left Wichita heading west to the California and Oregon coasts, with stops in Scott City, Denver and Yellowstone National Park along the way. It could be asserted that Yours Truly made the trip as well in vitro, since Vera Mae was by this time pregnant. This would be the first of many trips I would make to the West Coast and beyond.

The New Deal and the Works Progress Administration (WPA)

After their marriage, Norman would continue with the WPA in Wichita and Iola until he received his notice of termination in 1942, by which time he had worked for WPA for nearly the entire lifetime of the agency. Reading through Norman's employment files initiated reflection on what it must have been like during those days. As a youth I recall references to the hardships of the Great Depression in the context of remarks like, "Clean up your plate and be thankful you've had a full meal" or, "You're lucky you have a chance to work and earn money." But there were few details about what the Depression was really like. It was obviously not a subject to be revisited with any enthusiasm. Norman's files reveal that for seven years he was employed by the federal Works Progress Administration, although I have only the vaguest recollection of his ever mentioning it. In retrospect, it was the WPA that kept the wolf away from Norman and Vera Mae's door during the early years of their marriage. For the Roaring Twenties abruptly stopped roaring with the Crash of '29 when the bottom fell out of the stock market.

The Great Plains area, especially hard hit by the Dust Bowl, witnessed the mass exodus of destitute "Okies" bound for California, the fabled land of milk and honey. By 1932, the unemployed in the United States numbered more than 13 million. Many lived in the primitive conditions of a pre-industrial society stricken by famine. Into this grim picture strode Franklin Delano Roosevelt. Upon accepting the Democratic nomination for President of the United States in July 1932, FDR promised a "New Deal" for the American people, a phrase that would come to characterize his administration for the next 12 years. The New Deal consisted of a wide range of efforts to end the Great Depression and to reform the U.S. economy. While many of these failed, there were enough successes to establish it as the most important episode of the 20th Century in the creation of the modern U.S. state.

During the first 100 days of the Roosevelt administration there was a flurry of legislation designed to bring the economy out of the depths of depression. Among the first of these was the Agricultural Adjustment Act which was passed by the U.S. Congress in May 1933, creating the Agricultural Adjustment Administration (AAA). Relative farm incomes had been falling for decades and the AAA was intended to provide agrarian relief. The most important provision of the AAA was the provision for crop reductions—the "domestic allotment" system of the act, which was designed to raise prices for farm commodities. Norman's last job in Scott County was with the AAA as office clerk, and he was responsible for computing the acreage of fields under contract.

In January 1935, President Roosevelt proposed a gigantic program of emergency public employment which would give work to 3.5 million jobless (Leuchtenberg, 1963). At the time there were more than 10 million unemployed in the United States. The new agency that would manage the program, the Works Progress Administration (later Works Projects Administration, abbreviated WPA), created on May 6, 1935, was the largest and most comprehensive New Deal initiative under FDR. The WPA was a reiteration of the Public Works Administration of 1933, designed to employ middle-aged skilled workers on public projects. Since the WPA was not permitted to compete with private industry or to usurp regular governmental work, many WPA projects were "make work" assignments that provided jobs and income to the unemployed and were of limited value. WPA projects primarily employed blue-collar workers in construction projects across the nation, but also employed white-collar workers and artists on smaller-scale projects.

The WPA would be denigrated by its detractors as a bureaucratic boondoggle. They referred to it as the agency of "We Piddle-Arounders," owing to its alleged bureaucratic inefficiency. It would also be criticized for becoming too highly politicized. Nonetheless, the WPA served a vital function at a critical period in U.S. history. But not until the U.S. entered World War II after the bombing of Pearl Harbor on December 7, 1941 was the country finally able to pull itself out of the Great Depression. After only eight years of existence, with unemployment figures falling fast due to employment generated by U.S. involvement in World War II, President Roosevelt shut down the WPA on December 4, 1943.

Shortly after the creation of the WPA, Norman began his first job with the WPA office in Hays, Kansas on September 2, 1935, as Employment Officer in the Employment Division. From 1935 to 1939 Norman was posted to Hays and Topeka, where his job consisted of maintaining reassignment files and assignment procedures. His beginning annual salary with the WPA was $720, increasing to $1620 in four years. In November 1939 Norman was transferred to Wichita, Kansas, which represented not only a substantial increase in salary ($2100) but more responsibilities: he was promoted to Principal Employment Clerk, in charge of personnel in the employment division of the Wichita WPA office. In March 1941 Norman was posted to Iola, Kansas, where he retained the same title and a modest increase in salary.

However, after seven years Norman's WPA career came to an end on April 7, 1942, when he received a notice of separation due to reduction in personnel. Small consolation that it was, Norman received a nice letter from the State WPA Administrator (April 27, 1942) thanking him for all the years of "splendid service" he had given the WPA during the time he was employed by the Agency. The letter congratulated him on having been subsequently employed with Boeing Aircraft Corporation in the Accounting Division. At last, a job in the private sector!

Despite the lack of opportunity to obtain a university education, Norman doggedly pursued whatever educational courses he could. While in Topeka he took two six-month night-courses in accounting through the Kansas University's Extension Division. Then during the time he was employed at Boeing, Norman completed a three-month course in 1943 in Production Expedite Planning through KU's Engineering, Science, Management War Training Program. He received another certificate from the same department in 1944 for Engineering Drawing. The Boeing plant was closed at the end of World War II, costing Norman his job.

4K- 56134 2

Vera Mae & Norman—Wichita Days

We must assume that throughout these years of moving about various locations and job changes, Vera Mae was performing the role of dutiful wife. She was the original stand-by-your-man woman, forsaking whatever career thoughts she might have entertained to be Norman's helpmate and companion and raise a growing brood.

Ponca City, Oklahoma (1945-)

In 1945 Norman and Vera Mae moved again, this time to Ponca City, Oklahoma, with two young'uns in tow: four year-old Galen and baby Judy Ann. Here Norman would soon secure a job at Continental Oil Company (Conoco). The town of Ponca City (even today not really a "city") had its origins in the boom days of the Cherokee Strip. Probably the only town not staked out as a townsite by government planners before the Great Run of 1893, Ponca City was the brainchild of one man, Col. B.S. Barnes, who came to Oklahoma Territory from Michigan in the hopes of founding a new town. After driving for many days with a team and buggy around the area that now comprises several counties of northern Oklahoma, Barnes chose a spot on the Arkansas River. Deciding factors included the spring of water nearby and the proximity of a Santa Fe railroad stop. Barnes had no trouble selling certificates of lots for $2 each in Arkansas City; each certificate was good for one business lot or two residence lots.

From the early years of the 20th century, Ponca City became a company town in which nearly everyone either worked for Conoco or owed their living to it in one way or another. Ponca City would remain a small town in the years to come, in the 1950s and 1960s hovering in the range of 15,000 to 16,000. By 2000 the city had a population of just over 25,000. The racial makeup of the town was as follows: 84% white, 3% African American, 6% Native American, 4% Hispanic or Latino and 3% other. The per capita income for the city in 2000 was $17,732, while 16% of the population lived below the poverty line (http://www.fact-index.com/ponca_city).

In the 1940s and 1950s Ponca City society was not very highly stratified. The vast majority of the population was in the low to middle income range, derived primarily from Conoco or its suppliers. The Black and Indian population was consigned to the more modest income categories, while at the other end of the spectrum were the upper level Conoco managers and researchers. There was a small business class of shop-owners and merchants. The Hispanic population was negligilble. The Woolworth store downtown still had water fountains that featured signs saying "white" and "colored". In many respects Oklahoma was a southern state.

Ponca City in those days was overwhelmingly Protestant, the principal denominations being the Presbyterians, Baptists,

Methodists, Anglicans and Disciples of Christ. There was a fairly sizable Catholic community, which had its own parochial school. There was a small but dynamic Jewish community in Ponca that was primarily involved in retail business; not until several decades later would they have their own temple in town. The social elite tended to be members of the Ponca City Country Club. It was my pleasure to observe the more active members and their families at play during the summers when I worked as lifeguard at the club swimming pool. The Nickels family—of the Nickels Machine Shop—in particular seemed to dominate the scene. The four Nickels kids tended to take over the joint—pushing, running, throwing water balloons, all very much against the rules—testing the resolve of the lifeguards.

One of them, pudgy little Donny Nickels, would become the suave Senior Senator from the state of Oklahoma. He faithfully served his constituency, and his voting record in Congress was testimony to just how conservative the state had become.

The Ponca Indians and the Trail of Tears

The town of Ponca City owes its name to the Ponca Indian tribe, a branch of the Sioux nation. The Ponca were forced into Oklahoma Territory from Nebraska on the "Trail of Tears" during a period when persons of European extraction were also making their way in the same direction. While the immigration of the latter into Oklahoma represented the consummation of dreams of economic freedom, for the Ponca it would a journey into deprivation. What had heretofore been set aside as "Indian Territory" would soon be primarily the reserve of white homesteaders. The large Sioux tribal language group was originally made up of many smaller tribes such as the Ponca, Omaha, Osage, Kansa and Quaqaw. These five tribes once lived in an area east of the Mississippi River, but just prior to the arrival of Columbus they had begun moving westward. The Poncas and Omahas split from the other tribes sometime prior to 1500. According to traditional belief, the Omahas and Poncas followed the Des Moines River to its headwaters and moved northeast (http://www.nebraskastudies.org).

Eventually they crossed the Missouri River and drove out the tribe living on the west bank of the Missouri River in an area that would eventually be located in the state of Nebraska. Sometime later, perhaps as early as 1390 and as late as 1750, the Ponca and Omaha themselves separated. Certainly by 1789 the Ponca were living on lands of a tributary to the Missouri River. The Ponca Tribe was never very large—between 1800 and 1900 they probably never numbered more than 800. On their expedition Lewis and Clark estimated that the Ponca numbered as few as 200 people in 1804 but by 1874 they were back up to 700 individuals.

During this time the Poncas were led by their great chief Standing Bear who was born on the Ponca reservation around 1834. He signed an agreement with the government for the Ponca Tribe to move to Indian Territory (Oklahoma). The Trail of Tears began with a scouting mission. On February 2, 1877, Standing Bear and nine other Ponca leaders left for the Osage Reservation in Indian Territory to select a site for the new Ponca Reservation. Adequate preparations had not been made for the visit to the Osages and many of the Osage chiefs were absent when the Ponca arrived. Consequently, no serious business could be conducted and the land shown to the Ponca as possible sites for their reservation was not satisfactory to them. On February 21, Standing Bear and seven of his fellow chiefs decided to return on their own. It was midwinter and after a strenuous journey, the Ponca leaders arrived back at the Ponca Reservation in Nebraska on April 2, 1877.

The Ponca were divided in their willingness to leave. Those willing to journey south left on April 16. In May, Standing Bear and the remainder of the Ponca Tribe started the long journey to Indian Territory, prodded along by the U.S. military. They encountered bad weather almost from the beginning of the trip; by the time the tribe reached their destination, the summer heat had become oppressive and they were constantly plagued with insects and extreme weather conditions. Several died on the journey and were buried in Nebraska.

Therefore, in the summer of 1877, the Poncas were moved overland to the Quapaw reserve in Kansas, arriving there in June. The Poncas were not satisfied with the location so they were given permission to select any unoccupied land in the Indian Territory. The chiefs under the leadership of Standing Bear selected their present reservation at the confluence of the Arkansas and the Salt Fork Rivers, containing over 100,000 acres. The Poncas were moved from their Baxter

Springs reservation to Oklahoma in July, 1878. But the Ponca were again disillusioned with the Quapaw Reservation since much of the land was not suitable for cultivation. Government agents refused to provide adequate farming equipment, and many of the people died from malaria. Since leaving Nebraska, nearly one-third of the tribe had died. Scarcely 15 years later the Poncas saw the Indian Territory opened up to homesteaders and their lives were forever changed.

E. W. Marland and Conoco: The Hottest Brand Going

The story of Ernest Whitworth Marland (1874-1941) could not provide more of a contrast to that of the Poncas. Continental Oil Company (Conoco) emerged out of Marland Oil, founded by Marland. To this day he is easily the most famous native (small "n") son of Ponca City. Marland was born in Pittsburgh, Pennsylvania, and received his law degree from the University of Michigan at the age of 19. Marland's interest in geology and nose for business caused him to pursue a career in the oil industry at a time when black gold was becoming the elixir of the American economy. He made his first fortune in the oil fields of West Virginia, only to lose it all in the panic of 1907. The following year Marland arrived in Oklahoma, with little more than belief in himself and a letter of credit.

Marland's story is intertwined with that of the famed 101 Ranch, founded by Col. George Washington Miller in 1881. The 101 Ranch, just outside what would become Ponca City, billed itself as "the largest diversified farm and ranch in the U.S." At the time Ponca City was a small trading town no more than a wide place in the road. The 101 Ranch spanned 110,000 acres at its peak, and included three towns, schools, churches and miles of road. The 101 Ranch Show featured prominent Western stars of the period. Among them was Bill Pickett, a top "bulldogger" who was of African-American and American Indian descent, and Tom Mix who later became famous in the movies. The 101 Real Wild West Show left the ranch in 1906 with 126 performers, teams of horses and equipment, touring the U.S. and Europe (Banham, 2000).

Marland was a fervent believer in the science of geology, which he felt would revolutionize the nature of oil drilling. In 1908 he mapped out the terrain and secured a lease from the Miller Brothers on 10,000 acres of land to drill for oil. The agreement marked the beginning of the 101 Ranch Oil Company. But Marland also had his eye on a parcel of land owned by the Ponca Indians. The negotiations proved difficult. "We had a lot of troubles with the Indians, but after a lot of squatting, smoking and palaver, I obtained the right to drill," Marland would later write.

Marland worked feverishly at drilling, and after several dry wells, he hit gas. The 101 Ranch Oil Company quickly began marketing gas, generating enough income to continue the search for oil with his buddies Lew Wentz and W. H. McFadden. On one trip around the ranch with George Miller his trained geologist eye spotted a rock formation, which turned out to be some Ponca Indian graves near Bois d'Arc Creek. Marland smelled oil (as it were). Miller arranged a meeting between Marland and White Eagle, the Ponca chief. Although this was sacred ground to the Poncas, White Eagle gave his consent to drill along the slope because he liked and trusted Miller!

Marland obtained a lease to drill on the land from Willie Cry, the Ponca Indian who owned the land. On June 27,1911, the well came gushing, a major new field right in the middle of the 101 Ranch. Marland later wrote: "I remember White Eagle standing near the derrick of the first well when it blew with a terrific roar. He told me in the sign language that I was making 'bad medicine' for him and his people." Little could White Eagle imagine the nefarious effects this would have on his people! With this quote (and a handsome picture of the Ponca chief) the official story of Conoco relegates the Poncas to a footnote in company history.

In a few years Marland's 101 Ranch Oil Company operations dominated the fast-growing oil scene in northern Oklahoma. In 1911 he saw his first gusher and soon after he discovered two more wells, and then began finding oil everywhere he drilled. Marland established a refinery south of Ponca City in 1918 as a small skimming plan designed to produce gasoline and kerosene. Two years later lubricating oil was added to the product slate and other process units were installed to help refine heavy oils.

The company name was changed to Marland Oil Company, and by 1922 it was said that Marland controlled one tenth of the world's known oil reserves. More than a third of the working-age population of Ponca City was employed by Marland Oil. It was the Roaring Twenties, and Marland roared with them! For the next six years the E.W. Marland story took on legendary proportions. Amassing extraordinary wealth through the expansion of his company, Marland began to build a remarkable 22-room mansion in Ponca City on Tenth and Grand Avenues, which would become known as the "Palace on the Prairie." A frequent traveler to Europe, Marland became enamored of the Davanzati Palace in Florence, Italy. He decided that he wanted one just like it, complete with the Italian architectural design and imported Italian marble. Massive orders of imported Italian raw materials and skilled workers poured into Marland's project. Construction, begun in 1925, was finally completed in 1928 at a cost of $5.5 million! (http://www.marlandmansion.com).

Marland's lifestyle during the Roaring Twenties would have been the envy of European royalty: fine paintings adorning the walls of the mansion, manicured gardens, fox-hunting on the estate, opulent banquets and entertainment in the elegant ballroom. All of this was in stark contrast to the lifestyle of average Ponca Citians living outside the gates of the Palace on the Prairie. This was still a largely frontier culture, only a few years removed from a time when the buffalo roamed the prairies. Whereas the Davanzati Palace in Florence was the product of centuries of advanced civilization and international commerce, Ponca City was still barely on the map.

But 1928 was the year in which Marland scandalized Ponca City and all of civilized Oklahoma society by marrying his adopted daughter Lydie, (thereby hang many tales). No sooner had the couple returned from an extended honeymoon and taken up residence in the mansion than Marland's business affairs took a turn for the worse. The victim of a hostile take-over, he was forced to resign as president of Marland Oil on November 1, 1928. J.P. Morgan & Company gained control of the Marland Oil Board of Directors, leaving Marland powerless to continue managing the company. The new powers suggested that Marland leave Ponca City, for fear that he would start up a new company and that many of his employees would follow him. Marland had inspired the loyalty of his employees, pioneering in such benefits as paid insurance, health care and even company-built housing.

In fact, Marland did attempt to establish a new company, but his efforts were for naught. In 1929 Marland Oil Company was merged with Continental Oil Company, begun in 1875 in Ogden, Utah. Continental had already become a top marketer of petroleum products in the Rocky Mountain region. Demand for gasoline increased as automobiles became more and more numerous. Continental had built the first filling stations in the West and invested in a fleet of delivery trucks. When Marland was replaced by Dan Moran as President of Marland Oil, the latter oversaw its merger with Continental Oil Company. It seemed like a good fit: Continental needed a steady supply of crude oil (Marland's strength), while Marland Oil needed more marketing outlets. The new corporation, headquartered in Ponca City, was known as Continental Oil Company (Conoco) and was immediately a force to be reckoned with: nearly 3,000 oil wells and thousands of retail outlets in 30 states.

In 1932, at the height of the Great Depression, Marland was elected to the U.S. Congress. Two years later he ran for and was elected the tenth Governor of the State of Oklahoma; he and Lydie moved to the capital in Oklahoma City. His one notable accomplishment as Governor was the successful leasing of state property at the capital building for oil production. Today Oklahomans can still see oil wells pumping on the grounds of their state capital. However, this was to be Marland's last hoorah. He would subsequently run for the U.S. Senate twice, losing both times. In 1939, far less wealthy than before and unable to maintain the mansion, the Marlands moved back to Ponca City, taking up residence in the artist studio before eventually moving into the chauffeur's house. In 1941 Marland finally was obliged to sell the mansion to the Carmelite Fathers for the measly sum of $66,000. Six months later he died of a heart attack in the same chauffeur's quarters where he and Lydie had lived. After Marland's death Lydie continued a reclusive existence on the Marland property, the subject of whispers and rumors.

Meanwhile, Conoco continued to grow and expand under the stormy but productive rule of Dan Moran during the 1930s. Moran introduced new products such as the first lubricant to reduce engine friction. On Christmas Eve of 1937 he handed out 5,000 bonus checks worth $770,000, one of the largest bonus programs of any company in the U.S. that year. To fill jobs previously performed by men absent during World War II, he hired more than 1,000 women and gave them blue denim overalls with the trademark Conoco red triangle. When the war ended Moran was replaced by Leonard McCollum, a more genial but equally ambitious president. By the time Moran left, Conoco had diversified into coal, chemicals, plastics, fertilizers and minerals. It had been transformed from a small regional oil company into an integrated, worldwide enterprise with more than $2.5 billion in assets. Conoco was going global long before it was fashionable! Conoco: The hottest Brand Going! This was the Conoco that awaited the Hull family upon arrival in Ponca City in 1945.

Rockin' Our Souls in the Bosom of Conoco: The South Oak Era

With the closing of the Boeing plant in Wichita at the end of World War II in 1945, Norman was once again obliged to look for work. Homer and Mabel were now living in Ponca City, some 100 miles to the south of Wichita, where Homer was employed as a janitor at Conoco. The Hull family, now numbering four with the new addition of Judy Ann, trekked back into Oklahoma. Norman first found employment at the Thompson Parker Lumber Company. But after a short time he was hired to work in the Purchasing Department at Conoco, which would prove to be a big break- through in an otherwise checkered career history. About the same time, in 1946, Homer was retiring from Conoco. The Hulls took up residence in a modest white frame house at 438 South Oak, next door to Grandma and Grandpa in a house Homer owned, just two blocks north of Conoco administrative headquarters and a whiff away from its refineries when the wind was in the south.

So from 1945 to 1956 the Hull family—with the addition of Everette in 1950—lived a typical Ozzie and Harriet routine on South Oak. For the first time in their lives Norman and Vera Mae could experience the semblance of stability, if not prosperity. Norman's job was a white-collar office job where the attire was shirt and tie, not the blue collar of the refinery. This would make a considerable difference in how he would define himself: not as a laborer but as a member of the white-collar administrative structure of Conoco. Norman was fastidious in arranging files and carrying out his responsibilities. His job was enhanced by the fact that his immediate supervisor, Clarence Spiller, was very supportive of him. The Spillers lived across the street on South Oak and the two families would remain life-long friends. Work and social relations provided a happy convergence of interests. However, Norman would be involuntarily "retired" with fellow workers after 26 years of service for having lost productivity!

Conoco had by 1945 installed a full range of amenities for its employees, including an indoor swimming pool, gymnasium and a minor league baseball field. Conoco became my second home. It was a world unto itself down there, all those facilities, just two blocks away from our house. On weekends the gymnasium was turned into a family movie theater featuring our favorite Disney characters. On Saturday mornings the gymnasium would serve as a skating rink and chocolate bars were handed out as prizes to winners of skating competitions. Conoco hosted basketball and badminton tournaments in the gym from time to time. Summer nights might find me attending a Ponca City Dodger game, rooting for the home team. I became a Brooklyn Dodger fan early in life because our team was a Dodger farm team. Even before I knew who the Boston Red Sox were, I learned to despise the hated Yankees because they caused our Dodgers so much grief! Dad taught me how to swim in the Conoco pool where I would eventually spend countless hours as a member of the Conoco Swim Team as did Judy. Surely this was a blessing for Mother, since she could pack us off to Conoco and not have to worry about what we were up to.

Not only did Conoco provide for leisure enjoyment and a place to grow up, it also organized annual gala Christmas parties in the gymnasium for employees and their families. Santa could always be counted upon to show up right on cue.

Conoco offered a full range of benefits to its employees and their families. Its corporate generosity included a college scholarship program for the sons and daughters of its employees. Beginning in 1956, Conoco established a scholarship committee charged with reviewing applications from graduating high school seniors. In July 1959, when The Conocoan announced 18 winners of $500/ year renewable scholarships, my name was among them. What a blessing!

I could be assured of a college education without having to burden my family with debt.

The year 1956 would be a red-letter year for the Hull family. In the first instance, we were finally able to move into a brand new home on the north (high!) end of town, just a stone's throw from Ponca City Senior High School. (For the three of us who matriculated through that institution, it would be very convenient to scurry home for lunch on school days). For months Norman and Vera Mae were engaged with a local architect in the design of a three-bedroom "ultra-modern" suburban home. For weeks on end we would go to the site and observe progress being made toward the construction of the new home, making sure everything was done to specification. It was beige brick, with sleek sloping lines that put the family squarely into the second half of the 20th century! The year was also a big one for me since it would feature a trip to Japan. Then, too, it was the year when Vera Mae became pregnant with Kurt Todd, her fourth and last child.

Parenting

Although Vera Mae did not wear her religion on her sleeve, she was a paragon of virtue and duty to family, grounded in her Christian faith. She had a clear sense of right behavior, which she managed to impart to her children without too much preaching. She placed high value on cleanliness, honesty, discipline, punctuality and fairness. (You know, "Be nice to your brothers and sister.") Her love for family and friends was manifested in countless ways. One of her most endearing habits was coming into the bedroom to tuck us in at night, whispering a brief prayer and always remembering to give thanks for a wonderful husband and father of her children.

Vera Mae was the disciplinarian, perhaps by default, but also because of her sense of right behavior and how to avoid bad behavior. One of the basic principles she dispensed to her children was self-reliance: do for yourself. This was especially relevant to income-generating activities. Yes, there was a modest allowance each month that came from her purse. But from early on she made us aware that if we wanted new clothes or to go on a trip in the summer, we would have to find ways to pay for them. Her admonition to stay on the job until it was finished was summed up in her exhortation to use "stick-to-it-ive-ness," which the dictionary defines as "unwavering pertinacity; perseverance." This term often comes back to me whenever I'm in the midst of a seemingly hopeless task.

Vera Mae's was a policy of tough love. During my five years delivering papers for the Ponca City Daily Disappointment, the hardest part of the job was getting up early on Sunday mornings, trudging downtown on my Schwinn bicycle to pick up the papers and delivering them to my 110 customers near our home. Vera Mae was my alarm clock, making sure that I didn't oversleep. On those mornings when the temperature plunged well below freezing and the wind chill factor was even worse, I would beg to be taken downtown by car to pick up the papers. That never worked. But I always had a cup of hot chocolate waiting for me when I got home, to help thaw me out and ease the pain. My sense of responsibility was reinforced once a month on Saturday mornings when I had to go around to each customer and collect for the paper. Whatever I didn't collect came out of my profit, a lesson in entrepreneurship.

Punishment for bad behavior varied depending upon the severity of the act. Withholding of monthly allowance for chores around the house was on the low end of the spectrum, as was grounding from attending social events. A swat on the rear was the extent of physical punishment, and that became more and more rare the older the miscreant was. The court of last resort was Norman, whenever Vera Mae reached her limit in dealing with sibling quarrels and other wayward behavior. But inwardly we would heave a sigh of relief if she said, "Just wait 'til your father comes home." We knew that he was hopeless at dispensing justice and meting out punishment, and that we would likely get off with another scolding.

If Norman was a miserable failure as a disciplinarian, he was a fine role model in many respects. There was never a hint of philandering; his devotion to Vera Mae was unshakeable. He gained strength from her, probably more than she gained from him. His personal habits were (mostly) impeccable: his pants were always creased and his shirts neatly pressed, his shoes polished and lined up on the floor of the closet, his personal hygiene above reproach. He kept all his personal and family files in order and paid the bills on time. He paid careful attention to the maintenance of the family car. In a word Norman was fastidious, you might even say fussy. He was punctual on business and social occasions. He was a dutiful father, taking a keen interest in the affairs of his sons and daughter. And while he didn't preach the virtues of such behavior, we kids seem to have inherited a gene for fastidiousness from Norman, as reflected in our habit of picking up our clothes and putting them away.

But Norman did have a few bad habits that were the subject of sometimes heated exchanges with his exasperated wife. He loved to work in the yard and at his workbench in the garage. Whenever Vera Mae would announce that dinner was ready, he could never manage to pull himself away from his project. After the third or fourth call to eat, Vera Mae would give up and call the rest of us to the table.

Norman's later arrival would be greeted with a cold stare. A rather more serious indictment of Norman was his smoking habit. Before the Surgeon General and Philip Morris discovered that smoking could endanger your health, Vera Mae was on the case. Long before public establishments began to ban smoking on the premises, the ban was in effect in the Hull house. Sadly, the ban was not effective in inducing Norman to give up his cigarettes, eventually resulting in a long bout with emphysema and his eventual demise. And let us not even mention abstention from alcohol. Vera Mae considered drinking one of the Seven Deadly Sins. Not only did the Hulls live in a dry county, we lived in a dry house!

But the point of contention with most substance had to do with Norman's reluctance to march into the boss's office and demand an increase in salary. He was not one to pick a fight, or for that matter to assert his rights. Vera Mae was keenly aware of the meager income available to the family and often reminded him that he should fight for a raise for the sake of his family. Apparently this came to no avail, and the Hull family income remained modest.

If Vera Mae had bad habits, we kids were not aware of them, busy as we were trying to live up to her standards. To be sure, she was rambunctious, a term she liked to use on us kids whenever things were getting out of hand. She was generally full of energy and liked to get things done. Vera Mae tended to be impulsive about things in general. Whatever the task at hand, it was her notion to get on it right away and not waste time. This trait was associated with one bad habit we heard about from time to time from Norman. It was her driving. Let's not say that she was reckless, but she often turned corners a little too sharply and occasionally pushed beyond the speed limit a tad. While there was no record of speeding tickets or accidents that I can recall, Norman felt obliged to reign in on what he considered Vera Mae's excessiveness. He was a by-the-rules kinda guy. Truth be known, he was probably concerned about avoiding scratches and dents on his car.

Vera Mae lived for her husband and children. She was the veritable image of the person who hid her light under the bushel, full of talents that never quite came to full fruition. So she dedicated her life to transferring her aspirations to her offspring. She had a lovely soprano voice, which was on display in church and at social occasions. She learned to play the piano as well, although this was not her signature talent. But she was determined that at least one of her children would learn to play a musical instrument and thus fulfill her ambition. The first candidate for this undertaking would be the eldest son. However, after several years of dutiful lessons and practice sessions, this effort would end with a whimper. Shortly before I was to play in my first piano recital I managed to slip and fall outside the Ponca City library, breaking my right wrist. Not only did I miss the recital, this episode effectively ended Vera Mae's aspirations for me to become a pianist, since I didn't renew my lessons thereafter. Judy took up the viola, and managed to earn a music scholarship to attend the University of Oklahoma. The two younger sons would turn to playing snare drums with rock groups, but I suspect that this was well outside the parameters of what Vera Mae had had in mind when she launched us on musical initiatives.

Another of Vera Mae's skills that she rarely had time to indulge in was sewing. She could patch up holes in worn out socks, mend a rip in a shirt, as well as design and sew together a costume for a special occasion. Fortunately for me, when I started to build my Indian dance costume the transfer of some of these elementary skills came in very handy. She taught me how to thread a needle, sew on buttons and rosettes and how to finish the job with a series of knots to hold things together. From there I was on my own with the tedious beadwork that was the basic ingredient of the costume.

Perhaps because she had grown up in the rough and tumble of a farm culture and had witnessed its seamier sides, Vera Mae tried mightily to shield her offspring from what she considered to be bad influences. For some reason this seemed to include country music, which we rarely heard in our house. But next door in Homer's house it could be heard on demand. I understand that in his younger days Homer played traditional music with a local band. By the time we kids came along, his playing days were mostly over. But he loved nothing more than to take down his fiddle after dinner and launch into tunes such as "East side, west side, all around the town..." My earliest recollections of music on the radio were of tunes like Tea for Two and the sounds of the big bands such as Glenn Miller. But Vera Mae clearly had a preference for church music and the classical tunes offered up by piano teachers of the day.

Homer loved to tell tales, the taller the better, preferably with a punch line that would allow him to launch into gales of laughter or at least a guffaw or two, regardless of whether others joined in. The tales were mostly for Homer's own entertainment; he always had a story or two at the ready. His language was especially colorful. Common curses were so much a part of his diction that he scarcely distinguished the profane from the ordinary. Painfully aware of this, Vera Mae monitored the more profane epithets. She felt obliged to protect her offspring from them. Since we grandsons were often as not around him when we were working on a project involving hammers and nails, his colorful epithets frequently filled the air. With a stern admonition from Vera Mae, his preferred exclamation of "God Damn!" would be turned into a less damning "God Darn" or "Gol Damn" in order to take the edge off and therefore pacify his poor daughter. The distinction was of course lost on us kids, but it appeared to pacify Vera Mae. Early on, I became aware that one of the Ten Commandments had to do with NOT taking the Lord's name in vain. So I sensed what Mother was up to!

There was a particular expletive I frequently heard as a tender youth that only later would echo in my ears. It seemed to come most often when Homer was hammering a nail into a shingle and missed. He would let out a yelp that I have never heard anywhere else: "Plague take it!!!" I have had occasion to reflect on the meaning of this strange curse in recent years. It must have come ricocheting down through the generations from a time when the bubonic plague was ravaging Europe in the Middle Ages. Whatever you wished to disappear from your life, you simply asked that it be swept away by the plague. How appropriate! Homer could get away with this epithet around Vera Mae since he wasn't taking the Lord's name in vain. Plus, we kids didn't have a clue what he meant!

Vera Mae's Cookin'

Vera Mae's culinary skills were pretty much limited to straight-ahead meat and potatoes fare. A typical evening meal would consist of some type of meat, vegetables and occasionally a salad—often served on TV trays in front of the tube. Liver and onions was one of Dad's favorite dishes, a taste I also came to acquire. Chicken fried steak and fried chicken were standard offerings. Hamburgers occupied a favorite place on the menu with the kids, usually reserved for weekends and holidays. On special occasions we would indulge in steak and mashed potatoes. Vera Mae's pies—cherry, apple and pumpkin—were popular items with the family. On cold winter evenings soup or chili and crackers would often be on the table. Corn or apple fritters were featured on Sunday evenings, especially when we were having guests. Lunch would usually consist of sandwiches: lettuce, tomatoes, pickles and mustard (no raw onions!) accompanied by potato chips. And washed down with milk, lots and lots of milk.

In the back of the garage there was usually a vegetable garden that provided fresh produce during the growing season. The backyard also provided the venue for preparing a chicken for the dinner table. On special occasions Vera Mae demonstrated skills she likely learned while Homer managed his hatchery by dispatching a chicken, chopping off its head and letting it flop around until the body was limp. The chicken would then be submerged in boiling water in order to soften the feathers, which would be plucked and the chicken readied for the oven or skillet. Although I have long since forgotten how these chickens tasted at the table, I often reflect on this basic process when eating a chicken dish.

Of course, holidays such as Thanksgiving and Christmas would invariably consist of turkey and dressing and all the trimmings, the product of several days' effort by the ladies of the extended family. This was consistently the high point of our culinary calendar. However, noticeably missing from the Hull family menu was seafood, likely a function of our living considerably inland from the ocean. Whenever fish was on the menu, it was probably a variety of local catfish. My first meal of shrimp and French fries, at the age of 13, was on a swimming trip to Houston at a place called Ship Ahoy.

And there was the frequent admonition to "clean up your plate" at the end of the meal. "Think of the starving children in India and China," Vera Mae would say. So we kids became members of the Clean Plate Club, a membership I have retained throughout my life. I have a vivid image of Grandpa Homer taking a piece of bread and wiping his plate clean to cap off his meal.

To my recollection, nothing Vera Mae cooked was ever identified with any ethnic cuisine. Well, okay, I suppose we were aware that the spaghetti or macaroni and cheese she served from time to time was Italian. But Vera Mae had a certain bias against the use of garlic ("gives you bad breath"), an essential ingredient in all Italian cuisine. Judy reminds me that Vera Mae's spice cabinet was limited to seasonings such as cinnamon used in baking pies. Indeed, I don't recall salt and pepper shakers being on the table most of the time. Vera Mae's kitchen may have had one cookbook. But perhaps she was simply a reflection of her element. Ponca City did not have an abundance of ethnic eateries, apart from the odd Chinese and Mexican restaurants, so our palates were not attuned to exotic cuisine. Our notion of a night out was more likely at Sonic's, A&W Root Beer or the Dairy Queen.

But for some reason that I can't really fathom, the one dish from Vera Mae's kitchen that most readily comes to mind is her goulash. It was especially common on cold winter nights. I always assumed that goulash was as American as apple pie, since we had it so often. Only much later did I come to learn that it had its roots in Hungary. The Free Dictionary defines Hungarian goulash as "a rich meat stew highly seasoned with paprika." According to Pat Soley, in an essay on goulash soup http://www.soupsong.com), goulash—or gulyásleves— goes back to the intrepid Hungarian horsemen who swept into Europe on horseback from the Ural Mountains in A.D. 800s. A 14th century Italian chronicler described how, in medieval times, these restive nomads adapted goulash into the world's first instant soup (this was before Campbell's). They would boil heavily salted beef in huge kettles until it fell off the bone—then cut it into small pieces, dry it in the sun or in an oven, grind it to a powder and carry it in bags so that all they had to do was boil some water to make a proper soup.

And it was Hungarian herdsmen—cowboys, really—who perfected the goulash form. From the Middle Ages on, the great Hungarian plain—the puszta—was home to vast herds of cattle. Herdsmen—or gulyás—would feast on gulyáshus ("herdsman meat") and onions, which they would cook up in a kettle (bogrács) that was hung up over a fire on a tripod. They would eat the soup straight from the kettle with big wooden spoons. Originally, Hungarian goulash did not contain the main ingredient that it came to be associated with: paprika. In fact, Soley points out that this dried and pulverized form of chili peppers wasn't even a glint in the Magyar eye until the 16th or 17th century. Pepper plants (chilies) were introduced into Hungary, either by the occupying Ottoman Turks or by Bulgarians who had fled north around that time trying to escape invading Turks. Chili peppers were resting comfortably in the New World—and didn't move until Christopher Columbus brought some seeds back to Europe from his voyage of discovery there in the 15th century.

Why this dissertation on the Hungarians and goulash? Well, it has occurred to me that Vera Mae must have learned to serve up goulash when she was cooking for the farmhands during harvest. Yes, cowboys, even if they weren't Hungarian. But her rendition of goulash more closely approximated the original variety, that is, without paprika. Recall that Vera Mae's kitchen had a very modest spice cabinet, which certainly did not include paprika. American cookbooks tell us that Hungarian goulash is one of those dishes that may have entered the United States in its ethnic form but has since been absorbed into the American mainstream, taking its place alongside such other "ethnic" dishes as pizza and French fries. Sadly enough, in recent months Hungary has been hit with a culinary crisis, prompting a government ban on paprika. The health ministry ordered all food retailers to withdraw the staple crimson spice from their shelves and also banned cooks from using it in their recipes after a high level of alfatoxin was found in warehouse supplies. Alfatoxin, caused by mould, can be carcinogenic in large amounts and can lead to liver damage and a weakening of the immune system (can't almost everything?).

Another reason for ruminating upon Vera Mae's cuisine: with travel abroad and exposure to exotic cuisines: my own tastes in food have gravitated further and further away from the mild menus we were treated to at home. Today the capsicum that forms the basis of chili pepper is for me a preferred ingredient in any dish. So needless to say, I would prefer my Hungarian goulash with paprika! All of this is not to say that I am lacking in fond memories of home-cooked meals from Vera Mae's kitchen.

The Church

For Norman and Vera Mae the church was a vital part of family life. Norman was born and raised in the Christian Church (Disciples of Christ) and Vera Mae was raised in the Baptist Church. However, from the time of their marriage onward they were staunch members of the Christian Church. The careful reader will have noted that Vera Mae had gone to a Baptist Church function when she first met Norman, but there the conversion apparently began. At the First

Christian Church in Ponca City both sang in the choir for many years. Vera Mae served as a deaconess, member of the Christian Women's Fellowship, as well as superintendent of the junior department where she also taught Sunday school. In addition to regular attendance at Sunday school and Sunday morning worship service, often as not we were back at church on Sunday evenings for Bible study or social events. Wednesday evenings were for choir practice, a ritual that Vera Mae and Norman rarely missed. As is customary with the Disciples, we were baptized by immersion at the age of 12 after weeks of Bible study focused on the meaning of baptism.

The Disciples of Christ, a Protestant denomination of approximately 800,000 members in the United States and Canada (down from over one million in 1900, however), came to be one of the largest faith groups founded on American soil. Throughout my life, whenever I have told people I was a member of the Christian Church they would almost invariably say "Which one?" So here's the story, in brief.

Mark Toulouse (1997), a noted historian of the Disciples movement, describes the period after the American Revolution as "the democratization of American Christianity." It was a period in which ordinary people took matters of faith into their own hands, rejecting the power and authority of the elite religious establishment. Toulouse argues that groups like the Baptists, Methodists, the Disciples and the Black churches "did more to Christianize American society" than anything before or since.

One thing the majority of Americans seemed confident about was their common distrust of institutional authority. The frontier attitude discouraged those in the educated eastern centers of power from attempting to establish themselves on the frontier. The new social conditions brought forth a new school of religious leaders who were able to tap into the interests and concerns of the common people. The established churches such as the Congregationalists, Episcopalians and Presbyterians had difficulty achieving success in this kind of environment. This was the context for the development of numerous religious groups and social experiments: the Mormons, Brook Farm, New Harmony, Shakers and the Oneida Community all emerged during these years. Such an environment, says Toulouse, was tailor-made for the emergence of a new religious group like the

Disciples. All the cultural trends of the day fit into the religious package they offered. He claims that the Disciples were the "quintessential American denomination."

There has been a long-standing tendency in Disciples history to avoid elaborate theological statements. The early Disciples believed that theological opinions too often led to division, so they were best left to the realm of personal opinion. The Disciples were born in the context of a resurgence of freedom among the common people. In religious life, this freedom had been curtailed for centuries by a hierarchical church life that required uncritical assent to creeds and clerical authority.

The founding Disciples were, like most Christians around them at the time, committed to the divine inspiration of scripture. For them the Bible represented God's message to humanity. So Disciples strongly asserted the authoritative nature of the Bible. They depended upon the Bible to tell them the truth about themselves. No more remarkable illustration of this faith is to be found than that of Ada Norman Hull. Ada, Norman's mother, was always a devoutly religious woman and a lifetime member of the Disciples of Christ. However, in her late eighties she began to believe that the Disciples were straying away from the Bible. So she took it upon herself to leave her church and join the Church of Christ, a denomination she felt was hewing more closely to the letter of the Good Book! Had she lived her life in Sweden, Ada would no doubt have become an Akian (a term we shall revisit in the chapter on the search for Swedish roots).

During the late 1940s and 1950s, the First Christian Church of Ponca City was actively involved in the worldwide missionary effort. A portion of each week's tithes and offerings went to support the work of our missionaries in the Belgian Congo. At the time, this was a Belgian colony, an area the size of the United States east of the Mississippi, much of it covered by tropical rain forests. The mission our church supported was in a town called Coquilatville, located on a bend in the Congo River at a point where the Equator bisects the globe. Pictures of the mission and the Africans always seemed to be enveloped by dense forest, so unlike the plains of northern Oklahoma.

These presentations represented my first exposure to a world beyond the oceans, of people different from ourselves. I was not so much drawn to the mission of saving souls as I was intrigued by the awareness that there was a big wide world out there. I wanted to know and experience it. As it turns out, a couple of decades later, in 1966, my travels would take me to this very place (now called Mbandaka after the campaign to Africanize the Congo). I would see the school and church buildings that my Sunday tithes and offerings helped to build. There I would step out onto the soccer field of the mission compound, where at half-time the competing teams would change hemispheres since the midfield stripe was also the Equator. I witnessed the missionaries working with Congolese to develop appropriate technologies for local farming and industry. The missionaries were more eager to talk about these development activities than about attendance at church on Sunday! They told me about a university that had been created with support from the Disciples of Christ in the town of Stanleyville (eventually to be known as Kisangani), on the other end of the Congo River. I would subsequently spend several years there as a professor.

The Whole Hull Family Christmas, 1963

Clouds over Ponca City: environmental issues at Conoco

For several years there had been suspicions that Conoco Oil Company's operations were not entirely environmentally friendly. But folks in Ponca were reluctant to bite the hand that fed them. But the story finally leaked out and not surprisingly the Ponca Indians were among the primary victims. Today the Ponca tribal homeland, known as White Eagle in honor of its chief, is located just south of the Conoco crude oil refinery. For over a century the Ponca have lived both literally and figuratively on the fringes of the local social order. Unlike the Osage Indians in neighboring Osage County, the Poncas leased the land that might have made them rich to E.W. Marland. While struggling to maintain their traditions and customs, the Poncas have high rates of unemployment and alcoholism as well as infant mortality and death rates.

When the Ponca arrived in Oklahoma they chose the highest spot on the southern plains landscape for their tribal cemetery in order to have a view in all four directions. Now buried next to it is Ponca City's municipal landfill, a gargantuan man-made mountain blocking a great portion of the view. In 2002, feeling trapped and overwhelmed by industry and environmental contamination, a diverse group of some 150 people rallied in a tour of the major industrial facilities adjoining tribal lands. The rally and walking tour was an effort to bring attention, they said, to environmental injustices facing the Ponca people (Dowell, JoKay, 2002). Ponca Tribe members and environmental staff, student groups, environmentalists and union members gathered together in the Standing Bear Memorial park on the south side of Ponca City across from the Conoco-Phillips crude oil refinery.

Conoco's contributions have not always been positive. During a year of heavy rains, basements in what was a housing addition across the road from the refinery began to flood. Residents complained of smelling gasoline and having headaches, respiratory problems and other ailments. Investigations by some homeowners found that the problem was the groundwater that flooded the basements and seeped up through foundations, causing fumes to accumulate in the home's living areas. The groundwater, contaminated by Conoco's refined product leaking from the nearby Conoco tank farm, formed an underground plume that moved off-site and under the homes north of the plant. Conoco was taken to court in 1990 and a settlement was reached in 1992. The company bought some 200 homes, and residents in the area were paid damages. The company then leveled the neighborhood and planted trees in the southern portion of the area now known as Standing Bear Park.

How and why did Vera Mae Die?

On March 20, 1965, Vera Mae Hull succumbed to Hodgkin's lymphoma cancer in the Ponca City Hospital. Scarcely four months earlier her family doctor had told her that the headaches she was experiencing were symptoms of menopause. I had just settled into my role as a secondary school teacher in the remotest corner of Malawi, in the region of Africa farthest from home, when I received a message from the Peace Corps office in Blantyre that my mother was ill and that I should return home as soon as possible. Few details were given about her illness and I didn't question the directive; I packed my bags and jumped on the next available lorry (truck) heading toward the capital city. The Peace Corps had been remarkably efficient in arranging for my air travel home, considering that I was starting from such a distant location. Within 36 hours, after four different flights through three continents, I was bouncing along the road from the airport in Oklahoma City to Ponca City.

I rushed straight to the hospital where I found Norman, Judy, Everette and Kurt, gathered around Mother. In the three months I had been in Malawi I had grown the regulation Peace Corps beard, which I had never had before during my clean-cut days in Ponca City and in college. Vera Mae had tubes attached to her body going in all directions. Her lymph nodes along the insides of her arms, which were all we were allowed to see, were horribly swollen and discolored. She winced as I walked into the room and saw the frightful beard that had cropped up on my face. She managed a wan smile recognizing my presence. I really felt bad. The least I could do was to get rid of the beard. So that evening I rushed home and shaved it off and tried to catch some sleep.

The next morning we all went back to the hospital. But it was already too late. Vera Mae breathed her last breath. I remember Norman breaking into uncontrollable sobs, the rest of us just too numb to emulate him. Only 48 years old! It seemed unfair for such a dynamic woman with so much to live for to go so soon. The funeral was just a few days afterward, and within a day or so after that I was on an airplane on my way back to Malawi. It was surreal. Perhaps I was the lucky one in the family, to be so far removed from the reality of Mother's departure and thrust back into a totally different world. I felt secure in the knowledge that she had done her best to raise me.

I have long since wondered whether the fumes from the Conoco refineries were a contributing factor in her death. Quite obviously, there was little reliable information available about cancer in the 1960s, either its causes or treatment. For several years after reading Bernie Siegel's best-selling book, Love, Medicine & Miracles (1986), I contented myself with an explanation for Vera Mae's death that seemed to make sense and didn't take a lot of detective work. Dr. Siegel was a practicing physician for several years before he began to reflect on the psychological dimension of his patients. In 1974 he began keeping a diary in which one of his earliest notations was, "It seems like the world is dying of cancer. Every abdomen you open is filled with it." He started a therapy group called Exceptional Cancer Patients to help people mobilize their full resources against the disease.

In his book Siegel sketches the psychological profile of cancer, starting with a quote from Galen, the 2nd century physician. Galen noted that melancholy people were more likely to get cancer than those with more sanguine dispositions. By the 18th and 19th centuries many physicians were realizing that cancer tends to follow tragedy or crisis in a person's life, especially in those whom today we term depressed. Despite the 20th century's far-reaching discoveries about the mind, Siegel says, medicine has been reluctant to apply them to an understanding of cancer. He quotes a 1926 study of cancer, which concluded that, "Cancer is a symbol, as most illness is, of something going wrong in the patient's life, a warning to take another road."

Today, according to Siegel, we are now able to sketch a fairly complete psychological profile of those people who are most likely to develop cancer. The typical cancer patient is one who has experienced a lack of closeness to his parents during childhood, a lack of the kind of unconditional love that could have assured him/her of intrinsic value and ability to overcome challenges. Having been a compulsive giver since childhood, the future cancer patient continues going through the motions with whoever remains in his/her life until depleted and exhausted.

Siegel then says that over and over again he hears friends and relatives of cancer patients say, "He was a saint. Why him?" But the truth is that compulsively generous and proper people predominate among cancer patients because they put the needs of others ahead of their own. Siegel calls cancer the disease of nice people. They are unconditional lovers, giving only in order to receive love. If their giving is not rewarded, they are more vulnerable to illness than ever. Siegel cites work at Johns Hopkins University beginning in 1946 and continuing for several decades aimed at constructing personality profiles of medical students. The study concluded that the profiles of those who developed cancer were almost identical to those of the students who later committed suicide. So that was it! Vera Mae had simply sublimated herself to the aspirations of her family. That was certainly plausible. I was willing to ignore the less plausible side of the profile having to do with the lack of closeness to her parents in childhood.

With the passage of time, however, the Siegel personality profile explanation cries out for more data. What is lymphoma and how does one acquire it? Today, of course, the World Wide Web is replete with information about its symptoms, causes and treatment. (http://www.cancer.org). Hodgkin's Lymphoma or Hodgkin's Disease—two terms for the same thing—is a malignant (cancerous) growth of cells in the lymph system. Hodgkin's Disease is the better known form of lymphoma; the other lymphomas are grouped into what are called the Non-Hodgkin's Lymphomas. The incidence or number of cases of Hodgkin's lymphoma (about 7880 cases, 4330 men and 3550 women in the United States) is significant, although less than the number of cases of Non-Hodgkin's lymphoma (over 53,000).

Although she was never in a workplace environment where she was exposed to chemicals, for over 10 years Vera Mae lived within less than a mile of the Conoco crude oil refinery which gave off toxic fumes on a regular basis. And we were only a couple of blocks away from the water contamination described above that eventually resulted in the forced evacuation of 200 families and the court action against Conoco in 1990. In truth, we will never really know what caused Vera Mae's cancer. Within a few months after her death, Homer passed away. He had suffered from a variety of ailments during much of his life, including hay fever and allergic reactions to golden-rod and the chicken feathers (the latter especially debilitating when he was managing a hatchery). While living in Ponca City, whenever the wind was blowing from the south, from the direction of the Conoco refineries and their foul fumes, he would remark on how they affected his hay fever and other allergies. If he had trouble getting around he would say that he had a "hitch in my git-a-long." Unfortunately, this seemed to be increasingly the case as he got older.

Today Vera Mae's memory is reflected in our custom of naming our house—wherever it happens to be—Vera Mae House. I am told that this it is a custom among some Asian peoples to name their homes after a deceased mother. In any event, Vera Mae's exemplary life would seem to merit such a distinction.

Hull Siblings with Vera Mae, December 2005

References

Banham. Russ (2000) CONOCO: 125 Years of *Energy,* Lyme, Connecticut: Greenwhich Publishing Group, Inc.

Beighle, Laura Houser (2001) Laura's Story: *A Private Gift From Laura Houser Beighle to My Children* (manuscript).

Dowell, JoKay (2002) "Poncas join chemical workers to protest neighboring pollution," in *Indian Country Today.*

Hull, Dale W. (no date), *Hull-Randall & Irwin-Purviance: Ancestors & Descendents,* Dodge City, Kansas (self-published genealogy).

Moberg, Vilhem (1951) The *Emigrants,* New York: Warner Books. The sequels to *The Emigrants* include *Unto* a Good Land, *The Settlers* and *Last Letter Home.*

Shull, Eunice (1932) *Interview with George Norman, pioneer of Western Kansas*, granddaughter of the interviewee (manuscript).

Siegel, Bernie (1986) Love, Medicine & Miracles, Harper & Row Publishers.

Toulouse, Mark G. (1997) *Joined in Discipleship: The Shaping of Contemporary Disciples Identify,* St. Louis: Chalice Press.

Websites

http://digital.library.okstate.edu/Chronicles, *Documents from the Cornerstone of the Nez Perce and Ponca Indian School*, Chronicles of Oklahoma, Volume 12, No. 3, September 1934.

http://www.cancer.org, "What is Lymphoma?"

http://www.nebraskastudies.org, "The Story of the Ponca."

http://www.soupsong.com, "Who Put the Paprika in Goulash...And Other Hungarian Tales."

Chapter 2

Japan and Hawaii, 1956:
In the Land of the Rising Sun

Neba hatchi, loosely translated: it will never happen.
        - English corruption of Japanese phrase to be used in
bargaining

At an early age I became involved in Cub Scouts while a student
at Jefferson Grade School in Ponca City. Having dutifully completed
all the requirements for my Webelo badge, I graduated into Boy
Scout Troop I of the First Christian Church. Scouting became my
passion, and by the age of 13 I had earned the Eagle Scout Award,
God and Country and was inducted into the Order of the Arrow. In
1953 I attended my first national Scout Jamboree in Irvine Ranch,
California and in 1955 I traveled to Niagara-on-the-Lake, Ontario,
Canada, for the World Scout Jamboree. So by the age of 14, I was
a veteran Boy Scout with a sash full of merit badges and a vest full
of patches swapped with scouts from around the world at various
jamborees.

It was at this point that the Regional Scout Executive for the Will
Rogers Council covering Northern Oklahoma decided to nominate
me for a once-in-a-lifetime trip to Japan because of my scouting
exploits. He and other scout leaders were organizing a goodwill
exchange between the Boy Scouts of America and the Boy Scouts
of Japan. The idea was to bring 25 Japanese scouts to the U.S. to tour
the country and stay with families of American scouts and to send an
equal number of American scouts to Japan. They managed to enlist
the logistical support of the U.S. Air Force as the carrier and co-host
for the American scouts. Thus it was that in the spring of 1956, during
my 9th grade year in junior high school, the letter came inviting me
to participate in the First Boy Scout Asian Airlift. (I have no idea
whether there was a second one.) Since the proposed travel would
be for three weeks during school time, the Scout Executive had to
negotiate my absence from classes. The rest is a blur—obtaining a

passport, getting required vaccinations and purchasing a camera—all had to be done in a short period of time. Since no one in our family owned a camera, a special collection was taken up to buy a Ricoh 35 millimeter camera for me to record the trip. And since the Japanese were already known for making good cameras, I was given funds with instruction to also buy a Minolta while in Japan!

Ponca City to Hensley Air Force Base   *23/March/1956*

On the morning of March 23rd I boarded the Santa Fe train at the Ponca City station, southward bound for Dallas, Texas. After a five-hour ride we arrived at the Dallas train station and then were taken directly to Hensley Air Force Base. I noted that the air in the Dallas area was rather warm compared to Ponca City. The grass was already a bit green, in contrast to the parched brown of northern Oklahoma. There were 10 scouts gathered at Hensley headed for Japan, and each of us was assigned to his respective barracks (I later learned that B.O.Q. meant Bachelor Officers' Quarters) and began to get acquainted with the other scouts from all over the U.S. Never having had any exposure to the military, I found this to be an eye-opening experience. For the next several weeks we would lead the life of the military, at least in so far as meals and accommodations were concerned. They told us that supper would be served in the mess hall at 1700 hours and explained that in civilian language this was 5:00 PM. We would have to get used to this way of reckoning time. Actually, after the first couple of days it started to make sense. Why should we have an AM and PM instead of counting the hours of the day from one to 24?

Hensley Air Force Base   *24/March/1956*

At 600 hours we were dragged out of our bunks and taken to mess for breakfast, which by now was already beginning to look familiar. By 830 hours we were boarding the C-47 bucket-seat Air Force plane and were being briefed by the pilot on the use of parachutes. Although our destination was San Francisco, the plane stopped in the afternoon for refueling at Williams Air Force Base near Phoenix, Arizona. Even though I had hardly any flying experience, the trip seemed especially bumpy to me. Williams AFB was a very attractive base. Here we met with the Region Eight Boy Scout leader and enjoyed a tour of the base which included a sizeable number of F-

86 jets and weather instrumentation. I was amazed to see that the temperature at Williams was 95 degrees Fahrenheit! And it wasn't even summer yet. After supper we checked our gear, elected crew leaders and watched a movie.

Who were these guys I would be traveling with for the next several weeks? Half (about a dozen) of the group would be going to the Philippines and the other half to Japan, but all would be stopping off in Hawaii. It seems that all of us were from the states of the Midwest, Southwest and the Pacific. Judging from the biographical notes each of us wrote about ourselves, nearly everyone was an Eagle Scout (the highest rank in scouting) and most had previously participated in jamborees and the ultimate in scouting experience, the Philmont Scout Ranch in New Mexico. There were scouts from Colorado, Oklahoma, Texas, Kansas, Nebraska, Iowa and Oregon. In our group headed for Japan there was Bunky Jordan, who would become my best buddy, from Dallas. Bunky signed my notebook with the comment: "Texas: Best state in the whole wide world." Others from the great state of Texas included John Jennes (Waco), Morris Smith (Uvalde) and Willie DuBose from LaMesa. The Oklahoma contingent included Richard Maule, from Sandy Springs, Bill Reinhardt from Bartlesville, and Howard Campbell II from Tallequah. The Washington was Jerry Solberg (Seattle) and the Oregonian was Tom Sherman (Portland). The others were on their way to the Philippines.

Williams Air Force Base   *25/March/1956*

Our C-47 arrived at Travis Air Force Base outside of San Francisco around 1200 hours Pacific Standard Time. We were treated to a tasty lunch in the mess and then ushered into the embarkation briefing room where we met more Air Force and scout leaders who provided further briefing about our trip to Japan. There followed another tour of the base, which included some C-97s and C-124s, the latter being among the largest aircraft made for the Air Force. The C-124, whose tail wing stands about three stories off the ground, can carry up to 400 men (a battalion). After supper we attended service in the base chapel before going to bed. By now we scouts were getting pretty well acquainted with each other.

Travis Air Force Base   *26/March/1956*

We were up again at 600 hours and had the usual hearty breakfast at the mess. There were further briefings concerning our passports and immunizations. Col. Bailey, MATS Commander at Travis, called us together for a group photo in front of the C-124 cargo plane. He also showed us the C-97 transport plane that would take us across the Pacific the next day. Travis is a SAC base with about 3,000 personnel stationed here. Drawing upon the wealth of experience that U.S. military have in Japan since the war, Sgt. Moorehead gave us a brief orientation to Japanese culture. For example, when we are shopping in Japan, if we don't agree with the price quoted to us we are to say, Neba hatchi, which loosely translated means, it will never happen. The sergeant also told us that the Japanese have hated Koreans for many generations.

We ate dinner at the commissary and then rested until 1500 hours when we were briefed on what and how to pack for the trip. Our propeller-driven C-97, equipped with no-so-comfortable bucket-seats, left at 2200 hours, on our way at last toward the Land of the Rising Sun. We would have a total of 39 hours of flight before reaching Japan, traveling at an average cruising speed of about 240 MPH.

First Asia Boy Scout Airlift, 1956

On board the C-97 to Hawaii   *27/March/1956*

An hour after departing from Travis Air Force Base we were provided with box lunches which we quickly devoured and then promptly fell asleep in our bucket seats. Upon awaking at about 600 hours, we found ourselves at Hickam Air Force Base in Hawaii. We were disappointed that the local scout field executive presented us with leis, the traditional Hawaiian greeting, instead of Hawaiian girls. We were then ushered into a waiting room in the terminal where we were served an exotic fruit called papaya. My diary recorded that this was a digestive agent that tasted to me something like I would imagine a flower to taste. I also noted that a single papaya in Hawaii costs only twelve cents, whereas on the mainland it goes for $1.25! Outrageous!

The local scout executive took us on a small tour of Honolulu, which of course included the world-famous Waikiki Beach. Back at Hickam Air Force Base, we prepared to board our plane for Japan. The Air Force band played a farewell tune for us and then we headed out around 1100 hours. I'm really looking forward to returning to Hawaii on return from Asia. At 600 hours the following day we landed on Wake Island, having crossed the International Date Line on the way.

On Board the C-97 to Japan   *28/March/1956*

You could say that today began at 300 hours when we crossed the International Date Line. Very confusing! All I can figure is that we have lost a day somewhere along the way and we'll gain it back on the way home. On Wake Island we were greeted by two local boy scouts who served as our hosts on a tour of the island. I was impressed with the coral reef.

Haneda Air Force Base—Japan   *29/March/1956*

Somewhere around 100 hours we landed at Haneda International Airport in Tokyo. Here we were ushered into the MATS section where we went through a lot of red tape, getting our passports and papers checked. A Japanese bus driver took us across town to the Air Force Base and we got to bed around 500 hours after a good hot shower. One of the first things I noticed is that the Japanese drive on the wrong side of the street, but they seem to avoid accidents! After a few hours' sleep we were awakened at 900 hours in order to change some currency for use in the military PX as well as some into Japanese yen. In the afternoon we went over to the University Club where I bought $16 worth of kimonos and a light meter for my Ricoh camera. After dinner we played a little ping pong and then sent messages home via MARS.

Tokyo, Japan   *30/March/1956*

After breakfast we took a bus to the New Kaijo Building, U.S. Air Force Headquarters in Japan, where we met Four Star General Kuter who welcomed us to Japan. I looked for a Minolta camera again in the PX (military commissary) but couldn't buy it here. After lunch we went to the University Club. Four of us then took a taxi to the world famous Ginza Market, which we found to be very colorful. With a wide variety of goods, it is very much what I imagined New York's 5th Avenue to be like (although I've never seen it). We couldn't resist buying things; they were so cheap and colorful. We took a taxi for 80 yen back to the New Kaijo Building.

At 1700 hours we met with the Japanese scout executives who were to be our hosts for the tour of Japan, including our guide, Teddie Murase. Teddie is 23 years old, a very brilliant and personable fellow. He is a Prefecture Scout Executive. We learned that Japan's scouting program is organized along three levels: District, Prefecture and National. We were presented with invitations to the 4th National Japanese Jamboree to be held in the summer. At 2200 hours we boarded a Gekko Train at the Tokyo Station. We had very nice berths and Teddie provided us with lots of information about Japan. Mt. Fujiyama is the tallest peak in Japan and is the country's national emblem. So Fuji rank in Japanese scouting is the equivalent of the Eagle Scout in the U.S. A scout must earn 20 out of 38 merit badges in order to earn the Fuji Scout award.

Kyoto   *31/March/1956*

Our train arrived in the ancient city of Kyoto about 830 hours. Here we were met by a local scout troop at the station. It was a very impressive welcome ceremony. We were then taken to Nijo Castle, which is huge and is more than 600 years old. The emperors used to live in this castle when the capital of Japan was Kyoto. Our next stop was the breath-taking Golden Temple, a gold-gilded Buddhist shrine set in the middle of a lake. It looked like a mirage. Apparently the original temple had burned down and this magnificent structure was built in its place by a general in 1953. The bus then took us to Heian Temple, a Shinto Shrine painted orange.

Golden Temple, Kyoto

Just a few hundred yards away from there we visited the Tatsumura Silk Mansion where we saw silk textiles being manufactured and sold. There were goldfish as big as basketballs swimming in the Tatsumura pond! At noon we were invited to lunch with the Mayor of Kyoto, who is also the President of the Kyoto City Council. After lunch we were again met by Kyoto Boy Scouts who presented each of us with silk handkerchiefs. By now we were beginning to feel a bit like celebrities! We were then split up into five groups, each one with Japanese Scouts as hosts who took us on a tour of the Kyoto shopping districts. At 1500 hours we boarded a train for the city of Nara where we were loaded onto a bus that took us to the 70-year-old Nara Hotel. This was a beautiful building overlooking the city. After our evening meal in the hotel we had our first traditional Japanese bath which was very different from our baths at home. They appeared to be large wooden barrels full of steaming hot water. To our amazement, a geisha girl was assigned to help us bathe! The hotel gave us kimonos (kind of like pajamas) which we wore to bed. Definitely not what I was accustomed to at home!

Notes on today's travel: The Japanese drivers are very reckless. As a result more people are killed on the roads than in the U.S. We see many more bicycles and scooters than cars in the streets of the cities. It seems that buildings in Japan are either very very old or brand new. There has been a lot of construction in the country after the end of World War II. A Shinto building is called a Shrine, whereas a Buddhist building is called a Temple.

Nara   *April 1, 1956*

Today was Easter Sunday, an Easter unlike any other I had ever experienced in my life. After breakfast in the handsome hotel dining room we were taken to a Catholic Church where we attended Mass. This was quite an experience for me since I had never even been inside a Catholic Church at home. Instead of sitting in pews everyone sat on mats on the floor. The priests were speaking in Latin and Japanese so we didn't understand any of it! The smell of incense which they swung back and forth in the air was very strange to me.

Nara is the ancient cultural capital of Japan and it still has a lot of very old buildings. Our first stop after church was to visit Nara Park where we saw deer grazing in the drizzling rain. Then we visited the Todai-ji Temple, the edifice that houses the greatest bronze statue of The Buddha to be found anywhere in the world. Constructed in 752 A.D., the Japanese call the temple Nara-no-Daibutsu.

The dimensions of the Buddha statue are as follows: body height: 60 ft; length of the Buddha's face: 15 ft.; length of his eye: four ft. Although I carefully recorded these figures, I really did not understand who or what the Buddha was. In Sunday school we were taught that non-Christian people worshipped idols, and I guessed that this is what they were talking about. Still, it was very impressive. But if this was a Japanese church, I wondered where the people were supposed to sit. We saw people walking up to the statue with flowers and putting incense sticks into big pots. The air was heavy with the smell of incense. It was certainly different!

The Buddha at Nara-no Daibutsu

For lunch we went to the Kasugano-so House which was furnished very lavishly. This was the first time for us to try to eat with chop sticks and it was a real ordeal. I was afraid I was going to go hungry for the rest of the day!

Back at the Nara Hotel we checked out and headed to the station where we boarded a train bound for Kobe at 1400 hours. Located on the southern coast of Hokkaido, Kobe is a major ship-building port. It was a very short ride, even though the train stopped three or four times on the way. Upon our arrival in Kobe there was a very large and enthusiastic crowd of Japanese scouts on hand to greet us, waving flags and cheering. We went from the station to the Yamamitsuwa where we were guests of the Mayor of Kobe and the President of the Kobe Prefecture Council. Now we were beginning to enjoy our role as celebrities. Here our first sukiyaki party awaited us. We had been told that sukiyaki was a traditional Japanese dish, a kind of soup that is considered to be a delicacy. So we were looking forward to the occasion. But when I tried to eat the raw egg that they plopped into the sukiyaki, it wouldn't go down. I began to yearn for mother's meat and potato dishes! At least I could eat the rice, something I could recognize for what it was.

Then on to Union House in Kobe where Japanese scouts had

organized another reception in our honor. That evening three of us were guests in the home of Mr. Kabayashi, a wealthy cotton merchant. His son was a scout. Their beautiful home was located in Ashiya, a suburb of Kobe. The Kabayashis made us feel very welcome and we enjoyed the evening very much. Again we were treated to a traditional Japanese bath, this time assisted by a geisha girl who poured water on my back and scrubbed it. This was...well, very different! Again kimonos were provided.

Kobe   *2/April/1956*

We were awakened early and treated to another hearty breakfast. The three of us met the other American scouts at the train station. The first stop on the tour today took us to the most important port in the Orient, Kawasaki Dockyards. This is the life and soul of Kobe, constructed around the middle of the last century. After a brief tour of the ship-building facility, we went to Koshiyen to see the All-Japan High School Baseball team try-outs. Those selected for the team would travel to the U.S. We were surprised to learn how very popular baseball is in Japan. On the way to the next attraction, an electronics plant, we sang songs with the Japanese scouts on the bus. We also traded scout patches which is a popular thing to do at jamborees.

Osaka   *2/April/1956*

The next site we visited was Osaka Castle, formerly known as Golden Castle, built around 1400 A.D. The castle is so huge that it took 50,000 workers and three and a half years to build. Although the castle has been damaged many times throughout the years, it has always been repaired. We had lunch on the bus on the way to a Shinto Shrine that now serves as an orphanage. Dinner that evening was another meal featuring sukiyaki, followed by a tea ceremony and a traditional dance by a geisha girl. That night all of us slept in the same room.

Hakone National Park, Japan   *3/April/1956*

This morning we were awakened very early since it would be a very long day. We traveled on the express train Tsubame for Numazu where we were welcomed and given the usual celebrity treatment. But much of the rest of the day was taken up with traveling to a place called Atami. From there it seemed like we went almost straight up mountain roads until we reached Hakone National Park. Along the way we began seeing snow on the ground and it became colder. Our lodging was at Green Gardens Hotel which is at an elevation of more than 10,000 ft. I was fascinated by the heating system in the hotel; they bring a thing called a hibatchi with coals in it and place it under the table. This is really quite effective. At the hotel there were hot springs (ohnsen) where people go for bathing. The water is naturally warm and the steam rises off of the water. We scouts were amazed to peer through the steam and see that both men and women bathed in the same place and…that they wore no bathing suits! This experience had us guys talking amongst ourselves for days afterward. We did not get to bed until after midnight, exhausted but happy after an eventful day.

Nikko National Park, Japan   4/April/1956

After breakfast at the Green Gardens Hotel we traveled by bus back to the train station. On the way we could glimpse Mt. Fujiyama, although it was pretty cloudy. The train from Atami was an electric express which seemed to travel very fast. We reached Nikko National Park around 1700 hours and were greeted as usual by the Mayor and local Scout Executive. After supper we American scouts were taught traditional Japanese folk songs and dances by local scouts. We were assigned sleeping quarters in the Nikko Palace Hotel and after another nice hot bath went to bed.

Nikko National Park, Japan   5/April/1956

Here we were housed at another elegant facility. We were told that the Prince of Wales used to entertain guests in the Nikko Palace dining room. Formerly it was the summer home of the Emperor of Japan. A morning bus tour took us around Nikko National Park, including the spectacular Kegon Waterfalls, Lake Chuzenji, Mt. Nantai and a Shinto Shrine. Nikko is famous for its many shrines and temples, and especially the Yomeimon Gate. The area is thickly populated by cedar trees. We took a cable car up the mountain, then got on yet another train to the Nikko Copper Works for a tour. The next stop was the Toshugo Shrine, built by Temitsu Tokugawa to enshrine the ashes of Tokugawa, one of the greatest leaders in

Japanese history. In the afternoon we checked out of the Nikko Palace and boarded another bus to the train station.

At 1800 hours our train left Nikko, and within a short time we were back at the Tokyo train station. Once again we were met by a welcoming committee and assigned to our host scout families. I went with Dr. Sashida, a medical doctor whose house in the suburb of Tenashi contains his clinic as well. The doctor and his very large family treated me like royalty! By now I'm feeling really spoiled and worried about how ordinary my life back home will be! My host while in Tokyo is Mr. Nobukazu Komine, a scoutmaster.

Tokyo   *6/April/1956*

It took an hour for us to drive through traffic from Tenashi to the New Kaijo Building, our point of entry to Japan, where we met with the rest of our group. Here we managed to sort out dirty clothes to be laundered, for the first time since arriving in Japan! Then we rushed to have tea with the top brass of Japanese scouting, feeling more and more like celebrities! Then off on a bus tour to see the Imperial Palace, home of the Japanese Emperors and their families. We passed through the Scared Archway and Ueno Park. Lunch was served on the bus on the way to Nippon Television Station, one of five stations in Tokyo. Yashikuni Shrine was our next stop, at which point we were again split up into groups for the remainder of the day.

It was time to go to the Ginza, the famous Japanese shopping center. My group went to Matsuya, the largest shopping center in the city, where I was planning to buy kimonos to take home for my mother and sister Judy. Here I was interviewed by a Japanese journalist. Innocently, I inquired of the sales ladies whether they wore anything underneath the kimono. This brought a round of embarrassed giggles, and of course it became the focus of the article, together with a picture of me wearing a kimono, which appeared in Tokyo papers the next day. Needless to say, I never got an answer to my question.

At 1800 hours we all met again at the Kabuki Theater where we had dinner. None of us had any idea of what or who Kabuki was. My notes for the day indicate that we went backstage before the presentation to meet with the main actors. They explained that Kabuki was like our opera, except that it focused on Japanese history and culture. I was surprised that the actors we spoke with were actually men, since they all looked like women. After the Kabuki performance, Komine took me back to Tenashi, this time to his home, which is actually a Buddhist Temple. His father is a bishop (monk?) in the temple.

Tokyo   *7/April/1956*

There I was in a very strange environment, waking up in the morning on the grounds of a Buddhist Temple to the sweet aroma of incense, thinking this was the most exotic thing I could imagine. What are those people doing outside my window? It looked like they were placing sticks of incense into large metal bowls. But then, I had been in Japan for 10 days now, and every day was a new experience. Then, off to the National Scout Headquarters of Japan for another briefing. Then another bus ride to the New Kaijo Building again where we met the contingent of U.S. scouts who had traveled to the Philippines while we were in Japan. We swapped stories about our experiences and got reacquainted. I was pleased to have been assigned to Japan, since it seemed much more interesting.

The whole contingent was then taken to the Japanese Diet (Parliament) Building, their equivalent of the U.S. Congress. Here we met Crown Prince Takamatsu, brother of His Royal Highness the Emperor. The Chief Scout Executive of Japan gave welcoming remarks and then we presented the Crown Prince with goodwill pins. As usual, we were served tea in yet another government building where we had a briefing about the structure of the Japanese government. I was amazed to learn that the Emperor has no veto power over legislation in the Diet, even though he is highly regarded by the Japanese people. We also met with the President of the Upper House of the Diet.

We were told that since World War II a new constitution was drawn up under Gen. McArthur which has significantly changed government in Japan.

Afterward we went to the University Club where we again met the contingent of scouts who had visited the Philippines, followed by shopping at the Air Force PX. We ate supper at the Marunuchi and returned to the New Kaijo Building which we were beginning to feel was our second home.

Tokyo   *8/April/1956*

After breakfast in the New Kaijo snack bar we went to the second floor of the building to attend a non-denominational church service with the chaplain. We then went by bus to the United Nations Building, formerly the "Japanese Pentagon" during World War II. We were served a delicious lunch, followed by a round of speeches by scout leaders and presentation of scout patches and slides. We split up again and went in different directions for shopping. Four of us were driven to a store specializing in cameras. Here I bought a Ricoh 35 mm for 16,000 yen, which seemed to me to be the best value available. We returned to the New Kaijo Building, ate supper, packed and turned in early.

En route to Hawaii   *9/April/1956*

We were rousted out of our beds at 400 hours and rushed down to Haneda Air Force Base for a scheduled non-stop flight to Hawaii. And then we waited, and waited and waited, annoyed because we could have been sleeping! We said goodbye to our Japanese friends who had provided such a wonderful tour of their country. However, not until 1400 hours did we finally board a Constellation-121, a U.S. Navy plane with combination of Air Force and Navy crew. Our traveling speed was 310 MPH. Needless to say, not long after take off most of us were sound asleep, having already been awake for ten hours and exhausted from a couple of intensive weeks of touring in Japan. At about 1740 Tokyo time we crossed the International Date Line. After Midway we traveled another 13 hours before arriving at Hickam Air Force Base. Here 17 of us again took off in a C-47 bucket seat, this time headed for the Island of Maui. We dropped off nine of our crew here and the rest of us headed on to Hilo on the Big Island of Hawaii. Along the way we had some spectacular views of the islands.

At the Hilo Airport we were met by Hawaiian scouts and presented scrolls as a welcoming gift. I was assigned to stay with the Jim Andrews family who lived in the Kinney Heights section of town. Despite the American-sounding name, the Andrews family is half native Hawaiian. We learned that 20% of the Big Island population were full-blooded Hawaiians, 30% Japanese and the rest were mostly of mixed race. Hilo, the largest town on the Big Island, had a population of about 20,000.

Hilo, Hawaii   *10/April/1956*

At 830 hours we assembled at the Hilo Scout Headquarters and from there drove to the Puna Eruption Area, the remains of a 1955 volcanic eruption. We learned that the Island of Hawaii has two big volcanoes, Mauna Loa and Mauna Kea, still capable of periodic activity. A short distance from here is the Kalapana Black Sand Beach, which as its name implies features black instead of typical white sand because of volcanic activity. A short distance away are the famous Warm Springs, truly a paradise. Our hosts informed us that several movies have been filmed here. We had a refreshing swim in the pond at the bottom of the springs and a box lunch. I could imagine a movie taking place here! We then visited a tree nursery featuring the specialty of the Island: orchids. Some of the guys bought orchids to send home. We took in Rainbow Falls after that and then all of us convened at the Maniloa Hotel as guests of the local Lions Club. After a great meal and rousing fellowship with the Lions, we headed home and straight to bed. The travel was beginning to catch up with some of us!

Hilo, Hawaii   *11/April/1956*

Jim Andrews woke me up at 700 hours and we had a typical Hawaiian breakfast in his home, including papaya. The first stop on the day's tour included the Hilo Sugar Mill, where sugar cane is processed into raw sugar, an important Hawaiian export. We visited the Hilo High School and the intermediate school across the street. At noon we went the Yacht Club for a very nice lunch and a cold swim in the club pool. The afternoon was dedicated to shopping. I bought material for a Hawaii shirt and some macadamia nuts, both items for which Hawaii is famous. In the evening I went with the family to a restaurant called Zane's for a traditional Hawaiian chicken hekka dinner.

Hilo, Hawaii   *12/April/1956*

Today we toured the docks where we saw a boat that had sailed from the mainland. We drove up the mountain and visited volcanic areas. At the park headquarters we viewed films on the 1955 volcanic eruption. Mauna Loa is the largest volcano on the Island. However, Mauna Kea is the tallest mountain in the world, when measured from the ocean floor to the top. We toured the crater of the mountain and tried to imagine an eruption!

In the evening we went to Kurtistown for a social where we were treated to some swell food. More important, we were presented with leis in the Hawaiian style, accompanied by a kiss from the young Hawaiian ladies! This is what we were hoping for all along!

Receiving a *lei* in Hilo, Hawaii

Hilo, Hawaii   *13/April/1956*

We got up early and had a quick breakfast at the Andrews home. I took pictures of the Andrews family in their Muu Muu's and Lava Lava's (Hawaiian attire). They drove me out to the Hilo Airport where we said our alohas.

At 600 hours our C-47 left the Big Island and one hour later we landed at Maui where we picked up the other group of scouts. Upon landing in Honolulu, we were greeted by Japanese and Philippine scouts who were returning from their tour of the United States. We all had big tales to tell!

Our morale dropped as we boarded buses for a tour of Maui since we were all expecting a tour of Waikiki on the main Island. We had no appreciation of what the Island of Maui had to offer. The afternoon was then spent flying from Maui to Pearl Harbor. Once again on the main Island of Oahu, we went on a tour of the city of Honolulu. After a refreshing dip in the ocean, we went to a flower shop. That evening we had a big dinner at the Golden Duck, a Chinese restaurant. After dinner we went up to Round Top for a view of the city and the beach. This was the end of our tour, as buses took us to Hickam Air Force Base for the flight home.

En Route from Hawaii to U.S.   *14/April/1956*

At 140 hours we boarded a Navy C-54 and said aloha to Honolulu. No sooner we were on the plane than we were fast asleep. After a 10-hour flight we landed once again at Travis Air Force Base. We checked our baggage and then went to the same barracks we had occupied on the way out. Here we began to go our separate ways, some toward Oregon, others to New Mexico. The rest of us learned that we would not leave until Sunday morning.

Travis to Hensley   *15/April/1956*

Arrived at Hensley Air Force Base, cold and tired, at 1900 hours from Travis. Home to Ponca City by train the following day and very happy to be met at the station by friends and family. This trip exposed me to the U.S. military on a very intensive level. Never again would I be this close to the military life. It was a culture quite different from that which I was accustomed to at home. More important, however, this trip exposed me to a culture very strange and different from my own. We were graciously received everywhere in Japan. It was hard to imagine that this was a country with which the United States had recently been at war.

Welcome Home from Japan, April 1956

Chapter 3

Oklahoma to Texas, 1956-1963:
Crossing the Red River

Son, you need to know how to tell whether a Texan is shootin'
straight with you. You have to look real close when he's talkin'
to you. Watch his lips...and if they're movin', he's lyin'!
                              - Homer Beighle to his grandson Galen

Crossing cultures would not always involve traveling to another
country. In one of my first college courses in sociology I learned
of the concepts of "in-group" and "out-group" used to describe
social groupings. The in-group is what you belong to; the out-group
consists of the other guys. Tribal and ethnic identities are defined
by these basic notions. Often as not, in-group identity is defined or
reinforced by exposure to an out-group. As long as you live in relative
isolation from other groups, your own social identity remains weak
or vaguely defined by tribal myths about the founding fathers. But let
an out-group cast aspersions on your group and it readily reinforces
your sense of belonging. That would come to symbolize for me the
relationship between Oklahomans and Texans. My identity as an
Oklahoman was relatively weak (undeveloped?) until I crossed the
Red River separating Oklahoma and Texas. This was an introduction
to a culture other than my own, to an "out-group".

Okla homa = red earth

Oklahoma territory was the land that the U.S. government
promised to the Cherokees, Seminoles, Creeks and other (civilized)
American Indian tribes in the eastern part of the United States—
if they would only agree to re-locate to the area known as Indian
Territory. In any event, they came to Oklahoma on what came to be
known as the Trail of Tears, from Florida, Georgia, North and South
Carolina. Although I would like to think that my ancestors were

blissfully ignorant of the deal that had been struck with the Indians that eventuated in their resettlement to Oklahoma in the late 1800s, it seems unlikely. It soon became clear that even this patch of land would also have to be opened up for "development" to the dominant culture.

By the 1940s and 1950s, there could not have been a more nurturing environment for a young white male than Northern Oklahoma. It was largely monocultural, a sort of bland European vanilla extract with no pronounced ethnic or national flavoring. There was little awareness of ethnic distinctions within the white community, no big parades on St. Patrick's Day, no Little Italy or other hyphenated groups. The defining moment in Oklahoma history was the opening up of the Territory for settlement in 1893, celebrated once each year in September. If there was any visible social stratification, it was more along the lines of religious affiliation. Ponca City was overwhelmingly Protestant—Baptist, Methodist, Presbyterian, Disciple, Episcopalian, Lutheran and assorted Pentecostals. The Catholic population was large enough to warrant a parochial secondary school. And there was a modest Jewish population, distinguishable by its prominence in the business community and of course excellence in the classroom. Our Jewish classmates were known as the curve-breakers.

The most distinct social stratification in Ponca City, however, was between White and Non-White. The latter consisted of a highly marginalized Black population on the south end of town (known as Dixie Hill) and the Indian population, limited to the White Eagle reservation and a few streets, also in the south end of town. The drinking fountains in the local Woolworth store, with their signs indicating White and Colored, were but the visible symbols of the era of segregation. Segregated schools were the order of the day until 1954 and the Brown vs. Board of Education court decision. By 1957 the Ponca City sports teams, basketball and wrestling in particular, reflected a modest trend toward social integration. The basketball team counted on a player by the name of Booker T. Washington to vanquish the opponent. No one in Ponca City could then imagine that Blacks would eventually OWN the National Basketball Association. That was then, and this is now!

In the post-Roosevelt era we were only vaguely aware of conflict outside our borders. The Korean Conflict (it was not a war, of course) touched far fewer families than had World War II. In Ponca City, most folks were unaware of how many Ponca Indians enlisted to serve (and die) in the Korean Conflict, out of a sense of patriotism. We were deep inside America, and we took a great deal for granted. We were so far inside, in fact, that we were largely oblivious to the rest of the world. At least so it seemed to me.

That is, until television came along. I distinctly recall being invited to a friend's house in 1953 where there was a television set, as rare then as a personal computer would be in the early 1980s. Two televised events that year stick out in my mind. One of these was the inauguration of Elizabeth as Queen of England, viewed then by Americans as an esteemed figure only once removed from our own culture, and thus meriting our respect. The second event, even more momentous, was the inauguration of General Dwight David Eisenhower as President of the United States. Gen. Eisenhower was a hero of World War II and immensely popular. As President, his administration ushered in an era of stability and prosperity that those of us in my generation would take for granted. But in the early Eisenhower years the nation came to be preoccupied with the Soviet menace. With the Chinese Communist threat in Korea we entered the Cold War era, which would endure for the better part of half a century.

As I reflect on my youth, there were few factors that served to bond us with an Oklahoma identity in those days. We had no Paul Bunyan or Pecos Bill, larger-than-life figures who made our history come alive. There was, however, Will Rogers, a real-life native son who rose to national and international prominence for his dry wit and political astuteness. He hobnobbed with presidents, prime ministers, kings and queens, captains of industry and movie stars but never lost his homespun character. A cowboy with Cherokee Indian blood, Will Rogers came to embody the best in American culture. Even today he is probably as close to a state icon as any Oklahoman could be.

Interestingly enough, it was a Broadway musical that probably did more than anything else to provide us with an identity. Thanks to Rodgers and Hammerstein's popular Oklahoma!, the whole world was singing and humming the lines from the musical set in our beloved state. It went something like this:

Oklahoma!, where the wind comes sweepin' down the plain,
And the wavin' wheat can sure smell sweet
When the wind comes right behind the rain!!

We know we belong to the Land,
And the Land we belong to is grand,
We're only sayin' "You're doin' fine, Oklahoma!"
Oklahoma! OK!

You couldn't sing these words in Oklahoma without getting a little choked up! It became our unofficial state anthem. We would as readily come to attention for the singing of Oklahoma! as for the national anthem. It never occurred to us to wonder whether Rodgers or Hammerstein ever came to Oklahoma or actually watched a hawk making lazy circles in the sky...Imagine! It was a Broadway musical that actually gave a sense of identity to a whole generation of Oklahomans!

Another factor that gave Oklahomans a sense of tribal identity was the University of Oklahoma football team. In the 1940s it had been the basketball program of Oklahoma State University that strode upon the national stage. But in the mid-1950s the University of Oklahoma Sooners football team under coach Bud Wilkinson became larger than life. For three perfect seasons (1954-1956), the Sooners won every football game they played. Wilkinson recruited the first Black player in major college football in the South or Southwest. The whole state went into mourning when the Fighting Irish of Notre Dame brought the Sooners' 47-game winning streak to an end. We could hardly believe that our mighty Sooners were capable of losing. Alas, they were!

I mentioned the nurturing environment. My participation in church and scouting activities provided me with both primary social groups and channels for my energies. Scouting especially absorbed much of my time and attention. I went at the requirements for merit badges with gusto, receiving the Eagle Scout, God and Country and Order of the Arrow Awards by the age of 13. I became a regular feature in the local paper. For example: "Eagle Scout Award for Grandson" (Ponca City News, February 11,1954).The article took note of the fact that I was the grandson of Ada Hull of Scott City, Kansas, and great grandson of Mrs. Mary Norman of the same city. Such was the nature of news in Ponca City!

However, it was my involvement in the Oto-Ponc Indian Dance Team, an offshoot of scouting activities that came to take up much of my time...and money. The primary source for financing my dance costume was the Ponca City News paper route which I maintained for five years. It entailed building my own dance costume, which in turn demanded investment of resources. I learned to sew, a skill necessary for beading the various items of my costume. Whenever I had a bit of extra money I would go out to White Eagle and pay an Indian woman to do the beading. Our dance team would sometimes go the reservation to dance on special occasions such as honoring Poncas returning from U.S. military service. Once a year in August there was the Ponca Indian Pow Wow featuring the world championship fancy dance competition. Of course we were never quite good enough to win, but I believe the Poncas appreciated our efforts. The Oto-Ponc dancers achieved a certain amount of local renown, culminating in a trip to Minneapolis where we appeared at the annual Junior Chamber of Commerce convention.

Scouting afforded me numerous opportunities for travel in addition to the Japan trip through attendance at jamborees at Irvine Ranch in California, Niagara Falls, Colorado Springs and Valley Forge, as well as the requisite epic camping trip to Philmont Ranch in New Mexico. All of which served to whet my appetite for travel and exploration! The World Jamboree in Niagara Falls in particular exposed me to scouts from all over the world. Swapping patches with scouts from as many countries as possible was the order of the day.

My career as an athlete took two rather divergent tacks, one as a swimmer and diver and the other as a wrestler. I joined the Conoco Swim Team at a very early age. Quickly finding that I was not among the swiftest swimmers, I began practicing on the one- and three-meter diving boards. By the time I reached junior high I was winning diving medals at swim meets in the area. However, my interest in and dedication to diving began to wane as my involvement in wrestling came on stream. The latter required a different set of muscles and stamina. In fact, Oklahoma was one of the few states in the U.S. where amateur wrestling was a popular sport. Year in and year out, our state universities produced NCAA championship teams. Besides, the cheerleaders came to cheer for us wrestlers just as they did for the football and basketball teams! I never managed to attain more than 123 pounds in high school, the weight I wrestled my senior year when the Ponca City Wildcats won the state championship. That tournament effectively ended my career as a competitive athlete since I did not pursue college scholarships in either of those sports.

I must say that participation in sports competition was decidedly character- building. I owe a debt of gratitude to my two coaches, George Harmon in swimming and diving, and Grady Penninger in wrestling. These men shared a common trait: while they taught techniques for mastering their sport, they were also teaching life skills, with discipline as the centerpiece. Even today Coach Penninger's homespun aphorisms still ring in my ears:

"No pain, no gain."

"A hint to the wise otta be sufficient," and,

"There never was a horse that couldn't be rode; there never was a man who couldn't be throw'd." (With apologies to English teachers!)

In addition to my athletic exploits, I was active in student organizations in Ponca City Senior High School (affectionately known to us as Po-Hi). Having served on a variety of committees during my sophomore and junior years, I decided to run for President of the Student Council my junior year. My campaign motto was "Smooth sailin' with Galen." Kinda catchy, but very little substance, right? Still, it was enough to win. I was elected and served as President my senior year. I was also selected as Citizen of the Month and Senior Rotarian that year. At Oklahoma Boys State I managed to get myself elected Secretary of State, which would be about as far as my political career would go.

Graduation from Po-Hi in May 1959 was followed by a brief period of uncertainty and anxiety. Could I afford to go to college, even if admitted to the institution of my choice? I didn't know of anyone in our extended family who had ever gone to college, and our family resources were quite meager. I had applied for a Conoco scholarship, along with several of my Po Hi classmates. The company traditionally awarded grants of $500, renewable each year, to sons and daughters of Conoco employees who were planning to pursue university degrees. In June the scholarship committee met and decided upon 18 awards, eight of them to Po Hi graduates, myself among them. We all received personal congratulatory notes from

Conoco Vice President R. L. Bosworth. There had been a total of 115 applicants throughout Conocoland. It was certainly an occasion for rejoicing! Thus it was that in the fall of 1959 I was off to college at Texas Christian University (TCU) in Fort Worth, Texas.

— — —

One of my earlier experiences in crossing cultures came when I chose to go to TCU, only three years after my maiden voyage to Japan. My Grandpa Beighle had often traveled to Texas to avail himself of the hot spring baths in Mineral Wells. When I told him of my intention to go to Texas to pursue my college education, he got that twinkle in his eyes that appeared when he was about to tell another ribald story. Grandpa allowed as how Texans were different from us Okies. Here it must be recalled that the term Okie was popularized in Steinbeck's epic Grapes of Wrath. Steinbeck used it to describe those people from Texas, Oklahoma, Kansas and other Plains States who found their way to California during the Dust Bowl of the 1930s. It was a term of opprobrium used by native Californians that tended to catch non-Oklahomans in its wake. But in Texas there was no confusion about the meaning of the term: "Okie" referred to those uncivilized hicks north of the Red River in Oklahoma.

Grandpa took me aside and gave me this word of advice:
Son, you need to know how to tell whether a Texan is shootin' straight with you. You have to look real close when he's talkin' to you. Watch his lips…and if they're movin', he's lyin'!

Grandpa's Okie identity was clearly reinforced by his exposure to out-group Texans. He wished to pass on to me the significance of his experience in a foreign land. His folk wisdom was related only half in jest, for he would always conclude his comments about his Texas experience by saying that he was glad to be back home in Oklahoma. However, I don't think the trips to Mineral Wells succeeded in curing Grandpa's ailments, since he finally succumbed to an accumulation of them after a lifetime of struggle.

Today everyone knows of the out-sized cultural and political ego that is the State of Texas, at one time in the 19th century standing on the world's stage as an independent country: the Lone Star State.

For several decades after Texas joined the Union. Texans could brag about being the largest state, and they did. But when Alaska achieved statehood status, surpassing Texas as the largest state, Texans were obliged to come up with a rejoinder. Which they did! Whenever anyone would mention that Texas was no longer Number One, the patriotic Texan would remark, "Jes' wait 'til the ice melts up there!" Other evidences of the Texan mindset are reflected in license plates that say: "American by birth, but Texan by the grace of God." And "Don't mess with Texas."

The myth of Texas grandiosity has been kept alive by at least three occupants of the White House. Well, okay, two of them: Lyndon Johnson and Bush the Younger. Bush the Elder, although a resident of Texas when elected President, never managed to affect genuine Texas manners despite concerted efforts. Bush the Younger, however, was pure, rough-hewn Texan. His braggadocio style has even proved an embarrassment to some of his fellow Texans. As the Iraq War dragged on and disaffection with the U.S. grew around the world, the American image abroad tended to be fused with that of Texas.

But I digress...When I entered TCU in the fall of 1959 I was greeted by an atmosphere of institutionalized friendliness. During the first week of the academic year, as we were registering for classes and finding our way around campus, everyone was obliged to wear name tags that said "Smile and speak, it's Howdy Week." If you didn't know how to say "howdy" with a Texas twang, you were marked as a stranger to be socialized into the Texas culture. A broad smile was expected to be accompanied by a firm handshake and an introduction. As I reflected on Grandpa's admonition, I began to think that Texans couldn't be all that bad!

Still, I would find that not a few Texans tended to view Oklahoma as a province of Texas, somehow culturally underdeveloped. Some feigned genuine sympathy for those of us who came from the hinterlands. Others were less kind, implying that we were somehow not quite as developed as were the citizens of the Lone Star State. (It WAS true that Texas highways were much better than ours, and things in general seemed to be bigger.) These Texans viewed students from other states with only slightly less condescension. Not to mention international students of whom there were but a few on campus in those days.

I would eventually learn that there was even a pecking order within the Texas culture. People in the Ft. Worth-Dallas megalopolis tended to look down their noses at those in West Texas. For that matter, Dallasites even had a tendency to look askance at Ft. Worth, a cow town lacking in refinement. Not for nothing is Dallas known as Big D, capital of hyperbole. Whenever we at TCU wanted to emphasize the importance of an event or the size of somebody's ranch, it sufficed to say that it was "bigger'n Dallas." The whole world would come to have an outzsized image of Dallas and its culture owing to the hugely popular television series by that name.

I doubt that this syndrome was really on my mind during those early years at TCU. The truth is that I was just a face in the crowd there. I plodded through my freshman year feeling somewhat lost on a campus of 5000 students. My primary association initially was the Disciple Student Fellowship (DSF) group at University Christian Church. It was an extension of my active involvement in youth activities in my home church, with a much wider range of social and cultural offerings. There were frequent retreats, conferences and lectures, as well as a thespian group that presented plays with contemporary social and religious themes. Within the first semester I could honestly say that a few of my best friends in DSF were... Texans!

For most DSF'ers this was the only social group to which they belonged. While I felt quite at home there and made a number of close friends in DSF, I still felt the need to belong to a social group. I decided to pledge a fraternity. I admired a few of those whom I knew were members of certain fraternities, although the Greek alphabet was, well, Greek to me. Needless to say, my independent friends in DSF and elsewhere in the non-fraternity community suggested that I had taken leave of my senses. The Greek world, they pointed out, was decadent and clannish; why would I want to taint my character, not to mention my reputation, by subjecting myself to their foolish ways?

Later in the fall semester of 1959 I pledged Phi Delta Theta. It is fair to say that I wasn't very well informed about Greek life. But I would soon learn that it was all about in-groups and out-groups. Being a pledge was an intensive exercise in reinforcing one's identify as a prospective member of the fraternity, while minimizing, if not denigrating, the attributes of other fraternities. Thus, the Sigma Alpha Epsilons (SAEs) became Sleep and Eats, and so on, while the Phis could do no wrong. Pledgeship would bring about intimate familiarity with one's pledge brothers, and in several instances friendships that would last a lifetime. The actives, on the other hand, made it their business to remind us of our pledge status. They could of course, harass us at will, but there were special occasions when harassment was formalized and pledges were all subjected to ritual hazing. Some actives would lick their chops at the prospect of giving the pledges grief on these occasions. We were given odd-sounding "gump" nicknames and were regularly reminded of embarrassing personal features or weaknesses. One of those in my case, as you might expect, was my Okie identity. But after I became an active there were fewer and fewer references to my Okieness.

Within a few days of my pledging, Ken Kellam, one of my pledgemates, sidled up to inform me sotto voce that we pledges were staging a "walk". We were "kidnapping" a hapless active and taking him to Lake Pontchartrain Bridge near New Orleans! Green as I was, I had never heard of such a thing! I was appalled, and quickly let my informant know that I couldn't go. I was your basic stick-in-the-mud, a goody-two-shoes. I had papers to write and classes to attend. He said, well, I didn't have much choice if I wanted to remain a pledge. We were ALL in this together, he added. I didn't really know my fellow pledges, but it sounded like a serious threat. So I meekly acquiesced and joined in the plot. We piled into several cars and drove through the night, straight to New Orleans. I couldn't believe my eyes when we went to the middle of the bridge, gave the Phi brother change to make a phone call, and then headed on down to the town of Hammond, home of "Bear" Schneider, one of our pledgemates, to have a good time. That weekend I began to bond with my brothers. Of course, we were all vaguely aware that we would catch hell from the actives when we returned to campus, and hell we surely caught late night sessions featuring calisthenics on Benbrook Dam! But it was all worthwhile.

Truth be known, I was attracted to the prospect of participating in the social life of the fraternity. As much as I thought the hazing of pledges was unnecessary and foolish, I bit my tongue and stuck it out. I looked forward to the monthly parties when the Phis would hire a band and rent a dance hall. It was always a Black band, musicians who knew how to raise the roof. Groups with names like Ray Sharpe and the Razor Blades. I had not had this exposure to such live bands in Oklahoma, but these guys taught me to love the blues. These parties opened up a whole new sensory dimension in me that I would carry through life. I always managed to enjoy myself without the benefit of alcoholic beverages.

To supplement my scholarship income I began washing dishes in the TCU cafeteria my freshman year. I came to know two students from Mexico who also worked there. One of them in particular, Rafael Ruiz, would become a very close friend and eventually my roommate. Rafael was outgoing, affable and charming, and well known throughout the campus. He was a member of DSF and very active in church activities, so we spent a lot of time together. Rafael was quite small and had distinctly Spanish features, unlike most Mexicans whose bloodline is mixed Spanish and Indian. He was a very sensitive young man, concerned about the application of the Social Gospel. I must credit Rafael with awakening in me a sense of social justice.

It was the spring of 1960, and Rafael became involved with a group of students who were planning to picket local cinemas to urge them to admit Blacks. This was the South, and the traditions of segregation died hard. Other students pointed out that we would be breaking the law and disrupting the normal flow of commerce! I must confess that I, too, was hesitant. Was this really my responsibility? After all I didn't know any Black people. But Rafael persuaded me to go with him. As we walked back and forth in front of the cinema carrying picket signs, cars would slow down long enough for the occupants to shout, "Go home, nigger lover! Shame on you, nigger lover!" This was probably my first real awakening to the race issue. My recollection is that the cinema in question remained off limits to Blacks after that. In retrospect, it is indeed ironic that it would be a person from a developing country (this was before the term Third World came into vogue) who would introduce me to social inequality in American society!

Rafael was from Acapulco, where his father managed a hotel and restaurant. He was planning to go home for a few weeks in the summer and asked me to come along. This time it didn't take as much persuading as the protest. We began the lengthy journey in the Greyhound bus terminal in Ft. Worth. This would be my first foray into a developing country, and I was fortunate that I would see Mexico through the eyes of my good Mexican friend. As we headed south across the border from Nuevo Laredo, the roads became rougher (even rougher than in Oklahoma!) and the drivers more careless. We would buy tamales and soft drinks from vendors who ran alongside the bus when we rode into another town. It was a seemingly endless trip that went on for a couple of days. We stopped to spend the night in the city of Puebla where Rafael had relatives. Then it was on along the winding roads of the highlands and down the escarpment to Acapulco Bay. The cool crisp air of Puebla gave way to the warm humid breezes of Acapulco.

We stayed with Rafael's parents in the Hotel Acapulco and went on excursions in and around the resort city, including a boat ride around the bay.

I did my best to resurrect my high school Spanish. Besides wandering along the sandy beaches, we watched the famous divers plunge into the ocean from rocky promontories. It was a wonderful visit, marred only by the occasion hazing by young Mexican boys not happy to see gringos in their midst. The bus ride back to Ft. Worth seemed even longer than the trip down.

Besides joining religious and social groups on campus, I again became active in student activities and government. My sophomore year I served as chairman of the Select Series Committee on the Activities Council. This was my first exposure to the world of planning and logistics for major events, entering into contracts with big name speakers and entertainers, and mounting public relations campaigns. That year we hosted Eleanor Roosevelt and Paul Harvey as guest speakers as well as numerous entertainers such as comedian Brother Dave and the Kingston Trio. I learned the importance of careful planning and follow through, making sure that the plan went smoothly. For my stewardship as an apprentice manager I was rewarded with the position of Director of the Activities Council my junior year. I became an established functionary within student programs, generally associated with both the successes and the failures of those programs.

So naturally I decided to run for Student Congress President in the spring of my junior year. I figured I could count on friends in the Greek as well as independent communities since I had one foot in both. To my knowledge, I didn't have any sworn enemies. On the surface it appeared that I would have a lock on the election, on name recognition alone because I entertained good relations with senior university administrators. A loyal band of supporters helped get out the word and I went about campus glad-handing with a firm handshake and a Howdy Week smile. But when the votes were counted in the primary election I was stunned to learn that I trailed a relative unknown (from another fraternity). Seemingly from out of nowhere he ran a campaign critical of the status quo, charging that I was too closely tied to the administration and demanding an independent student voice. In my naiveté, I was oblivious to the existence of such sentiment. I was devastated, and ready to throw in the towel. But my band of supporters was not ready to quit. They renewed their efforts to get out the vote. Lo and behold, we vanquished the upstart opponent in the run-off! Upon reflection in the years after my tenure as Student Congress President, I have reminded myself that the political culture of Texas is pretty conservative. The students of TCU were not quite ready to follow a Pied Piper into the unknown.

Even after four years as a student in Texas where I felt pretty much at home, I still wore my Oklahoma identity as a badge of honor. In our neck of the woods it was all about football: the epic 100-year old annual Red River Rivalry between the Longhorns of the University of Texas and the Sooners of Oklahoma University. Often as not more than the game would be on the line, since the winner would go on to win a national title. Since 1950 the two teams have won a combined 10 national championships, seven of them going to Oklahoma.

On the day of the Big Game I would tend to forget who my own TCU Horned Frogs were playing. For long periods of time we Okies tended to enjoy the edge in the Red River Rivalry. Furthermore, it is well known that many of the best players on the Sooner teams are recruited from.....horrors....south of the Red River! Hard to swallow for patriotic Texans!

But then, I can no longer afford to be too smug about my attitudes toward Texas and Texans. All three of my siblings followed me across the Red River and have long since taken up residence there, raising their children as Texans. It is fair to say that their own

Oklahoma identify has been substantially watered down, if not entirely diminished. The modest Ponca City property left to us by dad upon his death has been sold, leaving us little reason even to visit Oklahoma. Family reunions these days are most likely to take place on sister Judy's Rambling Oaks Ranch south of Ft. Worth.

Chapter 4

Europe, Summer 1962: Discovering Old Europe and Working in Greece

"I sometimes feel not very useful, carrying stones from here to there, and then from there to here..."

- Jean-Pierre, French participant in the World Council of Churches
- work camp in Greece, in his heavily accented English.

In the summer of 1962, after my junior year at Texas Christian University, I was fortunate to have the opportunity to travel in Europe. The primary objective of the travel was to participate in a World Council of Churches work camp in Greece. It would appear that my itch to see the world that appeared as early as 1956 with travel to Japan had to be scratched again. It should be noted that I had completed a second year of study of the German language, and I felt that I needed to immerse myself in a German-speaking environment. Furthermore, I had just completed a very intensive course in English history and I was conversant in the importance of such arcane subjects as the Council of Whitby in 664, the role of the Angles and Saxons and the Norman Conquest of 1066. Strangely enough, my immersion into English history failed to evoke any particular curiosity about my English (Hull) roots. And the Swedish roots were still tucked into the back of my mind. I was far more taken with the course in the French Revolution, probably because of charismatic Prof. Vardaman than the subject matter per se. I felt that I had a pretty firm grasp of what Europe was about and was ready to see it firsthand.

I was aware that the World Council of Churches sponsored a variety of programs abroad, so I started looking into them. To my chagrin, there seemed to be no programs in Germany available for the period which interested me. So I looked into the alternatives. As a history major, I had always been fascinated by ancient history, the more ancient the better. So when Greece emerged as an alternative I was not altogether disappointed. The historian in me had been awakened early on in Coach Grady Penninger's World History class in High School. No sooner had I learned of my acceptance into the work camp in Elassona, Greece, than I began to plan a European tour to complement it. The organizing principal was to identify friends along the way on whom I could drop in, sign-posts along the way as it were.

New York City   3/July/1962

The first leg of the journey was by Greyhound Bus from Ponca City to New York City. We drove into the Greyhound terminal in midtown Manhattan just as dawn was breaking over Gotham. Richard, my Negro traveling companion from the Bronx, pointed me in the direction of the nearest subway and I was on my way to Columbia University. For a country boy like me, even one who had spent three years in the mid-sized city of Ft. Worth, Cow Town, the City was rather daunting. The subway system was noisy and dirty. There were strange citified looking people seated across from me. I was relieved that it was not night time! Joe Short, my long-time home town friend, had preceded me at TCU and was now in graduate school in Political Science at Columbia. He had invited me to stop in on him before taking off for Europe. I hoped to see two other close friends who were also in the City: Bob Glover, from our church in Ponca City now at Union Theological Seminary, and Rafael Ruiz, my roommate at TCU, from Acapulco, Mexico.

I strolled around with my 35 mm camera snapping scenes right and left: the Interchurch Center, Columbia University's International Houses, the Jewish Theological Seminary, Union Theological Seminary, Julliard School of Music, Grant's Tomb and Barnard College. Two hours later I returned to 170 Claremont and pushed the right button this time, succeeding in getting Joe's attention. The morning agenda proved quite interesting. I attended Joe's class with him, a course in the Political Development of Sub-Saharan Africa. We then headed to the Interchurch Center where I was to register for the work camp in Greece. After paying all my transportation costs, I still had about $500 left for the balance of the trip, a sum I thought should be sufficient. My information packet included a copy of *Europe on Five Dollars a Day* (the traveler's Bible of the day) and I quickly began to familiarize myself with it; this was to be my guide for the next month.

That afternoon found Bob, Rafael and me on a tour of downtown: the United Nations, Grand Central Station, Chase Manhattan Bank, the Empire State Building and Times Square: all icons of American culture known to school children in the farthest reaches of the republic. We stopped off to buy tickets ($3.80 — almost a day's expenses in Europe, I thought to myself) to the Broadway hit of the season, Camelot. Later in the afternoon Rafael captained a group of YMCA "seminarians" on a tour through Harlem. He was his usual effervescent self, perfectly at ease in yet another cultural environment. Here we met with a veritable sea of black faces, more than I had ever seen in one place before.

New York City   *4/July/1962*

Independence Day began with a 9:00 AM orientation session at the Interchurch Center. Three of us underwent a briefing on the mission of the Church, Americans abroad and the World Council of Churches. We then left for Idlewild Airport (later to be known as JFK) from the terminal on 38ᵗʰ Street. After a mad dash to Idlewild through heavy traffic, we were informed of a three-hour delay in our propeller flight on Icelandic (*Loftleider*) Airways. This gave me time to collect my wits and write a few letters. Icelandic was by far cheapest fare available to Europe ($328 compared to $525, the second cheapest). It still seemed to maintain high standards. The food the first night was excellent, and I even allowed myself to try the shot of brandy that followed dessert. I was happy to be on my way to Europe.

We students appeared to be a distinct minority on the flight. I was seated next to a deutsche lady and got a chance to test my German language skills. It was painful to realize how little would come out after two years in German class at TCU! She had been living in Oklahoma City and was more interested in speaking in English than in German. The stewardesses, all blond Icelandic nationals, were very multilingual. The first stop was in Gander, Newfoundland

(Canada), ostensibly for refueling. Three hours later we were still on the ground, wondering how refueling could take so long.

En Route to Europe   *5/July/1962*

At 2:00 A.M. "Gandar Standard Time" we took off. As we landed at Reykjavik Airport in Iceland, there were rumblings of discontent. We trouped through customs and were informed that we would be in Iceland for a while. It is much shorter to fly over Iceland on the way to Europe than to follow the latitudinal line straight east from New York. We learned that Reykyavik was the home of Leif Erickson, the voyager who preceded Christopher Columbus by several centuries in venturing to North America. Today the city has a population of about 70,000. Located 2,675 miles from New York, it is only a short distance from the Arctic Circle. As we descended onto the tarmac, I thought: "This is my first glimpse of Europe." The first hints of European civilization were in evidence as we began (an unscheduled) bus tour of the island: foreign cars driven on the wrong side of the road, people with ruddy complexions and blond hair. Then finally our flight took wing from Gander, landing precisely at noon local time in Reykjavik, Iceland. By now some of the more savvy travelers suspected that we were not following the scheduled flight path. It was a bright sunny day, and I rather enjoyed being out of doors for a while.

Upon returning to the Reykjavik Airport, we began to realize why Icelandic Airways might be the cheapest means to Europe. There would be another three-hour delay before departure for Europe! Another tour of downtown Reykjavik would follow, eliciting comments from the discontented about missing appointments in Europe. Finally, at 2:30 PM we said goodbye to Iceland, anticipating arrival in our destination (Luxembourg) in five and a half hours. We took comfort in the information in the Icelandic brochure that said the company's record was accident-free since its inauguration in 1948. But, alas, the wretched craft again coughed and sputtered and gave up an engine, forcing a landing at Prestwick Airport near Glasgow, Scotland. What began as a novel, non-threatening experience now appeared very disturbing. We were informed that no one would be allowed outside the Prestwick Airport since we were in transit. Another four hours of waiting, without really knowing what was going on! Then, about midnight, we were transported to plush quarters at a Glascow hotel and fed a rush meal. It was announced that the plane would NOT be continuing on to Luxembourg as scheduled. To bed!

Amsterdam, Holland   *6/July/1962*

I was jarred out of my deep slumber by a telephone call informing me that I needed to be downstairs. I made my way down the (Scottish) plaid carpeted stairway for breakfast. A bus took us through the streets of Glascow, back to Prestwick. After a walk around the village of Prestwick, we learned that we had almost been left behind. Behind what?: A Royal Dutch Airlines flight to Amsterdam, our new destination. Since Luxembourg was no longer on the flight schedule, we were all being packed off to various alternative destinations, mine being Amsterdam. Tempers had by now grown very short. Me, I was just along for the ride. Where I landed in Europe was not of particular concern. I stood around, letting my beard grow. My originally flexible plans became even more flexible! An hour later we were on the ground at the Amsterdam Airport.

Icelandic Airways treated us to our last favor, providing dinner and a bus ride into the city. Here a glad-handing American from Chicago introduced himself as a medical student at Leyden University, on his way back to the U.S. on Icelandic Airways. However, due to a delay (sound familiar?) he was in town another day, and so offered to take us on a tour of Amsterdam. At Icelandic Airways' expense, he checked into Hotel Suisse and we left our luggage there. Thence to the bright lights of Amsterdam, down Kalverstraat, across Damstraat to Rembrantspein. The city of Amsterdam is named after the river Amstel that flows through it. Our good fortune (and his always open mouth) led us into a lively conversation with two traveling English school teachers. They, in turn, suggested a pub known as the Bamboo on a very unobtrusive side street that literally swarmed with people, mostly Americans.

The gods again smiled upon us. Beers in hand, Bill and I felt a bit out of place in the Bamboo. At this point two charming Dutch students—Douwe and Eric—rescued us. Striking up a conversation, they suggested that we could stay at Dower's flat. I rode on the back of Eric's motorcycle to a quaint old triangular-shaped room on Leidsekaade Strasse. We were literally wined and dined in extraordinary style until the wee hours. Eric was studying Latin and

Greek and Douwe political science. I felt at once comforted by their hospitality and at the same time uncomfortable with how much more knowledgeable they were about world affairs than I was. Today I spent 10 guilder on a pipe and 10 cents on a phone call today. Bed felt very good tonight, my first in continental Europe.

Amsterdam, Holland   *7/July/1962*

The day began at 10:00 AM as Douwe mapped out a few sights for us to explore. Our first stop was the Stedelyke Museum of Modern Art, not far from Douwe's place. With little understanding of art, I was struck by the Van Goghs and especially the famous painting entitled Night Watch. In the afternoon I hiked over to the rondevaart for a tour of the city by boat. Our guide spoke in English, German and French. Out itinerary included the home of Anne Frank and the tallest church in Amsterdam (285 ft.). I confess that I knew little about Anne Frank and the horrors of the holocaust. None of my courses at TCU had introduced me in any detail to World War II. Our rondevaart cruised into the harbor where we were informed about the Dutch engineering feats involving the construction of dykes to hold back the North Sea. I was reminded of a childhood story of young Peter who held his finger in the dyke and saved his country from inundation! On the way back we saw a Russian-style church and an ocean liner carrying Norwegian school children. For the first time since setting foot on European soil, the sun peaked out from behind the perpetual layer of clouds for a few minutes. I was ecstatic! But as quickly as it appeared, the sun resumed its hiding place.

Back at Douwe's place, we went on a walking tour of his neighborhood. The city is composed of a grid of canals that criss-cross an area that has been reclaimed from the sea by the systems of dykes. In the evening we ate dinner at a Chinese restaurant and then did a bit of pub-crawling. There seemed to be more people on the streets at midnight than at mid-day!

Westeremden, Holland   *8/July/1962*

It had been my intention to visit the village Westeremden if I managed to get to Holland. But not even the travel agency in Amsterdam could tell me exactly where this place was. He thought it might be somewhere in the north of the country, but wasn't sure.

And this, one of the smallest countries in Europe! Why would I want to go to such a place? This is where my TCU classmate Terry White was assigned to a work camp similar to the one where I would be in Greece. Finally, a man in a bookstore got out his map and showed me that Westeremden was located about 20 miles north of Groningen, near the North Sea. It was not without some difficulty that I found a bus going in that direction.

My elementary German was sufficient to converse with the bus driver and confirm that he was going to Westeremden. The countryside was verdant and scenic, although not exactly the picture of Holland I had in mind of tulips, windmills and wooden shoes. The weather was...cold. Very un-summer-like. Upon arrival in the village, we learned from a local couple that the work campers had gone to a neighboring village and would be back in the evening. Meanwhile, they took pity on us and invited us into their home, affording a wonderful opportunity to taste the typical rural fare of Holland. The food they served was delicious and the conversation pleasant. It seems that quite a few Dutch people speak English.

Terry White and his fellow campers soon arrived and we talked of the work they were doing. The group consisted of eight boys and 10 girls from various countries. Their sleeping quarters were in a bauernhof and the conditions were rather rustic. The wretched cold weather had given Terry a touch of bronchitis which he was fighting. In the evening the camp members discussed the work of the day and held Bible study. It seemed to be a rather ecumenical group, held together by a common sense of purpose despite hardships. I was shown to my stall where I was to sleep on a cold floor. Summer in Oklahoma was never like this!

Westermeden, Holland   *9/July/1962*

The grey haze grew lighter and by 6:00 AM we were out in it. The work camp would be completed by July 20, and I was encouraged by the prospect of traveling with Terry after that. We planned to meet up in Berlin on that day. Today I got my first experience in a work camp which seemed to consist of building a hill on the *speergarten*. All of Westeremden converged on that popular site and much of the work consisted of avoiding the scampering children under foot. The work was neither intense nor well organized, but it was the spirit that counted after all! An excursion to Groningen was planned for the afternoon, so the work stopped early. We all bicycled the five kilometers to the train station and were in Groningen by mid-afternoon. A local work camper acted as guide for the camp contingent and we trooped in and out of antique and souvenir shops.

In the evening I took the train back to Amsterdam, saying goodbye to Terry and his crew. The remainder of the day was spent in a leisurely fashion, now that I was feeling increasingly familiar with Amsterdam. Since arriving in Europe, I have not spent anything on lodging, so I'm ahead of the *Europe of Five Dollars a Day* formula. Douwe proved to be a gracious host and insisted on my staying longer. He gave me a nickname—steckelmus—something like sticky bird—because of my crew cut hair and prickly beard, which by now was itching fiercely.

Amsterdam, Holland   *10/July/1962*

Today there was time for a bit more sight-seeing at the Rijksmuseum before departing for my next destination: London. At the Rijksmuseum I spent five guilders on a reproduction of the world's most famous painting, The Nightwatch. Standing on a corner at Leidseplein, the Times Square of Amsterdam, I was amazed at the river of bicycles and scooters that mixed seamlessly with cars and trucks without any apparent loss of life. The major portion of the day was taken up with travel arrangements which would take me via The Hague, Rotterdam, Hook von Holland and Harwich. The entire trip would cost 75 guilders (roughly $21), leaving me a balance of $440. And this was a first class ticket, affording me a sleeping berth for the night. The boat was scheduled to leave Hook von Holland at 10:00 PM. I was to take a train from the Central Station to Hook von Holland departing at 8:30 PM. Although I left with what I imagined to be ample time to catch the boat, I arrived at 8:33 PM, in time to see the Hook von Holland train leaving the station. I recalled my German professor, Herr Wyatt talking about the precision of European trains. But before I had to panic, I learned that there would be another train leaving shortly that could also take me to Hook von Holland by way of The Hague. Good fortune smiled on me again.

London, England   *11/July/1962*

Our boat docked on time at the East Anglian harbor of Harwich (the English pronounce it Harridge) and we quickly disembarked. Here I was for the first time touching ground on which King Arthur had walked and near where William the Conqueror launched his conquest, also the land of Shakespeare. A jumble of historic dates and figures committed to memory in Dr. Potter's English History class came rushing to mind. I proceeded to Chelmsford and then on to London. Liverpool Station, on the east side of London, is one of a dozen train stations in the city, serving both inter and intra-city transit. My first move was to locate the youth hostel headquarters and buy a membership card. The remainder of the morning was spent in a fruitless search for lodging in YOH hostels as well as YMCAs. No room in the inn, so I stashed my luggage in a locker in the train station at Charing Cross Road and resigned myself to sleeping in Trafalgar Square with the rest of the bums.

Just as I stepped outside near the square London Bobbies began congregating along the sides of the streets. Throngs of people lined up, surely in anticipation of some dignitary. Rumor had it that the Queen would be passing by, but it turned out that it was an entourage from some African commonwealth country instead. Nonetheless, it was a momentary diversion that took my mind off my predicament. After a brief lunch I headed over to the American Express where I picked up mail from home waiting for me, then purchased a ticket to School for Scandal at the Haymarket for Thursday night.

Soon afterward I discovered that I was having trouble with my camera and probably had lost a whole role of film. Not a good first day in the Kingdom. Plus my feet were beginning to hurt. What a miserable introduction to London! In the evening, in an effort to forget my troubles, I took in an Italian film near Piccadilly Circus. Finding myself by now thoroughly exhausted, I took a tram to Great Russell Square to look for one of those myriad cheap bed and breakfast places Arthur Frommer promised me in Europe on Five Dollars. By now it was past midnight and I managed to find a B&B that would take me in.

London, England   *12/July/1962*

A late breakfast at 9:30 AM and then another search for cheaper lodging. With a pocket full of coins I began calling around. Success finally came after conferring with the YMCA office on Great Russell Street. I took a room at Mackay's House on Greenville Street for 19 shillings and six pence, about $2.75. Walking back along Great Russell St., I couldn't help noticing the British Museum covering one full block. I decided to spend some time there, especially since admission was free. Perhaps the most famous object in the museum is the Rosetta Stone, confiscated by Napoleon from the town of name in Egypt in 1799. In 1804 it was taken to Britain and since has become renowned because of the three languages inscribed on it. It concerns a decree of Ptolemy VI in 196 B.C. The opening lines list titles belonging to the Pharaoh, followed by a listing of the benefits he conferred upon Egypt. Another famous section in the British Museum, one that appealed to me particularly, is the Elgin Marbles, contributed by the Duke of Elgin. These are remains from the Parthenon, friezes from both east and west pediments. In a short time I would be seeing from whence they came!

The remainder of the afternoon was dedicated to shopping for a sport coat in Soho Square. None of the styles, however, appealed to my American (plebian?) tastes. I decided to save the money for something I really needed.

After a brief nap I set out a bit early to see School for Scandal at the Haymarket. In its present state the Haymarket was constructed in 1821, but it remains well preserved. My seat was on the very last row. As the play progressed, I was sorry that I had not read it more carefully in English Literature class. However, the main scenes were still stuck in my mind. The "scream scene" was well played and the characters in general were superb. Restoration drama came alive from the dusty pages of the text book!

London, England   *13/Friday/1962*

After breakfast at Mackay's House I was greeted with a pleasant surprise: Ms. Johns, the proprietor, informed me that I could stay on another two nights. Bless her heart! I paid her two pounds for the two nights. I had an American roommate who was teaching school in rural Canada. For some reason the sun was shining and the forecast was for an increase in the temperature, up to 70 degrees Fahrenheit. I took my laundry across the street and was obliged to pay an outlandish sum to have a suit dry-cleaned and jeans laundered: one pound for both! My intention to visit Oxford and Stratford on Avon was diverted today when I checked train schedules at the Express. But while there a very pleasant English chap fixed me up with a ticket to My Fair Lady at Drury Lane. He recommended it highly, based on the 36 times he had seen it.

Wandering along Whitehall Street, I was approached by a shabby old man who offered to show me some sights. In all my naiveté I assumed that this gnomish, servile creature just wanted to do me a good turn. Two hours later I realized that this was his way of eking out a living. It cost me a few pence. He did manage to show me a few sights, despite his lack of knowledge of English history, of history in general. At one point my guide knowingly informed me that the Crimean War occurred sometime before World War I! Our tour included 10 Downing Street (under reconstruction), St. James Park, Westminster Abbey and the changing of the guard at Buckingham Palace, all sights that every tourist to London must see. Passing by Victoria Station, I had an impulse to go into an army and navy store to browse, which resulted in my purchasing a raincoat on sale for five pounds ($14). Well, after all, I needed one. After standing in line at Victoria Station for some time I managed to buy a ticket (four pounds) to Paris for Sunday night.

Back at Mackay's House, I rested to the sounds of rock 'n roll on the BBC station. At 6:30 PM I was off to Drury Lane. I found to my surprise that Theater Royal is not actually on Drury Lane, although its stage door faces it. The first impression of the theater was depressing, viewed from the exterior. But once inside, it was a palatial sight, much more impressive than Haymarket. My Fair Lady, the greatest musical of all time, had already been running for five years and was booked at least through the end of the year. The performance could only be described in superlatives. I sat with chills running up and down my spine, especially during the scene in which Liza Dolittle sang about the rain in Spain.

London, England   *14/July/1962*

Today began at the early hour of 4:30 AM, with preparations for travel to Oxford. The constant drizzle outside gave me the opportunity to try out my new English raincoat. I took a taxi (five shillings) to Paddington Station on the West End where I began the journey to the ancient and revered seat of English higher learning. The pastoral countryside was a rich green, owing to all the rain. Still, I would have traded a bit of sunshine for all the moisture. I was missing July weather in Oklahoma: hot and dry. Upon reaching the queen of medieval English university cities, I set out on foot. My perambulation of the town took me around the various colleges (28 of them in all) that comprise the university.

I stopped in at the Church of Virgin St. Mary and at Christ Church College. And I thought perhaps Pete Dawkins (All American Army football player) would appreciate my visiting him, but unfortunately his next session wasn't to start until October.

After a two-hour stay at Oxford, I boarded the train again, and headed toward Stratford on Avon, home of the great Bard. I guess I was surprised by how small Stratford is, given its outsized reputation as the home of William Shakespeare. But it well deserves its reputation for scenic beauty, and beneath the façade of Shakespearean era architecture, it is really quite a modern, even industrial town. At 2:30 PM I attended the matinee showing of Measure for Measure at the Royal Shakespeare Theatre on the river. There being no seating tickets left, I paid three shillings to stand in the back. And although I didn't relish shifting from one foot to another, the performance really made the Old Bard come alive. This play, described as one of his darker comedies, is almost a tragedy. The comic relief was excellent, the tragic situation typical of Shakespeare's existential questions.

As with all English stage productions, the performance was closed with singing of God Save the Queen. I must say that the high point of my stay in Merry England has been these superb stage productions.

London, England   *15/July/1962*

As I was dressing for another day of sight-seeing, I looked outside and concluded that it would be another bloody nasty day of drizzle and cold. I made my way down Holbarn Street to the "City", the part of London that is the financial and commercial center, to St. Paul's Cathedral. I was just in time for the 10:30 AM matins and sermon. Sitting under the dome of the most famous church in all of Protestantism, I felt the majesty and power of 300 years. Looking about at the large number of people awkwardly going through the matins, I suspected that perhaps 90% of us were tourists. The choir was magnificent, their voices filling the whole cathedral. The sermon had as its theme unrestrained pacifism, a la Bertrand Russell.

The pastor insisted that the churches must not persist in building material might, since history has shown that nationalism and an obsession with materialism have always led to war. Churches, he argued, are custodians of a better way. Then he leveled a direct charge at the Archbishop of Canterbury who had said, "Pray for peace, but keep your powder dry." The pastor indicated that he had just returned from a Moscow peace conference where he had a private conversation with Mr. Khrushchev. He described the Soviet leader as congenial and personable. In effect, he concluded, if our faith is anything it is realism. I concluded that this must be the spiritual home of the Fabian Socialists.

I took another brief stroll down to Tower Hill and London Bridge, then caught a boat ride back up to Westminster. Here I stumbled onto another church service in progress and wandered in. The sermon here was rather moralistic and the prayers seemed to be for anybody and everybody in England with royal blood. After the service I made a tour of the Abbey observing the marble tombs of England's' revered. The size of the tombstones seemed disproportionate to their service to country or genius. Charles Darwin, for example, rated only a tiny marker. On the way back to the hotel to pack I stopped off for a Wimpy burger, which I felt paled by comparison with a good old American hamburger.

The train for Paris left at 9:00 PM and I said goodbye to England. On board the ship from Newhaven to Dieppe across the English Channel, a good time was had by all, except of course those trying to sleep. I found myself engaged in conversation with a U.S. Air Force mechanic and a pint-sized English paratrooper. The latter was pure Cockney, straight out of My Fair Lady, with a conspicuous absence of his "h's". We in turn got to joshing with a group of English elementary school boys on excursion until we docked at Dieppe around 3:00 AM. I reckon that England is about $50 richer for my having sojourned here for four days.

Paris, France   *16/July/1962*

Parisians had just had their annual celebration of the greatest event in French history on the 14th of July: Bastille Day. So I missed it. By 6:00 AM we arrived in not-so-gay Paris, bringing with us the soggy English weather. I spent a considerable amount of time trying to obtain French francs, deciding what to do and where to go first. I took the metro (underground) across town from St. Lazare Station to the Left Bank *(Rive Gauche)* to look for a youth hostel (listings, of course, in *Europe on Five Dollars)*. I was nearing desperation when fortune once again smiled on me. As I wandered along *Rue St. Michel*, two Californians detected my forlorn appearance and invited me to accompany them to the UNESCO-sponsored hostel on *Rue St. Jacques* in the heart of the Latin Quarter, where, presumably, it all happens. Lodging at the UNESCO hostel was four francs (the equivalent of 80 cents) a night, breakfast included and dinner was two francs. Some 60 international students are maintained for a maximum of four nights each, representing a true melting pot of transients from East Germany to Italy and beyond. Once settled in, I did a bit of window shopping in the vicinity. My ordeal of the day brought physical fatigue and guaranteed an early bedtime.

Paris, France   *17/July/1962*

The hostel breakfast consisted of bread and coffee. At least today promised to be partly sunny for a change. My first order of business was a stop at the American Express, hoping for mail from home and to purchase a train ticket on to Koln, Germany. There was a letter from the Hulls and I bought the ticket for 42 francs (about $8). Without much of a game plan, I struck out toward the Sorbonne, the Parisian university that seemed to attract American students. Already my lack of French language skills proved to be a problem. Fewer people are inclined to countenance non-French speaking Anglophones here. I made a desultory effort to locate a TCU student who was supposed to be studying there. Failing that, I stumbled upon a class being held in a large auditorium in French.

I invited myself in for a while, but managed only to ascertain that the topic had something to do with Renoir and Velasquez. The remainder of the day was taken up with a cursory tour of the Right Bank (Rive Droite), including Notre Dame Cathedral, Hotel de Ville, the Tuileries, the Louvre and then back to the UNESCO hostel. Dinner was preceded by a hot shower and hand-washing of personal items. Counting my coins and anticipating the remainder of my journey to Greece, I forewent the temptation to go out on the town and taste the tantalizing night life of the Latin Quarter.

Paris, France   *18/July/1962*

I hitched a ride to the American Express (my home away from home) on the back of a scooter with a fellow hostelier. No mail this time. I then headed straight for the not-to-be-missed Louvre Museum which opened at 10:00 AM. My visit here lasted four hours, and even that was not nearly enough time. According to the pamphlet I bought upon entering the Louvre, this is the largest palace in the world, an amalgam of various architectural types. The most well known displays in the museum include the Venus de Milo, the Winged Victory of Samothrace and the Mona Lisa, all carted off by procurers from their original homelands.

At lunch near the UNESCO hostel, I happened onto another Californian, this one a UCLA sociology major. Since he, too, was traveling alone, we decided to join forces for the day. Neither of us had yet seen the Eiffel Tower (another must see) so that was our first stop. This famous structure, at 900 ft. in height, is allegedly the third highest structure in the world. (I neglected to inquire which were the first two!) We jammed into the elevator and made the obligatory ride to the top. Helas, the dense fog (smog?) obscured our vision of the city. But then, one is apparently supposed to visit the Tower with a lover, so I will have to return some day.

Back at the hostel, I had a hearty dinner of omelet and rice in the company of another Californian, this one Jewish and returning home after of year of study in Israel. Later I talked my friend into accompanying me to the Place Pigalle, the section of Paris known for its world famous night club, the Moulin Rouge. The ladies of the night, plying their trade along the sidewalks, were less than subtle. We spent most of our time watching a would-be Houdini work his way out of chains...mainly by working up a sweat! At the top of the highest point in Paris is its newest cathedral, Sacre Coeur, which is very distinctive for its Arabesque architecture and maintains a commanding view of the city. We were told that the French don't really like the Sacre Coeur because it is not French enough. We arrived back at the hostel just in time for the midnight curfew.

Paris   *19/July/1962*

Again the day began with a trip to the American Express where letters awaited me. This was the day for visiting the famous Versailles Palace. I took a train from Mont Parnasse to get there. With all my worldly experience on urban subway systems, I am now prepared to make a comparison. The London underground is better than either the New York subway or Paris metro, surely faster than the latter and cleaner than the former. But the Amsterdam tram system beats them all for its efficiency and cleanliness. I found the advertising in the French metro to be rather risqué, showing more skin than I was accustomed to seeing. I was about to encounter my first real snafu on an urban train system.

As I mentioned, my destination was Versailles, but due to some misunderstanding I missed the Versailles exit and went to St. Cyr. After a couple of rides back and forth along the line, I gave up and hiked some three miles back to the Palace. The back of the Palace is a splendid sylvan scene, an intricate network of flower gardens, shrubbery and walkways; the playground of King Louis XVI and his retinue. Without spending money on tour tickets, I walked the grounds of Versailles and tried to soak up the richness of its history. Back on the train, I managed not to miss my next destination, which was the Invalides Palace. Here I paid homage to the greatest of all Frenchmen, Napoleon Bonaparte. I wandered down the Champs de Mars, across the river to the Champs Elysee, thence to the Arc de Triomphe. Surely this boulevard deserves all its renown as the penultimate in chic.

My train left at 11:20 PM, and it proved to be excruciatingly slow. What with all the stops along the way, it was a rather sleepless night. My objective was to meet Terry in Berlin on the 20th, which meant that I should be there by the following day.

En Route to Berlin, Germany   *20/July/1962*

For a couple of hours after arriving in Koln I strolled around, looking for the great Cathedral that was the subject of a travel poster that had been tacked to my wall at school. Sure enough, it was even more imposing than it looked on the poster. I decided to take the

Rhine boat up the river to Bonn, a pleasant trip through industrial flatlands. It is said that the most scenic portion of the Rhineland is up toward Koblenz, but time didn't allow me to go that far. By noon I had arrived in the capital of the West German Republic, a smallish city nestled at the foot of its fabled seven hills (reminiscent of Rome?). It was a bright sunny day, the first really sunny day since my arrival in Europe. Bonn was so new and clean that it looked as though it had sprung full grown overnight as the goddess Athena. So my first impression of Germany was much better than the previous countries I visited.

Since Terry was not due to arrive until mid-afternoon, I toured the town am fuss as usual. Bonn is well known as the birthplace of Ludwig von Beethoven. His historic home must be the only really old building left standing besides the church. My spirits did an about-face when Terry didn't show up at the appointed time. But as fortune would have it, he had only been delayed by missing a change of trains in Koln and arrived on the very next train. Hence, my narrative resumed the plural and my spirits soared, pleased to once again have a familiar traveling companion. We decided to have a real full-sized meal for a change to celebrate our reunion, and then to take the night train to Berlin. There followed another restless, sleep-deprived night on the over-crowded train. Although the German trains seemed considerably faster than elsewhere in Europe, they didn't offer the second class traveler much comfort. We spent most of the night in the aisle!

Berlin, West Germany   *21/July/1962*

By 3:30 AM it was already daylight when the train stopped at the border between West and East Germany. This was the infamous Iron Curtain that Churchill had referred to in his speech at Westminster College in Missouri. Fully armed soldiers boarded the train and began to scrupulously scrutinize every inch of every berth, including the toilets. It was rather unnerving since we really didn't know what they were after. Then we were obliged to purchase a visa for entry into East Germany, even though the train was to arrive in Berlin, West Germany. The remainder of the trip trough East Germany was uneventful, but the villages along the way had a rather gloomy and shabby appearance. The volpos (armed military) everywhere gave off an ominous air.

We arrived in the city of West Berlin about 6:30 AM at the Hardensberg Bahnhof, just down the street from the famous old battered Lutheran Church which was left by Berliners as a symbol of the destruction and devastation the city had suffered in World War II. The booming West Berlin economy was everywhere in evidence in the shiny new sky-scrapers and expansive boulevards full of late-model cars.

Nowhere was the prosperity more greatly manifested than in the smart new U-Bahn (subway) system that put New York, London and Paris systems to shame! And there were no tacky advertisements on the walls! After considerable difficulty, Terry and pooled our ignorance and managed to locate the Ecumenical Headquarters in suburban West Berlin. Our objective was to have a brief taste of another church-sponsored work camp. The lady who greeted us there, a Domine in the Dutch Reformed Church, graciously arranged for us to stay with the group that was engaged in the renovation of an old folks' home. And a wonderful reception it was, too, in a stylish new youth center owned by the Lutheran Church! We learned that the project was sponsored by the Church of the Brethren, a denomination with a long history of pacifism both here and in the U.S. Although rather small, the government allowed Brethren conscientious objectors to participate in church-sponsored projects like this in lieu of military service.

Again with some difficulty, Terry and I managed to find the project site—a jungenheim (youth hostel)—in the eastern sector of West Berlin, close to The Wall. So we could now look forward to three nights of free lodging in clean beds and wholesome food, provided we would do our share of the work. Already we could sense the ecumenical spirit of camaraderie and fellowship. We melted into bed, secure in the feeling that this was going to be a positive experience.

However, being so close to The Wall, it warranted further comment in the historical context of our visit to Berlin. The Berlin Wall had been erected not quite a year before, during the night of August 13, 1961. It was a weekend and most Berliners slept while the East German government began to close the border. In the early morning of that Sunday most of the initial work was done and the border to West Berlin was closed. The East German troops had begun to tear up streets and to install barbed wire entanglement and fences through Berlin. The first concrete elements and large square blocks were used first in the first two days. Within the next months the first generation of the Berlin Wall was built up: a wall consisting of concrete elements and square blocks. A second Wall had been built just the month before in June, in order to prevent East Germans from escaping to the West. The first Wall was improved during the next years and it would become difficult to distinguish between the first and the second generation of the Wall.

Then, after closing the border on August 13, 1961, the only persons allowed to enter East Berlin via the crossing point at Friedrichstrasse were tourists from abroad, diplomats and the military personnel of the Western Powers. Soon the U.S. military police opened a checkpoint at Friedrichstrasse. The other two checkpoints were Helmstedt and Dreilinden at the border between West Berlin and East Germany. Based on the phonetic alphabet, the Helmstedt checkpoint was called Alpha, Dreilinden Checkpoint Bravo and the checkpoint at Friedrichstrasse was given the name Checkpoint Charlie. The latter would acquire the most notoriety during the years of the Cold War.

West Berlin   *22/July/1962*

We were awakened by the clanging of church bells outside our window and a bright sun streaming through. Breakfast was very refreshing and nourishing...and free. I wondered whether work camp life in Greece would be more frugal. We were joined by a Moslem boy from Turkey, making the group even more ecumenical than before. We trooped downstairs to the church service, since our quarters were actually in the church. Attendance at the service was very sparse—as it apparently is everywhere in a very secular Europe—although this church had a "membership" of some 22,000 people. We were given to understand that in Germany everyone is obliged to pay "taxes" (tithes) to the church, whether or not they go to church. The sermon, in German, gave me an opportunity to practice my language comprehension. It was surprisingly easy, since the text was taken from the New Testament and told the story of St. Peter's conversion.

The city of Berlin had arranged to provide a bus tour for the group which began after services. Our guide explained that the city had originally consisted of many smaller villages clustered along the Spree River. Now it contained a population of 3.3 million inhabitants. Our trip along die mauern was the highlight of my European travel thus far, bringing as it did the whole East-West crisis into vivid, symbolic focus. It was hard to comprehend how The Wall had already disrupted families, businesses and commerce in the city, not to mention world politics. Our bus went north along Karl Marx Strasse where we caught our first glimpse of The Wall. The guide explained that the only West Berliners allowed into East Berlin were professionals such as doctors and of course members of the Communist Party. Perhaps the most striking portion of our tour was along Bernauer Strasse where thousands had already escaped East Berlin by jumping out of houses before they were cemented shut. The guide informed us that the material used in them, as well as The Wall itself, could have been used to construct 8,000 apartment buildings.

We then drove through a district featuring avant guarde architectural structures designed by men of all nationalities. We passed by Kongresshall, known affectionately by the Germans as "the pregnant oyster" because of its shape. The building was donated to West Germany by the Ben Franklin Foundation. We saw a sort of depot where the West Berlin government was storing provisions: food and emergency supplies in the event of a crisis. It was hard to imagine that West Berliners lived in a perpetual state of danger and uncertainty.

West Berlin   *23/July/1962*

In the morning our group took the U-bahn to the brand new European House for a couple of films and indoctrination about the Berlin crisis. The films dramatically illustrated the training of East German youth and the construction of The Wall, places we had seen the day before. To recap the information in the films, the current crisis is retraced (pretend now that I am an eighth grade social studies teacher). Germany surrendered unconditionally on May 8, 1945. Zones of occupation were drawn up in the London Protocol. An Allied Council composed of zonal commanders was established as a loose coalition with each commander having a veto. Churchill, Stalin and Roosevelt met to divide Germany into occupation zones, at which time Stalin's plan to divide it into three parts prevailed. Each power was to have complete control in its zone, a plan that fit Stalin's purpose just fine. However, when the West proposed to give France a zone the Soviets opposed the idea. At the time, the

Eastern region of Germany counted about 16 million inhabitants. Since the beginning of the Cold War and Soviet domination of East Germany, however, some three million people have escaped to the West through West Berlin. Roosevelt accepted the plan but Churchill wanted further division for assurance.

The Western powers wanted to institute a democratic state with membership in the United Nations. The Potsdam Agreement of 1945 provided for a democratic German state with free political parties, no centralized government and a judicial system. It was hoped that this decentralization would help prevent the rise of another Nazi regime. In the Western zone the spirit of Potsdam was incorporated into the planning. In the Eastern zone Stalin pursued his own course of establishing Leninist structures. The East German state was put under a Soviet puppet head of state run by the Communist Party. The Marxist notion of class struggle and the dictatorship of the proletariat were put into effect and by 1950 the party was in complete control. In 1958 Khrushchev would declare the Potsdam Agreement null and void.

In the light of Marxist ideology envisaging a world proletarian revolution, it became necessary for the Soviets to build The Wall in order to protect the interests of the working class. As early as 1917, Lenin had written that Germany must be taken by the proletarians because of its industrial power that should be harnessed to socialist objectives. In Marxian terms, when historical conditions are ripe for revolution it is inevitable, but this does not mean that the revolution should not benefit from a little armed might. All actions may be justified in the name of the working class, regardless of the consequences. Free elections are today non-existent since the "unity list" gives the voter only the choice of voting yes or no on whatever the issue might be.

The current relationship between East and West Berlin has been defined in several important ways. Since 1947 the only way for East Berliners to go to the West has been limited to Berlin. People in the East have had no objective information about public affairs since it all emanates from the state. So before August 1961 there were some 80,000 East Germans coming to West Berlin daily, simply to have access to different sources of information (and probably to shop!). That has been stopped cold with The Wall. In 1948, one of the first crises erupted over Berlin as a result of a Soviet blockade which resulted in the Berlin Airlift, drawing Western powers closer together in a united effort. Not only did the airlift succeed, it precipitated a free trade agreement aimed at keeping West Berlin in the Western camp.

The East German economy in 1962 is less than robust. Whatever existed at the end of World War II was to be demolished and a new socialist economy built in its place. Conditions of a dictatorship of the proletariat have largely been fulfilled through a centralized government controlled by the Soviets. The East German economy is successful in only a few sectors: the optical, photographic and mechanical industries. The most dramatic aspect of the East German economy are its imports with West Germany, critical to its survival, with a view toward development of military and nuclear power. The East German economy is still dependent upon the West.

Each and every change in world politics is felt in vulnerable West Berlin, cut off as it is from the rest of West Germany. The separation from the rest of West Germany has had a tremendous effect on the West Berliners. They expected President Kennedy to go to war over the construction of The Wall, but that did not happen. Not until 1963 did the President come to Berlin and make his now-famous speech in which he stated emphatically, Ich bin ein Berliner. (I'm a Berliner). And even then, Kennedy said he would fight only over the rights of the West Berliners.

West Berlin   *24/July/1962*

We were up at 5:30 AM, greeted by a bright sun. This was the first work day of the camp, begun by dividing into groups of three and four. We packed ladders, paint and paint brushes and hiked for half an hour to our work destination. Within the group was a Swedish girl, Birgitta, who was very reserved and shy, but quite attractive. She had never been south of her home north of the Arctic Circle before, but spoke five languages and could read Greek! Such genius! I reflected momentarily on my own Swedish roots, but then couldn't think of anything we had in common. The sprightly lady for whom we were working (we called her Brunhilde) was anything but reserved. She recounted, in German, her tribulations in East Berlin before coming to West Berlin to settle. Her recitation was tragicomic: when we weren't crying we were laughing at her story.

Meanwhile, Terry had managed to come down with some sort of

ailment and was undergoing tests at the hospital. So it appeared that I would have to linger on in Berlin a while longer if I were to travel with him. In the evening the youth from the church conducted a bilingual Bible study on the Beatitudes.

Eva Balardich, the co-leader of the work camp, did a remarkable job of translating. Afterwards, two boys from Lebanon (University of Beirut) suggested that I accompany them to some sort of telecast at The Wall. We soon learned that this was the first "telstar" production from Berlin. As far as I was able to ascertain, this was a live program featuring NBC's Pearce Anderson and being transmitted to London and on to New York. We watched until 1:30 AM as tension mounted. The East Germans were apparently loading guns with water bombs and tear gas for use along The Wall. I never understood quite what it was about.

West Berlin   *25/July/1962*

Our redecorating work began as it had the day before, but we were held up because the wallpaper was considered too drab. While attempts were being made to procure a better color, I decided to visit Terry. An hour's ride on the U-bahn from the extreme southeast to southwest took me to his hospital on Bussealle. I have yet to see anyone pushed or shoved while getting in or out of the U-bahn. Terry informed me that he would be released by Friday, so we decided to leave for Frankfurt then.

It had been my intention to see East Berlin since I came to the city. So in the afternoon I set out with a couple of friends from the work camp on the U-bahn to Check Point Charlie. Here I changed five West German deutschmarks into East German currency for subway fare and from there we went straight to Alexander Platz in East Berlin. Since we had no particular destination, we wandered along until we stumbled upon an anti-West Berlin exposition. Here we were presented with lots of brochures of East German propaganda and a guide who was especially friendly. On our walk-around we encountered a worker who was quite proud of his work as superintendent of a street-cleaning crew.

But the striking aspect of our brief tour through East Berlin was the city itself. For all we could determine from the condition of many of the buildings, World War II might have ended last month.

We walked down to Marx-Engels Platz, along Unter von Linden to the Brandenburg Gate. Nothing but eery silence, a few cars and a handful of other tourists! At Checkpoint Charlie we had promised the guard we would be back by the 9::00 PM curfew so we started early just to make sure we didn't miss it.

West Berlin   *26/July/1962*

Meanwhile, the Berlin work camp project continued its task of wallpapering, which I joined while waiting for Terry to be roadworthy. I had been informed that he would have to stay until Monday so I again went to visit him and take him some personal items. We both agreed that I should go on ahead since Terry was not feeling strong enough to travel. We said goodbye and went our separate ways. I was sad, both for him and myself because I had enjoyed our times traveling together.

Back at the work camp project, I checked on my laundry and paid another outlandish sum of $3.00 for two pair of pants and a shirt. I arrived back at the jungenheim just in time for "national evening" under the direction of the Swedish girls. Our supper of Swedish blueberry pancakes was superb! Birgitta gave a very interesting presentation about Swedish culture and cuisine. Now that my "tour of duty" here in Berlin was coming to a close, I felt that this had been the most positive experience thus far in Europe. The personalities represented in the project were varied and fascinating. I could only hope that my work camp in Greece would be as fruitful.

West Berlin   *27/July/1962*

It had been my intention to leave Berlin on the 10:19 AM train. But when Denny, a fellow work camper, asked if I was interested in going to East Berlin with him I decided to have another look. This time we went to Marx-Lenin Strasse, the former Stalin Allee, renamed for reasons I wasn't quite clear about and lined with apartment buildings. Walking westward, we came to Alexander Platz, then Rathous Strasse and back to Marx-Lenin Platz. From there we passed Humbolt University and the State Opera House. My lasting impression of East Berlin was of a very somber, rather shabby ambiance and very few people. Of course, I did not get back in time for the 10:19 AM train, but I had already begun to feel nostalgic about my experience in Berlin so my emotions were mixed.

En route West Berlin to Frankfurt

28/July/1962

Today marked a month away from home. I was awake at 5:30 AM and on my way to meet Terry by 8:00 AM to say goodbye once again. And lo, he was now in much better shape and pronounced hiself ready to travel! The weather in Berlin had been almost a taste of Texas: thunderstorms, gusty winds and clouds interspersed with bright sunshine. After purchasing our tickets to Hannover (we could only go into West Germany through that corridor), I still had over $300 in my wallet. I was still within budget.

As before, we found the trains through East Germany packed with people and slow as well. But Terry and I were undeterred. We had stocked up on fruit and bread and ate gluttonously along the way. At Hannover we were fortunate to catch a snellzug (fast train) to Frankfurt. For the first time I really enjoyed the train ride in comfort, enhanced by beautiful scenery. The train arrived in Frankfurt by 9:00 PM and we began to encounter the usual complications of finding a place to stay. Consulting my Bible, Europe on Five Dollars, we decided on a couple of places which were already full. In desperation, we finally pulled into a nice hotel just off Bahnhof Strasse and paid 10 DM (deutschmarks) a piece. It hardly seemed possible that this was only the third hotel I'd stayed in during the month of traveling. And this was the nicest and cheapest by far.

We tested Frommer again by going to eat at the International Grille and were pleasantly pleased. However, the price he quoted in the book was rather lower than we paid. We sat down beside a young Greek man who was a student of philosophy in Frankfurt. We were subsequently engaged in conversation over the merits of Marxism and the proletariat. His contention was that there would be a war soon unless the working class were accorded equal economic rights to the bourgeoisie. Terry countered him somewhat persistently, but the language barrier proved to be too great. We were in bed shortly after midnight. One month without a haircut, I was feeling a bit shaggy!

En route Frankfurt to Rome

29/July/1962

Again we fought the crowds on the train but finally succeeded in finding good seats all the way to Milan, Italy. By noon we were in Basel, Switzerland and a few hours later in Lucerne. Here, surely, is the most magnificent stretch of railway anywhere to be found. The Alpine scenery was truly spectacular. In Switzerland there was a mixture of German, French and Italian being spoken, but as we headed south into northern Italy it was all Italian. The Lake Lucerne region was breath-taking, with tiny mountainside chalets and clear running streams down from the Alps. Just on the other side of the lakes the sun burst forth through the clouds and stayed with us from there on. The air became warmer the further south we went.

Coming into Milan, there was magnificent view of a highly industrialized city and modern sky-scrapers. Regrettably though, it was obscured by a series of tunnels. Once on the ground in Milan, Terry took charge and we found a nice hotel one block from the station for about $2.00 (1300 lira). As we walked down toward the great cathedral of Milan, Terry was seized with the impulse to wander into a big pastry shop, so we ended up eating sweets for dinner. We took time exposure pictures of the Piazza Duomo and La Scala Opera House. It was interesting for me to try to carry on conversations with people in Spanish, assuming it to be similar enough to Italian that they would understand me.

Rome, Italy   *30/July/1962*

We began the third leg of our trip to Rome with another early morning departure from Milan. The train passed through the famous Renaissance cities of Parma, Bologna and Florence. I was sorry that in my rush to get to Greece we would not be allocating any time to this area so rich in history. The warm air and bright sun provided a welcome relief from the general gloominess of the lands north of the Alps. I felt that I was going home! We crossed the Tiber River several times as it meandered through plains lined with rugged mountainous terrain. By this time we were becoming tired of trains and anxious to get to Rome.

Our arrival in the Eternal City was in the most ultra-modern train station I had ever seen. Our first move, as usual, was to seek out accommodation. We settled on a modest ($1.60, one thousand lira) pension house near the Coliseum. Naturally, our first impulse was to visit this ancient ruin known throughout the world. I could already sense that this city exuding history was likely to be my favorite European city. Even though I had never taken a university level Roman history course, I was an avid student of both Greek and Roman history. As we were walking toward the Coliseum I noticed a billboard advertising the Opera Aida at the Caracella Theater, alleged to be the largest outdoor theater anywhere in the world. We asked our landlady about how to get tickets for Aida and then managed to get reservations for a 9:00 PM performance. Terry and I were bowled over by the grandiose production of Aida, said to be the greatest opera ever written by Verdi, considered by many to be the greatest of all operas. And we were amazed by the abundance of Americans in the audience.

Rome, Italy   *31/July/1962*

Terry and I were awakened from a deep slumber by the constant flow of traffic on the street below our window. Looking out, we could see the Cathedral of St. Maria Maggiori, the largest church dedicated to the Virgin Mary. We made the ritual trip to the American Express, walking down the Spanish Steps to the Piazza Spagna. The scene was straight out of travel brochures: bright sunlight, pigeons flocking toward outstretched hands hopeful of food, and a veritable swarm of tourists like ourselves. I was disappointed after standing in the mail line (mine is always the longest) not to have received a single letter. Then there was another line for cashing traveler's checks, another for getting tickets to Greece. On the upside, I learned that my whole fare would be less than $20.00, including a night in the seaport of Brindisi. This American Express was more packed than all the others and some of the Americans had a very shabby appearance.

The morning having been taken up with red tape and misinformation, we then set out to do some serious sight-seeing. This was really the first time I felt that being a tourist was not a task: we assured ourselves it was going to be a real Roman Holiday. The many fountains in the piazzas give the city a special aura, different from all the others I had seen. Rome is surely the worst place in Europe for pedestrians. If there are street lights anywhere, no one pays them much attention. For lunch we bought some fresh bread, cheese and fruit, then went into a wine shop for a modest-priced Chianti—a feast all for only 50 cents a piece. We sat on the steps of the Fontana de Trevi of three coins-in-a-fountain fame. Finishing our feast and washing it down with wine, we walked toward the memorial to the man known as the father of Italy, Victor Emmanuel. The view from there looking out over the Eternal City was itself worth the price of admission.

Map in hand, we negotiated the traffic and tourists to the Pantheon with its awe-inspiring open-air dome 30 feet in diameter. With well developed map-reading skills, I directed us to the ruins of the Roman Forum. Somehow we seemed to have arrived there just in time for a spectacular sunset that illuminated these ancient remains. Across the street was a Metro stop which we decided to take back to the pension to give our weary feet a break. Not being in the least bit familiar with the Roman Metro system or conversant in the Italian language, we failed to get out at the right exit. For a while we were like Charlie on the MTA, going back and forth until we finally reached our pension exit. Happily, for some reason there were few passengers on the train so it could have been much worse. This is surely is the most aesthetic urban transit system we have seen yet in Europe, with its ornate and gilded walls.

Back at the pension, we enjoyed a steaming bath and I tried to scrub off three weeks' worth of dirt that had accumulated on the bottoms of my feet. By 10:30 PM we were ready to step out on the town for dinner, fitting into the rhythm of Roman life. Again we took pot luck and wandered into an Americanized ristorante. A house band played a mixture of typical American songs and Italian folk songs and flirted with a table of older women. Within the hour and a half or two that we were there three or four American Express bus tours disgorged American tourists. Our luck with the prezzo fisso (fixed price) was not quite as good as it had been the night before. We heard a rumor this evening that Pope John would make an appearance at the Vatican the following day, so we started making plans to be there.

Rome, Italy   *1/August/1962*

Working on the rumor about the Pope, we were up early and off to St. Peter's, the largest church in all Christendom. Immediately I felt that this was the most beautiful of all cathedrals I had seen thus far, especially the frescoes in the interior. Of course, the thousands of milling tourists were something of a distraction to anyone bent on spiritual inspiration. Sure enough, the rumor proved to be true. Pope John and his entourage were in a funeral procession for a recently deceased cardinal.

We stopped in at the Vatican museum to look for mementos of our visit. I was taken with the open porticos and outdoor gardens, but especially with Michelangelo's Pieta and the Sistine Chapel. We hurried back to the American Express to cash traveler's checks, only to find it closed. So we had sandwiches and shared a bottle of wine on the Spanish Steps. We dedicated the remainder of the afternoon to visiting the Appian Way and the Catacombs, burial grounds for Christian martyrs during days of the Roman Empire. We made it back to the American Express before it closed and I was pleased to see two letters from home waiting for me that they neglected to tell me about the previous day.

Terry and I were now coming to a parting of the ways, this time for sure. We packed our belongings and checked out of the pension in time for Terry to catch his 8:30 PM train back to Switzerland and two more weeks of travel. Now the saga reverts once again to the singular. And a sad tale it is indeed. The train ride from Rome to the seaport of Brindisi was excruciatingly painful. As is often the case, I was misinformed or perhaps misunderstood the departure time. I arrived a little after midnight, just as the train was about to leave, and found no seats available. Sleeping in the hallways with people stepping over and around me was no fun at all. As I prepared to leave Rome, I paused to reflect on our brief stay here. Italians, in my view, are boisterous and argumentative, always seemingly at each other's throats. Mama mia! And I have to make this observation about European women in general, not just Italians: they don't shave their legs. To my American way of thinking it was a bit off-putting.

En route from Brindisi to Patros, Greece   *2/August/1962*

The beautiful bustling seaport town of Brindisi on the southeasern coast of Italy was a welcome relief after the miserable train ride. Here is the terminus of the famed Appian Way, the birthplace of the immortal poet Virgil, and Rome's gateway to the east. It was here in the natural harbor that Caesar blocked Pompey's fleet and thus gained sole control of Rome. All of which appealed to my keen sense of history. Because of all the free time at my disposal before leaving on the good ship Atreus of the Epiriotiki Lines at 7:00 PM, I decided upon a haircut, the first since leaving home. On the way down to the docks I was told of a beach just on the other side of the canal. So I took a boat over there and spent a pleasant afternoon snoozing on the sand. A juke box nearby was playing Chubby Checker songs over and over.

Another strange bit of luck came my way as I was checking out my luggage at the train station. A tall, shabbily-dressed man next to me was also scheduled to leave that evening on the Atreus. Geoffrey was an Australian who described himself as a freelance writer. He had spent quite a bit of time in Greece before and was eager to return there. While waiting for the ship to set sail, we ensconced ourselves at a sidewalk café where we traded life stories. Geoffrey was an avowed atheist and he smiled wryly when I told him I was on the way to a World Council of Churches work camp in Greece. After an hour of discussion on the subject of religion, Geoffrey noted that I was only the second "sensible Christian" he had ever encountered. I wasn't sure whether to take this as a compliment or not.

However, Geoffrey was decidedly passionate about Greece and things Grecian. He became my window onto Greece. He was a very perceptive and sensitive fellow, and when he began talking about his experiences in Greece

I sat in rapt attention. My understanding of Greece was limited to the classical period and I really didn't have much notion of modern-day Greece. I had a gap of about two millennia to fill in. Geoffrey's perspective was very contemporary. He asserted that the Greeks of today were quite congenial, fiercely nationalistic, but very poor. He described them as the most opinionated people on earth, stemming from their deep-seated sense of independence.

We set sail from Brindisi at 7:30 PM on the Atreus, loaded to the hilt with students from all over Europe in the second class section. Surprising enough, there were few Americans. Within a few hours I was ready for bed, which in my case was a wooden bench and a raincoat. A few feet away on the deck there were four South African girls curled up in sleeping bags on deck chairs. Although it got rather cool as the night wore on, I slept soundly, unmindful of everything around me. This was my first time at sea, and I liked the sound of the waves gently lapping against the Atreus.

En Route to Athens, Greece   *3/August/1962*

The sun came streaming down on us on the deck of the Atreus and within a short time the air was warmer. Even at mid-day the heat of the summer was scarcely noticeable because of the stiff dry breeze from the Mediterranean Sea which was a dazzling blue. Breakfast on the Atreus consisted of Greek coffee, grapes and bread. It was rather close quarters, so we got to know each other rather quickly. There were several Britishers from London on board and for the first time I came to appreciate how witty their sense of humor can be. Meanwhile, Geoffrey gave me a couple of books on Greek vocabulary which kept me busy for a while. By 8:00 AM we had passed Corfu and on the right we could see the island of Ithaca, home of the fabled Odysseus. From then on there was land visible on both sides of the ship as we sailed southward toward Patros.

We docked at Patros around 3:00 PM and a Pullman coach awaited the ship to transport us overland to Athens. Again there was beautiful scenery as we traced the coastline along the northern edge of the Peloponnesus to the New Testament town of Corinth. The rugged countryside was almost devoid of any crops except olive trees. At Corinth we crossed the isthmus onto the mainland. Here, through the canal separating the isthmus from the mainland both the Aegean and the Adriatic Seas were visible. Arriving in Athens, I was presented with my first impression of the enigmatic Greek personality. Geoffrey asked two men where Omonia Square was located and they pointed in opposite directions! But then they agreed to take us there themselves. We followed Socrates Street down to Sophocles where we found a modestly-priced hotel.

It was readily apparent to me, walking through the streets of the 5,000-year-old city of Athens, that this was no ordinary European city. The pungent odors emanating from the bazaars were exotic and the music had a zing to it that was quite different than any I had heard elsewhere in Europe. For dinner that evening Geoffrey and I went to a charming little place at the foot of the hill leading up to the Parthenon. Here I had my first taste of Greek cuisine, a three course meal of lamb, rice and Greek salad for less than a dollar. Geoffrey insisted that I sample the Greek national drink, stuff called ouzo that had a liquorish-like taste. It was fire-water!

Athens, Greece   *4/August/1962*

My instructions had been to take an early bus up to Elassona, but I overslept (intentionally, I think) and missed it. Since this would likely be my last chance to see Athens, so I decided to take a 9:00 PM bus to Elassona. Geoffrey was happy to continue serving as my guide to the city, so we mapped out the day's activities over a breakfast of thick Greek coffee and sweet rolls. Then we headed to Syntagos Square for the obligatory changing of money at the American Express. Geoffrey suggested that we visit the Parthenon first before it got too hot in the afternoon; already at 8:00 AM it was well on the way. The Acropolis was truly an unforgettable experience. From high on the hill the view of the city is breath-taking, the smog from the vehicles below notwithstanding. At the foot of the Acropolis were the remains of Aeropagus, the Agora and Hephestus. Images from my readings of Greek history came washing over me like the waves lapping against the Atreus.

We took the train out to the seaport town of Piraeus, known as the site of the popular Never on Sunday film, for lunch. If I had any notion at all about what Greece would look like, it was derived from seeing that film. Open-air markets lined the waterfront for several miles. I tried to imagine Merlina Mercuri lounging at one of the many cafes. Geoffrey headed back to the hotel to observe the time-honored Mediterranean siesta. Since I had so little time and so much to see, I set out with my map of Athens to take in as much as I could. I walked down Stadiou Street where I came upon some imposing buildings in the classical style that included the city library, the Academy of the Arts and the University of Athens, with an enrollment of about 4,000 students. Besides these buildings and the Acropolis remains, I saw few ostensible manifestations of classical Greek style in modern-day Athens which otherwise seemed like a modern city.

As I prepared to leave for Elassona, a review of my financial portfolio revealed that I was on fairly sound footing, a few drachmas shy of $200 dollars in my balance. I expressed my appreciation to Geoffrey for his services as a tour guide and bid farewell. The bus ride to Elassona at night deprived me of any images of the Greek countryside.

Elassona, Greece   *5/August/1962*

Elassona (variously spelled Olosson) is first mentioned by the venerable Homer in his Iliad as being the finest dwelling place in Thessaly. The original town Acropolis, built around 1000 B.C on a hill overlooking a valley, has long since disappeared. The village of Elassona was basically carved out of the side of a mountain and the buildings constructed of stone. Life in Elassona is defined by the Greek Orthodox Church: the pillar of religious, cultural and social affairs. The Bishopric, of which Elassona is the chef lieu, has a population of some 60,000 inhabitants. It was a middle-sized division of the Orthodox Church during Turkish occupation from 1453 to 1821. The Bishopric suffered severe suppression of its Greek culture, including the Church building itself. During the Turkish occupation resistance movements often began and were put down in the Thessaly region.

There are few fond notions of the Turkish period among the Greeks of Elassona. And sad to say, today the Church does not have very good attendance at services, as seems to be the case throughout most of Europe. According to a local authority who addressed us at the center, the climate of the region of Thessaly is very favorable, the land is fertile and there are abundant forests. German excavation teams have unearthed evidence of human habitation in the area as early as 100,000 years ago. The Dorian invasion swept through this area from neighboring Macedonia, and from that time onward there have been many isolated pockets of people retaining their independence in the surrounding mountains.

Our World Council of Churches project was housed in spartan dormitory quarters located on the very ground on which the Elassona acropolis had stood, now shrouded in the mists of antiquity. In the valley below, a community center was already under construction. The project leader was Father Graham Dowell, an Anglican priest from England, with a long beard and lean chiseled features. He wore a robe whenever he was not working. Father Graham not only looked like he had sprung full-blown from the Old Testament, but he had the demeanor and earnestness of a biblical figure. We all liked him and he proved himself a good leader.

Our group—a veritable kaleidoscope of nationalities, cultures and personalities—consisted of about 30 youths from Europe, Lebanon and the U.S., including several Greeks. Michael, from Austria, was perhaps the most extroverted and fun-loving of the group. He was born in the minority German community in Romania but had lived most of his life in Vienna. His sense of humor often kept us in stitches. Perhaps reflecting his German heritage, Michael regularly complained good-naturedly of the lack of beer in our daily diet. The other German in the group was Hartmund from Dortmund. He, too, was talkative and outgoing, proud of his German identity. Jean-Pierre represented the great Gallic culture, speaking English in his heavily accented but charming French.

He made us laugh when he lamented that:

"I sometimes feel not very useful, carrying stones from here to there, and then from there to here..."

Chantale, the other French worker, spoke only minimal English which limited my conversations with her. She chose to dedicate her language learning to Greek instead and succeeded admirably. Marguerita, the only Dutch girl, arrived late because her luggage got mixed up on the train. Although very young in appearance, she was one of the oldest workers at the ripe age of 23. Her language skills were the most advanced, as she regularly exhibited fluency in German, English and French as well as Dutch. As with many of the other Europeans, Marguerita informed me that she rarely attends church services at home but was very pleased to have this experience.

Gihad, the only Lebanese person in the group, was originally from Beirut now studying at the University of Athens. He was a deacon in the Orthodox Church in the Patriarchate of Antioch, preparing for the priesthood. Our first contact with Gihad was on Sunday morning at church where he sang the Divine Liturgy in a beautiful, resonant voice.

Barbara, a Greek-American from the Boston area and the only other American, brought considerable Greek cultural baggage with her to the work camp. Already conversant in Greek, she made a point of practicing her Greek on the locals. Barbara and I were the first ones to be assigned to kitchen duty where we were supervised by Yanni the cook whose English was marginal. So Barbara was obliged to dust off her Greek in order to communicate. Yanni wasted little time in inquiring of Barbara whether she would be interested in marrying a Greek and taking him with her to America. He quickly eased her mind by noting that he himself was already married. Marisa, a Greek Orthodox student, was our Greek teacher, providing us with basic words and common expressions. We learned to say den pirasi (a phrase connoting general agreement) and entoxi (everything's okay). She also managed to teach me the Greek words to Never on Sunday. My efforts to sing it delighted our Greek hosts.

We arrived in Elassona to find a partially finished building and grounds which were apparently to be surrounded by a stone wall. Our task during the month to come was to take part in the construction project. The area of construction, just below the hill and along the stream running through the town, covered about 100 square yards. The property belonged to an Orthodox monastery, and the plan called for building a youth home, equipped with a library, gymnasium and soccer field.

At first my work did not seem clearly defined. My first day assignment consisted of cleaning the johns and preparation of meals. It also involved transporting meals from the housing quarters down to the work site. By the second day, however, I got a taste of the real work. With pick and shovel in hand my work gang worked to tear down old existing walls to make room for the new one. The construction of the new wall, then, involved breaking up large rocks, hauling them from one place to another, and then putting them in place for the mason doing the actual construction. The project included laborers from the local area who were being paid a total of 50 drachmas (about $1.66) per day for 10 hours of work! I could imagine how the use of heavy machinery could have accomplished the task in short order. Alas, such was not available in this up-country setting.

The first couple of days we threw ourselves into the work with zeal. At the end of the day we fell into bed from sheer exhaustion, scarcely able to roll out in the morning. By the third day we had learned to pace ourselves somewhat. By the end of the week, the blisters on our hands and feet were turning into calluses. The sore muscles were giving way to firmer biceps and triceps.

Elassona Community Center under construction

However, it was also noticed that our clothes were becoming infested with fleas, and some of the workers had red spots emerging on their ankles and around their beltlines. It was not until one girl became sick from scratching them that we finally managed to smoke the little devils out of the dormitory.

The saving grace that rewarded our hard labor was the veritable feast awaiting us at the mid-day meal. This was usually a wonderful array of Greek salad (fresh lettuce greens, olives, tomatoes and feta cheese), fish or lamb, fresh vegetables, all cooked with generous portions of olive oil, one of the principal agricultural products of the country. Each meal was capped off with generous helpings of cantaloupe or watermelon, always accompanied by bottles of ouzo and retsina. The latter, which resembled nothing so much as what I imagined turpentine to taste like, was to be avoided. On the other hand, ouzo, a drink with a sort of liquorish flavor which was served on virtually any occasion, both before and after meals, in between meals, at festivals and most any other time, was not so bad. On celebratory occasions, the Bishop himself or other church authority would bring glasses around, ask whether we wanted ice or not, then come with the ouzo bottle to fill it up. When ice or water was added to the ouzo, it turned from a clear to smoky appearance. There are clearly certain differences between the Orthodox Church, and say, your standard Southern Baptist Church! After such a meal and liberal imbibing of ouzo, the afternoon siesta was a wonderful respite for the day's labors. The evenings were dedicated to chatting, singing, dancing and recuperating. Zorba the Greek would have fit right in. Sleep always came quickly.

Elassona, Greece   *9/August/1962*

On Thursday of the first week we reached a climactic point when we were able to force the roof of the empty wine cellar open so that excess earth could be thrown in, thus obviating the need to haul it elsewhere. By this time the skilled masons had begun building some of the walls for the new rooms. The Bishop himself was the architect for our project, and at least once every day he would come to check on our progress. There were generally five or six Orthodox monks from the Bishopric assigned to work with us, always attired in their conservative black robes. The other local workers were often young boys who loved to kid around and tell jokes. One of them took to calling me John Glenn, the American astronaut who had recently pioneered in outer space and enjoyed enormous worldwide popularity. This was in apparent reference to Glenn's high forehead and receding hairline, features which I possessed. This nickname stuck, and soon the whole village was calling me John Glenn. When the news of the death of Marilyn Monroe and William Faulkner— icons of American culture—arrived in Greece during our stay there, people offered me condolences, as though they had been members of my own family.

I was given a new assignment as "special worker", helping the brick-makers by going down to the creek-bed for sand and mixing it with cement. There were three of us on the special detail: Gihad, Hartmund and I. Hartmund was our "spokesman". He liked to say that he had "contracted" for our special work with the Bishop, an indication of our special status! Hartmund, however, had a bad habit of referring to the fact that his uncles had been here in Greece during World War II as part of the occupation force and had also enjoyed "special status". He always failed to mention anything about how the war turned out! One day Hartmund and I weighed ourselves on the scales and we were both exactly 64 kilos (140 lbs.).

By the second week my sunburn had turned to a robust tan and the soreness in my muscles had disappeared. Having adjusted ourselves to the rhythm of the work, and taking frequent breaks while standing in the shade away from the torrid sun, we learned to pace ourselves.

There was still a great deal of heavy-lifting to be done. But one day, miraculously, a bulldozer appeared on the scene and we all watched with our mouths open, marveling at how much it could accomplish. Then it disappeared, not to return again. Obviously we were not to be able to regularly count on its miraculous powers.

Elassona, Greece   *11/August/1962*

The intensity of the project work was occasionally broken up with excursions into the countryside, usually on Sundays or Wednesdays. However, the first one came on Saturday. We went to swim in a small lake nearby, a most refreshing respite from the heat of the ever-present sun. Not since our arrival had we seen so much as a cloud in the sky. But no sooner had we dipped our toes into the water than a brisk wind arose, clouds formed and drops of rain began to fall on us. That would have been fine, except that there were bolts of lighting as well. We scurried back into the bus, just in time to see the sun re-appear and the wind subside. And of course, that was to be the extent of the rain.

Elassona, Greece   *15/August/1962*

A second day of rest and recreation. The Bishop had arranged for us to visit an ancient monastery in his district near Mt. Olympus called Sparmos. He informed us that this monastery was about the same age as the one in Elassona and had produced many well known monks throughout the ages. It had been instrumental in spear-heading the revolt against the Turks in 1821, a pivotal date in modern Greek history. Today the monastery is used as a summer camp for boys up to the age of 12. Although it was very dirty and run-down, we were treated to a delightful talent show by the boys themselves. We could not help but admire their strong spirit in the light of adversities.

At Sparmos we also attended a service of Divine Liturgy for St. Chrysostom. It was slightly different from the service we witnessed the Sunday before because there was a choir and chanting. We stood for nearly two hours, first on one foot and then another, attempting half-heartedly to follow in the liturgy books. The European Protestants reacted rather negatively to what they considered as too much ritual. For that matter, most of them were not accustomed to attending church services at all, even though they were ostensibly in the work camp under the auspices of their churches.

The Greeks say that there was only one Christian Church until the 8ᵗʰ century A.D. when the West broke away from the original Church and vowed allegiance to the Pope in Rome. This has come to be known as Roman Catholicism. The Orthodox Church, headquartered in Constantinople, placed heavy emphasis on apostolic succession and a strong reverence for Virgin Mary and numerous saints as did the Roman Catholics. Religious icons are very prominent in the Orthodox tradition. The priests conducting the service this day wore long black robes, curved black top hats, large metal crucifixes and they swung incense around, filling the air with a strong sweet scent. For us garden-variety Protestants, this was different!

Mt. Olympus, Greece   *19/August/1962*

Today was the mountain top experience of a life-time! The Bishop announced that we would be going on a trek to Mt. Olympus. Now, several of us had never been mountain climbing, and we didn't know much about this particular mountain. So we were a bit anxious, to say the least. Would we need hiking boots and gear? Oxygen masks? But then he said that the local people climbed it often and rarely did anyone disappear as they did on Mt. Everest. That was most encouraging! Of course, being young and impressionable, we were all ready to go.

We were loaded onto the back of a vegetable truck and transported to a small village at the foot of Mt. Olympus. With light packs on our backs, we climbed for a couple of hours until dark. Here we pitched camp. The guide said that we should try to get some sleep since we would continue our ascent again early in the morning. And sure enough, at 2:00 AM, we were rousted from our slumber!

"What kind of madness is this?" we asked, blinking in the dark.

"You'll see," said the guide.

This was mid-summer, sunlight came early, and there was little likelihood of frostbite. We fell in line, following the guide. It was a relatively modest incline, with few really challenging passages. Then, a couple of hours later, we couldn't go any further. We were at the top of the highest peak, Mytikas, at 2918 meters (9570 feet, close to two miles), just in time to see the sun rising majestically out of the Aegean Sea. Exhausted, but exhilarated, we realized that it had been well worth the effort. We now understood that the whole idea was to be on the top of the mountain exactly at sunrise.

Traditionally regarded as the heavenly abode of the Greek gods and the site of the throne of Zeus, Mt. Olympus, the tallest mountain range in Greece, seems to have originally existed as an idealized mountain that only later came to be associated with a specific peak. Homer's early epics, the Illiad and the Odyssey, composed around 700 B.C., offer little information regarding the geographic location of the heavenly mountain and there are several peaks in Greece, Turkey and Cyprus that bear the name Olympus (variously spelled Olympos). The most favored mythological choice, however, is this Olympus massif, 100 kilometers southwest of the city of Thessaloniki in northern Greece.

On Mt. Olympus at sunrise, summer 1962

The deities of the Greek pantheon that dwelled upon the mythic mount were Zeus, the king of the gods; his wife Hera; his brothers Poseidon and Hades; his sisters Demeter and Hestia; and his children, Apollo, Artemis, Aphrodite, Ares, Athena, Hermes and Hephaestus. These were archetypes representing idealized aspects of the multi-faceted human psyche. Worship of the deities among the Greeks was a method of invoking and amplifying those aspects in the behavior and personality of the human worshipper. Zeus was the god of mind and the intellect, and a protector of strangers and the sanctity of oaths. Hera was the goddess of fertility, the stages of a woman's life and marriage. Apollo represented law and order and the principles of moderation in moral, social and intellectual matters. Aphrodite was the goddess of love and the overwhelming passions that drive humans to irrational behavior. Hermes was the god of travelers, of sleep, dreams and prophecy. Athena, the goddess who gave her name to the city of Athens, represented spiritual wisdom incarnate. Hephaestus was the god of arts and fire. Ares, for his part, symbolized the dark and brooding aspect of human nature.

While all of these gods and goddesses may not have actually resided on Mt. Olympus, this was their mailing address. Collectively, they represented a metaphor for the power of the sacred mountain. This spiritual power had drawn hermits and monks to live in the caves and forests of the mountain since long before the dawn of the Christian era. With the coming of Christianity, however, the myths and legends of the old Greeks were suppressed and forgotten, and the holy mountain was seldom visited. Our history books now record that the religion of the ancient Greeks was a pagan religion, full of superstition. I would prefer to believe that these gods and goddesses helped to sustain for several centuries the most highly developed civilization the world had seen in ancient times.

Elassona, Greece   *25/August/1962*

Today the whole village turned out for an official ceremony of dedication for the newly completed portion of the community center that had been the subject of our labors. There were speeches and congratulatory remarks by all the secular and religious dignitaries of Elassona. Father Graham spoke for all of us when he observed what a rich and rewarding experience it had been for our working group. We would all remember the hard work, the festive occasions and the mountain-top experiences as well as the intimate relationships we had formed with fellow work campers in a short time.

Elassona Community and workers

Let me attempt to distill from the Greek work camp experience some enduring impressions. My notes from the summer of 1962 make frequent reference to the Church in Europe. Throughout my travels in Holland, England, France, Germany and Italy I was struck by how relatively inconsequential the Church in Europe seemed to be. And this was confirmed by my fellow European work campers in Elassona, who were a very secular lot. We Protestants in the U.S. were accustomed to attending Sunday services on a regular basis and to seeking ways of living out the lessons imparted by the preacher on Sunday morning. Well, yes, I was shocked! The Protestant Church in Europe seemed moribund to me. Everywhere churches were empty on Sunday morning. Somewhere I read that attendance at Sunday services throughout Europe was in the range of 5% of the membership! This phenomenon appears to date especially to the post-World War II period. The Church becomes increasingly irrelevant to them, replaced in many instances by adherence to Communist or Socialist ideology. This is not just true of Protestant counries but in France, where the Protestant population numbers only a minute portion of the population.

Chapter 5

Malawi, 1964-1966:
The Peace Corps Experience

Ask not what your country can do for you; rather ask what you
can do for your country.
　　　—John F. Kennedy, Inaugural Address, January 1961

The goal of man should be a life of pleasure regulated by
morality, temperance and serenity..."
- from Epicurus, attached prominently on PCV John Dixon's
bathroom door in Ncheu, Malawi

Training at Syracuse

In January 1961, John F. Kennedy assumed the presidency of the
United States. It was the golden age of American idealism. Thousands
of people applied to the Peace Corps, at least in part because they
were responding to the call to service. Within a short period of time
he had assuaged the fears of most Protestants that the Pope would
be calling shots in the White House. One of his earliest initiatives—
in March 1961—was to launch the Peace Corps, the hair-brained
idea of Senator Hubert Humphrey of Minnesota, into which the
new administration bought. Sargent Shriver, a Kennedy extended
family member, was appointed Director of the new agency and he
went about the country trying to sell the program. Two years later, in
my senior year in college, I applied to the Peace Corps in the spring
of 1963 and was accepted into a training program for Tanzania in the
summer. But by the time I received the invitation more mundane
considerations had prevailed. I opted for the road most traveled—
graduate school—instead and headed to Washington, D.C. with
fraternity brother Kenneth Kellam and his girlfriend, Elaine Valencia.
I entered American University in the fall of 1963. Shortly thereafter

President Kennedy was assassinated. It was a period of sadness for the nation as well as personal disillusionment. My Washington experience was not at all what I had imagined it would be.

Back at home on holiday in the spring of 1964 I was expressing my unhappiness with graduate school to Vera Mae. Whatever residual misgivings she had about Kennedy the Catholic, she saw the Peace Corps as a worthy cause. "You should go back and tell the Peace Corps you want another assignment," she said. Across the country at the same time other mothers were pleading with their sons and daughters NOT to join the Peace Corps. It was a venture into the unknown. What could you possibly expect to come of it? Your classmates would be out there gaining advanced degrees or getting a good start on their careers. But Vera Mae seemed to know her son well. And so it was that I was persuaded to re-apply to the Peace Corps.

After renewing my application and making numerous phone calls to Peace Corps Washington to find out what was happening to it, the invitation finally came for a training program for Nyasaland. This time I accepted. It was a decision that would change my life in fundamental ways that I could scarcely imagine. Several weeks later a packet came in the mail providing background information on......Malawi. This was explained, not by the all-too-common Peace Corps mix-up, but rather by the fact that during those few weeksthe British Protectorate of Nyasaland had become the independent nation of Malawi on July 6, 1964. I was to enter training at Syracuse University on August 31 as a member of Malawi V—Secondary Education, the fifth group to be trained to go to the country. It was said that PC Director Sargent Shriver had promised the Congress 10,000 Volunteers and Trainees in operation before September 1, 1964.

Syracuse   *5/September/1964*

Moni Azimai ndi Azibambo!

The greeting—"Moni azimai ndi azibambo'—in Chinyanja, the national language of Malawi, roughly translated means Greetings Ladies and Gentlemen. Shorlty after our arrival on the Syracuse University campus in late August I began keeping a diary and eventually sending mimeographed copies of my notes out to family and friends.I reported that there were 240 prospective Peace Corps men and women who had established residence at Vincent Apartments in Syracuse, which had become a permanent training center for Syracuse University. Of those, 140 of us were in the Malawi V group, an exceptionally bright and personable lot. Several were transfers from other training programs, where in most cases they had trouble learning the language. The other 100 trainees were bound for Tanganyika and were being trained in Swahili.

Check-in procedure began Sunday evening and most of Monday was taken up with the assignment of bicycles, an absolute must for every trainee regardless of race (there were no more than ten Negroes, one Asiatic), sex (over one-third female), or previous condition of servitude. Our housing was situated about seven minutes by bicycle from classes and meals. There were numerous complaints owing to saddle sores from the hard seats on our bikes; we suspected that all this cycling mileage was calculated as part of the shaping up program. We ate in a place called Slokum Hall, which sounds like something out of Dogpatch, U.S.A., but was one of the more ancient ivy covered buildings on campus. Besides having the number three ranked football team in the country Syracuse was widely known for its African Studies program, which provided a clue to the reason why trainingn was here instead of TCU or Slippery Rock State.

As my suitemates arrived we readily became acquainted. These guys were regular Americans, straight from the mainstream of American youth. Jeff, with whom I shared a bedroom, just graduated from Wisconsin (beer on tap in the student center) and he was quick to reveal that he was an avid Lambda Chi alum as well as Jonathan Winters fan. The latter he mimicked to perfection and frequently entertained on the spur of the moment. Jeffie exuded enthusiasm, instigating the very first social affair of the whole shootin' match the first week.

The next day our suite was well known all over Vincent Apartments! This soiree set the pace for the next three nights and soon I was able to associate 50 names with faces. Another co-resident, Phil, was a graduate of New Mexico University, with a Masters in English. He was jolly at times but more inclined to the sedentary life. He was vowing to give up smoking and take the phys-ed courses seriously. Bob, the fourth member of our suite, was a graduate of Wooster College, the least inclined to extroversion of us all, but very pleasant and compatible. In sum, I would say that we had the cream of the so-called crop; not even one ostensible beatnik and only a few misguided Goldwater enthusiasts. Nearly everyone was conversant in politics, both domestic and international. Everyone had a special field of academic interest, hopefully one which Peace Corps intended to exploit for the next two years.

I must also add that the program in the beginning struck most of us as being a little flat. To say the least there was little of the rigid discipline which we were all geared for upon arrival from all the publicity about training. The staff, individually interesting types, seemed to be helplessly disorganized, which they contended was due to misdirection from Peace Corps/Washington. For example, we would not receive our first stipend until the second week, and most of us arrived financially threadbare. Even the language instructors, straight from Malawi, were not yet paid. Officially, language classes were due to start September 1, when the regular Syracuse faculty returned to campus. But there was no syllabus to indicate what our training would consist of. My group was scheduled for first aid instruction at 8:00 A.M. Sunday morning! We "sheep" generally reacted with good natured patience and only occasional barbs at the bureaucracy. Of course, everyone inwardly lived in deathly fear of the mysterious process of selection about which we had heard so much and yet knew so little. It was an atmosphere not unlike Kafka's Trial.

Although I thought my selection for the Malawi teaching program instead of Latin America, after a year of graduate study in that area, was unique in its irony, I encountered other cases equally strange. There was the girl from Hawaii who had majored in French and was selected out of a Francophone Africa program for language deficiency. Not to mention scores of other "rejects" from other programs. Peace Corps used a dubious euphemism in the selection process; you do not fail, you are "selected out". Who was it who said, "Ours is not to reason why..."? Nevertheless, Peace Corps continued to make giant steps forward under the patronizing arm of a benign Congress. The one thing which seemed certain, regardless of the outcome of the Presidential election in November, was the continued existence of the Peace Corps. The American public had bought the idea and was impressed with its successes. The first week we were scheduled to take our fist battery of written personality tests and to try to out-psyche the psychologists.

Syracuse   *5/October/1964*

As we sat watching a series of films on the promised-land, featuring Lake Malawi, one of the trainees was heard to remark, "It must be wonderful to be an underdeveloped country." Each new exposure to the history, people of the "land of the flames" seemed to bring Malawi one step closer to reality. We filled out our first peer-rating sheet which made us all rather uneasy. I was pleased to be able to tabulate 75 acquaintances out of a total of 103 Malawi teachers. We also completed the first academic plateau, taking "finals" in special methods and TEFL (Teaching English as a Foreign Language). The former had to do with methods in teaching social science in my case, which supposedly would prepare me for two months of practice teaching. We began settling down to the apparently serious business of teaching in Syracuse public schools. My group was assigned to Smith Jr. High, a veritable palace of an institution with mostly upper and middle class students. There were a few classes of under privileged students to which we were assigned.

At one point Peace Corps Director Sargent Shriver swooped down on Syracuse for a political fund-raising speech at a local labor union. It was rumored that he would be out to Vincent Apartments to address us as well. But when it turned out to be just a rumor, we were herded onto buses at the last minute and taken to the local hotel where he was speaking. As two hundred trainees crowded into the room, Shriver's comments became less political and more focused on his role as Our Leader. He was impressive, with a gift for stump speaking to match his reputation as an organizer. This would be the last time we would see him as head of the Peace Corps since his new job of Poverty "Czar" was taking more and more of his time.

My "pledge class" in training was a colorful agglomeration, heterogeneous in background as well as personality. Severin Hochberg, sometimes known as Mike, wais 25, Jewish and resident of the lower East Side in Manhattan. He referred to 125th St. as "up-state New York". On a couple of trips to the City with him we were introduced to his world. Walking the streets of the neighborhood where he had taught school, Severin remarked,

"Consider all the things a man needs to live and enjoy life, then take away fresh air and trees, and you have New York."

At another street he reflected, "Name anything you want to do in New York and there is a city ordinance against it."

Even though I had lived in the city a few weeks during the summer, I felt this was my first personal introduction.

Jim Jones, the outstanding graduate of Wilkes Barre College (Pennsylvania) shared my own small town origins. We discovered that we were both in the Order of the Arrow Service Troop at the Boy Scout Jamboree in Colorado Springs in 1960. Small world!

Dave Bush, another Pennsylvanian who wrestled six years in the same weights in which I wrestled, joined Jeff and me most often in off-hours carousing. Dave was a real mover with the young ladies and well trained in the art of beer-drinking. He and I found time after classes to unwind in a one-on-one game of basketball.

Jamie Kunz was a magna cum laude Yalie with a tinder-dry wit. He frequently livened up our living room with his home-spun humor. He was the one trainee who had more bike trouble than I did!

Richie Kornbluth, graduate of Rutgers, was another city boy with a strong New Jersey accent. Richie had typically boisterous city manners and a big heart. He seemed more concerned even than the rest of us about deselection because of what he considered his unorthodox past.

"Tosh" Mitchell, was a Smith graduate who we figured would be voted most likely to succeed. She broke the curve on practically every exam and approached every aspect of training with deadly earnest. Tosh wore a left- handed pig tail, causing me to chide her good-naturedly for looking like an old schoolmarm.

Joyce Lewinger, a graduate of Syracuse itself, reluctantly came back to her alma mater for another stint. She emerged from the social whirl of Syracuse unscathed and thoroughly informed on East Africa. She graciously hosted our gang on a recent trip to New York in her Bay Shore home. While we seemed to have a compatible relationship, we sometimes had trouble communicating because of the disparity in our regional accents!

There were a couple of staffers worth mentioning too. As luck would have it my long time Ponca City friend, Joe Short, had left Columbia University to do his doctorate at Syracuse, and was engaged as discussion group leader for our program. The boys in his group, the coop project, held him in high esteem, which was par Joe. I had the privilege to fix him up with a date with one of my fellow trainees and hewent back for seconds. Dave Hutchison, our cross-cultural discussion group leader was an ex-Volunteer from the very first Peace Corps group sent overseas in Ghana I. He injected a somewhat cynical and yet realistic note into our training. His candidness was especially reflected in a discussion on the matter of sex, or lack of sex, for healthy, red-blooded Volunteers. Needless to say, he was short on solutions. He did suggest, half in earnest, that Peace Corps should assign male-female teams to isolated areas.

The scenery here in upstate New York typically becomes really breath-taking. The leaves turn violent shades of red and orange as the autumn air becomes nippier. Each day founnd us all the more determined to complete training, in spite of all the seemingly meaningless exercises and inquiring psychologists. There were nevertheless many meaningful experiences to offset the morc negative ones. I attended a Rosh Hashanah service with some of my Jewish fellow trainees, my first time to enter a synagogue. I was beginning to understand how important Jewish culture was in New York.

Extracurricular activities were enhanced by a hither-to-well-kept-secret: my 1959 pea green VW Beatle. A word of explanation is in order. Shortly after I received my invitation to training at Syracuse in the spring I decided to spend the summer on the East Coast. Packing some personal belongings and a modest bank balance, I said goodbye to the Hulls and drove the bug to New York City where I stayed with my old friend and roommate Rafael Ruiz in an apartment on the upper West Side. He had a job with the Columbia Men's Faculty Club while pursuing his studies at Union Theological Seminary. Summer in the City was in itself a cross-cultural experience. Small town boy goes to the Big Apple! My pleasantest recollection from that period was of driving the bug up and down the streets of Manhattan accompanied by native New Yorker Susan Meltzer shouting at taxi drivers: "Hey Chief, how d'we get to toity-toid and toid street?" It was a hoot!

I had already been accepted to work as a volunteer at the Democratic Convention in Atlantic City in early August. So I hopped in the VW bug and drove down for the big event. Not that I was a hard-core Democrat or an avid fan of then President Lyndon Johnson, but I truly lived in fear of the possibility of Barry Goldwater, the Republican candidate, becoming President. I donned my red-white-and-blue Youth for Lyndon outfit and did whatever chores I was assigned. And at the moment of his coronation (his nomination was a fait accompli as sitting President) I was standing not more than 30 feet away on the convention floor. As a four year resident of the great state of Texas, I was too familiar with the political shenanigans of Landslide Lyndon to be too excited.

Upon arrival at the Vincent Apartments in Syracuse, I parked the bug on a side street well out of sight and locked it. But after the second or third party in the apartments and the question of how to transport cases of beer, I mentioned that we might use the bug just this once. At TCU I was a well known teetotaler, a real blue-nose, but I was about to be pulled into the vortex of peer pressure. Not only did my peer-rating soar amongst my fellow trainees because of my dare-devil willingness to drive the bug against training rules, but I learned to relish the beer-drinking sessions. Weekends might often find us down at the Orange, a pub popular with Syracuse students, and occasionally attending a college football game.

Syracuse   *12/November/1964*

Armistice Day is Syracuse came nearly a year after the assassination of President Kennedy, and all trainees were given a vacation from practice teaching. This was a presidential election year, and in order to vote I was obliged to drive back down to the City with my Native New Yorker fellow trainees to register. Since this was my first time to vote, I had to establish residence, and somehow my brief sojourn in New York City served that purpose. Driving near China Town, we noticed a huge billboard picturing Barry Goldwater (with slightly slanted eyes!) that announced, "In your heart, you know he's right." And we muttered to ourselves, "Yeah, far right." I was not the only trainee who feared that he might lead us into a nuclear war with the Soviets.

Nevertheless, Landslide Lyndon, whose constant refrain in his Hill Country twang in the campaign was, "I need yer hep!" was re-instated in the White House with the largest plurality in history. Bobby Kennedy, whom we heard speak on the Syracuse campus during the campaign, cracked the Republican wall in upstate New York in gaining election to the U.S. Senate. Even in my native Oklahoma, the Republicans lost an opportunity to send football coach Bud Wilkinson, who enjoyed god-like status, to the Senate. In his acceptance speech Johnson used the refrain "let us continue" but nobody I knew was quite convinced that he could take the place of John Kennedy.

There were other earth shaking events which made this fall noteworthy. Harold Wilson came to power in Britain with the Labor Party while Khrushchev was eased out of power in the Soviet Union. Out of Africa the headlines were carrying news of the Simba Rebellion in Stanleyville and its aftermath. The Communist Chinese announced their first nuclear bomb. In Malawi the cabinet crisis between Dr. Banda and his ministers resulted in the sacking and resignation of most of the younger ministers. Our language instructor, Dearson Bandawe, was called back to Malawi, informed by the Malawi Embassy that his wife and daughter had been shot and seriously wounded as a result of the political tension.

Hardly less earth shaking for the trainees at Syracuse was the first round of selection known as "midboards". Everyone was in a state of hyper-tension, although we knew it was coming. The Malawi teachers program was reduced from 115 to 91; the co-op program was heaviest hit with a 20% loss. I myself received an ominous little note (yes, a pink slip) during a practice teaching class, instructing me to report to the psychiatrist's office. Most of us who had been considered borderline cases for selection had already had at least one psychiatric interview under the belt. The selection officer from Washington, hat in hand and very apologetic, was first to greet me. Speaking very much like a recording, he regretted to inform me that the board had decided that I should leave the program. He handed me a one-way ticket to Ponca City! The selection officer said that the head psychiatrist would be happy to explain to me the basis on which the decision had been made. My heart sank!

I entered the office of the head psychiatrist, feeling like anyone would who had just been told he was not going to Africa after months of eager anticipation. He explained to me in very sympathetic tones that my written psychological tests and oral interviews revealed a serious state of depression which they were afraid would not allow me to function properly in a foreign culture. And wasn't it true that I had begun drinking beer only since coming to training? This was probably an indication of the tension under which I was operating! The psychiatrist conceded that the other aspects of my evaluation were well above average: peer-rating, practice teaching, language ability: everything which came under the heading of skills. This was simply a decision taken on medical grounds — for your sake as well as the Peace Corps. You do understand, don't you?

Numb at first, I managed to keep my cool. I knew what they were talking about when they mentioned "depression". I had been very open in discussing the frustration I still felt in the pit of my stomach from the emptiness of my graduate school experience. I could agree with their analysis. It was their prescription I had to question. Wasn't it just possible that with all their professional knowledge about what made me tick, with all that they knew about me from the background evaluation, exams, brain-picking and peer ratings...wasn't it possible that I still knew what was best for me? A key element missing from my year of graduate school was a sense of challenge, a sense of purpose. That, I was certain, was what the Peace Corps experience would provide.

Then I heard myself telling the head psychiatrist that I wanted to stay in training, that I would fly to Washington to appeal my case to the medical board. He reminded me that 99 out of a hundred medical appeals were turned down. Without blinking I suggested that I might very well be the one who made it. After about an hour the head psychiatrist, very phlegmatic and unsympathetic, announced that there was nothing else he could do or say. He said that if I was determined to appeal the case I should go see Paul Miwa, the Training Director. Miwa, a Japanese-American political scientist from Hawaii, was a sly sort of fellow, considered by everyone to be inept as administrator but nevertheless human in what seemed an inhuman system. I told him I wanted to stay in the program and he nodded knowingly. The board was still meeting, so he told me to come and see him after midnight. I wandered off, like a shadow, feeling very much in limbo. I found my way to a flick downtown — Seven Days in May. It was bizarre, Dr. Strangelove ordering the destruction of the world to defeat the Ruskies. But at that point what was happening on the screen became real, and what was happening to me was just make believe.

I went back to Vincent Apartments and hung around shadow-like, waiting until well after midnight for Dr. Miwa. Finally, after what seemed like a year since I talked with him just that afternoon, Miwa motioned me into his office and closed the door. His face was expressionless. He walked back and forth across the room a few times. Sue Urbonas, a trainee working in Miwa's office, gave me a sympathetic smile. I should wait, Miwa said.

"But wait for what?" I demanded, the tension of the day at last unwinding.

"Don't pack your bags just yet," he said.

The next day my shadow took its place in line with the other trainees waiting for the weekly meal ticket. Sure enough, there was one with my name on it! I ate lunch just like all the real trainees. By now everyone was asking where I had disappeared the night before. I mumbled something about having a date with the head psychiatrist. They began telling about all the guys who were gone, the ones whose shadows had disappeared during the night in keeping with the policy not to condone tearful goodbyes. Again that night I was summoned to Miwa's office. This time he announced that I would be having another psychiatric interview the coming Friday, and then every week until the end of training!

So here I was, still at Syracuse along with the other 90 teacher trainees for Malawi. The only thing I knew for sure was that I would be under the microscope from now on. I had to walk the straight and narrow if I wanted to get to Malawi! I would be less inclined to talk straight with the psychiatrists than before, knowing now that they were not necessarily there to help us along but to make decisions for us. Looked at positively, this was perhaps the greatest challenge of my tender life, and if I measured up to it then I would become a man. And if I made it through I would know for sure that I am the only one who should decide which road my life should travel.

Soche Hill, Malawi   *28/December/1964*

Kornbluth and James aptly described the entry of the largest single Peace Corps contingent in Africa in the December/January issue of the Migraine: "The morning of Monday, December 28, a daring invasion of Malawi in southeastern Africa took place at Chileka Airport, an invasion unprecedented in Malawi history. The Malawi V group arrived. Green as pubescent mangoes, we descended shakily from the airplane." Eager to test our Chinyanja, we greeted Jim Blackwell, Country Director, with hearty Moni bambos. Our greenness became a dazzling chartreuse when he replied, 'Hi, welcome to Malawi. (We were to learn quickly enough that he just didn't know any Chinyanja.) Jeff James, the co-author or the article and my roommate in training, had kept repeating on the trip over, "I still don't think they're serious; we're not really going to Africa." And Dave Bush was heard to say, "Well, we fooled 'em again didn't we Jeffie?"

Shortly after our arrival at the airport we were given our post assignments. There mine was: Mt. Mlanje Secondary School. Visions of fabled Mt. Mlanje danced in my head! All during training we had been told of the grandeur that is Mt. Mlanje—the highest point in Central Africa—of its beauty as well as its near-perfect climate. There were other nice assignments in this country known for its beauty, but none better than Mlanje. I would be one of three PCVs teaching in a brand new school. Two of our fellow trainees were to be stationed at Chisitu Mission, some four miles west toward Blantyre. Mlanje wasn't just a place; it was Valhalla.

It was a somewhat rare sunny day during Malawi rainy season. We were driven pa basi (by bus) to our in-country training center at Soche Hill College, said to be the best secondary teaching training college in the country. We bounced along the paved road toward Blantyre and on to Soche Hill, chatting excitedly with Chuck Wallace, Syracuse liaison and sometime cupid. Our eyes soaked up the greenery of the countryside, the countless people shuffling along the road invariably carrying articles on their heads. Chinyanja words such as mudzi (village) and mbuzi (goat), learned painfully during training, skipped through my mind. We arrived at Soche Hill just south of Blantyre, where on a clear day you can see Mt. Mlanje. There we spent the rest of the day being assigned to one of two dorms, Kamuzu and Chilembwe Halls.

Jeff and I retained our roommateship for the nine-day training period. The first day we were subjected to our first sampling of in-country food which the students at Soche Hill usually eat. Some Volunteers tbecame promptly ill and others went on self-imposed diets. Fortunately the food was by no means typical of that to which we would become accustomed in our own homes. The other aspects of training were pleasant enough, apart from the seemingly extraneous staff orientation. The consolation was that at least we were now across the ocean, away from the specter of de-selection. However, I was still officially on "hold" according to PC/Washington and I couldn't help feeling a bit uneasy. It was as though I had never really been selected in although I hadn't quite been selected out.

The annoyances of classes and orientation sessions aside, in-country training gave us a chance to go into Blantyre for shopping and kibbitzing with the old Volunteers. It was good to see Dearson again, alive and well. We were introduced to all the PC/Malawi staff, including Wes Leach who had come to Syracuse to urge us to learn Chinyanja. (We found out soon enough that he didn't speak the language either.) One day there at Soche the Ministry of Education hosted us on a trip to Likabula, the garden spot of the country, for a picnic and swim. We also attended a rally at Colby Community Center on the occasion of the presentation of a mobile health unit by Prime Minister Ngwazi Dr. Kamuzu Banda, our first time to see him in person. Several VIPs from the Malawi government came out one evening for a reception in the assembly hall. Notable among them was Aleki Banda, the golden boy of Malawi politics at 25 and reputedly the second most influential man in the country. There was also Mr. John Msonti, Minister of Education. American Ambassador Gilstrap was on hand to extend the official greetings of the establishment. A personal appointee of President Johnson, the Ambassador wasn't an especially big hit with our group.

January 5th dawned early as the scheduled day of dispersion of 86 teachers to our respective posts. We scurried about briskly getting our katundu (luggage) onto trucks and buses, and then settled back to wait the rest of the morning for connections to be made. It would take the Likhoma Island boys several days by boat to get to their post. We all went out of our way to offer our condolences to the Port Herald and Karonga contingents since they were going to hard ship posts. We had been told of Port Herald, the scourge of Malawi, repeatedly in training. We had also been told that no one would be sent there unless he requested to go. Unfortunately that was a promise the field staff didn't keep. Our most gregarious PCV, Severin, was off by himself to Nkotakota on the lake shore; two Jewish girls, Joyce and Harriet, would be teaching at Chisitu, a Catholic mission.

Before heading out to our respective assignments a few of us paid a visit to the home of our language instructor, Dearson Bandawe, whom we all called masharubu because of his luxuriant mustache.

Because of his political support of the exiled ex-Ministers Dearson would soon find himself locked up in Zomba Prison. (A few months later I would go with his wife Jean to the prison to take Dearson food, possibly risking my own standing as a Volunteer.)

Dearson *Masharubu* Bandawe & family in Kanjedza

Mlanje   *5/January/1965*

Four of us were taken by truck on an hour and a half ride to Mlanje, via the Protestant Mission at Chisitu. The southern route, although the longer of the two, is paved all the way. One of our sentence drills in Chinyanja class had asked the question:

Kodi njira yopita ku Mlanje ndi tara? (Is the road to Mlanje paved?)

Yes it is, and it passes through the scenic tea estates which bring Malawi its largest source of hard currency revenue. My two roommates-to-be were attending a conference of Malawi III teachers, so I was left to my own devices. I wrangled an invitation to stay with the girls at Chisitu, probably going against the rules of propriety in the eyes of the Catholic Sisters. But they were overwhelming in their hospitality toward both their new teachers and me. Chisitu is an idyllic place with its 50-year-old church and grounds lined with palm trees against the backdrop of Mt. Mlanje. It is no wonder that a volunteer from Malawi I, Linda Millette, has signed up for her third year as a Volunteer.

Yes, the Road to Mlanje is Paved

The week I stayed at Chisitu was marked by several curious incidents, at least curious to newly arrived mzungu (white person. Joyce asked a local bambo (man) to bring us chicken for Sunday dinner. And sure enough he appeared the next morning with an nkhuku ya moyo—a live chicken—flopping energetically. After the initial shock and fuss about who was going to take care of it, the chicken was eventually beheaded, plucked and cooked. Another time I was sitting on the porch reading when the air was pierced with shrill wailing. From the village only a few yards directly behind the house came the mournful sounds of a family lamenting the death of a small child.

The next week I began settling in, getting ready to begin classes while the girls were enjoying another week's vacation at the lake. By this time I was joined at Mlanje by my two roommates, Pete and Carroll. Our house, one of the new government-constructed projects connected with secondary schools, was spacious, beautifully situated at the foot of Mt. Mlanje, but still unfinished. We had no electricity, little furniture and two beds for three people. Therefore Carroll went to stay with a friend in town until another bed arrived. The first couple of days Pete and I invested a good many hours and more than a few shillings in painting floors, getting acquainted talking very much like a recording and breaking in the house boy. Suedi was a Muslim Yao from Fort Johnston who once worked for Colin Cameron, the only European in the Banda cabinet, before the crisis.

Pete and Carroll were fresh from a year in Port Herald, for which they had volunteered. Pete spoke of his experience down there in moderate terms, admitting that he enjoyed the year in some respects. But he allowed as how one year was enough. Carroll, on the other hand, recounted how he told Mr. Blackwell to either send him out to some other post or send him home...basi! (enough). Pete's physical attributes were well known, even to new Volunteers: the goatee, long curly blond hair and one ear ring reportedly acquired during a state of inebriation in Port Herald. He was presently hobbling about with a broken leg and says that he is always breaking a bone somewhere. This was one guy who really knew some Chinyanja and conversed handily with Suedi in it. Two other identifying features should be mentioned: Pete's motorcycle and his girl Lil. The motorcycle was officially his since he had been commissioned by PC/Malawi to keep the Malawi IV health workers' Hondas in good repair. Lil was acquired only recently while he was recuperating in the hospital from his accident. She was a health Volunteer stationed at the hospital.

Both hailed from the South and they spoke with a smooth lilting drawl. Carroll was one of the very few Negro Volunteers in Malawi. According to the story, Pete and Carroll became good friends in training and asked to be stationed together. When one decided that Port Herald might provide an interesting challenge, the other agreed to go along. They were inseparable; at the end of the first year they asked to be transferred together. These days it seemed that Lil was taking more and more of Pete's time and Carroll was finding the social life in Mlanje more favorable than in Port Herald.

Mlanje   *20/January1965*

I started on my 24th lap toward old age on Jaunary 20th while
Lyndon Johnson was being inaugurated President of the U.S. for a
second term. That same day marked my first day in the classroom
as a teacher in Form One English, history...and French. I had never
studied French, so I asked the French Canadian Sisters at Chisitu to
teach me enough to keep me one step ahead of the students. There
were no French texts for any of the classes, but they were promised
for the near future. So the first week was spent in getting acquainted,
associating faces with strange sounding names. I assigned my English
class a composition about their villages. It was also their first year
in secondary school. The freshness and cautious determination
they displayed was a source of encouragement to me, and I kept
reminding myself how lucky I was to be stationed at the best post
in the country.

Jeff came all the way down from Lilongwe for a weekend and
helped me celebrate a belated birthday with a bottle of Portuguese
wine. The next Thursday Frances Jones came roaring down from
Mlanje town on her Peace Corps-issue njinga ya moto (motorcycle)
to relate an urgent telephone message from Dr. Blackwell. Frances
was one of the Florence Nightingales of the health project stationed
at Mlanje, known for her earthy humor. We rode back into town and
I got on the phone. It was Blantyre. Dr. Blackwell's voice was crisp
and cheerful but business-like.

"We have decided to send you to Port Herald...next Sunday," he
announced with no trace of hesitation or apology.

I said something like "No thanks, I'm happy here and besides
they need me to teach French."

Blackwell replied, "Sorry but the decision has been made; we're
sending a truck out for you Sunday."

He sounded very definite. I hung up and told Frances the news.
True to form, Frances provided me with a thought for the day.

"Just remember" she said, "that life is just a shit sandwich and
every day's another bite."

The logic was clear enough. One of the two girls in our group
stationed at Port Herald had already gotten a little under the
weather and demanded to leave. She was being transferred. Mlanje
was said to be over-staffed at the same time. My qualifications for

Port Herald, according to the Director, were just what the doctor ordered. I had grown up in the rugged frontier country of Oklahoma and my teaching field was the one needed to replace the departing Volunteer. I reminded the Director that they had found me emotionally unstable in training and that this might put me under greater strain. They hadn't received that information from Syracuse, he said, but he was sure that I'd do just fine.

I was packed and ready to go when the carryall arrived. The feeling of being on "hold" slowly returned to me. It was 1984 and Big Brother was coming to get me. My protestations in Blantyre were once again dissolved in the nature of the bureaucracy which allots the administrator final authority. We had a pleasant weekend in town although we weren't invited by the staff to join them in a game of tennis at the Blantyre Sports Club. Sunday afternoon I joined the Port Herald gang, in town shopping during the weekend, on the bed of the Ministry of Works lorry which was headed back down into the lower Shire Valley to y new home.

Port Herald Day Secondary School   *31/January/1965*

Port Herald, with a reputation as the armpit of Malawi, received its name from the historic H.M.S Herald which used to make its way upriver from the mouth of the Zambezi. The Shire River has its source at the southern end of Lake Malawi, passes through the Shire Highlands, and eventually forms the border between Malawi and Mozambique before joining the Zambezi. Our lorry wound its way down the escarpment from an elevation of over 3,000 ft., to less than 200 ft. within 30 miles. A few miles outside of Blantyre the tarred road peters out, giving way to a treacherous trail which follows the Shire River down to Port Herald. It was still the rainy season and the air became heavier and more humid as we descended. The graceful blugum (eucalyptus) trees of the highlands were replaced with swampy marshes and then tall deciduous trees, followed by prickly shrub. It was another world. The driver pressed on and after 130 miles and five hours we arrived in Port Herald.

The first couple of days I tried to sort out fact from fiction. It was quite warm, as legend had it. Although the middle of the rainy season, it didn't rain often, but when it did it poured, ridding the air temporarily of its oppressive humidity. The temperature ranged in the mid nineties in the afternoon, dipping to the low eighties by early morning. Common garden variety house flies were voracious during the day. On our way to school in the morning dozens of flies congregated on the back of our shirts, as though looking for a cheap means of transportation. But then they were merciful compared to their nocturnal counderparts, the mosquitoes. No sooner did the sun set than these udzudzu move in, relentless in their search for a drop of human blood. Even though our houses were well screened, a few hardy ones always managed to invade our sanctuary. Texans could not even boast of a healthier breed of mosquitoes! Although all Volunteers are instructed to take anti-malarial prophylactics; in Port Herald no one questioned it.

Port Herald Day Secondary School

The flat area surrounding Port Herald was covered in February with tall, green grass, punctuated by a wide variety of trees. Huge pelicans squatted in the upper reaches of the tallest and brilliant-colored smaller birds darted to and fro. A family of bats made its home in the railroad station house. The soil was a poor sandy loam which lent itself to a meager living for the local gentry. Sunsets were reminiscent of those back home when the skies were cloudless all day. Days seemed to drift by with a steady sameness, giving the place a kind of south-of- the-border atmosphere. The slightest breeze was heartily welcomed.

It was said that the greater metropolitan area of Port Herald numbered some 10,000 inhabitants, but the number of commercial and residential houses in town was negligible. An inventory of the town would include the pink pastel boma—government building— in the center across from the square. The railway station provided the main link with the outside world. A few yards away was Baghat's general store where everyone who is anyone came to drink beer in the afternoon. The Hindu community controlled a large portion of the local economy and they stuck very much to themselves. They made enough money to send one or two members of the family to India nearly every year. In addition to the handful of other Indian stores, our inventory would mention the post office, the district council, the police station, the dispensary and the Catholic mission across the tracks. There were no more than seven telephones in town. A brief demographic study would reveal that a majority of the local people were Asena tribesmen, who spoke Chinyanja mixed with Portuugese expressions drawn from the peoples of Mozambique (officially known as Portuguese East Africa).

In fact we were surrounded on three sides by Mozambique, at the farthest point only 20 miles away. Several of the officials in the Malawi government stationed in Port Herald were from the north. A dozen or so political detainees were being severely punished by their presence in Port Herald. The European community numbered only four: the two Dutch fathers at the mission, the Portuguese stationmaster and the Scottish customs agent. The two Malawi IV health workers preceded the teachers by only a few months. At Chididi Mission, 13 miles up into the hills, two families—American and Canadian—ran the non-denominational fundamentalist church and primary school. Only a few weeks before I arrived a clash between Portuguese soldiers and Frelimo, the Mozambique liberation movement, had taken place near Chididi.

Port Herald didn't lack for personalities. Notable among them were the Volunteers from Malawi III who lived on in spirit. Students talked about what a good teacher Mr. White (Carroll) was, and any number of legends had grown up around Pete. Folks said he could do everything but walk on water, and that he refused to do only because of the danger of the snail-born bilhartzia disease! He left a mighty big pair of sandals to be filled. The G.A. (Government Agent) was the principal figure in town, in size as well as importance. Nhlane was a native of Mzimba in the north, industrious, personable and especially accommodating to us. Peter, the assistant police chief, was another friend of ours, also from the north. He also spoke of being "detained" here because of his job. John, the Scotch customs agent, was our most frequent visitor and a very charming fellow. The Dutch fathers had the longest term of residence among the azungu (foreigners). With their typically long beards, ever present pipes and deeply tanned faces the fathers seem to belong to the land itself.

Lastly, I should make mention of my four Peace Corps colleagues. My roommate, Tom Smith, a Malawi V "add-on", was quite a change of pace from Jeff and Pete. A total abstainer (including everything but water and Coke), Tom was from Ohio and claimd to be an individualist-a-la-Goldwater. And that after the election! Tom was pretty much a loner and liked to tinker a lot. He could build, repair, plant or modify anything. And that's what he was usually doing. A garden with a 30 ft. well, an insect collection and a temperature chart were among his projects.

Rick, Artie and Barton shared the other Peace Corps house. Rick, the Woodrow Wilson scholar from Stanford graduate school via Reid College, was in the lead for the number of sick days due to malaria. He said you could tell you had it when you felt like you'd just as soon be dead. Barton had also been sick and was about to overtake Rick in the lead. He liked to drink; by his own admission Bart could become an alcoholic before leaving Port Herald. Artie, the Bronx kid who made good, was running third. I guess that's proof enough that our mosquitoes were tough. Artie wrote in a recent letter home that we had adopted "we shall overcome" as our motto. Artie and I were together most often, whether engaged in a strenuous bao game (played with a wooden board and pebbles) or being paddled up the Shire River in an indigenous bwato (dugout canoe).

Port Herald   *15/February/1965*

Our professional endeavors were halting in the beginning at Port Herald Secondary School because of administrative difficulties. Our headmaster, a local product with a B.A. in geography from Roma University in Basutoland, was likeable enough but slow. Moved slow, thought slow, acted slow. I'm sure that we were faced with no more insurmountable teaching problems than anyone else. It was just a matter of overcoming our cultural differences. Should it really have mattered to us if he had the habit of inviting the prettier school girls into his office for long periods of time in the afternoon after classes? And then there were the simple joys of teaching. There was always that handful of students who managed to give you the feeling that you might be accomplishing something. There were exciting times... well, one that I can remember off-hand. One evening a crowd of about 1,500 fought off the mosquitoes after dark to watch the USIS film on JFK, Years of Lightning Days of Drums.

I reflected on a quote from the Peace Corps Volunteer Handbook:
"...Your survival as an effective Volunteer...will depend on your ability to remember why you volunteered, your ability to keep doing the things you believe in."

Nsanje   *1/August/1965*

There are no fixtures in nature. The universe is fluid and volatile.   Permanence is but a word of degrees.
                                        - Ralph Waldo Emerson

Some time in the early days of my service in the southern tip of Malawi the name Port Herald was nationalized to Nsanje, which was a Chinyanja word for jealousy. A strange name for a town, but given the continuing ethnic and political animosities in the region, perhaps fairly apt!

Just as life seemed to stretch out in a never-ending succession of days with little variation, I experienced a series of events ranging from fantastic to surreal, from tragic to sublime. On March 17, I received a message from Peace Corps Director Blackwell, which by this time had already become something ominous in itself. A few weeks before word had come from home that Vera Mae was hospitalized with what was originally diagnosed as symptoms of menopause. It was far more serious, and now Dad was asking that I be called home on emergency leave. I managed to hitch a ride from Nsanje to Blantyre the next day on the back of a Ministry of

Labor lorry. Within a few more hours I was winging my way home on an Alitalia flight from Salisbury, Rhodesia. Within 36 hours of my departure I arrived home in Oklahoma. As I have recounted in more detail in chapter one, Vera Mae died the following day. The next few days our family virtually re-enacted page by page the tragedy that was depicted in the "American Way of Death" by Jessica Mitford. My Peace Corps idealism caused me to react negatively to all the materialist trappings which accompany the American funeral.

Upon arriving back in Blantyre I was informed that I was two days over the allotted two weeks emergency leave and therefore not entitled to reimbursement. However, I was grateful that the Peace Corps had arranged to get me home so quickly, as it happened only just in time. It was even good to return to Port Herald, to throw myself back into things real which could absorb my energy. But I could still feel the trauma of the last couple of months knotted in my stomach. Something of the puritan had died in me with Vera Mae and yet it was hard to foresee the consequences.

Spring vacation was upon us in a matter of weeks, and I found myself being urged by Jeff to come to Lilongwe. He had bought a motorcycle recently, as had a good many other Volunteers, and he suggested I do the same. Although PC policy officially prohibited owning motorized vehicles, implementation of it was nebulous. There were warnings sent out from time to time, but the bark was presumably bigger than the bite. So I did it. I bought a little "scrambler" used for climbing up and down tea plantations. Of course we would have to steer clear of PC staff but most of them were at the lake for a conference. And thus began an odyssey which would bring me no end of grief. Jeff was in Blantyre, so we started off together toward his place in Lilongwe, ostensibly for the purpose of taking Chinyanja lessons during the vacation. We picked up Bush at Ncheu and continued on our way. But naturally, since it was I who bought the cycle, it developed a hitch in its git-a-long. We limped into St. John's Secondary School where Jeff lived near Lilongwe 200 miles later, exhausted but still exhilarated by the experience.

We did in fact have a few Chinyanja lessons but there was time for goofing off too. Jeff and Dave and I toasted the old days and went on a trip to Salima on Lake Malawi. After the Malawi V conference at the lake I decided to push my luck a little further and ride around to visit Fort Johnston. This was a very colorful place, as much for its madcap Volunteers as for its political heritage. A thousand miles later I arrived back in Blantyre for our own teacher's conference, ending a vacation that was too good to be true. Once again I was confronted with the summons to Dr. Blackwell's office. This time my misfortune was self-induced. He had seen me on the cycle, and this was against PC policy. I was instructed to sell it, immediately if not sooner. Well, at least by the time he got back from the regional conference in Addis Ababa where the cycle policy was to be reviewed. I had managed to set the all time record for the shortest number of days of ownership before being detected.

My devil-may-care attitude then led to one further bit of bad luck. In the few remaining days before the June 15 deadline I decided to take the cycle down the escarpment to Nsanje. Sure, it wasn't a very rational thing to do but it was a great challenge. Beautiful scenery, passable roads, waving moni bambos to the villagers, functioning on all 259 cc's. But halfway down the escarpment it happened, although I don't remember what. The next thing I remember, some passersby were picking me up off the road and taking me back up the escarpment to Queen Elizabeth Hospital. In addition to multiple lacerations from head to toe, X-rays revealed that I had a fractured clavicle. Anxious not to be sent home with dishonorable termination, I sneaked out of the hospital after two days with my arm in a sling and took the 12-hour bus ride back down the escarpment to Port Herald. The third day I was in front of my class going through the motions of teaching.

I arrived home to find a letter waiting for me from you-know-who charging me with 30 days unsatisfactory service for possession of a cycle. It appeared that I was the only PCV being penalized. I didn't even stop to wonder why. Apparently the Director decided it was time to crack down and let the Volunteers know he meant business. In the Scottish phraseology of our friend John, I went about "buggered up" quite some time. There followed shortly afterward a fresh five-stitch wound incurred when Mafuta ran in front of my bicycle. Mafuta was one of our household dogs, so named because when he was young he was chubby. The other dog, Sakonzeka, earned his name by being ungrateful to his masters. Their favorite past-time was chasing chickens and squirrels.

Artie aptly summed up what could only be an existential predicament in his breezy Bronxese:

"I don't believe you Hull...things just seem to happen to you. At least you're not a Peace Corpse yet."

There is a Yiddish expression which Artie said applied to people like me: Moishe Chupoya, in apparent reference to some mythic Jewish guy who was always courting disaster. When the news filtered up to Lake Malawi, Severin wrote back referring to me as a "living bundle of catastrophe."

— — —-

Somehow, woven into this story of funny and not-so-funny things which happened to me on the way to the Forum, there is another story which provides a striking contrast. It is the story of Nsanje, the Africanized name for Port Herald. The change of seasons around May brought temperatures plunging to as low as 60 degrees fahenheit and with that a whole new mood, almost a new raison d'etre for our lives as Volunteers. It is a story set amid endless sunny days, cool evenings, countless hours of reflection, busy mornings in school, the simple joy of students visiting our house, good food prepared by our cook Grayson, friendly squabbles, taped Beatle and Barbara Streisand music, nights of marathon bridge games, voracious reading and soul-searching discussions that sealed the bonds of friendship.

The story can be narrated in the first person plural instead of singular. It is at once brighter and easier to write. It concerns a threesome: Catholic (Bart) and Jew (Artie) and Protestant, (me) under one roof. We began living together when a clash of personalities reached storm proportions in the other house and I was aksed to trade with Rick. Happily, three more compatible roommates than ourselves could not be found. On the surface it would appear that the only thing we had in common was our having come from the wrong side of the tracks; none of us was from an especially well to do family. Our cultural and religious backgrounds were decidedly different. But the Peace Corps experience gave us a kind of common denominator.

Bart, the non-Catholic Catholic with a southern Baptist father and Italian Catholic mother, was a favorite with students. His compulsion to talk out what he referred to as his "metaphysical crises" made us all prone to confession. The slightest annoyance or surprise often elicited a not-too-irreverent "Jesus, Mary and Joseph" from Bart. Artie, the Jewish side of our unholy trinity, was somewhat less lethargic than Barton and considerably less accident-prone than I. He was an accomplished raconteur. He made us laugh when he got started on the times when he used to sell hot dogs at Yankee Stadium. Artie's Chinyanja featured the ubiquitous word, ujeni, which is used to mean anything from whatshisname, whachyamacallit, to Mr. So and So.

With the coming of the cool season in May we began to undertake several projects. First of these was the renovation of the old colonial tennis court in back of the girls' boarding. Our first and wisest step was to solicit the good offices of Brown Nhlane, the Government Agent. He not only served up a score of penal laborers for us but often as not he was on the spot with his considerable common sense. One month, 25 bags of cement, and 30 Malawi pounds later we put the finishing touches on it. Two months later we were still waiting for the tennis equipment promised from Peace Corps/Blantyre. Also on the waiting list for the same amount of time: a movie and slide projector. In order to complete reparations for the opening of Nsanje Tennis and Swimming Club, we also spruced up the less-than-Olympic-sized pool in the G.A.'s backyard. We had surely done our part to destroy the image of the "bland Volunteer", if only out of collective self-interest.

PCVs Relaxing at the Nsanje "Swimming Club"

Among our professional extra-mural endeavors was the clearing of a football and track field and the publication of the second annual edition of the school newspaper. In order to provide the school with its own playing field we literally had to clear out 100 yards of bush in back of Form III. Rick was coaching a track team that was to make its debut in a meet in Blantyre in July. My own efforts were poured into the incipient school literary digest, which we named Nsanje Secondary Speaks. Beginning with the student leadership of Editor Truzao, we formed a committee of representatives from each of the three Forms. Within a month we had received some 60 articles ranging from barely legible English to rather perceptive essays which the committee then whittled down to 25. Finally came the gigantic task for us of editing, typing, and mimeographing 250 copies. I wonder whether Henry Luce could have had anymore headaches publishing Time Magazine!

PCV Hull working with students to clear brush for a track

We also found time to scour the countryside, absorbing African culture at the grass roots while being closely scrutinized ourselves by the local populace. One of the first of these forays consisted of a 13-mile hike up into the hills to Chididi Mission, which we learned had some affiliation with the South African Reformed Church, although run by Americans. The missionaries were never seen in town and we could not understand why. The higher altitude of the Chidid Hills afforded great relief from the heat of the valley. Another strenuous trip by bicycle took Artie and me across the border south of Nsanje over 20 miles to Villanova in Mozambique. This small town had little to recommend it except Portuguese wine and a slight touch of European civilization. Because of my insistence on returning early in the afternoon Artie was stricken with sun stroke and we had to stop at an infirmary about halfway.

Another colonial artifact was the antiquated railway running from Beira on the Mozambique coast through Nsanje to Blantyre. When all other transport failed we could take the midnight special, which took 10 hours to go 100 miles to Blantyre—that's right, an average of 10 miles per hour! But the scenery was magnificent and if one was allowed to ride with the driver it was even more interesting with a bird's-eye view of the tracks.

More frequent, and even more grass-roots-ish, were our trips to adjacent villages. The occasion might be a visit to Forty's home, the clerk at school to whom we owed much of our practical exposure to Nsanje. Or it might be a search for vegetables and fruit such as papaya, tomatoes, beans and corn which were not always available at the market. One of these ventures was prompted by the legend of the Mbona, related to us by a student. The Mbona was a sort of Christ-figure who went about performing miracles, especially gifted with the power to bring rain in times of drought. Although the Mbona was no longer alive, the cult lived on. It was my good luck to be conducted by a couple of chiefs to a small forest in which his spirit was said to reside. Each year a young maiden would go to his hut to keep him company. Barton undertook to write an epic poem about this local saint. Occasionally we stumbled onto traditional dances in the villages. One time I came away with a drum for which I paid ten shillings.

The second school term also saw the passage of some memorable events in the life of the community. First of these, so delightfully described by a couple of students in the newspaper, was the opening of the Community Center in May. It was notable for the presence of Mr. Chakuamba, one of the cabinet ministers and probably the most influential man in the Lower Shire Valley; Mr. Malamba, the local M.P., recently returned from Europe; and Simoni, the greatest of all Malawi tribal dancers. With the opening of the Center we now had another place to drink beer (besides Baghat's) and most every

Saturday evening there was a local penny-whistle combo to liven things up with South African style kwela.

A month later an event of less universal but nevertheless intense interest was the arrival of Nsanje's first two female Volunteers: Ester and Mary Jean. They were to work with the health project, bringing the total number of Volunteers in Nsanje to nine. A third event was the local celebration of Malawi's one year of Independence and the change to status of Republic. If it had been reported in the Malawi News the article might have gone something like this: "Thousands of people thronged the field in front of the boma (government building) today to help the Ngwazi, Dr. Kamuzu Banda, celebrate Malawi's first year of politically stable government as an independent state." Whether or not independence was uppermost on their minds, the people did celebrate, wth tribal dancing, songs, boxing matches and marching by the Young Pioneers, the youth wing of the Malawi Congress Party. In the evening we were formally invited to a banquet at the District Council which consisted of rice, roast beef and beer.

These were the notable events. But days were more often than not, not composed of events. An ordinary afternoon might be spent reading from our Peace Corps library. Among the books which were of particular interest to me included: Zorba the Greek, The White Nile, Citizen Tom Paine, Africa Unbound, African Image, A History of Central Africa, and especially Memories. Dreams, and Reflections by Carl Jung given to me by my TCU roommate and aspiring psychiatrist, Rafael Ruiz. This domestic routine was about to be broken with a much-awaited trip to East Africa.

East African Safari

East Africa   *August/1965*

East Africa is the traditional playground of the tourist, drawn by the prospect of seeing and hunting the wild game that roam the broad plateaux. It is the region where Swahili is the lingua franca, one of the major languages of the world. According to the evidence being unearthed at Olduvai Gorge, East Africa may have been the home of the earliest predecessors of man. The coastal area has known the impact of Arab traders for centuries. East Africa has seen the colonial powers contending for dominance over its land and its people, culminating in British rule. It has been the adopted home of tens of thousands of white settlers who came to bask in the perfect climate of the highlands and to claim the rich, fertile land as their own. The Europeans brought thousands of Asians—predominantly from the Indian sub-continent—to aid in his "civilizing mission". Indeed, one of the great British imperialists argued that East Africa was, and should be considered, the New World for an over-populated Asia. The Asian came and prospered, becoming even less loved as exploiter of the native African than the European colonizer.

Then the colonial empires began to crumble. Uhuru (freedom) came first to Tanganyika, the poorest but probably most politically united colony of East Africa, in 1960. Then came Kenya's Independence in 1963 after a decade of turmoil which the Europeans called Mau Mau. It was in Uganda where the British dreams of a white-dominated federation of East Africa were dashed. The Baganda, the traditionally advanced tribe of Uganda, would have no part in such a scheme and resisted British domination. But they lost their hegemony and had to settle for a federated independent Uganda in 1962 which they did not control. The loose federation formed by the independent states of East Africa—Tanzania, Kenya, and Uganda—with its common currency and customs, was the first hopeful step toward complete federation.

The Peace Corps Volunteer turns tourist during vacation. For many of us in Malawi V, this would be our first big excursion since coming to Africa. East Africa was a must, and we looked forward to this safari for months with eager anticipation. Having applied for 21 days of vacation leave and the $7.00 daily Peace Corps allowance, I began my East African safari in the company of three of Malawi V's most sanguine and hedonistic Volunteers: Bush, Dixon and Artie. It was a trip which proffered rest and relaxation on a grand scale, one of the true rewards of Peace Corps service. The only note of uneasiness about the trip was the group's knowledge of my own propensity for misfortune which they feared might extend to them. Bart was remarking as we departed that he wouldn't get on the same plane with me! But I somehow felt that I was leaving all my misfortunes behind in Malawi.

Dar es Salaam   *10 /August/1965*

After a typically close call, arriving in Blantyre from Nsanje at the eleventh hour, Artie and I joined John Dixon and Dave Bush in the ride to the Chileka (Blantyre) Airport on August 10th. Our flight was on time, so by 2:00 PM we were winging out way over the Shire Highlands, eastward first with the green peaks of Mt. Mlanje peeking through the billowy clouds. Three and a half hours later we landed in Dar es Salaam, the city of peace. We stepped out into a balmy breeze. It was the cool season and the air was mild. At this point all our organized plans ended; from now on we were playing it by ear. We hopped into a five-bob (English slang for shilling) taxi and drove the six or seven miles into the city. Along the road there was a maze of palm trees, assorted types and sizes, and rows of industrial complexes which seemed to indicate a more pronounced economic development than in the Blantyre-Limbe area. We went first to the New Africa Hotel. It was by no means "new" nor was it particularly "African". The preponderance of patrons in the hotel were European and on this day there was a rather diffident group of Tanzania PCVs who were able to provide us with little information about accommodation in Dar. Finding the New African a bit too "dear" for our Peace Corps tastes, we wandered over to a place called the New Metropole (which was also not very new) where we paid only 35 shillings a head for one room.

It became apparent very quickly that we each had different goals in mind. Bush contended that he was strictly interested in the museum-library-church tour. Dix, in his familiar lecherous leer, said he doubted that. Sure enough, within a short time the four of us would go in different directions, which ever way the wind blew us.

The city of Dar es Salaam surrounding the natural harbor which looks out on the Indian Ocean is a melange of Arab, Portuguese, German, British and African cultures as well as Indian. There was little resemblance to the continental flavor of Beira or the antiseptic air of Salisbury. The senses were first assaulted by the exotic odors of spices and coffee sold from brass urns on the streets and by veiled women dressed in flowing black robes of the coastal Swahili. One was reminded of this being an old city full of history. There were sail boats and big ocean steamers lulling in the harbor against a clear blue sky. Where there might have been a church or cathedral in Blantyre there was a mosque in Dar. The sound of the muezzin issued from each minaret, regularly calling the Muslim faithful to prayer. Everywhere we heard Swahili, a trade language born of the mixture of Bantu and Arab languages common throughout East Africa. We were tempted to answer in our familiar Chinyanja, also a Bantu language with a similar structure. Although German was occasionally heard, English was the predominant language in the formal sector. The clothing seems to be of better quality than that worn around Blantyre, and the Muslim women were in all-black attire with their heads covered. The constant sea breeze wafting in from the bay gave Dar respite from the heavy humid climate, especially during the (relaltively) cool dry season.

The first evening in town we sat around the dinner table after a good meal at Margot's wondering where the action was. We were informed by a local that Dar was a "eunuch" as far as entertainment was concerned. So we strolled through the streets and then stopped in to see an Indian film, my first ever. Then back to our hotel where gay-blades congregated. Talking to a couple of other Malawi PCVs, we were told that Banda Beach was the place for late-evening fun. It was! There I was invited by Mnkonda, a young African student, to visit University College the next day.

Dar es Salaam   *12/August/1965*

Morning brought a very pleasant surprise when we tracked down a lead on travel to Zanzibar at Keasey's Travel. The desk clerk signed us up for a tour of the island for 115 shillings, with no strings attached. Tanzania had only been indepdent a short while, and although Zanzibar was part of the Tanzania Republic, it still enjoyed considerable autonomy frolm the mainland. It was viewed from the outside as being even more "radical" than Tanzania, under the influence of the communist Chinese. We were told that there were rather tight controls on foreign tourists to Zanzibar and that there was normally a lot of red tape involved in getting a travel permit to go there. We were to learn that however radical-sounding the Zanzibaris were, they were nevertheless interested in tourist dollars. We were to leave for Zanzibar in three days.

Meanwhile, a five-bob taxi fare took us six miles out to the newly opened but expanding University College of East Africa. The campus was one of three University Colleges in the region, the others being the well-established Makerere in Kampala, Uganda and in Nairobi, Kenya. Enrollment at present was just 500, projected to double to 1000 in a year. Here we ran into our old mentor from Peace Corps training, Dr. Carol Fisher, who had told us in training that if we were ever in her neighborhood in Tanzania we should drop in. She looked quite chic, fresher than I remembered her in Syracuse.

We climbed up the hill on which London Hall overlookeds the Dar harbor, then took an elevator up to the 7th floor to Mnkonda's room which afforded a spectacular view of the city and the harbor. He explained that the academic program at University College was designed for three years and that the most popular course of studies there was law. He expressed a coolness toward Malawi President Banda but a very high regard for his own President Nyerere.

Back in the city, Joe Short, now teaching at Kurasini School for Mozambican refugees outside of Dar, came to the hotel and invited us to visit his place. On the way we became ensnared in a miniature traffic jam and Artie got all excited. He said it reminded him of home in the Bronx, horns blowing, people cursing, cars whizzing around. He wanted to get out and yell, "Hey mac, move yer..." Joe was a gracious host, treating us to an epicurean dinner, after which we retired to the veranda for reminiscences of our days in training at Syracuse. A rollicking good time was had by all!

Dar es Salaam   *13/August/1965*

Normal people would perhaps have bad luck on Friday the 13th, but today turned out to be a real triple-header for us. It was marred only by one incident. Dave had gone down to the beach near Joe's house to take a few pictures, when I arrived on the scene to find a dozen or so Africans squabbling with him. They were unhappy about his having taken their picture without their consent. Unlike Malawians, they seemed very sensitive about tourist exploitation, especially if they consider themselves not properly dressed for the occasion.

Browsing through the shops in downtown Dar, we came across the casual clothing sensation of Tanzania, already spreading to the U.S.: the Uhuru shirt featuring colorful African designs. We cleaned out a dozen or so, with plans to flood the Malawi market. Bushie and I then took a bus out to a riding stable where he plunged with gusto into a one-hour lesson in horsemanship. Lena, the instructor, was a colorful white settler from Kenya, dressed in lean riding pants and surroundnded an air of authority. Having finished her task of teaching Dave how to handle the horse, Lena recounted her days in Kenya during the Mau-Mau rebellion in the 1950s.

In the meantime I made an excursion around the ranch. A quick inspection of the flora and fauna of the area revealed numerous similarities with our home in the Lower Shire Valley: the abundance of palm and mango trees, and the occasional stately baobab. But I also remarked upon the relative absence of mosquitoes, perhaps owing to the constant sea breeze. In the evening we treated ourselves to a live performance at a place called the Little Theater in exclusive Oyster Bay. To my personal pleasure, the show we saw there was an amateur presentation of the ever-popular play Oklahoma! As I sat there in far away Africa, being treated to images of my own culture, the goose-bumps came in profusion. Oklahoma! apparently had played to a sell out European (expatriate) crowd of 200 or so every night for several weeks. Amateur it was indeed. I scarcely recognized the lines, as they were sung with a sometimes Cockney or Oxford accent.

Later we went back out to Banda Beach where I engaged our waiter, Hassan, in a lengthy discussion. In impeccable American argot ("big deal, you guys") he was Mr. Cool. We didn't have this sort of conversation with Asians in Malawi. However, beneath his extroverted surface, Hassan was a very disillusioned young man. Raised as Pakistani Muslim in Uganda, he had moved to Zanzibar where he claimed to have been active in politics. As a Youth Leaguer, he was sent to Russia and China. But as an Asian who helped to overthrow what he considered to be the Arab aristocracy in the recent election, he was later imprisoned by the Zanzibari authorities. With only a two-year primary education, Hassan sees little chance to achieve his ambition of entering the university.

Dar es Salaam   *14/August/1965*

In the afternoon we went to a party organized by the Syracuse "vllage-i-zation" Project. Headed by Prof. Carol Fisher, this group includes about a half dozen Syracuse graduate students whose contract with the Tanzanian government calls for setting up pilot villages with model health, agriculture and education facilities— the ground level for socialized nation-building. The project, which was to last for 18 months, was one-third complete. Carol painted a very sympathetic picture of the Mozambican ministers-in-exile here in Dar. Edouardo Mondlane, the first leader of Frelimo (the Mozambican Liberation Movement) had been at Syracuse and was well known and beloved by the Syracuse community. She and other Syracuse staffers frequently saw the Mozambicans and socialized with them. Joe, Dave and I returned home for an extended session featuring a recitation by Joe from a book called The Unfair Sex.

Zanzibar   *15/August/1965*

A 30 minute plane ride and 333 shillings took us from the Tanzanian mainland to the island of Zanzibar, whose dimensions are a scant 25 by 50 miles. With a population around 300,000, Zanzibar was now federated with the Republic of Tanganyika in a union known as Tanzania. The bloody revolution that overthrew the Arab aristocracy and caused a mass exodus of Europeans was now in the hands of the Revolutionary Council, headed by Vice President Karume. Following the revolution there had been a mass exodus of the Arab aristocracy and Europeans. Even now after the establishment of federation with the mainland, the Revolutionary Council maintained considerable autonomy from the central government. Naturally, because Zanzibar had accepted aid from the East, their revolution was being labeled "Communist" in the West.

Having consulted with various people about the trip to Zanzibar, we figured our chances of getting there would be slim or none. If we did manage to make it, it would be at the risk of life and limb. However, far from being barred from visiting the island as capitalist Americans, we were met at the airport by an official for the Ministry of Tourism. He waited on our every command, like a genie out of A 1001 Arabian Nights. We were assured that all those stories about anti-Americanism on Zanzibar were so much rubbish. Whether our guide was there to keep an eye on us or just to see that we enjoyed ourselves, the end result was the same for us. If I was still questioning at all why I suffered the indignities of training, the all-seeing eye of the Peace Corps bureaucracy, the alienation of Bwana Blackwell; all of that was quickly dispelled. This exotic isle—and it was indeed exotic—could only be described with superlatives in its physical beauty. The air was heavily scented with spices, the sea of palm fronds waving softly in the breeze. For us, indulgent "ugly Americans", it would answer all matters of indulgence.

We were taxied to the Africa House Hotel, a British establishment now abandoned by the former colonial masters. The only other foreign faces to be seen consisted of a couple of Tanzania PCVs! In the hotel lobby one could see nothing but news and magazines from China, the USSR, the German Democratic Republic and other peoples' republics—and posters of Chou Enlai who had recently visited the island declaring Africa "ripe for revolution." There followed a taxi tour of Zanzibar Town, passing the waterfront and its harbor full of dhows. There was Livingston House, where the good doctor outfitted his expedition into the interior of East Africa in 1866. We stopped for a drink of coconut milk along the road. Ambling through the luxuriant tropical palms, we were introduced to Zanzibar's premier export: cloves. There were also mangoes, oranges, coffee, bananas, papaya and a palm oil factory. The tour ended at the Zanzibari Museum.

Zanzibar   *16/August/1965*

The next morning we were finishing a leisurely breakfast on the balcony overlooking the ocean when I looked up to see a vaguely familiar face, although I couldn't readily distinguish the gender. It moved closer and a woman followed just behind. The figure was lean with a gaunt, bronzed face and lively eyes. It spoke, in a crisp British accent, asking if I was a young American who had been in Greece in 1962. By this time I recognized him as Father Graham Dowell, the Anglican priest from Great Britain who had been the director of our World Council of Churches work camp in Elassona. Same prophet-like appearance: long hair, goatee, shorts and short-sleeved golf shirt. But he had put away the priest's habit and was now married. We talked briefly, mentioning others who had worked with us in Greece. It was one of those times when one says over and over "It's a small world." He said he was now working with the Coptic Church of Ethiopia. We swapped stories about our experience in Elassona and wished each other well. Then he disappeared with his wife and we went about finishing our tour.

In the morning we took the tourists' tour of the city of Zanzibar, through the narrow, winding streets that seemed older than anything I had seen in Africa. Our guide named Ali was typically dressed in a Muslim skull-cap and galabeya (traditional robe). We followed him through the narrow, winding streets, stopping frequently to listen to his explanations. He showed us the renowned carved doors dating back centuries to early Arab days and smiled as we took his picture standing in front of them. We climbed to the top of the Anglican Cathedral, built it is said, on the very spot where the slave market had stood before the British came. There were other interesting places such as the mansion built by the Aga Khan, the remains of a Portuguese fortress, a Hindu temple, a government house which was originally the palace of the Sultan of Zanzibar Mnkonda and an infinite number of curio shops selling ivory trinkets made in Hong Kong.

There was a potpourri of people on the streets. The veiled Moslem woman was even more predominant here than on the mainland and the men were dressed in cap and gown. There were Hindu women in bright silk saris with the spot on the forehead and Hindu men dressed like any European. There were Africans, too, who seem to be absorbed in the mixture. We looked for Chinese faces since the impression given by the Western press was that Zanzibar was overrun by Red Chinese following the revolution. And we found one, that of Chou en-Lai, on posters peering at us from buildings and trees. They had been distributed on the occasion of a recent diplomatic visit. Perhaps there were Chinese technicians around but they were not very visible. We said our kwaheris (good-byes) to Zanzibar, taking the afternoon plane on to the Kenyan seaport of Mombasa. In 24 hours we had exploded the myth about the difficulties of travel in Zanzibar, leaving the island without a trace of remorse in our minds.

Mombasa   *17/August/1965*

With all the anticipation of a bunch of girl scouts going to Disneyland, we flew into Mombasa, sin city of East Africa and fleshpot of Kenya. Situated on an island just off the mainland, Mombasa appeared to be more affluent (i.e. more Europeanized) than our previous stops. This was undoubtedly due in part to the swarms of U.S. sailors who drop anchor here and dump U.S. dollars at every turn.

Richie and I were to leave for Moshi, Tanzania, together with my ultimate destination being Kampala, Uganda. We had decided on the bus that left every morning at 8:30 AM, but this was 30 minutes before we got up! Having missed the bus, I instead went through 100 shillings on curios, film and odds and ends. We then decided on an excursion to the east side of the island to Fort Jesus, built by the Portuguese during their hay-day in Africa. It commanded a very imposing position overlooking the channel. The recently opened museum contained artifacts and notes on the history of East

Africa. We again piled into a taxi and returned to Nyali Beach for the afternoon. I lost myself once more in reading Heller's Catch 22. Richie and I had a meal of chow mein at the Splendid Hotel, washed down with saki and ginger. Another early night in anticipation of a long trip the following day.

Mombasa-Moshi   *20/August/1965*

Finally, after a three-day profligate spree of lavish spending and extravagant living, Richie and I bid salaam to Mombasa and hit the open road, heading west toward fabled Mt. Kilimanjaro. Within five minutes our bus had a flat tire. An hour later we were off again, climbing the 200 miles to Moshi. After 25 miles we had left the palm-covered coastland and were in the midst of prickly, scrub brush and unyielding Oklahoma-red soil. The air became cooler and more arid. After the town of Voi the tarmac faded into dirt on the roller-coaster type hills. By 4:00 PM (normally tea time) we had crossed the Tanzania border and were soon in Moshi at the foothills of Kilimanjaro. Standing in the bus depot, bodies limp and minds a bit vacant, we were suddenly accosted by Eloise Choi-he (known as "Cho Cho" by fellow Tanzania volunteers). We had trained together with her at Syracuse. She was in transit from Nairobi and an art project, heading back to Korogwe where she lived.

After only slight inducement she persuaded us to stay over one night, which was certainly the right decision. Familiar as she was with the town, Cho Cho took us out to dinner. Rather, we accompanied her there. We were finishing the meal, taking in the spectacular view of the mountain, when Richie motioned for me to turn around. Doing so, I was startled by the grey, blinking horizontal lines of a television set. It was a Nairobi station, our first glimpse of a TV since leaving the States. Pulling our eyes away from the TV set, we went looking for a place to stay and found rooms at a place called Mlay's for a meager five shillings: clean beds and a real bonus: hot water!

Moshi/Arusha, Tanzania   *21/August/1965*

We saw Eloise off at the bus station and hitched back along the main road, up to Marangu. To get there, the lowest station on Mt. Kilimanjaro, we took one of the many minibuses, climbing up to the 5,000 ft. level. Again the scenery changed: to leafy green forests and crisp mountain air. At Marangu, in Chagga territory, Richie and I stopped at a small art museum which featured some of the finest works of African tourist art we had seen. Climbing to the summit of Mt. Kilimanjaro was not on our agenda, however, and we headed back down to the main road toward the town of Arusha, some 50 miles away. There we were, having decided to hitch-hike and throwing ourselves at the mercy of any vehicle that would take us, we were immensely relieved when John Nellis of the Syracuse village-i-zation project slowed to a halt and offered us a ride. We gratefully accepted, and John and his wife dropped us in Arusha.

Arusha, located at about 4,800 ft. at the foot of Mt. Meru, is said to derive its name from the Warusha tribe, cousins of the stately Masai. The Warusha could be seen on the streets of the town with their lobed ears and brightly-colored but scant attire. Accommodation was secured abruptly when we ran into a Tanzania Volunteer who was managing a hostel in his home! We walked back into town for supper to a place which very nearly simulated a Sonic drive-in hamburger stand in Oklahoma. Its proprietor, who went by the sobriquet of "Cha Cha," was an Asian of the Ismaili sect of Islam who had fled South Africa three years before. Now, it seemed, he was doing a land-office business. Effervescent and witty, Cha Cha said he now knew Swahili inside out, greeting his Mzungu customers with a hearty jambo as they entered and a cheery kwa heri when leaving!

Very earnest in his religious convictions, Cha Cha held forth about the Aga Khan, both secular and religious leader of the Ismailis, and their commitment to economic development. We learned that Ismailis number some 20 million worldwide and have their origin in Persia. Having lived in South Africa most of his life and being familiar with its multiracial population, Cha Cha quickly spotted Richie as being Jewish and had only good things to say about the Jews of his former home. Of all the Asians in East Africa, the Ismailis seemed the most outgoing and approachable to us Westerners.

That evening was spent in the friendly company of five female Volunteers from Ethiopia who happened to be going to Ngorongoro Crater the next day in a rented vehicle. This was on my must-see list. However, I had felt it coming for some time, and sure enough Richie announced that he would not be going on to Kampala. After Ngorongoro, we would go our separate ways, he back through Dodoma and thence to Zanzibar and I on Kampala via Mwanza and the Lake Victoria steamer. Even though I was sorry to lose a traveling companion, I at least had the satisfaction of knowing that I likely talked Richie into visiting Zanzibar instead of Uganda!

Arusha to Ngorongoro Crater, Tanzania   22/August/1965

After lunch in Arusha our swinging safari of seven got under way, crammed into a Peugeot sedan. The 110 mile ride to the Ngorongoro Crater provided an opportunity for us to compare notes with the Volunteers from Ethiopia. They told us that there were so many Volunteers in that country that some of them had chartered planes to West Africa for vacation. The road to the great crater reminded me of our own escarpment road from Blantyre to Nsanje, with its abundance of baobab trees and flat scrubby plains. Occasionally we were engulfed by clouds of dust from passing cars. The ascent up to the rim of the 8,000 ft. crater provided a panoramic view of Lake Manyara to the south. At the youth hostel overlooking the crater we found Malawi Volunteers Jim Jones and Teddy Konen and ate supper with them, swapping tales and plans for the rest of the vacation. Jimmy decided to spend his last five pounds and to accompany me onto Kampala. For the first time in Africa that night I shivered from the cold air, even though we were quite close to the Equator.

Ngorongoro Crater   23/August/1965

After a hearty breakfast at the hostel we got into open-topped Land Rovers and began the winding descent into the crater. The tourist pamphlet described Ngorongoro as Africa's "Garden of Eden", claiming that it contained the largest constant stock of wildlife in the world. Only in the recent years had hungry-eyed tourists begun to invade its natural beauty. We readily began to see that this claim might not be over-stated. Once down on the floor of the crater, 2,000 ft. from the rim, one could survey the immense variety and abundance of flora and fauna. No tourist could be disappointed; here was the very image of Africa with which we had all grown up. The crater was teeming with wildlife: thousands of wildebeests with heads like buffaloes and bodies more like horses, zebras, gazelles, rabbits, cranes, ostriches, guinea fowl, as well as hyenas and vultures. But the main attraction was initially a lonely rhino that charged our Land Rover as if on cue, almost playfully and then backed away. The driver hunted up a couple of lionesses with cubs and a huge male lion. We scrambled through the open-top to take pictures. Near the forests along the side of the crater was a small herd of elephants foraging among the prickly trees. Only once was my enthusiasm momentarily dulled when I discovered that I might have ruined a roll of film while rewinding it. But only one misfortune in a two-week period would be a record for me, given my recent history!

Toward the end of the tour in mid-afternoon we drove onto a grassy knoll. As the driver came to a halt a stately Masai man appeared (again as if on cue) dressed only in elaborate plumage in his hair and a cloth draped around one shoulder. We half expected him to hold out his hand for money, which very poor people often did in Malawi. But he seemed almost oblivious to our presence, perhaps annoyed that we were disturbing the pristine natural environment of which he was a part.

We said goodbye to the Ethiopia PCVs and soon Jimmy and I resumed our all-too-frequent posture: hitch-hiking back to Arusha. Close to giving up hope, we were finally picked up by a truck loaded with Indians. Back at Cha Cha's, worn to a frazzle, we munched on his Dagwood sandwiches and collected our wits. An embittered American coffee planter engaged us in conversation, pouring out his woes. It seemed that he was slowly being squeezed out of business (and out of the country) by the threat of government confiscation of his property. He didn't elicit much sympathy from us since we saw ourselves as being on the side of the Africans.

On the Road to Mwanza, Tanzania   *24/August/1965*

Jimmy Jones and I started out together on the next leg of the safari, which more than any other made me aware of the vastness of East Africa. We were headed to the port town of Mwanza on Lake Victoria, but in order to get there by bus we had to go 90 degrees off course, due south. It was an 800 mile grind, 32 hours on end. We might have caught the bus going straight through the Serengeti Plain, but for the common foe of all who travel abroad: misinformation. On more than one occasion we found ourselves in a situation where English was not spoken at all, and our Swahili was not yet sufficient for communication. That, coupled with an unmistakable coolness toward us wazungu,(Swahili for foreigners) gave us a distinctly unwanted feeling and caused us to miss the desired bus. It was most unusual in our Africa experience, making us all the more uncomfortable.

According to the map, we traversed the Masai steppes and the Great Rift Valley some time in the middle of the night. The next afternoon we finally arrived in Dodoma, a fair-sized town, seemingly close to nowhere but on the rail line to Dar. With a couple of hours' wait before our next bus to Mwanza, Jimmy and I wandered around town and bought sandwiches to fill our empty stomachs. Soon we were on the road again, bumping and grinding our way in a northwesterly fashion across land even more vast and un-peopled than before. It was still the land of the Warusha, and they were seen moving across the parched plains with studied disregard for our bus. Somewhere in the black of night at one stop the bus took on a person who appeared so frail as to be on the verge of starvation. The person, whose sex was hard to determine, sat directly next to me, eyes listless and boney fingers wrapped around the handrail. I was suddenly seized with the stark realization of how privileged we Americans were, and how easily it must be for Africans to be resentful of us. Somewhere in the course of the long ride from Arusha I managed to complete Catch 22, following Yossarian's wild and absurd adventures to their bizarre conclusion.

Mwanza   25/August/1965

As the bright equatorial sun began to scorch the land in the morning, we saw more wildlife, mostly giraffe and ostriches, and an abundance of exotic birds. As we neared Mwanza I stood up, since by now there was no portion of my posterior that was not tired of being sat upon. For the past two days we had subsisted on bread, scones, Fanta and Coke. Mwanza, the third largest city in Tanzania, was a sight for sore eyes. Since there were hundreds of PCVs in the country, the Peace Corps maintained several district hostels. Happily, one of these was in Mwanza and we readily availed ourselves of it. If there was no catch to the information we received this time, Jimmy and I would be off across the equator the next morning toward Uganda.

Lake Victoria   26/August/1965

Jimmy and I scurried down to the East African Railroad harbor office early in the morning to purchase 2nd class tickets, only to be assured initially that were no tickets available for the steamer that day. Before our despair managed to set in, the one chance in a hundred for tickets somehow materialized. We boarded at 9:30 AM for a scheduled 10:30 AM departure...and finally set sail on The Victoria at 3:00 PM. There was no reason for us to be out of sorts, however, since we were too busy being happy not to be bouncing along on the bus! Second class was, relatively speaking, the lap of luxury. The Victoria was the largest and fastest steamer on the lake. At 4,000 ft. above sea level, Lake Victoria is the second largest fresh water lake in the world and the largest in Africa. The moderately high elevation gives the lake and its shores a nearly perfect year-round climate.

The Victoria took on passengers like Noah's Arc, an exotic mélange of all sorts. There was a handful of Europeans, an American missionary family, a few Asians, hundreds of Africans jammed into 3rd class below in the hold, as well as a bewildering assortment of live fowl and animals. As we finally took leave of the Mwanza harbor I settled back in the sun to read, reflecting that the nightmarish bus trip might almost have been worth enduring to arrive at this moment of calm. I had bought a copy of Transition magazine, a literary journal published in Kampala by Asians. The lead article by Norman Podhoretz was about growing up poor and Jewish in Brooklyn. It was a sort of white man's version of James Baldwin's The Fire Next Time, popular at the time. Hungry for intellectual stimulation, I was determined to visit the Transition office.

At one point I became aware that one of the few African women in the 2nd class deck was staring at me. It was not at all uncommon for Africans to stare at us wazungu but this time it set me thinking. Thinking about what goes through the mind of the Africans as they regard Europeans (we Americans are usually lumped together with them). Why do we, with our pale complexion, sit in the sun in order to make our skin darker? The glasses, the watch, the clothes, the fancy luggage and other accoutrements bespeak an easy lifestyle. Perhaps there was some remembrance of injustice at the hands of similarly white-skinned hands.

I glanced back at the Transition article where Podhoretz was recounting his experience with gangs on the streets of Brooklyn. Then I reflected on the absolute authority we had over those who work for us, our cook, our gardener, the deference our students pay to us as teachers as possessors of all knowledge. I thought about how often the mzungu waiting in line with Africans is motioned to go toward the front, a clear sign of privilege even after Independence. And we came to immerse ourselves in their culture! How will we escape a sense of cultural superiority? Will we ever manage to converse with an African peer on an equal footing? How can we possibly understand the nationalist pride in a young country trying to regain its self-esteem after decades of colonial rule? Is it possible we will leave Africa with a heightened superiority complex, happy to have spent two lovely years in Africa but glad not to be one of them?

Kampala, Uganda   *27/August/1965*

The majestic Victoria docked at Port Bell about mid-morning and we sauntered out into the dazzling sunlight. Although there didn't seem to be distinct rainy and dry seasons here on the equator, the land was clothed in absolute greenery, in striking contrast to the drab brownish hues on the other side of the lake. Only minutes before we had crossed the equator into the northern hemisphere. In another hour Jimmy and I were in downtown Kampala looking as usual for a cheap place to stay. Jimmy was anxious to get to Nairobi in time for a promised ride back to Malawi and I was running low on money. So we had time to take in only a few of the highlights of Uganda. Located only about 20 miles north of the equator, Kampala is named for the seven hills on which the Baganda grazed their herds of impala and planted matoke (the banana-like staple) before the coming of the European. It seemed remarkably modern to us, without all the excesses of a modern city. The roads were well laid out and clean, the lawns well manicured and surrounded by luxuriant foliage. In part, it must be the near-perfect climate that gives Kampala the appearance of freshness and cleanliness.

Jimmy and I checked into a modest hotel near the center of Kampala and I drew out more cash at Barclay's Bank. Our first venture was to the neighboring town of Entebbe, the administrative capital of Uganda. It seemed one continuous stream of suburbs between the two cities. We were told that the Baganda had traditionally been a "suburban" people, organized into counties—sazas—all owing allegiance to the Kabaka or king who lived in Menge Hill. Since political Independence in 1962, however, the Kabaka's power had become rather more symbolic than real. Every family seemed to have its patch of matoke. In Entebbe we visited the aviary and animal farm which contained samples of Uganda's bountiful wildlife. Dix would have been interested in the slovenly warthog! As my students would add in summation in their essays: that is all I can tell you about Entebbe.

Back in Kampala, Jimmy and I began to seek out the major attractions. The first of these was the resplendent Parliament building in the middle of the city, with it Independence Gate and beautifully carved wooden paneling inside. The official guide informed us that President Milton Obote's ruling party, the Uganda Peoples' Congress, was represented by a large majority in the Parliament (76 seats out of 92). But his real opposition, the Kabaka, was not really a party leader but the traditional head of state of the powerful Baganda. At 39, Obote was the youngest of the East African Prime Ministers, and he had just returned from a tour of China. In the West this was seen as a sign of a possible breach of a stated policy of non-alignment in international relations and leaning toward communism. I thought about all the signs we had seen in Zanzibar of coziness with the East and imagined this to be a real possibility.

Having just been introduced to Transition journal, I was intent upon visiting its office just across the street from the Parliament building. There I decided to subscribe for one year. While at the Transition office I bumped into Paul Theroux, a Malawi PCV who would become famous as a travel writer. He was already at it, collaborating with the Transition staff. This was our first—and last—meeting and Paul did not show much interest in small talk about Malawi or travel in East Africa for that matter. He was likely busy on his next publication.

In the afternoon I went out Kampala Road to pay a visit to Makerere University, the first (1948) and most prestigious of the three East African universities. It was here that many of the present leaders of the three East African countries had received their university education. Its reputation reached far beyond East Africa and it was considered by many to be the best in Sub-Saharan Africa in some fields. I spent several hours in the library (Bushie, with his interest in museums and libraries, would surely have been jealous!), impressed with the number of volumes and the card catalog system.

Kampala to Nairobi   *28/August/1965*

Jimmy and I resumed our familiar stance at the side of the road in Kampala with the intention of reaching Nairobi. It was a well traveled road, so we didn't experience the usual trauma in securing a ride. The first couple of lifts took us through the rich forests and coffee plantations which ring the northern edge of Lake Victoria. Just before reaching Jinja we passed Owen Dam, the largest hydro-electric installation in East Africa and among the largest on the continent. Here also is the source of the Nile River which flows out of Lake Victoria on its long journey toward the Mediterranean. On the other side of Jinja we continued our search for another lift. Eventually a cream colored Ford Galaxy pulled over. It was an elderly Scotsman dressed in the traditional colonial uniform: white short-sleeved shirt, white shorts and white knee-length socks. It was as though the European sought to accentuate the symbol of his authority with whiteness. He was rather sanguine and affable, soon telling us of his birth in South Africa and his subsequent 40 years in Kenya as a very successful white settler and surveyor.

And if his attire indicated the old established order, his narrative was even more indicative. For he was, by his own definition, an unreconstructed colonialist, a living remnant of the past and vivid symbol of the neo-colonial present. He had scarcely concealed contempt for "Communist-leaning Nyerere" whom he claimed to have admired greatly at first. But Nyerere was guilty of "hypocritical" dealing with the West at least and a dupe of China at the worst. Ugandan Milton Obote, although not quite such a scoundrel, was just a cut above Nyerere. But when it came to Kenya and Prime Minister Jomo Kenyatta, the old settler became effulgent with praise. After all, Kenyatta "thinks like a Britisher." The white settler explained further: "Mzee (Kenyatta) has held back the contending forces of tribalism which would otherwise be rife." In his view, Kenyatta was not a tribalist, although he was recognized as a leader of the Mau Mau rebellion, considered to have been a Kikuyu conspiracy. The old settler also had kind words for Tom Mboya, referring to him as level-headed and pro-British. (Although Mboya was a Luo, he was considered to be perhaps the second most influential man in Kenyatta's cabinet).

Our host stopped to buy the wife at home a basket of oranges. He continued his appraisal of the African political scene. The old settler described the Federation of East Africa as being further from reality than at any time since colonial rule. This he ascribed to Nyerere's foot-dragging, his fooling with the currency policy and his generally "reddish" tint. Obote, too, with his recent trip to the

Communist countries, would surely cause more trouble. And then he sounded a final note on the whole of Africa. He considered Emperor Haile Selassie of Ethiopia the pretender to the leadership of the Organization of African Unity and "highly amusing." Rhodesia, he observed, could be the flashpoint for all of Africa, and he hastened to add that his sympathies lay with the settler minority. As so many times before, my conversations with the European revealed a strong feeling for his "investment" in his home in Africa and his reluctance to part with it.

He let us out near Tororo at the southeast edge of Uganda and we thanked him for the ride. At this point our hitching success once again took a turn for the worse. Eventually we gave up and went across the road to the Tororo Girls' School to beg for lodging. An American couple agreed to put us up for the night. This was a truly palatial affair built with USAID funds as a model secondary school. I imagined that with the money spent on this school, the Ugandan government could have built half a dozen modest schools in the bush.

Nairobi   *29/August/1965*

Our luck the next morning was no better than it had been in recent days. Jimmy began to wonder whether he would make it in to Nairobi in time to catch his ride back to Malawi. I was just plain tired of hitching! At the eleventh hour we found ourselves in the back of a truck and yet another Indian driver, on the go again. The next 300 miles into Nairobi afforded some of the most spectacular scenery in Africa. The first third of the way was a climb up to about 10,000 ft. through green fertile plains. Then the road dropped down into the Rift Valley where the white settlers found their paradise. This wedge-shaped depression extends some 40 miles and contained rich fields of wheat, coffee, tea and grazing land. The Rift Valley has its origins in the Red Sea and cuts all the way through East Africa, right to our doorstep in the Shire Valley.

Even more abruptly than it began its descent, the road now climbed the eastern escarpment up to Nairobi at about 6,000 ft. As we had heard from all accounts, Nairobi is in a class all by itself among East African cities. While it may not have the exotic charm of Zanzibar or the rich history of Mombasa, Nairobi has the appearance and the smell of affluence. Cars move in and out of the center city in a neatly gridded pattern. We found our way to the University College men's dorm where lodging was available during school vacation. Here was once again found some of our Malawi PCV peers. In the evening we attended a movie version of My Fair Lady. Rex Harrison as "enry "iggins" was just great. Jimmy was in time for his ride to Malawi and we said goodbye.

I settled down to see a bit of the city before moving on. At last I was really on my own and could make mistakes in judgment without worrying about it affecting anyone else. I had only to let the left hand know what the right hand was doing. I found that Nairobi has frequent periods of grey days when a heavy fog descends over everything. This was one of those periods. I roamed through the numerous bookstores in the city, letting myself unwind from the tedium of hitch-hiking. In the evening after dinner the residents of the university dorm gathered in front of the television set in the lounge. TV was still pretty much of a novelty for me after nearly a year of settling in to read a book by candle-light at night. Mzee Kenyatta was featured holding forth at a political rally, trade-mark fly whisk in hand, exhorting his people with a mantra of harambee (let's all pull together). This was followed by a re-run of I Love Lucy, followed by cowboy films.

At no time during our sojourn in Africa was I more aware of the relative affluence a Volunteer enjoys than on our East African safari: Ethiopian Volunteers chartering planes to Nigeria, Malawi PCVs criss-crossing East Africa with the ease of business executives (at least in the eyes of many Africans), and for the first time in my life spending money as though I really had it. And I did. How ironic that it should be on the modest Volunteer salary!

Nairobi to Mombasa   *31/August/1965*

Today marked the one-year anniversary of my association with Peace Corps, having entered training in Syracuse on this day in 1964. The world was turning on its axis. The mop-topped Beatles had burst on the scene, first in England, then the U.S., and now in the farthest reaches of Africa. The Rolling Stones were wailing about not getting any satisfaction. The Cold War was reaching its apogee, with the Soviets and the West engaged in a regular dance of saber-rattling and slogan-mongering. The U.S. troop build-up in Vietnam increased and the anti-war movement gained steam. Here in Africa we felt somehow removed from all of these developments, although we were vaguely aware that there would be days of reckoning.

I was up early and on the road, busy with the dismal business of hunting for a lift. I noticed that amidst all this affluence I now had only five pounds to get me all the way back to Malawi! So I summon up my old frugal ways. I reflected on all the benchmarks on this trip: this has been my fourth time to pass through Nairobi, my fifth crossing of the equator and with my stay at University College a visit to all three branches of the University of East Africa. And all this without the usual litany of blunders and misfortunes that had become associated with me!

I needed to get to Dar where I would take a return flight back to Malawi. The fist car that stopped was headed, not toward Tanzania, but for Mombasa. Anxious to be moving and knowing that it was a bit of a detour, I took it anyway. Better than roasting in the equatorial sun! The driver was a British fellow whose main concern seemed to be with his source of wealth: his mother. He was afraid his allowance might be cut off. Kenya, he complained, had not been too kind to him—taxes and all that—so he would soon be off to the Bahamas on a business venture. He had little good to say about either Africa or the Africans. The road, which was rugged all right, he allowed had been built by the devil himself. It could well have been, with its roller-coaster hills and frequent clouds of dust kicked up by passing vehicles.

And so I had come full circle, back to Mombasa just as the three East African heads of state were meeting in town in a summit conference. With a bit of time on my hands I wandered down the street from the New Hotel where I was staying to take in a very exotic sight which turned out to be a Hindu Temple, very colorful and unlike anything I had ever seen. The bronze statue of a calf reminded me of the many statues of the Buddha I had seen in Japan. These Eastern religions remained very much a mystery to me. Dead tired from the travel, I turned in early to conserve energy for the trip to Dar.

Hindu Temple in Mombasa

Tanga   *2/September/1965*

Just outside of Mombasa my hitching-hiking fortunes took yet another disastrous turn for the worse. I was marooned for the better part of the morning (or rather the worst part) in an attempt to reach Tanga. Seasoned hitcher that I had become, I hunkered down and began reading, with one eye on the passing cars. But even such predicaments can be made worthwhile. I finished reading Lolita (another selection from our Peace Corps book locker), recognizing some tangential points in my own life described by Nabokov, and then got well into Uhuru. This book was purported to be the definitive novel on the life of East Africa's white settlers and African elite. It has probably drawn more than one wealthy white matron out to the bush in search of an affair with a virile safari guide. We will still have to wait for a novel that describes the emerging post-independence society through the eyes of the African.

And then the winds came, the lightning flashed, the heavens opened up and I looked up to see a truck slowing down. "That petrol lorry has stopped for you and wants to take you to Tanga," I muttered to myself, still unbelieving. Well, not quite, but most of the way. The last leg into Tanga was with yet another old colonialist who had been District Commissioner of Tanga in the 1950s. He mused that in the years before 1900 Tanga had enjoyed even more importance as a port city than Dar. While it was still the second city of Tanzania, Tanga relies primarily on the large sisal plantations in the area which it serves as a port. But as sisal becomes replaced by synthetics in the manufacture of rope, Tanga may lose its economic raison d'etre.

In the five hours I had before the bus to Dar was to leave I took a walk around the town of Tanga, thankful that the day's lorry ride was over but dreading the all-night bus ride ahead. There were throngs of people out in the streets taking in the soft evening sea breeze. The sweet smell of frangipani trees filled the air. My sense was that the coastal area, with its lazy palm trees and Arabesque culture, was the most fascinating part of East Africa. It was quite a different world from the vast plateau and the temperate lake region, as well as the majestic White Highlands. Along the Kenya and Tanzania coast there was the pervasive Swahili culture that gave the area uniformity. Here it seemed that the measure of a man was faith in Allah.

The island of Zanzibar seemed the essence of the coastal culture, more "coastal" than the Tanganyika coast itself. The old District Commissioner had speculated that the growing power of Zanzibar was such that the Zanzibaris might well take over the mainland of Tanganyika. This seemed highly improbable, given that the population of the mainland was around nine million and that of Zanzibar only 300,000.

Half past eleven, going toward midnight. The bus finally departed. This was no more pleasant than most bus trips on this safari. I endured the entire journey skwunched (the term seems ever so appropriate) between an Indian man on the one side and an African woman on the other, symbolic East African bookends. One or the other managed to doze off on my shoulder at regular intervals, then occasionally into my lap, all through the night. I spent much of the night sitting upright, my arms drooped over the rail of the seat in front of me. As with many nightmares, this one ended at dawn as we bounced into theh station in Dar, the Haven of Peace. I climbed down from the bus on rubbery legs and claimed my katundu (luggage). There were two PCVs from Nigeria on the bus—a long way from home—who wanted to know if I knew of a place to stay.

Joe Short winced a little when I appeared at his place with two strangers and asked if there was any room in the inn. He obliged and we plopped down exhausted. I filled Joe's ear with stories about the last couple of weeks up- country. The next day Joe and I went for a ride on his motorcycle—pure joy for one who had been confined to such torture on buses and crowded cars for the past several weeks. By noon I was on the way to the airport, already beginning to reminisce over a momentous safari.

Altogether too soon I was bouncing along the bank of the Shire River in a Land Rover to the end of the world, to the Peace Corps post farthest in the world away from Oklahoma, with much the same feelings a convict must have going back to his cell after having been out on parole. But still it was a better feeling than I had had on that first ride down the escarpment in January, sulking at the prospect of living in Port Herald. Now it was spring and the valley was once again beginning to turn green; the air was still cool. Whatever the Lower Shire Valley was now, it was home, and I was going to resume the job I was sent to Africa to do. Having seen a large portion of East Africa, I now realized there were places more desolate and much less habitable than Nsanje.

Nsanje   *5/October/1965*

For the eight months that I was in the Shire Valley I grew to understand and perhaps to appreciate it. As a teacher of geography I frequently showed my students that rivers traditionally support large populations. And so it was with their own Shire Valley. Cotton, the chief cash crop of the area, was harvested and loaded in sacks to be sent to Beira (Mozambique) by rail. The recent scheme to make Malawi self-supporting in sugar production was well under way at Makanga and Nakalu. The Europeans who ran the experimental sugar stations told us that irrigation from the Shire could transform the whole valley into an oasis of green, growing things, given the technical know-how and capital investment.

But the present picture was rather grim. The long dry season left the land parched and sterile. The age-old practice of burning the scrub to prepare for the rains created a smoky haze that hung in the air for miles. Virtually no crops were grown during this time, and the result was chronic seasonal depression. This year the Shire had been dammed upstream and the usually rapid current slowed to a trickle. The long stretches of elephant marsh had become desiccated, happily reducing the breeding grounds of the pestiferous mosquito. At the same time water became a scarce commodity. Lines of women and children queued up at the wells.

Surely 1965 would be remembered as the year of unseasonably cool weather in the Valley. In Nsanje temperatures remained moderate throughout most of usually notorious October. There were even several week-end showers. But inevitably the heat set in, bringing enough unpleasantness to remind us of where we were. For the record, Tom's thermometer registered daily averages hovering at 105 Fahrenheit degrees with overnight lows down to the high 80s during November. But the heat was more appropriately measured in the rising number of students whose heads slumped on their desks by the third period, and the number who left for the hospital after the fourth period, "the whole body paining" as they were wont to say. Or the frequency with which we teachers came home after school and flopped down to lunch muttering "Oh Gawd." The freeze (refrigerator) worked overtime to keep us in supply with essential ice cubes.

Nsanje   *15/November/1965*

As we began to reflect on another term in Nsanje Secondary it seemed to have been marked by innovation and intrigue. As early as last term the growing rift between PC staff and headmaster was indicated in his negative report to the Ministry. This was due to alleged irregularities in our teaching habits, not completely unfounded. From our standpoint the difficulty stemmed from the headmaster's feckless administration. Nearly all our attempts to bring the school abreast of the times had been met with either intransigence or monumental indifference. Perhaps this was too stereotypical a Peace Corps experience to belabor.

So, without attempting to solicit sympathy, I will move on to I what I considered to be our considerable achievements. At the outset it must be said that so far the innovations were procedural rather than substantive. Whether they would become institutionalized and endure, it was too early to determine. It may be, as Artie asserted, that we would be judged by posterity as los patrones, PCV's described in the August issue of The Volunteer as those whose sin was "over-involvement" rather than blandness. That is to say, those things which looked tangible might only be written in the sand....

In the beginning of the term I experienced a burst of enthusiasm for giving students some sort of structure for extra-curricular activities. As a product myself of the student council system in my high school, I wondered if the idea of a student government might catch on here. The interest at first was marginal. But soon some of the more ambitious chaps were asking questions about the idea.

There wasn't a science club, a social club or newspaper at their school. And, quite clearly, these were the ones who fancied themselves already to be junior leaders. Several weeks later we struggled through the awkward process of a democratic election which was very new to most of the students. This was reflected in the rebellion among Form III students after a Form II boy had been elected president. Form III would elect its own president! Somehow I felt they had been following their own government's politics too seriously. But a school-wide debate on the matter successfully unveiled the wounded egotism of the few who had initiated the rebellion. After the first few faltering steps the student council grew into a fairly responsible organization with a real constitution.

The queer business of parliamentary procedure and committees was clumsy at first, but it didn't seem to stifle their enthusiasm. Most significantly the council gave students a sense of identity with the school that was heretofore vague. One of the real tangibles to emerge from its deliberations was the idea of students finishing the leveling of the new school football field. Despite the incredible aversion (to us Volunteers) most students had for manual labor, the project was completed.

The most popular innovation was Artie's film presentations. After having finagled both a slide and moving projector, he showed no less than half a dozen films taken on loan from USIS and British Information Service. Naturally, the "badness" was that the kids came to expect a film every Friday and they would undoubtedly feel deprived when the projector leaves. The football team continued its exploits, emerging as the powerhouse of the lower Shire. In addition, the girls' netball team won all of its initial games.

The week of November 15-19 was marked by notable sobriety among staff and students. We PCVs made the ultimate sacrifice by wearing ties. The occasion was the dual visitation of first the Chief Inspector, and secondly the Minister of Education himself. The inspector went about peeking in student notebooks and teacher lesson plans when he could find them and striking fear into the headmaster's fluttering heart. Afterwards the headmaster consoled us with the news that the inspectorate found our school "about average", although they wanted to say "below average." The next day we were honored by the presence of the Hon. John Msonti, Minister of Education. His two and a half hour tardiness was owing to the "urgent matter of UDI (in Rhodesia) in Zomba" at the time. He urged the students to work hard, be courteous to their masters and pass their examinations. Appropriate words, indeed!

On the domestic front we deviated little from the previously established routine. Sakonzeka, the dog with the propensity for killing chickens, finally became obsessed with the idea. After nearly a dozen convictions, I asked the veterinarian to give him capital punishment. Mafuta, by contrast, became even more lethargic while Katudzi, our kitten, provided us with much comic relief. For several weeks I indulged in a superficial cram course for the Foreign Service Test which 20 of us took in Blantyre. It was like studying for one of Dr. Potter's English history finals: no place to begin or end. (Note: I didn't quite make the cut on the Foreign Service Test.) News of the outside world seeped down to Nsanje via Time, Newsweek and the occasional PC staff visit.

Speaking of PC staff, it often occurred to me that the story of Peace Corps in Malawi — mine in particular — read like a paraphrasing of Joseph Heller's Catch 22. It was a chronicle of absurdity. I was sometimes Yossarian, the non-hero who copes with the illusory world of regulations and commands with cynical resignation. Take for example the recent episode. Some time ago I received a letter from Dr. Blackwell assuring me of a transfer at the end of the academic year. Then he left Malawi, replaced by Big Mike McCone. The new Director soon made his initial tour of the country to acquaint himself with Peace Corps problems, even coming all the way to Nsanje (something the former administration never got around to). I reminded him as he sat in our living room drinking our wine that I had been promised a transfer.

"Well," he said, "We've decided not to grant any transfers except in case of emergency." His would be no wishy-washy administration.

"Fly more missions," Yossarian was told. "Remember, you are a Volunteer."

Then Big Mike McCone put his own neck on the line by defending a Volunteer, Paul Theroux by name, who had written a critical article in the Malawi Peace Corps Migraine about the "feckless Johnson administration." McCone was called on the carpet by Johnson's Okie friend, Ambassador Gilstrap, in turn. Soon McCone himself was banished to a limbo of consultations in official Washington. Freedom of speech? Well, yes, if you say the right things.

Nsanje   *8/December/1965*

Mike McCone never returned from his consultations in Washington. But Will Lotter, Deputy Director, acting in his stead, relented and confirmed that I would be transferred after all, although it was not initially known where! I could begin to see my Malawi experience measured in more pluses than minuses. The really big plus would prove to be Dr. Will Lotter, his wife Jane and their three boys. Will was recruited into the Peace Corps from the faculty of the Physical Education Department of the University of California at Davis. He would forever be to those of us who served as Volunteers under him the very model of a PC Director: committed, engaged and attentive to the concerns of both Volunteers and Malawians as well. Pancake breakfast at the Lotter house for any Volunteer who wandered into Blantyre would become an institution, a haven of fellowship. And in the Peace Corps office, it was always nice to see the friendly face and words of encouragement from Sue Urbonas, now in her second role as office secretary.

Goodbye Nsanje!

Dedza Day Secondary School

The word came from the Peace Corps office in Blantyre: my assignment for the second year of service would be Dedza Secondary School, one of the top boys' schools in the country. But first, there was to be a pleasant respite from teaching in some of the most lovely spots in Malawi.

Likhoma Island and Malindi   *December 1965*

Having left Nsanje in early December with ambiguity of feeling toward my one-year residence, I set out again with Artie on an extended in-country vacation which was to rival the East African safari. Carolyn Brook, it seems, was the trainee who popularized a phrase in Syracuse which recurred to me frequently on our tour of Malawi:

Ndidzakhala wokhondwa kukhala kuno ku Malawi moyo wanga wonse.

This Chinyanja phrase roughly conveys the idea that I would be happy to live in Malawi all my life. However hyperbolic this may sound, it did reflect a much-heightened sense of appreciation for a beautiful country.

Groping for a required service project to fulfill our Volunteer obligation, we chanced to meet with Roy Frazier who solicited our help in the renovation of the hospital at Malindi, north of Fort Johnston on the lake. He was hosting a dozen PCVs in something more than just a project as we were to see. Malindi was an Anglican Mission whose history reached back to the early part of the century. Its thatch-roofed buildings had seen Henry Chipembere—one of the most prominent of the Young Turks chased out of Banda's cabinet— come and go. Its clear waters and sunsets across the lake provided a travel poster setting. The work group was peopled with a wide assortment of Malawi Vs from Livingstonia to Nsanje. There was an atmosphere of reunion; many of us had not been together since training. There were afternoons of swimming and cavorting about, evenings of bridge, idle chatter and good jazz. Even the work, which consisted of cleaning and white-washing the infirmary complex, was romanticized by the conviviality and earnestness of the whole crew. It was like a big Join the Peace Corps at the post office in Anywhere, U.S.A.

Jeff & Galen in Lake Malawi, Malindi

Artie and I took our leave at the end of the work camp to set sail on the renowned Ilala which traverses the length of the lake. We were first subjected to a 50-mile, five-hour bus ride to the port of Monkey Bay, uncomfortable even by Malawi standards. The entire voyage on the Ilala was to cover 355 miles and three full days to the northern-most port of Karonga. One of the first stops was the railhead at Chipoka, after rounding Cape McClear. There we waited 12 hours for cargo loading—and Jamie Kunz. He boarded the Ilala after a day's train ride from Blantyre, his usual jovial self, also on the way to visit students.

Once more the Ilala was cruising along the western shore of the lake, the hills cascading down into its blue waters. There is something about the leisure of a sea voyage that is more leisurely than any other kind of leisure. Almost an enforced leisure: a daily repetition of sun-bathing, eating, absorbing the scenery, trying to remember when the bar opens. We eventually arrived at Likhoma Island, site of the largest cathedral in Africa south of the Sahara, home of about 3,000 people (all Anglican), and two isolated PCVs. I promised myself I would come back to the island when I could stay a while. Other routine stops included Nkhata Bay, Florence Bay, Ruarwe and Miowe at which point Jamie disembarked for his venture into the interior—and finally Karonga.

The earliest evidence of human settlement in Malawi was during one of the drier climatic periods nearly 100,000 years ago, and it was on this flat lake-shore plain of Karonga that stone-age hunters lived. At one time Karonga served as an Arab slave trading post; in World War I it was the scene of early skirmishes between British and German troops. It was now an outpost of Peace Corps activity, over half a dozen strong. One of these, Tom Popp, was incidentally parked in a PC vehicle at the port five miles from town when we docked. He served as our host for a three-day stay. It was with Tom that I witnessed the most striking event of the trip: Christmas Sunday at the local C.C.A.P. (Scottish Presbyterian) church.

Accustomed to seeing congregations numbered by the handfuls in Nsanje, I was amazed as we watched thousands of brightly clad Africans gather under a huge baobab tree outside the church. They were addressed by a most articulate African minister. We were invited the next day to visit the construction headquarters of the Germans south of Karonga who were building the Great Kamuzu

Highway all the way along the lakeshore. These men were hospitable toward us and asked us to stay for dinner which we readily agreed to. They were a rugged lot, obviously interested in building the road and little else concerning Malawi. However, they demonstrated a despicable display of blatant racism toward their cooks. And then, for good measure a few anti-Semitic comments were thrown in. I pinched myself to see if it was real, to recollect what decade it was.

Driving back along the construction of the highway, we were beset with large puddles left by heavy rains. The Great Kamuzu Highway was still in the midst of humble beginnings. Another side trip took us out to a secondary school, easily the most isolated post in the country. Just as Artie and I began to fret over the prospect of hitching overland all the way to Kongwe we met with a singular stroke of luck. A British homecraft extension agent was preparing to return to Lilongwe in a government Landrover and she invited us along. We followed the lake road back to Deep Bay, up the 2,000 ft, escarpment to Livingstonia, hence to Mzuzu for the night. Mzuzu Secondary School was an impressive sight, certainly by comparison with the few secondary schools I had visited heretofore. Pushing south around the Vipya Plateau, we passed through Mzimba, Kasungu and Dowa then finally to Kongwe Secondary School.

There they all were at Kongwe—Hazel, Holly and the Harrods— fellow trainees in Syracuse. They provided us a unique and happy yuletide, with all the trimmings. There was a Christmas tree, fireplace full of stockings with goodies and a sumptuous dinner. The only thing we could have asked for was snow! And there was a truly ecumenical flavor including several brands of Protestants, a Catholic, and Artie representing the Jewish community.

Zambia and the Congo

The scene changes to Lilongwe again, to St. John's Teacher Training College, where I was visiting with Jeff after much ado about visas for my trip to the Congo. After a little arm-twisting Jeff decided to make it a twosome. The next day we were flying over the green hills of Africa in a bucket-seat Skybus on its last scheduled flight to Lusaka. It was to be a short vacation full of impressions. The first of these was a reflection of the Rhodesian crisis which greeted us at the Lusaka airport in the form of hundreds of barrels of petroleum standing to the side of the runway. They were being flown into Zambia in big transport carriers. No sooner had we muddled through customs than we noticed a truck-load of British soldiers, RAF troops, recently arrived to keep the peace.

That was our transport into town. Although the streets of the capital city were not paved with copper Lusaka did reveal the comparative affluence that copper had brought to the country: neatly-gridded streets, modest sky-scrapers, well-dressed citizens. However, it was noticeably lacking the cultural charm of East Africa's seacoast cities or the scenic beauty of Malawi towns.

Lusaka, Zambia   *31/December/1965*

Jeff and I allowed ourselves a little luxury by registering at the expensive Lusaka Hotel. It was the afternoon of New Year's Eve and we were taking in the town when we stumbled onto a small bar called the Pig and Whistle. An RAF chap happened in about the same time, insisted on buying us a round, and thus began a six-hour session ranging from motorcycles to Anglo-American relations. By evening we had settled nothing in particular and our benefactor suggested that we adjourn to a New Year's celebration. The scene was the social center of St. George's Church where one of the white tribes of Africa was trying hard to live up to Richard West's description of it. We found this pretty much a drag and so left, wishing we had followed our own noses elsewhere.

A long and rather monotonous train ride found us in the temperate woodlands of the Zambian copper belt near Ndola. Here we made a pilgrimage 13 miles out of town to see the site of Dag Hammarskjöld's fatal plane crash of 1961. Then on to the Congolese border where Jeff dusted off his high school French to get us through an interminable customs procedure at Sakania. Shortly afterward we were in the Katanga capital of Elizabethville, a city which readily revealed something of the erratic fortunes of the Congo. Copper-rich, "E'ville" had the easy old world charm and grace of a European city and a large number of Europeans still around. At the same time the biggest and most imposing building, now only a few years old, was barred and overgrown with weeds. It is symbolic of the violent disarray in the Congolese economy. The black market flourished;

the Zambian pound was highly prized. And I saw my first Cadillac in Africa in downtown Elizabethville.

We witnessed a parade through the middle of the city in celebration of some holiday in which the dress for the occasion was, de rigueur, top hat and tails. Some of the local whites noted that there was still a feeling of racial tension, five years after the chaotic assumption of Independence and the attempted secession of Katanga Province. This was nowhere apparent to us, especially in the appropriately named Black and White nightclub. Here there was a thorough co-mingling of white and black which I had not seen as yet in Anglophone Africa, with an emphasis on Congolese music and chicly dressed African women decked out in flamboyant print cloth.

Little did I know that the Democratic Republic of the Congo would have such an enduring allure for me. It was to draw me back again and again over the next 11 years, first as tourist, then as adventurer, teacher, researcher and university professor.

Dedza   *February 1966*

Back in Dedza, I logged another 5,000 miles of travel both in and outside of Malawi. The only "badness" (a Malawi-ism) to arise from this vacation was the loss of most of my clothes. Our house in Dedza had been burglarized. Dedza Secondary School was by now my third post and Severin Hochberg my sixth room-mate. Dedza's reputation for excellence was perhaps as well known as was Port Herald's notoriety. Naturally the juxtaposition of these two posts in my experience invited comparison. The most obvious difference was geographic: most of the discomforting things with which God seems to have cursed Nsanje he has graciously withheld from Dedza. The school is ensconced on the side of Dedza Mountain (7,212 ft.), itself over a mile high, temperatures rarely climb above 70 and on a July morning frost may be found on the mountainside. Tropical Africa! Rainfall measures better than 80 inches a year. It is a hardy mosquito that can survive the brisk mountain air. In the near perfect climate, the sweet smell of cedar and the sound of the wind whistling through the pines enveloped our house.

It is said that Dedza received its name from early settlers who found groundnuts growing along the mountain range, (mtedza).

These early tribes were probably Chewa, driven into the highlands by the warlike Angoni from South Africa, who entered Malawi west of Dedza township in the 1830s under Chief Zwangendaba. The invaders eventually settled and today Dedza became highly populated by the Angoni. Then came the Yao invasions which forced the Chewa along the lake up the escarpment to the plateau and as far as the Lilongwe Plain. David Livingstone passed near here on his first expedition opening up the area for British expansion under the banner of Christianity and Commerce. Dedza Secondary students are predominantly Angoni and Chewa from the Northern and Central Regions.

Dedza township, four miles from the school on the other side of the mountain, was once a colonial outpost. The Angoni Highlands Hotel was a relic of the past, the golf course only used by our secondary school staff and the airstrip only occasionally used by the doctor. The Catholic diocese claimed some 90,000 souls and there is a Mosque that served a substantial Indian community. The boma, built in 1947, was set against Dedza Mountain and surrounded by a luxuriant growth of trees. In addition to the groundnut crops, Dedza District produced 80% of Malawi's potatoes. Other cash crops included tobacco, some cotton along the lake, rice also near the lake shore and of course every family had its maize patch.

The reputation enjoyed by Dedza Secondary (popularly known as Box 48, from its mailing address) matched that of the town. Formally opened in 1951, it was one of the few government boarding schools in the country. Its former students and staff were often the Very Important People of Malawi; the social scientist would call them the elite. A School Certificate from Dedza was a key to the future. Out of 89 5th Form students who took the Cambridge Exam in 1965 75 received the School Certificate, three of them first class passes. We began the year with about 320 students, 20 teaching staff and a first class headmaster. Mr. Justice Kanyuka was easily one of the best headmasters in the country and he had impeccable credentials. A graduate of the University of Rhodesia and Nyasaland as Head Boy, he spent two years in Britain on a teacher training program. More important he commanded the respect of our European-packed staff. Indeed, as is usually the case, we Americans were considered among the "Europeans"; all together we constitutd an overwhelming majority of eighteen.

Dedza Day Secondary School, "Box 48"

There were almost as many variations of the King's English in the staff room as there were teachers: two Welsh, two Irish, one Scot, one South African, a preponderance of English whose accents ranged from Oxford to Cockney. Jean Jacques teaches French while doing his alternative military service. The staff ranged in age from 17 (the Bolton School Volunteer) to semi-retirement, in temperament from erratic to imperious. Half of them owned cars, only three were married and one was the captain of the Lilongwe rugby team, considered the best in the country. Severin and I taught exactly the same subjects, English and history, in the upper forms.

The students, generally speaking, were models of enthusiasm and self-discipline. There were those, however, who were there not so much on merit as through the good offices of certain members of parliament. The boys' boarding houses (all students were boys) stretched up the side of the mountain in steep procession. The usually neat rooms reflected a rather sophisticated sense of humor. Their clothes cabinets carried such inscription as: May God Bless

Thy Humble Servant, Nganje the Unbreakable, A Fan of Laurel and Hardy—Mphande, Secret Agent 007—Gondwe, and a liberal smattering of Elvis Presley and Beatles pictures. One of the fifth form boys sported a Playboy foldout!

As one entered the school compound on the road from town there was a brightly lettered sign directing the visitor to the residence of Hochberg and Hull. And as one approached the house of sturdy brick he would notice a small but vigorous garden, a legacy of the two Malawi III PCVs. It contained a wide assortment of delicacies such as strawberries, sugar cane, carrots, cabbage, lettuce, melons and coffee plants. James, Severin's Man Friday from Nkhota-khota, kept the weeds out as well as doing the cleaning and ironing. Our cook, Richard Kapangaziwiri, whom we inherited with the house, was a good cuisinier, given his British training. He was also a bit eccentric: he talked to himself incessantly. One of his favorite refrains which we were likely to hear coming from the kitchen was "One Zambia, One Nation!" He kept us wondering. We did our interior decoration in African modern, nearly resembling a curio shop, with ivory carvings of Zanzibari dhows, Masai masks, a Sena drum and a set Angoni spears and shields.

The only dark spot in the foreseeable future was the long arm of the Peace Corps coming to retrieve our fridge. After all, Dedza was not a hardship post so we were not entitled to one. But then, it wouldn't be Peace Corps if we allowed ourselves to become too comfortable.

Likhoma Island   *l5/July/1966*

The last five months saw the furrows of experience deepen and broaden. It was a period of intellectual stimulation and growth, rewarding satisfaction in my profession as a teacher and most of all a period of a gratifying sense of community with others. In sum, many of the seeds of expectation planted in training had long since taken root and germinated in my African experience. The first term at Dedza reached its conclusion as we began to plan another project, long anticipated and talked about. The idea for a day camp on Likhoma Island had been bantered about by a half-dozen of us months ago and subsequently taken up by Lonnie and Rick who promised to host it. Soon there were a dozen enlisted to share their island existence for 10 days. The ingredients of the camp would include instruction in sewing, singing, swimming and sports for primary students. We gathered at Nkhota-khota on the mainland across from the island to wait for the Ilala. Terry and Bill, the local Health Volunteers were on hand to greet us with tall tales about their life in the bush. They could easily lapse into near fluent Chinyanja at any time. Probably no two Volunteers in the country had made more of their experience than these guys.

As we disembarked from the Ilala into the crystal-clear waters of the bay and made our way through the baobab trees and rocky soil to the mission on Likhoma Island, we were met by our hosts and a sea of happy African faces. Here, it seemed, was a microcosm of the family of man, people who for years had made their home on this island of only a few square miles and had made it widely known throughout Central Africa. They were almost entirely Nyanja tribesmen. Many had left home to travel and settle on the mainland, not only in Malawi but all over Central Africa. It must be said that Likhoma Island remained their spiritual home. In the course of time the Islanders had gained a reputation for diligence and achievement. Recently the population of the island had been increased by a stream of refugees from Mozambique seeking out family ties or at least refuge from the war in that colony. In fact, the island was so close to the Portuguese East African territory that Portuguese gunboats could be seen ominously patrolling the waters. The history of Likhoma Island since the turn of the century had been written mainly by the Anglican Church Mission which commanded one's immediate attention by its massiveness. It was the focus of the lives of the faithful as well. And this was virtually everyone on the island.

Rick and Lonny had done their homework and we could quickly see that the camp would not lack organization. Jeff, Artie, Bush and I were quartered in the quaint brick house overlooking the Cathedral which had been the home of Archdeacon Chipembere, father of Henry. On the second morning after our arrival we were awakened by the tolling of bells for the Easter service. I had a vague remembrance of an Easter morning 10 years before when I awoke in a Buddhist temple in Japan.

Each day on the island dawned bright and clear, with never a hint of clouds. And each day was fun and often eventful. Bush and I put our considerable experience as aquatic instructors to work, a job envied by everyone else. We soon found that teaching an island boy to swim was a rather presumptuous thing, tantamount to teaching an island girl how to pound chimanga (corn). But at least we introduced some orthodoxy to their strokes. Afternoons were often taken up with excursions or special projects. Three of us paddled pa bwato (by dugout canoe) on an ambitious round trip to Madimba village toward the end of the island, but the highlight of the week was our participation with the permanent secretary for the Ministry of Community and Social Development in Operation Santa Claus. He was there to dispense free maize and candy to the refugees. And he came in earnest too, with the good ship Noheni loaded to the hilt. A few of us accompanied him to the sister island of Chizumulu to unload the final portion. Here we beheld an extraordinary display of biting the hand that feeds. The local politicos were so insistent that they deserved more than 10 bags of maize that they refused at first to unload any of them. Despite this somewhat unsettling experience, it was with a great sense of refreshment and satisfaction that we closed the camp and set sail once again on Lake Malawi.

As the second school term was launched you could almost peer down over the edge of the Peace Corps tour into the future. This was the home stretch. And if you were not inclined to look toward the future, there were disturbing omens that told you to do so if you happened to be a male Volunteer. Despite pronouncements that the U.S. "seeks no wider war in Vietnam", President Johnson began calling up more and more able-bodied young men to stop Communist aggression in Vietnam. The Hon. Senator from Mississippi speculated that there might have to be 600,000 American troops deployed in the non-war by the end of the year. Hubert Humphrey returned from a tour of Asia talking about a strong prosecution of the war effort. Emmet John Hughes, a close advisor of Eisenhower at one time, reported from Asia the pitfalls he saw in American policy in Southeast Asia. And Senator Fulbright waged a lonely war against the war in the Senate, warning of the "arrogance of power".

Escalation of the Vietnam War and all its ramifications led to something amounting to a Vietnam syndrome among Malawi Volunteers. For each of us (males) was susceptible to be hustled from the Peace Corps into the war corps via the selective service system upon return. Every week we were likely to be confronted with an article in Time or Newsweek pointing up the vagaries of local draft boards or the deployment of more troops in the field. At least once I felt that Lt. Gen. Hershey was leering at us from the pages the magazine. So I attempted to cope with the specter of the draft by writing to my board. From local board #36 in Oklahoma I was told simply that men over 25 were being taken, that my Il-A deferment expired before my Peace Corps termination date, and that "the board would not care to state its position on deferments in the fall". The irony, of course, was that not too long ago the threat of de-selection (from Peace Corps) was imminent but now it is the threat of selection that loomed large.

At the same time I was fully aware that my situation was not the bleakest since I had been re-admitted to graduate school and would have reached 26 years of age one month after returning home. (Presumably the cut-off age for the draft.) Others not so fortunate were faced with low grade averages in college and uncertain acceptance by grad schools. Frequent conversations about post-termination plans tended to end in glum resignation. Everyone assumed the immorality of the Vietnam War, heightened at least in some degree by the feeling of having just contributed something positive to the American presence in the world. The sense of moral indignation ran deeper in some than in others. Richie Kornbluth vowed never to serve in the military and intended to fight the draft tooth and nail. Most of us tended toward the same stand. But then without a complete willingness to suffer the consequences, talk was cheap. There were occasions when more happy topics were discussed.

Jeff James, that relentless organizer, institutionalized a kind of bi-weekly seminar at St. John's Secondary in Lilongwe designed to stimulate intellectual batteries. The usual procedure was for one of us to present a paper, open the floor for discussion, followed by a more casual beer-sipping session in gloves off style. Basic themes of disagreement had a way of cropping up at each session regardless of the original topic. The range of subjects was as broad as the personalities involved. For example, Jeff gave a scholarly analysis of Japanese foreign policy; Tracy, a critique of Zorba the Greek, his hero; and Phil presented an introduction to music appreciation for those of us with more or less philistine tastes. My own presentation, a paper on Afrikaner nationalism borrowed from the South African staff member at Dedza, provided the impetus for my decision to travel to South Africa. Senator Kennedy's recent triumphant visit there also served to focus my attention on the land of apartheid.

While most of my weekends centered on the social life in Lilongwe there were occasional visits to the delightful world of Ncheu. Here lived Epicurus, alias John Dixon, whose motto appeared prominently on the chembudzi (toilet) door:

"The goal of man should be a life of pleasure regulated by morality, temperance and serenity..."

The whole Ncheu Peace Corps community worked hard at defining and pursuing the good life, and that included the young Bristol Volunteer. This was not to minimize the intellectual activity there as revealed in a paper submitted by Dix to our regional conference, questioning the direction of the young educated elite in Malawi and the role of Volunteers who taught them.

But the pursuit of happiness prevailed. A peculiar vocabulary grew up among the Volunteers in Ncheu which attempted to measure pain, or the absence of pleasure. "The pain factor" especially applied to the irksome business of hitching-hiking. A quick ride in a Mercedes going directly to the desired destination might only involve a pain factor of one. (Zero would be limited to owning a car.) A long wait on the road in the rain pushed it up several points. The record for waiting in Ncheu on the main road to Blantyre was nine hours. A lift on the back of a fish truck with a reckless driver might go as high as nine. But the calculators of the "pain factor" informed me that Severin and I may have reached near infinity on a recent trip. Having jounced for several hours to Dedza on the night compost we were forced to climb the additional five miles from the town around the mountain to the house. Arriving at 3:30 A.M., we found the door locked as it should have been, but no key!

When a situation such as that occurred one was said to "be hurtin". Afternoons at Ncheu were invariably devoted to "catching a few zzzz's" (I'll just lie down a bit and rest my eyes.) "A little action at Happy's" meant a night at the local bar. A really big weekend turned in by the Big Kahuna (Dixon) was referred to as a "streak". And then there were the less genteel terms that described the good life. "To do a job on something" indicated that one had completely outdone himself. Without offending anyone, it is probably safe to say that Epicurus' number one disciple, Dave Bush, was the most successful practitioner of the life prescribed by his mentor.

Another happy post was aptly named Mtendere (meaning peace in Chinyanja). While not so homogeneous a community as Ncheu, the Mtendere Volunteers—five under one roof—were a dedicated lot. One was serving out his fourth year, two were considering extending for a third year; as a whole they engaged themselves in full scale philanthropy for needy students and extramural activities. They put together the regional championship track team that also routed our Dedza boys in a dual meet. The several times that Richie invited me out to Mtendere were times of fun, fellowship and generous helpings of good food. I also managed trips to neighboring posts such as Mkhoma and Mlanda. In the African vernacular, I was said to be "too movious."

There were experiences of a different sort too. In Ncheu I witnessed a Caesarian section on an African woman at the hospital. The indigenous medicine which she had been given before coming to the hospital caused her to suffocate from a green mucous which filled her lungs. Both mother and child died. Such occurrences, according to the doctor, were commonplace. At Dedza Hospital a similar emergency called for a blood transfusion. In Malawi there was no blood bank. From my rather extensive experience in college of selling a few pints of blood, I knew that I had a universal donor type, so I willingly donated a pint when no one else could be found. Two days later the doctor informed me that the mother and twins were doing well.

Interwoven into my African experience was my relationship with an astonishing person. He was the diminutive African whom we called masharubu—man with a mustache—in training. As our language instructor at Syracuse, Dearson Bandawe kept our classes lively with his quick wit and candid air. He was our real introduction to Malawi, but we were mistaken if we assumed that this man was typical of those who inhabited Malawi. With only a primary school education, he had worked as a civil servant for 17 years under the colonial government. His uncanny self confidence had gotten him into, and out of, many predicaments. His expansive personality allowed him to be at ease in nearly any situation, with any group.

But not long after he had greeted us upon our arrival at Chileka, Dearson was whisked away to jail from his home in Kanjedza township. The charges were unspecified. Soon it became known that he was being held as a political detainee. And since all Volunteers were strictly forbidden to meddle in political affairs, my legitimate association with Dearson was thereby ended. Several of us had visited his home, met his wife and houseful of children (including the small girl who still bore the scar of a bullet on her forehead), and had eaten with them. Within a few weeks of his arrest I received a telegram from his wife asking for my help.

My reaction to this plea was spontaneous, and only afterward did I weigh the possible consequences of political involvement. At what point, after all, do personal relationships cease when merged with the political? That, too, was a period of my life governed even more than at other times by impulses. I determined to help the Bandawe family financially as much as possible since the large family, including several of school age, now had no source of income. Several of the other PCVs from our language class became regular benefactors as well. For 11 months I visited the house in Kanjedza whenever I was in Blantyre for the weekend, asking about recent news from Dearson. Then one day he was off to Nzeleka, the last stop for detainees. Hope for his release faded. At long last we heard the announcement over MBC that Dearson and one other detainee were being released.

It was May 1966. Again I received a letter, this one from Dearson, requesting my presence in Blantyre. He was even thinner than before, but a picture of indomitably high spirits. The girls at Mlanje had invited him and his wife and me to a "coming out" reception for him. Here he spoke to us with his usual eloquence, with not even a trace of bitterness about the past year. He admitted that the physical conditions had been harsh, the food usually inedible. But one simply had to believe him when he said it had been a valuable experience. He was most effusive in his thanks to us for aiding the family. I remembered his saying during training that he had never been invited by a European to his house nor had he ever invited one. That was the way things were in Nyasaland (the old colonial name for Malawi). He had no reason to trust a European and it had apparently been a mutual feeling. It was certainly gratifying to know that our efforts had been worth whatever risk was involved. The same scene was enacted when we were invited to dinner at a Volunteer's house in Zomba, down the street from the prison where Dearson had spent the first 11 months.

As to the nuts and bolts of everyday life in Dedza, we settled into a routine that consumed both my energies and my interests. Teaching in the upper Forms (grades) lent a sense of immediacy, especially as the Form Vs neared the Cambridge Exams which would make or break their future. One could hardly escape the notion that much of what was taught was not particularly relevant to that future. In English literature class we studied the prescribed material for this year's exam: Romeo and Juliet. My own grasp of Shakespearean drama was never profound, and I had to scramble to dig out the metaphors and similes in the passage to be covered each day.

Next was another book on the Cambridge Exam list which was a brief biography of Albert Schweitzer that indulged in the usual deification of this saint of the Western world. Naturally the students had been conditioned to think of him in just this manner, so I spent much of my time in class talking about the nature of paternalism. With the Form IV English I had a wider range of choice as to what could be covered. Students enjoyed Chinua Achebe's Things Fall Apart after their initial reaction to it as being second class literature since it wasn't part of the standard repertoire. They were also enthusiastic about Commonwealth history which I taught also. Some students wondered aloud why they were not taught any history of Russia or China.

In a large boarding school such as ours with 15 years of tradition there were a good many extra-curricular activities. Since I had always had an extracurricular bent I became involved in several of these. Early first term I became editor of the newspaper, The Dedza Weekly News, by default. The old hands considered it a thankless job. It was customary for the staff sponsor to do most of the work. My first task, then, was to attempt to instill in the half dozen students who worked on the paper the idea that it was their paper. I assumed the role of advisor. Some of the following issues were a little shoddy and even included some critical comments about teaching staff. For which I caught hell as sponsor! I stood by the newspaper staff and they dug in to make their publications tidier. It was a good experience for them. In fact two of the older boys declared their intention to follow careers in journalism.

I also assisted in coaching track and basketball but we managed only mediocre records in both. The object of my greatest endeavor, however, was the publication of the highly acclaimed school magazine, Sapere Aude, again by default. We three senior English masters sorted through over 100 articles submitted for the essay and poetry sections. Also included were hostel, society and sports reports as well as a thumbnail sketch of each staff member. Total cost for printing in Blantyre: 50 shillings.

The school was a whirl of activity in many areas. The British Volunteers directed a first class production of the play Medicine for Love which they presented to an enthusiastic audience at Lilongwe Girls' School. They also hosted geography and history conferences which gave the school university-like sophistication with numerous visiting professors. The whole school turned out en masse whenever the football (soccer) team took the field. They were accustomed to undefeated seasons but this year was only moderately successful. They suffered two successive defeats at the hands of Likuni Boys School.

There was a great deal of intrigue among the staff members, at least among those who took part in school activities. For several weeks we were without the weekly film showings on Friday evenings after a tiff brought about the resignation of the staff sponsor. But the popularity of the program necessitated finding a new one as soon as possible. No sooner was that resolved than another storm broke out over the showing of a USIS film on the wonderful progress of American soldiers fighting in Vietnam. Sure, the students liked the action. But some staff members questioned the value of such open propaganda.

Here on the Dedza compound we lived in a kind of British ghetto. Manners and customs, attitudes and language of the British staff prevailed. While we non-British resisted Anglicization, I find words like "bloke", "chap", and the phrase "bloody hopeless" creeping into my vocabulary. I had to smile whenever young George, the Bolton Volunteer, went about the staff room frantically asking, "Where's mi boook?" While the older contract staff were still stand-off-ish toward us and we Americans had no use for them, we weve on increasingly good terms with the young British Volunteers who did not share their colonial mentality. Our most frequent companion was the Frenchman, Jean Jacques.

There were several images that would stick in my mind for years to come. One of them was the view of Dedza Mountain on the way to school each day. Sometimes I would embarrass myself by imagining its two rolling peaks to be the breasts of an African woman. And there was the neurotic dog next door that yelped at us every day until we made friends. There were mornings when I would wake up during "winter" under two blankets shivering in a fetal ball. And there were days of bright tropical sun, and days when the firmament would turn grey under a covering of army-blanket clouds. There would surely be mixed feelings when it came time for departure in the fall.

Summing Up: Two Years in the Peace Corps

Dedza   *l5/November/l966*

Nearly two years came and went in Africa and now I found myself in a bare room with all my earthly belongings packed and ready to be sent away. Already a feeling of nostalgia set in, coupled with the anxiety of returning to the jet-age pace of American society. Here one was constantly aware of the physical world, the world as perceived by the senses rather than the mind. Outside the crickets and the mournful dove heralded the beginning of the rainy season. Even long before the heavy rains began the hillsides turned into luxuriant leafy greenery. Every month the countryside was washed by a shimmering full moon just as Carol Fisher had promised us in training. I suppose there were full moons back home but I don't remember them being quite this bright.

But surely the most memorable image of Malawi is that of the Malawian himself. He is a picture of unalienable good humor, unconcern for the troubles of tomorrow, unsophisticated joy in the simple pleasures of life unhampered by the pressures that the Western world seeks to impose. Having said this one immediately thinks of the unhappy result of exposure of the select few to the material blessings the European has brought. All too often they are ill-equipped for the role that such exposure brings to them: the supercilious cabinet minister who owes his position to political subservience, the secondary school student who flouts his education in the villages, the "been-to's" (a play on the term Bantu) who become "experts" after a six month course abroad. And quickly oneremembers that these attitudes are certainly no worse than our own as we help to implant the values of a culture we know to be imperfect itself.

Perhaps the most perceptive description of Malawi culture and Africa in general was written by an African himself. Dunduzu

Chisiza, until his death in a car accident several years ago, was one of the most gifted and influential young men in Malawi. An article of his appeared in Modern African Studies (Vol. 1, No. 1) in which he attempted to describe the uniqueness of the African. To Chisiza the people of the East are given to meditation, Westerners are inquisitive and rational, while Africans rely instead on intuition. He believes that Africa's great contribution to the world lies in the field of personal relations. He contends that in the West the essential ethic is that man "lives to work," whereas in Africa man "works to live." One does not attain salvation in Africa by hard work as in the Western world. (This maybe accounts for the lethargy that descends on students required to do "estate" work!)

With Africans, Chisiza says, "life has always meant the pursuit of happiness rather than the pursuit of beauty." (Paraphrasing of Jefferson is probably not unintended.) And in his religion the African has tended to be eclectic. He has adhered to a religious faith "only so long as it is the only faith he has known". He clings to a faith so long as he has faith in it. Rather than showing a fickle nature, this is an indication of his acceptance of the basic elements of truth in every religion. At a time when the very basis of society, the family, is being corroded in the West, it seems strongest in Africa. Examples are abundant. A student always relies upon his father, brother or uncle, maybe even a distant member of the extended family for payment of school fees. He knows at the same time that as soon as he brings home his first paycheck it will be absorbed by family needs.

Chisiza characterizes the basis of human relations in Africa as thinking in terms of "we and our rather than I and mine". If you give a boy a new shirt he will wear it every day for weeks, but you may one day see that his brother or cousin is wearing it. When it comes time to build a new house a man can usually count on relatives to drop everything and come to help him. There is not the compulsion to show possession that pervades in the West. Chisiza's example rings very true. "It is a society", he says, "where if you found seven men and one woman amongst them, you might never know, unless told, whose wife she was."

The African, however, is very adept at copying certain manners and values of the European. Those exposed to the acquisitive spirit and taught to believe in its necessity reveal the weakness of such an ethic. One of the most conspicuous symbols of status among the literate in Malawi is the ownership of one's own books. That probably explains why so many of them disappear from the Dedza Secondary library each year. Every young man who tastes affluence has designs on a new bicycle and a suit. To own a pair of glasses supposedly increases one's knowledge automatically. But, then, this is progress in a developing society.

To me one of the most striking traits in the African personality is his complete extroversion, his flare for showmanship. There is no place for a brooding intellectual in a society which places so much emphasis on communal activities. In Malawi an African often addresses a fellow African who is a total stranger as achimwene — brother. It is quite uncommon for an African to manage to look depressed very long. As Chisiza puts it, "our conception of life precludes, as far as possible, the accommodation of dejection." One only has to be around African children for a while to believe they all are born with a gift of rhythm. Completely devoid of inhibition unless in the presence of strangers, they can twist as though they invented it instead of Chubby Checker. Even as one waves to people walking along the road a young boy may break into a momentary "shake — shake" to show his recognition.

One thing continued to puzzle me more than anything in my two-year acquaintance with Africans. In a country where zikomo is interspersed in every conversation and thank you is a way of saying hello and goodbye, there seems to be little that passes for gratitude. The most prodigious effort or most out-of-the-way thoughtfulness usually goes unnoticed—or at least not acknowledged. But of course this is the relationship between African and European. (We Americans are inevitably lumped together with our Old World kith and kin.) It is probably in the nature of things for those who have nothing or little to expect something from those who seemingly have everything. It is difficult for an American Volunteer to overlook the decision made after our departure by Dr. Banda to send Peace Corps home because Volunteers had become "scruffy, unkempt and immoral." At our termination conference some Volunteers suggested that Peace Corps leave the country entirely. But it is not the nature of Peace Corps to withdraw from a country until told by the country's government to do so.

The other side of this coin, however, is the African's unfailing generosity. I will never forget the time when the Peace Corps carryall which I was driving stalled on the road to Nsanje to pick up our luggage. After being passed by two speeding Europeans I managed to flag down an African driver with a truck-load of 15 or so men who were working on telephone lines. It was near lunch time but the driver insisted on checking every inch of the carryall gas line to fix the problem. Finally after two hours, I was on my way again, and not a single complaint from the hungry workers. We alendo (strangers) in Malawi were usually shown great courtesy. One never walked far with luggage in hand without an African offering to carry it for him. The best seat on the bus was reserved for us, although that didn't exempt us from the raucous discussion between two friends just reunited.

Malawi was a developing nation. Everywhere in the bomas, the market-places, the community centers, signs proclaimed that Malawi "is at war—against poverty, ignorance and disease". The national anthem mentioned these same enemies that all Malawians were enjoined to do battle against. A quick glance would seem to reveal a losing battle; the enemy was so deeply entrenched. Malawi supposedly had one of the lowest per capita incomes of any country in Africa. There were skirmishes along the front line and Malawi sometimes came away with hard-fought victories.

Physical signs of progress in the last two years, in fact, were unspectacular. Blantyre-Limbe, now incorporated into one city, sported a new eight story skyscraper, the Malawi Development Corporation building. The USAID gift of the Polytechnic branch of the University of Malawi was complete, and the arts and science college had enrolled its first class. Bunda College of Agriculture was finishing its first term of classes with 35 men at the Dedza compound, waiting for the completion of its own buildings near Lilongwe. At Nkhula Falls hydro-electric power was harnessed from the Shire River for the first time. It was only after a disaster at Liwonde Ferry that a barrage was constructed there. A bridge also now spanned the Shire at Matope and another would cross the lower Shire at Chikwawa within a year.

Farther downstream the sugar schemes at Nchalu and Chiromo were expanding. It was commonly accepted among development planners for Malawi that guerrilla tactics must be employed against the enemy in agriculture if hunger was to be rooted out. Toward this end new schemes for cotton were springing up at Salima and for rice at Karonga to supplement the main money crops of tea, tung and tobacco. There had been one quite spectacular innovation as a result of UDI (Unilateral Declaration of Independence) in Rhodesia: VC jet service to Blantyre from Johannesburg to London. And yet this country of four million people had a GNP of barely $150 million, barely enough to pay for a squadron of U.S. fighter jets.

On other fronts there were notable advances. Malawi had been blessed with a stronger sense of national unity than most other African nations partitioned by European powers. Chinyanja was understood by nearly everyone in the country from north to south and serves as a common lingua franca. (President Banda himself did not speak the language, at least publicly, since he left the country at a very early age not to return for 60 years.) The country was not beset with the tribal and regional strife which plagued other countries. In three giant steps Malawi had come through self-government in 1958, to independence in 1964, and to republican status the following year. Dr. Kamuzu Banda had accomplished what he came to do: "To break the stupid Federation (of Rhodesia and Nyasaland) and to bring self-government." Unfortunately this had been at the expense of the young nationalists who invited him to come back and help them during the 1950s. They were gone now and there was no room for dissent in the ruling Malawi Congress Party.

For most of the masses in Malawi the personality of the Ngwazi (his self-proclaimed traditional title) was inextricably bound up with their idea of the free nation of Malawi. Middle-aged and elderly women who were the staunchest conservators of the national heritage bought millions of yards of "kwacha" cloth with pictures of Banda for their dresses. Malawi Broadcasting Corporation's air time was taken up, half with rock 'n roll and country singer Jim Reeves, the other half with songs of praise for the Ngwazi. (In fact Jim Reeves might have been Dr. Banda's major rival for popularity!)

Newsweek pointedly described the tune of Malawi politics as a "one man Banda." So successfully had Dr. Banda consolidated power in the last eight years since his return to Malawi that he felt free to play the maverick in African politics. He stoutly defended British policy on Rhodesia while Kaunda of Zambia was among the chief critics. Malawi alone among the African nations abstained on the General Assembly vote to take Southwest Africa away from South Africa jurisdiction, while 110 nations voted for the measure. At the same time the International Commission of jurists condemned Malawi as a "police state" because there were allegedly 500 in political detention there. No wonder Dr. Banda was a favorite among the South Africans. Following several months of domestic calm after the cabinet crisis the Malawi News, the organ of the Party, headlined that Henry Chipembere was back in Dar preparing for the overthrow of the Malawi government. There could be no doubt that Dr. Banda had the national interest at heart, but his tragic flaw might well have been that he was not preparing the nation for the time when he would not be President.

Our role as Volunteers in Malawi V was fast drawing to a close while the Peace Corps seemed to be expanding with success. The hunch that most of us had when we plunged into training that these two years would be meaningful and exciting had been proved true. We had seen the Peace Corps stuck in the mud of human failings and witnessed the faltering steps of an emerging nation. We made life long friendships—some leading right to marriage—and experienced a fraternity of common interests and concerns. We had been described as a part of the New Left in the American society. If this was so we would probably be uneasy about things as we found them back in the United States. Maybe that's what the Peace Corps experience is all about.

Return to the U.S. — December 1966

Mbandaka, Democratic Republic of the Congo   9/December/1966

My last departure from Chileka Airport was on November 28, 1966. As the city of Blantyre-Limbe receded into the distance, the feeling came over me that my two years in Malawi had brought a lasting change in me. I wasn't sure exactly what it was. It was my inner self more than anything. But it had to do with Africa, with new horizons, with people.... Since the earliest flight to the Congo would be December 2, I settled down in Salisbury, Rhodesia, for the remainder of the week.

The British government had laid down the ultimatum, such as it was, to the rebel UDI regime of Ian Smith: if no agreement was reached by the 30th the matter would be taken to the General Assembly. UDI was already a year old and Smith wasn't showing any signs of disappearing. On the same day I arrived in Salisbury, he flew out to meet Harold Wilson near Malta in the Mediterranean. The hue and cry went up from black Africa that Wilson was about to sell out. They suspected, and rightly so as it turned out, that Britain would not be as willing to send force against kith and kin as to protect other vital interests such as those in the Suez Canal.

At Ndola we transferred to an Air Congo plane since that was now the only line which the government allowed to enter the country. The TV technicians cautioned me not to fly over the Congo, reminding me that it was full of "savages". I thanked them for their advice and boarded the plane for Lubumbashi. A year ago when we had visited the capital of copper-rich Katanga Province it was Elizabethville. But with the proclamation of June 30, 1966, it was now called Lubumbashi. As I sat in the lounge of the airport waiting to board the 707 Boeing jet to Kinshasa, I noticed the well heeled cosmopolitan clientele and the buzz of French being spoken by most of them. Customs check was quite painless; my eight-day visa was not even questioned, nor did they ask for my international health card. No hint of the chaotic Congo my Rhodesian friends had promised me. I did feel a little uneasy about not checking to see that my luggage changed planes, but...everything was going smoothly.

Only upon landing in Kinshasa—formerly Leopoldville—did I begin to see how the Congolese could be master practitioners in the art of confusion. At the airport terminal my passport was taken and I was motioned aside to another desk along with a French-speaking Swede in transit to Lagos. A recent regulation required tourists to exchange $20.00 worth of hard currency for Congolese francs for each day that they were to be in the country. Since I had an eight-day visa

I was compelled to cash $160.00 in checks, with the vague understanding that whatever currency was unspent at the end of the week could be readily exchanged for dollars. What I was not told here was that I was being paid the official rate, 150 francs to the dollar, a total of 20,000 francs—with a slight charge for commission. And what I painfully learned the next day was that a dollar on the black market was worth 500 francs. In reality I now had $148.00 worth of Congolese currency which not even the Banque Nationale du Congo would exchange for dollars at the regular official rate!

The second chapter in the story of how to lose friends and stultify tourism concerns missing baggage. The next hour was consumed in a frantic search by the clerks for my suitcase, around the terminal and inside the jet about to depart for Europe. I was kicking myself for not having checked it at Lubumbashi. A telex message was prepared to inquire at the point of departure. The plane was leaving. The last bus to town was also about to go. Panic! Then, lo and behold, the missing suitcase was found—right where it should have been. I scurried to the bus just in time for the long ride though the vast suburban sprawl into the city and the Sabena Guest House. But, helas, the manager informed me I would not be able to stay there because I had not been given a paper to indicate that I was en transit. It was after midnight; by now my bones ached and the humid air closed in around me. After much palaver in a kind of universal sign language and a few broken phrases in French, I was finally granted a room. I was soon to learn that such situations must be met with simple resignation—"C'est le Congo."

My primary motive in coming to the Congo, apart from a great curiosity, was to visit my old TCU friends Dan and Sandy Owen in Mbandaka (formerly Coquilhatville). Saturday morning, then, I attempted to get a flight to Mbandaka. At Air Congo I was informed that I would have to pay for the ticket in hard currency since I did not possess a carte de sejour (visitor's permit). Not eager to be taken in again, I marched to the nearby American Embassy to avail myself of their services, at least to find someone who spoke English. Closed! Ready to throw myself again at the mercy of the Congo, I resolved to buy a ticket in dollars. Now I was informed that there were no seats available until the following Friday. I was ready to admit defeat and fly on to Lagos on Monday.

Before dawn the following day three of us, including Rev. Jean Bokeleale, the first Congolese director of the Disciples du Christ du Congo (DCC), were at the Ndjili Airport ready to board. The immigration officer checked our passports and then asked for our health cards. Health card? But I had mine in my attaché case at the hostel thinking it would not be needed for an internal flight. They hadn't even checked it at Lubumbashi when I entered the country. Again quiet desperation set in; this time I had only myself to blame. Then I noticed Rev. Bokeleale in a huddle with the officers, gesturing and speaking to them in Lingala. He motioned for me to pass on through. By now, accustomed to crisis conditions, I didn't even have to ask what had happened; this too could be answered with "C'est le Congo".

One minute we had crossed the equator and the very next we taxied onto the Mbandaka runway. It was still a heavy rainy season in the Congo basin and puddles were standing all around. We walked toward the terminal through a light drizzle. Looking out past the parking lot one could see the tall dense forest standing silent and majestic. Sunday school visions from childhood of the heart of the Congo merged with reality. Within a few minutes I was listening to the familiar Texas twang of Dan and Sandy. Mbandaka, the capital of Equateur Province, is perhaps the fourth or fifth city of the Congo. The home district of President Mobutu, it was among the poorest with an almost entirely agricultural economy.

While Equateur Province had provided the country with large numbers of military men, it had seen the least political turmoil in comparison with the other regions. The chief domestic crop was manioc and the two important cash crops exhibited by the Belgians had been rubber and palm oil. Shipping had also developed as a vital industry under the Otraco monopoly with Mbandaka being the half-way point between Stanleyville and Kinshasa. Now that the constitution of the Congo had been suspended since the military coup of November 24, 1965, the province was run by a colonel in Mobutu's army.

The missionary effort in the Mbandaka region had been largely divided between the Belgian Catholics and American Disciples of Christ. Since many of my own nickels and dimes used to be enclosed in the envelope marked for our church's missionaries in the Congo I was particularly interested to find out what they had been doing here. The center of Disciples of Christ activity was at Bolenge, about 10 kilometres west and south of Mbandaka on the Congo River. According to an account by an early missionary, H.M. Stanley was besieged by unfriendly natives in 1877 on the island across from the present site of Bolenge while he was on his historic mission. But just as things looked hopeless, friendly natives appeared on the scene and his life was saved. This proved a good omen for the missionary effort that was to follow.

In the 1880s the Disciples brotherhood, self-conscious about its lack of missionary zeal, determined to establish a mission in Africa. By the end of the 1890s the Foreign Missionary Society had sent two fearless Disciples to explore the Congo region and secure land for the site of a mission station. One of them was a graduate of Add-Ran College, later to become Texas Christian University. In 1899 the first building was erected at Bolenge, and thus began Disciple history in the Congo. The Protestants had been fairly successful in the competition with the Catholics for African souls. From their toehold of a handful of converts in the beginning, the Disciple membership had expanded—at least nominally—to over 130,000. Because the Catholic Church had traditionally been aligned in the unholy trinity of administration, church and industry in the Congo, Protestants were not been especially welcomed.

Bolenge was now comprised of an infirmary, a church, a garage, housing for at least a dozen missionaries and families, and the secondary school begun in 1928. l'Institut Chretien du Congo (ICC) was interdenominational with a staff of 13 teachers and 150 students. In Mbandaka the church maintained headquarters and another half a dozen mission families lived there including the full time pilot. Recently the Congolese had gained almost complete autonomy in the direction of the DCC, and the missionaries served rather like a team of UN technical assistants. Congolese were urged to do their own teachin' and preachin' and not to rely on missionaries. This policy was in striking contrast to the Catholic Church which did not yet train African priests. Although the 10 DCC bush posts had Americans there most of the pastors were now Congolese. With this kind of liberal orientation it was no accident Rev. Bokeleale, a product of DCC, was influential in urging the organization of a united Protestant church in the Congo under Congolese direction.

My initial insight into mission life came upon my arrival Sunday morning. No mention was made of church service, until after lunch. Several families didn't attend regularly because the services were two hour marathons designed to bring salvation with sheer volume of religion. Sunday evening, however, the missionary community gathered at the chapel for its own service; the Congolese did not meet on Sunday evenings at all. This custom of maintaining a closed missionary community was especially prominent in Kinshasa where at least 12 Protestant missionary groups attended one church. At this evening meeting I was surprised to see a familiar face, that of a fellow Okie, Dean England, who spoke in my native tongue, from

Phillips University. We would be tourist mates on several occasions during the next week.

The Owens family saw to it that my week was pleasant and eventful. I was delighted when they issued me a small Peugeot mobilette on which to get about town. No sooner had I driven around the block than I was called to a halt by a policeman's whistle. What was it? Had I been speeding? Run a stop sign? Turned the wrong way on a one-way street? Three policemen on bicycles ushered me to the nearby police station, asked for my passport (but not my driver's license), and then we waited for the verdict. The sergeant informed me that I was being fined 3,000 francs ($6.00) for violating article 53 of the city ordinance which prohibits riding a bicycle without both feet on the pedals! Surely few tourists could boast having contributed as much to the local economy as I had in such a short time.

The week rushed rapidly to an end; soon I was back in Kinshasa ready to fly on to Lagos. The people at KLM mentioned that the flight was sometime in the afternoon, but that I should stop by the next morning to check for sure. At 9:00 A.M. the next morning when I strode into the office ready to confirm my flight they sheepishly told me that it had left at 8:15 A.M! The next flight to Lagos would be Monday afternoon. How about that one? I nodded agreement and my reservation was booked once again.

As I boarded the Nigerian Airways flight to Douala and Lagos a hefty, handsomely bearded young African sat down behind me. A brief introduction revealed that Chris was Ghanaian, on leave from the new University of Zambia where he taught political science. As we were both planning to stay in Lagos that night, we took a bus in to the Mainland Hotel, passing through street after street teeming with people. Even though it was nearly midnight the air was still heavy and sultry and the people had their doors and windows open to catch the slightest breeze. Even now "mammy wagons" rushed through the streets always crammed to overflowing with people and usually embellished with aphorisms such as "God is Able", "High Boy", "Pay the Boy Now", and "Who Knows?". Here, as I would see elsewhere in West Africa, the men rivaled women in colorful garb with their long graceful robes, bright skull caps and sandals. Although Lagos proper is on an island, the city of well over one million reached far into the mainland. And while it was located in Yoruba territory, Lagos had witnessed the co-mingling of many tribes and races. White-turbaned and bearded Moslems from the North were frequently seen carrying their staffs along the streets.

Chris and I checked into the Mainland Hotel, a luxury affair recently built in a not-so-luxurious neighborhood. The next day could not have been planned and yet could not have been spent more fruitfully. Chris invited me to tag along with him to see old friends on the faculty at Lagos University, pleasantly located on a lagoon looking out toward the ocean. The first of these was a fellow Ghanaian who teaches in the faculty of law, who in turn introduced us to Dr. B.A. Williams in the political science department. His study was lined with American classics in politics and history, and he was, so he said, on first name basis with the likes of James Coleman (UCLA) and Gwendolyn Carter (Northwestern). He spoke in very analytical, professorial terms which even sounded American. He was Yoruba, a native of Lagos itself, and had earned his PhD at Chicago.

Outside our hotel I decided to take a stroll down into the jungle that was the market nearby. There was row after row of tin-roofed open-air shacks where market mammies peddled an infinite variety of goods. Accustomed as I was to East Africa, these authentic West African capitalist market mammies were an intriguing sight. It was mid-afternoon and some of these stout women had succumbed to the heat, slumping languorously over their tables. Some were clad only from the waist up in brightly colored brassieres. This certainly wasn't East Africa! There was something...something less reserved, less formal about these people. A transaction was as much a social encounter as a business deal. I soon figured out that the "hssst!" coming from all sides was their attempt to get my attention to buy their wares.

"You buy nice cloth for wife?" No wife.

"Girlfrien' at home?" No girl friend at home. Pause.

"Friend in Lagos?" winking, and finally bursting out in titters.

Even though I showed them I had only a few coins, there ensued a huge palaver and I received a mock scolding. For a while I felt very much the Ugly American, but then it became apparent that it was all in good fun. I had provided the occasion for these happy people to indulge in their national pasttime—palaver. It was the kind of scene that would be repeated often and become a lasting image in my African experience.

The next morning ended my brief stay in Lagos as I boarded the eighth flight of my return trip, on to Accra in Ghana, a city strewn with public works. Black Star Square, located right near the ocean, was designed for massive demonstrations much like the Marx-Lenin Platz I had seen in East Berlin four years before. At the entrance to the Square was the Freedom and Justice Monument which commemorates the Independence of Ghana in 1957. Just across the street was the national stadium used for football, boxing and other sports. There is also Black Star Circle and National Liberation Circle, the latter re-named after the February coup which toppled Nkrumah. It seemed as though there was an embassy building on every corner which reminded one that Accra considered itself the diplomatic capital of Africa. To this end also, there was an array of OAU buildings with office space that might never be used. Missing from in front of parliament was the statue of the Osagyefo (Nkrumah, the great leader), torn down by rampaging citizens in the wake of the coup that brought him down.

In the four days I stayed in the capital city of Ghana I fell in with folks in the U.S. Embassy. My first night in town we went to eat at the really "in" place, the fashionable Continental Hotel. I had never seen such an agglomeration of well-heeled, jet-set Africans. Traditional dress vied with European, men as well as women. The service was fashionably slow, or maybe it was simply that a very small cadre of waiters was commissioned to serve droves of people. After dinner we drove out to the Lido and soaked up some real Ghanaian "high-life". I recalled the first time I had ever been exposed to this West African rhythm at the Kenya independence celebration in Washington when the African student community took part.

The program varied from night to night. One evening I was introduced to a middle-aged Negro in charge of the Embassy building and maintenance. He did his work with efficiency but he got no special favors from the higher echelons. He was by no means part of the Embassy establishment. You would not find him waving the red-white-and-blue very often. But when it came to talk about Peace Corps in Ghana he took the straight embassy line. His attitude was by now very familiar to me.

"Why is it you Peace Corps are always so goddam dirty and unkempt?" he demanded, obviously not attempting to antagonize me but expressing a real concern.

"Sometimes I'm ashamed to have to defend Peace Corps when foreigners criticize it. In my opinion the U.S. still hasn't got below the surface in African countries. There needs to be more investigation at the grass roots level."

Denying my meek assertion that Peace Corps was accomplishing this at least in part, my friend arrived at the real crux of his argument:

"Why, I can learn more in five minutes here in a local compound in Accra than you can in five weeks with your white face."

Heading Homeward to the U.S.   *18//December/1966*

In Accra, I climbed once more into a plane that would take me to Dakar, Senegal, via Monrovia's Roberts Field in Liberia. Stepping from the stifling night air into the plane, we were met with Christmas carols a la muzac. The captain wished us all a very Merry Christmas and Happy New Year, then repeated it in French for the francophone customers.

We landed in Las Palmas for a fueling stop. Las Palmas is the chef lieu in the Spanish-owned Canary Islands. My only lasting impression of the Gran Canaria is the swarm of Scandinavian tourists who flock to the islands like New Yorkers to Miami Beach. Also here I was hit, only for the second time since Blantyre, with a charge for over-weight luggage. Generally, whatever one can carry in hand went unweighed but the Iberian Airlines agent insisted that my book-filled attache case be weighed—a rather costly business.

San Juan, Puerto Rico   *21/December/1966*

Seven hours later we landed at the San Juan, Puerto Rico, airport. Brochures claimed that this airport was one of 15 international terminals that processed over two million people a year. That was not hard to believe, especially with holiday traffic at its peak. In the course of one day in Puerto Rico I saw my first mini skirts (my sister Judy would be wearing one of these?), over-sized belts and bell-bottom trousers on teen-age boys as well as girls (brother Kurt would probably be sporting one and Ev might even have one to hand down

to me), and ate my first Whopper at Lum's. The place was swarming
with people in mod attire. After trying to keep up with trends in
American society by reading Time and Newsweek for two years, I
suddenly became aware that there was a sub-culture of youth in the
American society. If someone had told me they had taken over in a
recent coup I would have had to believe it. In fact, it occurred to me
that one of these youths probably spent more by himself in one year
than the average Malawian did in a lifetime.

Caracas, Venezuela   *22/December/1966*

And so on to Caracas because it's there and because I had done
a paper on the Venezuelan political system in graduate school. But
the idea of being home for Christmas for the first time in three
years began to outweigh the prospect of lengthy stops in each place
I had planned to visit. I had now only three days to make it back
in, but Caracas was a must. The American establishment pointed to
Venezuela as a model of social democracy since the overthrow of
dictator Perez Jimenez in 1958. The playground of Nelson Rockefeller
and the Latin American country with the highest per capita income,
Venezuela under Romulo Betancourt was said to be firmly secure in
the "Free World".

But the always tenuous balance of political power, with the
military and foreign interests on the right and militant students
and Castroites on the left, had been recently threatened with the
assassination of two top military men. It was immediately attributed
to the FALN, the national liberation front. As an act of reprisal
President Leoni, Betancourt's successor, sent 2,000 military troops
onto the campus of the Central University, traditionally considered
a sanctuary for political extremists of all persuasions. It was an
awesome sight for me to see the University grounds shut down and
armed militia patrolling the inside. Elsewhere around the burgeoning
city I was greatly impressed with what oil wealth had wrought.

Caracas, which would soon celebrate its 400th anniversary, is
nestled in a valley up in the mountains, a ways from the Caribbean
coast. A cable car lift to the top of the mountain range provided a
stunning panorama of the city and its suburbs. Down on the western
end of the city was the magnum opus of Perez Jimenez: la Plaza
de los Precurceros. As I stood gazing at this beautiful mall with

Romanesque statuary and monuments to national heroes such as Simon Bolivar, it was impossible not to notice the wretched favelas (slums) that crowded the hillsides.

Ponca City, Oklahoma   *25/December/1966*

From Caracas I flew to Miami and after what seemed forever finally caught a plane heading to Tulsa. At the Tulsa Airport I learned that all flights to Ponca City had been cancelled during the holidays. Buses weren't running because of the blizzard conditions that gripped the state! So close and yet so far away! It would certainly be a white Christmas, but it looked like I might not be home for Christmas after all. Just as I was about to call Dad to say that I was stranded the announcement came that the midnight special (bus) to Ponca would be running after all. Relieved and excited, I called home to report that I was on my way there. After my first couple of sentences there was a long pause on the other end of the phone. Dad wanted to know who it was talking. He was stumped by the peculiar accent I had picked up in the last two years! Apparently, after standing up in front of classes in Malawi and speaking distinctly in order just to be understood, my diction had been permanently altered. For years to come, Americans as well as foreigners would frequently ask me what country I was from! At home two surprises greeted me. A letter from Local Board 36 requested me to report for physical examination, although I was one month away from my twenty-sixth birthday, presumably the cutoff for the draft. And Dad asked me to be the best man at his wedding the following week.

I joined the Peace Corps at a time when the agency was in its infancy, the butt of many jokes and much skepticism. Over the years Peace Corps would become the gold standard for achievement. Testament to this fact is to be seen in the number of initiatives that attempt to trade off the name: Mercy Corps, Story Corps, Americorps, Teacher Corps, and so on. I'm proud to have served!

Chapter 6

Bringing the World Back Home—Part I, 1967-1969

Promote better understanding of other people among Americans at home.

> - Third goal of the Peace Corps

American University, Washington, D.C.   *Spring 1967*

The invitation from the draft board instructed me to report for a physical exam and induction into the army, a proposition I had spent long hours with my fellow Volunteers in Africa inveighing against. We had spent two years waging peace in the name of Uncle Sam. It didn't make sense to undo our efforts by then going and waging war. But Uncle Sam needed more soldiers to prosecute the War in Vietnam, by now in high gear. I pointed out to the Board that I was about to reach the age of 26, presumably the cutoff for the draft, and that I had been accepted back into a graduate program at American University (AU) School of International Service that I had begun in the fall of 1963. In its mercy, the Board agreed to have me report to the army base nearest the university for the physical after resuming graduate studies.

I had a semester of course work and a thesis paper left to write for the degree. So I started classes in January, and in March took a bus up to Ft. Hollobird, outside of Baltimore, where I underwent the physical exam. The doctor noticed that I had an ear infection, so he denied my availability for military duty temporarily, indicating on my file that I would be notified again in six months. That awful feeling with which I left Peace Corps training in Syracuse, of still being "on hold", returned to me. But the notification never came. I had successfully failed the physical, and my file apparently began collecting dust in the Ponca City draft board, as files are wont to do!

The brief period at American University in the spring and summer of 1967 would be a great time in my life, a time of transition from the life of a Volunteer in Africa—to what, I didn't exactly know, of reconnecting with American society at a time of social and political ferment. Happily, the nest-egg of $75/month that Peace Corps put aside during my two years in Africa was nearly sufficient to cover tuition and a bit more. And it was my good fortune to run into a couple of classmates who were looking to rent a room together somewhere in the AU vicinity. They asked me to join them in the search, and we eventually found a small two-bedroom walk-up apartment on Wisconsin Avenue across from the National Cathedral. The last one to join the group, I was left to occupy a couch in the living room. The kitchen table was our study. My mode of locomotion was a 50 cc motorcycle that whimpered at negotiating the slightest hill and didn't like cold weather any more than I did.

Kenneth Bedford Hatcher had been a Peace Corps Volunteer teacher in Saganetti, Eritrea (northern Ethiopia). Amazingly, Ken was bi-lingual in both Amharic, the national language of Ethiopia, and Tigrinya, the language of Eritrea. He would dazzle both Amharas and Tigres at parties with his gift of gab and charm in both languages. James Karioki, known to us as Jimmy, was a Kikuyu from Kenya. He was equally charming, articulate and decidedly a ladies' man. We were all studying international relations, so we had a lot to talk about besides all the socializing. We styled ourselves the Kennedy brothers: Ken was brother Jack, I was brother Bobby and Jimmy was Teddy. The three of us formed a close bond of friendship and in our tiny apartment managed to host some of the most popular multi-cultural parties in the city. Our soirees were animated by the soulful sounds of Aretha Franklin: the Queen of Soul, James Brown (number one Soul Brother), Sam and Dave, Wilson Pickett and Otis Redding. It was also a time when African rhythms were becoming popular in the U.S. as well. Miriam Makeba and Hugh Masekela not only entertained us, but raised our awareness of the injustices of apartheid in their native South Africa.

In the midst of all this merriment I managed to complete all the requirements for a Master's degree in International Relations in the summer of 1967. I submitted two "non-thesis option" papers, one on the Development of Malawi Nationalism and the other on the South African Government's Public Relations Campaign. All the while I was exploring possibilities of re-joining the Peace Corps and going back overseas as a staff member, which I thought of as my calling. However, falling short of that objective, I accepted an offer to work as a Peace Corps recruiter out of the southern regional office of the Public Affairs Department in Atlanta. I was disappointed, but then I held out the possibility that this assignment would open doors to my objective of going back overseas. Well after all, I told myself, the third goal of the Peace Corps was to "bring the world back home to the U.S.", telling fellow Americans about our experiences overseas.

Atlanta   *Fall 1967*

After an orientation to Peace Corps programs and regulations in suburban Virginia and a big send-off by Peace Corps brass, the new batch of recruiters was deployed to the four regional offices in September 1967 just six years after the first group of Volunteers had entered service overseas. Our job was to encourage college students to consider a two-year stint as a Volunteer, regardless of their career objectives. It was a time when the public perception of the Peace Corps was that you needed to be a little wacko to join.

There were about 30 of us in the Atlanta office, located in the Federal Building near the futuristic Hyatt Regency Hotel with its revolving restaurant on top, our favorite place to unwind after work. Mike Hanrahan, a former UC Berkeley student and Volunteer in Bolivia, and I decided to rent a modest house on Cambellton Road. Although we would only be there for one week out of every four, we out-fitted the house with minimal accoutrements including beds and kitchen utensils, and the requisite Hi-Fi system. Mike was infused with the culture and the music of the counter-culture, having experienced Berkeley even before it was Berkeley! Mike introduced me to the sounds of Janis Joplin, Jimi Hendrix and the West Coast psychedelic sounds. So I guess I owe my introduction to the budding counter-culture to Mike. When we all converged on San Francisco in December 1967 for a national recruiters' conference, I was able to experience for myself the font of the counter-cultural revolution.

For the next nine months or so during the academic year we were on the road, traveling three weeks out of every month to campuses, preaching the gospel of the Peace Corps experience to students across the Southland, yes, bringing the world back home. We would arrive on campus, set up our Peace Corps booth, hand out brochures and rap to anyone who happened by about the challenges and opportunities of being a Volunteer. We were fresh from the Peace Corps experience, so we didn't have to rehearse our lines.

During the fall my visits took me to campuses in Florida, Maryland, Virginia, Alabama, Texas and Oklahoma. Many of those we visited were Historically Black Colleges and Universities (HBCUs) such as Tuskegee in Alabama and Texas Southern in Houston. We were invited to attend football games, where traditional rivalries were on display, and other campus events. It was a sub-culture about which many of us white folk who had grown up in the dominant culture were blissfully unaware. We enjoyed the gridiron rivalry, an aspect of campus life we could identify with, but we were ignorant of the social and cultural dimensions of HBCU campus life, especially the importance of Greek organizations and the significance of "rappin". This was long before "rap" became a prominent feature of American pop culture.

It was a time of high dudgeon for anti-establishment organizations on black campuses, fueled by anti-war and anti-white sentiment. Groups such as the Black Panthers and the Students for Democratic Society were beginning to articulate a program of violent resistance to the established order. In this environment we were not always welcome as representatives of the U.S. government on university campuses. Occasionally a scruffy youth would run alongside our government vehicles and shout epithets about fascism and racism. At Tuskegee in Alabama Socialist radicals made a point of burning our Peace Corps booth and its contents, to show us just how unwelcome we were. All of this was BEFORE the assassination of Rev. Martin Luther King Jr. in Memphis in April 1968. Then, after the assassination, on the campus of Howard University in Washington, D.C. our recruiters were asked to leave for their own sake.

Stillwater, Oklahoma   Fall 1967

My fall travel agenda took me to Oklahoma State University, only a few miles from my home town in north-central Oklahoma. As on other campuses, we met with those students who had submitted their applications to the Peace Corps and were still awaiting an invitation to a training program. We recruiters were supposed to cut through the red tape in Washington with our contacts there. In Stillwater we were invited to mix and mingle with a group of graduate students at a student apartment. There I met an attractive young lady named Becky Brown, a political science graduate student from Oklahoma City who had applied to the Peace Corps and was expecting to enter a training program in Africa. I took up Becky's cause, attempting to push it through the bureaucratic channels in Washington, hoping as usual to move her file up to the top of the pile. We got on well, continuing to communicate and exchange visits after I left OSU and returned to Atlanta. Although I would be spending much of the time traveling, initially in the U.S. and later back to Africa, Becky and I managed to see each other on several occasions. It seems that I got my personal and professional priorities mixed up in the months to come, paying less attention to the application process and more to the applicant!

The Brown family was very hospitable toward me. Margie and Bill were to my mind model parents, and together with their four children comprised a remarkably close-knit nuclear family. Becky's younger sister Mikel was especially friendly, bright and inquisitive beyond her tender years. After spending the past several years away from my own home, the Browns provided me with an opportunity to re-connect with my roots. Even so, my eyes were fixed on the world out there. Oklahoma no longer held my attraction even though it had defined me socially and culturally. I told the Browns of my interest in going back overseas whenever the occasion presented itself. They, of course, were more interested in knowing what my intentions toward their daughter were.

Chapel Hill, North Carolina   *Spring 1968*

Then, in January 1968 I was asked to set up a new statewide recruiting office in North Carolina, considered to be especially fertile grounds for bringing in applicants. I was fortunate to be invited to stay in the Wesley Foundation Center on the campus of the University of North Carolina (UNC) in Chapel Hill, together with my fellow recruiter "Doc" Long who had been a Volunteer in Sierra Leone. The Center would serve both as a place of residence and a temporary recruiting office. During the spring semester we found Chapel Hill to be a most receptive place for our mission as well as a great place to live. There was a vibrant student culture, one that had produced the highest number of Volunteers anywhere in the South. After a short while I understood why God had made the sky Carolina Blue!

Doc was a big fan of Wes Montgomery, so my ear became attuned to his distinctive sounds. He would occasionally take me out to clubs in the Black community, where I would never have thought of going before. I was by now already a jazz and soul music enthusiast so I enjoyed seeing the ambiance in which it was generated. During my two years of living in Africa I became accustomed to being a minority White in an overwhelmingly Black social environment. Yet exploring the African American culture seemed in some respects more adventuresome than Africa since I had grown up in an essentially segregated society in which we were taught to keep our distance from people of color. All around in the late 1960s there was abundant evidence of the resentment Blacks felt toward Whites. "Burn, baby, burn" was in the air. We were, after all, only a few years removed from Brown vs. Board of Education that was supposed to have done away with inequality in education.

Springtime in Chapel Hill was glorious in its Carolina Blue. Furthermore, the spring of 1968 was a presidential election season and the Vietnam War was the over-riding issue. President Johnson was highly unpopular on campus and students were looking for a Savior to rescue the country from the morass that was Vietnam. The person who fit that bill on campus more than any other was Sen. Eugene McCarty (D-Minn). Shaggy-haired hippies and radicals shaved themselves and went campaigning "clean for Gene." (Happily, a few of them had the good sense to sign up as Peace Corps applicants as well.) Although Robert Kennedy was also campaigning for the Democratic nomination, he was considered a little too "establishment" for the activist UNC students. In any event, he was gunned down that spring by a deranged assassin. That, coupled with the assassination of Rev. Martin Luther King Jr., cast a dark shadow over Carolina and the entire nation in the springtime of 1968.

UNC Chapel Hill Campus, Spring 1968

My job as director of Peace Corps recruitment for the state of North Carolina, however, also involved soliciting applicants on Historical Black Colleges and Universities (HBCUs) campuses. As it turns out, North Carolina abounds with HBCUs, many of which I visited during my semester in the state. They included St. Augustine University, Shaw University, Bennett College, North Carolina College, North Carolina Agricultural & Mechanical University and Winston Salem University. Although several of my recruiting colleagues were African-Americans, the fact was that only two percent of the Volunteers who served in the Peace Corps were Black. Recruiting volunteers like them was a hard sell. Most Black American students felt a strong obligation to family and community, a commitment to make money and assist their families upon graduation. They were generally not inclined to spend two years in a developing country on modest income.

I sensed that one of the surest signs of unease within the Agency was the feeling of ambiguity with which my Black colleagues recruiting on Black campuses attempted to sell the Peace Corps. Deep down I believe they felt it was Charlie's organization. In any case, the voice of the Black Revolution often drowned them out.

And for many of us, recruiting on predominantly White campuses, the experience was much the same: we found that a lot of young Americans just didn't believe in Santa Claus any more. Vietnam overshadowed everything. I don't recall whether we achieved anything like the numbers of applicants projected for the state of North Carolina that year. Likely not, for it was an extraordinary period of turmoil in American society.

Peace Corps, Uganda/Tanzania Desk Officer   1968-69

From my role as recruiter out of the Southern Regional Office in Atlanta, I was able to parlay my interest in a Peace Corps position into an offer to go to Washington, D.C. as Operations/Training Officer for Uganda/Tanzania in the Africa Region of Peace Corps. Shortly after being hired in the summer of 1968 my division chief decided to send me to Africa to get a sense of issues pertaining to the two country programs. In those days the Peace Corps operating budget was such that new desk officers could be sent to the field for orientation and familiarization of their country programs. These are notes kept during that trip:

West Africa   9/July/1968

This trip to Africa began in Philadelphia where I joined 131 trainees on a charter flight to Sierra Leone. Even as we took flight on July 5 it was uncertain just what kind of reception we would get in a country teetering on the brink of political turmoil. A few days before it was questionable whether the group would be allowed to train in-country as planned, or in fact whether it would be allowed to come at all. Two of my own recruitees were among the group from North and South Carolina, which evinced a calm sense of satisfaction in seeing the end result of our crusading efforts. The group went through customs in Freetown and out to Forah Bay College. Here the trainees were to receive orientation before beginning "live-ins" and practice teaching. My mission, however, was to get on to Uganda. I waited five long hours at the airport for Nigerian Airways to take me to Accra where I was to catch an Ethiopian Airways flight to Addis Ababa. Since it was delayed so long I arrived in Accra too late for the only flight to East Africa until the following Tuesday. That meant a lay-over of several days in Accra, which I didn't mind much at all.

Kampala, Uganda   *10/July/1968*

I was to depart for Kampala via Addis Ababa in Ethiopia, so I sent cables to the respective Peace Corps offices of my ETA. Arriving early in the morning at Entebbe, Uganda, then riding the bus 20 miles though the mist rising from the lush forest to Kampala, I was at the Peace Corps office long before the first secretary came in. Country Director Del Lewis, (a fellow Jayhawker) had arranged an itinerary for us which included a trip up north beginning that morning. Bob Kelley, a fellow ex-Malawi PCV, joined us for my initial orientation. I soon learned that the proposed livestock tick control project had finally fallen by the wayside in much the same way the co-op program had died in the spring: strong Ministry of Animal Industry backing, but denied by the Ministry of Planning for political reasons.

In the afternoon Bob took me out with him to inspect one of the four school partnership projects, six miles outside of Kampala. This was a primary school being constructed under the supervision of an African minister, Rev. Kasozi, in memory of his son who had died recently. All the cement blocks were being made at the site by local parents of the students. Work had already begun on the construction when Rev. Kasozi approached the Peace Corps about helping finance it under the School Partnership Program. Bob had worked with him ever since, obtaining support from two schools in New York. This was a school obviously very much needed in the community. And it was a classic example of self-help, to which the Peace Corps has been able to give assistance.

Bob volunteered to chauffeur me down to the Ankole and Kigezi Regions himself. As the junior staff member in Uganda, Bob was soft-spoken and quite serious about his job. He was absolutely dedicated to Peace Corps. He was adamant in his view that the "grass hut image" of the Volunteer was a sham, that the manner in which he lives need not in any way hamper his effectiveness. As a married man with a boy named Rafiki (friend), Bob frequently had Volunteers in his house. But he also maintained that lack of privacy was the greatest problem staff men faced.

Kisoro, Uganda   *13/July/1968*

We began the 650 mile round trip to the southwesternmost edge of Uganda on Thursday. Crossing the equator and skirting

Lake Victoria to the south, the first Volunteer post we came to was Masaka, among the largest towns in the country and an important center in Buganda. Several years ago, Masaka was the stronghold of Baganda resistance, which resulted in the Kabaka's exile. The Aga Khan Secondary School in Masaka was considered by PCVs teaching on its staff to be an ideal school, with a completely integrated student body (Asian and African) and at least 10 nationalities on the teaching staff. Pushing on through Buganda territory we came to a somewhat isolated post at Kitunga Secondary, now in Ankole District. The married couple here took us in for the night; we sat up into the wee hours chatting under a tilly lamp.

One topic dominated evening discussions: the British headmaster, not a man to be described briefly. He required anecdote after anecdote to illustrate his character: intolerable, vain, inconsiderate, rude and incompetent. In short, he was mentally unstable. The students disliked him and the staff ignored him. He in turn accused the PCV teachers of stirring up a student strike. He locked himself up in his house, afraid that the students would stone him. As for the Volunteers, they went about their work as teachers, not altogether unhappy but rather lethargic about anything else. The headmaster was anxious to enter Cambridge to study archeology after leaving Uganda. He readily admitted that PCVs rarely left the compound to go anywhere because it involved too much effort. They concentrated on being good teachers.

The next morning Bob and I went to talk with Headmaster Perkins. He was indeed eccentric, his eyes darting around the room as he talked, his voice booming like a fog horn. Here was a man recognized by everyone as crazy, but as he talked it became obvious that he wasn't stupid. Fourteen years in East Africa as an economic geographer had given him an awareness of where priorities for development should lie: it was unquestionably in agriculture. He talked of integrating agricultural science into the East Africa Examination curriculum and starting a commercial tea or coffee scheme on the school compound so that students could defray school costs. Perkins knew his soils and geographic conditions well, and what would grow where. Had he talked with anyone in the Ministry about his ideas? Well, no, because he was known to be eccentric and no one would listen to him anyway. Perkins said that they had tried to get rid of him several times and that he had had to battle for his very job. What a sad, sad case! I noted the books on agriculture which he gave me for training and then he took us on a tour of the compound.

By nightfall we reached the town of Kisoro, situated in the finger-like projection of Uganda toward the Congo and Rwanda. Kisoro faces a row of majestic volcanic mountains along the Rwanda border that reach as high as 13,000 ft. We stayed at a rest house owned by a Belgian who had been there 15 years and was so tired of the adversities confronting him that he talked of packing up and leaving. He kept a pygmy on hand to serenade the tourists which he complained were few these days. He was a friend of the three Volunteers, however, and they were planning a birthday party that evening in the restaurant of the hotel.

It wasn't a very festive occasion as birthday parties go — no candles, no cake, no dancing. The only woman there was the honored guest. After supper we drank coffee and talked. It reminded me of similar nights in Port Herald when our little community got together; it was a special event. We worked to strain every drop of festivity from the gathering. The three Volunteers at Kisoro, Mutolere Secondary, were not a very happy lot, or at least so it appeared. The headmaster, an African who held firmly to the tenets of his Catholic order, was concerned about their failure to adhere to the religious nature of the school. He also indicated that the Volunteers showed little interest or appreciation for the local culture. One of them had not performed well as a teacher. From the Volunteers' point of view the headmaster was not to be trusted; he paid no attention to their suggestions. They had been accused of apostasy in teaching anti-religious literature, and of having provoked a student strike. (The threat of such strikes appeared to be bubbling under the surface in several Uganda schools and at least once recently erupted into a demonstration against expatriate teachers.)

On Saturday we drove up to a market just on the Congo border before returning to Kampala. It was hard to imagine that not far from this mountainous, temperate region of elegant eucalyptus trees lay the vast Congo rain forest. We then headed back to Kampala.

Kampala, Uganda   *20/July, 1968*

On Monday I met with Del Lewis, the PC Country Director. We made the official rounds with U.S. Embassy and Uganda government offices related to Peace Corps operations. First of these was the U.S.

Ambassador, whom I already felt I knew because of his prominent role in getting the health project through. I struggled to overcome my prejudice toward embassy personnel derived from my Malawi experience and travels as a Volunteer. It wouldn't go away. Ambassador Stebbins is a genial man who speaks with a distinctive New England Brahmin accent. He had been Ambassador to Nepal before coming to Uganda and showed unusual enthusiasm for the work "his Volunteers" had been doing there. He revealed the same personal interest in PC operations in Uganda, referring to several PCVs by name and exulting over the final approval by PC/Washington of the health project.

The other visits were far less interesting. We talked with the number two man at AID, a career man past retirement age who viewed each African country according to the degree to which it fit the American ideal for development. Uganda, then, was a relatively good country because it pursues a stable—i.e., common sense, sound economy—path toward development. He talked about the AID contribution to the Ankole cattle project with pride, saying that he had just bought several pounds of experimental beef himself.

In the afternoon we went to see the senior education officer whose office was in the Parliament building. He had no particular complaint about PCV teachers, but then he conceded that he had little to do with them. In fact, he went so far as to praise Volunteer teachers in general for the work they had done (perhaps to let us hear what we wanted to hear). He thought that perhaps some time in the future Volunteers might be requested for private schools and primary schools in Uganda. The latter seemed highly unlikely since Tanzania had just "dis-invited" Peace Corps out of its primary school system, with bruised feelings on both sides.

Moroto, Uganda   *25/July/1968*

Thursday, Del and I packed up and headed north toward Moroto in the Karamojong Region on a second safari. The trip to Moroto would prove to be the highlight of my stay in Uganda. The staff who had visited this post before described it as one of the most remote, the least frequently visited in the country. The road to Moroto goes along the lake past Jinja to Mbale and then cuts northward through the marshy lowland and shrub to Soroti. From there on the way becomes more and more arid, with a broad expanse of flat land much like West Texas. Multi-colored birds dart in and out of the bush, and farther on one begins to see herds of cattle presided over by small boys with sticks.

They were Karamonjong, a people so culturally insulated that the British colonial administration didn't bother to try to "civilize" them. The Karamojong are of Nilotic stock, tall and stately, similar in their cattle-centered culture to the Masai. They are feared by neighboring tribes in Uganda but are themselves fearful of the Turkana of Kenya who have managed to acquire rifles. Cattle-raiding between the two tribes is common. The dress of the Karamojong men usually consists of one piece of cloth tied across one shoulder, and little else. The women are more concerned with fashion. They wear a loin cloth made of goat skin, often beaded, and sometimes a longer goatskin piece in the back which extends past the knees. They are nearly always adorned with necklaces of beads or brass ringlets, and just as often they sport large metal earrings. For the women the cloth tied across the shoulder appears to be optional.

We arrived in Moroto toward sunset, suddenly driving along a four-lane paved street. A sign to the left said "Welcome to the Heart of Africa" and you could almost believe it after the long ride. The town and school were nestled in the crotch of a 10,000 ft. mountain which affords a pleasant climate the year round. The secondary school had about 160 students, half of whom were Karamojong. The three Volunteers, two of them with shaggy beards, greeted us heartily, surprised that we had gotten there at all. Along with two British teachers and an American student working on his thesis in political science from Makerere, we all gathered in one house for supper. It was, in contrast to the "party" at Kisoro, a happy occasion.

These guys liked their post; they would not trade it for any other. One of them was extending for an additional term and another asked to re-up for a third year to devote full time to the orphanage he worked with part time. The next morning we got a hearing from their British headmaster. Peace Corps, he stated, had been indispensable in the functioning of Moroto Secondary since its opening four years ago. Involved in the community? They were so much involved that the headmaster worried about the loss of one Volunteer to the community entirely (to work with the orphanage). He discussed with me the inspectorate's report on Moroto.

Strangely enough the main criticism of PCV teachers had been that they spent too much time in preparation, concentrating on the text book too much, and doing too little to instill in students a spirit of self-reliance and discipline! Exactly what most PCV teachers would say about their British colleagues! The headmaster himself was critical. The students, he contended, were complaining that inexperienced and. young teachers would hinder their chances of passing the Cambridge School Certificate. They were too lax in disciplining the more unruly students, he added, but on the whole they were "a good lot".....

A refreshing appraisal after the other two schools we had visited in Uganda.

The next day we followed the watershed road south out of Moroto around the mountain, back into the expanse of fierce thorn bush and eventually around another mountain about the size of the first. On the right one could see the low-lying Lake Kyoga which we had skirted in coming, and to the left in the distance the beginnings of the Kenya Highlands. At first scattered clusters of Karamojong huts dotted the bush, then none at all. Finally in the southern part of Karamojong Region the villages begin to look more permanent and better built. The terrain became less formidable and the leafy matoke plant regained its prominence.

We had now entered Bugisu Region. Along the roads there were bands of young men with bells on their legs, beads across their chests and sisal fiber plumes on their heads. They shuffled in cadence to drum beats. We were to learn that this was the year of circumcision rights, and that this hell-raising, as it were, was part of it. Every even year such as 1968 the rights are practiced in Bugisu. Any young man who reaches the age of 20 or 21 without having been circumcised is considered with scorn in the villages. During the season relatives of a reluctant youth may even round him up to be circumcised in order to avoid the embarrassment he would otherwise cause the family. These roving bands of youths are usually in a rowdy spirit and can cause the motorist considerable grief.

Back in Kampala, having only partially recuperated from the safari, I went with Bob and family to a farewell party Saturday evening given in their honor. Bob was finishing his tour here so he was being wined and dined frequently. This party was a colorful mix of non-official Americans, Asians and Africans with soul flavoring. An evening of hard partying was rounded out with a session at the fashionable Susanna Club. Sunday, then, was necessarily a day of rest.

(Note: The next time I would see Bob would be in Nashville, over 30 years later. He was still re-living his Peace Corps experience!)

Sometime during the week I had been at the USIA office where the visiting president of Lincoln University was introduced to me by the USIA director. One of the few remaining White presidents of a major Black university in the U.S., he proudly noted that Lincoln had yet to experience student violence. From my experience recruiting on campuses, both Black and White, I guessed at the reason for this. Often the Black bourgeois administrations of Black campuses were more conservative and afraid of intimidation than their White counterparts.

Kampala, Uganda   26/July/1968

My plans were confirmed to leave for Tanzania. The past two days saw heavy rains in Kampala despite the fact that this was supposedly the "dry" season in southern Uganda. The week began with an afternoon visit with Del and Rev. Kasozi to a community near Kampala called Chitezi. It was no ordinary visitation for we were the honored guests during a full program that included a Church of Uganda service, inspection of school grounds, demonstrations by the scout troop and various sporting activities, ceremoniously capped with tea and formal speeches. In order to appreciate the occasion it must be noted that this industrious community, like most of southern, "suburban" Uganda, was Baganda. One readily learned that the Baganda sense of grievance against the Obote government since he chased the Kabaka from Uganda in 1966 was profound and pervasive. The Baganda were not just without a leader, they were without a king who represented an institution hundreds of years old. Talking with a very articulate Muganda person recently, I was informed that the Uganda situation bore many similarities with the Biafra secessionist conflict in Nigeria. Many Baganda, he said, were sympathetic with the Ibo cause. Were not the Baganda so "docile", he concluded, there might have been civil war in Uganda by now.

The next day I spent at Makerere University where I met one of the most notable political outcasts from Malawi, writer David

Rubadiri, who had served as Malawi's first Ambassador to the UN. He had now joined the dozens of young Malawians in exile as a result of Dr. Banda's urge to go it alone. In our brief conversation he seemed very subdued, content to let me do most of the talking.

I told him we were planning to use his recent novel, No Bride Price, in our Peace Corps training program; he nodded his approval. It was sad to hear that he had broken off all communication with Malawi. Another outcast from Malawi, former PCV Paul Theroux, was at the University. His most recent article, "Tarzan is an Expatriate," had just appeared in Transition Magazine. It was a clever parody of the White tribes of Africa who, like Tarzan, had come to live in the jungle as master. It was the "liberal" Tarzan who came in for the most damning comment. He had come to a liberal's paradise where he could "hold leftist opinions in a lovely climate..." It was the liberal Tarzan who says, "Here! Here!" when preventive detention legislation is passed, while the Tory Tarzan keeps silent. In all, Theroux's article struck too close to home for one to chuckle very loudly. (It was to be banned and the editor detained by the government shortly thereafter).

Bukedi District, Uganda   *30/July/1968*

On Tuesday Del, George—the PC doctor—and I embarked on the most informative visit of my stay in Uganda: three days in Bukedi District where the health project we were designing would have its origins. In addition to his responsibilities as PC doctor, George would be heading up the project, and he seemed eager to get started. George had a dry sense of humor and a compulsion for driving at break-neck speeds on sometimes treacherous roads. And as was often the case with PC doctors, George brought to Uganda the kind of conservative social values common to his profession.

During lunch at the Rock Hotel in Tororo, the three of us plunged into a heated discussion about the intense subject the state of American society. Our views nearly reflected a generation gap although we all belonged to the same generation. Del (29) and George (28) assumed the role of apologist for Americanism in its current form, allowing for certain modifications. Hull (27), on the other hand, defended the student revolution and the need for a basic change in the system (a reflection, no doubt, of my intensive exposure to the militant student voices on campuses while recruiting). Del, the lawyer Catholic, Negro, Democrat—convincingly argued that ours was still a society in which almost anyone could "make it". His own rise in so short a time from part time porter on the railroad to PC country director was of course exhibit A. The lines were drawn on a very personal basis. They both said they would fight in Vietnam; I contended that one should refuse to fight an unjust war. The debate subsided over coffee and we went off to examine the prospective sites for health Volunteers.

Bukedi District was known to have a very high incidence of eye disease, and we observed several diseased persons at each post. The population was most heavily concentrated in one sub-district, but in most of the district villages it was rather widely dispersed. At each stop, which included such exotic names as Butaleja and Iki Iki, we looked for possible locations on the compound for houses that would have to be built. We drew up a floor plan for very modest dwellings, with a living room, bedroom, kitchen and shower. A bid for about twenty such houses would go out to local contractors. We spoke with the principal of the School of Hygiene in Mbale about participation of his staff in the in-country training segment, and he assured us they would be willing to help.

While my work was cut out for me in giving support to PC/Uganda, I felt that my trip provided valuable insights which would help when I returned to Washington. It had given me a feeling of being a member of a team rather than just a bureaucratic functionary.

Dar es Salaam   *2/August/1968*

Although my work in Washington would continue to be mainly concerned with Uganda, it was the prospect of visiting Tanzania again that turned me on. My admiration for President Nyerere, which began during my training at Syracuse, had increased with my growing awareness of the experiment in African socialism upon which Tanzania had embarked. Among the very first countries to request and receive PC Volunteers in 1961, Tanzania had also had among the highest total number, at the peak well over 400.Then came the decline in Volunteers, inevitable as a result of Nyerere's emphasis on self-reliance and Africanization. It was a principle that was hard to argue against. In fact it underlay the basic assumption of the Peace Corps itself. We were in the business of supplying middle-level manpower, only until the host country considered itself ready to supply its own manpower.

I boarded the East African Airways flight at Entebbe early on Saturday morning. In the shuffle of passengers vying for seats I found myself across the aisle from a long-haired, sloe-eyed, mini-skirted young woman. She introduced herself as we took to the air as Janice Jamal, a Tanzanian by birth, of Indian parentage, but obviously quite British in her speech and lifestyle. She was now living in London and working as a journalist for Young and Rubicam. It occurred to me as we talked that I had never really carried on a conversation with an Indian woman. Our discussion touched on a wide range of topics, from Franz Fanon to the women's emancipation movement. Ms. Jamal would be writing an article on UNICEF in Tanzania as well as visiting her family in Dar. I was invited to drop by and see her there sometime during the week, and I promised to make every effort to do so.

I was met by the PC driver and taken directly to the office where the Peace Corps Director, Gene Mihaly, was on hand to take me into his custody. The spacious two-story office which I remembered as housing a sprawling PC operation before was now only partially utilized. Upstairs dust had collected on some of the bookshelves and medical supplies. The staff was down to only three, in addition to the secretarial help and a PC physician still awaiting immigration clearance. The pace was rather less hectic than in Kampala. The mood was somewhat more sober as Gene and his staff presided over the dismantling of what was once a vast program. By December it was anticipated that only eight soil surveyor PCVs would remain in the country, and possibly a half dozen extending teachers. This is not to say that there was an air of pessimism here; rather it was an awareness of the political considerations which inhibited any expansion of Peace Corps programming.

Gene was a jaunty, self-confident fellow, although not quite as effusive as Del. He belonged to a sizeable number of ex-navy men who had been recruited into the PC, which perhaps accounted for his directness in dealing with crises. One such crisis had arisen a few days before I arrived concerning a Malawi PCV who was being held in the Songea jail for failure to report to immigration at the Tanzania border with Malawi. Nothing more specific was known, so Gene was planning for us to fly out to Mbeya on Monday where the Volunteer was being remanded for trial.

Meanwhile, hotel reservations had been made for me at the new ultra-modern Agip Motel, just as in Kampala they had wanted to put the man from Washington in the most luxurious accommodations. But I figured that the money I could save staying in a cheaper place, which was considerable, could be more happily spent elsewhere. Anyway, I was familiar with the old relic called the New Metropole across the street. And Margot's restaurant downstairs still served about the best food in town, so I made the move. By now I was accustomed to ordering fresh leafy salads with my steak and French fries, against the rules in the Peace Corps handbook. But not once had I ever gotten sick from food in Africa, so I was willing to take the chance!

Mbeya, Tanzania near the Malawi Boarder   *5/August/1968*

Monday morning five of us, including an Indian lawyer hired to handle legal problems which might arise, and an Israeli pilot took off from the Dar airport in a Tim-Air Cessna. For the first 10 or 15 miles the view was of palm trees interspersed with villages, then dense forests and soon the grassy plateau where the pilot dipped down to within a few feet of the ground and every now and then flushed out a couple of giraffe and an occasional elephant. We passed over the Great Ruaha River and mountains surrounding Iringa, and the remainder of the way covered parched brown earth and shrubs. It was a spectacular trip!

Mbeya is the main town in the southwest of Tanzania, located near a mountain range that leads right down to Lake Malawi. It is roughly midway on the famed road from Lusaka to Dar, a distance of over 1000 miles. Heavy transport trucks stop here to refuel and rest. At the Mbeya Hotel where we stayed there was an assortment of British, Italians and Chinese. The Italians had just finished laying the Tan-Zam pipeline under the giant Agip Oil Company contract. The British had been around Tanzania ever since they kicked the Germans out in the 19th century. But the Chinese contingent in Tanzania represented the most extensive investment of Peking in Africa. The technicians here were surveying the Tan-Zam Railway, one of the most ambitious projects undertaken in Africa by any government. Having been turned down in its request for aid by

Western bilateral donors and the World Bank, Tanzania finally approached the Chinese government who agreed to do the job. The Chinese, who were coming in increasingly larger numbers, were known for their discreetness and their non-involvement with Tanzanians. They had a job to do and they were doing it, no time for socializing.

The PCV Smith case by now had involved cable traffic and telephone calls to Malawi and Songea. It threatened to become an international incident. I could picture Time magazine verbally slapping the Tanzanian's government hand for putting an innocent Volunteer in jail. We waited for his arrival in Mbeya, checking with the police and magistrate to find out what they knew. Nothing was certain. The lawyer was anxious to return to Dar for engagements and the official permission for the aircraft was for one day only. The other three left, while Gene and I sat on our thumbs. Fortunately this afforded me the opportunity to meet most of the eight PCVs in the town. As usual there were the problems with the headmaster and concern about not being accepted. The two soil scientists were most encouraging, assured that their soil surveys were going well despite the indifference of local officials. However, they were somewhat pessimistic about the development of new crops in this region because of poor soil. The experimental wheat schemes in the Mbeya area did not seem to be faring too well.

At long last, on the evening of the second day, PCV Smith appeared at the hotel looking like the "fugitive"—tall, gaunt, reserved, sporting a heavy black beard and clutching a copy of Doctor Zhivago given to him by a PCV while in the Songea jail. His story filled in the picture we already had. He had left Kapoio, a small village near the Tanzania border where he was a health worker, with his faithful houseboy on July 19th. They dutifully stopped at the port village of Itungi to present their official visas and then proceeded to sail along the eastern shore of the lake in a boat full of Africans. PCV Smith was the lone mzungu. All of which sounded like the kind of vacation any enterprising PCV might plan. That is, if one did not take into consideration the sensitive nature of that area. He claimed to have been unaware of the tension in northern Mozambique and southern Tanzania. In the Nyassa region of Mozambique the Frelimo rebels had been very successful in wresting control from the Portuguese.

And in Naohingwea, southern Tanzania, there was a training base for freedom fighters from all over Africa. Needless to say, white faces were not especially welcomed in these parts, since they were likely seen as the face of the colonial oppressor. Even regular flights of East African Airways had drawn a hail of bullets in the area near the coast of the Indian Ocean.

The immigration "officials" apparently had second thoughts about Smith's entry and notified the authorities in the nearest town. Several days later, at one of the stops along the shore, the two travelers were apprehended by Tanzanian police and escorted to Songea, the point at which our story began. When I left on the following day there was hope of his being quickly tried and sent back to Malawi. But at least, whatever steps were to be taken, it appeared that an international incident involving possible charges of spying had been averted.

Back in Dar, I had two days remaining before my departure. Gene was still out working on the Smith affair, which left only the deputy director in the office. There was none of the camaraderie in the Dar office that I found in Kampala. The PCV secretary crisis persisted, with only one out of three remaining. The other two had left because of the emotional stress caused by personality clashes within the office. There seemed to be a legacy of bad blood between secretarial staff and administration unresolved from previous administrations.

The high point of my visit in Tanzania was an unofficial conversation with a very official person. Janice Jamal made good her invitation to lunch at the house of her brother, Amir Jamal, who, as it turned out, was Minister of Finance in the Tanzania government. The Jamal family, I had learned, was one of the most prominent in the country, with roots a couple of generations deep. It was their father who had first identified with the African nationalist cause and had been instrumental in arranging Julius Nyerere's education. He was a prosperous merchant in Mwanza. His sons had taken up his cause, even to the extent of alienating their own Asian community.

Amir Jamal, now 40 years old, had slightly graying hair and a sober countenance that reflected the tensions of his office and his personal life. He was wearing a white Nyerere (safari) suit that had become the style of most of Tanzania's public officials. Since Independence he had held a number of portfolios in the Nyerere cabinet and was at present the only Asian representative. I was introduced as a PC staff member from Washington by Janice. Jamal then explained that as Minister of Communications in 1969 he had made the official request himself for Tanzania's first group of PCVs in the feeder roads scheme. He had also attended a conference of Peace Corps in Puerto Rico that same year and was an admirer of JFK as well as Sargent Shriver.

Then, reflecting on the present precarious state of the Peace Corps program in the country, he became even more serious. Simply put, he said, it had to do with the "unfortunate business" the U.S. had got itself into in Vietnam. That was difficult for any country to ignore, and especially a developing country that saw such a war as the result of neo-colonialist involvement. It was not, he hastened to add, that Tanzania no longer needed or wanted Volunteers. The hint was there that Mr. Jamal had not given up hope of the amelioration of the American society and a more palatable foreign policy. But it was quite clear that Peace Corps was part of the bigger picture, and it was not a very pretty one at present. I wished that Mr. Jamal could have attended the recruiters' conference in San Francisco in January to see how we in the Peace Corps wrestled with issues of U.S. foreign policy. Maybe we hadn't lost the admiration of the Third World completely as yet, but there might be a time soon when the reservoir of good will among leaders of developing countries would run dry.

UCLA Uganda Training   Fall/1968

Back in Washington, I resumed the mundane business of writing memos, pushing paper and attending staff meetings. Outside the office the American society was a seething cauldron of ferment, what with the civil rights movement, the anti-Vietnam War movement and now Flower Power. A definition of my job which I tacked above my desk mirrored my frustration with the bureaucratic world:

"The desk officer: one part authority and two parts responsibility."

Charged with the responsibility of coordinating a fall training program of some 60 Volunteers for Uganda at a UCLA facility near Oxnard, California, one of my first tasks was to recruit and hire a dozen "language informants". Because the Africa Region conceived itself to be in the vanguard of innovation and "cultural sensitivity", regional rhetoric stressed that the language instructor become something more than an "informant". I subscribed to this notion, so I adopted it as a working principle.

As it turned out, however, powers within the agency meant for this principle not to be taken too seriously. I went about signing on my African staff for the Uganda training, telling those who had experienced insensitivity in former Peace Corps programs that a new day was dawning. In the process I became personally acquainted with most of them, the majority of whom were to teach Luganda, the language of the Baganda. During each of my three visits to the training site in Oxnard, I spent much of my time with the Ugandans, listening to their grievances with the program director. Often I sided with them, and assuming that responsibility as training officer also meant authority. I reported my attempts at resolving problems in their favor to my Division Chief in Washington. However, he was disturbed, not by the possibility that we were allowing "cultural sensitivity" to creep into Peace Corps training, but rather by the prospect of irresponsible language "informants" trying to "take over" the program! It was here on this issue that I earned my reputation as the most immature and "unprofessional" desk officer in the region. My Division Chief was concerned to avoid any "radical" disturbance.

Meanwhile, one of the first and most enthusiastic countries to ask for Volunteers—Tanzania—quit asking. We waited for the slightest hint of a new request, and watched while the number of Volunteers from Finland and Sweden increased in Tanzania. Occasionally Tanzanian government officials complained that there were too few Afro-American Volunteers in the Peace Corps. At the peak in 1965 they never represented more than three percent. Yet most of the top administrators within the Africa Region were themselves Black. With these factors in mind I wrote a memo proposing a predominantly Black program to be recruited and trained upon Tanzania's request. It met with sudden bureaucratic death. This, I was told, smacked of segregation and was against Peace Corps principles. So much for thinking outside the box!

Our Uganda training program in Oxnard was unexceptional in most respects. Our field staff members came from Uganda to participate in their respective components of training and to offer critical comment. One of them became a bit upset during a discussion of American policy in Africa. A couple of the Ugandans were offering uncomplimentary remarks concerning US policy in East Africa, daring to suggest that Peace Corps in Uganda should change or get out. And some of the trainees joined forces with them in the debate.

During the remainder of his stay at the training site, the PC/Uganda staff member kept his distance from the African staff until he returned to the field. Shortly thereafter he sent in his evaluation of the program, directly to the Director's Office, rather than through regular channels (through me). He was incensed over the impudence of these ungrateful young snobs. It was much the same language that Spiro Agnew would use on the under 30 Americans a year later. Unfortunately the report came very close to stating the reality of Peace Corps attitudes toward training, despite all the cathartic tea-group sessions and self-denials.

Who were these effete snobs? As was usually the case in Peace Corps programs, most of them were students who were taking a semester out of school to earn a little money. They were mostly Baganda, with names like Musoke, Nagenda, Mukasa, Ssemakula and Kibaya. Most of them had traveled extensively in Europe as well as the U.S. Nearly all of them had spent from three to five years in the U.S. and were hip to the social revolution going there. So there was nothing "country" about these language informants. They were not unschooled in the issues gripping their respective universities and the community at large. They had long since ceased being over-awed by the greatness of America. And most important, they belonged to a new breed of African students who were coming to understand and—yes—to identify with the Afro-American. Secure in their own cultural identity, their Kiganda-ness, they were reaching across the traditional gap between Black American and African. They were into a soul thing. The tactics of confrontation being used on the college campus were not lost on these Africans during the training program when their personal interests were at stake.

Oklahoma City   *December 1968*

Back in Washington after my East Africa safari, I renewed my relationship with Becky. Then in the fall of 1968 I received a call from Margie Brown, Becky's mother, in Oklahoma City. Subject to debilitating allergies, Becky had become quite sick. But it was fairly certain, although they weren't sure, that Becky was pregnant.

It was clearly my handiwork, and I didn't go to any lengths to deny it. Becky and I had been together on several occasions, including the likely period of fertilization in the early fall of 1968. We had had a very mutually compatible relationship. However, my professional and personal objectives were clearly confounded. I had been hoping that Becky would be accepted into a Peace Corps training program as a result of my efforts. I was not oriented toward marriage and domestic tranquility. Rather, I was scheming to find my way back to Africa with the Peace Corps.

In December 1968, having visited our Uganda training site in California, I stopped in Oklahoma City to meet with Becky and the Brown family. As might be expected, they were anxious to have me accept my complicity in Becky's pregnancy and declare my intention to marry her. It was an unpleasant experience for all of us. The family had engaged the services of a lawyer to explain to me the legal implications of my complicity. John Lacy, a friend of the Browns, was from a prominent Oklahoma City family. John was the master of ceremonies for the occasion, a very tall man with a booming voice and most intimidating manner. He summarized for me the options at hand. I don't recall what all the options were. But I agreed to a marriage, coupled with annulment, accompanied by a commitment to pay Becky child support payments.

As it became increasingly clear that the Peace Corps would not be the vehicle for me to go overseas again, I began to explore other avenues in the spring of 1969. One such venue opened up which would see me on the way back to Africa, this time back to Kinshasa, in the Democratic Republic of the Congo in April 1969 (chronicled in another chapter). Then, on May 31, 1969, a child was born to Becky Brown whom she named William Christopher Hull. I received word of the blessed event in the Congo in the village of Lutendele with a mixture of elation and remorse; remorse, because I had turned my back on paternal responsibility, a wonderful woman and a certain family support system.

In 1971, after I had returned to graduate school, I traveled to Washington state to visit Becky and young Chris, now two years old. It would be the only time I would see him until he reached voting age. When Becky subsequently married John Lacy, they officially changed his name to William Christopher Lacy. John would be the only father Chris knew as he was growing up. However, events would conspire for me to become re-acquainted with Chris in 1990. It would prove to be one of the most gratifying experiences of my life. It was readily apparent that John and Becky had done a splendid job of raising young Chris.

I found him to be exceptionally articulate, well educated, intellectually alert and curious about the world beyond the campus. Well, all right, he was a Northwest chauvinist, of the firm belief that the quality of life in his native Washington state was superior to all others, especially with regard to its natural bounty. (A belief that is in any case difficult to argue with!) He was already just a few semesters away from a degree in forestry from the University of Washington in Seattle, a reflection of his passion for the great out-of-doors. He had a keen sense of humor, a generally secular outlook on life and a huge appetite for sports, both as a participant and as a spectator. He had a special attraction to basketball and skiing and excelled particularly in the latter.

To my immense relief, I found that Chris shared my interest in cultures other than his own and in travel. Thus, I would have little difficulty persuading him to come and visit me for a week in Sri Lanka. Later on Chris would go to Hawaii to live and work for several months his longest residency outside the Great Northwest. I was relieved, also, to observe that Chris seemed to harbor no bitterness toward me for having been absent from his life during his formative years. We have gotten together on numerous occasions, on skiing and white water rafting trips and family gatherings. I believe it is fair to say that we have become good friends.

Following his graduation from the university Chris embarked upon a career in forestry management which has remained his primary livelihood and area of expertise. He would marry Tami Dunlop, one of nine children reared on a farm in northern Oregon. Tami and Chris have two daughters, Moorea and Siena, apples of their father's eye.

William Christopher Lacy in his prime
(Courtesy: Ms. Mikel Brown Myers)

Our relationship has been nurtured by the continuing blessing of the Brown family, in particular Chris' aunt Mikel and her husband Craig Myers. Following a career in the Marine Corps, Craig and family settled in the Washington DC area where he works as an attorney specializing in environmental issues. Mikel has a remarkable skill as a portrait photographer (see above). Mikey and Colin, their two offspring are of the finest order. Both have excelled in their academic pursuits. Mikey is becoming a gifted linguist and Colin, God bless him, is becoming a world traveler! One proud uncle here!

Chris with daughters Moorea and Siena

Chapter 7

Democratic Republic of the Congo
1969-1970:
In The Heart of Darkness

Tambolana mokili...omona makambo. (Lingala: meaning travel around the world and you'll see things).
- popular song of Johnny Bokelo in Kinshasa, 1969

Omono wapi?...Na Lutendele   *June/1969*

It was the saison seche (dry season) in the Bas (lower) Congo River basin. The mornings were usually overcast and cool, the sun shone brightly in the afternoon, and it could be quite nippy at night. Looking down from the porch of our farm house in the village of Lutendele outside of Kinshasa, one could catch a glimpse of the mighty Congo River rushing swiftly toward the Atlantic. Vegetation in the gentle hills outside Kinshasa was occasionally dense with majestic palms, dotted with splotches of manioc fields and tall grass. Everywhere one went, in the city of Kinshasa or surrounding villages, he was likely to hear the distinctive sounds of Congolese music emanating from radio Kinshasa, frequently punctuated by recorded speeches of President Joseph Desire Mobutu—and his incantations of nye, uye...nye (listen up!).

Col. Mobutu, a career military man, began wielding political power in the years leading up to independence from the Belgian Congo on June 30, 1960. He was from a small Lingala-speaking tribe in Province Equateur. Since he did not belong to one of the major tribal groups, Mobutu nurtured a tribal-regional grievance against the Balunda, Baluba and especially the Bakongo (spelled in French with a k, not c)—tribes that were seen as being favored during the colonial era. Having participated with the CIA in the demise of Patrice Lumumba, the martyred nationalist hero, and having marginalized all other political figures, Mobutu assumed power in a military coup on November 24, 1965. He would soon become one of the most dominant and long-lasting political leaders on the African continent.

Mobutu set about systematically consolidating power in his own hands, leaving little authority to traditional chiefs or to the legislative body. His main instrument of political power was the Mouvement Populaire de la Revolution (MPR), whose main task was to mobilize the masses to do his bidding. He became known to the citizens of the country by a myriad of titles: Pere de la Nation, Guide Clairvoyant, le Grand Leopard, in addition to his official title as President of the Second Republic (the first republic having been interred at the time of the 1965 coup).

Mobutu was the architect of an ambitious nationalist movement which he entitled nationalisme authentique. The basic premise was that everything the Belgians had done during the colonial era had to be un-done. Starting with the easy part, Mobutu decided upon a thorough-going program of name-changing to reflect authentic African values. Christian names (read European) were to be jettisoned in favor of indigenous African names. Mobutu himself set the example: henceforth he would no longer be Joseph Desire, but Mobutu kuku gbenda wa zabanga—roughly translated as "the cock who leaves no hen unruffled." It is most likely that Mobutu knew that this appellation would not meet with the approval of the Catholic fathers! Nonetheless, he did his best to live up to his new name in most flamboyant ways. The entire Congolese nation was obliged to drop given Christian names and take up African ones. Thus, Jean Felix Koli would become Koli Elombe Motukoa. Prof. Pascal Payanzo would become Payanzo Ntsomo. Even birth certificates as well as passports had to be changed. Que vive la revolution!

But why stop there? Let's change the name of the country and get at the root of things! Congo, after all, was a name given to the country by the Belgians because the Bakongo were the first people they encountered as they worked their way inland from the Atlantic Ocean. It was not fair that one tribe should see its name emblazoned as the name of the entire country. So let's dig deep into history and look for a more authentic name. And there it was, right there in the history books: Zaire. This was actually a name the Portuguese had given to the area around the mouth of the mighty Congo River.

When they asked the Africans what they called the river, they replied "nzedi" (river).

The Portuguese said, "Huh?"

Finding it difficult to pronounce, they said, "You mean Zaire?"

The Congolese gave up, and from then on Portuguese accounts of their exploits in the area referred to the region of Zaire. So much for authenticity!

And while we are at it, all the cities and towns need to have authentic African names as well. So Leopoldville becomes Kinshasa; Elizabethville is Lubumbashi, Stanleyville is Kisangani, Katanga Region becomes Shaba and Bukavu becomes...well Bukavu gets to keep its name. An even more important, less symbolic issue concerns the national language. The Belgians insisted on two languages of instruction—French and Flemish—reflecting their own tribal differences. But how to replace these languages with authentic African ones? There are over 250 different languages and dialects spoken in the country. Lingala wins the popularity contest since it is the language of both the military and popular music and is spoken throughout the country. But then there are millions of people whose main language is Kikongo, Chiluba or Chilunda. What to do? As in many other developing countries, the language issue would rage on for several years. French retained its official status while Lingala easily retained its standing as the language of the masses.

Clothing was a very important matter to Congolese, both men and women. The latter generally had a good track record of maintaining traditional attire. But the men! Helas, they had taken up bad habits foisted upon them by the Europeans, wearing uncomfortable three-piece suits and ties, even in this tropical environment. So let's do away with this decadent style and replace it with an authentic one. A bas les costumes! Down with suits! We'll create a new African style and call it abacost. Henceforth, all Congolese (that is, Zairean) men will wear the national attire: an open-necked, sleeveless suit with no tie. There, that's much more comfortable anyway, isn't it? (This would prove to be a rather enduring policy, at least until Mobutu's demise.)

Then on to the harder part: nationalization of property. Communism? Certainly not! But the Mobutu government had a commitment to spreading the wealth, taking it from the foreign elements and giving it to the indigenous Africans. Beginning in the early 1970s, an extensive program of nationalization was instituted across the country. The massive Belgian copper mining interests were taken over by the state and Africans appointed to the highest managerial positions. Even mom and pop operations run by other foreign groups — the Portuguese, Greeks, Pakistanis and Lebanese, were declared to be property of the state. And what is the state to do with all this property? Why, they'll give it to the most deserving: friends and business associates of those in the sole political party, the Mouvement Populaire de la Revolution (MPR) of course. The latter, lucky fellows, would become popularly known by the appropriate title of acquereurs (acquirers).

Mobutu's rise to power corresponded with an increasingly global economy that had need of the critical minerals with which the Congo was blessed, copper and cobalt in particular. Thus, by the beginning of the 1970s the world demand for these minerals was such that the Congolese economy experienced something of a boom. The price of copper and cobalt soared, and with it the fortunes of GECAMINES, the nationalized mining company in Shaba (formerly Katanga Province). For a brief period the new currency, known as the zaire, was worth two U.S. dollars, making it one of the strongest currencies in the world! This was at a time when cartels of raw materials-producing developing countries such as OPEC began to play a key role in international economics.

— — —

I left Washington, in the idiom of the Now Generation, to do my thing. I had been reading Eldridge Cleaver's best-selling book, Soul on Ice, before making my decision to return to Africa. While Cleaver had become a fugitive from American "justice", I felt somewhat of a fugitive too—from the excesses of American "civilization". Richard Nixon in the White House was a symbol of all that the US might NOT have become: humorless, soulless, the button-down Omnipotent Administrator. The scene from The Graduate in which Dustin Hoffman was fervently exhorted by his elder to consider "plastics" as a lifetime vocation remained stuck in my mind, symbolic of the stranglehold of material values in American society. While final plans were being made for Apollo XI to put the first Americana on the moon, the new administration was making feeble attempts to extricate itself from Vietnam, the American Waterloo.

In many respects my going to the Democratic Republic of the Congo marked a radical departure in my life's pattern. A product of the traditional Midwestern America, I was taught the importance of thrift, diligence and clean living as the key to success. Conditioned by participation in, and acceptance of, basic American institutions, I had always managed to achieve "success" measured by these institutional standards. Two years as a Peace Corps Volunteer in Africa exposed me to a culture quite different from that of the American Midwest, to a people whose values challenged my own. At the same time I was part of an experiment rooted in the American psyche. Apart from the noble JFK vision of providing a fresh form of foreign aid to developing countries, the Peace Corps was born out of the fundamental belief that the same basic ingredients of hard work and organization that fashioned the American society could be employed to boost "under-developed" areas toward the same standard. It was the conviction that, given enough good old technical know-how, and to be sure a measure of goodwill, Western man was capable of bringing the rest of the world out of the darkness of poverty, ignorance and disease into the bright light of technological society.

Not incidentally, the Peace Corps was conceived of as a positive way of staving off the inevitable push of Communist influence into the Third World. But what virtually every returned Volunteer could tell you is that the real value of the Peace Corps is derived from his own awakening to another culture on more than merely a superficial level, which in turn often leads him to question tenets of his own society. He learns quickly that problems of "development" are much more societal than technological. And he returns to the U.S. to find the American society itself ravaged by the most acute societal problems while Americans continue to worship the god of technology. Yes, the Omnipotent Administrator—the corporation-democrat-capitalist—managed to construct a technological miracle while his neglect of social and racial inequalities has produced a veritable nightmare.

My decision to return to Africa, after a year and a half of employment with the American government, represented in a sense a rejection of the "success" to be achieved by faithfully adhering to protocol and the party line. It was a rejection of apprenticeship for the role of Omnipotent Administrator and, perhaps more important, a search for identity with the Super-masculine Menial. It was a rejection of the myth of the "superiority" of Western civilization coupled with the hope that the moral force of non-Western societies might yet be strong enough to overcome the myth.

But why the Congo? In the eyes of most of the world the Congo was a symbol of irrationality, associated with Joseph Conrad's Heart of Darkness. My feeling was that perhaps the darkest thing about the Congo was the Western man's ignorance of it. The history of the Congo had been marked since its precipitous Independence in 1960 by frequent periods of crisis. It had been the battleground of contending forces of capitalism and communism, in which the Congolese people suffered most. It may be, then, that my return to the Congo was a flight from (family) responsibility and the coldly rational world of computers and systems analyses to the irrational.

Okay, there was an element of rationality about my decision to return to the Congo. My friend and classmate at American University, Ghislain Kabwit, a Congolese, had talked about a Protestant university in Stanleyville and I wanted to see about teaching there. But none of my letters to the university authorities were answered. Telephone communication was out of the question. So I would just have to go there.

So there I was in the sprawling capital city of Kinshasa in late April 1969, having taken the existential leap of faith, having left a $10,000/yr job and ignored the possibility of higher paying jobs. After all, I felt, one must not be motivated solely by monetary considerations. But after a month and a half of unemployment in Washington and three weeks in Kinshasa, I was still without employment. It was three weeks spent shuffling in and out of the wrong offices and being introduced to the wrong people. At every turn I was told that my services were sorely needed in the Congo where the government policy was tailored to entice foreign-hire teachers at salaries considerably higher than Congolese themselves garner.

Meanwhile my only source of income was a stint of substitute teaching at the American community school for a couple of days. It was a school that mirrored the large and conspicuous American community in its American-ness. The headmaster's pre-occupation with preserving a clean image had led to confrontation with some students over their long hair. Living at the American missionary hostel, courtesy of my old friends Dan and Sandy Owen, only heightened my urgent desire to find employment. The missionary clientele there often reflected a heavy paternalism at best and a dark cynicism of the Congo at times.

After three weeks I was certain I did not want my French to sound like that of most Americans here. Language learning can be a very humbling experience, especially so if you are attempting to learn two at once. The first several weeks of initiation to French and Lingala were indeed humbling. Frequently I was called on to explain my presence in the Congo, so I worked out a couple of awkward sentences indicating that I was a chomeur (unemployed), that I had come from the U.S. to seek employment. Congolese suggested occasionally, and not altogether facetiously, that I must be a CIA agent then if I could offer no better explanation. They would sometimes smile knowingly since it was common knowledge that Americans were rich. Besides, who ever heard of an unemployed mondele (white man) in the Congo? It was hard for me to find any humor in this after a while. The real truth hurt. I wondered whether I might become a statistic in the urban unemployed. It was Hemingway, I believe, who said the only way you really get to know a country is to earn your living there. I would amend that slightly by saying you may learn a lot about a country by living there and NOT earning a living.

My introduction to Reverend Dick Prosser brought me an occupation, if not employment. Rev. Prosser, whom Time would call "left-leaning", was a missionary. But he was one of a kind in the Congo. His job was to develop a youth program for the Conseil Protestant du Congo (CPC), the rather fragile organization grouping all Protestant churches in the country. It was under the direction of Congolese, but its unity and power were severely hindered by hard-line missionaries—the majority—who perpetuated denominational differences and refused to believe Congolese should run their own churches. There were still over 2,000 Protestant missionaries in the country whose denominations had sunk roots in all regions, usually corresponding to tribal areas, for over a hundred years. Dick Prosser liked to help some of the hard-liners out of the country. He was about as popular with the missionary community as a skunk at a garden party.

A former disciple and trainee of Sol Alinsky, Pastor Prosser brought with him several years of experience in community development, mostly in Black ghettos in the U.S. One of the earliest efforts of the Church, that is to say the Congolese Protestant Church, to relate to the real needs of Protestant youth was the establishment in 1964 of a youth center known as Carrefour des Jeunes. With a center located in the middle of Kinshasa, Carrefour resembled a YMCA in most respects. Pastor Prosser oversaw the operations of Carrefour as technical consultant, in effect a kind of lightning rod for its problems, and in turn was responsible to the Comite Executive, composed mostly of influential African businessmen.

With a great deal of foresight and wisdom, the Comite also decided to establish an experimental farm for young Congolese to develop practical skills. The motto for this bold initiative was retour a la terre (return to the land). The notion was that by enticing young unemployed urban youth to live and work on the farm, the problem of unemployment would be reduced and a taste for rural life could be instilled in them. This pilot farm had its beginnings in April 1969, with the purchase of an abandoned Belgian farmhouse and a few hectares of land near the village of Lutendele, about 20 kilometers from Kinshasa. In its first few weeks the farm consisted of thick foliage covering virtually every inch of the farm area. The first task was to reclaim from the forest a small piece of land, which it constantly threatened to consume. After that they were to make of it what they could. For this task Pastor Prosser hired a young Congolese, Victor Lusawovana, to manage the farm.

It was at this point that the aspirations of the fledgling farm at Lutendele were for a time joined with my own. Having walked the streets of Kinshasa in fruitless search for work and having spent a big chunk of my meager funds on lodging, I was easily persuaded by Pastor Prosser to spend a few weeks on the farm. The Lusawovana family kindly provided me with a room in the farmhouse which they occupied and I shared meals with them. My justification for being there would be to teach the director how to drive the newly-purchased Fiat tractor. That would take a few days of practice myself, since my experience along those lines was greatly limited. And while

I would not be solving the problem of unemployment, I could at least try to be useful.

Days became weeks, and after one month I was still here, with my mission of teaching the director to drive the tractor long since accomplished. While I wasn't driving it into town on errands, I worked with the rest of the youth, clearing the brush and planting. Each week brought a new generation of blisters. By 8:00 P.M. I was usually sound asleep with exhaustion. There seemed to be a kind of marriage of mind and body as the tensions and frustrations from day to day were dissolved in physical labor.

Lutendele was a small and not especially prosperous village peopled by the Banibwe. Their family ties reached across the Congo River to the former French colony of Congo-Brazzaville. In the vicinity there were quite a number of Angolan refugees, and frequently the Congolese army would send units here on manoeuvres. Not far from our farm was a farm of the Kimbanguists, an indigenous Protestant sect whose origins dated back to the early part of the 19th century amongst the Bakongo tribe. Suppressed by the colonial government until the death of its leader, Simon Kimbangu, the sect flourished with over three million members. As a movement whose emphasis was on self-reliance, hence African nationalism, the Kimbanguists had set up kibbutz-type farms in several areas of the Bas-Congo.

The Salvation Army, too, had a church and school in Lutendele, run by a widely respected African capitaine. Most of the livelihood in the area was based on the cultivation and preparation of the principal crop, manioc. Fishing was also a major occupation of the men of Lutendele since they lived near the Congo River. There was even a resident sculptor who marketed his pieces in town. Probably the most prosperous and popular man in the village was Samuel, the one who sold beer. Virtually every afternoon would find a congregation of beer-drinkers chez Samuel, seated under a big tree discussing the affairs of the day. Still the most influential men in the area were the traditional chefs du village and chefs du terrain.

The big news these days at Lutendele was the Carrefour des Jeunes farm which was gradually becoming integrated into the community. One could only hope that this pilot project would be a window into the future rural development of the Congo. Heretofore, during the present regime whatever passed for animation rurale had been lost in rhetoric. It was no secret that the primary emphasis of the Mobutu government was concentrated on the development of urban-centered industries. Recently several hundred Fiat trucks and tractors were presented to the Ministry of Agriculture by Fiat to be dispersed into the interior. It was unfortunate that they would not all find their way to farms such as this one where the beginnings of a modest revolution paysanne (peasant revoulation) seemed to be taking root.

Talk of a real peasant revolution of course was pre-mature. But a description of the young man who directed this farm and his vision of the Congo will serve to illustrate its beginnings. Victor Lusawovana, known by all in Lutendele as Messr. Victor, was not yet 30 years old but had already spent several years as animateur. He once worked as an assistant to the Minister of Agriculture not long after Independence. While his grasp of agriculture was comprehensive, it was Victor's view of the need for social revolution that was most extraordinary. Son of a chief of a Bakongo clan, Victor had a strong sense of tribal identity but was dedicated to the cause of Congolese nationalism. First among his heroes was former President Kasavubu, leader of the Bakongo and architect of Congolese Independence. Part and parcel of this tribal identification was Victor's religious fervor. According to him, the basis of Bakongo unity was Biblical, with the 12 clans corresponding to the 12 tribes of Israel. The Bakongo viewed their spiritual force as a progressive weapon against the forces of fetishism in the rest of the Congo. The one must win out over the other in order to bring unity and purpose.

At this point social scientists, my fellow Africanists, will be prepared to argue that it is this very tribal ethnocentrism that cursed the Congo, and that it must be replaced with a broader identity. I would say, however, that tribalism in Africa is no more likely to disappear than is Zionism, or for that matter American chauvinism. What the Western social scientist often fails to acknowledge is that tribal identity is the spiritual and social force, the elan vital of the African community. We had best look at our own de-tribalized, homogenized society and recognize the effects of the loss of any such identity. To what do Americans belong? Where is the sense of community, of belonging, that is so essential to the nature of man? Is it possible that the basic social unity for American society in the near future will be the country club and the bridge club?

But before I have marked Victor as a reactionary conservative tribalist, I must hasten to justify my description of him as revolutionary. From his profound belief in God, if not the God of the Catholic Church certainly the God of the Old Testament, Victor derived a supreme self-confidence. (For if God is with me who can prevail against me?) It was his penchant for decisiveness and self-assurance that explained Victor's admiration for such men as De Gaulle, the Kennedys and the state of Israel. The latter he had visited and especially admired the Israeli success in agricultural development. If Mao Tse-tung, the greatest of all peasant revolutionaries, was missing from Victor's list of heroes it is probably because the Chinese Revolution was lacking in the spiritual force he believed was needed to develop Africa.

So what made Victor revolutionary after all? It is this: that the Biblical injunction in Genesis for man to earn his living from the soil is to be taken quite literally. Victor's lifestyle was a reflection of his single-minded idealism. Using his own standards to judge other people, most everyone else fell far short of perfection.

"The problem of the Congo is the problem of man," Victor frequently remarked with a philosophical air.

He was disdainful of Whites who were not sympathetic with the cause of African nationalism but reserved great respect for those like Pastor Prosser who had proven themselves. But he disdained even more his African brothers who had become Uncle Toms, and the weak at heart who continued to mimic European ways. Although he had spent a year and a half in Belgium, Victor prided himself on not owning a single tie. He was likely to wear the same shirt four days in the same week. His sense of frugality extended to the rest of us on the farm. Our diet varied little from traditional fish and chikwanga, the heavy, sticky substance made from manioc roots. Almost as inevitable at mealtime as fish and chikwanga was a discussion of the evils of mercantilism or the psychology necessary to deal with eight student workers on the farm. As my French has improved I became increasingly able to make these into discussions more than just Victor's extended soliloquies.

If he was notably lacking in humility, Victor was decidedly generous. On his paltry salary 22 zaires ($44) per month he managed to treat everyone of drinking age at Samuel's two or three times a week. In addition it was often necessary to press a few zaires into the palms of policemen for alleged violations of the law, or of villagers who helped get our tractor out of the mud. Whatever was left over went for food and clothes. Such generosity is not universally appreciated, however. Victor's wife was a very beautiful, buxom woman who, like most traditional African women, was very subservient to her husband. Rarely did she speak to him in public unless first spoken to. She seemed quite content to be the mother of her husband's two young boys and to be the wife of a man of affaires.

As an unsuspecting foreigner, I little realized that in recent weeks there was a gathering storm beneath her calm facade. And then one day she erupted with all the fury of a woman scorned. For a night and the following day she raged, flinging beer bottles, raising machetes threateningly in the air and finally ripping to shreds most of Victor's prized books. When we menfolk sought refuge at Samuel's, she followed. The whole village became engulfed in her wrath. Victor refused to raise his hand against her.

The next day she was gone, with the baby on her back. Bewildered, I began asking what was going on. She was reportedly resentful of her husband's use of family funds for communal affairs. And because of Victor's frequent absences from the house, he was suspected of philandering. Nevertheless, Victor maintained his cool, saying that he understood his wife and that he was sad it had happened. He called on the traditional chiefs for advice and invited the capitaine of the Salvation Army to pray for him. After four or five days the wife returned from her father's house where she had fled. As quickly as the storm had come, it now subsided. The same day we found the table set and food prepared, an apparent sign of reconciliation. Since there was no professional psychiatrist in Lutendele to send her to for analysis, we may never really know whether Victor's wife was psychotic or just mildly neurotic. At any rate, from beginning to end it was a community and family concern, and was resolved through their good offices.

The most striking illustration of the problems confronting Victor in the development of the farm—and his tenacity in dealing with them—was to be found in the farm's relation to the Carrefour des Jeunes office in town. The farm was financially and administratively responsible to Carrefour and therefore directly affected by decisions made there. Unfortunately Carrefour mirrored many of the problems of the Congo itself. Nominally under the direction of an African secretary general, much of the actual administration of Carrefour was in the hands of two Europeans. While there was nothing sinister or oppressive in this per se, it amounted to one thing in the minds of the Congolese: neo-colonialism. It was double-edged. On the one hand the African staff was lacking in self-confidence and initiative. At the same time the two expatriates were perfectly willing to perpetuate the myth of African incompetence, and to act in the conviction that without their own efforts things would fall apart.

For her part, the Swiss woman of carrefour was a model of omnipotent administration, familiar with all aspects of the Carrefour operation and skillful in asserting her influence. She was a "liberal", to be sure. She lived very modestly, had become fairly conversant in Lingala, and even picked one of the Congolese staff to marry. But her manliness was a matter of unspoken scorn among the Congolese and her assumption of the role of administrator was resented. The case of the German comptable (accountant) was rather more pathetic. A conscientious objector, his three-year tour in the Congo was considered an alternative to military service. His mind completely overshadowed his body and soul. His personality was the very antithesis of that of the African. He was adrift in a society which placed little value in intellectual prowess. Charged with great responsibility as treasurer for both Carrefour and the Conseil Protestant du Congo, he carried his briefcase to and fro as though all the cares of the world were contained in it. Above his desk was a neatly lettered sign:

"Respectez le budget."

Often confounded by budgetary restrictions as interpreted by the comptable, Victor once blurted out his response:

"Respectez le budget ou acceptez la mort, l'argent vit' (respect the budget or accept death; money lives).

Nothing better symbolized the tension that lay just below the surface of Carrefour des Jeunes. Victor had elaborate plans for expanding the farm which were provided for in the projected budget; he was anxious to have funds dispensed without having to depend on someone else's judgment, especially one who knew little about agriculture. There remained, however, one single common denominator between the comptable and Victor: dedication to hard work. Still, Victor was determined to declare financial independence from Carrefour as soon as the farm became self-sustaining.

So what was really happening at Lutendele? The essential goal was to train a cadre of young Congolese in the elements of farming. But more important, and surely more difficult, was to instill in them the primacy of agriculture as the key to economic and social development of the country. While most of them came from rural areas, others had lived in Kinshasa for some time and were by no means convinced that rural life was for them. Victor's evangelistic ardor for farming left little room for hangers-on. Two of the original number had already left the farm. Those who stayed would complete nine months and then return to their respective homes, presumably to put their skills to use.

Most of the work on the farm consisted of wielding a shovel or hoe. A vegetable garden which stretched several hundred meters along a small river was carved out of the thick bush. Nearly two hundred platbonds (elevated mounds) were producing an exotic array of legumes (vegetables) such as radishes, green beans, lettuce and cabbage. Exotic, that is, because they are not commonly grown or consumed by Africans. That which was produced on the farm was generally marketed in town where the Europeans in their affluence were willing to pay dearly for fresh vegetables. As chauffeur, it was my job to drive into town a couple of times each week with one of the older boys with our produce in search of clients. Often our program included purchasing needed items for the farm. Gradually each of them would have the experience of marketing to complement their knowledge of production. At first we managed to sell only about 20 zaires worth of vegetables each week. But somewhere I read that a journey of a thousand miles is begun with a single step.

A typical day in the garden consisted of two parts work and one part discourse (speech-making). Victor was never so lost in his work that he didn't have time to stop, lean on his hoe and pursue a vital point being debated. Such debates often concerned football, a subject every Congolese seemed obliged to have an opinion on. And small wonder. The Congo had boasted the All-Africa championship team, for two years in succession, Tout-Puissant Englebert of Lubumbashi. And the national team, the Leopards, had once accomplished the impossible by defeating F.C. Santos in Brazil and its immortal Pele. There was a profusion of local teams in each region, each with its Jim Brown or O.J. Simpson whom every village boy idolized.

Nevertheless, the work got done. Each worker was usually given a quota such as two platbonds a day, which he must finish before eating lunch. Afternoons were sometimes used for working on odd projects, such as building outhouses, painting or repairing maisons des poules for the chickens. We would also receive about 300 chickens that added a new dimension to the program of the farm. And, always keeping in mind that the farm was a part of the community, Victor occasionally went into neighboring villages to distribute packets of seeds to people interested in starting their own gardens.

The farm itself developed a sense of community with its own esprit de corps. Nicknames seemed to indicate when one had "arrived" as a full-fledged member of the community. Marteau—the hammer— was known as the strongest and most hard-working. Mandebvu was so called because of his goatee. He was the only one who had already completed secondary school, and he planned to return to the Kasai where his family owned land. He liked to be referred to also as le colonel Ojukwu, after his hero, the leader of the Biafrans in Nigeria. He also invited comparison between the cause of the Ibo and that of his own Baluba tribe. And then there was Ambassadeur, one of the older six whose family was from Kisangani. A veteran of the rebellion there, Ambassadeur lost his parents and most of his brothers and sisters. As his name would imply, Ambassadeur was a popular figure in the garden debates. But his unreliable work habits and his extramural village activities led to his early departure from the farm.

Sometimes I myself saluted Victor as mon general, in jest since he was not especially fond of the military government. And while the workers showed their proper respect by calling me Messr. Galen, to most people of Lutendele and surrounding villages I was simply mondele (white man). Mondele is a subject of curiosity, especially to the children of the villages. One can never forget his mondele-ness since mondele is always expected to have more moyens (means, resources, money) than anyone else. Then, too, he is accorded special privileges most everywhere, such as the biggest helping of chicken or the last beer. My own arrival came, I felt, when the workers began calling me grand frere—big brother.

Living in the microcosm of rural Lutendele and commuting regularly to Kinshasa gave me an awareness of the distinctive flavor of Congolese life. While the Congo was often said to have been the most thoroughly "colonized" colony in Africa until the Belgian behemoth came tumbling down in the early 1960s, Congolese culture seemed very much intact to be in many respects. The popularity of Congolese music throughout Africa was a striking example. School boys in Uganda semmed to be more familiar with Franco and O.K. Jazz, le Seigneur Rochereau and African Fiesta, Docteur Nico and African Fiesta Sukisa thans their own musicians. Top Congolese musicians were among the wealthiest men in the country and the competition among them was fierce. Since most of the records were in Lingala, this helped to account for the almost universal familiarity of the language in the Congo.

If the sound of Congolese culture was very much alive today, so was its appearance. Congolese women, even those who flocked to the cities, retained their colorful traditional dress. This consisted of two or three layers of bright print (the best imported from Holland) known as elamba, which they swooshed about them in ritual fashion as they took to the dance floor. The increasingly popular abakost (safari suit) worn by the men of the cities, vied with the coat and tie of mondele. The sights and sounds converged nightly in literally hundreds of boites de nuite (night spots) in the city such as the Sans Souci and the Vis-à-vis. Those who could not afford the cover charge at the bigger open-air clubs would often stand outside, packed against the walls, when a popular orchestra was playing. On the inside people danced to the easy rhythm of the soucous, mambeta or whatever was en vogue.

If one uses the word in its popular connotation, l'ambiance might be said to characterize the life-style of the Kinois, people of Kinshasa in the late 1960s.

It is an ethic of hedonism: man should live life to the fullest and be happy. Take care of today's needs and tomorrow will take care of itself. There is little notion of savings and investment involved, except in so far as immediate goals are concerned. It is an attitude that the evangelical missionary considers sinful. It simply does not concern itself primarily with the Hereafter. A man is judged not so much by his adherence to Divine Law as he is by his ability to relate to the community of which he is a part. If he does manage to lay up for himself treasures on earth, it is almost certain they will be shared by family and friends alike. The man who forsakes the interests of family and community for the pursuit of self interest is the object of greatest scorn. Moise Tshombe, leader of the secessionist Katanga Province who represented to a large extent European mining interests, was eventually ostracized by the entire African community. While often forgotten in the Western world, it is still literally true in Africa, that one is his brother's keeper.

The leavening of l'ambiance in Kinshasa was beer, or in the villages, masanga ya mbila (palm wine). It seemed there was hardly an occasion or time of day inappropriate for beer drinking in the Congo. The first Sunday I was in Lutendele several of us were on the way to attend the Salvation Army church service. It had not yet begun, so it was suggested that we stop across the road at Samuel's for a beer. Two stayed there drinking beer while two of us went to church after the first beer. Three hours later when the service was over, our friends insisted that we join them in another round before lunch! Which we did! There was, of course, a ground rule for beer-drinking: one should never drink alone. A rule easy to live by, since one could always find a drinking partner.

The most memorable occasions in Lutendele were the times when we sat at Samuel's after a hard day's work, our Primus and Stanor bottles perched on upside down crates, sometimes until the moon rose, singing Congo manda maluti (Congolese are fighting the good fight) or "Swing low, sweet chariot." Story telling was a big part of the Lutendele scene. Each one took turns playing the griot, the traditional African story-teller. The bigger the tale, the more guffaws it would elicit and the greater the applause. The story was often punctuated by mock incredulity with the question:

"Omona wapi?" (Where did you see that?)

And without giving the story-teller a chance to respond, there was a chorus from the listeners:

"Na Lutundele!" Right here in Lutundele! The implication being that such fantastic things could only happen in a place like our village of Lutendele.

Often there was a refrain from a song on the pop charts. The one that would become the Lutendele theme song was a Johnny Bokelo tune that took the country by storm after Apollo Eleven and the walk on the moon:

"Tambolana mokili...omona makambo!" Travel around the world and you'll see things. There was a vague awareness in Lutendele of a big wide world out there, brought home by the news of the moon walk.

Missionaries talked disdainfully of the fact that during the entire period since independence the industries which continued throughout rebellion and counter-rebellion in Kisangani were the two breweries! A song propagated by the ruling political party intended to exhort people to work went something like this:

Salongo, Congo alingi mosala—people of Congo like to work.

Here at Samuel's we sometimes gave it a more realistic interpretation:

Congo, alinga masanga—Congolese like beer.

Another important element of l'ambiance had to do with les femmes, and more specifically les femmes libres (unattached but available women). In a city of over a million and a half, there was an abundance of young unattached women. They caome from all corners of the country, often as not from areas where the male population had been reduced by conscription practices during colonial rule and more recently by a combination of mercenaries, ANC (Armee Nationale Congolaise) and inter-tribal feuding. They came to Kinshasa expecting life to be less harsh than in the villages, and no doubt, with the idea of finding some able-bodied young man with a job to support them. But too often they would find that over half of those able-bodied young men weare unemployed. Those who did make money seemed most willing to spend it on les femmes libres.

Among the femmes celibatrices (single but presumably not available) in Kinshasa there was a kind of sorority known as ndumba, a Kikongo term which refered to a girl who has reached the age of puberty. In the urban setting it took on a more or less pejorative meaning. Still, the ndumba society was lent an air of respectability in an article in Presence Congoaise in which Miss Congo was interviewed on the subject. She spoke of ndumba as a cooperative for mutual aid and companionship among single women, and as such asserted a growing demand for respect and independence. Certainly it indicated disaffection with restraints of traditional marriage in which the woman enjoyed few rights but many obligations. The urban Congolese man was becoming keenly aware that he was losing the firm dominance he once enjoyed in the village. The forces of modernization had been unleashed and were bound to gather momentum.

But modernization is always tempered with traditional values.

One of these, many-faceted and described by African and non-African alike in different ways, is a sense of togetherness. Kenyatta refered to it as harambee (pulling together). Nyerere talked of ujamaa (familyhood. I was always struck by this whenever our Fiat got stuck in the mud. Since getting stuck seemed to a fairly regular occurrence, I noticed a pattern that developed each time. After the first several attempts at gunning the motor makes the rut all the deeper, we climb down out of the cabin, depressed and discouraged. By this time a few passersby have gathered. One of them takes it upon himself to cut down palm fronds and grass to put under the tires for traction. The driver, often myself, stomps on the gas again and the truck lunges back and forth, flailing mud in all directions — to no avail. The wheels are now hopelessly embedded in the muck.

Now most of the neighboring villagers are on the scene, ranging from pre-school children to ageless old men. One by one the new arrivals take their turn at engineering new devices for remedying the situation. This includes an endless variety of pulleys, levers, shovels and massing of manpower. Meanwhile a spirit of involvement has taken hold. The cheering section hails each concerted effort and groans with each failure. Then, after hours of strain and stress and near-resignation the tide turns. The cry goes up in unison:

"Errrrrrrr...yah! Errrrrr...yah."

A mighty heave and the beast trudges onto safe ground. The cheering section goes wild, the engineer of the successful effort is congratulated and the driver reaches into his pocket for a matabishi (tip) to give those who have stuck it out. In many respects urban Congo was as much in the mainstream of the twentieth century as is, say Seattle.

A sure sign of "progress" were the clogged thoroughfares of Kinshasa during rush-hour. The popularity of imported Japanese cars was such that Toyota became a byword for chic or clever. Over 250 Toyotas were being sold each month in Kinshasa. Several taxi-buses sported signs saying Apollo XI, and with each moon-shot the old numeral was crossed out and the new one written in. During the week of the moon-landing throngs of people gathered outside the USIS Center to watch the progress of the flight monitored on TV. USIS officials, harassed for the latest information, readily acknowledged that it was better to be besieged with questions than with rocks and epithets! And as a token of appreciation for Mobutu's steadfast compatibility with the U.S., Kinshasa was chosen as the only African city to be visited by Apollo XI astronauts.

The summer of 1969 witnessed another memorable event: FIKIN—Foire Internationale de Kinshasa. With dozens of countries—nearly all in the capitalist camp, presenting exhibits—and several heads of African states attending, the fair was a symbol of the Mobutu regime's t determination to exploit the Congo's vast economic resources. It was said that some $10 million was spent on FIKIN. Although the Second Republic was described everywhere as "revolutionary", the emphasis at the fair was clearly on wooing foreign investors with the prospect of stability and favorable conditions for investment.

The year 1969 brought to a close one decade in Congolese history in which Congolese themselves had been the principal actors. It was here in Leopoldville (now Kinshasa) in January of 1959 when a totally unexpected demonstration of Congolese marked the beginning of the end of Belgian colonial rule. The year 1969 saw the death of two chief antagonists during that period: Moise Tshombe and Joseph Kasavubu. Their lives represented polar opposites in the drama of the first years of independent Congo. Tshombe, in his bid for secession of Katanga and his heavy reliance on Belgian mining interests, embodied the real "darkness" of Congo to many Africans. And while Kasavubu was not the arch-nationalist Patrice Lumumba was, he, more than anyone else during the first half-decade, was the instrument of national unity. Then, with the two forces of political power still contending, Colonel Joseph Desire Mobutu "neutralized" them in a bloodless coup of 25 November 1965, thus ushering in the Second Republic.

There was certainly change in the Congo since then, whether it warranted being called revolutionary or not. In the Manifeste de la N'Sele, published by the ruling MPR, it was stated that the Republic "renounces capitalism as well as communism." The revolution in the Congo had nothing to do with that of Peking, Moscow or Cuba, nor was it founded on their ready-made theories of borrowed doctrines. Rather it was "revolutionary" in the people's will to support it and in its aim to change the former state of things. The Manifesto pointed to decisive reforms since the coup, such as the reduction of the number of provinces, installation of the presidential system (the former parliamentary system patterned after Belgium's proved very unwieldy), the declaration of economic independence through the Congolisation of l'Union Miniere (henceforth to be known as GECAMINES) and the etatisation (nationalization) of insurance.

It was claimed that 80% of the means of production in the Congo was by now under national control. Perhaps the most revolutionary aspect of the four-year-old regime, as the Manifesto proudly pointed out, was its ability to hold the country together, "a real revolution in comparison with the former regime". The Manifesto made no secret of the cement used in establishing order: it was the MPR, the "only organization which since 1960 has remained loyal...to the ideal of the Fatherland..." The Manifesto, then, was to be the Bible of Congolese development.

Notably missing from the proclamation, however, was the role of the university in the development of the country and its relationship with the MPR. Not too surprisingly this is where the Party's alleged popularity had been most seriously challenged. Less than one month after the public proclamation, in June 1969, a student demonstration was held at Louvanium University near Kinshasa to protest the government's inattention to their requests for an increase in student stipends—living allowance. A rather mundane sounding issue! But Mobutu used the rigid shoot-to-kill reaction of Chicago Mayor Daley. Para-commandos were sent to dispel the demonstrators, and having done so followed their prey into the communes of the city. Papers the next day reported six students killed; the streets were very nearly deserted. With the campus closed and occupied by troops, students continued to be hunted down for several days.

A medical student from Rhodesia whom I saw a week or so later said he knew of at least 60 students who had died. Some estimates were even higher. No doubt the government's overreaction was due to its intense desire to avoid ugly protracted demonstrations during the visit of prestigious foreigners to the FIKIN. Ironically, this was the same Mobutu, who in the turbulent early days after Independence intervened in the Lumumba-Kasavubu dispute to set up a government of composed ot students, a college des comissaires. He launched an appeal to all Congolese students and technicians in Europe to return as quickly as possible to assume the administration of the country. It was a unique experiment which lasted only a few months. Nevertheless, viewed in the light of the events of June 1969, it was a sad commentary on the tendency of power to corrupt.

Free University of the Congo

Kisangani—Boyoma la Belle   *11/August/1969*

While still in washingtonm D.C., it had been suggested that I
might be able to get a job teaching at Universite Libre du Congo (the
Free University of the Congo) in Kisangani, the third largest city in
the country. But my initial efforts to communicate with the University
had been frustrating. Then, after seemingly endless months of
waiting, word came from on high the very day that Neil Armstrong
set foot on the moon; I was offered a position at the University to
teach English beginning in October. Two months remained before
I was to begin at the University, so I decided to spend what little
money I had left on a vacation to Uganda, as though I hadn't been on
"vacation" the last five months. My stay at Lutendele was brought to
a pleasant end with a farewell party and Victor's presentation of two
symbols of his mission: a Bible and a miniature hoe.

On August 11, 1969, I left Ndjiii airport on a flight to Kisangani,
formerly Stanleyville—very nearly the heart of the African continent.
A sign at the Kisangani airport reminded the newcomer that this was
le Berceau de la Revolution (the cradle of the revolution). Another
sign of the building adjacent to the terminal, Foyer Estudiantin,
introduced the visitor to part of the scattered campus of ULC.
Within a few minutes I was settled in the University guest house
where I spent the next week and a half looking for a lift on to
Uganda. During that time I was able to confirm that I really had
been hired by the University; it wasn't just an administrative snafu.
This brought me an intense sense of relief, followed by a keen desire
to find out more about my adopted home!

I had already begun reading up on Stanleyville and the history of
the region. Literature on the topic of Northeast Congo, especially
relating to the 1964 Rebellion, already abounded. Most of it had as its
theme the evil and darkness of the Congo, an image very successfully
conveyed to armchair observers in the Western world. Headlines in
the press around the world spotlighted imminent danger faced by
the couple of hundred White hostages held by the rebels, of whom a
handful eventually died. But little attention was paid to the fact that
thousands of innocent villagers were killed. Scores of accounts by
missionaries of their harrowing experiences rendered them martyrs
in the eyes of the Christian world.

But seldom did one run across a sympathetic reading of this Simba Rebellion and its genuinely populist roots. A particularly odious account was given by the leader of the mercenaries himself, Mike Hoare. Sanctimonious in his defense of White mercenary intervention on behalf of the Tshombe regime, Hoare maintained that he was here to "fight communism". Often as not this meant blasting unsuspecting villages to bits and pillaging every town that fell to his mercenaries. Having ravaged every corner of Province Orientale (Eastern Province) and helping crush the rebellion, Hoare's gang was acclaimed in many circles in the West as heroes. His admirers were to be found in the British House of Commons and the American Congress. He closed his story of adventure with a re-print of a letter sent to him by Mobutu himself praising Hoare for his service in. helping the Congolese army bring law and order to the Congo.

Another, more objective and subtle version of Stanleyville during the 1964 rebellion, was David Reed's 111 Days. Commissioned by Readers' Digest sometime after the events of July—November 1964 to reconstruct them for the American public, Reed put together a Zane Grey thriller. The main difference here is that in this story the good guys wearing white hats were the American and Belgian consular officers who managed to survive the savagery of the primitive Simbas. The final act in this drama involved—deus ex machine—the dropping of hundreds of Belgian paratroopers from American planes onto the beleaguered Simba stronghold. Not without great soul-searching and deliberation on the part of the American government. American lives were saved, and at the same time the threat of "communism" was forestalled as the back of the rebellion was broken. Meanwhile Uncle Sam incurred the helpless wrath of even the mostly moderate Western-oriented African governments.

Colin Turnbull, a well known anthropologist respected as a kind of mystic apologist for the traditional African, wrote a book called The Lonely African in which he described his experience among the pygmies of the Ituri Forest. He succeeded very well in his attempt to see the world as did his pygmy hosts. He seemed to capture the spirit of pygmy life when he wrote of the "seductive informality about everything the pygmy does", and his "always unexpectedly casual, carefree attitude". Unfortunately, Turnbull was compelled to use the neighboring Bantu people as a cultural whipping boy in his zeal for praising the unadulterated pygmy. The "negro" was pictured usually as believing in evil spirits and discriminating against women, both supposedly uncommon among his hosts. The Lonely African defended this same traditional "negro" in a very worthy cause—against the hypocrisy and decadence of Western culture. But his description of the "native" communes of Stanleyville as "drab and sordid" showed both a lack of familiarity with the town and a distorted disdain for anything having to do with modernization. In any case, Turnbulls' book was a useful introduction to the pymies that would serve me on my safari to Uganda.

On Safari with Bwana George   *August 1969*

Meanwhile, back at the University guest house, my search for a ride to Kampala was successfully resolved. An American missionary also staying there was preparing for a trip to Nairobi in his International truck. He was on the way back to the U.S. for a year's home leave, via Nairobi, and would be making several stops along the way to minister to his mission's faithful. His invitation for me to come along was not readily extended. He suspected me of secular ways and was anxious for me not to set a bad example for his parishioners in the bush. The ground-rules were explicit: no smoking, no drinking and no "messin' around" during the safari. With little choice and considerable resolve to make the trip, I agreed.

Bwana (Swahili term of respect) George spent several days, along with another passenger, buying up food stuffs and fitting out the all-purpose truck for the safari. This was no ordinary truck; it was a veritable bwana-mobile. Its most elaborate device was a ham radio set, seemingly indispensable to all American missionaries in the Congo. Every night without fail the call-letters and "Chancy Hotel" went out to parties standing by in the U.S., Kinshasa and Bukavu. Another essential item was a tape deck and a selection of tapes which put one in mind of the muzac in Safeway stores and dentist offices back home. Appropriately enough among them was Bert Kampfert's "Swingin' Safari", and then Pat Boone singing his favorite hymns. There were also half a dozen demijohns of wine to be dispersed for communion services, strange I thought for a mission with such conservative orientation. There were cans and cans of corned beef and soup, since we surely should not hazard eating food prepared in the villages.

Bwana George was a relative old-timer in the Congo, a native of the American Midwest who first came out to pioneer in establishing a remote mission station in the Ituri Forest 16 years before. His theological and social outlook were representative of those who had characterized a segment of the American missionary effort in the Congo, especially in this area. He was unabashedly evangelical. Any deviation in church organization and practice from fundamental truths imparted in the New Testament were to be shunned. Therefore, he viewed recent efforts by the Conseil Protestant du Congo (composed mainly of mainstream Protestant denominations) under African leadership to unite the myriad Protestant sects in the Congo as politically inspired, a danger to the evangelical cause. Implicit in this attitude was the belief that missionaries themselves were the only ones who could be trusted to see that the Church survived the onslaught of nationalism, which was really another word for communism. And of course, communism was the root of all evil, regardless of what the scriptures said about material possessions.

It was this unshakable faith in the Christianizing, i.e. civilizing, mission of the Church that had sustained Bwana George throughout all the troubles in the past 10 years. He was also sustained by a wry sense of humor and a kind of cynical awareness that the native might never be "civilized". But there was the Biblical injunction that said one must try ("Go ye therefore into the world and preach the Gospel...."). While many missionaries had fled for their lives never to return to the Congo, Bwana George stayed on. As we traveled from one remote church to the next, where small bands of the faithful carried on despite the departure of missionaries, one began to understand why he did. He belonged here. In the world of the forest people he was the Bwana.

He was in the world but certainly not of it. With a command of the forest dialect of Swahili he could discuss problems that had developed in his absence for hours.

After one such session he turned to me and said, more serious than not, "I've been here too long; I'm beginning to think like them."

With all his understanding of his flock, Bwana George scarcely trusted any one of them:

"The main industries in this village," he announced as we drove into the first one, "are palm wine and stealing."

During a meeting with the church elders in the guest house they had built for him, he remarked in English to me:

"This is one of two men I trust here; he thinks like a white man."

He told of how revolted he had been once while traveling alone in that area among his churches, when an elder had offered him a woman to take care of his needs during his stay.

"That," he told the elder emphatically, "is not the way we play the game!" It's one thing to fail in civilizing the natives, but it would be quite another to succumb oneself to their uncivilized ways!

Bwana George's authority in church matters among the Basenji a term which can mean simply people of the bush, or more pejoratively, monkeys (from the French word for monkey—singe—was absolute. At each stop a kind of kangaroo court was held to review the moral standing of each church member. He had a dossier tucked away in his head of past misdeeds on everyone. On one occasion a man who was chief of the village was unceremoniously "excommunicated" from the church for having acquired two wives. Those who fared most smoothly in these investigations were frequently the most kizungu-ized, those who accepted the ways of the white man. There was, of course, a democratic structure within the congregation which operated in the absence of Bwana George, but it was quickly put aside upon his arrival. Those who remained faithful to Bwana's admonitions were duly rewarded, sometimes with money for work on the upkeep of church property, sometimes by the granting of greater influence within the church community by Bwana George's personal grace. Although he feigned weariness with the frequent request for saidia (help) Bwana George clearly relished the role of feudal baron in his fiefdom.

We stopped in at a duka (small shop) there run by Greeks who spoke hardly any French and did business only in Swahili. After all, the couple of Greek families in town were the only remains of the large European community before Independence. In fact we would find Greeks to be the predominant merchant community along the remainder of the way to the border. They had been the last Europeans to evacuate during the rebellion and the first to return, armed with guns and ready to defend their lives and property. Of all the foreign "tribes" that have settled in the Congo, the Greeks seem to come closest to assimilating with African culture. They share the same expansive spirit and strong family ties. Their businesses usually cater to immediate needs such as food and drink. And yet because the Greek lives so close to the African, below the other European tribes, he is most apt to play the Bwana.

From Bafwasende we left the main road, traveling several hours deep into the recesses of the Ituri Forest. The trees seemed to grow ever more silent and tall. Reaching Bomili, which had been Bwana George's mission redoubt for years, we arrived at the banks of the Ituri River and the end of the road as well. Nothing was left of the mission and the coffee plantation which had employed over 70 workers at one time. The mission houses had been burned and all the missionaries had long since fled. We spent the night in Bwana George's special guest house. The next day after a sermon exhorting the faithful and excoriating the faithless, as well as a lengthy meeting with the elders, we were on the road again. Bwana George reminisced over the trouble he'd seen. Having gone home on furlough in 1963, he and his family had been saved martyrs' deaths. Upon return, they had moved to Bukavu on Lake Kivu, only to have their home pillaged by Congolese soldiers in the wake of the mercenary rebellion in 1967. The last couple of years they had spent mostly in Nairobi, still maintaining ties in the Congo.

The International truck, Bwana George's bwana-mobile, was stuffed to the gills now with the addition of two young men on their way to our next stop where the mission was establishing a preacher's school. This was the village of Olina, just on the road that turns north toward Isiro, where we were to stay for three nights. Here I went looking for a place to buy a bar of soap, but there were no dukas to be found. While wandering around, I came across a large house facing the road. It was the home of the young chef coutumier who welcomed me in. He said that he had once belonged to the mission church but had had a falling out. He then asked whether I would be interested in returning that evening to watch a traditional dance. I told him I'd be there.

And sure enough, before we were finished eating supper the staccato sound of drums filled the evening air. With no great show of enthusiasm, Bwana George announced he had decided to come along with me. The scene at the village was wild...maybe not as exciting as Hollywood could make it...but it was real! We were seated next to the chef just in front of a row of tiny women not much more than four feet tall. They were young Bambuti (pygmies) with typically light skin and large soft eyes, full bare breasts bouncing as they kept time with the drums. The rest of the ensemble consisted of the usual-sized Bantu, no less exuberant and singing at top volume. With men ranged on one side of the circle and women on the other, the object was for a dancer to go bounding over to someone of the opposite sex and do his/her thing, a bump-and-grind, then race back to his place. Without warning, the mistress of ceremonies charged over in front of Bwana George and gave him the works!

This was too much. Here was a man of God, charged with stamping out licentiousness, being confronted with sin itself. Within a few minutes he excused himself saying it was past his bedtime. I stayed on, not quite as concerned with Bwana George's moral dilemma, and somewhat mesmerized by the shrill chanting and the frenzied rhythm of the drums. After all, I might not have another chance to observe pymies again.

It was a long day's drive from Olina to Nyankunde. We stopped for lunch at Epulu, where Colin Turnbull had done his famous study of the pygmies. As we passed Mambasa the forest became less dense, the air a bit less humid. Long after dark we rolled into Nyankunde Mission, cold and tired. We had left the rain forest and were now well over a mile high. In 1888, the great explorer Stanley passed near the foothills of Nyankunde Mountain. Then, in 1923, ground was broken for an independent American mission station. The compound now consisted of two dozen missionaries, a 70-bed hospital, the largest printing press in the Province (its periodical, Neno La Imani, reached all of Swahili-speaking Congo and East Africa), a tennis court and swimming pool now under construction. In his book describing the evacuation of all the missionaries shortly after Independence, the dean of the mission gave us a picture of the work of the missionaries.

After a good night's rest and an all-American three-course breakfast, we were on the road again toward the Uganda border. Another day's travel found us still in the Congo about 100 miles from Nyankunde at another mission station called Rethy. Headquarters of African Inland Mission, Rethy, rivaled Nyankunde in every respect: in size, influence, amenities and particularly in evangelical fervor. Here, as at Nyankunde, were a sizable number of second-generation American missionaries who were not really pioneers any longer, but rather comfortable administrators of a mission establishment. Their living allowance depended solely on their ability to secure contributions in the U.S. from like-minded patrons during furloughs.

As best I could tell there was no mainstream denominational link although most of the missionaries belonged to some conservative sect. They were, in effect, the prototypical entrepreneurs in their field. American children from all over Eastern Congo were sent to the mission's grade school where they were safe from the possible de-Americanizing effects of public schools. Here they learned the elements of Americanism; they become aware of the civilizing mission among the heathen, to which their parents had dedicated their lives. And along with this, they acquired attitudes that might allow them to become third generation missionaries. Riding across the compound in a mini-bus with several of the younger children, I was struck by a little chant they had composed for themselves:

"Wouldn't he hate to kiss a Congolese, wouldn't you hate to kiss a Congolese..." The mother smiled back at them approvingly.

We pressed on the next day, with the prospect of at least crossing the Uganda border. Our passing through customs and immigration at Mahagi on the Congo side went smoothly. A few miles farther was the Uganda customs post, near Goli. Here the plot thickens. I had left Kisangani without a Uganda visa, hoping something could be arranged at the border, knowing my chances were at best 50-50. I had first attempted to get a visa at the Uganda Embassy in Kinshasa, but had found all the embassy personnel involved in FIKIN. Then, when I found no Uganda consulate in Kisangani, I decided to try my luck. My patron, Bwana George, was privy to all this. He clearly said from the outset that if we encountered any visa trouble at the Uganda border he would have to leave me there. Fair enough.

The bwana-mobile cleared customs, the other two passports were stamped and then the official looked disapprovingly at mine. No, I couldn't purchase a visa there; I could only return to the Congo. I pleaded. Finally, not anxious to have a stray tourist left on his hands and at least a little sympathetic with my cause, the official said I could "cross over in the bush" so long as he didn't see me do it. I would therefore not be his responsibility. Gleefully, I sneaked over to where Bwana George was poised for departure and explained to him the story and told him I was ready to take my chances. I piled into the truck and waited for the sound of the motor. But Bwana

George wasn't prepared to take chances with me. He suggested, instead, that I stay there and that he take my passport to Kampala to request a visa.

My spirits sank. God only knew how long that might take; there was no restaurant, no hotel, not even a duka within three miles of the border. And without a passport I would be confined to quarters. With atypical largesse, Bwana George offered me the remainder of his tinned food and bread in the box, as well as a two-week supply of assorted pills! And then the bwana-mobile was gone, on its way to Kampala and Nairobi. Miserable as hell, I dumped my stuff on the ping-pong table in the customs office and treated myself to a can of beans for supper. The customs agent was a bit surprised to find me still around.

"You mean to say" he asked incredulously, "Your brother just left you here?"

Yes, I said, that was more or less what happened. And I must have been a rather pathetic sight, because shortly thereafter I was offered food at the house of one of the customs agents and a mattress at the police lines. It was the same policeman who had checked the truck.

My host insisted on taking me down the road to a little bar whenever he was off duty. Life was going to be tolerable here after all. Next day the man in charge sent word to Kampala, vouching for my identity and requesting that the visa be granted. Time dragged on; the big event each day was a bao game which all the customs staff played expertly. My sense of frustration was somewhat assuaged as I learned that most of these guys were here against their will too. Goli was an outpost, far removed from just about everything. One was from Teso in Eastern Province, another from Kenya (since East Africa had a common customs union, an agent might be sent to one of the other two countries outside his own) and a third had been "exiled", as he put it, for helping to organize an abortive union strike. Misery, it seems, really does love company. Days passed, and finally a telegram arrived from the office of immigration authorizing them to turn me loose. They asked the next vehicle headed toward Kampala to take me along, and with that I was once again on my way. My friends at Goli good-naturedly suggested I come and spend my next vacation there with them!

Many decades had intervened since a British Protectorate was established in Uganda. Acknowledging the similarities between the

Baganda institutions and their own, the British conferred special status upon Buganda within the Protectorate. Giving with one hand, but withholding in the other, British policy encouraged the Baganda to think of themselves as a most-favored-nation as long as they maintained proper respect for British administration. Thus, with imperial magnanimity, the British government arranged for the return of their traditional king Kabaka to Mango Hill toward the end of 1955. By the time of Uganda Independence in 1962 the power of the Kabaka had become submerged under a government headed by a northerner named Milton Obote. By 1966 Obote had consolidated enough power of his own to chase the Kabaka from his throne once again, never to return.

I enjoyed my stay in Kampala, however brief, revisiting some of the same places I had seen while on assignment with the Peace Corps. But I was eager to get back to Kisangani and begin a new chapter in my life. This time I made a point of going out to visit Makerere University, one of the outstanding universities in Africa. As if in tandem with the eternal springtime of Uganda, as elsewhere in Africa I found a spirit of inclusiveness; whatever or whoever is of interest or concern to a member of the family becomes — whether for better or for worse – the concern of all. After a few days in the Kampala area I started looking for a way back to Kisangani.

As luck would have it, I managed to connect with another Christian missionary who was leaving Kampala to return to the Congo. A Britisher with wife and family, he was different in temperament from Bwana George but every bit as evangelical. He would be making several stops on his safari, but he allowed as how he should be able to get me to Kisangani. Well across the Congo border we stopped in Bunia to spend the night and tend to some church business with fellow missionaries. To my chagrin, it was announced the next day that I would need to look for other transport on to Kisangani, since some unexpected luggage was being loaded onto the truck. I was assured, though, of room and board with the American missionaries until something developed.

With the end of the week approaching there was still no transport on the horizon. I suggested that perhaps I would have to borrow some money for an air ticket. Could my hosts think of anyone who might be able to help?

A flurry of consternation..."We would, of course, love to help," they said, "but we just don't have it."

I made the rounds of the missionary community and met with the same hesitation. Apparently I wasn't a very good credit risk. Don't you have a bank account? Well, yes, but they didn't have a branch in Bunia, besides which there wasn't much left in my Kisangani account.

"How would you manage to pay it back if we loaned you the Z15,00 ($30.00)?" "I should be starting to work within a month or so; perhaps I could send you a check," I offered lamely Eventually my creditors agreed to take collective responsibility for me. As I climbed aboard the plane that afternoon it was with a great sense of relief. It promised to bring to a close six months of wandering and uncertainty.

Kisangani—Boyoma la Belle   *September/1969*

Upon my return to Kisangani, I was assigned an apartment in the University Complex on the opposite side of the city from the University. These dozen or so three-story buildings owned and maintained by the University were certainly the choice location in the city. My place was a one-bedroom unit on the ground floor looking right out at a stand of papaya trees and assorted exotic varieties. Within the first couple of weeks I interviewed candidates for a cook/guardian/Man Friday. The winner was Honore, a stout, light-complexioned fellow with a broad smile and big laugh. With the program of nationalization, Honore—his French name—would become Gelige—his African name. Some of the Africans in the complex warned me not to hire him because, they said, he had been a simba (rebel) during the rebellion and was not to be trusted. They said he was headstrong and belligerent. But his papers had good references from previous Belgian employers and he seemed very eager to please. So I took a chance.

The first order of business was to find a common language in which to communicate. As with many of those in menial jobs in Kisangani, fluency in French was at a premium. Gelige's French was virtually non-existent and mine was still in incubation. Like most Africans in Kisangani, Gelige spoke both Lingala and Swahili. Although I had picked up some Lingala at Lutendele, I reckoned that Swahili would serve me better in the long run than Lingala.

So I got out a little pocket Swahili dictionary and started giving basic instructions to Gelige. The problem here was that the Swahili spoken in eastern Congo was not exactly the classical Swahili of the coast. People referred to their language as Swahili ya poli, or bush Swahili. For starters, since it is a more Bantu-ized language, the prefixes are slightly different from the coastal variety:

Watu wanasema Swahili becomes Batu Banasema Swahili.

People speak Swahili.

In fact, Gelige would become my Swahili teacher. At first there was a lot of pointing and gesturing to arrive at an elementary vocabulary we could both understand. At the same time Gelige insisted upon learning a few words of Kingereza (English) in order to show off to his fellow cooks. It took a while for Gelige to realize that I was more interested in African cuisine than the Belgian cuisine he was accustomed to cooking for his mondeles in the past. Fortunately he was very good at concocting pili pili, the hot sauce for which Congolese cuisine is famous. Everything else tended to fall into place as we worked out enough verbs and nouns to carry on a conversation.

I would take Gelige on the back of my Lambretta motor-scooter with his shopping bag and drop him at the market on my way to the University. He would find his way back to the apartment in a kombi and my meal would be waiting for me when I returned. In the back of my mind, however, was the comment of the neighbors about Gelige's simba past. I was on the lookout for any telltale signs: missing sugar or flour, bottles of beer or items of clothing. Nothing. On the contrary, Gelige went out of his way to please me. Sometimes I would find my shoes all shined and polished, without having said a word to Gelige about them. Gelige demonstrated remarkable loyalty to me. He was, as they warned, however, rather strong-willed. And whenever I scolded him about some oversight or forgetfulness, Gelige's response would be to argue first, then sulk and often go on a drinking binge and not show up for work the next day. All things considered, Gelige rendered good service and never once showed any simba-like behavior.

— — —

A man without any nationalist tendencies is a man without soul...what we have to avoid in our country is false nationalism, the cramped nationalism that conceals forms of racialism and hatred for those of another race...This struggle against racialist nationalism can be effective only if we are able to abolish its causes.

    - Patrice Emery Lumumba, Ie Congo: terre d'avenir, est il menace?

It was in 1890 that Joseph Conrad made his epic voyage up ther Congo River in his search for the man he called Kurtz in the Heart of Darkness. It is Conrad's work that contributed greatly to the image of the Congo as a place of darkness. An even greater contribution to this image was Belgian colonial history beginning under King Leopold II who claimed the Congo River basin as his personal fiefdom. The Belgians ruled the Congo with an iron fist until 1960 when they abruptly declared the colony independent. Pacification of the interior was achieved in the early 20th century and in 1906 the 125 km. of railway from Stanleyville to the site of the first cataracts at Ponthierville on the Lualaba River was completed. This was an essential link between the interior and the Congo River since the rapids prevented direct passage to the capital city of Leopoldville. The railway allowed Stanleyville to become an important center even before roads had been built through the immediate forest area.

The first Europeans in the vicinity of what is now Kisangani (formerly Staneyville) were met by a robust people who called themselves Wagenia. Their livelihood was centered on the very rapids which hampered the "progress" of European civilizers. For several miles along the Congo River near Stanley Falls their villages stretched on both banks. Their economy was based on the fish which they trapped in baskets suspended over the rapids from a scaffolding of poles. As a function of their trade the Wagenia are expert swimmers and boatsmen. Livingstone himself wrote of the Wagenia tribesmen he encountered in the Manyema to the south of Stanleyville that, "...the Wagenia women are expert in the water as they are accustomed to dive for oysters..." Although the Wagenia steadfastly resisted integration into the urban community, including inscription into the Force Publique under Belgian rule, they had had no qualms about exploiting tourist interest in their unique culture.

Even today there are Wagenia hustlers who scour the town in search of Wazungu (white people) interested in a pirogue ride through the rapids or a Sunday afternoon at the wrestling matches. And I'm one of those who attended. The weekly wrestling competition called kabobo is an event which absorbs the total community. Kabobo very closely resembles the classic Greco-Roman style and is always preceded by a rather elaborate display of the opponents who prance about to the wild acclaim of their supporters. Usually the rive gauche (left bank of the river) is pitted against the rive droite (right side) each with its coterie of young girls chanting and dancing. And to make sure the visitor living in town does not lose perspective, the Mugenia guide proudly noted that it was his people who gave Kisangani its name. It refers to the sizeable island near the right bank which is the center of the Wagenia community.

By 1920 the population of Stanleyville had reached over 7,000, of whom perhaps 100 were Europeans. This number had risen to a total of 18,000 and 1,000 Europeans by 1938; many immigrant Africans were now settling in the town permanently. In addition there were a few thousand Arabises (Islamized Africans, some with Arab descent), in an adjacent village. The African population grew rapidly with the economic expansion in the late1930s to around 10,000 by 1952. In the immediate post-war years Stanleyville quickly became a minor boom town, with an ethos of high prosperity and urgent activity. There were several factories including a brewery, an oil mill, a cigarette factory and a water factory; a large hydroelectric plant was under construction.

Industry had become the largest single employer of Africans, followed by building, administration, transport and commerce. By 1952 the Europeans and Asians at the top of this boom numbered nearly 5,000. The most striking feature of the population of Stanleyville was its ethnic diversity. It was said that every tribe in the Congo and many from outside the colony's boundaries were represented in Stanleyville. More important, there was no dominant tribe or tribal grouping that would plague other urban areas in their intense rivalries. Of the 66 tribal groupings, 50 had fewer than 500 members in the town. Only five were represented by 2,000 or more, and no tribe counted much more than 5,000. Nine principal tribes made up together about two-thirds of the total African population of the town.

Patrice Lumumba: Favorite Son of Kisangani

The tragedy of the Congo and that of Patrice Lumumba himself is illustrated in the book which he wrote while in the Stanleyville prison under Belgian administration. Published posthumously in Brussels in 1961—le Congo: terre d'avenir est il menace?—was a plea for human dignity full of optimism for the future of the Congo. In December of 1956 Lumumba began a lengthy exchange with a Belgian publishing house in an attempt to have his book printed. Given the hostile attitude of the Belgians toward the development of African "intellectuals" and the mildly critical approach to Belgian rule in the Congo taken in the book, it is understandable that Lumumba should have been coolly received.

What strikes the reader of this book is the good will with which the author presents the problems of the Congo to his Belgian overlords. Had he not died a martyr to the cause of radical nationalism, one might easily accuse Lumumba of Uncle Tomism from reading this book. In his letters to the publisher, Lumumba pointed out his aims in writing the book. First, he said, he was attempting to "translate the thinking and aspirations of Congolese" and to "explain the causes of discontent". He suggested "reforms to the authorities (Belgian colonial administrators) if a crisis is to be avoided." He drew the attention of Congolese to the "bad propaganda (anti-Belgian) which has separated Congolese and Belgians," insisting on "the harmony of the two." And most significantly he wrote to "the sovereignty of Belgium in Africa". Realizing that the chances of publication might be slim, he added that he hoped the publishers would "take account of the confusion which has reigned in the Congo within the past few years."

Although he described the future of the Congo as "cloudy", Lumumba hoped for a "fraternal entente." Obviously proud of his standing as an évolue (educated person) in the Stanleyville community, and perhaps to let the publishers know that he was Somebody, Lumumba also wrote out a biographical sketch. It included membership in no less than five organizations. As early as 1951 he became a member of the Association des Evolues de Stanleyville, and in 1955 was elected its president. Also in 1951 he was appointed secretary general of APIPO (Des Postiers de la Province Orientale) the professional organization of postal workers. By 1953 he was also founder of an inter-racial group designed to bring Belgians and Congolese together. And in 1955 Lumumba became chairman of an office of equal employment opportunities.

Other identifying comments Lumumba made in his correspondence with the publishers hardly gives one the picture of a radical. He noted proudly that his three children were attending l'Athenee Royale, a school for European children in Stanleyville. He said that he had pursued a correspondence course in French in 1948. And finally, he noted that he had had a long meeting with the Belgian King Baudouin himself during his visit to Stan in 1955. If all this was designed to convince the publishers that Lumumba was "establishment", Lumumba himself clearly realized that he wasn't. He was painfully aware that his colonial masters looked upon all Africans as children to be civilized.

Although he dared to raise questions heretofore unspoken by Congolese, the tone of Lumumba's book was apologetic. He still had faith that the system might change itself. He tried to explain to the Belgians the uniqueness of the African; he wanted them to understand. He frequently talked about soul. His avowed intention at the beginning of the book was to clarify for Belgians the "mysteries of the black, so as to explain what Congolese think".

Again he says,

"Do not destroy the soul of blacks in wanting to make a superficial African, a caricature of a European with black skin."

And in the most eloquent statement of African nationalism Lumumba wrote:

"A man without any nationalist tendencies is a man without soul..."

He listed grievances which any evolue of Stanleyville might have had at the time. The first of these was that salaries of Congolese employees should more closely approximate those of Belgians engaged in similar positions. This, then, led to a plea for more and better educational opportunities for Congolese. Lumumba even quoted the American journalist, Carl Rowan, in raising the question of equal voting rights for qualified Africans.

But he was even more concerned with the breakdown of

traditional African values under colonial rule. He deplored the rise of prostitution in the cities among African women, the direct result of the European's civilized ways. He argued for the emancipation of Congolese women, saying that "to educate a woman is to educate a whole nation!" In retrospect, Lumumba's most wishful statement was to fall tragically short of being realized:

"If others have obtained their independence by atomic bombs and bloody wars, we shall obtain ours by the mouth, by intelligence and reason."

Political scientist Rene Lamarchand provides some biographical information on Lumumba in his book on the political development of the Congo. Born in 1925 in Kasai Province, Lumumba was a member of the Batetela tribe. After completing his primary education in a Catholic mission, he went to work as a clerk in Kindu, in the Manyema district. Shortly after moving to Leopoldville to attend a vocational school, he was sent to Stanleyville to work as a clerk in the post office. Here Lumumba became editor of l'Echo Postal a publication of Amicale des Postiers. He also made frequent contributions to the local papers such as la Stanleyvillois as well as to more widely read publications such as l'Afrique et le Monde.

The emphasis in his writings was usually on racial, social and economic discrimination rather than on tribal heritage as with other Congolese writers. During 1952 Lumumba worked as a part time research assistant for a French sociologist. Although Lumumba was especially eager to continue his formal education, he was denied admission to Louvanium University which opened in 1953 on the grounds that only bachelors could be admitted. Added to this disappointment was the sudden interruption of his career as a clerk when he was arrested on July 1, 1956, for embezzlement of postal funds and condemned to two years in prison. Nearly a year later the sentence was commuted to twelve months after the sum in question had been reimbursed.

Just before Lumumba was jailed he had returned from a visit to Belgium with a delegation of 16 Congolese at the invitation of the Minister of Colonies. He had been most impressed, and upon his return urged that more Congolese be able to explore the mother country. But his year of imprisonment in Stanleyville must surely have seen the gestation of radical nationalist sentiment which characterized his career from there on. After his release from prison he again went to Leopoldville where he eventually found employment as sales director of the Bracongo Brewery. For the next three years until his assassination in 1960 Lumumba was to be the central figure in the drama of Congolese Independence.

Voicing the discontent of Congolese elites with the Belgian administration, Lumumba quickly rose to a position of preeminence among the nationalists. In December 1958 he attended the All-African People's Conference in Accra as president of MNC (Mouvement National Congolais). A few months later he was in Brussels attempting to rally support for the nationalist cause. His speeches there were still of moderate tone, although he decried "the bastardization and destruction of Negro-African art" and "the de-personalization of Africa." In May of 1959 Lumumba returned to Stanleyville where his efforts at organizing for MNC met with astounding success. Astounding, that is, for students of African politics who assumed that the masses were conservative and apolitical and must be prodded by self-serving elites. Lumumba eventually became the first Prime Minister of the Democratic Republic of the Congo in 1960 but was assassinated in early 1961, shortly after taking office. The country was subsequently plunged into political chaos, pitting Western capitalist interests against Eastern Communist interests.

Rebellions in the Congo

Following Lumumba's assassination, Antoine Gizenga, his Deputy Premier, returned to Stanleyville and took control of the city. On February 15, 1961, eight countries recognized the legitimacy of his "lawful government". But in January of 1962 Congolese and UN troops took Stanleyville and Gizenga was arrested and imprisoned. The year 1964 would see the name of Stanleyville splashed across the headlines of world news. It became as much a symbol of East-West confrontation as Berlin or Havana. Early in the year rebellion broke out in Kwilu Province and eventually spread over most of the country. Its origins were largely rural and popular, a massive reaction against the unequal distribution of the rewards of independence. In short, there had been a large gap between aspirations raised by the fallen Lumumba and the realities of life under a succession of regimes.

As the last of the UN military forces were being withdrawn, the

Congo was faced with the horrible irony of former Katanga rebel leader Moise Tshombê being invited by President Joseph Kasavubu in July to form a "transition government of national unity." While the rebel bands of Pierre Mulele soon lost ground to the Congolese Army in Kwilu Province, by May of 1964 rebels began to meet with success in eastern Kivu. Emboldened by their baptism with mai Mulele (Mulele water), thousands of rebel recruits who called themselves simbas (lions) joined the liberation army under "General" Nicholas Olenga. A.N.C. soldiers dropped their guns and fled, believing that mai Mulele turned their bullets into water. By July the rebels had overrun much of North Kivu Province and moving toward the Lumumbist capital of Stanleyville.

With the capture—virtually by default—of Stanleyville by Olenga's army on August I, the rebellion fanned out, fed by the fury of the wretched of the earth. Within a month Olenga set up a rebel state. The West made much to-do over the supposed Communist inspiration of the rebellion. Noting that the rebellion derived its force from the martyred Lumumba, it was then recalled that Lumumba had turned to Communist countries for support in his last desperate efforts to hold the Congo together. Ergo...And hadn't Pierre Mulele returned from Red China steeped in Maoist doctrine? Had not Chou En-lai just declared Africa "ripe for revolution" during his visit to Africa in December 1963?

Meanwhile Prime Minister Tshombe acted predictably by calling up some of the same mercenaries who had aided him in the past. A campaign was underway to recruit whites in Johannesburg, Durban, Salisbury and Bulawayo to fight communism and defend Western civilization. Soapy Williams, Under Secretary of State for African Affairs, expressed official American distaste for such a policy, adding however, that the U.S. could certainly understand the considerations which led the Congolese Government to use mercenaries, which it has every legal right to do to defend its sovereignty. He was concerned with the controversy which the presence of the mercenaries had caused. Although the rebel leaders would hold out until the end of November—the fabled III Days of which David Reed wrote—the ANC mercenaries began recapturing areas in Equateur and Kivu as early as September.

The Europeans taken hostage by the rebels in Stanleyville, among whom the American missionary doctor Paul Carlson, became the cause celebre of the Western powers. There was a flurry of international intrigue, the rebels seeking to garner support from the more radical African states and the great powers seeking ways to throttle the rebellion's momentum without the stigma of open intervention. William Attwood, U.S. Ambassador to Kenya at the time, gives us an illuminating—although unintended—account of American diplomatic duplicity during this period in his book, the Reds and Blacks. Finally, the State Department decided that a tiny bit of intervention—a humanitarian rescue mission—could be undertaken without the use of any American combat troops. So on November 20, 1964, Belgian paratroopers were flown into Stanleyville by U.S. Air Force planes.

Beginning in 1965, with Mobutu's seizure of power in Kinshasa, a Pax Mobutu seems to have finally settled on this troubled town. But Kisangani was still to be the scene of yet another crisis. By the end of 1965 Mobutu claimed a tenuous hold on the reins of power while Tshombe had gone off to exile once again to lick his wounds. Nevertheless, he cast a long shadow over the Congo. In September 1966 Katangese soldiers stationed in Kisangani initiated a rebellion of their own, killing their commanding officer and mutinying against the Mobutu regime. With the Katangese in control of Kisangani, Mobutu called again on the trusty mercenaries to put things in order.

The leader of the 6th Corps of foreign "volunteers" was none other than the Frenchman Bob Denard who had fought for Tshombe during the Katangese secession. The situation was soon re-established in favor of the government. Mission accomplished... or so it seemed. Denard and Jean Schramme, a Belgian plantation owner-turned mercenary, set up their headquarters at the University in Kisangani, already forced to take refuge in Kinshasa once before, and struggled to stay alive. The mercenaries made themselves at home in University housing and quartered their troops in a building complex nearby. That complex housed the Faculty of Economic and Social Sciences. Then, on July 5, 1967, the trusted 6th Corps did an about-face, crossing over to the side of the Katangese. They declared themselves "the army of liberation" and took possession of the Kisangani airport.

True to their word, the rebels routed the hapless ANC (the Congolese army), again throwing Kisangani into chaos. With their chief Denard convalescing in a Rhodesian hospital, and lacking any noble objective whatsoever, the rebels held Kisangani only a few days before fleeing to Bukavu. Left in the hands of ANC troops, the city of Kisangani fared little better than before. The wary Asian population remained barricaded in their homes for fear of reprisals. The city's economy was once again brought to its knees. Meanwhile, Schramme and his boys held out in his native Bukavu, where the spirit of white supremacy had perhaps the deepest roots in the Congo.

A counter-government was declared in Bukavu in early August "to save the Congo from chaos". World opinion, and that of the African nations in particular, provided the rebels with little succor, and the mercenary rebellion eventually petered out. The name of Schramme became synonymous with villainy itself. At the same time Mobutu was scoring a great diplomatic success as 37 member countries of the Organization of African Unity met in Kinshasa for its fourth session. While many of the African states had expressed reservations about even sending delegates to Kinshasa, the representatives were of one accord in voting support "without reservation" to the Congo to fight the mercenaries if they did not leave immediately. By 1969 when I arrived in Kisangani the last vestiges of the mercenary rebellion had petered out and there was a semblance of order in the city.

Boyoma la Belle: The Revival of Kisangani.

The city of Kisangani lies 50 miles north of the equator at a point where the Congo River begins a gentle arch westward toward Mbandaka. In any direction from Kisangani one may travel several hundred miles and still be enveloped by dense equatorial forest, except where man has carved out a portion of it in which to live. The elevation being well over 1,000 ft. above sea level, the heat is never as oppressive as it becomes in the lower Shire Valley in Malawi in November. A downpour during one of the "rainy" seasons may bring a pleasant cool spell in its wake, lasting for several days. One is never more than a few days away from a bright sunny day, nor for that matter, more than a couple of weeks from rain. Kisangani gained a good reputation early in the colonial days. Visitors then spoke of its beauty, and the extraordinary competence of colonial administrators in Stanleyville was well known.

A journalist representing Le Soir on a 1922 visit described Kisangani as the highlight of his stay in the Congo. Sometime in the colonial past the town was given a nick-name by the people of the region. Boyoma indicated a quality of excellence, of something unbeatable. It belonged in the same lexicon as Apollo and Toyota. By the late 1960s there was a Boyoma Taxi Co., Boyoma Editions of recent recordings by the Rock 'n Band and le Renouveau (the Revival, the city's newspaper) incited civic pride by referring to Kisangani as Boyoma-la-belle..

The revival of Kisangani was very recent indeed. The New York Times Magazine carried an article in the fall of 1969 on the Congo. As with most hurried journalistic accounts, the picture of tristesse painted by the author was deceptive. Plans for the renewal of Province Orientale were underway at the time of the author's visit to Kisangani in the spring of that year. To illustrate his concern for this revival, President Mobutu arranged to celebrate the second anniversary of the founding of the MPR in May of 1970 in Kisangani. The town underwent a vigorous face-lift for the occasion. It was pregnant with promise.

The Kisangani of August 1969, however, still bore the deep scars of rebellion and counter-rebellion. The downtown area looked very much like 13th and 7th Streets in Washington DC after the Martin Luther King Jr. assassination. The buildings were nearly all still pock marked with bullet holes. Many of them had been gutted by fire and were left with only an occasional piece of windowpane and a charred shell. Often as not, someone had made practical use of the remains.

Small businesses set up shop, carpenters plied their trade and a good many vacant buildings were taken over by squatters with no money to make repairs. The streets were not especially over-crowded with cars; a pathetic fleet of '57 and '58 Fords and Plymouths served as taxies, charging outlandish fares. Buses were not to be seen. My initial search for razor blades and shaving cream was futile. Any luxury item one could find was sure to bear a fantastic price. Contraband goods from neighboring Uganda provided a lively income for a number of enterprising merchants.

But even the physical appearance of Kisangani was not all that bleak. Nature herself was the greatest conservator of the city's beauty. No matter what season of the year there is eternal verdure which minimizes some of the ugliness brought by events of the past. In this, the Congo's third city, there was little in the way of air pollution which was becoming the bete noire of the civilized world.

Dominating the center of the city was the mammoth neo-Gothic post office completed just a couple of years before Independence. A sign in front of the building on the grass — Defense de faire le pipi (don't pee on the grass) had only recently disappeared. It was a reminder of the Belgian will to dominate every aspect of the life of the African. Across the street was a building only less imposing which was the governor's mansion, now the site of administration of the city, referred to as Hotel de Ville.

Only a few hundred meters away, past Hotel des Chutes, was the port of OTRACO on the river front which linked Kisangani to the interior and in turn to Kinshasa and the world beyond. Looking across the river from Avenue Tshatshi, in front of the Catholic cathedral, one could see Stanley Falls to the left and directly across on the left bank the spire of the Catholic mission. It is said that this is where The Nun's Story was filmed in the early 1950's as well as portion of the Bogart classic, The African Queen.

There were numerous reminders in Kisangani of the economic progress wrought by Belgian rule. In its 1958 publication commemorating 50 years of colonial rule, the Belgian establishment gave a glowing account of the material progress of the colony and of Kisangani. With a population of over 60,000, the city had become the second busiest center of air traffic in the Congo after Kinshasa. The very first regular airline in the colony had linked the two cities in 1920. At the time of Independence the Kisangani airport provided 10 direct lines including flights to Cairo, Brussels, Rome, Khartoum, Athens, Tripoli and all parts of the Congo.

By the late 1960s nearly every major company operating in the Congo was represented in Kisangani; most of them had now begun to operate again since a condition of normalcy was settling over the city. A partial listing of enterprises in Province Orientale compiled in 1968 by the Office des Services Economiques shows about 100 companies which were already functioning. Their operations include 20 oil mills, 16 rice mills, 10 sawmills, 19 coffee plantations, five carpenter shops, five construction companies mainly concerned with road repairs, four soft-drink factories, four soap factories, two breweries, 13 bread and pastry shops, and various producers of aluminum and plastic ware, paint, cement and cold storage. It was readily obvious that the economy was still mainly based on agricultural production, with the major exception of the gold extracting company of Kilo Moto in the northeast corner of the Province. Of all these enterprises, roughly half were located in Kisangani itself, and many of the others are centered in the second city of the Province, Isiro.

While many of these represented single-owners (often Greek or Cypriot), it was the large commercial societies with home offices in Brussels and elsewhere that were most in evidence in Kisangani. These included the three banking houses, Belgika (whose sprawling investments included a tobacco factory still out of order), Socophar (pharmacy), Solbena (export-import), CEGEAC (Ford agent), Difco (VW agent), Interline (general commerce), Jouret (steel products), Phillips (radio and appliances), SEDEC (British-owned company among the first and largest established in Kisangani) and Agence Maritime Internationale. Some of the giants had yet to regain their operations in town, such as Prokivu (import-export), CFAO (the big French company dealing in heavy road equipment and motors). Bata (the multinational shoe store), as elsewhere in Africa, was doing a land-office business in the city. Four oil companies—Texaco, Shell, Mobil and Fina—were operating in the city although many of their stations remained vacant.

A few enterprises were now in government hands, such as Regideso (water and electricity), Caisse d'Epargne (savings association for mainly low income earners) and Air Congo. The numerous labor unions which grew up in the past had now been fused into the national labor union (UNTC). It appeared to have little power either in dealing with these companies or in alleviating the still high rate of chomage (unemployment). The Mobutu government was intent on clearing the way for massive infusions of foreign capital investments and signs of it were increasingly abundant in Kisangani.

Surely the most spectacular sign of the revival to be seen in Kisangani was the number of vehicles in the streets. Toyota alone had invaded the town with a vengeance. The installation of Toyota sales and service was under way in September of 1969 although it was not until a few months later that business really picked up. A smiling Greek manager told me in April that he had sold over 60 Toyota trucks, 50 cars, 11 land-cruisers, and one ambulance already. He was selling an average of two to three trucks each day and the requests for cars, five a day, was more than he had on hand. Still the operation was so well oiled that one only needed to wait a few weeks after putting in an order, and all spare parts were available in Kisangani. The aged

Ford and Plymouth taxis were giving way to chic Toyota Corollas. No self-respecting ndumba would ride in anything but a Toyota taxi! Our block of university apartments was also well represented by Toyotas. No wonder Wilbur Mills was trying to get legislation to protect American manufacturers from Japanese imports.

Even more popular among university staff was the VW. The University used Volkswagon minibuses to transport professors without cars of their own. The university parking lot often resembled a VW dealer's lot. The VW agency in the Congo, Difco, had recently run into legal troubles with the government for unscrupulous business practices. The Congolese who ran the local office informed me that he had sold 15 cars, five kombis and four camionettes since the beginning of the year. His main difficulty, he said, was simply a lack of spare parts.

Perhaps a better gage of the overall revival of the economy was the number of bicycles and scooters appearing on the streets. A small private business which opened in December 1969 had already sold 50 Peugeot mobylettes, 16 Italian Vespas, and 36 bicycles. One of the most prosperous Pakistani families in Kisangani since 1962 was for a time the only bicycle and scooter dealer. Their business in "wax" cloth and other goods was going so well that they turned their concession over to the European firm Cyclor. In the last year the family sold 96 mobylettes and 100 bicycles. Cyclor, on the other hand, was a large company with an assembly plant in Kinshasa and a professional staff and a big publicity campaign in Kisangani. In September the STK (Societe de Transport Kinois Kisangani branch) inaugurated its service with five Mercedes Benz buses. But it was two steps forward and one backwards. The umbilical route linking Kisangani to the breadbasket of the Eastern Province—a distance of 700 km—became a veritable nightmare. At one point the route was completely closed due to impassable stretches in the middle. The only meat available in the Kisangani market for some time was local goat.

And what of the American presence in the Congo and in Boyoma la belle? It appeared that President Johnson's decision to send American planes to fight the simbas was entirely vindicated. American interest in the Congo was rather more strategic than commercial although American financial interests were larger than in most oother African countries. Belgium, Italy, West Germany and France were reportedly the chief commercial partners of the Congo. According to the British journal, African Development (Jan., 1970), American business tycoons were planning an unprecedented "raid" on Africa. An exclusive club of representatives of the biggest corporations who call themselves Business International met in Addis Ababa in November in a round table with delegates from interested African countries. This venture corresponded with the gradual down-grading of USAIDs development assistance programs in Africa and the Nixon Administration's aim of winning the world through private investment. It also corresponded with a law in the Congo granting exceptional conditions for foreign investors in a favorable climate. A modest U.S. gesture toward the Congo was the decision to send Peace Corps Volunteers there for the first time.

In the fall of 1969, for the first time since the 1964 rebellion, the U.S. Information Service appointed a full-time director of the Cultural Center in Kisangani. Bob Palmeri would play a very active role in the life of the city, building up the Center library, providing English language books to schools and generally showing the positive side of the American presence. The Center rode the crest of the Apollo publicity, featured a sizable library and frequent film showings. Bob would become a life-long friend and our paths would cross on many occasions over the years.

The revival of Kisangani was taking place within the population as well as its physical appearance. The past year had seen the first nationwide census in the Congo since Independence. Figures from the Ministry of the Interior revealed a total of just over 2 million inhabitants for the four districts of Eastern Province. The population of Kisangani, including five communes, was just under 200,000, of whom only 1,000 were foreigners, one-third of them from 25 other Africans countries. No one country was predominant but the largest number of immigrants came from West and Central Africa. There were 625 Europeans, one-third of them Belgians. Greeks were listed as both Hellenique and Cypriot, an important distinction. They were primarily involved in commerce.

While representing less than one percent of the population of Kisangani, the foreigner was often the most conspicuous. He was usually at the top of the company, the school, the hotel, and visible in the best night spots. In a few instances he was born here and had no other home. For example, the young Pakistani who called himself Bobby Nasser who was not yet 25 but was probably the town's number one capitalist. His family left India 300 years ago, long before there was a Pakistan, and settled in East Africa. They built up a thriving business in Tanzania only to lose everything during World War I because they bet on the Germans. The first president of Pakistan when it was formed in 1947 was a relative of the family. A quarrel between the head of the family and the Aga Khan resulted in the family's breaking ties with the Ismaili leader. Bobby (the nickname which the young Pakistani acquired as a student in the U.S.) proclaimed himself an atheist; his most profound loyalty was to his family. He had great antipathy toward the British and considered the British government very hypocritical.

Presently, however, he was back in Kisangani taking care of the business of liquidating the family's holdings in town. Why, then, was a young man who knew the Congo so well pulling out? Bobby's goal was to complete his studies but his plans were unclear. He knew the economic prospects in the Congo and considered that, given proper government policies, there would be a favorable climate for the entrepreneur. He was at once sentimental and coldly realistic. Schemes for investment in abandoned plantations in the Province filled his mind. But, he noted, there was no support from the government, especially for Asians. The government was making it tough to make a profit; some imports were charged 100% duty.

So what of the future? Wherever there wais money to be made Bobby would go because that is what he knew how to do. Maybe back to France where the family also had business interests. But he also kept a close eye on Pakistan. It was his opinion that the more populous but poorer East Pakistan would eventually gain political control over the more prosperous but presently dominant West Pakistan. If and when that happened Bobby felt certain there would be a split between East and West Pakistan. He wanted to be there when it did, partly because of his loyalty to his ancient homeland but also because of his hunch that it might very well be a good time to make money in the event economic ties were cut between the two Pakistans. (All of this was just before Bangladesh was born.)

Even more conspicuous than the Pakistanis were the Greek and Cypriot communities. To the outsider they were all Greeks. But one quickly learned that not only was there a difference; the two communities are to one another as cats are to dogs. Cypriots could be distinguished in several ways. As Cyprus once belonged to Britain, many of the Cypriots retained Commonwealth citizenship and most of them spoke English. The Cypriot holds that his is a distinctly superior breed. He views the Greek mainland in much the same way in which the West Pakistani views the East Pakistani. And to show his superiority the Cypriot could point to a more favorable position in the economic life of Kisangani. This is not to say, however, that the Greeks themselves were poor.

The most well known Cypriot in town was George, the owner of the Olympia restaurant and night club. Just as the Olympia of Paris was a symbol of excellence, so was the Olympia of Kisangani the center of the town's social life. George had been in the restaurant-hotel-night club business all his life. In his early days he ran a restaurant in London where he met his Cockney wife. By the early fifties he was in Kisangani where he built a hotel and cinema house. Later the building which housed the cinema was converted to a dance hall and to that was added a large open air "garden" with a circular concrete dance floor. The "garden" was planted with tables and chairs underneath a natural umbrella of trees and ringed with colored fluorescent lights. It had the air of perpetual festivity. Several hundred people could be, and often were, seated in the garden surrounding the dance floor facing the orchestra.

George himself was a rather sober, unfestive fellow who worked day and night to keep the Olympia in top shape. He was forever trimming a tree in the garden or planting another vine around the outdoor restaurant. In some respects the Olympia suffered from over-popularity; local MPR officials were always holding private parties there and then forgetting to pay the bill. The Olympia was not just another bar; it was considered public domain by the people of Kisangani. George claimed to be constantly harassed by tax collectors and police threatening to close the place down. He talked of selling it and moving away. Of course he was criying all the way to the bank. But George accepted the inconveniences of success quietly. He knew that as long as there was a Kisangani people would drink beer there and that it would earn him money. He was proud of his Commonwealth citizenship and British wife, but he shared a closer identity with the Rhodesians. On March 2, when Ian Smith declared Rhodesia a republic under white rule, George remarked: "They built the country; they should own it."

The Olympia was such an institution that it was referred to by my students and faculty of the university as "The Temple." One went there to pay homage to the great god Bacchus. Its star quality was derived from the group that played there seven nights a week and called itself the "Rock 'n' Band". Its chef-fondateur was Garcia who left the fiercely competitive world of Kinshasa some years ago and became King of Kisangani. The Rock 'n Band was versatile and catered well to its audience. During dinner hours they would play Greek music since a large percentage of the regular customers were Greek. Then they would glide into a medley of pop songs which might be French, Portuguese, American or what-have-you. Then there would be a tribute to James Brown and the New Breed...the soul sound. Congolese music was hardly in danger of being undermined by any exported variety, but American soul seemed to be taking its place among the mini-skirt set. Garcia became an expert in adapting other genres of music to his own style, but the closer to home the better. The next segment was usually Afro-Cuban whose rhythmic origins may be detected in the drums of the Congo. Until now only a few couples have taken the floor to do their special thing, but it is their own Congo music which brings the rest to their feet and onto the floor like lemmings to the sea. The rest of the night, until morning, belongs to the people.

The Temple was the great social common denominator in Kisangani. The Governor and his party were often honored guests. For the European community it was the one place visitors must see if they were to know the town. For some of the university community the Temple was a second home. But it was the ordinary people who kept George in business, who come regularly to the Temple because this is where life was. The femmes libres seemed to be a distinct majority. There were students, chomeurs and workers. And there was nearly always a chiwelewele or two (people who for one reason or another have lost touch with reality) who characteristically would drink and dance alone. It might be a woman in shabby clothes and no shoes or a man who some times squawked like a bird. They were recognized as being mentally deranged but there was no attempt to chase them away. No one thought of locking them up, and they could usually depend on a free beer or two from someone. It was a vivid example of the inclusiveness of African society.

There was a big sign in neon lights above the 15-piece band which said D'abord, Stanor. It advertised the local beer which sponsored the band and had exclusive selling rights — exclusive not of expensive imported beer or whiskey, but of its number one local rival, Primus. Stanor sold for 13 makuta — 26 cents a bottle and the establishment made its profit on sheer volume of sales. The manager of the giant German company of Unibra (Stanor) brewery sometimes came to help drink up his profit. He claimed that Stanor, which was made from manioc, had 70% of the market. Its several hundred employees made Stanor one of the largest employers in town. It was the preference of the masses. Primus, with the other 30% of the market, was brewed with maize and was generally considered the choice of outsiders and the odd local type. But as with football teams and orchestras, one was obliged to have a preference, as a matter of sociability. A full hour could be consumed with a discussion, even an argument, as to the merits of one's own preferred brew. The Primus people had their own public relations man too, whose job was to arrange exclusive concessions with well known bars.

l'Ambiance was not the sole domaine of the Olympia by any means. It existed wherever one or two were gathered together. For those with money it was the Congo Palace Hotel, renovated in the spring of 1969 for Mobutu's visit. There you could really spend your zaires if you had them, or if you were a high fonctionnaire of the MPR (Mobutu's political party). Occasionally there was a Congolese combo at the Congo Palace that catered to European tastes. A couple of other more intimate spots catered to the free-spending European community. But for most of the citizens of Kisangani l'ambiance was more often found in literally more bars than one could count scattered throughout the city and its communes. Across from the marketplace, which was the physical and social center of Kisangani, was a row of bars which filled up after the noon whistle ending the day's market activity. Here was humanity in its purest social form. Thirsty market mammies after a hard day's work mixed with policemen (sometimes still on duty) and soldiers who come in big trucks. Relative would met relative and whoever had 10 makuta would buy the beer. In the evenings the scene changed to the communes where almost everyone with a little extra cash opened his own bar. A typical place had its open-air dance floor and a listing of available drinks written on the wall, and a name like Morvie's, Bebe 69, or Alexis.

Kisangani was a crossroads of cultures, rivaling Kinshasa as a melting pot. Here the Swahili-speaking people from the east and south converged with the Lingala-speaking tribes to the west and soldiers of the ANC. Africans who were here for a certain length of time usually spoke or at least understand both. It would probably be safe to say, though, that Lingala was in the ascendancy; Swahili being viewed as the language of the old days whereas Lingala was associated with modernization. It was the language of Mobutu. Still radio broadcasts were given in both Swahili and Lingala.

During the troubles of rebellion and counter-rebellion many of the townspeople fled to the bush where they were relatively safer but suffered from hunger and exposure. Nowadays they were pouring back into the communes from all parts of the interior, looking for family ties to help them along. And, too, Kisangani acted as a kind of funnel for many who moved on to Kinshasa which represented an even greater prospect of social and economic advancement. There was, nevertheless, an increasing degree of civic pride among the people of Boyoma-la-belle and talk of making Kisangani the second city of the Congo (replacing Lubumbashi).

The third anniversary of the MPR on May 20, 1970 was a milestone in the consolidation of Mobutu's power and that of the Mouvement Populaire de la Revoluation (MPR). Over 1,000 MPR leaders met in Kinshasa to proclaim Mobutu their sole candidate for the first national elections since the November 24, 1965 coup which brought him to power. Delegates from Eastern Province attended the congress in which resolutions were passed institutionalizing the MPR as the only legal political party and "the supreme institution of the Congolese state". The official ideology of the MPR was reiterated by Mobutu as "authentic Congolese nationalism." In proclaiming this doctrine of nationalism Mobutu paid his respects to Lumumba for having first showed the way toward its expression. He added his own interpretation:

"In a word our nationalism is a communal humanism." And he described nationalism as the "force of development and the most formidable weapon against the reactionary forces on our continent."

The popular slogan which characterized Mobutu's regime and placed his own stamp on Congolese nationalism is:

"Actes et non blah blah blah". Or "Blah, blah, blah...jamais. Action!"

Mobutu was unquestionably a man of action determined to do away with the rhetoric of the past and translate words into action. The corollary to that slogan was a second one, now a popular song: Salongo alingi mosala. There was supposed to be something contagious in singing a song which exhorted one to work.

As Head of State Mobutu made a point of visiting the interior of the country regularly, secure in the feeling that he drew strength from the people. And whenever he was not abroad on a state visit he was receiving his counterparts from other countries. Two of these occasions have Mobutu back to Kisangani. On one occasion he came all the way from Kinshasa in the presidential boat, stopping at numerous towns along the way. Arriving at the OTRACO port, he was given a 21-gun salute as dozens of fishing boats paddled up to extend their greetings. Then he was carried several kilometers down the main boulevard strewn with palm leaves and cheering crowds to the Governor's mansion. The next couple of days saw a full round of public appearances. Sunday morning the President attended an ecumenical church service which even included the Muslim community, an example of ecumenism never aspired to or desired in the old days of mission domination.

The President also managed to visit the University and address a group of students who had not been especially favorable toward the government since the events at Louvanium in which students were killed by government soldiers. In fact, they commissioned their student MPR secretary to issue a bold request for direct Presidential aid as proof of his good will toward them. It was precisely the kind of request the President was in a position to grant, to prove himself to doubting students as a man of action and not blah blah blah. The students were not asking for any kind of social reform or reorientation of government policy; they were concerned with personal needs. Because many of them lived away from the campus in the communes they asked for buses to facilitate transportation to and from classes. Five months passed and the more skeptical among them were saying "I told you so." Then finally they came: five brand new air-conditioned buses with tinted windows and muzac with Congolese music. It is safe to say that this gesture made believers out of a good many potentially anti-government students.

Another measure of student sentiment regarding the President's visit to the University appeared in an article in the satirical student journal of the Faculty of Philsopy and Letters, lampooning the University's reception of the Congo's first citizen. It was noted that the University was of "Calvinist inspiration" and that here one must be content to drink orangeade and Coke. So when the Grand Leopard himself was offered a soft drink he refused. Everyone knew, however, that he wais "animated more by authentic Congolese nationalism than by Calvinism." This was not merely an insult to the Grand Leopard, not to be offered the beer of his choice, but it pointed to a deeper problem:

"In effect the African has been considered as one who couldn't drink moderately and so it has been judged well to tell him that to drink is to sin."

The article ended with a plea to the ruling powers of the University to "let the future come."

Kisangani   25/June/1970

In June 1970 the city of Kisangani welcomed Bwana Kitoko— King Baudouin I of Belgium—in what was billed as the event of the decade. The two-week royal visit to the Congo coinciding with its 10th anniversary of Independence was the ultimate expression of the entente toward which the Congo and its former colonial master had been moving in recent months. President Mobutu was reciprocating for the royal invitation he had received for a state visit in Belgium the previous year. The Congolese press exuded goodwill towards His Majesty and spoke of ever greater horizons for the relations between the two countries...a new era.

It was recalled that this was the same Baudouin who had personally come to Leopoldville on June 30, 1960, to grant Independence, that he was loved by the people of the Congo then as he was now. Pictures of Baudouin and Mobutu together on several occasions bespoke a kingly comradeship, two men born only months apart in 1930, whose "profound friendship" was the basis of the excellent Belgo-Congolese relations. For Kisangani, the royal visit was especially eventful for it was here that Baudouin, on his first trip to the Congo as King in 1955, was given the name Bwana Kitoko, a title of endearment. He had been preceded by King Albert in 1928 and Prince Leopold (who would become King Leopold III) in 1925, both of whom were received in royal fashion by the Wagenia chiefs. Here it was in 1955 that Baudouin met an enthusiastic young postal clerk named Lumumba who would soon claim the loyalty of the Congolese in the King's place.

Again the town flowered like the desert after a rain, in an array of soft pastel colors. Tons of paint found their way onto just about every building in town, including those still abandoned. The middle of town was blocked off by a wall of palm leaves for a week-long fair, centered on the very same park where the Lumumba monument had stood and hundreds met their death during the Rebellion. The King arrived in the company of his proud host at the same airport from which he departed to Belgium 15 years before. The four-hour visit in Kisangani took the royal court first to an orphanage built by the Congo government to accommodate children of the rebellions. And then Baudouin and Mobutu were gone, downriver in the elegant Presidential boat.

L'Universite Libre du Congo (ULC), Kisangani   *August 1969*

"Blessed are the meek for they shall inherit the earth..."
- Matthew 5:5

The brief history of l'Universite Libre du Congo (The Free University of Congo) was hardly less dramatic than that of Kisangani itself. At the time of Independence in 1960 anyone who bothered to acquaint himself with elementary facts about the Congo knew that there were only a dozen Congolese who had achieved university degrees. The Belgian policy of development had been a sound one according to Belgian logic: don't over-educate the African and his level of expectation will not rise beyond his education. The African wasn't invited to go and study in the universities of the metropole as he had been in other colonies.

But pressures for higher education mounted, and in 1953 the Catholic establishment opened Lovanium University near Kinshasa with direct ties to its namesake (Louvain) in Belgium. Within the first nine years the University awarded over 1,000 degrees and continuied to expand its facilities. To counter the influence of the Catholic Church in preparing its elite cadre the Congolese government established the first state university known as l'Universite Officielle du Congo (UOC) in Elizabethville (later named Lubumbashi).

By 1969 they both had an enrollment of between two and three thousand students.

In keeping with its desire to keep up with the Catholics, the Protestant community began to talk of starting its own university. The impetus was provided by the need to form Congolese pastors for their churches. The first meeting to this end was held in Kinshasa in 1962, and a national committee was formed to come up with a plan. Stanleyville was chosen as the location and the first pre-university classes were begun with 20 students on October 22, 1963. The founding institution, Protestant Council of the Congo (CPC), naturally chose a former Methodist missionary as the first Rector. The official opening ceremony on November 23, 1963 was presided over by the Minister of Education. The following year the Free University of the Congo received official recognition by the Organization of African Unity as the 33rd University in Africa.

The campus was composed primarily of the group of buildings which had served as the secondary school of the European community before 1960. The provincial government also gave the new University a block of nine three-story luxury apartments on a long term lease which had been abandoned after Independence. No sooner had the University opened its doors than the Simba Rebellion broke out, a movement that grew out of hatred for the very educated and moneyed elite that the University was attempting to train. Some of the students and professors were held captive during four months of rebel occupation but only one student died.

So the University moved all its professors and students to Louvanium in Kinshasa, where they merged into one academic community. The enrollment grew modestly from 84 in 1964-65 to 110 the following year. ULC was still alive, if not flourishing, due to a unique example of cooperation between Protestant and Catholic. During the second year at Louvanium a few activities were revived back in Kisangani, with the hope that a new period of calm would be ushered in under the strong arm of the new military regime.

After two years of exile, preparations were made to return the entire operations to Kisangani when once again mutiny broke out in Katanga in September 1966. The decision was then made by the harassed administration to evacuate again, this time to Luluabourg in Kasai Province. Students and professors, already skittish of the situation in Kisangani, had begun to desert what was apparently a sinking ship. For a second time it appeared that ULC was doomed to extinction. But for the energetic aid of the Congo government and the stick-to-it-iveness of a few of the faithful, it might well have been. Through the direct influence of President Mobutu, anxious to see the province pacified, ULC returned to Kisangani in early 1967. To underscore his interest the President came to the campus in March and was decorated by students. The debate as to retaining all university operations in Luluabourg was resolved by the persistence of the government.

The third trial by fire was yet to come. And again it coincided with the misfortunes of the city itself. Bob Denard and his mercenaries decided to go on their infamous ego trip in July 1967. Commandeering university buildings for their use, the mercenaries were not altogether unwelcome by some of the white members of the university community. In fact when the mercenaries pulled up stakes and left town quietly for Bukavu after only a few days of occupation, many of the Europeans fully expected a massacre at the hands of the ANC troops.

We have already seen how the mercenary rebellion dissolved in pockets of resistance on the eastern border. The ANC was busy chasing them out and establishing law and order well into the following year.

But the city of Kisangani had at long last turned the corner. The University had not only survived during that period, its administrators became influential in affairs of the city. The University served as a rallying point for the rest of the town; as long as it was alive and pumping there was hope that the patient would live. The inauguration celebration of the academic year in November 1967 was a joyful occasion. There were 250 students at Kisangani and another 100 at Luluabourg, which had created a serious housing shortage. There were five Faculties within ULC: Theology, Liberal Arts, Social Sciences, Education and Natural Sciences. There were plans for a Faculty of Medicine and Agronomy, both of which would be quite costly. There had been many repairs and purchases with the funds accorded by the President during his recent visit. The University had become the largest single employer in town with nearly 400 heads of families. This worked as a multiplying factor in the city's weak economy. A plea was made to the Congolese government to aid in the construction of dormitories. And if anyone was tempted to forget, it was reiterated that ULC was "openly based upon the Christian faith in its original expression". Students were urged to think, not of the obligation of the government to pay their scholarship, but of their own obligation to the people of the Congo to serve them in the future.

The following year witnessed the greatest increase in student enrollment to 570 and of teaching staff to a total of 50. One of the stated aims of the University was to proceed as rapidly as possible toward nationalization. By the 1968-69 academic year there were 15 Congolese nationals teaching on the University roster, which included those studying abroad with positions promised upon their return to the Congo. Half of the top administrative positions were occupied by Congolese. And finally, to help resolve the complex of academic inferiority which the University had always felt, a bona fide academician with a Doctorat d'Etat (the highest French academic degree) in anthropology was installed as Rector in June of 1968. As a Frenchman, he was a symbol of the highly regarded French education system, and a staunch Protestant.

The revival of the Eastern Province ushered in a period characterized as "consolidation" by University authorities. In July 1968 the first two students to receive their B.A. degrees were graduated, appropriately enough from the Faculty of Theology, in partial fulfillment of the dream of the missionaries who founded the University. The teaching staff at the beginning of 1969-70 numbered at least 64 on the Kisangani campus (others were to arrive later in the year). They represented 22 countries, among them 14 from France, 13 from Holland, 10 Congolese nationals, and nine from the U.S. In addition, there were now 12 Congolese graduate students pursuing their studies abroad.

There were professors from just about everywhere in the "free world", including South Vietnam, Jamaica, Spain, Switzerland, Germany, Britain and several African countries. The one professor born in mainland China was listed as South Vietnamese, having lived there more recently. One of the Congolese had studied in the USSR. Only 15 of the entire teaching staff had doctorates, and some of these as it turned out were of a dubious nature. The lower echelons of the administrative staff were entirely in the hands of Congolese. Although the pre-university at Luluabourg was ceded to the Official

University of the Congo, the total number of ULC students had risen to 676.

Physically and financially ULC was growing as well. In addition to the long-term loan for the construction of the buildings which formed the skeleton of the physical plant, the government supplied fully 80% of the University's working budget even though it was a private institution. It had also allocated funds for a science building and water tower. The U.S. Agency for International Development (USAID) provided funds for an administration building which was under construction off and on (mostly off) since 1966 due to contractual and bureaucratic snags. Two new dormitories directly adjacent to the administration building were going up, also with USAID money. In addition, USAID donated several scholarships each year for Congolese students and staff recommended by the administration.

The Dutch were second only to Americans in their involvement in the University. A direct link with the Free University of Amsterdam provided a large number of professors as well as the Academic Vice-Rector. The Dutch government gave the money for the construction of a Technical Services workshop which in turn provided maintenance for university housing and grounds. The British government sent one technical assistance professor and promised to finance the construction of a library. A bureau of development was established and an American architect was commissioned to draw up plans for future use of university land.

The organization of the University strongly reflected its Protestant and American origins. The Administrative Council was composed of 15 to 20 members, of whom about half were businessmen, both Congolese and European, and the other half associated with the Protestant establishment. Three were Americans. Most all of them were of the more liberal Protestant community. Of the three most influential members, all had close ties with the American community, including the Minister of Education who was a former Ambassador to Washington. The Council met in a regular session once a year. The day to day administration of the University was theoretically the collective responsibility of the Executive Committee whose five members included the Rector, two Vice Rectors—for Academic and Student Affairs—the Secretary General and the General Administrator. The Interim Rector was American, the Vice Rector

Dutch, and the other three committee members, Congolese, were products of the Protestant mission community. They meet weekly whenever two or three of them were not traveling abroad either to raise money or to Kinshasa to straighten out kinks in the University Representation Office. Each of the five Faculties has an academic Dean, charged with its operations and elected by its professors. The Dean is responsible to the Academic Vice Rector.

There existed an organization of professors whose purpose was to relate the interests and grievances of the teaching staff to the Executive Committee. All student organizations were banned after the June 1969 demonstration at Louvanium. Instead, students and Congolese professors were required to become members of the University branch of the MPR. The practical administration of ULC was a veritable "missionaryeaucracy" with 10 American missionaries and missionary wives in administrative positions. Decisions of the Executive Committee were reflective of the Protestant ethos, whether in hiring new professors with a religious orientation or in placing Congolese in positions of responsibility who have had proper Protestant training. The missionaries, whose relationship to the Interim Rector was personal rather than institutional, enjoyed authority relative to their personal relationship with him or with members of the Administrative Council.

There was a pronounced form of tribalism within the University, although not the tribalism usually described by social scientists. Rather it concernd the white tribes of Africa. Applied to "civilized" nations, it was more often referred to as chauvinism or jingoism. At the University it was most pronounced among the largest communities, namely French, Dutch and American. The conflict dated back to the hiring of the French Rector in 1968. He had had long years of experience in Africa as an anthropologist-missionary and only recently served as Rector of a university in Malagasy. In short, he possessed all the academic and executive experience one could have asked for in a Rector. But perfect credentials do not a perfect Rector make. Especially since he was a lone Frenchman, attempting to work within a predominantly American-run University. His greatest achievement of which he boasted was the acquisition of 14 French teachers furnished as technical assistants by their government. The majority were to teach in lieu of military service. The Rector was imbued with a Napoleonic civilizing mission which he honestly believed that Africa needed. Richard Wright might well have had him in mind as he wrote in Black Power:

"Frenchmen feel that they have worked out in the last two thousand years just about the most civilized attitude on earth."

And this may well have applied to the Rector's attitude toward his African subjects when he wrote:

"In French eyes nationalism implies a rejection of French culture, whereas they regard communism as a temporary aberration of youth."

It was natural, then, that he should wince whenever he heard these countrified Americans butchering the language of Voltaire and that he should bend every effort to bring more of his own countrymen to ULC.

All of which set the French Rector on a collision course with both the American community and his African subjects. He was singularly lacking in diplomacy and insisted on his own way. By the end of his first year he had resigned several times and threatened to resign several other times. He managed to alienate just about everybody, including non-francophone professors. In establishing the classification of teaching staff according to their degrees and experience the Rector ranked those with degrees from French universities highest since, as everyone should know, the French educational system was innately superior to others. (He did allow room for exceptions, such as those with degrees from the top five American universities which he had heard of. But then, we didn't have any professors from the otp five.) He wasn't entirely politically insensitive though. He worked at a coalition with the students and was partially rewarded with demonstrations in his favor on occasion.

Thus, the stage was set for the inauguration of the academic year on November 8, 1969. The occasion was a bit tense, as a result of the student demonstrations five months before at Louvanium in Kinshasa, and the expression of sympathy by students at ULC. The recently-appointed Minister of Education presided over the ceremonies and delivered the keynote address on behalf of the President. His tone was somber. At the very outset he reminded the student audience that Mobutu had given amnesty to the student leaders at Louvanium responsible for the events there. And he noted that they had gained their objective: an increase in student stipends. He went on to talk about their "apprenticeship responsibility and the exercise of authority." The Minister was cordially received by his audience.

Then the Rector delivered a homiletic discourse in his impeccable French tongue, ranging over the civic duty of students and constantly referring to the foreign aid accorded to the University. Two days later a lengthy editorial in Le Renouveau, the local newspaper, entitled "Doucement, Messr. le Recteur" delivered a broadside which proved to be the handwriting on the wall. In whose name did the Rector think he was speaking, his own? In deploring the state of under-development of the University, the Rector had spoken of the "few realizations we have been able to manage thanks to our foreign friends." But not a word of thanks to the Congolese government or to President Mobutu, who provided 80% of the university budget.

Within a week the Council, meeting in Kisangani in a regular session, decided to accept the Rector's long-standing resignation, thereby ending the game of cat and mouse they had been playing. But the Rector didn't really want to resign; he quickly used one of his old tactics, arousing the students to demonstrate for him. It didn't work this time, despite his vows to them that "I will be with you till death; I have supported and will support the majority always." The Rector thus refused to leave, and demanded that the Council "negotiate". The Council remained adamant.

Le Renouveau had meanwhile begun an inquiry into the matter which appeared in the following days. Even allowing for the usual hyperbole, it was a resounding indictment. Rumors that had run through the university community now reached print. It was alleged that Messr le Recteur had used some of his substantial salary ($36,000 a year) to bribe the students, and that two French professors had served as spies for him. The Rector showed scarcely veiled contempt for the black race, using variations on the same theme on various occasions:

"The Congolese have chaos in their blood....they have anarchy in their blood."

With their categorical refusal to consider again his resignation, the Council itself became the object of his contempt:

"The Administrative Council is a band of savages with anarchy in their blood," he raged.

For his curtain call Messr le Recteur had parting words for his erstwhile allies:

"All the students are ingrates and sauvages endimanches (savages in their Sunday best)!"

With the reluctant departure of the Rector, a new era began, or rather we should say the renewal of the previous era. It was marked by the return of American tribal domination, in coalition with the Dutch. The latter shared many of the tribal traits of the Americans, including uneasiness in the face of a "superior" French culture. Quite unlike the French tribe, however, the American-Dutch coalition could call upon a leader who was crafty and wise in the ways of the African world. He was the Omnipotent Administrator. Born and raised in the Congo, he belonged to a second generation of missionaries with a semi-liberal theology and social orientation. He spoke the language (Lingala) fluently and understood Congolese culture. After receiving a B.D. in the U.S., he came back to the country which was home to him to help in the founding of a Protestant university, after being named interim Rector. Once again, with the departure of Messr. le Recteur, the Omnipotent Administrator assumed the title of Rector ad interim for the second time. He himself contended that the University would have to continue its search for a Rector with proper academic and administrative credentials.

But it was no secret that it was his own administrative acumen, bred through decades of missions and missionary life that had held the University together in its first tender years. It was he, and a handful of others, who had seen ULC through its crises and refused to let it die. Like the jungle itself when chopped down immediately takes over again, his resolve was strong. There was to be a ULC, no matter what. Except for a year of sabbatical leave in the U.S. to study business administration, the Omnipotent Administrator had served as General Administrator from the beginning whenever he wasn't Interim Rector.

Although he now devotes himself full time to the University as its head, the Omnipotent Administrator thought of himself first and foremost as a missionary in the truest sense of the word. As was said of Kurtz, who preceded him into the heart of darkness,

"We want for higher intelligence, wide sympathies, a singleness of purpose..."

Perhaps it might be said that the interim Rector was a latter-day Kurtz, bent on bringing order and light where there was none before.

And like Conrad himself on his venture into the interior of his own mind, the Omnipotent Administrator found "no joy in the brilliant sunlight"; the Congo was rather "brooding and gloomy." His mission was a very serious one indeed and it commanded all of his energies, which were considerable. He worked hard, only to see the frequent violations of some principle of administration or slackness within the University. He once remarked wistfully:

"Sometimes I like to go down and watch the river go by; it doesn't need anyone to push it."

The Omnipotent Administrator knew that the meek were destined to inherit the earth. His mission was to see that they weare morally and administratively competent to do so when the time came. He was at the University to set the example and to see that other Christians, both Congolese and foreign, did their part. The keys which he wore fastened to his belt at all times may not have been the keys to the Kingdom of Heaven but they did symbolize to Congolese something of the work and discipline required to achieve salvation. They had to understand that in order to maintain impersonal bureaucratic standards every letter must have five carbon copies. But even more important than the ability to run their own University was the need for the meek to develop as persons — to become mentally awake and morally straight. This is where the Omnipotent Administrator found the greatest challenge.

The administration assumed that a Congolese would embezzle until he managed to prove himself innocent. The administrative staff — typists, secretaries and mail-sorters — also felt the pinch of the tight-fistedness of the Omnipotent Administrator. Even for special occasions such as a birth or marriage (which might cost the ordinary city-dweller $100 and $400 respectively) there was no provision for receiving an advance from the University as there was in most companies. But if the University didn't take care of marryin' it did accommodate buryin'. Technical Services had a supply of coffins available which it supplied upon the death of a member of a University family.

If the Omnipotent Administrator sometimes wondered "why the natives didn't eat him" (Conrad) if he felt "like a hyena on the battlefield" after the war (Conrad again), his mate and faithful companion lived an essentially innocent life, honestly trying to make people happy. She was every bit as American as her mate but she represented the America of pot-luck dinners, bar-b-ques and ice cream socials. When they invited groups of professors over from time to time the Omnipotent Administrator saw it as an obligation to be sociable, or perhaps a chance to keep his finger on the pulse of university life. For her it was an opportunity to spread a little good will. She was a positive purveyor of American culture. But she too was raised with the Protestant ethic, in the American South, and taught to fear the wages of sin.

Before condemning the whole missionaryaucracy, it must be said that there were some who did not march to the beat of the established order. In fact, the missionaryeaucracy has its own Martin Luthers who in one way or another took their stand against the system. They might simply be piqued by the Omnipotent Administrator's high-handedness. Or they might have really begun to escape the confines of Calvinist convention. Rather than viewing their mission as the conversion of the heathen to the American way of life, they immersed themselves in the life of the Congolese and found their salvation in it.

In sum, the American presence at the University in Kisangani mirrored all too clearly the American presence in the world. It was the logical culmination of the Wilsonian injunction to make the world safe for democracy, combined with a distorted interpretation of the Biblical injunction to go into the world and preach the Gospel. It was the manifestation of an outworn liberalism which assumes that the world should be remade in the image of the corporate-liberal-democrat—the Omnipotent Administrator. In trying to save his soul, the Omnipotent Administrator was in danger of loingt it.

There were those whose essential aim was to save souls, at least figuratively speaking, and those whose motivations were more mundane. Sometimes it was difficult to tell which was which. The missionaries continued to retain the highest positions in the University administration and were the recipients of the best of the material goodies available. On the other hand, there were non-missionaries who have portrayed a most missionary-like zeal in their attitudes toward the Congo and Congolese. There had always been, it seems, a clash of values between missionaries and "mercenaries" (expatriate faculty and staff who came to the Congo mainly for adventure). In the beginning, the administration attempted to discourage smoking among its staff (not to mention drinking). Unfortunately the moral force of this intended regulation was greatly weakened by the fact that the Dean of the Faculty of Theology could not give up his pipe. The mercenaries came in ever greater proportion each year and successfully defended their secular rights to these minor sins.

There was no "publish or perish" pressure; those who did publish were by far the exception. Most of my colleagues would have to agree that life in Kisangani was almost unadulterated leisure, even for those who set for themselves academic tasks. No one taught more than the standard 10 hours per week and the average seemed to be about five or six. And there were still some who complaind of heavy work loads! My own teaching assignment consisted of required courses in practical English for students in several faculties. My Peace Corps teaching experience in Malawi stood me in good stead. For the majority of us the position of professor in Kisangani carried far more social prestige than would the same position at home (if indeed we were able to find the job).

While life in Kisangani had much to offer, I became increasingly aware that if I were to pursue an academic career I would eventually need to acquire a doctoral degree. Furthermore, I was quite certain that I did not want to continue my profession as a teacher of practical English into the indefinite future. By the end of my first full academic year at the University in Kisangani I had decided to return to the U.S. The fall of 1970 would find me in Evanston, Illinois, at Northwestern University.

References

Hull, Galen Spencer Hull (1970), "The Revival of Kisangani," *Africa Report.*

_____ (1974), "The Nationalization of the System of Higher Education in Zaire", PhD Dissertation, Northwestern University, Department of Political Science.

Lumumba, Patrice Emery (1972) *Lumumba Speaks: The Speeches and Writings of Patrice Lumumba, 1958-1961*, New York: Little, Brown Publishers.

Pons, Valdo, (1969) *Stanleyville: An African Urban Community under Beligan Administration,* printed for the International African Institute *for* Oxford University Press.

(le) Renouveau, November 11, 1969 (newspaper of the city of Kisangani).

(le) Renouveau, June 25, 1970, West, Richard (1965) *The White Tribes of Africa*, J. Cape Publishers.

Chapter 8

The Graduate School Experience, 1970-1973

A sense of commitment is required of the new Africanist. Indeed, it may be that any effort on the part of the American scholar amounts to cultural imperialism, however pure the motive. The very least that is being asked is that he have a sense of empathy toward African problems as perceived by Africans.

- Galen Hull, in The Pan-Africanist, 1971

Evanston, Illinois   *September 1970*

My time in the Congo in 1969-1970 was both exhilarating and sobering. Exhilarating because it was a deeper cross-cultural experience than I had had in Malawi. I went there entirely on my own, without the institutional cushion of the Peace Corps, and became rather more immersed in the local culture. I was obliged to learn French in order to function in the University and acquired proficiency in Swahili. French fluency, in particular, would serve as the key to many future experiences. The experience was sobering, however, because the longer I remained in the Congo, the more I realized that I would need to pursue a doctorate if I wanted to stay in academia. So by the middle of the academic year in Kisangani I began applying to graduate schools in political science, targeting those with African Studies or international relations programs: UCLA, Columbia, and Northwestern. Sending out applications from the middle of the rainforest, however, was risky business. Sometimes mail never reached its intended address, and I missed several deadlines.

When the dust settled, my choice was pretty much limited to Northwestern University in Evanston, Illinois. Northwestern was renowned for the famous anthropologist, Melville Herskovitz, founder in 1948 of one of the first African Studies centers in the United States. This appealed to me since I felt myself already something of an Africanist with nearly four years of experience on the continent.

But first let us look at the social and cultural environment into which I was thrust after several years of wandering about in Africa. The term reverse culture shock comes to mind. The American society in the fall of 1970 was in full dudgeon. It was being asserted that the National Guard operation at Kent State University the previous spring marked the decline of what had come to be known as the "counter-culture." According to one of its self-styled prophets, Abby Hoffman, the counter-culture represented a truly revolutionary era in American society. Consciousness III was a state of mind which would usher in a new cultural lifestyle and thus change the American way of life in fundamental ways. Long hair, bell-bottom trousers and acid rock were but the visible accoutrements of the new culture. Historically, the counter-culture had its roots in the alienation grown out of the Vietnam War and the excesses of a materialist society.

While it was occasionally couched in terms of radical leftist political ideology (Black Panthers, Peace and Freedom Party, etc.), the counter-culture was more often expressed in a vague philosophy of "do-your-thing-ism" which was simply the radicalization of the fundamental American value of individualism.

(The Isley Brothers summed it up in their anthem, "It's yo thang, do what you wanna do.") One need only recall that individualism was a core value of the westward movement across the American frontier in the 1700 and 1800s. Consequently, the system would prove itself quite capable of absorbing, through a process of co-optation, the disparate elements of a movement that was essentially within the mainstream of American politics.

Still, by the fall of 1970 it was not yet clear to all, especially to the fervent ideologues of the New Left, that the counter-culture was but an ephemeral phenomenon — a parenthetic pause as it were — in the history of American society. Even among the less ardent followers of "the Movement", there was a wisp of hope, fueled by the continuing follies of Uncle Sam's involvement in the Vietnam War and the repressive rhetoric of law 'n order espoused by the Spiro Agnews of the Nixon Administration, that the counter-cultural revolution would ignite the population and bring about the Millennium. Evidence of the sad state of affairs could be witnessed every evening on the 6:oo PM news, could it not?

Something would have to give...if only the counter-culture could produce an eloquent spokesman who could articulate its basic truths to the masses, its disparate elements could come together and thus show the lethargic middle class the Way Out.

Such was the situation as I interpreted it upon my return from "the bush" to continue my education in the fall of 1970. To be honest with myself, I should say that my expectations upon returning to academia were marginal. I was firmly convinced that my life experiences outside of academia had been more educational than the education dispensed within. I wasn't expecting any kind of intellectual fulfillment in graduate school. The most that could be hoped for was a relatively benign environment in which to serve my time and emerge within the shortest possible time with the "union card" required by academia to remain within its hallowed halls. As it became readily apparent, however, a benign environment was too much to ask. The University was no longer a place in which to seek truth and experience a community of seekers, as it might have been at some idyllic time in the past. Rather, I would find that it was a place where one was trained for a given profession, initiated into the rites of "scholarship", and pronounced in the end either competent or incompetent to fulfill a particular professional role.

I cannot claim to have been entirely ignorant of the environment I was entering in the fall of 1970. There was my previous graduate experience that had exposed me to the range of approaches within The Discipline. Intellectually, I had felt rather at ease at American University, but then the School of International Service in those days was still pretty much in the backwater of traditionalism. Lectures tended toward the anecdotal recounting of brushes with the political and diplomatic set (e.g., "when I was Jack Kennedy's advisor at Harvard..."). There were references to the Behavioral School, but it was clearly out there somewhere, not at American University. I knew something of Northwestern's reputation in political science, but then I was there because of the African Studies Program. Nosing around the department the first few days, inquiring about individual professors, I began to sense that this was a different tribe. I was a

Lulua entering a Luba compound in the years just after Congolese Independence.

Anticipating that I would find the environment rather unsettling, I sought out professors during the pre-season round of coffee-klatches and presented my case. I was usually assured that there was a wide diversity of interests within the department and that I would surely find my niche. Occasionally the response was candid. In one discussion I described myself as something of an existentialist. That line of thought, my respondent replied, would have to be shelved, at least temporarily during the period of introduction to The Discipline. And he knew exactly what he was talking about, as it turned out, since he conducted the introductory course.

I should have taken his comment far more seriously than I did. Nevertheless, they succeeded during those first few weeks in conveying to me, and I suppose to most of my peers, the idea that we were to be one big happy academic family. The Department encouraged an air of familiarity. It was not to be Dr. So and So, but just plain Jim, John or Dave. After all, we graduate students were "junior colleagues", soon to become full-fledged members of the community. In some cases I was dealing with professors younger than I was, having come back out of the bush at the ripe age of 29. But it was an uneasy familiarity, for we all knew that our "senior colleagues" would have the power of deciding our academic fates.

I would learn within a few weeks of my arrival at Northwestern that it was to be an uncomfortable fit for me. Graduate school was certainly no place to go with pre-conceived notions about society or how to study it. All that would be taken care of for the initiate in the introductory courses. In fact, all those pre-conceived notions would be considered a positive hindrance to be banished, wiped clean to start with a tabula rasa. It was no dishonor to admit to one's peers or to those charged with dispensing education that one's prime motive was to acquire the union card. But it would have to be conceded eventually that there were certain canons of comportment to be followed, certain values to be absorbed.

First, a word about my "pledge class" in Political Science at Northwestern University in the fall of 1970. Nowhere does the law of supply and demand apply more rigorously than in the production of PhDs in the American economy. There were only 21 of us, down from a high of 50 two years previously, the reflection of a general decline in the American economy and a corresponding decrease in the market demand for political scientists. We were in some respects a microcosm of what was being referred to as the counter-culture; the obvious exceptions were there to prove the rule. There were five Blacks (two of them Africans), two women, two Jewish-Americans, and a preponderance of long-haired mid-western WASPs (White, Anglo-Saxon Protestant). The two military men, one still on active duty and the other shortly to resign, were rather more clean-shaven than the rest of us, both in appearance and in expression. We were bound by two required core courses, designed to introduce us to The Discipline, and thus thrown together several times each week.

Some in our class were there because they had received generous grants from the University or other sources, others because of the relatively sound reputation of the department, and others like me who were also attracted by the reputation of the African Studies Program. However, we were to learn quickly that the interdisciplinary African Studies Program was of only marginal interest to the Political Science Department. Few of us had a clear notion of becoming what the Department had in mind for us: research-oriented political scientists. A few, having already received training in The Method, took to the program as ducks to water. Some of us, however, were forever questioning assumptions.

A glimpse at the composition of our pledge class, compared with those preceding and those succeeding it, reveals the social analytic skills of the admissions committee. In previous years the Department had been largely composed of students from the surrounding Midwestern states. What with the social ferment of the late 1960s, however, the ethnic variable was manipulated to admit a substantial number of Jewish students from Eastern states. The number of Blacks varied between one and none. For our class, it is obvious that the race variable was manipulated, to include fully one-fourth Blacks in the class. It proved to be more than the Department had bargained for, since for the most part the Black students brought with them a significantly different set of values; not surprisingly, most of them were attuned to the unique concerns of the Black community. They did not have to be taught the virtue of relevance in social science research.

The Department, on the other hand, was not quite prepared for what it was wont to consider "ethnic politics" which was indeed ironic when one considers the "enlightenment" that brought about manipulation of the ethnic variable. The next year, therefore, brought the manipulation of yet another variable in the selection process: nationality. The class of 1971 brought an influx of foreigners to the Department, although those whose socio-economic background and previous training by and large made was thought to have made them more amenable to the prevailing value system.

What was the prevailing value system anyway? A good social scientist defines his concepts before he makes them operational. Let us attempt to define the value orientation of the Department as it was presented to us in the series of core courses known as D-01, D-02 and D-03. The over-arching philosophical concept that was the key to all that followed was the notion of a social science constructed on the model of the physical or "exact" sciences. Our Bible was Kuhn's Structure of Scientific Revolution and his thesis that each succeeding generation of scholars constructs its own paradigm within which it seeks to build upon a given body of theory, until it is replaced by a new paradigm. With this as a given, it remained for the humble student to find out where the paradigm was and dig in. We were forewarned that new paradigms were usually arrived at only incrementally through the painstaking process of "falsifiability": investigation of all plausible rival hypotheses. In fact, you weren't to be too discouraged if, often as not, you succeeded in proving the null hypothesis. Beware the self-fulfilling prophesy, so prevalent in social science! It was open war on naïve common sense!

Although it was rarely referred to as such, the prevailing paradigm in the Department—and in The Discipline, it seemed—was behaviorism, or behavioralism (the distinction never became clear to me). For it was here at Northwestern that the behavioral persuasion had taken root in the 1950s. Some very big names in The Discipline had been made in our Department, most of them associated in some way with the development of behavioral methods. Most of those names were by now gone or were out to pasture. Consequently, the Department had slipped to a flimsy 14th in national standings. Pretend as they might to ignore it, the prestige factor weighed heavily on the minds of faculty. While there was some dead wood on the faculty, there was also a band of Young Turks bent on restoring the Department to its golden age. Prestige, then, counted for not a little among those who dispensed education to us.

As a citadel of behaviorist thought, the Department could be located within the ancient positivist tradition. Science operated at the level of religion. The spiritual fathers of this tradition could be traced back to August Comte, through the latter-day positivists such Lasswell, Kaplan, Pepper, Zetterberg and Guetzkow. Despite the presence of a handful of faculty who did not fit into the positivist mold, the basic framework was monocultural. There was little room for contending philosophical perspectives.

In my anxious search for terra firma on which to make my intellectual stand, I found myself drawn to phenomenology. Although Northwestern boasted one of the most renowned departments of philosophy dedicated to phenomenology anywhere in the U.S., there was absolutely no link with the positivists within our Department. An interdisciplinary approach would have to be sought within the confines of the behaviorist paradigm. I was drawn to the phenomenological approach. Its most prominent representative was Edmund Husserl whose manifesto was: "If men define a situation as real it becomes real in its consequences." But phenomenology was considered by the articulators of The Discipline to be too vague and old-worldish, and above all non-quantifiable. It really had no place in the modern world of technology and sophisticated methodological techniques. Furthermore, it was viewed as something of an intellectual smokescreen for the avoidance of the more "advanced" modern approaches. It was considered incapable of dealing with the problem of "unintended consequences". So there I was, standing outside the paradigm looking in.

What, then, was the prevailing notion of political theory in the Department? Again, it must be noted that it was a monocultural environment. Pluralist democratic theory was accepted as a given. Our D-01 reading list made no reference whatsoever to socialist, much less Marxist theories, even though outside the Ivory Tower there were legions of Marxists and neo-Marxists marching under their banner. Whenever the name of Marx was invoked, and it was invariably by one of us naïve, unsophisticated students, Marxist/ socialist thought was quickly put down as being an out-dated, deterministic 19th century model unworthy of serious consideration. This, too, was chalked up as an intellectual smokescreen thrown up by young would-be radicals to mask their alienation. What the world needs, according to the pluralist format, are increasingly sophisticated models of a democratic society to account for the ever-increasing complexity of interests. The economic variable (Marxism) was certainly incapable of explaining all, or even most, of the phenomena in the modern world. This theoretical approach was in keeping with the premise that each problem should eventually be subjected to multivariate analysis.

The student, then, was to be initiated into these notions within the Department. In the first instance he/she should be capable of separating fact from value, of living up to the Weberian dictum of separation of disinterested, objective research from the netherworld of individual bias and value orientation. Since political scientists are in the business of studying politics, this is all the more reason why they should be trained to check their personal values at the door when embarking upon a research project. Otherwise, it would be better to "just go do journalism."

And what of the problem of "relevance", the chief criticism leveled at the behaviorists by their traditionalist and neo-traditionalist enemies? Well, one should learn to wear two hats, one for conducting disinterested, objective research, and the other—after all the results have been tabulated -for proclaiming one's personal bias and prescribing policy choices to those in authority. The successful scholar allows his data to speak for itself. If faithfully followed, the canons of reliability, verifiability, and replication will lead to sound theory construction over time. Speculative theory must be condemned to the realm of metaphysics, a realm forbidden to all True Social Scientists. In this respect, an ever graver shortcoming of the Marxists than their economic determinism was their adherence to the vague metaphysical notion of the withering away of the state.

If the student has successfully absorbed the rules of The Method and learned to wear the first hat, that is, to have mastered the systems analytical approach, what is the nature of the second hat? It is relatively safe to argue that a majority of students who did stick with the core program and proceeded to the level of dissertation research and developed competence in The Method were quite happy wearing the first hat. On the other hand, the Department had in recent years admitted into the fold a number of students who were considerably more competent in The Method than many of the faculty. In fact, they had The Method down cold, spending countless hours in the computer center with reams of data. But much to the horror of the

Department, it awoke in the spring of 1970 to learn that it had re-created Frankenstein's monster. The Model Methodologists used The Method to beat the Department over the head in the name of rebellion. They chose to strike at what they considered to be the stodgy liberal paternalism of the Department. The second hat they chose to wear was anarchy. Their purpose was nothing less than the destruction of the Departmental decision-making process dominated by a handful of powerful professors, and the inclusion of students in that process. They went so far as to throw up barricades to the Political Science building. If their conditions were not met, the rebels were perfectly willing to bring down The System.

Linked as their action was to student protests throughout the country over Nixon's bombing of Cambodia and the killings at Kent State, the protests at Northwestern should be viewed through the broader lens of an American society in turmoil. Although these events took place a few months before my arrival at Northwestern, by the fall of 1970 the corporate structure that was Northwestern University remained largely unscathed. Armageddon had been avoided. Within the Department there were several visible repercussions. The Head of the Department retreated from office to resume his teaching duties. In any case, the role of the Department Head was mostly ceremonial, since real decision-making was not done transparently. The liberal-pluralist Departmental ideology had been shaken by the black flag of anarchy.

But just as American society managed to cope with the generalized student rebellion, so too did the Department recognize in the student rebellion the basic strain of radical individualism and thus attempt to co-opt the rebels. Their concerns were essentially personal, alienated as they were from society and from the University. Offspring of middle and upper-middle classes, the Young Methodologists could hardly be considered Marxists. They had little contact with the toiling masses, nor were their basic values all that different from the bourgeoisie against whom they protested. They were mainly interested in radicalizing individual freedom and exercising power.

So it was that by the time of our arrival on campus in the fall of 1970, the liberal Departmental machinery was busy implementing a program of co-optation known by the radical-sounding name of The Commune (ironic indeed!). In theory, The Commune was a mechanism whereby students were to be involved in deciding who would have what teaching assistant positions and how the Departmental financial pie would be apportioned. Its basic assumption was that by granting students more participation in decision-making, they would develop a greater feeling of belonging, indeed a spirit of "community". Unfortunately for us, first-year students were excluded from The Commune because assistantships were reserved for second-year students and beyond. We had to be content with hearing the members extol the virtues of The Commune which we would inherit the following year, if indeed we survived the initiation rites.

Political Scientists like to say that they study who gets what, when and how. In practice, The Commune worked something like a colony that had just received its political independence but was still bound economically to the metropole. Those who controlled la chose publique had already proven themselves loyal to The System and thus enjoyed a privileged position within it. The distribution of scarce resources went first to those closest to the real seat of authority, that is to say, The Department. It was not uncommon for fourth or fifth-year students, technically excluded from teaching assistantships, to continue receiving goodies from The Commune, since they were well established within the system. In our second year our class attained something of a majority. Having just suffered the humiliation of the first-year program, we set about attempting to democratize The Commune to include the incoming students, whose needs were usually greatest. Proof of this could be seen in the fact that only about half of each incoming class survived to the second year.

It was an excellent experience in the dynamics of underdevelopment. We fell to squabbling amongst ourselves and with the senior members of The Commune over questions of principle and purpose. The old-timers urged us to look to our own self-interest, not to cut off the nose to spite the face. Whatever feeling of community there might have been was dissolved in the pursuit of self- interest. The Commune drifted back to the status quo ante. My own feeling of belonging to The Commune must have corresponded roughly with the feeling a prisoner has toward serving on the prison library committee.

———

What was it that was so alienating about the Northwestern experience to me? There were of course the secondary factors that nearly everyone complained of: the cold social climate in the graduate school environment, the even colder winds blowing off Lake Michigan in the winter and the generally stultifying cultural milieu of Evanston. All of these could be dealt with, given the proper amount of personal adjustment. One simply had to keep in mind that this was not Berkeley or Madison.

There were other factors perhaps common to the graduate experience. In the first instance, graduate school is by its very nature a process of individuation. It is a time for personal intellectual development. To be successful in this endeavor one is compelled to limit all other aspects of personal development: physical, social, aesthetic and cultural. It is probably rare for the average graduate student to overcome feelings of social anomie in a big campus environment while spending a large portion of the time in the library or computer center. The typical graduate student rarely gets the gratification derived from seeing his research efforts published. Most often it would be under the professor's name in any event. He turns out papers with the suspicion that the busy professor will scarcely read them.

In a sense the graduate student is something like a factory worker, alienated from his labor. In most cases it is a period of forced unemployment, of accepting hand-outs from various funding sources or else going deep into debt. Like the factory worker, the graduate student does not own his own labor. He is rather like the indentured servant working off the years until he is "freed" by obtaining the sacred diploma. His fate is in the hands of professors who in turn owe their allegiance to the corporate structure that is the University. The fate of the professor is in turn determined by his connection with publishing houses and the departmental fathers who decide on whether or not he is to obtain tenure.

The graduate student, at any rate, is at the bottom of the pecking order, the "nigger" of the University. He may become the unwitting tool of a professor who uses his research talents for his own ends.

Worse still, he may not be shepherded by any professor, in which case he is let out to pasture on his own in a kind of academic limbo. This is often the department's way of letting the weak student—who hasn't figured it out for himself—know that the jig is up. Hardly anyone fails in graduate school. Rather one is more likely to deselect himself. There are numerous subtle institutional ways of easing out the student who doesn't "fit". The not so subtle first step may be the repeated question, "Well if you don't like our method, why did you come here anyway?"

As the weeks became months and we plodded through the endless reading list on the philosophy of science, I became more and more ill at ease. There was no subject matter that inspired my enthusiasm. The early conviviality of the classroom frequently turned toward confrontation. Any questioning of the nature and extent of the syllabus was treated as an affront to the very program. The usual response was that once we had endured all four of the core courses we would be free to choose the theoretical and methodological approach that suited us. Then would come the rather threatening question: if you didn't care for the orientation of the department, why did you bother to come here? (Implication: wouldn't you be happier in a second-rate department somewhere else?) The onus, therefore, was on the student to absorb the tenets of the behavioral stance before becoming worthy of critiquing it.

I must confess that this was an atmosphere that created a great deal of anxiety in me, if not to say a sense of inadequacy. Perhaps this was the very root cause of my alienation. Each of us dealt with the challenge at our own individual level. For some it was all very boring. The temptation for them was to sleep in on those cold mornings and do the minimum required for the course. A considerable number simply disappeared from the program within the year. Others embraced the behavioral paradigm with gusto and helped defend it against the traditionalists. Still others recognized it as a useful tool to be used with discretion. To me the entire format represented a threat to my intellectual well-being as well as my personal values. I could not help attacking it at a visceral level. The behaviorist behemoth with its emphasis on ever-higher levels of abstraction symbolized the de-personalization of society. It ignored unique events in human history. Its demand for the strict observance of objectivity required that the researcher be alien to the object of his study. Worst of all, there was the tendency to ignore the fact that science, however objectively conducted, was often at the service of repressive political forces. How could they pretend that a disinterested value-free social science could ever exist? I wondered.

As a result of my constant intervention as the devil's advocate in class, I earned the reputation of an unreconstructed intellectual Neanderthal. I was the proverbial square peg in a round hole. Others who had more fully comprehended the behaviorist enterprise and recognized its more blatant misuses were more credible in their criticism of it. They were listened to with a good deal more seriousness than I was. Mine was a knee-jerk reaction. They could be more "objective" in their criticisms. Such was not my case. My friends good-naturedly pointed out to me that my behavior in class was entirely predictable. Ironic, I suppose, since the ultimate goal of the behavioral persuasion was to predict behavior...

The anecdotal or case study approach to the study of social phenomena was especially frowned upon. One of the most denigrating epithets used to describe a bad example of social science was "journalistic". After one particularly heated class debate on the relative merits of less formal methods, including participant observation favored by anthropologists, the book was closed on the subject with a pointed comment by the professor. If you were "going to do a Norman Mailer (with reference to his eye-witness account of the recent march on the Pentagon) you should not be calling yourself a social scientist." Subjectivity went against all the canons of good social science.

The required course in statistics was my bete noire. Numbers of any kind had always posed a problem for me. Although the course was poorly conducted (even those who breezed through it said so) it was geared to the practical use of statistics in social science research. I had to concede that a firm grasp of statistics was a useful key to the comprehension of our technological society. This realization did nothing whatsoever to ease the pain of sorting out mean from median and fathoming the technique of factor analysis. Despite Herculean efforts, I had to face the very real prospect of failing a course for the first time in my life. But, by the grace of Science, or perhaps a simple miscalculation in the grading of my final exam, I received a gentleman C in the course. (Only later did I learn that in graduate school a C was roughly equivalent to an F at the undergraduate level.) Whatever! The C that I received in statistics, with humble gratitude, meant that I would not have to repeat the course. A couple of my classmates were not so sanguine. In fact, my good friend Ndiva Kofele-Kale glumly remarked that the course had been a threat to his manhood. To those of us who knew him (male and female), that was saying a great deal!

If one were to reach for a common denominator to describe the general sense of alienation that settled in on our pledge class of 1970, it would have to do with the lack of "relevance" we saw in the social scientific enterprise. We shared, I would say, a common sense of urgency about the need to address obvious social problems. Whatever our conception of social science was, we sensed that it was not a powerful enough tool for bringing about social change. We were being asked to be objective in our analysis of social problems without being committed to any particular program of social change. Social science proposes; the public power disposes. In effect, we were expected to place our personal values in cold storage for however long it would take to become technically competent to analyze social problems. It was the form of alienation that goes by the name of powerlessness. I recall having thought more than once, and finally having blurted out in one of those frustrating class sessions: "Here we are, fiddling while Rome burns."

That common sense of frustration finally reached a culmination during the winter quarter of our first year when a group of us got together and wrote a tract which carried the rather presumptuous title of Humanist Manifesto No 1. (To my recollection there was never a second manifesto.) It was written in the rhetoric of rebellion, and virtually all our classmates were signatories to it. The Manifesto presented a litany of complaints as well as demands (suggestions?) for curriculum reform. It was typed up, run off and presented at the next class meeting. The harshness of the language, as much as the content, produced a boomerang effect. We had intended that it be discussed in class with a view toward determining which, if any, of its proposals could be acted upon. Instead, the Manifesto was interpreted as a personal criticism of the two professors who were conducting the core courses. Discussion immediately degenerated into name-calling and personal insults. Three of our pledge-mates subsequently got up and quietly left the room. The rest of us sat limp in disbelief as Professor Jim's temper reached fever pitch. Then, in a moment of blinding irony, he turned to the blackboard and resumed his scheduled lecture on...the techniques for measurement of political alienation!

Frankly, I have no clear recollection of any concrete reforms which emerged from the Manifesto. We had no plans for backing up our "demands" with any type of boycott. We were far too disunited in our attitudes toward the program for that. The net effect rather was to harden existing attitudes and dispel any notions of creating one big happy family. From there on, each of us who stayed on went about the grim business of assuring our own academic survival.

A somewhat less alienating experience was my involvement in creating an African Studies journal of Northwestern students. Entitled The Pan-Africanist, the publication first saw the light of day in March of 1971 during my second semester. As an associate editor, I was a member of the executive committee, and of course a contributor to the first issue. The journal grew out of the confrontation between traditionalist and radical Africanists at the Montreal and Boston meetings of the African Studies Association. We associated ourselves with the latter group. The editorial stated that "we do not pretend to be 'objective,' and mere scholarship will not be our main aim."

There was a certain middle-classness about the Northwestern milieu that made me realize that I did not belong to this class. At best, there was an attitude of noblesse oblige, the notion that political science might be used as an instrument to help the less privileged classes in some vague way. At worst it was an intellectual smugness that proclaimed the right to make a living from the study of social conflict without the slightest commitment to social causes: the idea that the social scientist should be in the world but not of it. This attitude could usually be traced to a comfortable middle or upper-middle class background and education at prep schools and undergraduate work at the better universities. Northwestern seemed to be a haven for this type of social profile, both among students and faculty. It was accompanied, often as not, by a fat graduate scholarship in the case of students or research grants in the case of faculty, granted of course on the basis of merit rather than need.

It remained for my fellow students, the Model Methodologist-anarchists, to instruct me in the meaning of class differences. Their credo was a kind of Ayn Rand individualism under the banner of anarchy. They were disdainful of all traditional forms of authority and societal mores. They believed in the great I Am.

Their goal was to break radically with the traditional, aided by sophisticated technology. Their program included zero-population growth (ZPG) and a kind of communal life style of like-minded intellectuals devoted to the freest expression of the individual. I listened carefully, but didn't buy it.

Dissertation research

Having painted a rather bleak picture of my life in graduate school, I should hasten to add that it had its redeeming features. I made some good friends and enjoyed the company of my classmates. In the summer of 1971 I moved into graduate student housing on the Northwestern campus. Down the hall from me was a young couple with whom I became well acquainted: Bill Owen and his Ghanaian wife Aisatu (Ayi) and their four year old son Tchaka. Because of his fascination with trucks and cars I dubbed him "Tchaka the Truck" and it seems to have stuck. We have remained friends over the years, our paths crossing periodically.

With all of this angst as the backdrop, my first year paper represented a monumental effort to demonstrate my newly acquired understanding of The Method. I designed a questionnaire aimed at the African student population at Northwestern, examining their attitudes about the U.S. Well, after all, we Americans had been studying African societies all these years, why shouldn't the African have his word on American society? The survey was intended to shine the spotlight on the issues that appeared to be rending the American body politic, rather than exposing traditional African tribal societies. There was Vietnam, racism, the counter-cultural revolution and a growing awareness of class divisions here at home. What did African students think about all this? My questionnaire was carefully crafted to capture their opinions on these weighty issues.

So what did my study accomplish? In the first instance, more than one of the African respondents (and non-respondents) suggested that I was probably working for the Central Intelligence Agency! Horrors! Here it comes again! In the Peace Corps we Volunteers were frequently cast as CIA agents, a charge we often tried to answer with sanctimonious denials which were often as not met with a knowing smile, or sneer. But my own classmates? They should by now be aware of my own anti-establishment attitudes. Why should I have to defend my good intentions with them? So there you have it! The conundrum of social science is the distinction between the observer and the observed. Check your values at the door. Observers, don't let the observed see you sweat! Draw your sample, collect the data and split. Let the chips fall where they may.

That was not the bad news. No, the bad news was the casual acceptance of my first year paper. It was just okay, and was accepted for a Master's Degree (normally a termina degree for those not going on to the PhD). But my skimpy Chi-squares would not pass the test for work at the PhD level. If you insist upon forging ahead toward a doctorate, you should give up the charade of applying quantitative measures to your research and go for the traditional stuff. Phffff!

And so I did. I set about designing a dissertation proposal based on my experience in the Congo. Yes, proposing the very type of field research I had railed against the past year and a half that is, Africanists making a living out of studying Africa! But if I were to find my way to the finish line I would have to pick a topic I knew something about. In my case, that would entail looking back onto my Africa experience and trying to make something of it.

The government of the Congo under President Mobutu decided upon a program of nationalization of all property and institutions in the early 1970s, which came to include the system of higher education. I had taught at the Free University of the Congo, a Protestant institution, and was aware of the two other universities in the country, one created by Catholic authorities in Kinshasa and the other the creation of the Official University of the Congo in Elizabethville (soon to become Lubumbashi), a public University. All three were being brought into one national system under the control of the government which would be called the National University of Zaire (l'UNAZA) when Mobutu changed the name of the country. With this experiential base, an extended review of the literature and a dogged determination to persevere (what Vera Mae had called stick-to-it-iveness), I plunged ahead fashioning a dissertation proposal.

Having transferred credits to Northwestern from my Masters program at American University, I could now see myself on the fast track. After two semesters of intensive initiation into the Northwestern program, I dedicated the summer of 1971 to taking courses and preparing for comprehensive exams, a small matter that needed to be dealt with before defending a dissertation research. Fully aware that I would not be able to demonstrate the requisite quantitative skills on the methodology questions on the exam, I began to steep myself in an altogether different paradigm: phenomenology. Ironically, Northwestern University Press was well known for its publications on phenomenology, but it was largely ignored by the earnest quantifiers in the Political Science Department. I read and read, soaking up Edmund Husserl's works and latter-day phenomenologists (mainly anthropologists) who sought to apply this philosophy to social science research. My frequent references to the literature of phenomenology among my peers made me the butt of good-natured ribbing, often with the intentional mis-pronunciation of the term!

In the fall of 1971 I took the comprehensive exams and was pronounced fit to carry on. I was on solid ground when addressing the basic concepts of political theory, contending approaches and demonstrating my grasp of the philosophical underpinnings of paradigm shifts. Truth be told, my passing of the exams was probably a testimony to the Department's stated acceptance of diversity, for which I was certainly grateful! I could now glimpse the light of day. I then requested that I be allowed to defend my dissertation research proposal. Request granted. And so it was that I presented my dissertation design and plans for conducting field research in the Congo to an intimate gathering of faculty and peers in Africa House, a venue rarely frequented by most of the professors in the Department. It was a largely pro forma affair, with the toughest methodological questions coming from my classmates. It is likely that some might have been a bit jealous of me, since I was exiting the campus after a residence of no more than sixteen months. But I saw this as a testimony to my single-minded determination!

Well then, how to finance field research in the Congo? My dirty little secret was that the NDFL grant I received for the study of Swahili at Northwestern provided a nice little nest-egg for field research. A Tanzanian professor of Swahili tested my comprehension of the language, acquired while living and teaching in eastern Congo. He assigned me a B grade, which I happily accepted, realizing that the language I learned while in the Congo (Swahili ya poli, or bush Swahili) was considered by proper coastal Swahili speakers to be a kind of bastardized tongue. But the NDFL grant would not quite be enough to support six to 12 months of field research.

My luck seemed to take a giant leap forward when Dr. Gwendolyn Carter, Director of the African Studies Program and a member-to-be of my dissertation committee, casually asked me in the lobby of Africa House one day whether I might be interested in a one semester teaching position at the University of Southern California (USC). Interested??? Somehow the stars were aligned just right, since that job would allow me to save up sufficient funds to complement the NDFL grant money. California, here I come!

Marriage to Dawn Marie Kepets   *January 1972*

Sometime in the spring of 1971 my classmate Ndiva Kofele-Kale introduced me to Dawn Kepets, his erstwhile classmate at Beloit College. We were walking down Sheridan Road and she was on the other side, coming from her office at Kendall College, a small private University down the road. Kale and Dawn swapped a few war stories from their Beloit days, and we went our separate ways. Later that summer I chanced to meet Dawn again on the Lake Michigan beach near the Northwestern campus. She talked about her job as a recruiter and admissions counselor at Kendall, quite a nice position for one just out of college. Dawn drove a late model car provided by the college and lived in an attractive apartment...on Hull Terrace! All this was a jarring contrast to my bohemian life style: I was still riding a motorcycle and living in the attic of Dave and Sandy Horne, a private home in Evanston that had become my home-away-from-home, known to everyone as Horne House.

My social life since arriving in Evanston had heretofore been marginal to say the least. So the opportunity to spend time with an attractive young woman while entrapped in the pressure-cooker environment of graduate school was a welcome prospect. Within a short time we were dating, such as it was, given the heavy demands of study on my time and her professional commitments. I soon learned that Dawn came from a Jewish family with Eastern European origins and had grown up in Euclid, Ohio. An only child, Dawn's father earned his living as an insurance salesman and at one time had entertained ambitions of becoming an engineer. Instead, he flew missions "over the hump" from India to China during World War

II and never had the opportunity to go to college. Dawn's mother stayed in the home, tending to wifely chores and raising Dawn. It was a very close-knit nuclear family of three, plus a grandfather, an uncle and two male cousins. Indeed, the Kepets family name was in danger of extinction.

I was quite comfortable relating to Dawn's Jewishness, having formed close ties with several Jewish friends during my Peace Corps days. For her part, Dawn seemed to share my interest in other peoples and cultures. She was at Beloit College during a time of social ferment, and Beloit enjoyed a reputation for being on the cutting edge of the social and cultural "revolution". There was a high premium placed on experiential learning, especially for those like Dawn majoring in anthropology. Beloit provided her with a very intensive study abroad experience at Robert College in Istanbul, and she came away with some life-long Turkish friends and a fondness for things Turkish. The experience seemed to have enriched her life in a way similar to my Peace Corps experience.

Our relationship had scarcely been tested when the moment of truth arrived. That moment came when I announced that I had been offered a one-semester teaching position at USC. And then I would be off again to the Congo to do dissertation research. So we were at the cross-roads: it was either a time for tearful goodbyes or for a more permanent commitment. I was excited about living for a while in southern California, land of the Okies, and the prospect of returning to the Congo. For Dawn this would be a venture into the Great Unknown. She assured me that she was prepared to take that leap of faith. So it was that we decided to get married in Evanston, only a week before I was to report to USC to begin teaching for the spring semester. We had only a couple of weeks in which to plan the event that would take place on a bitter cold day in mid-January 1972.

The venue for the ceremony/celebration was quickly decided upon: it would be in the living room of Horne House. The Horne family was up for it. Any excuse for a party would do! The exchange of vows was conducted by none other than Rev. Richard Prosser, the very same preacher/social revolutionary whom I had encountered in Kinshasa nearly three years before. Kale (from Cameroun) served as Best Man while Aurora D'Souza, a Goan from Kenya and Dawn's best friend, was Bridesmaid. It was something of a cultural kaleidoscope.

Those present for the ceremony were our parents and a few close friends. The celebration that followed, also in Horne House, was attended by a lively contingent of Africans and my graduate school classmates.

To Southern California and back to the Congo   1972-1973

The very next day after our marriage we were off in a rental van packed with our modest earthly possessions, including Dawn's precious potted plants, for the cross-country trip from Chicago to Los Angeles. Our stop-over at the Grand Canyon constituted a close approximation of a honeymoon. My most vivid recollection of the trip was the close scrutiny given to the potted plants by the border authorities when we crossed the Nevada border into California. Within a few days we were ensconced in an apartment and I began teaching a course in international relations and another in comparative politics in the Political Science Department in the gilded ghetto that was USC. Dawn found a job teaching English as a second language. We motored around L.A. on my 150 cc Yamaha motorcycle that had survived Chicago winters.

The semester at USC came and went quickly. The first weeks I tried correcting the departmental secretary when she referred to me as Dr. Hull. After a while I gave up; in any case, it had a nice ring to it and I told myself it wouldn't be long before I would have earned the title! Much of my spare time was spent in the Africana section of the UCLA library, fortifying my literature review on African universities and government policies toward them. I managed to get myself invited to a (non-paying) adjunct faculty research position back at the Free University of the Congo, soon to become the Kisangani campus of l'UNAZA (l'Universite nationalize du Zaire), beginning in June 1972. That very transformation from private Protestant University to government controlled national institution would be the subject of my research. In place of the cast of Protestant missionaries running the University, I would find a new team of Congolese in charge, appointed by and serving at the pleasure of the Mobutu government.

My field research in Kisangani was a rather lonely task, entailing as it did scrounging for documents on the University's decade of existence and interviewing old-timers. There was no tidy archive room where such documents were kept by a conscientious archivist.

And the new Congolese administrators, several of whom I knew from my previous residency there, were not too keen to open themselves up to inquiry, a reflection of the nationalist sentiment that governed the University. By this time, the University was a highly politicized place in which all academic authorities were obliged to be members of the ruling MPR political party. Some of my old friends and colleagues were still around, but many of the expatriates were long gone. The University was not quite the fun place it had been for me two years before.

I should note that it was especially difficult for Dawn since she had no job or professional role. Most of the wives of university professors were themselves teaching or conducting research. Their roles were thus fairly well defined. It was a very male-dominated environment in which women had to fight for respect. Much to her credit, Dawn set about honing her cross-cultural skills. To the amazement of our friends, and to the derision of some, she began baking peanut-butter cookies and taking them to sell in the African market. This was of course not about getting rich! Rather, it was about being a participant observer in the fine tradition of anthropologists. And yet, it was not formal research that would eventually result in an advanced academic degree. The market women took her in and adopted Dawn, calling her their sister. They offered advice as to the setting of her prices and how to market her product. They would even tell their own clients that they had to try one of Dawn's cookies. Dawn and her cookies were a smash hit with the Africans in the Kisangani market. The Europeans—and that included many of the Americans who shopped in the market—tended to ignore her, seemingly embarrassed that one of their own should be engaged in such pedestrian endeavors.

After nearly half a year in Kisangani, we moved on to the second university campus in Lubumbashi. This was the capital of the Katanga Province famous for its abundant supply of copper and cobalt, once the seat of a secessionist movement. It was more of a city than Kisangani, with a distinct European flare about it. Here the climate was more temperate and there was a longer history of Belgian presence than in Kisangani. We stayed in the University guest quarters, such as they were, and made a few new friends there. By now we were already running tight on funds. It was clear that my field research would have to be cut short so we began to husband our resources ever more closely. After a concerted effort to procure university documents in Lubumbashi we again moved on, this time to the capital city of Kinshasa, home of the Louvanium University. Founded by the Catholics, Louvanium was intended as a replica of Louvain University in Belgium. Here we were also fortunate to be housed on campus, located on a hill high above the din and dust of the city. (Faculty and students referred to their University affectionately as la colline inspire (the inspired hill.)

The early spring of 1973 found us back on the campus of Northwestern University. I had carted off boxes of files and documents from my field research and it now remained for me to get on with the gritty business of churning out a dissertation. With no distractions other than this, I hunkered down in our apartment in North Chicago and assigned myself a daily production quota of five type-written pages. It was a long hot summer. But by the fall I was ready to present and defend my dissertation, which I did successfully just over three years from the time I entered Northwestern as a graduate student. The PhD diploma would carry the date of 1974. Almost as valuable to me as the degree itself was the Patient Tuchus (a Yiddish term referring to one's backside) Award provided to me by Dawn for the countless hours I had spent sitting at desk! I would soon find out exactly how valuable the doctoral degree was.

During the late summer and fall I began sending out applications for teaching and administrative positions to universities all over the U.S. The response was, to say the least, disappointing. There was scarcely a nibble, leading me to wonder whether it had been worth all the effort poured into obtaining the degree. Of course I knew that I was not exactly the Poster Child of the Northwestern Political Science Department, but it was to be hoped that a doctorate from Northwestern would somehow be recognized in the marketplace. And then, by some strange fluke, the Vice Chancellor of the National University (l'UNAZA) campus in Lubumbashi chanced to pass through Northwestern recruiting for teaching faculty. He was the same US-educated gentleman who was serving as Vice Chancellor of the Kisangani campus while I was doing field research there. He recalled that I had taught English when I first went to Kisangani and asked if I could come back and resume teaching English. The humiliation! After all that work to become a certified Political Scientist! I told him that I was only willing to return to Lubumbashi to teach Political Science. He demurred, and I thus began the tedious process of actually getting hired to teach Political Science by the University.

Lubumbashi, Zaire   *1974-1975*

Thus began my official career as an academic upon arrival back in Lubumbashi in January 1974. Once again I found myself surrounded by Americans, a veritable cabal in the Political Science Department under funding by the Rockefeller Foundation. The Dean of the Faculty was none other than Crawford Young, the distinguished Africanist from the University of Wisconsin and foremost specialist on the politics of the Congo. Several of his former students had joined him on the faculty in Lubumbashi. Indeed, several of the Zairians in the Social Science Faculty were American trained. It was clear that the Rockefeller Foundation aimed at having a significant impact on the University with its support for a critical mass of American academics. I was the lone American in the Political Science Department not under Rockefeller auspices. As a direct hire of the government of Zaire, my paycheck, when it came, was from the Rectorate of the National University in Kinshasa.

With my newly-minted doctorate, I took up my appointment in Political Science. Now what? All the classes at l'UNAZA-Lubumbashi were taught in French, the official language of the former colonial power, Belgium, and now the official language of Zaire. Okay, so I had developed relative proficiency in French during my earlier residencies in the country. And I was fully aware of the nuances between the French of the French and that spoken by the Belgians. But I had never had a course in French, so grammar and spelling were not my forte!

The courses I was assigned to teach included Introduction to Political Science, Theory of International Relations and Raw Materials in International Trade. Of course, these were all subjects that held a certain fascination for me and about which I had some knowledge. But I would quickly discover that there were no textbooks available for any of these courses, nor was there the semblance of a syllabus left behind by previous instructors. Furthermore, in the fine European tradition, the professor was expected to stand in front of the class and dictate, word for word, (cours magistraux) what the student should know that day. The serious student was expected to write down virtually every word out of the professor's mouth.

Within a few days I frantically set about putting together lecture notes, usually attempting to translate materials from my own English language sources into something resembling French.

And then there I was, standing at the podium in front of two to three hundred Zairian students in a large amphitheater where I could hear my voice echo off the walls. Needless to say, not all of them were pleased to be addressed by an American in a halting version of the language of Voltaire! Humor was my saving grace. If I could only manage to tell one or two funny stories to go along with the ponderous material on the political theory of Plato, Aristotle and Machiavelli, I could make it through the class. Sometimes there were loud cat-calls and hoots from the audience whenever I butchered the language. Some students would walk out when they were sorely offended by my egregious mistakes. Yes, they saw me sweat!

Not since my Peace Corps training days had I been so tested. I had to ask myself if I was really up to the challenge of teaching in French, never mind whether I covered material that was of any interest to the students or to which they could relate. Night after night I pored over whatever sources I could find in order to come up with lecture notes for the following lecture. So I was ecstatic whenever one or two students would come up to me after class and ask serious questions about the lecture. I shared a small office with Prof. David Gould, a fellow political scientist and Rockefeller grantee with sterling French language skills and a firm grasp of his subject matter. We became good friends and maintained contact long after our tour in Zaire was over. David would later run a very popular management training program for francophone Africans at the University of Pittsburgh for several years afterward. Sadly, he was among those who perished on the PanAm flight over Lockerbie in 1988 on his way back from a trip to Mali.

I must not paint too bleak a picture of the Lubumbashi period. Our living quarters were quite nice. Dawn and I found a very pleasant place to live, a portion of the former residence of an Italian family that had fled the country in the wake of nationalization. An urban farm, the property had been taken over by a Zairian national during Mobutu's campaign to return the country into the hands of native sons. The new proprietor, whom we never saw, was only interested in collecting his rent from the University. Many of my colleagues from Kisangani days were now in the Faculty of Social Sciences, following the consolidation of university functions under the nationalization program.

Dawn and I were fortunate in making several good friends, among them a young couple, Allen and Kit Roberts, who were anthropologists from the University of Chicago. Kit and Al were gearing up to head upcountry to conduct field research in a village on Lake Tanganyika. Several months after they left Lubumbashi and disappeared into the bush, I went on a safari to visit them. This entailed a 24-hour ride in a pirogue (dugout canoe) on the lake. It was quite the adventure, but well worth it to see the remarkable ingenuity they brought with them to their enterprise. We have remained friends through the years.

For her part, Dawn became involved with a group called Mwondo Theatre, African thespians and dancers directed and managed by Denis and Jill Franco. Denis was also Jewish, having grown up in Tunisia before immigrating to France. Jill was garden-variety American, raised in a military family and having lived in France for several years. They had three small children who helped teach Dawn and me French since they were not entirely proficient in their mother tongue. Denis and Jill were steeped in French language and culture and provided us a welcome window onto the world of the arts. Dawn spent countless hours with the Mwondo actors, helping out with the design of costumes and stage management.

During that time Lubumbashi was still a pleasant town with citified pretensions. During its glory days as Elizabethville, capital of the Copper Belt, the city enjoyed considerable prosperity. Even in the mid-1970s the nationalized copper company, GECAMINES, kept the local economy humming. Those fortunate to have jobs at GECAMINES were decidedly well off. But the process of nationalization—Africanization—of all private property boded ill for Zaire. As the foreign business people (mainly Belgians, Pakistanis, Greeks, Portuguese and Lebanese) were forced to hand over their property and enterprises, the Zairians who acquired them by virtue of their standing in the Party ran them into the ground. The local economy began to first show tattered edges and then serious decline. It was a highly politicized environment, and although we did not often experience personal animosity, we could sense the anti-foreigner sentiment engendered by the many speeches of President Mobutu. By the end of my second year at l'UNAZA-Lubumbashi, just as I was beginning to feel more comfortable lecturing in French, Dawn and I decided that it would be best to head back to the U.S. in the summer of 1975.

———— .

References

Hull, Galen Spencer (1971) "African Studies in Perspective," in *The Pan-*

Africanist (journal of students in the Program of African Studies at Northwestern University (No 1, Vol. 1, March).

Chapter 9

My Life as a Consultant, 1976-1998: Beltway Banditry and Social Entrepreneurship

"A consultant is a guy who borrows your watch to tell you what time it is."

Anonymous

So what's a returned Peace Corps Volunteer to do if his efforts to find a respectable job as a diplomat, professor, bureaucrat, or... lobbyist come to naught? This, alas, was the question I had to ask myself in the bleak days following my return from Zaire, after two years of teaching in the University there. Well, of course, look for a consulting gig with the Peace Corps itself! I had applied for jobs as Peace Corps Country Director, my ambition since my Volunteer days. At one point I got through several rounds of interviews for positions in French-speaking Africa. But then there was an election, ousting Democrat Jimmy Carter and bringing Republican Ronald Reagan to the White House. My chances of obtaining any Peace Corps staff assignment quickly evaporated as the Reagan folks began appointing their own people. This is the way Washington works.

Little did I imagine that my experience as a Peace Corps Volunteer would lead to a career as an international development consultant! Indeed, such a career path was never on my radar screen. Diplomatic service, university administration or teaching, perhaps work with an international organization, yes! But management consulting? I had never known anyone who professed such a profession, much less did I know what it entailed. Let us just say that I backed into working as a consultant by default, having knocked on the front door of numerous organizations and agencies I thought might have need of a person such as myself with cross-cultural experience and language skills to boot. To no avail! There were thousands of folks of my ilk walking the streets of Washington DC in the mid-1970s, and probably many more since. Indeed, it has been suggested that the Peace Corps cache has become nearly a pre-requisite for those wishing to pursue international careers.

There being no honorable jobs to come by for a PhD with glittering credentials in 1976, the winter of my discontent, I turned to the short-term fix. Thus it was that I found myself accepting short-term assignments and defining myself willy-nilly as a hired-gun, ready to pack my bags and travel to wherever.

I would venture to say that a whole generation of ex-Volunteers such as myself wandered into this profession, by default. Our resumes shared space in the files of multiple consulting firms and private voluntary organizations (PVOs) looking for expertise in the latest development fad. During extended periods I would work as an employee of a management consulting firm, a PVO or university consortium. These entities were distinguishable more by size than anything else. That is to say, small start-up consulting firms had much more in common with smaller private voluntary organizations than with large consulting firms. Often as not, I would find myself working for minority-owned firms eligible for "set-aside" contracts with Federal agencies. Our task was to keep an eye out for solicitations that specified the requirement of a minority sub-contract partner. At other times I would be shopping my services as a free-lance consultant to whichever firm or organization could use me.

As it turns out, the largest segment of my professional career would be spent in this grey area, vaguely defined as "consulting". To many folks consulting appears as a less than honorable profession. I would become a "Beltway Bandit", a person who earns his living in Washington DC as a consultant. It was only later that I would understand that the term "Beltway Bandit" included folks like us. The term is likely derived from the fact that many of the management consulting firms and contractors in the area are located along the corridors of Interstate 495 beltway that circles Washington DC Those that do business with the Pentagon, for example, are often strategically located within striking distance of the Defense Department.

As for the "bandit" part of the moniker, it was most likely derived from the image that hard-working civil service employees have of private sector operatives, always trying to squeeze out a higher profit margin in contracts. ("Hang on to your wallets; here come the consultants.") To be sure, Beltway Bandit has become a catch-all term that applies as much to the do-gooder private voluntary organizations (many of which are really located downtown along the K Street corridor or on Capitol Hill) as it does to the military-industrial hangers-on. The one thing they all have in common is that they hustle federal government contracts and grants. Some pay big bucks to lobbyists to represent their interests on Capitol Hill. Others rely on their networks of church or farm organizations to gain access to the Public Trough.

So while I'm throwing around the term international development consultant, I should perhaps define it. Simply put, international development refers to that process developing countries go through in order to become developed. So an international development consultant would be someone who is a catalyst in that process, and of course gets paid for it. Development takes place, for example, when the people of a country reduce their rate of illiteracy or incidence of HIV-AIDS, increase their gross national product or raise the standard of living through an effective program of micro-lending. The major purveyors of international development include such heavy-hitters as the Bretton Woods group (World Bank and International Monetary Fund) and bilateral agencies such as the U.S. Agency for International Development. They include a myriad of non-governmental organizations—more often known as PVOs in the U.S.—such as Oxfam, Save the Children, CARE, Catholic Relief Services and the Trickle Up Foundation as well.

And of what do consulting assignments consist? In the international development area work in the field usually falls into one of several categories: short and long term assignments, the latter consisting from a few months up to several years. Short term work generally averages between two and six weeks. First, there is the design of a new program or project that often entails a team effort. Second, the assignment may involve evaluating an existing program or project, either at the mid-point (formative), at the end (summative) or several months or even years later to gauge its impact. Short term assignments may also involve management training of project personnel. The more sophisticated consulting firms field staff on short term assignments (on overhead) to gather information aimed at the preparation of a proposal, to spy on competitors, or to schmooze with Mission personnel known to be friendly toward the firm.

Work in the home office of consulting firms and organizations entails managing and backstopping projects in the field and seeking new contracts or grants. In the first instance, the team to be deployed in the field must be carefully selected, oriented, fielded and supported. Housing must be secured and education arranged for dependents. Procurement of office equipment and supplies for the field staff is critical to its proper functioning. In the event of an accident or serious illness a team member may have to be evacuated and replaced. In truth, home office personnel are always marketing the firm's wares, both at home and abroad. The firm is constantly on the lookout for bidding partners. A competitor may become a partner, and visa versa. As in international relations, there are no permanent friends, only permanent interests.

The substance of development is defined by the funding source and is subject to paradigm shifts and fads. During the 1960s and 1970s development agencies focused to a great extent on physical infrastructure: roads and bridges, highways and school construction. Toward the end of the 1970s there was a paradigm shift toward integrated rural development, thought to be a kind of silver bullet for solving all the development problems of the population in a given area.

Government was considered the solution to problems of development, whether in agriculture, health, education or management.

Then came the Reagan Revolution and discovery of the private sector. Government was out and private enterprise in. Development projects and programs had to be designed with a whole new set of objectives and parameters.

There was a special emphasis on promoting policies that would remove the shackles of government and free pent-up enterprise initiatives, a focus on export promotion. The magic of the marketplace was preached throughout the hills and valleys of developing countries everywhere. A call went out for the promotion of entrepreneurs who would champion the new private enterprise paradigm.

It was within this shifting paradigm that I would find most of my consulting work from the early 1980s onward. Assigned to evaluate several small business development projects in East and West Africa during this time, I eventually became a proponent of this approach to development. Increasingly my resume began to reflect expertise in the promotion of small business policies and programs. My academic papers and monographs began to reflect that expertise. But as small business development came to be juxtaposed with micro-enterprise development, I became a strong proponent of the later.

Besides working for a number of consulting firms and consortia as an employee, I took assignments as a freelance consultant on projects funded by a wide range of for-profit and non-profit entities, and bilateral and multilateral agencies including the African Development Bank, the Asian Development Bank, the World Bank, the United Nations Development Program, U.S. Agency for International Development, the U.S. Information Agency, U.S. State Department and Peace Corps. Every now and then a consultancy would actually NOT involve getting on an airplane and traveling to country X. In which case, I would usually have to put on my political science hat and try to recall why I spent all those months laboring over a dissertation.

Looking back on this period in my life, I have often tried to sum up work as a consultant. It was very "episodic", disconnected and thus difficult to assign any meaningful value. Rarely could I connect the dots from one consultancy to another. The consultant mode of operation was occasionally punctuated by efforts to establish non-profit organizations. Truth be known, it is difficult to identify examples of missions that contributed to any tangible, positive impact. All told, during the period from 1976 to 1998 I would complete short-term assignments in some 30 countries. The following are vignettes from my 22 years of international development consulting.

Congo-Kinshasa (Zaire) Revisited   1976-1979

I managed to land my first ever overseas consulting assignment in 1976, as a member of an evaluation team sent to look at the Peace Corps program in the Congo (then Zaire). A major part of the program was education; perhaps a third of all the Volunteers in the country at the time were serving as teachers in secondary schools, as well as a few in the University. I was thinking of myself as something of an expert on Zaire, and especially its system of education, which was the subject of part of the evaluation. (A PhD dissertation on the Congolese system of higher education and four years of experience in the country!) But our team leader let me know that there were certain program priorities that should not be messed with in the evaluation report, regardless of my "professional" opinions. It was a sobering experience. I would soon learn that the consultant is always running into political and programmatic issues on assignments that cloud the picture. Truth for its own sake is not always the mantra of the consultant!

With that bit of wisdom under my belt, I went looking for my next employment. While there would be a variety of domestic sources of income over the next few years—including a year of teaching political science at Texas Tech University—my next overseas consulting assignment would take me back to Zaire in 1979. A minority-owned consulting firm in Washington DC was looking to complete an evaluation team that would examine the USAID-funded North Shaba Integrated Rural Development (IRD) project in the hinterland of Shaba Province (formerly Katanga). The IRD model was then viewed by USAID planners as the approach du jour that would address all the challenges to full and equitable development in a given area. In our briefing before departing to Zaire we learned that the very same consulting firm that had designed the elaborate multi-faceted project was the one that had been awarded the contract to implement it. Surprise! In later years USAID would come up with prohibitions against a firm bidding on a project that it had designed (something to do with conflict of interest). But not this one! Once in the country, we would begin to understand why the Mission and the consulting firm were in cahoots.

The consulting firm with the evaluation contract had trouble cobbling together a project team, attempting to find the right mix of technical skills and development experience. There were to be eight of us: four expatriates and four local-hire Zairians. We all arrived in the nether reaches of the Shaba project site at different times, courtesy of USAID-supplied transport planes. Two of us introduced ourselves to each other as the firm-appointed Chief of Party, a clue that there might be complications to come! However, that proved to not be a problem at all. No, there were much larger issues lurking around the evaluation. The exercise was fraught with politics.

At the time of the evaluation the Shaba Province was not quite firmly under the control of President Mobutu's army. There was a rag-tag band of rebels hiding out in the region, occasionally raiding villages and military posts, calling itself Marxist and preying upon the hapless population. The rebels lived by dealing in contraband diamonds. The IRD project was intended to bring economic, and thus political, stability to the region so as to blunt the rebel presence. In conducting interviews with project staff and project "beneficiaries", our team observed that the project was not being especially responsive to local demands to basic needs such as clean drinking water and access to medical services as articulated by the local "beneficiaries". When this was reported back to the North Shaba project staff they pointed out that the project was designed to increase the production of corn, not to solve ALL the problems in the region. Our evaluation report was somewhat critical of the North Shaba project for this and other reasons. This gained the evaluation team the ire, not only of the firm implementing the project, but the USAID Mission as well, since this was its flagship project. Much was at stake!

Back in the USA, I resumed my status as a development consultant, would-be scholar and sometime snitch. When I was asked by a staffer of the House Sub-Committee on Africa to testify at a hearing about the North Shaba project, I willingly agreed. This almost sank my budding career as a consultant. Because I went on record as criticizing some of the aspects of the North Shaba Project, I was black-listed by the implementing firm (friends told me my file there was contained in a black folder!) and considered as something of a pariah by the USAID Mission in Zaire.

Postscript: Not only did the North Shaba Project not succeed in dislodging the pesky rebels, but Laurent Kabila, the very rebel leader it was seeking to dislodge, would eventually become President of the country! Kabila brought with him to the capital of Kinshasa all the bad habits he had developed in the bush! The country descended further into a cauldron of political intrigue and economic devastation from which it has yet to recover.

Small Business Development   *1979-1992*

Early on in my life as a consultant I developed a keen interest in the promotion of small-scale entrepreneurship. I was evaluating projects of this type before the term Small and Medium Enterprise (SME) Development came into vogue. Although on paper I was more of an education sector specialist, most of my consulting assignments would come to involve design and evaluation of small business projects. Certainly this approach appealed to me much more than the over-designed and under-performing integrated rural development mega-project I witnessed in Zaire.

In October 1979 I was hired as a consultant to a non-profit organization (PVO) headquartered in Washington to evaluate its rural development enterprise project in Upper Volta (later to become Bourkina Faso). Funded by the USAID Mission in Ouagadougou, this was a pilot project under consideration for an extension. The project, located in the remote Eastern Region of the country, was an experiment to determine whether a similar project in western Kenya being implemented by the same PVO could be replicated in Upper Volta under different circumstances. The government agency operating in the region was focused solely on increased agricultural production. Its only provision for assisting small scale entrepreneurs was for animal traction. Facilities for obtaining small loans were virtually nil since the loan requirements of the development bank were very strict. This project aimed at filling the void of credit and advisory services available to small businesses.

During the first two years of the pilot phase the project had managed to accord 120 small loans to small businesses, half of them start-ups. The loans went to such activities as a grain mill, beehive, rice decorticator and a small tractor used for clearing land and planting. There was a 90% loan repayment rate, which was quite high when compared with the loan rate of commercial banks in the country. I recommended funding for another year of the pilot project. Little did I know at the time that this would be the first of many such projects I would see in the years to come. Repayment rates of over 95% were typical of group lending schemes. We would eventually come to recognize that small and micro-enterprise development was a new and largely effective development paradigm.

Political Risk Analysis   *1980-1981*

Not every assignment I undertook involved getting on and off of airplanes and working in foreign countries. Periodically I was reminded of my presumed skills as a political scientist. So beginning in1980 I plied my trade as a political analyst for the public as well as the private sector. In the early 1980s I was engaged to analyze political events and suggest what might transpire in the future in selected African countries. The U.S. Department of the Interior, charged with tracking the nation's needs for critical minerals, contracted with a beltway consulting firm to assist in predicting possible disruptions in access to those minerals. The firm identified and hired a dozen "Africanists" such as myself, thought to have special insight into the regions of the world that produced these minerals.

We were asked to do background papers on Central and Southern Africa, and I was assigned to write on Zaire (formerly the Democratic Republic of the Congo). The focus of my paper was on industrial diamonds, copper and cobalt, the latter produced as a by-product of copper. Cobalt in particular was critical to U.S. weapons systems, and there was no known substitute for it. At the time Zaire provided fully 60% of U.S. import needs in cobalt. We were then convened as a panel of experts and asked to speculate on various scenarios of disruption: e.g., East-West, tribal, regional or ethnic conflict. The end objective was to quantify our collective hunches and arrive at predictions that would help Interior determine what to do about the nation's strategic reserves. Did Interior get its money's worth? I have no idea what use the Department of the Interior made of our projections, but I got paid for my efforts and moved on to the next consultancy.

For several months the following year I was on retainer with the firm of Frost & Sullivan as a consultant to develop a World Political Risk Forecast which was then sold to subscribers, most of whom were interested in their overseas investments. One such assignment was for South Africa. My job was to gaze into my crystal ball, using my political science expertise, and predict what would happen in that country over the next 18 months. In a 40-page paper I suggested to Frost & Sullivan subscribers that the regime in South Africa was not likely to change substantially in the near term. The biggest threat to Prime Minister P.W. Botha's regime, I concluded, was the growing conflict within the Nationalist Party. I said that a buoyant economy and the promise of more support from the Reagan Administration in the U.S. would serve to sustain the regime in the medium term. Again, my pre-occupation was with making sure I received compensation for my consulting efforts.

With these seemingly related back-to-back consulting experiences under my belt, I began to mull over the possibility of pulling together my research papers into a publishable monograph. Although I was no longer in academe, I felt the compulsion to get my writing into print. I came up with a theme and a title: Pawns on a Chessboard: The Resource War in Southern Africa (1981). In the introduction, I noted that the term "resource war" was of fairly recent vintage, coined by those who maintained that the struggle for scarce mineral resources in the Third World was becoming one of the key issues in international affairs. It was a "war" between the Western industrialized "free world" and the Soviet Union and its Communist allies. The premise was that many of the Western "free" nations, including the U.S., depended upon imports of critical minerals for industrial needs. Chief among these minerals were chromium, cobalt, manganese and platinum group metals. The study was limited to Zaire, Zambia, Zimbabwe and South Africa— all pawns in the resource war between the East and the West.

In the concluding chapter of Pawns on a Chessboard I noted that the Reagan Administration was fashioning an Africa policy that had as its basic tenet rapprochement with the South African regime. It was predicated on a mutually shared view that the principal danger to the Southern African regime was the Soviet Union and its allies. I argued against the Reagan Administration's policy of "constructive engagement" toward the South African regime, suggesting that the long-term interest of the U.S. would be better served by supporting the African majority rather than the white supremacist struggle against the Soviet menace.

While Pawns on a Chessboard never reached the best-seller list, it was my first book, published in 1981. It helped me to connect the dots, if only temporarily.

Conakry, Guinea   1987-1990

During a four-year period from 1987 to 1990, I found myself on four different assignments in the West African country of Guinea-Conakry. (There were at least two countries known as Guinea, distinguished by the name of their capital city). I became quite familiar with the local government departments and funding agencies in the country. It is most likely that my French language expertise and familiarity with francophone institutions was the factor that kept me going back there. My first assignment in Guinea was with the African Region of Peace Corps. A wealthy business man had given the Peace Corps a gift which he said should be used to promote microenterprise development in Guinea. My task was to identify four sites and potential agencies or local organizations that would host the Volunteers assigned to the village. This was rather different from most Peace Corps programs, which typically amounted to responding to the host government's request to accommodate shortfalls in personnel of development initiatives. I would later have occasion to meet some of the Volunteers assigned to the project in Guinea, and they assured me that they had had a good experience.

Another Guinea assignment came about after I had joined a prominent Washington consulting firm. This was a World Bank-funded feasibility study on the possibility of promoting the export of non-traditional agricultural products from Guinea. During colonial times, the French had promoted the planting of mango trees to such an extent that the country became the largest exporter in the world. Now, three decades after the French left the country, mangoes were dropping to the ground and not reaching export markets. Funded by a World Bank loan, the consultancy was contracted with the Guinean Ministry of Agriculture and Animal Resources. The Guinea Agricultural Export feasibility study of non-traditional exports constituted the first step in the process of developing a $40 to $50 million project, including contributions from bilateral donors such as USAID. The study included 10 weeks of work in country and another couple of weeks of revision, followed by presentation of results to the authorities in Conakry. The Guinea Ag Export Team consisted of six members, three of them Canadian nationals.

Our firm was one of six short-listed by the World Bank project officer. While I was not senior enough to be involved in the contract negotiations with the Guinean Ministry of Agriculture, I was privy to one of the provisos that assured us of the contract. We would agree to provide the host Ministry with a shiny new four-wheel drive Pajero (wink, wink). It would simply be taken out of our contract fee. The firm wanted the contract, so we couldn't let a small matter such as this stand in the way. We said okay, and we were on the way! After all, the Guinean mango farmers wouldn't lose anything in the deal. The U.S. Foreign Corrupt Practices Act was intended to put the kibosh on this type of activity, but it has proved largely ineffective. Since its inception only a handful of firms have actually been prosecuted under the act. The assessment team eventually completed its task and submitted its report to the Bank. I do not believe that the export project envisaged ever saw the light of day, despite our valiant efforts.

Islamabad and Peshawar, Pakistan   *October-November 1990*

Of all the assignments in my illustrious consulting career, in retrospect perhaps the most bizarre involved designing a project for Afghanistan, a country inside which no American could set foot at the time. By 1990 Afghanistan had waged a decade-long guerrilla war against the Soviets who were now seeing their empire beginning to crumble. The USAID Mission in Islamabad, Pakistan was acting on behalf of the Office of the AID Representative for Afghanistan. The O/AID/Rep congressional presentation for FY 1991 included a plan for privatizing its program of providing goods and services to Afghanis remaining inside their country. It concluded that the free distribution of relief assistance was doing little to stimulate the resumption of normal economic activity inside the country, and in fact might be inhibiting private sector development because of the distribution of free commodities.

Afghanistan was faced with the task of rehabilitating and reconstructing its economy, in the absence of a viable public sector. Therefore, in addition to searching for ways to privatize already existing programs, the O/AID/Rep proposed to explore ways to promote private sector development in the eastern provinces of Afghanistan bordering Pakistan by assisting small businesses. The vehicle chosen to achieve this objective was a Commodity Export Program, whose activities included procurement, logistics, transportation and road repair. The underlying assumption behind our mission was that the Afghanis were eager to build a free market economic system with all the democratic trimmings. All of this at a time when the Taliban was incubating in the rugged Afghan mountains and Osama bin Laden was gaining stature as a rebel leader against the hated Soviet occupiers, apparently unbeknownst to Washington.

In October 1990 I participated as a member of the Afghanistan Private Sector Needs Assessment Team consisting of four persons: two Americans and two Afghanis who were U.S. residents. The consultancy was contracted by the USAID Mission in Pakistan, acting on behalf of the O/AID Rep, with another minority-owned Washington DC firm. Within the first week our team conducted meetings with the USAID Mission staff and relevant organizations in Islamabad before heading out to Peshawar where most of the work was to take place.

The scope of work for the assessment was guided by certain assumptions. The overall objective was to promote the transition from relief-oriented activities to long-term, sustainable development. The private sector would be the most effective vehicle for achieving development objectives. Training and technical assistance inputs were to take place in Peshawar, near the Afghanistan border.

Our assessment was to determine what type of pilot projects would be needed for the resettlement of displaced Afghanis and the initiation of private sector development in selected communities. The assessment would culminate in a project document that would lay out options for private sector development, proposed methods of operation, management, financing and technical support. Financing for pilot projects was to be mostly in-kind, that is in machinery, equipment, tools and raw materials.

The dangers facing our mission were everywhere manifested. A recent report of an emergency taskforce in Paktia Province prepared for a United Nations meeting had concluded that there had been too many surveys which had not produced results. The report said that people there were unimpressed by surveys and were demanding action. Our assessment was not to be just another survey, but an action plan for implementation. Even so, the conditions were not exactly conducive to fruitful development designs. There were no indications that our mission would be any different from previous ones.

Nevertheless, our team traveled to Peshawar to conduct interviews. Peshawar had served as a British military outpost during colonial times, and the town proper still had a distinctly garrison appearance. Surrounding the town itself there were now teeming Afghan refugee tent villages manned by literally hundreds of PVOs and NGOs. As a frontier town near Pakistan's lawless Northwest

Province, Peshawar had a reputation for trafficking in black market arms and drugs trade. The local market in town featured a full range of captured Soviet military paraphernalia from Afghanistan, including items such as hats and shirts, pendants and badges— souvenir attractions for visiting Western tourists.

Then the two Afghanis took their lives into their hands, traveling into villages in Paktia and Logar Provinces inside Afghanistan. We Americans remained ensconced in our hotel rooms awaiting their return. After harrowing scrapes with local warlords who were not interested in the proposed scheme, our colleagues found their way back to Peshawar. Back in Islamabad, we managed to piece together a draft needs assessment report, replete with caveats, that was submitted to O/AID/Rep in November. Discussions were held with the Office of the AID Representative to Afghanistan, but it quickly became apparent that there would be no need to formalize the draft into a formal project design. Better for the project to die in the formative stage than later on when massive resources would be poured into an empty vessel.

Social Entrepreneurship

By 1985 I was a confirmed believer in the small business development approach. More and more Private Voluntary Organizations (PVOs) began to incorporate small business into their program portfolios and development agencies were allocating line items in their budgets for SME development. I was propounding the virtues of this approach in my evaluation reports and public presentations abroad. In 1986 I published my second book entitled *A Small Business Agenda: Trends in a Global Economy.* While pointing to research showing that the small business sector in the U.S. was creating new jobs and providing for growth in the economy, I argued that the same could be true for developing economies, given the right mix of policies and business advisory services. Without overly tooting my horn, I would have to say that this book was ahead of the curve. It presaged a growing recognition that small business promotion could also be the motor for growth in developing countries. Within a few years development agencies were allocating more and more funds toward small business development.

I began looking for ways to give vent to my own latent

entrepreneurial urges. But it seems I lacked the critical desire to make money and run my own business necessary to be an entrepreneur. Back in the early 1980s I had been involved briefly with a group interested in setting up an Africa House in Washington DC. With such an influx of African immigrants into the country and the capital area in particular, the idea was to provide a point of contact for newcomers to Washington. We went through the process of registering as a 501-C-3 organization and looking for funding. Our efforts however, were for naught since we were unable to secure funding or a property to house the proposed Africa House.

Meanwhile, my work as a consultant in small business development would take me on assignments to countries as diverse as Niger, Togo, Senegal, Haiti, Indonesia, the Philippines, Ghana, Malawi, Pakistan and Lesotho. In 1988 I was hired by USAID to chronicle the agency's efforts to promote small business development, eventuating in a monograph on the subject. The Agency, however, was taking pains to point out that its focus was on established business entities, not on what was coming to be known as micro-enterprises of ten or fewer employees in the informal sector. This was ironic, in light of the fact that the projects the Agency had supported over the past 15 years or so were in the informal sector. In any case, I found myself on the other side of this bureaucratic argument, becoming a strong proponent of micro-enterprise development.

The Micro-Enterprise Institute: Stillborn

With my finger in the wind, I could sense that there was a growing awareness among development agencies and practitioners (PVOs and their local partners abroad) of the micro-enterprise or group-lending approach. In 1988, I collaborated with a former Peace Corps Volunteer, now business magazine publisher, in establishing what we called the Micro-Enterprise Institute. I was to be the operations manager and brain trust, he the fund-raiser and behind the scenes orchestrator. We approached nearby George Mason University about hosting a conference on micro-enterprise development. For the conference we invited Dr. Muhammad Yunus, at the time a little known Bangladeshi economist and founder of the Grameen Bank in Bangladesh. He was joined on the panel by several other practitioners and advocates of micro-lending, including George Stephanopoulos, then with a Congressional committee supportive of Dr. Yunus. (The

Grameen Bank did not use the term "micro-enterprise", preferring rather to say that the organization was in the "poverty alleviation" business). Several hundred people attended the affair, by all accounts a very successful event. We developed a mailing list which was to form the basis of our outreach from the newly formed Micro-Enterprise Institute. It seemed we were up and running!

Alas, it was not meant to be! Within a few days after the Big Event I left for a consulting assignment in the Philippines and much needed income. When I returned I discovered that my partner had not only dropped the ball but was considered persona non grata by the Dean of the George Mason School of Business, who was to have been our benefactor and institutional host for the Institute. All the momentum that had been built up by the conference was lost and we were adrift with no place of operations or source of funding. The big idea died a quiet death. Meanwhile, Dr. Yunus and the Grameen Bank burst on the development scene with increasing vigor. The success of Grameen's group lending scheme, with its loan repayment rates hovering just under 100% among poor women, became the model for development efforts around the world. A new development paradigm was born. Even the haughty World Bank, which had initially tried to ignore Grameen Bank's success, came to embrace mico-lending. It would eventually go so far as to adopt poverty alleviation as its signature development objective. Dr. Yunus went on to receive accolades around the globe for his pioneering efforts, refusing offers by the World Bank to underwrite the Grameen Bank.

For several years thereafter I remained on my micro-enterprise soapbox. I tried to sell the new paradigm to my new employer in the late 1980s, but there weren't quite enough development assistance contracts available yet to make it worthwhile. I was a voice crying in the wilderness. The micro-lending program was a little too grass-rootsy for the likes of high-end consulting firms. Not enough technical assistance built into the design to warrant hefty overhead rates. For a while I maintained contact with Dr. Yunus, inviting myself to visit the Grameen Bank on my way back from a consulting assignment in Pakistan in 1991. Unfortunately, my visit coincided with an all-too-frequent state of emergency, owing to political disturbance in Bangladesh. I spent the first 24 hours in my Dacca hotel room, hesitant to go out onto the streets. The following day I hired a rickshaw driver and asked him to take me to the Grameen Bank headquarters. Although I was not able to see Dr. Yunus then, I was pleased to be able to say that I had visited the Mother Church of Micro-Lending!

Friends of Malawi   *1987-1998*

One social entrepreneurial effort that did take root and flourish, however, was the formation of a non-profit organization known as Friends of Malawi which grouped returned Peace Corps Volunteers like myself who had served in that country. In 1986 I became actively involved in the planning committee for the 25th Anniversary of the founding of the Peace Corps in 1961. It was an exciting time, reviving the Volunteer spirit and re-connecting with fellow Volunteers. Among other activities during the celebration were country-of-service meetings intended to bring together those who served in the same country over the past 25 years. At the time there were only a handful of organizations of returned PCVs that called themselves Friends Of. It seemed like an idea whose time had come. So in our Malawi meeting we brain-stormed about the creation of such a group. As is often the case, those who made the proposal were given the task of putting it together. Tim and Susan Davis joined me and Jeff James in a committee to explore the formation of a Friends of Malawi non-profit organization. We collected names of those who attended the meeting and Susan added her list of those who came to a reunion in the Great Smokey Mountains a year before. With that database we were up and running.

By 1987 Friends of Malawi (FOM) was incorporated as a 501-C-3 organization in the District of Columbia. We began holding meetings and identifying program objectives. Initially the core group consisted mainly of the Malawi V group (1964-66) but we soon gained diversity with participation from other groups, most of them from the 1960s. Although I would serve as FOM president for the first 10 years of its existence, the organization really owed its expansion and success in large measure to the dedication of Linda Millette, a Volunteer in the very first group to go to Malawi in 1962. Once Linda purchased a home computer she undertook to build a formidable database of everyone who could be identified as having been Peace Corps staff or volunteers in Malawi. By 2000 Linda, with help from Damon Kletzien, had published the fourth edition of the Friends of Malawi Membership Directory. An FOM newsletter became the primary means of communicating with members. An FOM website (www.friendsofmalawi.org) was eventually up and running. The FOM organization raised funds from membership dues and fund-raising activities, established a grant program for worthy development projects in Malawi, occasionally lobbied the Congress and the Administration on issues affecting Malawi and organized trips back to the country. I relinquished my role as FOM president in 1998 when it became clear that I would be leaving Washington, proud to have left my mark on a worthy organization.

Friends of Malawi Board Members, circa 1992

Washington DC, Beltway Banditry Postscript   *April 16, 2004*

During the period from 1996 to 1998 I was employed as a consultant to Datex Inc., as were several others hired to work on the same evaluation contract. Elsewhere, in the chapter on my experiences in Central and Eastern Europe, I have recounted my work in that region as a consultant with Datex. As with so many of my employers, Datex, Inc. was certified by the U.S. government as 8-A, that is as minority-owned. This allowed the firm to feast on set-aside contracts intended to give minority firms an advantage. Datex was decidedly a Beltway Bandit, located as it was right on the beltway at Route #7 in Virginia. It was not an especially happy place to work, despite the trappings of a high-end enterprise. We consultants were treated as expendable second-class hired help. We were vaguely aware that the owner of Datex had a few other irons in the fire besides the contract we worked on, but this did not seem to have any bearing on our work. I left Datex in 1998 and headed west to Nashville, putting my consulting life behind me.

Then in 2004, Dina Towbin, a colleague in Washington, sent us the following email attachment of a press release issued by USAID, April 16, 2004:

The Office of Inspector General for the United States Agency for International Development (USAID) announced today that Ajit S. Dutta, President of Datex, Inc., was sentenced to 21 months incarceration pursuant to a January 2004 guilty plea of Obstruction of a Federal Audit. This result occurred pursuant to a 19 month investigation by the Office of Inspector General's Investigations Division in Washington, D.C. Dutta was sentenced in U.S. Magistrate Court for the Eastern District of Virginia. In addition to jail time, he was sentenced to make restitution in the amount of $861,089 — full payment of which was made the day of sentencing—as well as a $10,000 fine and $400 special assessment fee.

According to court documents, Datex, Inc. received approximately $71 million over the last six years in USAID contracts and fraudulently overcharged the agency by approximately $867,000. The investigation disclosed evidence that Dutta created and certified fraudulent costs for Datex, Inc. on annual reports submitted to USAID, enabling the company to garner inflated reimbursement. Dutta also lied and provided false documentation to Defense Contract Audit Agency auditors responsible for reviewing those annual reports.

Pursuant to this investigation, USAID Special Agents executed four simultaneous search warrants at Dutta's properties and interests in December 2002. Evidence developed from those searches confirmed that Dannix, which was identified by Datex as simply a consulting firm, was wholly owned by Dutta. Dannix did not actually do any work, though it received over a million dollars from Datex. The searches revealed that work statements and other documents "sent" to Datex from Dannix, some of which were later submitted to the U.S. Government, were in actuality created by Dutta. A search of the Datex, Inc. branch office in New Jersey confirmed that it was an unfurnished residential property owned by Dutta and his wife. Dutta's wife, meanwhile, was listed on Datex's books as a full time employee, which was false.

In addition to the above-noted actions by the U.S. Magistrate Court, Dutta and three of his companies—Datex, Tera Foundation and Dannix,—have been debarred from all U.S. Government procurement contracts.

References

Hull, Galen Spencer (1981) *South Africa: World Political Risk Forecast: South*

Africa. Frost & Sullivan: New York.

_____ (1981) *Pawns on a Chessboard: The Resource War in Southern Africa,* Washington DC: The University Press of America.

_____(1986) *A Small Business Agenda: Trends in a Global Economy,* Washington DC: The University Press of America.

USAID Press Office, April 16, 2004, "Ajit S. Dutta Sentenced to 21 Months of Incarceration," http://www.usaid.gov.

Chapter 10

Sweden, Summer 1985:
In Search of Swedish Roots

"I've heard about your intentions. Why do you wish to emigrate, Karl Oscar Nilsson?" asked the Dean.
"I have debts and hardships and cannot improve my situation at home," replied Karl Oscar.
- from Moberg's The Emigrants, 1951

It was Aunt Eva Norman Bemis, the youngest of Grandma Ada's seven siblings, who was inspired to explore her Swedish origins first-hand. She wrote the family of her pioneering efforts to connect with second and third cousins there. Through the good offices of the Alfta Lutheran Church minister she was able to obtain the names of those in the vicinity who claimed to be descended from her father, Eric Hansson, who had come to America from that town. Aunt Eva finally visited the parish of Alfta Socken (parish) with her niece Wilma and her husband, Karl Carson. Her Christmas letter of 1980 describing their trip in the spring of that year provided impetus to a notion that had been discussed in the family off and on for several years.

She recounted the wonderful welcome they had enjoyed on her visit to Alfta Socken that summer. Norman Hull, her nephew and son of Ada Norman Hull, Eva's older sister, received all her letters and passed them on to me. That represented the germination of the idea for us to follow suit, since Aunt Eva had already done the hard part by going through her father's old letters and checking with the Lutheran Church in Sweden. But the notion of traveling to Sweden would have to incubate several more years before being hatched. By the summer of 1985, we had contacted cousins, made our travel plans and bought our tickets. Dad had never been outside of the United States, and only on rare occasions had he been outside of the southwest. He and I were to be accompanied by his wife Thelma on the trip to Sweden.

So while the name Hull suggests English origins, it had always been the Swedish roots of Ada's Swedish ancestors that fueled the imagination. Grandma remained an avid amateur genealogist and keeper of family records well into her 90s. She often spoke to her grandchildren about her daddy's native Sweden and she struggled to retain the few Swedish words he had imparted to her. She must have also served as inspiration to sister Eva as well. While Ada passed away before being able to visit her father's birthplace, she helped keep the family's Swedish roots alive in our collective consciousness.

As it happens, we may have picked one of the best parts of the world in which to originate from a genealogical point of view. The official Lutheran Church in Sweden has for centuries kept careful genealogical records. And because Sweden has happily escaped involvement in international wars throughout most of modern history, those records have remained intact. Aunt Eva was able to obtain the names of a couple who claimed to be descended from the same Hans Jonsson as her own father. She began corresponding with Thure and Ingegerd Sundvall, who lived on a farm in Galvsbo, a few miles around the lake from the old family farmhouse in Galven. Thure's great grandfather, Jonas Hansson, was the older brother of Eric Hansson, Ada and Eva's father.

America: A Melting Pot?

High school history books describe the American society as a melting pot of peoples from all over the world who came in waves during the mid-to late 1800s and early 1900s. They eventually gave up their old-world tongue, customs and cuisine and adopted standard American ways. Their children are often the most avid devotees of McDonald's and Pizza Hut. They frequently resist efforts of their parents to teach them their mother-tongue. Their ambition is to fit right in with the other kids. In recent years there have been new waves of immigrants from Asia and Latin America. As with the earlier immigrants, the new Americans find that they are obliged to learn to speak English in order to find a job. Their objective is to become as inconspicuous as possible, to "melt" into the American cultural pot.

But there is a counter-trend, one being documented by

anthropologists and sociologists, toward a reassertion of ethnic and cultural identity. It is, in a word, the refusal to melt, a reaction against the homogenization process. Alex Haley gave voice to this attitude in his famous search for his own African roots. Americans of all races and cultures sat glued to their TV sets when the serialization of his book Roots came to the screen in the late 1970s. A whole generation of Americans is now drawing up genealogy charts, trying to recall the few words of Dutch, Russian or Yiddish that grandpa used to speak at home. They search the map to see where he might have had his origins. Often this is a generation that has no recollection of the pain and hardship attendant upon immigration to a new country and is only vaguely aware of those factors that led to emigration from the old country. I must admit to having fallen into this category.

To Sweden: A Midsummer Night's Dream

Norman, Thelma (his wife) and I flew from Ponca City to London, and from there took a flight to Gothenburg on the southwest coast of Sweden. From the afternoon of our arrival at the Gothenburg airport on a mid-June afternoon we were blessed with bright sunshine and mild temperatures. For the first four days it was a repeat performance. During our brief visit with my Swedish friend Lars Eric Hill, his wife Cyndy and his parents at their summer home north of Gothenburg, the Swedish summer was in full bloom. The view of the sea from their summer home as the sun was setting at 10:00 and 11:00 PM in the evening was spectacular. It never really became dark. The Hill family showed us a wonderful time, plying us with Swedish pastries and coffee on a table out on the grass.

From the time of our arrival we were mostly blessed with bright sunshine and mild temperatures. The good weather followed us overland in our rented car into the interior. For the first four days the weather stayed the same. We took to bragging that we had brought the weather with us from Oklahoma! We listened politely as Swedes promised us it would eventually cloud over and become cooler. This indeed happened. For most of two days there was a slow steady drizzle followed by another day of leaden clouds with an occasional glimpse of the sun. Jackets and sweaters became the order of the day. Whenever the sun shone, however, there was something most idyllic about the Swedish summer. We drove north out of Gothenburg into a patchwork of neat rust-red farmhouses with accompanying barns adjacent to them, usually surrounded by gently rolling hills planted in barley and oats and interspersed by stands of pine. And water... there were small ponds and big lakes around nearly every turn in the road. The farther north we went the more heavily wooded the countryside became. In its natural state, the ground was almost certain to be covered with rocks; the grain fields and pastureland were sure evidence of considerable human effort at clearing the rocks in order to make the land useful.

As we headed off onto secondary roads in search of a short cut, the asphalt gave way to winding, twisting, gravel roads, and fewer and fewer farmhouses. Dense forests allowed only slivers of sunlight to reach delicate patches of ferns and moss-covered rocks on the ground. The sylvan scenes from torn Elvira Madigan were called to mind. From time to time there were clearings which revealed efforts at uprooting trees and removing rocks for human productivity. After a long day's journey, just as we began to be a little apprehensive about being lost, the forest path wandered into the village of Alfta from the south. The steeple of the Lutheran Church presided over the town, a reminder of its history and culture.

The town of Alfta gives its name to the parish—or socken in Swedish—which was a farming area north and west of Stockholm, in Helsingland. Located farther north than Anchorage, Alaska, Alfta is still far south of the northern region of the country that reaches past the Arctic Circle. The region today has the air of stability and tradition about it, still very much the preserve of nature, unfettered by few intrusions of the industrial world. For generations farmers had tilled the soil at the foot of gently rolling hills, nestled beside a small lake facing southward, where wild moose roam even today. Once in Alfta we easily managed to locate the farm of Thure and Ingegerd Sundvall, Norman's second cousins on his grandfather's side. The hand-drawn map that Ingegerd had sent us was quite adequate in directing us to the Sundvall farm. Halfway between Arbra and Alfta there are two small clusters of houses—village would be too big a word to describe them. One of them—Galvsbo—consists of about a dozen houses near one of the lakes and Galven is just a few kilometers to the northeast, near the other lake. Neither community sustains even a convenience store any longer since the farmers do their shopping in Alfta or Bollnas, the nearest commercial centers of any size. Why would our ancestors have departed this seemingly pristine setting to venture off to the New World?

Swedish Emigration

There were four groups of people in traditional Swedish society: nobility, clergy, burghers and farmers of which the latter made up the largest part of the population. Farmers used the patronymic system of naming, so that a child is known as the son or daughter of the father. The son of a person with the first name of Anders would have as his last name Andersson and the daughter would be known as Andersdotter. The last time Sweden fought a war was in 1814 (lucky Sweden!) and each province had to raise, maintain and support a standing army. Each parish was divided into wards consisting of several farms. Each ward had to equip one soldier and then nobody living within the ward would be drafted. The ward repaid the soldier by furnishing him with a craft and a few acres of tillable land. The next few generations of the offspring of soldiers kept their fathers' military name.

Happily, the saga of Swedish emigration to America has been captured in a classic epic novel entitled The Emigrants by Vilhelm Moberg (1951) which, together with sequels, recounts the factors involved in the decision of a family to leave Sweden and to take up life in the New World. It is the story of Karl Oscar Nilsson, his wife Kristina and their children who joined the vast exodus from Sweden to America in the 1850s and 1860s. It chronicles a family typical of the thousands of Swedes who set sail for America from their homeland, venturing into the unknown full of hope.

The Nilsson family was among the first of more than a million Swedes who emigrated during that period! It is estimated that by the middle of the 1900s, one-fourth of the Swedish population was living in the United States. By January 1946, Ljuder parish in which Karl Oscar lived counted nearly 2,000 inhabitants. The population had increased threefold since the 1750s. Moberg describes the farm of Korpamoen where Karl Oscar was born, as consisting of sandy soil strewn with stones. "It looked as if it had rained stones from heaven during all six days of creation." Karl's father, Nils, had searched out every patch of soil that could be cultivated and attacked the stones with his iron bar and lever. But his best tools were his hands, with which he went after the stones deep in their holes. If he couldn't move a stone, he called for his wife. It was a silent struggle between Nils and the stone, a fight between an inert mass and the living muscles and sinews of a persevering man.

Karl Oscar Nilsson and his family lived in a world that was characterized by unchangeableness for generations, but that was to be shaken to its very foundations. Four personages governed their parish. There was Dean Brusander, "who in his capacity as minister represented the Almighty, King in heaven and on earth". Next to him in power was the sheriff who had his office from the Crown and represented worldly majesty, Oskar I, King of Sweden and Norway. The foremost man in the parish as to birth and riches was the owner of a freehold, of noble birth, the wealthiest man in the community. Representing the parish on the county council was the churchwarden and storekeeper, the second wealthiest man in the community. These four men governed the parish, holding the spiritual and worldly offices.

This order was typical of that of the other Swedish parishes at that time. Besides the elements, the most important factor affecting Karl Oscar's life was the church. The parishioners lived under "pure evangelical Lutheran religion" in accordance with church law of 1686, and thus were "protected" from heretical and dangerous new ideas. The parish engaged its own schoolmaster who was responsible for teaching children to read well enough to learn Luther's Little Catechism by heart. Occasionally such worldly and useless subjects as arithmetic, writing, Swedish history and geography were also taught. Most male adults could read fairly well and some could even sign their names. But very few women could write at all since no one knew what use a woman could make of the art of writing anyway!

Our hero, Karl Oscar, was named after King Oscar I who ascended the throne of Sweden and Norway in 1844. He was only 14 years old when he hired himself out as a farmhand away from his father's farm. He took possession of one-sixteenth of his father Nil's homestead after the latter became disabled. Nils had fallen face down on a large stone he was trying to dislodge. He finally lost the battle of the stones, after 25 years. During the first few years Karl Oscar enjoyed good crops and was able to pay his father the mortgage interest on time. But the third year he was full of anxiety. When the hay was cut in July, a heavy rain fell. When the flood subsided, the remaining hay was rotten and the animals refused to eat it. In the fall, potato rot spread to Karl Oscar's field and he went deeper into debt while his wife Kristina continued to bear children. The weather patterns bore strange portents: warm air in February and a snow storm in May after the cows had been let out to graze. The next year no rain fell. Karl Oscar sowed his winter rye on the fallow land, strewn with hard clods of earth.

The Swedish population of the time was fostered in the pure evangelical-Lutheran religion in accordance with church law. Children were instructed in Luther's Little Catechism. The typical parish schoolmaster managed to teach a few worldly subjects as well, such as arithmetic, spelling and Swedish history. Most men and women could read at the elementary level, but few could write much more than signing their names. Despite the fact that Luther's Protestant Reformation had shaken the absolute authority of the Catholic Church, the Lutheran (Protestant) order that replaced it was still highly authoritarian. This in turn engendered movements against the established order, which the church considered heretical.

As seen by Church authorities, the greatest threat to the established order, which was beginning to crumble as the waves of emigrants left their farms, was the Akian heresy. Begun by Ake Svensson of Elmeboda in the 1780s, the movement swept through Sweden. The followers of Ake Svensson tried to copy the early Christian church and return to the ways of the apostles. The Akians separated from the state (Lutheran) church and recognized neither temporal nor spiritual powers in their community. They attempted to live a completely communal life, claiming no personal private property. Clearly a recipe for danger! Ake Svensson and seven others were taken to an insane asylum in Stockholm and within two years Ake himself had died in 1788. Other dissenters were released and returned home, but the Akian heresy re-emerged in the 1840s and figured prominently in Moberg's Emigrants, woven into the story of the departure of Karl Oscar and his family for the New World.

. In the late 1840s one of the last remaining relatives of Ake, Danjel Andreasson, had a vision in which Ake came to him and urged him to resume his work on earth. Danjel heeded the call and began to preach the Akian faith. When news of the revival of the Akian heresy reached Dean Brusander he was angered. He was charged with guarding the purity of the Lutheran Church and watching over the flock that God had entrusted to him. The Dean heard that Danjel was making awful comments about him, calling him a "neglectful shepherd." For his part, Karl Oscar was not tempted by the heresy. He tended to remain loyal to the established church and the holy tenets of the Augsburg Convention. He was persuaded that the Dean was right in charging that many emigrants were driven by selfishness and lust of the flesh, but not himself.

There were several factors that motivated Karl Oscar and his brother Robert to think about emigration. Not least of these was the hard life of a farmer. By 1847 Karl Oscar had gone into debt and had to borrow money for the whole of his mortgage. The Swedish soil was rocky and stubborn, and the radical changes in the weather wreaked havoc on farmers. Moberg provides us a vivid passage in which Robert is working on a dunghill with his manure fork. He has a vision of two worlds, an old one and a new one. His home is the Old World where people are worn out, decrepit, old and weak. In their ancient villages time stands still. Children obey their parents and parents imitate them, doing the same thing their parents did before them. This Old World, Robert thinks, cannot go on much longer.

Eventually Karl Oscar and his brother would sell their farm and begin to count the dalers they reckoned would get them to the New World. Although by this time all Swedish persons of good character were permitted to leave the country without having to petition the King, the church was another matter. Thus, Karl Oscar dutifully went to Dean Brusander to request his papers in order to emigrate. This conversation between the two, which spoke volumes about the tension between the old and the new, thus ensued:

"I've heard about your intentions. Why do you wish to emigrate, Karl Oscar Nilsson?" asked the Dean.

"I have debts and hardships and cannot improve my situation at home," replied Karl Oscar.

"It has pleased God to send us a year of famine," said the Dean. "But a devout Christian does not complain in time of tribulation. You know your catechism, Karl Oscar Nilsson. You must know that trials and tribulations are sent for your soul's betterment... You are known as a capable, industrious farmer. Can't you find sustenance in your own community?"

In the end, the Dean succumbed, writing a few words in the parish register indicating that Karl Oscar Nilsson requested extracts from the records for himself and his household for emigration to

North America. The remaining pages in the register would be filled in the decades to come with the repeated notation: "Moved to North America." The remainder of The Emigrants is dedicated to the voyage from Sweden to America. On April 14, 1850, the brig Charlotta sailed from Karlshamm in Sweden for New York carrying 78 passengers. On the ship were Karl Oscar and his family as well as that of Danjel Andreasson, leader of the latter-day Akians. It was on a Midsummer's Eve that year when the brig Charlotta tied up at the pier in New York after 10 weeks of sailing from Sweden.

The House that Mats "Finne" Mickelsson Built

If we can now flash back to the story of our own Swedish roots, we can ask how similar their story might have been to that recounted in Moberg's saga. In contrast to customs in the United States today, where no local institution is responsible for maintaining family records, in Sweden the official Lutheran Church has kept this type of information for generations. A big thick book on Alfta Parish, published in 1947 and prominently displayed in many homes, chronicles all registered families within the parish. To appreciate regional history, it is necessary only to reflect on the fact that construction on the original church now standing in Alfta was begun in the 13th century! Of course, it was a Catholic Church for its first couple of centuries until Martin Luther came along to sweep away the papists and establish another official order. The earliest entries in the book date from the 1540s. Thanks to Church records we are able to reconstruct this tale of Norman Hull's family roots on his mother's side.

Surely some of the elements we have seen in The Emigrants must have been present in the story of Eric Hansson, alias George Norman. He was born the son of Hans Jonsson on September 12, 1851, in the village of Galven in the parish of Alfta. As it happened, the emigration of Eric Hansson to America in 1872 and thousands like him represents a rather abrupt turning point in the history of the region. For centuries before that, life in the Alfta region must have varied only slightly from one generation to the next. Swedish culture pays close attention to genealogy. So let's go back a few generations.

In 1640 Mats Mickelsson, a young man of about 25, arrived from Finland in the parish (or socken) of Alfta in central Sweden. Within a year he had built a handsome farmhouse in the village of Galven at the foot of rolling green hills, nestled against a picturesque lake. The young man became known in the area by the sobriquet of Mats "Finne" because of his Finnish origins. (It seems that Swedes are generally proud of Finnish roots, in contrast to other parts of Scandinavia.) Mats Mickelsson presumably settled down to the life of a farmer and joined the melting pot that was Sweden. Allowing for a few missing dates, the following bloodline can be traced:

and Mats "Finne" begat Mats Matsson	1648-1688
who begat Eric Matsson	1683-17??
who begat Mats Ericsson	1707-1766
who begat Jonas Matsson	1744-1791
who begat Jonas Jonsson	1780-????
who begat Hans Jonsson	1811-1866
who begat Eric Hansson	
(aka George Norman)	1851-1937

As far as can be ascertained, all of this begetting must have taken place in or around the house that Mats "Finne" built in 1641 since church records indicate that each of them was born in Galven or nearby Galvsbo. Even today the house is one of only a dozen or so in the area of Galven. Folks still go into Alfta to do their shopping and catch up on news from the outside world. We drove out to see the house that Mats Mickelsson built—still well preserved and affording a panoramic view of the lake and hills beyond and bathed in brilliant sunshine with a gentle breeze wafting through the trees. I could only ask myself: why did Eric Hansson leave all this to come to an uncertain future in America?

The house was still inhabited, although not by his offspring. Typical of the farmhouses of the area which date from that period, it is a sturdy two-story edifice with tiled roof, consisting of about eight rooms and a front porch. The wood siding is painted a rustic red, with white window frames. Surrounded by waving fields of barley and oats, the house is nestled at the foot of rolling hills beside a picturesque lake. A few yards to the left of the house there is a very large barn. A far cry from the sod houses put up by the pioneers on the prairies of the American Midwest!

The House that Mats "Finne" built, 1641

In an interview in 1932 with Eunice Shull, one of his grand-daughters, Eric Hansson, aka George Norman, recounted his life in Sweden and how he had come to America. Until the age of 21, his life must been very much like that of his ancestors. During summer months he worked on the farm, helping to plant and harvest oats, barley, rye, wheat and potatoes. In the winter he worked with a timber contractor, measuring and cutting logs from the abundant forests surrounding the farm. He earned about 50 cents a day plus his board. His primary education consisted of six weeks of instruction a year in the home of a neighbor. At the age of 15 Eric attended high school for three months, thus completing his formal education!

Eric's older brother had traveled to the United States before and returned to tell of the great possibilities the new land had to offer young farmers. His own father had died when Eric was only four and the family was struggling to make ends meet. Thus his mother, born Annie Olson, decided to take her four sons and two daughters and emigrate to America. They set sail from Gothenburg in 1872, landing first in Hull (yes, Hull) England, and traveling by rail to Liverpool. From there they sailed on the steamship Wyoming to New York, where they joined waves of other emigrants at Ellis Island in search of a new life. Here Eric changed his name to the more Anglo-sounding George Norman and began learning the language of the melting pot. The family first settled near Galesburg, Illinois, where they took up farming. We do know that the Norman family in the New World no longer belonged to the Lutheran Church, and by the second generation had embraced the born-in-America Christian Church.

We do not have the same wealth of information about Ada's mother's family. In another village near Alfta called Gundbo, Anders Jonsson was born to Jon Person, a farmer, and Christina Wilsdotter in 1804. When he became a soldier in the Helsinge Regiment, he was given the name Hjelm (later changed to Yelm). We know that it was customary for the military to give soldiers a one-syllable name such as Hjelm or Hill—replacing their given family name—which was easy to pronounce, thus lending itself to military parsimony. Anders Yelm was married to Anna Nilsdotter in the Alfta Church. They were among a group in the northern provinces of Helsingland and Dalecarlia that came under the influence of another heretical preacher by the name of Eric Jansson who became known as Bishop Hill. Jansson moved to Alfta, where he attracted such a large following that it is estimated that one-tenth (300) of the population of the town left with him for America in 1846. In any event, it was less difficult for me to imagine why a soldier would join the ranks of emigrants to America than a farmer!

Another group, perhaps 100, left Alfta at the same time. Ship manifest records show that Anders Yelm and his wife Anna took seven children with them when they sailed from Sweden on October 14, 1846. Rather than following the custom of taking the father's first name—e.g. Anders Anderson—the Yelm children kept that name upon arrival in America. In the U.S. they settled not far from the same site as Bishop Hill's followers, in Victoria, Illinois. An account of the Bishop Hill group is said to be the subject of a book (circa 1975) by Olof Issacsson. A subsequent search for the book in Stockholm's finest bookstores proved fruitless. It is to be noted, however, that the Stockholm phone book contains a column of Hjelms (Yelms), including three Anders Hjelms. The factors leading to the emigration of the Yelm family remain a mystery. Mary Yelm's marriage to George Norman and their life in Western Kansas has been recounted earlier.

The Sundvall Farm

The hand-made map that Ingegerd had sent us was quite adequate in directing us to the Sundvall farm. Halfway between Alfta and Arbra there are two small clusters of houses—village would be too big to describe them really—nestled alongside a couple of lakes. One of them—Galvsbo—is just a few miles to the north and east of the Sundvall farm, near the other lake. Neither community maintains even a convenience store any longer since the farmers do their shopping in Alfta or the larger commercial center in nearby Bollnas.

The Sundvall farmhouse, which has been in the family for a couple of generations, is a picture of prosperity and natural beauty. Recently remodeled with an abundance of furnishings made of pine and the latest appliances, the house features a picture window which looks out over the potato patch and a grazing area toward the lake a few yards away. On the other side of the house is the barn and beyond it more grazing land, following by a stand of forests that abuts the hills to the west.

All of the operations of the farm center on the production and storing of grain crops for the cows, and of course milking the cows. There are some 20 cows that are milked twice daily every day of the year. The barn is a model of Swedish ingenuity. Heat from the bodies of the cows is drawn by a fan and transported through ducts to the house. An intercom system connects the house with the barn. The milking machines pump the milk up into a tube which transports it into a large vat where it awaits the arrival of the milk truck every other day. The principal farm income is from the sale of milk to a government agency. Thure says that he averages about 110,000 liters of milk a year, for which he is paid three kronar per litre. Each milk pick-up averages between 300 and 600 liters, for an average of three times a week. This annual production computes to about 29,000 gallons a year at $1.36/gallon for a total income of about $40,000 from the sale of milk.

Other secondary sources of family income are from the occasional butchery of bulls, the sale of timber and Thure's assisting other farmers in filling out their income tax forms. The Sundvall family farm operation consists of Thure, Ingegerd and son Stephan (daughter Evelyn when she is at home) and no hired help. The family owns several sections of grain fields scattered around the area along the road to Galven. The single family farm is still the predominant unit of production in the northern part of the country, whereas in the south the farms are larger and more likely to be consolidated into a larger commercial operation.

Tradition is the operative mode in Galvsbo. For example, on Thursday mornings it is customary to eat Swedish pancakes (crêpes), with thick fresh whipped cream and preserves made from strawberries, linen berries and other types of berries that grow around the farm. W broke with this tradition by having pancakes on Tuesday morning instead. Family entertainment consists frequently of father and son playing the accordion or the piano, or watching an old western movie with Swedish subtitles on TV. It is also traditional to hunt moose in the fall. A census of the moose population is taken by plane when the snows begin to fall and it is possible to see them more easily from the air. Then a quota is set for each hunter. He takes up his hunting post at 9:00 A.M. and stays there until 3:00 P.M. The hunter cannot kill more than his quota. Like his father at his age Stephan was looking forward to obtaining his license, since he was turning 18 years old. The family's freezer contains enough moose meat to last a year. The wild, lean meat of the moose is eaten much more often than is beef from cattle.

Rainbow over the Sundvall home near Galven

Tradition is reflected in the ownership of property as well. It is a matter of the same houses remaining in the family generation after generation. You may not purchase property in the area unless you are a farmer intending to till the soil. The Sundvall family farms land that belongs to an uncle, and they hope to inherit the land some day. Young Stephan fully expects to eventually take over his parents' home when they move to the other property. The family tree is traceable back to the 17th century, nearly all branches within the Alfta parish. Primary social contacts are still to a large extent with the extended family, as they are in rural areas around the world.

Swedish Cousins

They turned out in their Sunday-go-to-meeting best—men, women and children—to meet us at the Galven Community Center, a few yards from the lake on the road from Alfta to Arbrä. A stone's throw away stood the house that Mats Mickelsson built. The Sundvalls had gone to considerable trouble to put out the word that there were visitors from America claiming to be descendents of Eric Hansson. On a bright sunny afternoon about 50 people came to the center out of curiosity, claiming a similar ancestry. Most of them were grey-haired, and only a few spoke English.

As our "relatives" arrived at the center, conversation naturally turned on how we might be related to each other. Many told about other members of their families now living in the United States. Some recounted their most recent visit there. The women had prepared cold cuts and salad and of course served coffee and pastries. After a few formal remarks on the occasion of the gathering, people began to excuse themselves to return home, some to milk the cows. It was then that our social agenda for the remainder of the week began to shape up. Invitations for each day of the week quickly filled the calendar.

The next day we went to the town of Bollnas, the largest in the area, to visit Christer and Gunhild Gunnarson, a couple who had become successful entrepreneurs. Over 15 years ago they had purchased a franchise from a US based company to sell home products: shampoos, lotions and various other aloe vera derivatives. Today they operate a network of over 100 sales agents in the region.

Cookout at the Sundvall Home with Stephan & Evelyn

The cultural high watermark of our week-long stay would probably have to be the traditional smorgasbord laid out for us at the farmhome of Thure's sister. This wonderful old culinary custom is one of the few that most Americans can associate with Swedish culture. Often a synonym for a cornucopia of things, the smorgasbord usually consists of such delights as pickled herring, caviar, and a variety of sliced meats, salads, cheese, meatballs and of course boiled potatoes. One of the most popular ingredients is gravad lax (dill-cured salmon). If ingested properly, each of the various courses must be washed down with Swedish vodka, aquavit or beer. From its origins in the well-to-do Swedish households of the 17th and 18th centuries, the smorgasbord has become a recognized institution around the world. In fact, there is an enterprise known as Smorgasbord, Inc., in New York which arranges festivals all over the North American continent. At the Waldorf Astoria, the company provided a Swedish yuletide table for 1000 people!

Everywhere we went we were graciously and warmly received among our distant relatives. Much of the time we had to rely upon the translating services of Evelyn, whose English had been polished during her stay as a student in California. We could only accept this hospitality and issue repeated invitations to one and all to come and visit us. Thure retorted, half in jest, that he would consider the proposition when the value of the dollar came down to six kronars (compared with the rate of 3.35 when we arrived). For her part, Evelyn would only remark that playing host to us was a token of her appreciation for the reception she had enjoyed with her American families when she was an exchange student in the U.S.

Summing Up Sweden

What is to be distilled from this pilgrimage to our ancestral homeland? What impressions are likely to stand the test of time? The pluses easily outweigh the minuses:

➢ *The scenery and weather*

At the risk of sounding rather like a spokesman for the tourist bureau's "Positive Sweden" campaign, I would have to say that I was overwhelmed by nature. This, from a seasoned traveler who has looked into many nooks and crannies of the globe. Mother nature herself accounts for most of this, but conscious public policy and a cultural tradition of cleanliness and conservation help a great deal. For example, the highways are uncluttered by a myriad of advertisements exhorting the motorist to stroke this or fly that. One simply cannot come quite prepared for the verdant pastures and forests and the seemingly endless array of lakes and streams. The motorist is rarely affronted by the spectacle of ramshackle barns and roadside junkyards or urban blight.

The flip side? Well, there is the rain and drizzle. Surely the statistics will tell you that Sweden is one of the wettest places to be found anywhere. That would be okay if the rain came in a tropical 30 minute downpour, making way for the sun. But no! Even otherwise taciturn Swedes voice their distaste for their weather. But let the sun burst through for a golden moment, maybe even a whole day, and the Swedes show their true sun-worshipping colors. They flock to the sea, the lakes or trim the roses in their yards. I even spied a well-endowed young woman cavorting about topless, playing badminton on the grass in her yard in Alfta. Now would that ever happen in Scott City, Kansas? On balance, however, this is not tennis weather. Now I ask you: did Bjorn Borg and Mats Wilander and a whole generation of Swedish tennis stars learn to play under these clouds? From an Oklahoma point of view, it almost seems unnatural.

> ### The Food

Maybe it's just my imagination, but it seems that the Swedish diet is healthier than that of the average American. Swedes eat more fish than red meat, and fewer fried foods. Our meals on the farm had to be more wholesome because much of the food was homegrown and therefore lacking preservatives. But, owing to the constant round of invitations, we often found ourselves eating four or five times a day, including the obligatory servings of pastries and coffee. It seemed that the belt was always a bit tight and buttons threatened to pop off. The fast food industry unfortunately is making inroads into this traditional wholesomeness. The Swedish equivalent of McDonald's offers up a standard fare of pomme frites (french fries) or three generous scoops of mashed potatoes to accompany a foot long piece of sausage. On the other end of the culinary spectrum, the Swedish smorgasbord appears to have taken its place among the world's great cuisines.

> *Religion and Culture.*

It is probably not appropriate for a one-time visitor to comment on so weighty a subject as official religion. But we're talking about impressions, so here goes. The stately Lutheran Church in Alfta serves as a point of reference. Centuries old, it is the physical and historical focus of the parish. The church and its surrounding cemetery, with its abundance of roses, are immaculately maintained. The sanctuary, which seats perhaps 500 worshippers, has been recently remodeled. It is a picture of impeccability, the wooden floors are beautifully finished and the walls are painted in soft natural colors with painful attention to detail. The pews are made of sturdy pine and equipped with plush cushions. As the visitor enters, a recorded message tells the history and mission of the church. The people of Alfta are clearly very proud of their church.

And what of the life of the church? Our hosts indicated to us that on a typical Sunday scarcely a handful of people attend services. It is as though the institutional church had long since outlived its moral authority, spent it perhaps in the vain attempt to keep would-be emigrants down on the farm. And yet one could hardly say that the spiritual values the church sought to impart were any less alive among the kindly folks in Alfta parish. Certainly the church structure itself is reflected in the workmanship and dedication of the people to aesthetic values. But the institution itself is no longer synonymous with community.

> *Politics*

It is probably even less appropriate for a trained political scientist such as I to hazard generalizations about the Swedish political order on so brief a visit. Perhaps a few impressions will suffice. On July 31, we drove into the sports Centrum in Alfta to attend a political rally featuring the prime minister, Olof Palme. He was born in Stockholm and received most of his education in the United States and then attended law school in Stockholm. He joined the Socialist Party in 1949, and soon became the leader of its youth wing. In 1955, he was elected to the Swedish Parliament. Eight years later, he became a member of the government, and in 1969 he became Prime Minister. Palme was a dominant figure in Swedish politics. A confirmed Socialist, he was committed to strengthening Swedish Socialist policies. Palme strongly criticized US involvement in Vietnam and was equally critical of the Soviet invasion of Czechoslovakia in 1968.

According to the local newspaper, there were about 830 people at the Sports Centrum, a large percentage of them grey-haired and, well, sedate. Boistrous would not be the word to describe this crowd; there was no foot stomping and cheering. They were warmed up by a violin ensemble followed by an accordion group, a la Art Van Dann. Palme took the podium wearing an open-necked powder-blue sweater. He began by noting that the last time he was in Alfta was 1963 and that the population of the town seemed to have declined slightly. He defended his administration's socialist-oriented policies, claiming to have reduced unemployment to only 2.5 per cent compared with an average of 11 percent in Europe. He remarked that Sweden now enjoyed a favorable balance of payments advantage in world trade and had a more modest national debt than other industrialized nations.

The Alfta audience listened politely, chuckled at the Prime Minister's occasional jokes, applauded whenever a point seemed to merit applause. But one was left with the feeling that this was not really a social democratic audience, that there was a kind of natural rural resistance to the statist policies that Palme has promoted over the years. But, then, with the general decline in rural population, the electorate is increasingly urban and industrial. Palme was assassinated the following year, in 1986, while walking home from a movie and his assailant was never apprehended.

———

References

Moberg, Vilhem (1951) *The Emigrants*, New York: Warner Books. The sequels to *The Emigrants* include *Unto a Good Land*, *The Settlers*, and *Last Letter Home*.

Shull, Eunice (1932) *Interview with George Norman, pioneer of Western Kansas*, granddaughter of the interviewee (manuscript).

Chapter 11

Brazil, 1989:

The Lure of the Berimbau

Bahia is more African than Africa...No one else in all the black slave world fought to keep their customs like they did here in Bahia, the soul of Brazil, the navel of the universe, the most mystical place in the world.
- Nelson Eubank, The First Thing Smoking, set in Bahia

Why Brazil? Several factors seemed to converge when Dawn and I discussed where and how to spend our vacation. I had had a long-festering fascination with Bahia, the state on the northeastern coast of Brazil whose name is often used interchangeably with its principal city, Salvador. An old Africanist, I had read and heard from friends that the strongest traces of African culture in the Western Hemisphere were to be found in Bahia. It was said to be the soul of Brazil as reflected in its people, music, religion and cuisine. An exotic blend of native Indian, Portuguese and especially African.

My fascination had been periodically fueled by people who know it firsthand. Judy King Calnek, host of WPFW's Saturday morning radio program, Berimbau in Washington D.C., served as one of the prime instigators. The sounds of the berimbau haunted me weekly. Dawn and I had hosted a Bolivian-born architect and artist, Manolo Miranda Campos, in our home. For many years he had lived in Brazil and was now retired in the Rio suburb of Niteroi. In appreciation of our hospitality, he later gifted us with one of his magnificent paintings. It was an impressionistic scene of the Pelourinho district of Bahia at night, looking down the narrow cobblestone colonial streets, with churches on both sides. It beckoned us to go and see for ourselves what had inspired Manolo the artist.

There was another factor that came along to clinch the decision:

our friend Theresa. We had met Theresa back in 1984 when she and her six year old son Ghilherme came to live with us in Kensington under somewhat strained circumstances. She had only recently come to the Washington area to be reunited with her husband, an erstwhile Zairian colleague of mine in Africa. To escape an abusive relationship with him, she and Ghilherme came to stay with us a few months, long enough to conclude that she should return home to Sao Paulo. We enjoyed their company very much; they were our window onto Brazil. Since then Theresa had importuned us to come and visit her in Sao Paulo. When we finally called to tell her that we were really thinking of coming to Brazil, but that we really wanted to visit Bahia, Theresa was not offended. She, too, was planning a vacation to Bahia and immediately offered to make in-country arrangements for us. That did it! I cashed in my PanAm frequent flyer mileage for a free ticket to Sao Paulo and the rest began to fall into place. It was late December and all around us the Washington area was locked in the deepest freeze in years. And there we were planning the Great Escape!

Inflation...it will be useful for the reader to retain one important fact of life in the Brazil of the late-1980s, one which was to have a significant effect on our own plans. It had to do with inflation. The Brazilian currency, the cruzado, had been wheezing heavily ever since it came to replace the defunct cruseiro. By the end of 1989 the rate of inflation in Brazil was running at 1500% per annum! Although considerably better than Argentina's 4000%, it was nevertheless a disastrous state of affairs, especially for the 95% of Brazilians who were not independently wealthy. Of course, inflation serves the interest of those who are in a position to speculate. The poor suffer the brunt of inflation. For example, a day laborer who agrees to do a week's work is obliged to calculate what his labor will be worth a week hence at payday, not today. An increase in the price of petroleum, not infrequent, has a ripple effect on all sorts of other prices, not just transportation. And what does inflation have to do with the Americnan tourist? Everything!

The exchange rate between the dollar and the cruzado (written NCz$) was changing almost daily. In early January when we bought our airplane tickets the official rate was NCz$11 to the dollar, while the unofficial rate was around NCz$ 20. By the time of our arrival in Sao Paulo on January 12th the unofficial rate was inching toward

NCz$ 30, and when we left at the end of the month, the dollar was fetching NCz$ 371. A jumbo-sized bottle of beer (either Brahmia or Atlantica) sold for as little as NCz$15, and an entire meal in a good restaurant cost between NCz$ 150 and 250. In sum, this means that everything seemed quite cheap to the tourist carrying dollars, deutschmarks, or imagine...yen! The Brazilian government aided and abetted this windfall by providing for a tourist (unofficial) rate of exchange window at most banks. Moneychangers in the streets, however, offered a few percentage points more, flashed on 3x5 cards for the non-Portuguese speaking tourist.

Sao Paulo: Setting the Stage

We arrived at the Sao Paulo airport in the afternoon of a bright spring-like day and were greeted by Theresa and Ghilherme with a bouquet of flowers. We were happy to be reunited after so longa time. For us, of course, it was an immense relicf to have our own personal guide to Brazil. We made our way by bus on long stretches of freeway which cut through the sprawling suburbs of South America's largest city. Sao Paulo, now celebrating its 400th anniversary, occupied rolling hills about a four-hour drive west of Rio de Janeiro. It doesn't take long for the North American visitor to notice something strange: the roads are filled with Fords and Chevrolets, but few Japanese products. Brazil must have a soft spot in its heart for Detroi; VW bugs more than 15 years old are popular among taxi drivers for their modest fuel consumption.

Theresa lived in a 6th floor walk-up apartment in the Pinheiro district of the city, not too far from downtown. It was a seemingly quiet neighborhood, surrounded on all sides by high-rises. Still, a small town ambiance held sway, where people took time to stop and chat on the street and swap child care chores. Although born outside of Sao Paulo, Theresa was a confirmed Paulista (citizen of Sao Paulo) so thoroughly urbanized that that she professed to miss the noise and pollution, the 24-hour life style, when traveling to 'rural areas" such as Bahia. She worked hard as an administrative secretary at Citibank to support herself and Ghilherme. Our brief stay in the city featured a welcome dinner in Theresa's apartment where we met some of her close friends and her mother. And we tasted a bit of cultural life, attending a show of the Ballet National de Senegal, followed by drinks at a newly opened piano bar featuring the jazz stylings of a pianist who went by the name of Tio Joao.

The Political Scene

Evidences of the recently held presidential elections were everywhere, on posters, graffiti on the walls...and newspaper headlines. Two candidates had emerged from the November primaries to face each other in the December run-off. Luis Ignacio da Silva, popularly known by the nickname Lula, represented the Socialist Workers' Party (Parti de Trabalho—PT). He was a metalworker from one of Sao Paulo's' industrial suburbs, a newcomer to the political scene. He had little formal education but was said to be gifted with a charismatic style. Lula's party (PT) was only 10 years old and was attempting to assemble the fractious political left under one tent. His support came from the trade union movement, intellectuals, and to some extent the Catholic Church. Lula's campaign was focused on restoring economic growth, redistributing the country's wealth and undertaking much needed social development programs.

Lula's opponent, Fernando Collor de Mello was an equally unknown politician, originally from the backwater state of Alagoas in the northeast. His National Renovation Party was also obscure coming into the primaries. But voters gave Collor 2.8% of the primary vote, versus 16% for Tale's PT and 15% for a third candidate, Leonel Brizola. The incumbent Brazilian Democratic Movement Party (PMDB) of President Sarney received a scant 4% of the total, as measured by the number of seats in the Congress. The mood of the country was clearly for change. The December general election brought Collor (pronounced as in ring-around-the-collar) to power. His administration was to take office in March 1990. Collor's campaign was characterized by populist demagoguery. He decried the prevalent corruption in government and its padded payrolls, calling for the adoption of radical free-market principles and the dismantling of state-owned enterprises, or privatization.

Collor himself was young at 40 and photogenic, scion of a wealthy land-owning family. His self-styled Camelot image was sometimes likened to that of another youthful presidential candidate in the United States in the early 1960s. Tabloids reported in excruciating detail the lavish post-election European vacation of president-elect Collor and his wife. Meanwhile, speculation centered on his likely choice of cabinet members. His chief economic advisor, Zelia Cardoso de Mello, was already installed as a media celebrity. At 35, Zelia (as she was commonly known in the press) was a professor of economics with a reputation for slightly liberal tendencies. During the campaign she advocated balancing the budget and reducing the deficit, likely to equal fully 5% of the gross domestic product. She talked of measures to achieve this, such as reducing the number of government ministries by half and stepping up tax collection by closing loopholes. She estimated that Brazilians pay only about 40% of the taxes they owe.

Shortly after our arrival the Sao Paulo newspaper, A Foiha, ran a lengthy editorial entitled Cheque de coragem, bluntly asserting that the Brazilian economic crisis could not be resolved without political courage, courage to destroy once and for all the failed parastatal structures. Courage to halt inflation, to break the vicious cycle of public irresponsibility and improvisation. The president-elect and his chief economic advisor deftly embraced the editorial, saying that it represented in itself an "injection of courage." Zelia now talked of reducing inflation by 4 to 5% within three months and attracting up to $2 billion (U.S. dollars) of foreign investment participation in the program of privatization within one year. She urged the liberalization of price and wage policies within three months, all part of an economic emergency plan.

The Collor team's task was daunting. The gaping inequities in Brazilian society during colonial rule had been re-enforced with elitist rule since independence. Nearly half of the total national income was accounted for by 10% of the population, while the bottom half of the society earned only 12%. In an economy that was the tenth largest in the world, more than half of the Brazilian population received less than $2000 a year and even that was ravaged by inflation.

Salvador, Bahia

In 1500, only eight years after Columbus' maiden voyage to the New World, the Portuguese explorer Pedro Alvares Cabral first set foot on Brazilian soil. His ship landed in Porto Seguro, on the southeastern coast of what is today the state of Bahia. Within a year a group of settlers sent by the Portuguese Crown arrived in the bay that was to give the region its name, All Saints Bay, (Bahia de Todos os Santos), and established the city of Salvador. For 233 years this was the capital of the Portuguese colony. It was the administrative, commercial and cultural center of the colony—including a flourishing trade in slaves. Portuguese settlers—known as banderantes came to open up the land and in the process took up occasionally with African slave women. There emerged a racial mixture known as mulatto, said to be derived from the color of the mule. Today over 40% of the population of Brazil is of mixed racial origin—African, European and Amerindian.

Salvador (often refered to as Bahia) is the third largest city in Brazil with a population of some three million, 85% Black. This is the heaviest concentration of people of African descent in the Western Hemisphere. Bahia is rich in colonial architecture although many of the ancient buildings are in disrepair. The city of Salvador is filled with over 365 churches, many of them concentrated in the old historic districts. The state of Bahia is also the cradle of many famous writers, artists and musicians, nurtured by the long cultural heritage. The section of the city known as Pelourinho (from the Portuguese) is the very heart of Bahia. It is on the Largo do Pelourinho where the infamous whipping post once stood for flogging unruly slaves. The best-selling book Dona Flor and her Two Husbands depicted a bawdy and colorful story set in Bahia. The movie version of Dona Flor entertained many North Americans, although few probably associate it with Bahia.

Bahia is the New Orleans of Brazil (or perhaps we should say it versa visa). While the popular boss nova style of the early 1960s emerged from the coffee houses of Rio, its rhythmic roots are traceable to Bahia. Its precursor, the samba, had been around in various forms for many years and is still the basic ingredient in carnaval dances. The samba in turn grew out of the informal dances of the descendents of slaves who formed a circle, clapped and sang and did the umbigades (literally, the belly button thrust). The most striking feature of the Bahian scene is capoeira, a dance and martial arts form brought from West Africa. It consists of frenetic whirling and kicking high into the air in rhythm to the drums and the strumming of the berimbau, usually a gourd strung with a wire that makes a percussive tone somewhere between a cello and a guitar. Before each match the two athletes kneel in front of the berimbau player, shake hands and then step into a circle.

As in the United States, much of the African music of Bahia

was born out of religious tradition, which in the case of Brazil candomble, still practiced today. This tradition gave rise to a generation of popular Bahian musicians, some of whom have attained international star status. Two of them, Caetano Veloso and Gilberto Gil, first burst on the scene in the late 1960s with styles that were steeped in the African tradition but drew upon the resources of pop-rock then sweeping through Western civilization. Their music was so irreverent and bombastic at the time that Caetana Veloso and Gilberto Gil were forced into exile in London by the military government of Brazil. Today both singers are riding the crest of popularity sustained by fervent Brazilian aficionados and increasingly appreciated by an international audience. Caetano's sister, Maria Bethania, has also made a big name for herself beyond Brazil. My own layman's awareness of this tradition was in large part the basis of my motivation to visitBahia.

Nowhere is African culture more in evidence than in Bahian cuisine. This was sure to appeal to our Africanized palettes. One of its basic characteristics is the generous use of dende oil, derived from the African palm tree that thrives along the coast. The Brazilian equivalent of the hamburger is the acaraje, prepared with batter made from fradinho beans soaked in water overnight and cooked in hot dende oil. Baihanas, (women of Bahia) dressed in traditional blouses and skirts, can be seen serving acaraje in their kiosques on the beaches and street corners. One of the most popular dishes is the mogueca, a casserole consisting of a shrimp or seafood base and a concoction of coconut and herbs, of course cooked in dende. There is always an abundance of pimenta to hotten up whatever you're eating.

Itaparica

Our actual destination was an island in the middle of All Saints Bay, a 45-minute boat-ride from Salvador. We had picked out a hotel from its description in travel books as a quiet retreat in a pleasant natural setting. We figured that we could have the peaceful rural ambiance and still be able to experience the myriad attractions of the city. This turned out to be the case, with certain important caveats.

Theresa's friend Gisele, a native of Bahia now living in Sao Paulo, was on hand to meet us at the Salvador airport. She and her family proved to be very warm and gracious hosts. While Theresa and

Gisele were a bit puzzled as to why we had chosen to stay in an out-of-the-way place, they were willing to accommodate our wishes. We had made reservations for two weeks at the Galeao Sacramento, and they had agreed to provide transportation from the airport to the boat launch and then a boat across the bay. After a lengthy wait and several phone calls to and from the Galeao we took a taxi to the marine terminal where a large in-board luxury cruiser awaited us. We were off on the next leg of our much anticipated adventure, not realizing that the little glitch in transportation communication presaged our only real inconvenience over the next couple of weeks.

Itaparica is the largest of several islands in the Bay of All Saints, extending about 18 miles in length. In the past it was the center of a thriving whaling industry. Today the main off season activities are artisanal fishing and small holder farming of fruits and vegetables. The travel books lured us to the island with such adjectives as "incomparable" and "glorious" to depict its natural wonders. One of the books goes so far as to assert that for "the first-timer the ideal vacation is to split time between the city and the island." So this was our strategy. The Galeao Sacramento was described as the "perfect retreat for a quiet weekend," during the off season which is any time other than December through February. Well, okay, we were going to hit Itaparica during the peak pre-carnaval tourist season, but how much difference could that make? We would soon find out.

Itaparica is indeed lush and tropical, with stately mango trees and coconut palms along the coast to greet the visitor. A constant breeze waiting across the bay tends to mitigate the tropical heat and humidity. Our luxury boat pulled up in the choppy waters in front of the seaside hotel and we waited for a smaller boat to take us ashore. And we waited. Something was amiss. Our driver shouted and gesticulated to another man on shore who finally came out in a flimsy kayak, offering to take us on in, with our luggage. Dawn took one look at the kayak bobbing cork-like in the waves and respectfully declined. Eventually our boat headed toward the end of the island to Bom Disapacho where the ferryboat docks. From there a taxi took us on the 10-minute ride to the Galeao.

This was our introduction to a most unreliable hotel service. When it became clear after several days that we could not count on the Galeao boat we threw ourselves at the mercy of the sundry forms of public transport, including the ferryboat, an umbilical cord to Salvador—and the system of VW kombis and buses that traverse the island. A typical day consisted of four to five hours of commuting into and out of the city jousting in a vast melting pot of humanity, lemmings to and from the beaches.

At the Galeao we were welcomed by Patricia, a French woman at the reception desk. She was to serve as our vital link to a bewildering morass of managerial incompetence. The sole person there who spoke a language other than Portuguese, she struggled daily to explain (and interpret) to us in French why this or that didn't work or why something wasn't on time. She was a saint. For that matter, all the hotel help were especially pleasant and cordial. But when Patricia was not on duty and crises arose, it was difficult. It was under these circumstances that my primitive Portuguese was forged:

"A gue hora saia a launcha hoje?" (What time does the boat leave?), I managed to ask.

"At 9:00 AM," was the response.

But each day a new set of explanations was offered for why it didn't leave at the appointed time. The manager, as it turned out, preferred to remain anonymous, for reasons quite obvious to us. Okay, I am probably making too much of this matter. After all, we were in a tropical paradise!

The Galeao in fact has much to commend it. The three and four story apartments are perched turret-like among the giant mango trees. Brightly colored parrots chat amiably with guests or screech at each other from their perches. A stable of horses provides recreation for the adventuresome. The sound system sends soothing jazz and Latin rhythms throughout the resort. The Galeao beach affords a panoramic view of the city shimmering across the bay. Except for the chattering teen-agers on the weekends, it is a quiet retreat. Along the beach was the village of Mar Grande, with its own boat launch, a picturesque church, snack shops and Baianas selling acaraje. In the evenings the village came alive with teenagers and tourists milling about the square.

Apart from using the Galeao as our base of operations, we also found Itaparica to be an interesting attraction in its own right. Barbara, a friend of ours from the old days in Zaire had reportedly gone to live on the island some years ago. We thought it might be worthwhile trying to look her up. We knew only that she taught French at the Itaparica Club Med and lived in the village of Moucambo. Anxious to see whether we could find Barbara and curious, too, about the Club Med, Dawn and I decided to rent bicycles and ride on over to the Club. It was said to be only a few kilometers away. In any case, I figured, Itaparica is only an island, so it couldn't be too far away. We set out bare-headed under the mid-day sun, peddling away. It was hot and we didn't seem to be getting any closer to the Club Med. The thought slowly occurred to me that Australia was also an island, but you shouldn't necessarily try to bicycle across it. Just as we were about to succumb to heat stroke, we came across a local entrepreneur with straw hats which he was willing to sell to us for considerably more than they were worth.

Fifteen kilometers later we staggered up to the front gate of the Club Med. The keeper of the gate confirmed that there was indeed a Barbara who taught French there. While waiting for her to finish teaching a class, we were accorded a walking tour of the grounds. It was a lush tropical setting amidst a thick growth of bamboo, a fresh water lake and a vast array of sporting facilities leading to the beach. We had left the Third World at the gate. This was another world, peopled by the International Jet Set. We learned that the original Club Med was organized by survivors of the holocaust in Europe who could not afford to go on vacation, so they offered their services to manage a Mediterranean resort for members only. The idea was so compelling that today there are scores of Clubs around the world, the staff are known as the GOs (gentil organisateurs) and the others as GMs (gentil members). The Itaparica Club Med was the first to be built in Brazil and catered mainly to wealthy Argentinians and Brazilians. Barbara came to greet us and seemed genuinely bemused that people she scarcely knew would hunt her down in her island redoubt.

Barbara invited us to visit her home at the other end of the island where she had lived for nearly 10 years with two of her own children and several adopted ones. She also managed to pay the school fees for 40 children in the area. Her farm consisted of several hectares of mango trees and grazing land for her 10 head of cattle. Barbara explained that in good years the sale of mangoes in the local market provided a modest supplementary income. She wais well versed in the art of maintaining the orchard and was acutely familiar with the vagaries involved. Last year, for example, there was an overabundance of rain, which retarded the blossoming of the trees. As a result, the harvest this year had been meager and Barbara's income therefore drastically reduced. One afternoon we walked with the kids down to the beach and fished for siri (small crabs) with a net. An hour or so later we were eating a tasty casquinha de siri cooked in dende oil and served with the ubiquitous farfofa (manioc) flour.

Baiacu—Africa in the Western Hemisphere

We had been hearing about a place called Baiacu on the same side of the island, where runaway slaves had established a free town deep in the rainforest as early as the mid-1600s. We asked to visit the place. Barbara obligingly rounded up a kombi driver willing to take us there. We bounced over rough roads and eventually into dense forest. Rounding a bend in the road, we came across a truly remarkable sight. There stood a 400-year old stone church built by the Jesuits shortly after the arrival of the Portuguese in Brazil, now entirely overgrown by the massive roots of tropical trees. It was a study in symbiosis, for neither the roofless church nor the trees seemed to have been able to survive without the other all these years. The recent remains of candles here and there were most probably from the practice of candomble than Catholicism.

We continued on down the road a little farther as it narrowed into the main street of Baiacu, coming to rest at the edge of the bay. Some of the homes were made of concrete blocks and tile while others were of mud and wattle. This traditional fishing village was populated overwhelmingly by dark-skinned people who could surely trace their ancestry back 400 years to those runaway slaves. Their complexion was distinctively different from the café au lait pigmentation of mainstream Brazilians. Our kombi finally came to a stop in front of the house of friends of Barbara's friends. This time we were treated to a feast of shrimp, dende and pimento washed down with cold Brahma beer. A sprightly gentleman—I guessed he was in his sixties—who had been sipping something he called cachcasu (a kind of home brew from sugar cane)—came around to regale us with homespun stories about how to grow old gracefully. I asked him to repeat what he called the drink, which he did. Sure enough, cachasu is the very same Bantu word used for the home brew concocted throughout villages in Zaire! It had survived for 400 years among the people of Baiacu. Furthermore, the gentleman's manner and bearing were unmistakably African.

The last foray during our stay on Itaparica took us to the town of Nazare, on the mainland away from Salvador. The main interest here was the market, which was said to feature pottery made in the region. Nazare is nestled in the hills bordering a river about an hour's drive from Itaparica. The market itself proved to be a disappointment, but our guide suggested driving farther up to a village (with an unpronounceable name) where the pottery was actually made. It was well worth the trip. We found scores of kilns surrounded by mounds of clay, interspersed with potters at their wheels. Each shed was stocked with hundreds of bowls, vases, figurines and plates. The entire village consisted of this series of cottage industries, constituting the largest production of pottery in the region.

Iguatemi

When we were not exploring Itaparica we were making our way across the bay to the city of Salvador. Gisele's family lives in a forest of high rise apartments in the northern suburb of Pituba. Our program usually involved taking the ferryboat to the terminal, then catching a bus for a 30 to 45 minute ride up to Iguatemi, a sprawling shopping center near their apartment. Gisele, Theresa and their entourage would pick us up in front of Iguatemi and we would be off. Each day was another adventure, within the rhythm of a typical bahiana family rather than the usual tourist routine. One trip through the labyrinthine Iguatemi shopping mall was enough for us to understand that Salvador is a major consumer market that compares with anything the Washington area has to offer.

The city of Salvador, like Rio, is located at the mouth and along the shores of a large bay. To the north of the center of the city on the Atlantic Coast there are miles and miles of white sand beaches. Salvador occupies two geographic levels. The lower city—cidade baixa—consists of wharfs, warehouses and commercial buildings, whereas most of the historical buildings are perched on a cliff in the upper city above the waterfront. The two levels are connected by sometimes sharp inclines known as lladerias, as well as an imposing complex of elevators that carry passengers between the upper and lower part of the city.

Near the elevator is one of the best known structures in the city, the Mercado Modelo. First installed in the old customs house at the port in 1915, the mercado was built on the site where the slave trade once flourished. Although the mercado was destroyed by fire several times, it has been completely reconstructed and now houses a maze of souvenir shops, a restaurant and stages in front for capoeira. Here one finds a full range of berimbaus in all sizes and colors for sale. Outside musicians pluck the berimbau and sing to accompany the stylings of the capoera fighters/dancers. My best find while wandering through the stalls was a sometime composer and merchant who was selling cassette recordings of traditional Bahian music. I loaded up.

Upstairs in a magnificent cavernous ballroom is one of the city's finest restaurants, the Camef en de Oxossi. We were seated near the windows, not far from a group of shirtless young men in dredlocks out on the terrace tapping on the table, strumming berimbaus and singing. As it began raining they moved inside and continued to play. While we were served a sumptuous repast consisting of the full gamut of moquecas, vatapa and accoutrements, the musicians went into an exuberant, full throated "serenade", which filled the room and spilled out onto the terrace. It was obviously part of the menu. The Camefeu de Oxossi was certainly unlike any restaurant I had ever frequented.

Just as important to an understanding of Salvador was stopping off at Gisele's favorite acaraje place, a kind of Bahian McDonald's, consisting of a mobile kiosk at the side of a square near the beach. It was apparently the favorite place of many Bahianos, since there was a long line. It was certainly worth the wait. We asked for lots of vatapa sauce and pimenta, washing it all down with tall bottles of Antartica, Gisele explained that we had now been officially initiated into life in Bahia!

One afternoon was spent browsing through Barra, a section of the city known for its beaches, bars, boutiques and interesting mix of people. It has been described as a kind of Bahian Greenwich Village, a bohemian quarter for artists, musicians and street people. At night Barra comes alive. Bars and restaurants spread their tables into the streets and live music blares from loudspeakers.

Our stay in Bahia did not include many of the cultural features for which the city is noted, for lack of time not interest. We did not manage to visit any of the ancient churches or see any religious festivals. And we were hesitant to attend any of the candomble ceremonies advertised for tourist consumption, for fear they would have a staged effect. In fact, we were to miss by a few days one of the important events of the year, the festival of Iomanja. The museums always seemed to be closed whenever we passed by. The last night in Salvador we stayed in the famous Convento do Canto, an imposing 300-year-old convent in the Pelourinho District that once served as home to Carmelite nuns. A short walk down the ladeiras from the Convento takes you into the colorful world of pimps, prostitutes and pickpockets that people Jorge Amado's novels. The gringo tourist is advised not to test his cross-cultural skills in this environment at night!

The Alakija Family

One of the unexpected pleasures of our visit to Bahia was the occasion to meet Gisele's family, the Alakijas. We were invited to lunch at the Alakija home where I spent much of the afternoon in discussion with her father, Dr. Jorge Alakija, a practicing psychiatrist. Fortunately he was quite conversant in English. Dr. Alakija proudly recounted the Yoruba origins of his family, reflected in the family name. His ancestors had come to Brazil as slaves and his grandfather managed to return for a visit to Nigeria as a free man. The Alakijas were a prominent family in Abeokuta, one of the most important traditional Yoruba cities.

Dr. Alakija's own interest in his origins was awakened and enriched during the 1970s when he was chosen to serve as a vice president representing South America on the organizing committee of the second worldwide Black arts and cultural festival in Lagos. Commonly known by its acronym, FESTAC, the festival was five years in the planning. Dr. Alakija's involvement in the process took him on several trips to Nigeria from 1973 to 1977 and reunion with members of his family still living there.

Dr. Alakija is an authority on hypnotism and uses it as a form of therapy whenever he considers it appropriate for his patient. During FESTAC, Dr. Alakija presented a paper on the trance state in candomble, in which he explored its therapeutic value. The cult of the orixas in Bahia is known as candomble; the same word applies to the place where the cult is practiced. The festival of the candomble begins with animal sacrifices, a tribute paid to Exu, a spiritual deity at the service of the orixas. This is to assure that the festival may take place in peace. This is followed by a chant to the orixas by the filhas de santo—daughters of the deity—who have undergone special training as novitiates.

The ceremonies are performed to the sound of special drums. When the group plays for a particular orixa, the corresponding filha de Santo begins to feel the influence of the specific rhythm and falls into a trance. She receives the entity which communicates through her to those in attendance. Dr. Alakija pointed out that this trance may be distinguished from others merely in terms of the external appearance, that is, the magic-primitive guise in which it is presented. It serves a similar functional unity in common with other neuro-physiological manifestations described in psychiatric literature sometimes termed the "kinetic trance".

This dispassionate explanation is of course a far cry from the image conjured up by the popular image of voodoo we Westerners enjoy making fun of. For example, when Manuel Noriega was recently being apprehended by the forces of the US army the press seized upon the evidence of his having been under the influence of a Brazilian voodoo agent. That did it! Most of us have accumulated too many layers of cultural bias to ever be able to recognize that the practice of candomble and assorted religious rituals might have any redeeming value.

Jaguaribe Beach and the Lambada

I must confess that much of our time in Bahia was spent on the beach. In this respect we were in good company. Bahianos themselves seem to appreciate their close proximity to the long stretches of white sand and surging surf. During the peak season they are joined by thousands of tourists from the interior and from around the world. Weekends in particular find a vast sea of bronze bodies worshipping the sun and enjoying the steady breeze from the Atlantic. Standard attire on the beach is the Brazilian bikini, or feo dental (dental floss), which aptly describes its dimensions! There is no point in feeling self conscious, unless one insists on remaining fully clothed. Bathers of all ethnic and racial compositions seem intent on becoming a shade darker, dobbing themselves with generous applications of tanning lotion. Theresa, for one, was pleased to be able to enhance her negritude.

The sights, sounds, and smells of the beach are truly sensuous.

The rich aroma of dende oil and cooking acaraje hang in the air. Everywhere clusters of people strum guitars, pound conga drums and sing samba songs from the recent carnaval with seemingly endless verses. Marathon volleyball and soccer games compete for scarce space in the sand. Merchants peddle everything from jewelry to suntan lotion and popsicles.

We had our habitual spot on Jaguaribe Beach, north of Pituba. Our "agent" kept us in regular supply of beer and soft drinks, essential ingredients at the beach. Sometimes he would bring drinks made from cachasu. More often it was the national drink known as caipirinha, a potent brew consisting of rum and a twist of lime. The caipiroska is made in a similar fashion...using, you guessed it, vodka! Not far from our spot on Jaguaribe Beach a band was playing rhythms our Bahiana friends identified as the lambada, with loud-speakers blasting for miles along the beach. An impromptu aerobics class did their exercises to the beat of the music. Whoever wishes to understand Bahia must grasp the importance of the beach, where it all happens!

Another confession: before coming to Brazil, I was not familiar with the dance known as the lambada. But I can now say that I have seen the best practitioners of this dance form. In keeping with her unerring sense of hospitality, Gisele and her friends took us one night to one of the most "in" places in Bahia, the Sabor de Terra (flavor of the earth.) Fortunately, we arrived before the dance floor was completely packed. For the first couple of hours in the evening we were treated to an exhibition of the most extraordinary display of dancing, equal parts energy and precision. Eventually the dance floor was crowded. Couples danced with something like a controlled frenzy, scarcely stopping to sit down or take a drink.

The room was full of steamy, vibrant energy. Dawn and I danced a couple of times and came away soaking wet. There was little space for rank Yankee amateurs. It seems that the dance we were witnessing was the lambada, a style that had already been in vogue for several years in this part of the world but was just beginning to catch on elsewhere. The term lambada is derived from the Portuguese word to whip which, well, conveys the essence of dance. It is in the tradition of the tango and meringue, and has become very popular in Europe and other parts of Latin America.

As we were leaving Brazil I happened to buy a copy of Newsweek and was treated to an article panning the lambada craze ("Lambada is a lot like sex, except more overrated"). Newsweek sniffed that "the lambada is cultural news so up to the minute that it hasn't happened yet..." This in spite of the fact that the Wall Street Journal and New York Times had already noticed the lambada craze! Upon return to Washington we found that the lambada was indeed gaining momentum. Thank you, Bahia!

Gilberto Gil

The highlight of a trip strewn with high points was the Gilberto Gil concert at the Concho Acoustical in Sara. The Concho is an outdoor arena in the shape of the Hollywood Bowl, surrounded on three sides by apartment buildings and located behind the Castro Averse Theater. The sound is obliged to reverberate around the buildings and back down to the audience before escaping into the air. The adjacent apartments must have been inhabited by music lovers or very grumpy people.

The audience was obliged to sit through a couple of warm up groups in eager anticipation of the arrival of Gil, an international pop star and the living embodiment of Bahia. Although originally from Bahia, Gil had spent much of his career living and performing abroad. His appearances in Bahia were therefore not as often as his public would like. Once he and his group came on stage it was abundantly clear that Gil was the master of the evening. A man in his mid-forties, Gil had the energy (that word again) and spunk of a teenager. His repertoire ranged from frenetic percussion in the African tradition, to lilting acoustic melodies and a borrowing from other artists.

He was the high priest of secularized candomble, constantly exhorting the audience to whoop and sing, urging them on to yet a higher level of involvement. People were on their feet the entire evening, struggling to keep up with their leader. When it seemed that he might be slowing down slightly, Gil paused after one song to ask his audience if they wanted more hock 'n holl. (the Brazilian tongue turns the English "r" sound into an "h". They roared their approval! In two and one half hours Gilberto Gil did not take a single break.

In the second half of the evening the group retired backstage and Gil took up his acoustical guitar. He sang a Portuguese version of the Beatles' Hey Jude, a song that was experiencing resurgence in Brazil. Gil paid tribute to Stevie Wonder with his own rendition of Wonder's compositions. But Gil showed slightly disguised scorn for Michael Jackson in a song that took the latter to task for running away from his black identify.

Saudade

Many Brazilian songs seem to be about saudade, a word that summons up a mood of reminiscence of things past. As a result of our visit to Brazil I believe I may have a better understanding of its meaning. I suspect I may have contracted a case of Brazilian saudade when reflecting on our experience there. It is rare in life that one's expectations are exceeded by experience. I think of how fortunate we were to have had such wonderful hosts, of how little time there was to absorb so much in Brazil. No doubt our experience there was sugar-coated by our privileged status as Americans. It is too easy to think of Brazil as a great racial and ethnic melting pot. But where are the black Brazilian politicians, members of the cabinet and presidents of corporations? True, black Brazilians have made names for themselves in the fields of music and sport. But, for that matter, where are the famous black women singers in Brazil? What is to become of the vanishing indigenous Indian population, the first to inhabit Brazil? What effect, if any, will the Collor government have on the abysmal conditions of poverty and inequality, so long ignored by its predecessors?

References

Galen Spencer Hull, "An American Goes to Bahia," in *The Brasilians*, May 1990.

Chapter 12

Sri Lanka and Vietnam, 1992: Immersion in Asian Culture

By self is one defiled...by self is one purified.
                                    -The Buddha in Dhammapada, v 165

The Buddha showed the path, and it is left for us to follow that path to obtain our purification. Self-exertion plays an important part in Buddhism.

Introduction

Sri Lanka is an island nation a few miles to the southeast of India, somewhat smaller than Ireland, with a population of over 17 million. In ancient times the country went by various names: Sinhaladvipa in the classical Indian literature, Taprobane to the Greeks, Serendib to the Arabs, Ccilao to the Portuguese and Ceylon to the British. In 1972 the official name of the country was changed from Ceylon to Sri Lanka. Even today, however, its most famous product is known around the world as Ceylon tea. The country's small size and close proximity to giant India cause Sri Lankans to be obsessed with everything India does and says. There is a constant preoccupation with asserting Sri Lankan uniqueness and independence from the mother culture, guarding against being swallowed up in any figurative or literal way.

The colonial era history of Ceylon lasted some 450 years, beginning with the Portuguese in the early 1500s. They came looking for cinnamon, the country's major product which gave it the name "Spice Island". At first the Portuguese were less interested in territorial possessions than they were trade. Eventually, however, through alliances with local kings and military conquests they became de facto rulers. Portuguese forts, houses and churches were built along the west coast of the island. The Dutch responded to an invitation from the King of Kandy—the last Sinhala kingdom to have held out against the Portuguese—to help drive the Portuguese out. This accomplished, the Dutch took up control of the country's lucrative trade from the middle of the 1600s. Unlike the Portuguese and Dutch, the British came not only to gain control of the existing natural resources but also to establish their own plantations. By the end of the 19th century the island had become a major exporter of tea, which remains its most important export crop to this day. The colonial period came to a relatively peaceful end in 1948 when Britain granted Ceylon independence.

My seven-month assignment in Sri Lanka in 1992 would prove to be one of the most intensive and educational experiences of my life. It became a search for understanding of the Sri Lankan culture, and an attempt to separate myth from reality. This search convinced me that living in other cultures and seeking to learn about them can somehow make a modest contribution to breaking down the cultural barriers and stereotypes that lead to discord and strife. Crossing cultures implies a moving from one cultural environment to another, perhaps even absorbing some part of another culture in the process. I cannot claim to have become in any sense Sri Lankan in the short period of time in which I lived in that country. But I do believe that I came away with certain insights and an appreciation of Sri Lankan life that will stay with me for a lifetime.

Sri Lanka is no longer the paradise island it was once thought to be, both by Sri Lankans themselves and foreign visitors. I was overwhelmed by the richness of the country's history and its cultural artifacts. I was taken by its natural beauty but struck by the fragile status of the ecology. At the same time I was also pained by the profound fissures in society that are manifested daily.

Certainly, while living in Sri Lanka one cannot help being aware of the protracted conflict between the majority Sinhalese and minority Tamils since the early 1980s. It is not so much between two basic civilizations—as between Hindu and Muslim in India—but two groups within the Hindu tradition. It pits the Sinhala population, descended from Bengalis from the north of India, and the Tamils, originally from Tamil Nadu in southern India. While the Sinhalese are mainly Buddhist and the Tamils are Hindu, it is often noted that they share at least as many cultural similarities as differences. The

Muslim population, an even smaller minority than the Tamils, seems to be more often than not the hapless victims of the conflict. It is not possible to understand the conflict in just religious and ethnic terms; equally important are differences in class and caste which are given far less attention by the press.

Having criss-crossed the island on several occasions and met people of all races and religions, economic and social status during my sojourn in Sri Lanka, I sensed that the prospects for the countrys future development were still quite promising. What I experienced was the multicultural diversity of a melting pot that refuses to melt. In sum, I felt richer for having experienced Sri Lanka. While I have tried to be balanced and objective in my observations, I am acutely aware that my Western biases will poke through upon every page. What I mean to convey, basically, is that there is much to learn from other cultures if one is open to that proposition. The consequences of this learning can be personally rewarding, and perhaps contribute to a better understanding of the sources of conflict.

Asian Development Bank Project, Sri Lanka   Spring 1992

In the spring of 1992 I arrived in Colombo, Sri Lanka, on a consulting assignment on the heels of yet another assignment in Africa. My life as a development consultant and travel enthusiast had already taken me to some 70 countries on four continents, but I was still something of a neophyte in Asia. This kind of work—a few months here, a couple of years there—can get tedious. Just as one starts to develop a certain empathy or even attachment to a place, it is time to move on. Occasionally the experience leaves an indelible impression that lasts for a lifetime. Some assignments, on the other hand, can be so harrowing and debilitating that you cannot wait to view the whole episode in the rearview mirror.

My mission as a consultant on an Asian Develoment Bank contract in Colombo, Sri Lanka, was to survey the problems and prospects for small and medium industries with a team of Sri Lankan specialists. I felt I had to try to understand how the Sri Lankan culture conditioned their activities, which prompted a self-education program. My cross cultural Peace Corps training had taught me to look at the world, not with rose-colored glasses or with the eye of a cynic, but simply to see the glass as being half full rather than half empty. This is easy enough to do in Sri Lanka where there is much to be enamored by as well as to be disconserted. My first impressions were of a mixture of the paradise island described in the tourist brochures, coupled with a nation struggling to maintain the richness of its culture while striving to become a Newly Industrialized Country by the year 2000. Even along the busiest streets there was a profusion of frangipani trees (here they were called aralias) whose fragrance competed happily with the exhaust fumes from passing trucks and buses. There was little sign of grinding poverty in the central city, and certainly not nearly as many panhandlers and people sleeping on the streets as in Washington, D.C.

Poya Day, or Full Moon Day, is the most common holiday in the Sri Lankan calendar. Each Poya Day marks a different episode in the life of The Buddha. My first holiday was Vesak in May, the most sacred of poya days because it commemorates the three most important events in the life of the Buddha: the day he was born, the day he attained Enlightenment and the day he died. It was a festive occasion. For several days leading up to the holiday street vendors sold an assortment of greeting cards with images of the Buddha and masks for the children. Each neighborhood constructed huge pandals depicting scenes from the life of the Buddha. At night the pandals were lit up in brightly colored lights and the scenes were narrated through a loud-speaker. For the newly arrived foreigner, Poya Day becomes a regular reminder of a significant cultural difference from life in the West. One must remember to do shopping in advance since all the stores are closed that day. For Buddhists it is a day to go the temple to hear bana preaching (sermons by the monks) or listen to the chanting of pirith (the verbatim discourses of The Enlightened One) in the original Pali language. Faithful Buddhists spend the day in meditation and reflection on the teachings of the Buddha and in observing "sil", vowing to follow the eight precepts of Buddhism.

I was struck by the gentle bearing and handsome features of the people of Sri Lanka. The women in particular are stunningly attractive in their multi-hued sarees, long-flowing raven colored hair, and ready smiles. Although generally shy and unassertive, their very demeanor is graceful and sensual. The men, too, are handsome in their traditional sarongs, although in the office setting they have long since given over to Western attire. Whatever "racial" distinctions exist between the Tamils, Sinhalese, Burghers (people of mixed race) and assorted others would continue to escape me. The same range of skin pigmentation from dark ebony to olive brown seems to be present within the same race. What is common among them is an unfailing politeness, friendliness and respect shown by everyone as a rule. Even-temperedness is the order of the day. On a few occasions when circumstances seemed to warrant a full blown argument and I started to raise my voice in exasperation, I was brought down with a comment such as, "Now, Doctor, you have misunderstood the situation."

Survey of Small Business Owners

My life as a consultant in Colombo took on a regular routine. Workdays consisted of checking into the National Development Bank where we had our project office. The bank staff were cordial and helpful to a fault and the working environment was quite pleasant. Tea was served twice a day at mid-morning and mid-afternoon, a soothing and civilized ritual. Our survey of small and medium scale industries was designed over a two month period and conducted from July through September 1992 by a team of local specialists recruited by the local affiliate of the Coopers and Lybrand accounting firm. My colleagues were specialists in food processing, wood, metal, rubber and electronics products. Working with them was educational and rewarding for the wealth of experience and knowledge they imparted. Our questionnaire was divided into two parts. The first was a profile of the company, drawing mainly upon information derived from the bank loan files. The second was a set of attitudes from the owners of industries themselves regarding the operation of their businesses.

On several occasions I managed to take trips "outstation" where I interviewed small business owners identified in our survey. After weeks and weeks of questionnaire design and testing, meetings and discussions with the Ministry of Industry, we were finally doing what we were hired to do: find out what problems small businesses were having and coming up with suggested strategies for dealing with them. On one trip to the town of Embilipitiya I interviewed the owner of a rice mill and a furniture manufacturer as well as a rubber mattress manufacturer in the coastal town of Matara. I had also arranged the trip so as to take advantage of witnessing an ancient religious festival at Kataragama which is observed every year by thousands of Hindus, Buddhists and Muslims. One of the features of the festival is the fire walk, which involves marching barefoot for about 10 yards over a bed of live coals. Pilgrims to Kataragama have done this for centuries as part their religious vows. The firewalk is only observed on one night of the festival, beginning at around 4:00 A.M.

On another trip north we interviewed an ice cream maker, a soft drink manufacturer and a producer of dried chilies in Puttalam, a predominantly Muslim town in the northwest. On the same trip I managed to visit the ancient ruins of Anuradhapura, Mihintale and the marvels of Sigiriya. As one raised in a small town in Oklahoma with a history of only a few decades, I could not help being awe-struck by the majesty of these ruins that tell of a civilization which flourished over 2,000 years ago.

The business owners who consented to the interviews which often lasted from two to two and a half hours were generally quite hospitable and accommodating to the members of our study team. The typical enterprise interviewed in our survey was family-owned, often involving sons and daughters, wives and brothers. Even those that had evolved from sole proprietorships into partnerships or limited liability companies often had the family as the nucleus of the business. Woman-owned enterprises interviewed nearly all had husbands as active partners in the business. All of the businesses interviewed were productive, that is, engaged in the transformation of a raw material into a finished product. None of them were strictly commercial or service industries. The vast majority of smaller companies had their factories and offices adjacent to their homes. This was in part a reflection of the fact that there were no effective zoning regulations that distinguished residential from industrial areas.

In our survey there were a total of 200 business owners in five sectors interviewed: food products (including tea), wood products, rubber products, metal products and electronics. They were located in most of the administrative districts in the country, although most were in Colombo and Gampaha Districts. Companies in the food processing industry were the most widely dispersed. Nearly all the tea factories interviewed were in Galle. The electronics companies interviewed were all located in the greater Colombo metropolitan area, from Panadura to Katunayake. While the wood sector was fairly well dispersed, there was a large clustering in Moratuwa, just south of Colombo. The main concentration of rubber companies was in Kalutara while metal companies were clustered in Colombo and Kurunegala.

Nearly half of those interviewed were registered as sole proprietorships, including most of the smaller units; a fourth were partnerships; while the others were limited liability companies, mostly the larger ones. In terms of gross annual sales, the range was from a few with less than 100,000 rupees to a few over 20 million rupees. There were equal numbers with sales below 500,000 rupees, (39%) and above 1.5 million rupees (39 percent) while the others were between 500,000 and 1.5 million rupees. With respect to the gross margin of profit, most companies were clustered in the range between 14% and 18%, while only 10% were below the 14% margin and the remainders were above 18%.

The number of workers employed by the companies in our survey ranged from fewer than five to 720. The food processing sector is characterized by a large number of very small units, whereas nearly all the electronics companies employ no fewer than 27 workers and an average of 100. Typical units in the metal and rubber sectors employ 20 to 30 workers. The wood products firms tend to be either quite large or very small. Most of the companies for which there was data indicated that none of their products was sold in the export market. Scarcely a handful of the food processing and metal products units have reached the export market, whereas all tea factories and more than half of the electronics companies produce for export.

The experience of driving around the exotic island of Sri Lanka, whether on the crowded streets of Colombo or along the narrow winding roads that run through the villages, can be unnerving. Sri Lankans themselves remark upon the sort of Dr. Jekyll and Mr. Hyde aspects of a people who are most courteous and mild-mannered in a face-to-face meeting, but who are transformed into monsters behind the wheel. Since I insisted on piloting my own ship on the road rather than relying on a driver, I quickly discovered that driving can be a truly hazardous business. There seem to be few rules of the road, other than giving way to the larger vehicle. The "buccaneers" of the road—as aptly described in a Daily News editorial—are the drivers of private buses. But drivers of all types of vehicles do not hesitate to approach you from behind, and if you are deemed to be going too slowly honk their horn frantically, then proceed to overtake and run your vehicle off the road. The price you pay for attempting to drive at a reasonable speed! A measure of the extent to which things have gotten out of hand was a bus which we noticed on the side of the road that had been overturned and burned to a crisp. The driver had run over and killed a village girl, so the villagers had taken appropriate revenge.

My stay in Sri Lanka was not dull. In many respects it was to provide me with the most challenging experience of my life in the crossing of cultures. Sri Lankans would prove to be generally friendly and hospitable. But the strong conservative influence of religion and family on their daily lives conditions their relations with outsiders, limiting the degree of intimacy in cross-cultural encounters. Throughout my stay in Sri Lanka I would struggle to fathom how such a seemingly gentle culture could harbor the virulent conflict that was also part of daily life.

Colpetty = Kol-lu-pi-ti-ya—a neighborhood in the city of Colombo

Within a week after my arrival in Colombo I managed to find an apartment to my liking on Sellamuttu Avenue just off Galle Road and moved out of the plush confines of the Galadari Meridien Hotel.

When I first moved into my apartment I told everyone I lived in Kollupitiya, an area within Colombo 3. I knew little about the city, but at least I knew where I lived. When I began shopping for things, people would tell me to look in Colpetty, just near my apartment. But I couldn't find Colpetty anywhere on my map. Then I began to notice Colpetty signs on buildings in my neighborhood. Well, wouldn't you know...Kollupitiya and Colpetty turned out to be the same place! Apparently the British had a tough time with the five-syllable Kol-lu-pi-ti-ya so they lopped off a couple of syllables and called it Colpetty. Now Sri Lankans imitate their imitators: Kollupitiya has become Colpetty to everyone except the publishers of Colombo maps!

A British chronicler of life in Ceylon in the mid-1800s described Colpetty as the most fashionable quarter of Colombo, consisting of large bungalows (dwellings on the ground floor) surrounded by highly-cultivated compounds or gardens. The neighborhood was just down the road from downtown, known simply as Fort, and Galle Face, the "Hyde Park" of Colombo. Every evening around five o'clock the area was quite animated. "there being many vehicles and horses in motion...and the eye of the stranger seeks in vain for the clear complexion, roseate hue of cheek and lip, vivacious expressive countenance and sparkling eyes, which are so pleasingly characteristic of Albion's daughters." These days there are many more vehicles, no horses, an occasional elephant, and a few more persons of European origin (only a handful of them Albion's daughters) traveling along Galle Road to Colpetty from Galle Face.

The same British chronicler of 19th century Colombo remarked upon the "immense flocks of carrion crows that infest Colpetty." While these birds abounded in every port of Ceylon, he was persuaded that their number and audacity were more manifest in this part of the island than elsewhere.

> These creatures are much larger than their European brethren, the plumage is thicker and more glossy and assuredly there is much speculation in their eyes. We think them very handsome-looking, intelligent birds. No sooner did the first glimmer of daybreak appear than their loud and incessant guttural kha-haa, kha-haa, used to break our matinal slumbers. The boldness, thievish propensities, and perseverance of these creatures are almost incredible.

Crows had been known to fly into the breakfast rooms, seize a slice of bread, and fly off with it, with people seated at the table. Reading this passage of the chronicle was for me deja vu. I did not need an alarm clock, such was the regularity of the "kha-haaing" of the present generation of crows in the early morning hours. Although I would not characterize them as "handsome", I noticed the "speculation in their eyes." And I witnessed a certain inhumanity among these carrion crows. On several occasions I watched a band of crows pin one of their "brethren" to the ground and literally peck the life out of him/her, as a chorus of dozens "kha-haaed" their approval from adjoining perches. What could he have done to deserve this sort of treatment?

The Colpetty area became the commercial center for the expatriate and well-to-do Sri Lankan set in nearby Cinnamon Gardens. The landmark building in my neighborhood was the Renuka Hotel, a three-star affair at the corner of Galle Road and Sellamuttu Avenue. Construction was underway for a sister Renuka City Hotel adjacent to the existing one. With all the five star hotels engaged in a price war in nearby Fort (downtown Colombo), it was not clear to me how the Renuka could hope to compete for that business. In Liberty Plaza you could buy almost anything, from the latest consumer gadgets such as video cassettes and tennis equipment to handcraft items and gourmet food. Air Lanka, the fifth fastest growing airline in the world according to a recent report, had just opened a branch office in Colpetty. A typical cottage industry in the area consisted of the privately managed telephone, fax, telex and postage outlets, many of them open 24 hours a day. They did a land office business owing to the scarcity of private phones. It took a minimum of six months to a year to get a phone installed in your home or business, when you were lucky.

Today Galle Road, the main north-south artery running along the coast to the town of Galle, has become a river of traffic full of bleating buses belching diesel smoke and three-wheeled bajajs swerving in and out and underneath them with seeming reckless abandon. Recently renovated into a dual carriage way with median lane, Galle Road has become the Sunset Strip and Champs Elysee of Colombo. Our neighborhood was awarded the prize for the most road accidents in a month, beating out such tough competitors as Bambalapitiya, Cinnamon Gardens and Fort. Kollupitiya (Colpetty) reported 110 accidents for the month, compared to 103 for Bambalapitiya. A familiar scene along Galle Face was a work crew wrestling to disengage a metal lamp post mangled by a wayward vehicle to replace it with another.

Colpetty certainly was more a commercial area than a residential one. Yet occasionally one was reminded of its social fabric. One night in September as I was reading in my apartment I began to hear a popping sound. I wandered outside and up to Galle Road, only to find a full-fledged temple-sponsored perahera (parade) going on. There had been no mention of it in the English language papers, nor had any of my neighbors said anything about it. Unlike the perahera in Kandy, there were few spectators lined up along the street. But it was a sure-enough perahera, what with elephants and dancers and drums and all. One notable difference: there were far more women and girls participating in this perahera than were to be seen in the great Kandy perahera.

The neighborhood was full of working class intellectuals. The man who sold me stamps in the private telephone/fax/postal agency up the street from my apartment insisted on engaging me in intellectual discourse with the purchase of each set of stamps. One day I scarcely had entered the office when he greeted me cheerily with the observation that today was the 25th anniversary of the assassination of President Bandaranaike. (This went unremarked upon, even in the opposition press). He recalled that the very man who had gone on the air to announce the death of the President was implicated in the murder, along with a Buddhist monk. He went on to point out that Mrs. Bandaranaike was then also standing for election as a Member of Parliament. She became the first woman Prime Minister in the world as a result of her husband's assassination.

The proprietor of my apartment building, Jimmy Rockwood, was a Tamil whose Christian family had moved from the Jaffna Peninsula to Colombo some years ago. He was a bright, entrepreneurial type who had constructed apartment buildings on the land he inherited in the section of Colombo known as Kollupitiya. The furniture, doors and window frames had been crafted by an artisan whose workshop was directly below my window. From the balcony of my second floor apartment I could watch the sun sinking into the Indian Ocean and hear the waves lapping against the shore. There was a perpetual breeze wafting in from the ocean, sometimes gentle, and at other times during monsoon season like a lion's roar. Always sufficient to keep the potentially pesky mosquitoes off guard and usually enough to make it pleasant sleeping. I was taken with the personality of the place.

Mr. Rockwood employed a young man named Raja as his apartment manager. Raja wore a bright smile and courteous demeanor and spoke in halting phrases, often omitting either subject or verb. But his sign language was excellent and he usually managed to get his point across. Raja was not exactly lazy, but he definitely took to certain tasks in preference to others. The apartment came equipped with a television of sorts which was frequently on the blink. Raja would come and tinker with the antenna or the knobs, and then for a while the reception would be better before reverting to its original behavior. Sometimes Raja would appear at the door with huge papayas or bananas as a token of his esteem for his client. When I presented him with a maroon-colored Washington Redskins T-shirt his smile was even broader than usual.

I lived on the second floor of a three-story apartment. Directly above me there was a succession of tenants during my stay in there. The one I got to know best was Tappani, a Finnish telecommunications technician who had formed a consulting group with some fellow Finns and a Sri Lankan partner. He had spent two years on the south coast at Hambantota where he and his colleagues installed a new telephone grid. One day he stopped into my apartment to introduce himself and noticed my key chain which carried a Finlandia Vodka pendant. Tappani asked whether I had any particular interest in Finland. I explained that while visiting Sweden with my father in search of our family roots several years before we had discovered that our ancestors may have originally come from Finland. Tappani took this as a good sign and we became fast friends. I enjoyed his wry sense of humor and insight into the local culture. We developed a pleasant habit of going out to a different ethnic restaurant—Korean, Chinese, Japanese, and Pakistani—every Sunday evening.

Sellamuttu, named after a former mayor of Colombo, was not so much an avenue as it was an alley which dead-ended at the ocean. In the daytime it was full of cars and vans related to the various commercial enterprises on the street. By night it reverted to a quiet residential area. Soon after settling into my new digs I was adopted by another Raja, an extroverted young man working in one of the Sellamuttu family enterprises next door to the apartment. His English was considerably more advanced than the apartment manager Raja, but even so rather convoluted and difficult to follow. At first he would stop by to say hello, and eventually began bringing me letters and postcards he had received from friends in the U.S. and Britain who had visited Sri Lanka. It seemed that he adopted any foreigner who crossed his path and he fancied himself an amateur travel agent. Raja told me of his village, Weligama, and the wonders of the coral reefs near it. He insisted that I go and visit his home one weekend. I put him off the first few months until I finally succumbed, inviting him to go along as my guide on one of my outstation missions. Our brief stay in Weligama was my first taste of Sinhala village culture outside the city and it was well worthwhile.

Within a few days after settling into my apartment I put out the word to anyone I met or worked with that I was looking for a cook who need only be skilled in making Sri Lankan curry and rice dishes.

In Africa I would have been inundated with candidates, camping on my door step with letters attesting to their honesty and work habits. Such was not the case in Colombo. Several people told me pointedly that it was unlikely I would find anyone willing to work on a temporary, part-time basis. (I anticipated no more than five to six hours of work a day for six months.) For the first few weeks I was discouraged by the luke warm response.

One day I mentioned my search to Joel, who worked at the Colombo Swimming Club where I went for my evening ritual of swimming laps. He said he had a cousin who might be interested and would check with her to see. A week later we arranged for her to come to my apartment and discuss the matter. Jacintha Jacobs was somewhat hesitant, saying that she was used to housework but not cooking for foreigners. I assured her I was interested in spicy curries and that seemed to put her at ease. But then she mentioned her main hesitation, which was that she was waiting for a sister in Kuwait to inform her about the prospects for work there. For my part, I wondered whether she would be reliable and stay the course. With these reservations on both sides, Jacintha came to work. For the next few months at least, the call to work in Kuwait did not come.

Jacintha was a Burgher, the term used to describe those persons in Sri Lanka who are of European, predominantly Dutch descent. Burghers account for less than one percent of the population, and as the name would imply, live mostly in urban areas. Like most Burghers, she was a devout Roman Catholic and spoke quite good English as well as Sinhalese, but no trace of Dutch. Not only did Jacintha prove to be reliable, she was a good cook and diligent worker.

Jacintha was immensely relieved when I explained that I wanted her to cook only the traditional Sri Lankan dishes she made at home, and the spicier the better. She took me at my word, and my palette soon became attuned to the rich texture of curried cuisine. She would cook once in the morning, making enough for both lunch and dinner, and then leave in the afternoon after cleaning up. Invariably she would make more than I could eat, and my entreaties to prepare less were taken lightly.

"Suh must eat properly. Looking too thin."

Despite my running around in the tropical sun and a regular routine of exercise, I began to put on pounds. Jacintha seemed pleased with her work!

Jacintha and her husband had two children, a teen-aged girl and a son who recently graduated from high school and plays field hockey. Her husband worked as a watchman—a major, although poorly paying industry in Sri Lanka—and is in poor health. A few years ago Jacintha had gone off to Singapore to work as a housemaid. There she earned the handsome sum of Rs. 4000 ($93) a month, double what she could expect in a similar job in Sri Lanka. In fact, one of the largest contributors to the gross national product is derived from remittances from Sri Lankans working abroad, mainly in the Middle East. It is not unusual for Sri Lankans who have returned from these jobs abroad to have substantial savings which they sometimes are able to invest in new ventures. But overseas employment has also contributed to an increase in marital tensions. Whereas traditionally divorce was almost unheard of in Sri Lanka, it is now not only heard of but increasingly common. Happily, Jacintha's family had weathered her two year absence in Singapore.

After she had been on the job for a few weeks, Jacintha noticed some of my papers on the table regarding small business development. She shyly remarked that she, too, was a small business person. She began to tell me of her family, her previous work experience and how the family made ends meet. Jacintha owns two candy floss (we call it cotton candy) machines and a generator. These constitute her basic capital assets. The business consisted of transporting the machines from her home by taxi and setting them up on weekends and holidays at church fairs and festivals and at Galle Face Park. At the festivals, which seem to occur every two or three weeks somewhere in the area, Jacintha could hook up her machines to electrical outlets. But at Galle Face park there was no outlet, so she had to have a generator to power the machines.

Jacintha needed an infusion of capital to invest in a new generator since the old one had burned up. Her modest income from the business, combined with the earnings from work for me, were not nearly sufficient. But she was reluctant to go into debt in order to purchase a new machine. Because of my work with small business owners, I began to notice advertisements in the newspapers for business loans at various banks. I eventually persuaded Jacintha to apply for a small business loan at one of those banks. She brought back the application forms and I helped her fill them out, listing her assets and describing her clientele.

I agreed to serve as co-signer on the loan and gave information about my bank account. The application was turned in and then the waiting process began. After numerous phone calls to check on the status of the application, the first bank finally turned her down, saying that they had just run out of funds for small business loans. I accompanied her to another bank where we got a friendly reception but similar response. Even as I was preparing to leave Sri Lanka, Jacintha had not been successful in getting a bank loan. Meanwhile, her family continued to operate the two machines without the benefit of a generator and I felt guilty for having dragged her into the unpleasant experience of dealing with banks.

Down along Galle Road there was a large Methodist Church complex including church, school and commercial building. Like most of the churches in Colombo, at least once in the year the church holds a big carnival that lasts for several days. I learned that this was one of the most popular cultural features in Sri Lanka. The typical carnival has a wide variety of snack foods ("short eats"), toys, games, rides and music. These carnivals were also a major source of income for people like Jacintha, who would set up her two candy floss (cotton candy) machines and sell candy floss for anywhere from three to ten rupees, depending upon the neighborhood.

A regular part of my daily routine was an early morning walk a few blocks down Galle Road from the apartment to buy a newspaper. The Daily News would tell me what the government wanted me to know, whereas The Island was mildly critical. Of course, I cannot vouch for the orientation of the Sinhala and Tamil language publications, but President Premadasa complained that they were unjustifiably critical of his government. There were no newspaper vending machines and few shops open at 6:30 A.M. My supplier was a grizzled old man with a wan smile and rather bloodshot eyes who dispensed papers in front of the neighborhood liquor store. He would have my paper ready before I was within a hundred yards. One day I arrived later than usual to find him gone. The next day he wasn't there either. I asked others standing around if he had come. One man explained that he had suffered a heart attack or something. I felt sad, not just because I was robbed of my daily fix, but that I would miss the old man.

Surely the most exciting episode during my stay in Colpetty was the visit of my son Chris. He had recently graduated with a degree in forestry from the University of Washington and finished an internship with Weyerhauser, the tree-growing company. Chris had grown up in the Great Northwest which was conducive to his developing two abiding passions: a love of sports and the great out-of-doors. Except for his occasional trips across the border into Mexico and Canada, and a visit to Hawaii, Chris had never left the continental United States. I managed to lure him to Sri Lanka with my descriptions of its natural beauty and the abundance of sporting facilities.

Chris and Galen in Sri Lanka, 1992

Despite my precautions, Chris was to suffer various forms of culture shock. I had explained to Jacintha that not all Americans had a taste for spicy food. So she practiced moderating her dosages of curries and even tried out a few Western dishes in anticipation of his visit. She was so anxious to please him. By the time Chris arrived she was well rehearsed, or so it seemed to me. After the first couple of days of dining on Jacintha's nouvelle cuisine, Chris developed queasiness in the stomach which didn't seem to go away. Rather than give up on eating altogether, we began frequenting all the restaurants that Tappani and I had sampled. Chris was relieved to find that the food in the Japanese and Chinese restaurants tasted very much like that he was familiar with in the U District of Seattle! His comment on the local Sri Lankan beers—Three Coins and Lion—was that they were "below average". A Northwest chauvinist, Chris was very much accustomed to the range of micro brewed beer at home.

Chris was also bemused by my friend Raja's tendency to camp in my apartment whenever we came home. I suppose I wasn't quite aware of the extent to which Raja had adopted me. He would always be at the door to greet and follow us in before the door could close. Raja would then regale us with stories and advertisements for cultural attractions he thought Chris should see. Because Raja's English was so difficult to understand, Chris claimed that he was starting to get a headache trying to follow him.

Then there was the matter of driving in Sri Lanka. Even coming into town from the Colombo airport on narrow, winding roads Chris anxiously asked whether it was like this everywhere. There were certainly no freeways or interstate highways and the roads tended to be full of bicycles, carts and animals darting in and out. The huge trucks barreling down the middle of the road with reckless abandon gave Chris the most cause for alarm. He probably didn't realize how tightly he tended to grip the arm rest. The drivers "are out of their bleeping minds," he remarked. By the end of his 10 day stay we had logged several hundred miles of travel around the island and he appeared only slightly more at ease on the road.

My friends and colleagues were eager to make Chris feel at home. We had several invitations to dinner—more than I had had the whole time I was in Sri Lanka. My tennis mentor, Dr. K.C. Fernando, arranged for us to spend a few days at Bentota, a popular resort area on a river that opens into the ocean on the southwest coast. There we stayed at a charming bed and breakfast, ate lobster right out of the ocean and water skied on the river. Chris and Dr. Fernando hit it off famously since they shared a love of sports. With just a few lessons from the master, Chris managed to dramatically improve his tennis serve. From Bentota we headed on down the coast to Weligama where we would visit Raja's home. He showed us to a nearby beach hotel appropriately named the Paradise Inn, nestled amongst swaying palm trees and adjacent to pristine sandy beaches. The clientele were mainly bohemians from Scandinavia escaping the arctic climes of their homeland and basking in the warm hospitality of the Sri Lankans.

One of the events Raja had been telling us we could not afford to miss was the Devil Dance, typical of the Sinhala peoples along the south coast. He had talked about it so much that I finally decided to add this to our travel agenda. The Devil Dance—as ancient as the Sinhala culture itself—is at once theater, entertainment and a form of communal therapy. It is supposedly performed to exorcise the evil spirits that have come to reside in a hapless victim. As the name would imply, the Devil Dance features dancers wearing a weird assortment of masks, some resembling the face of a dog or wild animal, designed to evoke demonic spirits.

Surely Chris would agree that this was the high watermark in so far as his exposure to a foreign culture was concerned. We arrived in the village where the dance was taking place just as it was getting started around midnight. The whole village—men, women and children— was gathered near the back porch of a woman dressed in white who lay on a bed of pillows and appeared to be in a sort of trance. The children were at first wide-eyed and attentive but eventually began to doze off as the night wore on. The scene was lit by an array of torches fueled by pungent smelling coconut oil. We were ushered over to a spot next to a French couple, the only other foreigners, where we were to remain the rest of the night. The dancers took turns going into frenzied tizzies, heaving and shaking, perspiring profusely, pausing to catch their breath and then repeating the cycle. They expended vast quantums of energy which never seemed to expire. Periodically they would charge up to the woman on the porch and shake violently in her face. She would wail, turn to others for comfort and then slump back down into her trance.

Raja had assured us that the dance would go until dawn. At

first the exotic combination of sights, sounds and smells was mesmerizing. But to the inexperienced and uninitiated, it was not at all clear whether the ministrations of the dancers were having their intended effect. As the night stretched toward dawn and our eyelids grew heavy, we begged Raja to be excused to return to the hotel.

Another event that marked Chris's stay in Sri Lanka was the U.S. presidential elections. Strangely enough, for the first time in the history of U.S. presidential campaigns, in the run-up to the 1992 elections, both Republican and Democratic candidates chose to pick on Sri Lanka. Both made what were interpreted in Sri Lanka as disparaging references to their country as an example of a nation in economic shambles. Arkansas Governor Bill Clinton warned voters at the Democratic convention that America would soon be like Sri Lanka in terms of its economy if the Bush administration continued in office. President Bush, campaigning in Bowling Green, Ohio, responded to Mr. Clinton's remark, saying that an island smaller than the state of Ohio could not be compared to America. From my perspective, neither of the candidates was justified in making these remarks about a country they knew little about.

On election day we went to the American Cultural Center where the results were shown on a giant TV screen. Nothing could quite make one feel more American in a foreign setting than watching U.S. election returns surrounded by other Americans and Sri Lankans who had lived in the U.S. By the time we left it had become clear that we were heading toward a new Democratic administration, a welcome relief to many of us who had suffered through 12 years of Republican rule. Chris could certainly say that he had had a novel civics education in this election year.

Colpetty was my initial point of reference for experiencing Sri Lanka and remained one of the most important. It was home to me, a neighborhood within the city. I suspect, however, that with the growth of Colombo it will eventually become entirely commercial and remnants of community will become increasingly frayed.

Images of Paradise Island

The Realm of Asian Kings and Parthian among these,
From India and the golden Chersoness,
And utmost Indian Isle Taprobane,
Dusk faces with white silken Turbans wreath'd.
                    John Milton, Paradise Regained, Book IV

Shortly after arriving in Sri Lanka I began to immerse myself in a steady diet of reading about its history and culture, feeling that I had a long way to go toward understanding my surroundings. I kept running across references to paradise. I discovered that until fairly recently the image of Sri Lanka was that of an unblemished paradise island. That image had to do with the physical features of the island itself, the flora and fauna, as well as its inhabitants and their culture. Indeed, some of the literary giants of our age have recorded their impressions of visits to the island, often contributing substantially to that image. Reading about their experiences in Sri Lanka gave me historical perspective on my own impressions.

Herman Hesse, the greatest German novelist of the 20th century, wrote the novel Siddhartha after his travels to the east. Following his visit to Ceylon in 1911, Hesse wrote of his pilgrimage to the lost centers of "primeval humanity" and "paradisiacal innocence." He described his encounter with the people: "the soft, sadly lovely gaze of the gentle Sinhalese, like the glance of a deer, the dazzling white of the eyeballs in the bronze-black faces of Tamil coolies...the shy and maidenly, the small slim people of Ceylon."

Hesse's Eastern safari reached its climax with a climb to the top of Adam's Peak, the highest point in Ceylon:

What I saw up there was not typically India. The wind had just swept clean the whole valley of Nuwara Eliya. I saw deep blue and immense the entire high mountain system of Ceylon piled up in mighty walls, and in its midst the beautiful, ancient, and holy pyramid of Adam's Peak. Beside it at an infinite depth and distance lay flat blue sea, in between a thousand mountains, broad valleys, narrow ravines, rivers and waterfalls, in countless folds, the whole mountainous island on which ancient legends placed paradise.

Hesse remarked that this primeval landscape spoke to him more strongly than anything he had seen elsewhere in India. "The palms and birds of paradise, the rice fields and the temples of the rich coastal cities, the valleys in the tropical lowlands steaming with fruitfulness, all this and the primeval forest itself were beautiful and enchanting." His journey to the East was in many respects a search for himself. Hesse may have spoken for Western man when he wrote:

We come full of longing to the South and the East, impelled by dark and thankful intimations of home, and we find here paradise, the manifold and rich profusion of all natural gifts, we find the simple, unpretentious, childlike people of paradise. But we ourselves are different, we are strangers here and without citizenship. We have long since lost paradise, and the new one we hope to have and to build will not be found on the equator or on warm Eastern seas; it lies within us and in our own northlandic culture.

Revolted by the militarism of his fatherland and the horrors of the Great War, soon after his return Hesse became a hermit in Switzerland where he lived until his death fifty years later. Today thousands of Germans flock to the shores of Sri Lanka, not a few of them mindful of Hesse's fascination with the country and, perhaps like him, looking into themselves.

Many of the great writers have been passionate travelers and observers of the human condition in societies different from their own. Nikos Kanzantzakis—20th century Homer, philosopher and author of Zorba the Greek—is among them. When asked what single thing had the greatest influence on his life, Kazantzakis quoted an ancient Egyptian:

"Happy is he who has seen the most water in his life."

Beginning in 1907 at the age of 24, Kazantzakis tried to see as much water and earth as he could in his lifetime. His first visit to the Orient, which included Ceylon, was in 1935.

Kazantzakis, too, remarked upon the people he saw in Ceylon:

Warm people, black eyes, long nails painted red, an easy balanced stride, large white teeth that light up in the narrow, half-lit little shops. And on another occasion:...lithe bodies, dark chocolate-colored; multi-colored pagnes; fiery, large, sweet eyes...The greatest delight is to see bodies and colors.... Everything we've seen so often in paintings is coming to life now in front of me...Flowers everywhere, red, mauve, snow white. A Buddhist altar in the middle of the street and a woman offering red flowers, intertwining her hands, gazing at the statue of the Buddha.

Pablo Neruda, regarded as Latin America's finest and most prolific poet of this century, went to Ceylon as a consul in the Chilean embassy in 1929 at the age of 24. He lived in a seaside chalet at Wellawatte, now a suburb just to the south of Colombo, where he wrote some of his best works. He quickly became involved in the city's avant guarde literary and artistic circles. Both the idyllic beauty of the island and the gentle character of its people were to leave an indelible mark of the lover and poet in Neruda. This is the way he described his neighborhood:

"I lived in a cluster of houses, among people and trees and a noble perspective; pavilions of passionate leafage, roots breaking the subsoil, plants bladed like oars..."

Neruda celebrated the southwest monsoon rains in a poem entitled "Monsoon in May." I was able to identify with Neruda's experience with the May monsoon, witnessing one of the wettest in history, although I dare say that the leafy foliage he enjoyed in Welawatte has probably given way to brick and mortar as it has in my neighborhood to the north.

For some visitors to Ceylon, it is the spectacle of ancient monuments that has afforded the most excitement and fascination. In the past hundred years, as the arts and crafts of travel began to bloom, the ruined cities of the East have drawn increasing attention from foreign travelers. Rose Macaulay, a popular English novelist and essayist of the early 1900s, was intrigued by ancient ruins, including those of Anuradhapura and Polonnaruwa in Ceylon.

Anuradhapura is perhaps the largest ruin anywhere...rivaling Nineveh and Babylon in size. It is one of the most religious cities that have ever been...The four great dagobas stand about it, solid domes, inverted bowls, some still grown with shrub, some containing relics, some merely commemorative; there are a crowd of smaller humps scattered over the green landscape, like a field of toadstools, and no doubt more in the jungle, as yet undiscovered...

Novelists figure prominently in the sparse field of literature produced by Indians and Pakistanis in the language of their former masters. Among them is Dom Moraes, born in cosmopolitan Bombay in 1938 to a doctor-mother and journalist-father of The Times of Ceylon. As a youth Moraes spent a couple of years in Colombo during a childhood that was marked by personal tragedy and maturation. Having been confined to the city of Colombo during his stay in Ceylon, Moraes observed that "the Singhalese are different from people in India; they have gold skins and small bones...The men have lilting feminine voices, but the women's voices are rather more husky."

Moraes eventually managed to quit Colombo and head outstation for a look at the country's ancient ruins. He, too, visited the abandoned kingdoms of Anuradhapura and Polonnaruwa, capitals of the first Singhalese kings:

Their temples had been burst open by vines, trees grew through their thick stone walls. Hidden in a clearing, with languors whooping round, an immense fractured Buddha lay on his side, sealed eyes calm...Yet to see these fallen monuments, invaded by the jungle, inhabited by beasts, made me aware of history. They were more alive to me because though the human life in them was dead, another prehistoric life had taken over. History to me was the way a spindly shoot sprouted through the Buddha's stone eye

The image of Sri Lankans as hospitable and gracious is not simply a thing of the past. Today's tourists attest to the hospitality of the people. Increasingly, Europeans are apparently persuaded that tourism in continental countries has become too commercialized and have started to look eastward for their holidays. One young German mother with her 13 year old son was interviewed recently while on vacation in Sri Lanka. The woman explained that she was in search of a more informal, hospitable and scenic environment. She said Sri Lanka was the paradise for which Europeans were looking. Contrasting her visit here with travel in Europe, the woman lamented that nowadays the emphasis there is on money and not hospitality. She said: "I have been to countries like Kenya, Tanzania and Egypt, but none of them compares with Sri Lanka. Your people are very kind, polite and hospitable. In fact I begin to suspect these virtues are the sole monopoly of Sri Lanka."

The image of an exotic paradise island is projected in various ways. Renowned science fiction writer Arthur C. Clarke made Sri Lanka the setting for one of his novels. In The Fountains of Paradise, Clarke uses its ancient name Taprobane, and acknowledges that country he has written about is "about ninety percent congruent with the island of Sri Lanka." He moved the island eight hundred kilometers south so that it straddled the equator, as it probably did twenty million years ago. The story draws upon the historical period of the reign of King Kasyapa (478-495 A.D.), the most intriguing of all the Sinhala kings. Kasyapa killed his father in order to gain the throne and then spent the next 18 years building one of the most remarkable kingdoms in history, atop Sigiriya (Lion Rock). Clarke calls the rock Yakkagala in his book. The frescoes painted on the sides of Sigiriya rock are its greatest glory, the object of fascination to generations of tourists.

Sri Pada in the book is actually Adam's Peak, a cone-shaped mountain that is sacred to Muslims, Buddhists, Hindus and Christians alike. Every year thousands of pilgrims journey to the top of the 2,240 meter summit. The view of the peak's shadow at dawn, which is a perfectly symmetrical cone visible only for a few minutes, is awe-inspiring. Clarke uses this as the setting for a seemingly fantastical story of the construction of a space elevator from the top of Sri Pada sometime in the next century. As readers of Clarke's work well know, his genius is in exploring the outer limits of imagination. What seems like a perfectly outrageous concept was actually presented in a scientific paper in the 1960s at Woods Hole Oceanographic Institution and by a Russian engineer about the same time. Clarke submits that the space elevator is quite clearly an idea whose time has come. And "Taprobane" might very well be as good a spot as any for such a project, considering what is known about synchronous orbits. Clarke himself is struck by certain coincidences surrounding The Fountains of Paradise. Years before he ever thought of the subject of the novel he purchased a beach house in Sri Lanka which is at precisely the closest spot on any large body of land to the point of maximum geosynchronous stability.

Sri Lanka's paradise image has also been enhanced by the movie industry. Two of the most successful films of all time have been filmed here: Bridge on the River Kwai and Indiana Jones and the Temple of Doom. In the 1950s director David Lean wanted to make the story of allied prisoners of war used by the Japanese to construct a bridge over the River Kwai in Thailand. At the time Thailand was judged to be unsuitable for filming so Lean selected Sri Lanka, where there was complete peace and tranquility. A bridge was constructed with wood in the village of Kitulgala. A steam locomotive was used in the final scene when the bridge was blown up. Bridge on the River Kwai went on to win eight Oscars and became one of the most memorable films of all time.

When Steven Spielberg was on the island in 1982 for the filming of Indiana Jones and the Temple of Doom, he remarked that "this is a film set made by God himself. Every type of film scene can be done here, whereas, in other countries I would have to travel thousands of miles to get the natural scene change." Although the film story and Spielberg's feats hit the cover of Time magazine, Sri Lanka was not able to reap the publicity benefits because the following year ethnic troubles engulfed the country. It is only recently that film and television drama makers have begun to return to Sri Lanka to make use of its paradise setting.

The image of Sri Lanka as paradise has, however, been subjected to a severe test in recent years. Indeed, it suggests paradise lost. Since the early 1970s, and especially during recent years, the country has been plagued with internal conflict fed by religious, ethnic and cultural differences. This sentiment—having to do with the innocence that is by now considered by many Sri Lankans to have been lost—was expressed in poignant terms nearly a decade ago. These are the opening lines from The Island's editorial of October 4, 1983, titled "The Island's Prayer" which appeared in its second anniversary supplement, superimposed on an impression of the map of Sri Lanka:

This was once a land where peace reigned and where compassion flowed. It was a land touched by the saffron robe, a country which bloomed under the gentle shadow of the dagoba; the land was rich and nature was bountiful. It yielded its rewards in abundance to the simple people who toiled to make the earth bloom but the people were not greedy...They were a simple, contented, ascetic people.

An Island newspaper columnist ("Men and Matters," August 30, 1992), writing about exorcising ethnic demons, offered a common plaint heard in various forms in Sri Lanka:

Sri Lanka is on the map, not because it makes some serious impact on regional stability or on the new global balance, but because it is Paradise Lost. It has so much going for it but Serendip is now close to the edge of anarchy.

Tongue-in-cheek, the columnist noted that Sri Lanka is blessed with a surfeit of internationally recognized expertise in matters of "ethno-nationalism". From Harvard and Yale to the ivory towers of Australia, Sri Lankan academics are "educating the benighted natives on the demons of ethnic identity that have cut loose in the world." But back in Sri Lanka, however, answers to the problems variously referred to as ethnicity, race, communalism and national identity are still being sought.

The years since 1982 have witnessed a civil war pitting Tamil separatists in the north and east versus the Sinhala majority government of Sri Lanka. The government has been preoccupied with winning the war against the Tamils. A reminder of what this could mean to the average person came to me in the mail soon after my arrival in Colombo. The letter from my bank stated that "consequent to the government's decision to increase the defense levy from 1% to 3%, we are reluctantly compelled to recover it from our customers". It reminded me of Lyndon Johnson's tax surcharge in order to prosecute the Vietnam War!

Sri Lanka continued to operate on a war-time economy. Six percent of the GNP in 1992 was going for military expenditures, as compared to only two percent in 1985. It had been virtually nil before the JVP (Sinhala) insurgency began in 1971. The country was spending more on defense than either health or education. Several of the current economic difficulties were due in large part to the high level of military spending. The government's defense budget was the single most important factor in the deficit, which in turn led to increasing rates of inflation. Military expenditures tended to raise prices, although they did not lead to an increase in the supply of goods and services which people could buy with the newly created money. Defense expenditures had negative balance of payments consequences, since the country relied to a large extent on imports. Ammunition, military hardware, aircraft and fuel all had to be imported.

While he was not the perpetrator of the war, President Ranasinghe Premadasa inherited the responsibility for prosecuting it when he came to office in 1989. Premadasa subsequently tried various approaches to ending it. He had ambitious plans for transforming Sri Lanka into another industrial success and was keenly aware that the war was hindering the achievement of those objectives. But he himself was to succumb to the conflict, assassinated within four years after taking office.

When I arrived in Sri Lanka the war was taking a tremendous toll in both innocent civilian and military lives on both sides. The population seemed numbed to the daily reports of casualties. However, there was one particular event which was the cause for an outpouring of national grief, pointing to a most insidious aspect of the war. On August 8, 1992, several of the Sri Lankan army's top commanders were killed in a mine explosion in Kayts Island in the war zone. Among them was General Denzil Kobbekaduwa, the highest ranking officer to die in the Northeast conflict. He was extremely popular among his troops and the general population as well. The circumstances of his death were the subject of speculation around the country and in the opposition press. It was rumored that the explosion may not have been the work of the Tamil Tigers or an accident but rather that it was planned by those in high positions within the government fearful of his popularity.

Thus the war itself was not the only element of tragedy. These under-currents of internal political intrigue within Sri Lankan society could not quite be comprehended by the casual visitor. Maurine Seneviratne, a well known Sri Lankan author, hinted darkly that something was rotten in the state of Denmark (The Island, August 31, 1992). She offered this lament:

On the beaches of the west and south the mini-season is in swing. But even the happy-go-lucky visitors, shedding their inhibitions and their clothes with impunity on the palm-fringed coast of far-famed paradise, pause a while to read the banner-black head-lines of the daily paper...to give ear to the rumors floating in the saltsea breezes. There is evil under the sun.

...In a land where killing is now the manner of life and where killers escape comfortably, doubtless to kill and kill again (and always the bold and the brave), who will apprehend, even identify the killers among those depraved killing bands that roam wild and free and evidently unfettered in our once-idyllic land? Under the murderous rays of the black sun that darkens Sri Lanka, who will dare? The daring ones went in one fell swoop to create a spectacle of mourning such as has not been seen in Lanka for a millennium.

During my stay in Sri Lanka the headlines of the local newspapers were daily filled with grim news from the front. Typical of these was that of October 16, 1992. As President Premadasa ceremonially opened yet another garment factory, "Tiger terrorists" were reported to have shot and hacked to death at least 145 civilians, mostly Muslim women and children, and wounded 70 others in simultaneous attacks on four remote hamlets in the region of the ancient capital of Polonnaruwa. Eight soldiers and nine policemen were also reported killed. A military spokesman said the attack was the biggest of the year.

Apart from the war, daily life in Sri Lanka provided other evidence that all was not well in the land of paradise. Not all tourists, it seems, were enamored of paradise island. A Danish tourist wrote to the newspaper to complain of the unpleasant experiences he had had in the country. "The traffic is terrible and chaotic, and we can't think that many tourists dare the experiment driving in Sri Lanka. Perhaps there are rules, but nearly all drivers broke the rules by Western standard in the most horrible and dangerous way." By contrast, the tourist pointed out that in such developed countries as Malaysia and Thailand people drive about "in a civilized way." His other complaints had to do with tourists being charged more than local people in stores and at tourist sites, as well as the profusion of beggars. "In these other countries you can move about without being bothered by beggars and swindlers all the time, like in Sri Lanka."

From the Sri Lankan point of view the tourist boom brought in its wake a host of problems associated with moral degradation. For example, the Ministry of Policy Planning and Implementation reported that there are 30,000 boy prostitutes in Sri Lanka between the ages of eight and 16. They were concentrated in the popular beach resorts such as Hikkaduwa and Negombo, but could be found all along the southwestern coast. Most of the boys were migrants, moving from one resort to another. Some were lured into prostitution after having worked as domestic servants. While male prostitution was not an altogether new phenomenon, it was becoming highly organized with pedophiles operating under guise of tourism along the coast. The ministry also reported an estimated 50,000 female prostitutes. Drug addiction was increasing at an alarming rate. According to a survey conducted by the Sri Lanka Anti-Narcotics Association, there were as many as 50,000 heroin addicts, many of them engaged in prostitution. Heroin addiction was on the increase among school children. Crack cocaine had been discovered in the southwestern tourist belt although the extent of addition was unknown. Other drugs in the form of tablets such as Valium and Seconal were the drug of preference of middle and upper class women.

In the vegetable-growing area of Nuwara Eliya a massive tomato glut led to reports of farmers who committed suicide after their bumper crops failed to earn them enough to pay back their bank loans. Apparently over-production was the sole reason for the unprecedented glut of tomatoes in the market. Farmers had been complaining that they were unable to dispose of their crops because the purchasing centers set up with government assistance failed to purchase them. It is understood that the marketing agents were granted bank loans on easy terms for this purpose, but farmers believed that the agents had used the loans for other purposes.

Mdeanwhile, the government of Sri Lanka proudly pointed to the 39-story twin towers under construction adjoining the Bank of Ceylon in downtown Colombo as certain symbols of the country's economic progress (now completed, see picture below). The towers would be the tallest and plushest in Sri Lanka. Echelon Square is a $110 million shop and office project bankrolled by S.P.Tao, a Singaporean property tycoon. The Greater Colombo Economic Council saw the project as evidence of the confidence of foreign investors in the country's future. For starters, Echelon Square was expected to stimulate the construction industry. But to some Sri Lankans, the Echelon Square project symbolized the misplaced priorities of the government. It was a declarative statement that bigness is better. The policies of liberalization implemented since 1977 encourage foreign investors and large industries with the hope that this will trickle down to the masses. The government was struggling to follow the free market, export promotion nostrums of the World Bank and International Monetary Fund. But the underclasses, subject to rising prices and inflation, were still waiting to see the benefits of these policies.

Downtown Colombo, 2003

There are unmistakable signs of environmental stress in Sri Lanka that have become cause for concern: loss of natural forest cover, contamination of waters, degradation of rural lands and rising levels of air, water and solid waste pollution. With a population of 17.5 million, Sri Lanka is already one of the most densely populated countries in the world. A projected population of 25 million by 2040 will create unprecedented demands for food, fiber, energy, land and other natural resources. Without prompt management action, these demands will aggravate the negative trends.

No less disturbing and debilitating for the country's development is the fact that for some time there has been a serious case of brain and brawn-drain. Australia has been the main country of attraction for Sri Lankan entrepreneurs, investors, although Canada and the U.S. are also high on the list. They took a combined one billion Australian dollars with them from Sri Lanka. Most of these entrepreneurs have started business ventures such as restaurants and agricultural enterprises. Hundreds of thousands of Sri Lankans have gone out of the country to work in the oil-rich countries of the Middle East or as house maids in Singapore.

Many Sri Lankans manage to disregard political affairs and most other indignities hurled at their country, remaining otherwise uninvolved. But an issue of truly tragic proportions for thousands of Sri Lankans was the defeat of the national cricket team at the hands of the Aussies in 1991. Cricket is the national sport, played for more than 160 years by small boys in villages throughout the island. The Australians have long been among the giants of the cricket world, so the Sri Lankan team was not expected to win even though Sri Lankan cricket standards have improved markedly in recent years. The nation was plunged into a state of virtual mourning one day in August after the Sri Lankan national team had risen to unprecedented heights during a five-week tour by the Australian team. They had mounted a commanding lead, dominating play on the first four days of a five-day Test Match. Then, unbelievably, they allowed defeat to be snatched from the jaws of victory, squandering what seemed to be an insurmountable lead. The heroes of the first four days became the target of public anger.

Buddhism in Sri Lanka

This island belongs to the Buddha himself...Therefore
the residence of wrong-believers in this island will
never be permanent...Even if a non-Buddhist ruled Ceylon
by force for a while, it is a particular power of the Buddha
that his line will not be established...
   - From the Pujavaliya, a Sinhalese prose work of the 13th

century

Buddhism was born in India (well, Nepal) and spread throughout Asia, even though it never really supplanted Hinduism as the principal religion in the land of its birth. Today, far from receding into some fossilized form, Buddhism claims more than 500 million adherents around the world. Sri Lanka, the original home of Theravada—or orthodox Buddhism—is a rich repository of Buddhist culture and as such affords a living laboratory for an understanding of Buddhism. Today Buddhism is an important factor in the daily life of some 70 percent of the Sri Lankan population. Even those who do not practice Buddhist precepts are touched by the observance of public holidays based on the life of the Buddha. Since independence, all of the prime ministers and presidents of the country have been Buddhists. Having never lived in a country with such a pronounced Buddhist culture, I resolved to study Buddhist thought and observe the behavior of those who practiced Buddhism, a modest search for my own enlightenment.

The images I carried with me with me to Sri Lanka were to be altered considerably by my reading and observation of daily life. I was familiar with the great stone statues of the Buddha with that inscrutable oriental expression on his face and the clean shaven monks in their saffron robes who provided a jarring contrast to the bustling modernity of the Asian countries where Buddhism still predominates. But I thought that surely the "worship" of these graven images was something like what the Lord had in mind in the Old Testament when He forbade the Chosen People to practice idolatry. Somehow I felt that Buddhism belonged more to history than to the modern world.

In Colombo I began to attend meetings on the teachings of the Buddha—the dhammapada—each Saturday afternoon at a temple in Bambalapitiya. These reminded me of Quaker meetings, in which there is an emphasis on developing a habit of meditation and looking into oneself. Although the meetings were conducted in English, not once did I see any other expatriates in attendance. The Sri Lankans were most cordial toward me, offering reading material and explanations to my many questions. Occasionally I would be asked to join others to drink tea or eat hoppers after the meeting. Thus began my introduction to Buddhism. I had to start pretty much from scratch in order to understand this "religion". There was a lot to learn.

The Buddha

On the full moon day of May in the year 623 B.C. Siddhattha Gotama (the name in the Pali language, in Sanskrit it is written Siddhartha Gautama) was born in Lumbini Park at Kapilavatthu, on the Indian border of current-day Nepal. His father was King Suddhodana of the aristocratic Sakya clan and his mother was Queen Maha Maya, who died seven days after his birth. Her younger sister, also married to the King, adopted the child. On the fifth day after his birth he was named Siddhattha, which means "wish fulfilled". In accordance with the ancient Indian custom, many learned Brahmins were invited to the palace for the naming ceremony.

As a royal child, Siddhattha certainly received an education befitting a prince, although few details are known about his early years. As a member of the warrior class, he received special training in the art of warfare. At the age of 16 he married his cousin, the beautiful Princess Yasodhara. For 13 years they had a happy marriage, leading the life of luxury, blissfully ignorant of the vicissitudes of life outside the palace gates. Of his luxurious life as a prince, he later said:

"In my father's house there were three lotus-ponds made purposely for me: blue lotuses bloomed in one, red in another and white in another..."

But Siddhattha's contemplative nature and compassion for humanity did not permit him to spend his life in the mere enjoyment of the pleasures of the royal palace. One day he went outside of the palace to a pleasure park, and on the way he came into direct contact with stark realities of the real world: a decrepit old man, a diseased person, a corpse and a dignified hermit. The latter signified to Siddhattha the means to overcome the ills of life and to attain calm and peace. After much deliberation, he resolved to renounce his life of privilege in search of truth and eternal peace. (Colorfully illustrated in Bertolucci's film The Little Buddha) But just as he was arriving at this decision, his wife gave birth to a son. As great as his compassion was for the two dear ones at his parting moment, greater was his resolve to seek truth.

It was thus in his 29th year that Siddhattha began his historic journey. He shaved his hair and beard and assumed the simple yellow garb of an ascetic, leading a life of voluntary poverty. He traveled far and wide, living on what little others gave him. He carried a bowl to collect whatever meager food he could eat and slept wherever he was offered shelter, always in search of truth, sometimes in the company of fellow ascetics. Siddhattha followed the teachings of a renowned ascetic, eventually mastering his doctrine and attaining a highlydeveloped stage of mental concentration. Still he felt that his quest for truth was not achieved. He was seeking complete cessation of suffering and the total eradication of all forms of craving, or Nibbana.

Disappointed but not discouraged, Siddhattha continued his search. He became fully convinced from personal experience of the utter futility of the self-mortification of the ascetics. He thus abandoned this painful extreme as he had the other extreme of self-indulgence which tends to retard moral progress. He conceived the idea of adopting the golden mean, or the Middle Path, which later became one of the salient features of this teaching. He recalled how when his father was engaged in plowing, he used to sit in the cool shade of a tree after absorbed in the contemplation of his own breath. Siddhattha realized that the enlightenment he sought could not be attained with an exhausted body. Physical fitness was necessary for spiritual progress. He thus nourished himself with wholesome food and concentrated on tranquilizing and purifying his mind.

After a struggle of six years, in his 35th year the ascetic Siddhattha succeeded in eradicating all defilements and ending the process of grasping, thus becoming a Buddha or Enlightened One. In the Pali language Buddha is derived from the root word budh, to understand or to awaken. Before attaining his enlightenment he passed through a period in which he was a Bodhisatta—a period of intensive exercise and development of the qualities of generosity, discipline, wisdom, energy and equanimity. He was not born a Buddha but became one through his own efforts.

After his enlightenment, Gautama the Buddha delivered his first sermon to a group of five ascetics, his old colleagues in the Deer Park at Isipatana near Benares in India. For the remainder of his long life, the Buddha went about teaching the way to enlightenment. He taught all classes of men and women—kings and peasants, Brahmins and outcasts, bankers and beggars. He recognized no differences of caste or social groupings, a notable break with Indian tradition. But he chose to speak in the Pali language (a form of Prakrit) rather than Sanskrit because it was the language of the common people. It was the language of menials, workers, hunters and farmers whereas Sanskrit was spoken by the Brahmins. Not only did he adopt the language of common people, he drew his metaphors and similes from the lives of farmers, cowherds and workers. He was an outspoken critic of organized Brahminical institutions which were dogmatic and oppressive. The Buddha died at the age of 80 on the Full Moon Day of the lunar month of Vesak in 543 B.C.

What the Buddha Taught

Among the founders of the world's great religions, the Buddha was the only one who did not claim to be other than a human being. Other teachers were either God or His incarnations in various forms, or were inspired by Him. The Buddha claimed no inspiration from any god or external power. He attributed all his attainments and achievements to human endeavor and intelligence. Any person can become a Buddha, as he or she wills it. As the Buddha put it in the Dhammapada which records his teachings:

"One is one's own refuge, who else could be the refuge?"

He admonished his disciples to be a refuge unto themselves and never seek refuge in or help from anybody else. If the Buddha is to be considered a "savior" at all, it is only in the sense that he discovered and showed the Path to Enlightenment, or Nibbana (Nirvana in Sanskrit). Thus, the "worship" of the Buddha is not a ritual as understood in theistic religions. People of ancient India "worshipped" their teachers and elders. It was a form of veneration but not the way to salvation as we tend to think of it.

On the principle of individual responsibility, the Buddha allowed freedom to his disciples. He never considered controlling the order of monks (Sangha) that followed him, nor did he expect them to depend on him. He argued that one's emancipation depends on realization of truth and not on the benevolent grace of a god as a reward for good behavior. This freedom of thought in Buddhism is in marked contrast to most other religions that require belief in certain articles of faith. It has been from the beginning one of the most cherished ideals of Buddhist culture.

In the third century B.C., the great Buddhist Emperor Asoka of India demonstrated this tolerance by honoring all other religions in his empire. He declared that one should not honor one's own religion and condemn the religion of others, but should honor all religions. In so doing one helps one's own religion to grow and renders service to the religion of others. Emperor Asoka had this edict carved into stone where it may be seen to this day.

It is often asserted that Buddhism is not in fact a religion at all since the Buddha did not speak of a god. Paramhansa Yogananda, an Indian spiritual leader who died in 1952, strongly contended that the Buddha was no atheist. But like every great master, his teachings had to offer correction to the misconceptions of his day. The people of that time were prone to let God do the work for them in a spiritual sense. Yet the Buddha stressed the importance of one's own effort in the spiritual search. Yogananda maintained that those who practice Buddha's teachings, and not those who merely argue about them, achieve their goal. As with any other religion, achievement of the goal is realization of the infinite Self, and freedom from the trammels of delusion.

The Buddha was not the founder of a religion with dogmas and rituals, although certainly rituals have grown up in the practice of Buddhism. The Buddha was a spiritual leader who founded a view of life based on religious perception and truth as he experienced it. But the question of belief or faith as understood by most religions has little to do with Buddhism. The question of belief arises when there is no seeing—seeing in every sense of the word. The moment you "see", the question of belief disappears. The Buddha, like all great teachers, was fond of using parables and metaphors. In explaining belief, he said that if one has a gem hidden in the folded palm of the hand, the question of belief arises because you do not see it yourself. But as soon as the fist is unclenched, then you see for yourself and the question of belief no longer arises. This is the way the Buddha urged his followers to adopt his teachings: only through experience.

One of the most well known parables the Buddha used was to explain the purpose of his teachings. It is the story of a man who built a raft in order to cross over a vast stretch of water. Having crossed over to the other side, he thought: "This raft was of such great help to me, it would be good if I carried it on my head wherever I go."

The Buddha then asked his disciples whether this would be a wise thing to do. Of course, they answered that it wouldn't. The Buddha then said:

"I have taught a doctrine similar to the raft; it is for crossing over, and not for carrying."

The Buddha's teachings are meant to carry a person to peace, happiness and tranquility. As a practical teacher, he taught only those things which were intended to bring peace of mind and happiness. He was not interested in metaphysics.

Practically all of the teachings of the Buddha during the last 45 years of his life dealt in one way or another with this Path. Together they constitute the Buddhist system of ethics. There is nothing of an essentially religious nature; it is a sort of moral psychology. He explained it in various ways and different terms to different groups of people, according to their stage of development and capacity to understand him. (Today he would probably rap with street people and address Republican women's clubs on the need to support AIDS programs.) The three essentials of Buddhist training and discipline are the Sila (ethical conduct), Samadhi (mental discipline) and Panna (wisdom). Sila is built upon the concept of universal love and compassion for all living beings, on which all the Buddha's teachings are based. Thus, following the Path is a way of life to be practiced and developed by each individual. It is self-discipline in body, word and mind: self-development and purification. It has nothing to do with belief, prayer, worship or ceremony.

Of course, in Buddhist countries there has grown up a tradition of customs and ceremonies for religious occasions. But the Buddha rejected the idea of mystic rites and ceremonies connected with the worship of God. During the Buddha's lifetime, his personality, the Path and the intense religious life of his disciples combined to create the idea of the holy in the hearts and minds of monks and laymen alike. After his death, religious symbols such as the stupa, the Bo tree, the Buddha image and other icons and rites connected with the worship of the symbols created a religious atmosphere in the temple. Under colonial British influence, certain educated Buddhists began to think that attending temple to worship Buddhist symbols was in fact a form of idolatry alien to Buddhism. But it is argued that this is to deprive Buddhism of the vital idea of the holy. The ritual worship of symbols at the temple is an aesthetic approach, still very important to simple folk and intellectuals alike.

History of Buddhism in Sri Lanka

Sri Lanka has shown a remarkably creative capacity to absorb diverse religious patterns. Religious pluralism has characterized the country's development since the beginning of its recorded history. Today four of the major religious traditions of mankind are present in Sri Lanka: Buddhism, Hinduism, Christianity and Islam. Of these, Theravada Buddhism claims by far the most adherents with two-thirds of the population, and the majority are Sinhala. The term Theravada might be translated school of the elders, or theras. It has replaced the term Hinayana, or "small vehicle", used to describe the original orthodox Buddhism practiced in Sri Lanka, Burma, Thailand, Cambodia, Laos and the Chittagong region of Bangladesh. The other major school of Buddhism—Mahayana, or large vehicle—developed later in China, Tibet, Japan and Korea. The Tamil minority in Sri Lanka (18 percent) are mainly Hindu. A small number of both Sinhala and Tamils belong to the Christian faith. The Muslim population amounts to about seven percent, many of whom speak Tamil but distinguish themselves by their Islamic faith.

The history of Sri Lanka is shrouded in legend and involves the intertwining of the Sinhala people with Buddhism. The word "simha" or "sinha" signifies a lion in most oriental languages and symbolizes the leonine paternity of the Sinhala people. The ancient chronicles known as the Mahavamsa, authored by Buddhist monks, date the settlement of the Sinhala people to 543 B.C. when Prince Vijaya landed in Sri Lanka from northern India, not coincidently the year in which the Buddha died. In the third century B.C. the great Buddhist King Asoka sent his son Mahinda to Sri Lanka to spread the word of the Lord Buddha. Mahinda converted King Devanampiyatissa, and from then on Buddhism was protected as the state religion.

Why did Buddhism continue to thrive in Sri Lanka and not in the land of its birthplace? Volumes of scholarly works have been dedicated to this question. Probably the most important factor was the lack of royal patronage after the reign of the great Buddhist Emperor Asoka. Moghul invasions into India from the northwestern passes surely undermined the development of Buddhist culture. In any event, Hinduism was deeply rooted in the Indian culture and the majority of the population continued to adhere to it. The spread of Islam further served to undermine Buddhism in India.

One of the more intriguing explanations has to do with the practice of Tantrism which developed among Buddhists in ancient India. The term Tantra is derived from the worship of Shakti, or female energy, which is worshipped in conjunction with male energy. According to this interpretation, one of the factors leading to the downfall of Buddhism in India was its mixing with occultism and sexual mysticism. Tantrism, which insinuated itself into Buddhism, degenerated into "a cult of women and wine", presumably infected with the seeds of its demise.

The Tantric phase of Buddhism spread all over India, Tibet and some other neighboring countries, penetrating into Ceylon in the ninth century A.D. In southern India the downfall of Buddhism came about in part because of sectarian quarrels and its involvement with Tantrism, gradually leading monks as well as laymen to participate in a form of worship in which "women and spirituous liquor were involved." There is evidence to indicate that Tantrism also prevailed in Ceylon during a certain period, judging from the Tantric symbols found on ancient remains. But the attempt to introduce this extreme form of occult Buddhism into Ceylon was apparently repelled by the monks who had been sternly disciplined by the austere tenets of Pali Buddhism.

Proponents of Buddhism point out that, alone among the world's great religions, Buddhism has not engaged in holy wars and over-zealous proselytizing. However, it must be conceded that the communal conflict in Sri Lanka between Sinhala Buddhists and Tamil Hindus has had much to do with religious and cultural differences. Tamils have inhabited the island, mainly the north and east, for thousands of years. They are said to belong to the Dravidian race prominent in southern India and therefore are considered racially distinct from the Sinhalese who purport to belong to the Aryan race. Tamils mainly practice the Hindu religion.

In 101 B.C. the Sinhala Prince Dutugemunu (sometimes written Duttagamani, Duttu Gemunu), the George Washington of his nation, killed the Tamil King Ellalan in an epic battle in the kingdom of Anuradhapura and succeeded in unifying the Sinhala nation.

The battle of Vijathapura was the greatest and decisive encounter that took place between the forces of Ellalan and Dutugemumu. According to the Sinhala interpretation of this event, Dutugemunu's aim was to unite the Sinhala people and free the country from foreign (Tamil) rule. Since the arrival of the Sinhala people into the country, there had been numerous invasions from southern India. Dutugemunu, a prince from the southern part of the island, came north to do battle with King Ellalan in Anuradhapura to free Rata (country), Deya (nation), Samaya (nationality) and (Sasana) Buddhist culture from foreign domination. During the period of foreign rule, considerable damage had been done to Buddhist places of worship. Protection of this cultural heritage was the duty of the Sinhala princes and kings. Following the battle of Vijathapura, King Dutugemunu began construction of a massive chetiya—or dagoba—to be built on the tomb of Elara. Completed after Dutugemunu's death, this great edifice may be seen today in Anuradhapura.

For Sri Lankan Tamils, this event over 2000 years ago is sometimes interpreted as a holy war waged against them. They note that Dutugemunu was accompanied by a contingent of 500 monks in his campaign against King Ellalan. The battle has been characterized as a "genocidal attack" since Dutugemunu's forces not only killed Tamil sub-kings but thousands of civilians, all in the name of the Lord Buddha. This interpretation of history could easily be left to professional historians were it not for the present tragic conflict in Sri Lanka which pits the Sinhala-dominated government against the minority Tamils in the north and east.

The Sinhala response was a revival of Buddhism which provided a framework for challenging colonial domination. One of the early voices raised in the revival was that of Angarika Dharmapala, born in 1864. Although he was educated in Christian schools, he also came under the influence of Buddhist monks and developed great admiration for them. Dharmapala was also influenced by Colonel Henry Steele Olcott, an American Civil War officer who founded the Theosophical Society. Theosophy advocated a universal mysticism favoring Buddhism and Hinduism, which helped Sri Lankan Buddhists to counter the influence of the Christian missionaries. However, Dharmapala eventually broke with the Theosophical Society because of its equally strong support of Hinduism. His anti-colonialist theme was based on the premise that the Sinhala are a chosen people with a special mission to rescue Sri Lanka from the British, whom he viewed as culturally and morally inferior to the Sinhala. Dharmapala served as a model for Buddhist activists and was one of the most influential leaders of Buddhist revivalism.

Religious identity and politics have remained interwoven in Sri Lanka since ancient times. In 1972 the government of Prime Minister Sirimavo Bandaranaika drafted a new constitution and declared a new Republic of Sri Lanka, replacing the constitution of Ceylon granted by the British at the time of independence in 1948. A constituent assembly was established for the purpose of drafting the constitution consisting of all members of parliament, including Tamil opposition. The assembly worked for nearly two years before producing the draft constitution which was then submitted to the parliament and accepted by a two-thirds majority, thus becoming law. From the Sinhala perspective, it was an entirely democratic process.

Nevertheless, some within the Tamil minority saw themselves marginalized in the new "nation". They saw politics as largely defined by the Sinhalese majority in terms of making Sinhalese the official language and Buddhism the state religion. This Tamil argument has it that the new constitution did not include a mandate from the Northern and Eastern Provinces, that the new republic was created with fraudulent intent to deprive the Tamils of safeguards provided under the previous constitution. The consequences of this unresolved conflict are the subject of studies on human rights violations and daily reports in the press of casualties by both the Tamil "terrorists" and government soldiers. The Tamil Tigers continue their struggle for Tamil Eelam, or a separate Tamil nation.

Nowhere in the world today is Buddhism more pronounced in the culture of a people than in Sri Lanka, entailing some seemingly curious contradictions. For example, Buddhist villagers do not rear fowls; eggs have never become an article of food with them and they still abhor the breaking of an egg. The egg has become taboo in Sinhalese culture because of the Buddhist precept that one should abstain from destroying life. Nevertheless, the fisherman of the same village who abhors the breaking of an egg daily destroys life in catching fish for a living. A villager will throw out a half boiled egg rather than swallow it, but the sophisticated Buddhist in the city enjoys his egg hoppers (a kind of crepe) which are a prominent feature on the breakfast menu. Sericulture, the growing of silkworms for the production of silk, is a fairly recent and promising industry in Sri Lanka. But some entrepreneurs who might otherwise be interested in investing in this business have not done so because it involves killing the silkworm once it has produced larvae. Again, ostensible concern for the reverence for life.

Buddhist thought is manifested in many ways. Although advertisements for marriage partners in the Sri Lankan newspapers are not a uniquely Buddhist tradition, they do offer insight into how important tradition still is in Sri Lanka. A few samples will suffice:

> ➤ An affluent Buddhist Govigama family from Colombo seeks for pretty daughter 29 years, height 4 feet, 11 inches; accountant in prestigious group of companies; monthly income 8,500 rupees; dowry three bedroom Colombo apartment, jewelry and cash worth over 2.5 million rupees.

> ➤ Aunt seeks for her Govi Buddhist 26 year old niece, height 4 feet, 11 inches; computer science graduate qualified in Australia, permanently residing in Sri Lanka; seeks professionally qualified partner below 31 years of age; should be tee-totaller and non-smoker; reply with family particulars and horoscope.

> ➤ Aunty seeks partner for Buddhist, attractive niece 36 years old; dowry two lakhs, jewelry, buildable block in Colombo, lands; caste immaterial. Details with horoscope.

The practice of Buddhist precepts among Sri Lankans extends well beyond the island's shores to the thousands who have gone abroad to seek employment. olombo newspapers reported that the Sri Lankan embassy in Muscat organized a sil campaign for the first time which was "attended by 70 Lankans of all religions." The Venerable Dr. Rastrapal Mahathera of the International Meditation Center who was on a short visit to Oman administered atasil. He was the first Buddhist monk to visit the embassy in Muscat. There was a dhamma (doctrine) talk on the importance of molding the lives of children according to Buddhist principles, followed by discussion with the children in attendance. Ven. Rastrapal also paid homage to the sapling Bo tree planted in the embassy premises.

Meanwhile, how is the visitor to Sri Lanka to understand the Buddhist villager who will not hurt a cobra by throwing a stone at it, but in a fit of anger will plunge a knife into the heart of his friend who he believes has deceived him? Or the docile Colombo inhabitant who becomes a monster behind the wheel when he goes to work as a bus driver? Or the young villager whose ambition is to join the Sri Lankan army and go north to fight the Tamil Tigers?

Sri Lanka and the Sri Lankans

Numerous scholars have dedicated their efforts to a search for the meaning of the name Lanka. It is apparently not a simple matter. The epic Indian poem, the Ramayana, is considered by some to be a quasi-historical document containing many riddles. One of these is the location of Lanka, an island fortress with its capital of Ravana. Rama, the hero of the epic, was an Aryan prince who went out to explore the southern peninsula of India when exiled by his father. In doing so he came in conflict with the tribe of Ravana of Lanka, whom he subdued. The location of Lanka has remained a subject of fascination to scholars. Some maintain that Ceylon is the ancient seat of Lanka while others say it was elsewhere, as far way as Indonesia, Malaysia or the Maldive Islands. The orthodox view has come to be that Lanka is Ceylon, at least to those who live on the island.

The country, known as Ceylon during colonial times, became known officially as Sri Lanka in 1972. Under President Ranasinghe Premadasa there was an official move to change the Sri to Shri—Shri Lanka—as though people were not having enough difficulty learning where the new Ceylon was. But of course there was a very important reason for this proposed change. It had to do with national pride, the constant struggle to move out of the shadow of the giant neighbor to the north. Sri is a common term in India, which carries the meaning of hallowed, honorable or venerable. So this was an attempt to draw a distinction between the Indian Sri and the Lankan Shri. The government-owned Lake House newspaper, The Daily News, used the Shri form, whereas other publications stuck to the traditional Sri.

Today Sri Lankan society is generally divided into four main socio-ethnic groupings: Sinhalese, Tamil, Muslim and Burgher. Regardless of their ethnic identity, they all seem to share a certain Sri Lankaness that consists of insularity mixed with a curiosity about the outside world, unfailing friendliness and deference and a sense of hospitality. Whatever their ethnic origin, most Sri Lankans seem equally proud of their national identity, especially as it relates to India. They are not in the least bit shy about approaching foreigners, striking up a conversation and inquiring about their country of origin. But this seeming openness comes together with a basic conservatism that focuses on the preservation of family and religious values. The foreigner should not expect to be brought quickly into the private lives of Sri Lankans, regardless of their ethnic origins. Amongst themselves Sri Lankans can be quick to anger, a trait that accounts in part for the ethnic-religious violence that seems endemic in the society.

The Sinhalese society has traditionally reflected the caste structure inherited from Hindu society. Of these the Brahmin caste was the highest. In the course of time Buddhist influence tended to diminish the influence of the Brahmins and modify the Hindu system; the rigid observance of members of lower castes by those of higher castes began to be relaxed. The power of the Brahmins was usurped by the bikkhus (monks). The four main groups that evolved in Sri Lanka were the farmers (govi), warriors (kath), traders (velenda) and assorted others (chandals). Each of these had numerous sub-divisions, amounting to some 30 in all. Most Sri Lankans have a ge name (pronounced gay) name, an important part of their identity which is bestowed at birth and denotes the paternal side of the family. In ancient times these names were related to the caste or traditional occupation of the male family members.

With a colonial history of over 450 years, Sri Lankans have had plenty of time to absorb the culture of their colonizers. The Portuguese dominated the country from 1505 to 1658. One legacy from that period is that a large portion of the Sinhalese population in the low country along the coast have names like Fonseca, de Silva, de Soyza, Perera and Fernando. Those who carry these names today may be Sinhalese or trace their roots to Tamil Nadu in South India. About the only remnant of Portuguese culture to be found among Sri Lankans with these names is their adherence to the Catholic faith. Even this is not a given, however, as many who took these names for social and economic reasons remained Buddhists.

Then came the Dutch, who ruled over the western and northern coastal territories from 1658 to 1796. In the east they controlled sea ports such as Trincomalee for trading purposes. They introduced the first commercial plantations of cinnamon, pepper, coffee and coconut, and developed a road and canal transport system. Their missionaries expanded the system of elementary school initiated by the Portuguese. Roman Dutch law and Dutch-style law courts were introduced into the island. They too left their legacy of Dutch names like Koelmeyer, Pollocks and Jacobs, as well as the Catholic faith. Those who trace their ancestors to the Dutch are known as Burghers. Typical Burgher names found today include Soysa, de Soyza, Jansz and of course most every name that starts with a van: Van Cuylenberg, Van Rees and Van Twest. Then there are those who carry English names such as Wilson and Rockwood, which may either indicate a Eurasian family of mixed origins or a family that has adopted the name of American missionaries.

Many of the names in common use today in Sri Lanka are derived from Buddhist or Sinhala tradition. Among the most popular male names is Ananda, a cousin of Lord Buddha who became one of his most faithful disciples. It was Ananda who persuaded the Buddha to admit women into the sangha (the priesthood of monks). Upali, a wealthy man who had been a follower of another guru, was so impressed upon hearing the Buddha that he asked to become his disciple. Vijaya is the father of the Sinhalese nation, arriving in Sri Lanka from northern India. Mahinda, the name of the son of the great Buddhist king Asoka, is quite popular. Family names derived from the founding father include Wijesekera, Wijetunga and Wijekoon. Gamini is another popular name, derived from a slight alteration of Duttu Gemumu, the great Sinhala king. "Singhe" is the word for lion in Sinhalese. Many Sinhala names are derived from this word, which came to symbolize the Sinhala nation. The lion is still used as a metaphor for traits of valor and courage. It has special significance to Sinhala people even today. President Premadasa made allusion to this in a speech at the opening of a Tamil college while reproaching detractors of his government:

We were very proud when we were told our forefathers were lions. They said they came from the direction of Bengal. However much a lion is hungry, it will never eat grass. Some who claim to be "Sinhala heroes" today will even eat cowdung for power and positions! When they want to attack their enemies they will take any dirt into their hands. At times like this, when they resort to such disgraceful actions, I am a bit suspicious about their Sinhalakama (their being Sinhalese).

Many Sinhalese names are from the Hill Country, the Kandy region which was the last capital of the Sinhalese kings. Kandy itself is a quaint British corruption of the Sinhalese word for "kanda", meaning hill. Singhe is perhaps the most commonly found element in Sinhala names. Thus we have: Wijesinghe — from Vijaya, (father of his nation); Amarasinghe — almighty (last standing) lion; Gunasinghe — good lion (good person); Wickremesinghe — adventurous lion; and Rajasinghe — king lion; or in the case of the forest preserve, Sinharaja. Frequently Sinhala names are derived from the social organization of the village and surrounding area. Another common element in Sinhalese names is the suffix — nayake, or leader. Thus the names of two of the country's most prominent political families are derived from this root: Bandaranaike — or chief leader — and Senanayake — group leader. Numerous other names are derived from the same root meaning: Dissanayke, Ekanayake and Ratnayake. Ratna refers to gems; thus Ratnapura is the city of gems; then Jayaratne, Indaratna and Gunaratne.

Other names indicate Low Country or coastal origin such as Jayaweera and Gunawardena (promoter of virtue), Jayawardene (promoter of victory) and Siriwardena. Place names are reflected in suffixes such as -pitiya and -gama. Bambalapitiya and Kollupitiya are locations within the city of Colombo. The -gama suffix refers to a village: Weligama owes its name to the wife of the god Kataragama; Kosgama — jac tree village.

The Tamils, consisting of some 18 percent of the population, are the second most important group in Sri Lanka. Tamil names are often fairly easy to identify since many of them end in -am, such as Balasingam, Ponnambalam, Vallipuram, Subramaniam, Paskaralingam and Gunaratnam. The Muslim names are also quite easily identifiable, the commonest being those like Mohammed, Mohideen, Siddique, Shafeek and Sheriff. Archeological and other evidence in Southeast Asia suggests that trade, religious and cultural contacts were common between Sri Lanka and the Malay-Indonesian Archipelago in ancient times. The Malays were a sea-faring people and are known to have reached the shores of Madagascar. Considering the strategic location of Sri Lanka on their searoute and the vagaries of the wind and waves, they could not have missed the island in the course of their long and uncertain voyages. The southern port of Hambantota, for example, derives its name from the Malay word for boat; that is, sampan. In the Sinhalese language the phonemes "sa" and "ha" are interchangeable. Thus the Sinhalese tota—harbor or bay—plus hamban (sampan) = Hambantota. Ambalantota, a village to the west of Hambantota, refers to a waiting room or rest stop.

Sri Lankans speak a curious language, a mixture of English adapted from the colonizers and local Sinhalese. When I first arrived in Sri Lanka I was determined to learn a few phrases of Sinhalese which is my standard policy when visiting other countries. So I started with asking how to say good morning.

I asked more than one person and I got the same response.
A long pause, then:
"Well, we just say good morning."
In fact, the most common greeting to me, with my foreign face, from the ordinary person on the street was:
"What country, Suh?"
They wanted to peg your country of origin so they would know how to direct the remainder of the conversation, if it went that far. Typically they would guess every European country before finally mentioning Australia and eventually the United States. Americans are rare in Sri Lanka. So much for my feeble efforts at learning Sinhala! I then concentrated on trying to learn street names (no small feat since the same street can have three different names depending on what end of it you are on.) And those terms I was obliged to learn because they had become part of Sri Lankan English.

This English includes body language and attitudes that go along with the language. Anyone who has been to the country even for a short time has been exposed to the head waggle. At first it seemed a bit like how we Westerners shake our heads in conveying a negative. The head waggle is slightly different, as the head is moved a short distance each way to the side while simultaneously moving up and down, in a sort of serpentine fashion. So you could easily mistake this for a "no" to your question when in fact it is an enthusiastic "yes". I think I incorporated the head waggle into my repertoire, but I was never sure whether I had it right.

Early on I began to notice that words being used in regular English conversations didn't register with me. Mahindra in the Coopers and Lyband office was telling me that such and such an item would cost me a hundred bucks; not much, he added. I was thinking, well that's bloody outrageous for such a thing. And then he said if I gave him the money he'd go buy it for me. I said well, I don't have any dollars on me. He laughed. "Bucks" is a slang term for rupees. End of story. Eventually, whenever people would speak of spending "bucks" on something I could smile to myself. And people were always talking about so many lakhs of money, or cost of machinery or acres of land. A lakh is 100,000 (one hundred thousand). This was a case of a Sinhala word insinuating itself into everyday English, so much so that everyone is expected to know its meaning.

There were also what one might consider Britishisms in Sri Lankan English that are quaint-sounding to the American ear. For example, a "garden" refers to a street in a neighborhood as often as it does a plot in which to grow vegetables. People live in "bungalows", which is a type of house. Attempting to grasp and follow directions given by a Sri Lankan for driving somewhere could be exasperating. Just go to Bambalapitiya junction, I was told on several occasions. Okay, I knew that Bambalapitiya was a section of the city of Colombo, like Kollupitiya, but there was no Bambalapitiya street. As it happens, the "junction" is the point where Galle Road intersects Bauddaloka Mawatha, neither of which carries the name Bambalapitiya. Everyone except me knows that's the junction, although you won't find the name on the map. Mawatha is a Sinhala word for street or boulevard, used more often than its English equivalent. Sri Lankans steadfastly resist giving address numbers, which are not considered particularly important, even though every business or residence has one. Instead, you are given directions to reach a destination with a description of well known buildings, or, say, a Bo tree, a statue of the Buddha or the beginning of a dual carriage way.

Rarely are distances given voluntarily. When they are, miles and kilometers are used interchangeably, a reflection of the changeover from the British system. A "roundabout" is a traffic circle, where the motorist must be at his/her aggressive best in order to get in, around and out without a fender-bender. When one speaks of going "outstation" it is with the intention of going upcountry or, as they would say in francophone Africa, en brousse. Before setting out on such a trip one needs to visit a "petrol shed", that is, a filling station.

My favorite term is "tinkering" which has to do with fixing things up. It appeared on my receipt for the left side of my rented car door. When we use the word it tends to carry the implication that the tinkerer doesn't quite know what he's doing. In Sri Lanka it is given a perfectly legitimate meaning.

My second favorite expression was one that cropped up regularly in conversation, whether it had to do with sports or the business world. You engage the adversary in competition and then do what you can, "bat on...or box on...." This is a sports metaphor that implies struggling on against seemingly insurmountable odds. Another one that always tickled me was "short eats", which are snacks served at afternoon receptions. Sometimes it is a question of pronunciation rather than the word itself that was confusing. Our survey of small businesses included the metal products sector. Whenever our metal sector specialist referred to machinery, it always sounded to me like he was saying "missionary". The words "garment" and "government", when spoken by a Sri Lankan, were hardly distinguishable to me.

Language is also reflected in cultural and social attitudes. Sri Lankans are generally conservative, not given to superficial informality. The hand-shaking ritual which is so important everywhere in Africa is not so common among Sri Lankans. In fact, it's the one cultural trait I found the most difficult to shake (as it were). Sri Lankans are reluctant to use first names of foreigners or those who are their elders. My Sinhalese staff of senior researchers as well as my administrative assistant, most of them with at least a bit of grey hair, persisted in referring to me as Doctor—no name, just Doctor. After four months I was still "Suh" to Jacintha, my housemaid. She would even refer to me in a conversation with someone else as "my Suh".

"Peopleisation" is a uniquely Sri Lankan term that is meant to imply privatization with a human face. It actually has a formal definition: privatization of a state-owned company in which a minimum of 10 percent of the shares are reserved for employees. In his May Day speech the President focused on "peopleisation", stressing that no employee in any "peoplised" venture would lose a job on that account. He stipulated that 10 percent of the shares of "peopleised" enterprises would be gifted to the employees, who would enjoy these benefits even if they chose to quit their jobs.

The Otters Club

When I first arrived in Colombo I was anxious to find a place where I could get regular exercise and perhaps make social contact. I eventually found an ideal place called the Otters Club I learned that it was primarily Sri Lankan in membership, although there was no apparent discrimination against foreigners. Established in 1933, well before independence, the club counted over 6,000 members. Its leadership in the early years was predominantly Burgher, with a substantial representation of Tamils as well as Sinhalese. There was a time when Sri Lanka was in the socialist orbit that the most visible expatriates were the Russians, but they were long since gone. The management committee was now a compatible blend that mirrored Sri Lankan society: Muslims, Tamils, Burghers and the odd European although it remained an exclusively male-dominated club. On the walls were pictures of Otter swimming teams over the years. Every late afternoon there were young Otters doing their laps in the pool and a small band of divers testing the boards, working on new dives.

I noticed that the tennis courts tended to fill up after 4:00 P.M. so I wandered over and began watching. The chaps playing were slightly balding, a bit paunchy, but surprisingly adept at getting the ball over the net. During a break in play one fellow recognized my presence and struck up a conversation. They introduced themselves and invited me to join them. There was Dr. K.C. Fernando, the 65 year old anesthesiologist recently returned to Sri Lanka after 15 years living in Zambia. "Casey" as he prefered to be called, was once one of the leading tennis players in the country and a well known water sports specialist. There were Bandu and Siddath, both lawyers. Siddath was a bachelor, who looked after his family's interests in an auction house while also doing legal work. He was politically active, involved in the opposition SLFP, as well as a variety of charity organizations such as the Young Men's Buddhist Association. The three Gomez fellows were from the same Burgher family. The unofficial chairman of the group was Akbarali, a north Indian Muslim and one of the largest tea exporters in the country. He collected the monthly dues of 200 rupees (less than five dollars!). Naresh came from a prominant Tamil family and was in the oil business. The group had been playing every afternoon for a decade and knew each other's tricks intimately.

The Otters Club became my second home. I took my place in this motly assortment of tennis hacks and found both a regular outlet for tennis and a source of camaraderie. My game improved immensely, despite battling to overcome my tennis elbow condition and getting my serve right. My language modified slightly as well. Instead of the usual "oh shit" after a bad play I learned to say aiyo, which conveys roughly the same sentiment. This was a jovial lot, as much dedicated to in-jokes and pleasantries as getting a bit of exercise. A typical game started with a comment to the effect that "we're going to thrash you buggers." The basic trick was to announce the score after a play, adding points to your side. If the opposition was not paying attention by keeping track of the score, you gained points. Usually, however, this would bring on a hail of hoots and corrections from the opposing team.

After my first few weeks of tennis and swimming at the club, I noticed that there was an area for table tennis as well. I started watching the matches while winding down from my usual routine. About the same time every evening there was an elderly gentleman who presided over the ping pong scene, leaning on the table with one hand and fiercely pouncing on any ball that came within his range. Although his style was rather awkward, he seemed to beat most comers against him. To my amazement I soon learned that this man was none other than Arthur C. Clarke of 2001 Space Odyssey fame, undoubtedly the most famous person in Sri Lanka, of Briisher origin but a resident here for several decades. At the time he was already in his early-mid 70s and had several physical handicaps. But he clearly didn't let them deter him from thrashing hapless opponents. I took my turn one time, thinking myself a fair to middling player. But I am proud to say that I was thoroughly beaten by none other than Arthur C. Clarke!

Politics and Conflict

One cannot read the Daily News or The Island a day without being made aware of the on-going plague that affects Sri Lankan society. A note in The News, September 3, 1992, was reminiscent of the evening news in the U.S. during the Vietnam War:

> While the overall number of war refugees has now declined from a peak of 1.2 million in 1990, the recent military operations in the Jaffna peninsula saw a fresh displacement of civilians. At

least 600,000 Sri Lankans are currently internally displaced owing to the present ethnic conflict, a senior UNICEF official told The Island. He said the number of displaced persons that was 1.2 million in 1990 had now decreased to 800,000 including 200,000 Sri Lankans who had sought refuge in India...Meanwhile, nearly 80,000 people had left their homes in the wake of Operation Earthquake launched by the security forces last month.

It is a conflict that would make that between the Hatfields and McCoys look like a little spat. It is similar in intensity to that in South Africa and Bosnia-Herzegovina. All I knew about it before coming to Sri Lanka was that it had something to do with the separatist sentiments of the "Tamil Tigers." The racial and ethnic mosaic that made up Ceylonese society at the time of independence in 1948 was intricate and complex. The majority Sinhalese were still classified in census returns as Low-country (coastal) or Up-Country (Kandy). Historically there had been rather distinct differences between these two groups, the Kandyans claiming to be more racially and culturally pure. Even among the Kandyans, perhaps only 10 percent could claim aristocratic origins.

Among the Tamils, however, the divisions ran deeper. There were the Tamils of the north, concentrated in the Jaffna peninsula. They had been on the island for at least two millenia and had a language and culture that was distinctly their own. From these people came the Tamils who settled in Colombo as well as other predominantly Sinhalese areas in the south. While they generally kept up their ties to the Jaffna peninsula, they were more cosmopolitan than those who stayed behind. Further down the social scale were the Tamils of the east coast, partially because of their admixture with other races. There was little social intercourse between the Tamils of the north and those of the east, even though both groups were classified as Ceylon Tamils.   Much farther down the pecking order were the Indian Tamils brought by the British to work on the tea estates whom had been disenfranchised and in effect debarred from citizenship. They derived no benefit from the educational and other welfare schemes available to other inhabitants of the island. While the rest of the population enjoyed relative prosperity in the decade after independence, the Indian Tamils remained on the margins, viewed as aliens.

To further complicate the picture, the term Muslim has been employed to denote race, as distinct from Sinhalese and Tamil. Though in census returns Muslims were distinguished as a race, they did not see themselves as such, rather as followers of the Muslim religion. There were indeed a number of Muslims of Malay origin, and traces of African or Arab blood, but by and large Muslims were assumed to be converts from among the Tamils or Sinhalese. In the east their first language was Tamil, while those who lived inland were mostly traders and tended to speak Sinhalese and assimilate into the majority population. The majority of those born after 1956 outside of the North and East have been educated in the Sinhala language and use it as their home language. Many Moors are conversant in all four national languages: Sinhala, Tamil, English and Arabic.

The All Ceylon Moors Association has lobbied against using the term Muslim as a racial category. Sri Lanka has Muslims of many different races, including a majority of Moors (of Arab descent) Malays, Indian Moors, Borahs, Memons, as well as Sinhalese and Tamils. The Association lobbies for the eradication of any reference to race or religion in forms used by the government for general purposes, particularly police stations. The Association is also strongly opposed to Eelam, the Tamil separatist movement, and in favor of preserving the unity and territorial integrity of Sri Lanka. While accepting the provincial council system of decentralized administration, the Moors are against any devolution of power on communal or religious grounds. The hapless Muslim population in the North and East has been the target of Tamil Tiger massacres.

Religion was also used in the census to identify the Christian minorities. Owning to the aggressive proselytizing of the Portuguese, there were many more Catholics than Protestants. The Anglicans were socially more prominent because of the continuing British influence. Finally, the Burghers were defined as a distinct race derived from the descendents of the Dutch mixed with the local population. Although few in number, the Burghers enjoyed administrative and professional influence out of proportion to their numbers because of their facility in the English language. Ironically, the people of Ceylon could congratulate themselves on a smooth transition to independence, unlike India where a communal bloodbath ensued.

The basic conflict is considered to be between Sinhalese and Tamil. The Sinhalese are said to belong to the Aryan race and are predominantly Buddhist, whereas the Tamils are of the Dravidian race and generally follow the Hindu religion. In 1958, 1977, and 1983 there were outbursts of anti-Tamil violence. Since then the Tamils have been fighting to create a separate state in the northern and eastern provinces of the island which they call Eelam. The ironies of ethnicity abound. The older generation of the Kandyan upper class maintained ties with a certain social class of Tamils in Jaffna. They were quite happy when their children sought spouses in the right Tamil families in Jaffna rather than with their own Low-Country Sinhalese. It seemed that the higher up one went in Kandyan society, the more contacts with Tamil society one could expect. This suggests a Sri Lankan society divided along caste lines as well as on ethnic and linguistic lines.

Indeed, the terms racial, ethnic and communal seem to be used interchangeably in Sri Lanka to describe this conflict. The intensification of the conflict in the 1980s and the unresolved war in the north have spawned considerable literature on the subject. Learned journals grapple with the fine distinctions in terminology. Apologists for opposing points of view invoke scientific and historical evidence to bolster their cause. Recent archeological findings serve to reinforce the evidence, one way or the other. Sri Lankan writer Serena Tennekoon notes that the violence of July 1983 marked a critical point in the conflict between the two groups. It was an important juncture in the redefinition of Sinhalese identity. The traditional image of Sri Lanka as a tolerant and peaceful society whose culture is nourished by Buddhist heritage was rudely shattered when the range and intensity of violence against the Tamils by Sinhalese were exposed in the international media.

The 2,500-year recorded history of Sri Lanka is bound up with that of India—its only neighbor except for the Maldive Islands— and is shrouded in legend. It has been marked by the intertwining of the Sinhala race with Buddhism. The word simha or sinha signifies a lion in many oriental languages and symbolizes the leonine paternity of the Sinhala people. The ancient chronicles known as the Mahavamsa, authored by Buddhist monks, date the settlement of the Sinhala people when Prince Vijaya arrived on the island from northern India in 543 B.C., not coincidentally the year in which the Buddha died. This probably symbolizes the consolidation of a wave of Aryan migrations rather than a single event. A more well documented period concerns the introduction of Buddhism into the country. In about 250 B.C. the great Buddhist King Asoka sent his son Mahinda from India to Sri Lanka to spread the word of the Lord Buddha. Mahinda converted the Sinhala King Devanampiyatissa, and from then on Buddhism was protected as the state religion.

The Sinhala version of history as presented by Prof. Nanadadeva Wijesekera goes something like this. Sometime around 1500 B.C. bands of Aryans entered India from the northwest. Whatever their physical characteristics may have been, their language was known as Indo-Aryan. One branch migrated along the Ganges basin as far as Bengal. By the sixth century B.C. these Aryan kingdoms had advanced considerably due to trade and contacts with the West. These were the ancestors of the Sinhalese. The Mahavamsa, a collection of ancient Sinhalese chronicles, mentions that the Buddha was the first Aryan to visit ancient Lanka, on three separate occasions.

Out of one of these Aryan kingdoms in Bengal came Vijaya, the founder of the Sinhalese nation. Vijaya was a rebel prince whose antics alienated him from his father. King Sihabahu ostracized Vijaya and sent him off to sea with a band of 700 men. They eventually landed on the northwestern shore of the island of Sri Lanka. Vijaya's arrival happened to coincide with the year of the death of the Buddha in 543 B.C. According to the legend, Vijaya bedded down with a local Yakka princess who bore him two sons before he got around to a marriage with a proper Aryan lady sent down from India, thereby raising questions from the outset about racial purity. In any event Vijaya sudued the Yakka king and founded the city of Tambapanni. The name of the progenitor Lion (Siha) was given to the island as Sihaladeepa and the people were called Sihalayo.

The important assertion which Wijesekera makes is that these Aryans who settled in Sri Lanka advanced to a highly civilized degree comparable to any contemporary kingdom in India within 300 years. The North Indian bonds with Sri Lanka remained close and lasted for many centuries. With the introduction of Buddhism into the island in 247 B.C. the religious and moral values of the Sinhalese were revolutionized, helping the people to withstand enemy attacks. A new civilization was born and the Sinhalese prospered. So much so that the kingdoms of South India, separated only by a mere 22-

mile strip of sea from the island, envied the growth and prosperity of the Aryans. Naturally, to these people who were the ancestors of the Tamils, Sri Lanka was a prize worth fighting for and there commenced a series of incursions from India.

Conflict between Tamils and Sinhalese can therefore be traced back over two millennia. An epic event took place in 101 B.C. when the great King Duttu Gemunu waged a war against the Tamils, killing their King Ellalan and 32 sub-kings, and thus uniting the Sinhalese people. Duttu Gemunu has been lionized throughout Sinhalese history and up to the present in a way that would make George Washington jealous. He built a capital city at Anuradhapura that was an architectural and engineering wonder. The remnants of his works are awe-inspiring. He propagated the Buddhist faith throughout his kingdom as reflected in the mammoth stupas that survive to this today. It might be argued that Duttu Gemunu was a better role model for young Sinhalese than his predecessor, the roguish Vijaya.

The Tamil version of Sri Lankan history is somewhat different, as Radhika Coomaraswamy tells it. Tamils living in Sri Lanka have been constantly subjected to the Sinhalese version of this "Aryan myth" which has been rammed down their throats ever since independence in 1948. As a reaction to the glorification of the Aryan race, there has been an increasing Tamil tendency to speak of the noble Dravidian past of the Tamil people. According to this version of history, one of the world's ancient civilizations flourished at Mohenjadaro in the Indus Valley as early as 2000 B.C. Mohenjadaro was destroyed by uncivilized Aryan hordes. The remnants of this majestic Dravidian civilization are to be found today in Tamil Nadu, in southern India, as well as among the Tamils in northern Sri Lanka. And the Tamil version of the Duttu Gemunu war has it that the Sinhalese fought with a contingent of 500 "bhikkus" (Buddhist monks), thus affirming that the conflict is officially religious as well as ethnic or racial.

The concept of Aryan as a racial category has been dismissed by some scholars over the years. In fact, the extension of this linguistic concept to convey a sense of race was a contribution of Hitler's Nazi Germany. The Tamil argument claims that the term Aryan was not even used in traditional chronicles of Sri Lanka and is a more recent invention. The Sinhalese have always claimed that they were the original inhabitants of the island, with the Tamil role being that of the invader. To combat this myth of origin, Tamil scholars contend that the Tamils are the lineal descendants of the Yakka people, who in turn migrated originally from South India to Sri Lanka.

Thus the assertion of the rights of one group, be it ethnic or racial, results in the need to "delegitimize" the other. Sinhala chauvinists, invoking the Mahavamsa, portray the Tamils as foreigners and invaders. The Tamil response is to assert that there is no such thing as Sinhalese. While the Tamils are the lineal descendants of the original inhabitants of the island, the Sinhalese lack pedigree. No matter what their racial origin, little remains of the original stock except belief in it.

A middle ground argument is that the Tamils, Sinhalese and Muslims are by now a racially mixed lot. Waves of immigration and internal migration have obliterated any legitimate claims to racial exclusivity. Articulating this point of view, Coomaraswamy observes that as a society Sri Lankans have tended to forget the deeply humane aspects of their respective traditions. "Instead, many writers and ideologues from various communities continue to emphasize those aspects of culture and history that accentuate differences and see ethnic loyalty as the supreme human value. Modern political categories are used as mirrors into the past and history is employed as a weapon in an ethnic war of words. The issues of justice and oppression get lost in a discourse of historical fact and counter-fact."

Letters to the editors of Colombo newspapers debate the issues of racial and cultural identity, heatedly defending or denouncing theories of the origin of the various races and pointing out the links with great and ancient civilizations. The Tamil argument generally assails alleged Sinhala superiority on the basis that there is little difference between the two races. Tamils, being of Dravidian stock are generally brown or black skinned people. And so are many Sinhalese people, who claim to be of Aryan stock. Sinhala culture, it is argued, is much like that of Kerala in southern India, including food habits, dances and even religious practices. One writer asked, "Why was Kandyan Perahara started as a Hindu festival?" And "how come names like Nayake, Chandrika, Chandran and Bala (common Kerala names) entered into Sinhalese life?"

One Sinhalese respondent maintained that where the Sinhalese people originated is not so important as to which racial group they belong. He invoked anthropological evidence to support his case.

"Anthropologists have divided mankind into three major groups and a sub-group: Mongoloid, Caucasoid and Negroid—and the sub-group being the Australoid...the Indo-Aryan group is a sub-group of the Caucasoids...people belonging to this group include Iraqis, Iranians and some north Indians and Sinhalese." The Shah of Iran, he noted, called himself the light of Aryans. On the other hand, "the Dravidians are descendents of the Australoid group. The original stock still survives in Australia. They are the Australian aborigines." A theory designed to fan the flames of racial animosity for sure!

Another, responding to the same article, conceded that the Sinhalese were of varied complexions:

Yes, the Sinhalese is a super nation comprised of people of various ethnic origins even European and Chinese. The land of Sinhalese may be of any ethnic origin. Furthermore, South Indians who came here those days from time to time got themselves absorbed into the majority resulting in national gains, contributions (setting an example to the present Tamils). Same way as Romans, Vikings, Saxons, etc. got interrogated (sic) with the Britons.

Yet another writer responding to the debate thoughtfully observed that;

...the theory of the Aryan-Dravidian dichotomy of origin the Sinhalese and Tamils was a conspiracy hatched by imperialist masters to drive a wedge between the two groups... Many foolish scholars have swallowed the bait hook, line and sinker, and helped to perpetuate the enmity to the great detriment of the Buddhists as well as the Hindus.

Strangely enough, during my stay in Sri Lanka I personally witnessed none of the racial, ethnic, and religious animosity reflected in these writings, nor did anyone seek to engage me in any discussion of the issues.

Ceylon Tea

If there is one thing most people know about Sri Lanka it has to do with Ceylon tea. Even since the changing of the name of the country in 1972, the country's principal agricultural export is still known as Ceylon tea. In Sri Lanka today there is no more sacred ritual than tea time. It is part and parcel of everyday life. Even the humblest office worker or auto mechanic is entitled to his or her mid-morning and mid-afternoon tea. And Sri Lankans are all aware that the tea industry was the foundation on which the modern economy was developed. In the early days, the development of infrastructure such as roads, harbors and railway lines as well as the main service industries such as banking, shipping and insurance were the direct result of the demands made by the tea industry. Later, the surplus generated by the industry was the main source of funds for the development activities undertaken by the state in other sectors. The services sector in particular made possible an exceptionally high quality of life of Sri Lankans relative to people of other developing countries with comparable income levels.

For all of this Sri Lankans can thank James Taylor, the founding father of Ceylon tea. Today Sri Lanka vies with India as the world's largest exporter of tea. In 1992 the country observed the 100th anniversary of the passing away of James Taylor, the Scotsman who pioneered the tea business in Ceylon. Taylor was recruited at the tender age of 14 from his native Scotland and trained by an English firm for a career in tea planting. He set sail for Ceylon in 1852 and spent the rest of his life dedicated to propagating tea. There were as yet no trains in Ceylon so Taylor set off on horse for a six-week journey to Kandy and another 26 miles to Loolecondera which he would call home for the next 40 years. Taylor built himself a log cabin covered with thatch in which he lived for the rest of his life.

In 1867, Taylor planted 19 acres of tea from seeds he had received from Assam in India, just two years prior to the "King Coffee" debacle. Heretofore, the main cash crop grown in Ceylon had been coffee. Less than 20 years later the entire coffee plantation industry of the island was destroyed by disease. It was as though Divine Providence had ordained that coffee must disappear to make way for tea. It is widely accepted that the pioneering efforts of James Taylor allowed the colony to hold its export economy together. Today, 125 years later, Taylor's 19 acres of tea have expanded to nearly 600,000, transforming the ecology of the hill country and providing a livelihood for two and a half million people. Taylor died of dysentery at the age of 57. He was a large fellow, weighing nearly 250 lbs. It is said that it took two gangs of 12 men to carry his coffin in turns from Loolecondera to the cemetery in Kandy. It is unlikely that he realized that he would someday be revered as the founding father of the tea industry in Ceylon.

The social and environmental consequences of tea estate development have been considerable, however. The traditional practice of paddy rice cultivation was accompanied by a family and clan social structure that has been undermined by the tea estate culture during the past several generations. The leader of the militant group Janatha Vimukthi Peramuna (JVP), Rohana Wijeweera, gave the humble tea plant highest ranking among the causes of the country's economic problems:

> The primary root of the burning economic problems in the country is the collapse of the simple self-sufficient economy. The birth of the tea plant at the expense of the kurakkan plant is the main cause of the economic crisis. These problems can be solved only by re-instituting the rice plant and the kurakkan plant at the expense of the tea and rubber plants.

Wijeweera's effort to topple the government failed and no one talks seriously about returning to exclusive paddy cultivation. But the problems of the tea estate economy remain.

Sri Lanka ranks as the third largest tea producing country in the world with nine percent of total production. It is the second largest exporter with a share of 22 percent of the global demand. Today, a century and a quarter since the beginning of the industry, tea exports generate the highest net foreign exchange earnings. In 1991, in spite of a 13 percent drop in tea export earnings due to low prices, the net earnings from the export of tea exceeded that from the export of garments by 25 percent. Currently tea is cultivated in an area of about two hundred thousand hectares. Eleven percent of the total employment in the country (600,000 persons) is directly attributable to the tea industry.

Tea plantations provide a livelihood for 2.5 million people, most of them Tamils brought over from India by the British planters. Pickers and their families usually live in cramped "line rooms" in one of the Divisions. Luckier ones are being provided with compact cottages with water supply and electricity. Life on a typical tea estate is arduous and demanding. The day begins at 5:00 A.M. and pickers are on the verdant tea slopes by 7:30. The average worker can pick 16 kilograms a day. Wages vary from estate to estate. With a regular six-day work week a typical picker makes the equivalent of about 35 US dollars a month. The highest wages range up to $100 a month. The earning differentiation depends entirely on the yield of tea per hectare.

Not too long ago the tea industry was considered to be the key to Sri Lanka's prosperity. In recent years, however, the industry has struggled to overcome problems of poor productivity, and other export products are being promoted to lessen the country's reliance upon tea exports. Until 1972 the private sector owned nearly all the tea in Sri Lanka, the bulk of it concentrated in large estates. In that year there were over 800 estates, averaging 100 acres. Then in 1972 the program of nationalization was begun. The actual transfer of land to the government began in 1974. The management of most state-owned tea estates was transferred to one of two corporations: the Janatha Estates Development Board (JEDB) and the Sri Lanka State Plantations Corporations (SLSPC). All other estates that were not nationalized were lumped together under the heading of small-holder estates. In 1982, tea represented 30 percent of the country's total earnings. Seventeen percent of all tax revenue was from taxes directly applied to the tea industry.

But after two decades of state management of plantations, the country learned a bitter lesson. The bureaucratic approach to plantation management had led to inefficiency and a decline in growth. Since 1980, the SLSPC recorded profits in only five years and the JEDB in only two years. The likely loss of the state-managed estates in 1992 was projected to be over Rs. 3 billion. The government was spending Rs. 400 million a month with the two corporations to meet their operating costs, funds that would otherwise have been available for investments in growth sectors of the economy. At the same time the private sector estates, comprised of both small holders and those who operate larger holdings, had consistently run at a profit.

The government was now engaged in a major restructuring of the plantation sector, the central focus of which were the state plantations. There was official recognition that the only solution to the problems of low productivity, poor profits and the absence of international linkages was to promote private sector development.

After several extensive studies, the decision was taken to form 22 government owned regional plantation enterprises to be managed by selected private sector companies. These would have government appointed boards of directors. But the government insisted that there would be no privatization of the ownership of land. In November 1991, applications were called from interested private firms for pre-qualification to bid on management contracts for the regional plantation enterprises.

If it is any consolation to Sri Lanka, the Indian tea industry was having problems of its own. The inability of Russia to meet its bilateral commitments in the barter trade with India resulted in a fall in the latter's export of tea to Russia. This in turn meant a decline in India's share of world tea trade by as much as 18 percent. Russia accounted for more than half of India's tea trade, and total tea exports had fallen over the past three years. According to observers of the tea industry, this could be due to the higher price of Indian tea. But even if India were to go in for tea bags and instant tea to capture the value added market, the Sri Lankan and Kenyan competition would be stiff since their teas are better suited for this use.

Sri Lanka's Export Development Board was mindful of these trends in the tea market. As a casual user, I would have thought that real tea lovers would insist upon the traditional tea leaf. But consumer preference in the affluent markets is overwhelmingly for tea in bags. This is a fast-growing market, since one of the problems consumers face is that of disposal of tea leaves after brewing. Tea bags represent the solution. As incomes increase, the market for tea bags will increase, at the expense of packeted teas. So it will be to the advantage of Sri Lanka to increase its exports of tea in the form of tea bags, thus increasing the value added in the bagging operation. Presently the country does not manufacture adequate quantities of CTC (cut, turn and curl) teas which are required for production of tea bags. Priority should be given to the manufacture of CTC teas. It might be to the advantage of the Sri Lankan entrepreneur to set up tea bagging operations in consuming countries abroad, thus saving on transportation costs and avoiding higher duties.

Totally soluble tea such as instant tea, which leaves no residue at all, appears to be the real answer to the problem of tea leaves after brewing. The gradual shift of consumption from tea to coffee can be attributed in large measure to the availability of instant coffee, which is considered a satisfactory substitute for ground coffee. It is noteworthy that Sri Lankan exports of instant tea have penetrated markets in many countries, much of it to the United States and Britain. On both the supply and demand side, instant tea seems to be a product which has the brightest prospects for Sri Lanka's future.

It has been suggested that sericulture, the cultivation of silkworms for the production of silk, could serve as a viable alternative crop on all denuded mid-country tea lands. No less an authority than Rene Dumont, the well known agronomist, has endorsed this idea. Sericulture involves the cultivation of mulberry bushes which are used to feed the silkworm. Cocoon production involves simple technologies and is easily adopted by farmers. The mulberry has a very short gestation period (nine months from planting to the first crop of cocoons. It is a perennial which needs replanting only after 15 years. A farmer can harvest eight to 10 crops a year. Sericulture is proposed as a response to the government's emphasis on poverty alleviation and rural employment generation. It is labor-intensive and can keep an entire family usefully employed. Sericulture was started in earnest in Sri Lanka only in the 1970s and in the 1990s was still predominantly in the hands of a state-owned corporation, Silk and Allied Products Development Authority (SAPDA). Most of SAPDA's silk fabrics are converted to batik dress lengths, scarves and saris, and sold locally to tourists.

Culture Shock?

Far from retreating into an expatriate subculture in Sri Lanka, I found myself almost entirely in the company of Sri Lankans during my stay there. Although I lived only a block away from the USAID office, I rarely stopped in there and made only a couple of visits to the American Cultural Center and Embassy. The American community in Colombo was quite small and it was possible to go several weeks without encountering another American anywhere. Even initially joining the mainly expatriate Colombo Swimming Club down the street from my apartment failed to bring about interesting social interaction with other foreigners. In fact, my only meaningful relations initially were in the work place, where I was the lone expatriate. There, I must confess, I rather appreciated the respect and deference generally accorded me as a project team leader (the big fish/small pond syndrome, I suppose). This situation fed my need to understand the people and culture that surrounded me.

I had come to Sri Lanka carrying nearly three decades of cultural baggage acquired from living and working in Africa and knowing Africans in the diaspora.

I was accustomed to a generally gregarious and affable society in which the ritual of shaking hands at the beginning and end of each encounter with others was a common denominator. Not that I found Africans inclined to be drawn into superficial "friendships" that seem to them to characterize American social relations. Sri Lankans, by contrast, I found to be rather more reserved, much less likely to extend a hand in greeting and certainly not in the ritual manner of Africans. After a while I trained myself to wait and see whether a hand was being extended before offering mine. A polite nod of the head and smile would suffice in most cases, especially when it involved introduction to the opposite sex. The head waggle, of course, had a special significance that the expatriate was obliged to fathom sooner or later.

What struck me from the outset was the universal cordiality and civility with which Sri Lankans of all races tend to treat the expatriate. Perhaps this is because expatriates have always been a small portion of the total population and therefore something of a curiosity. I'm not able to vouch for how they treat each other. Colleagues and government officials, business owners and fellow club members, as well as casual acquaintances tended to be most courteous in their dealings with me. (The notable exception is when they were behind the wheel of the car!) And granted, their motive sometimes seemed to be to work a tourist deal with my presumed deep pockets.

But I would continue to have trouble reconciling this distinctly positive impression with that of a society riven with ancient animosities and capable of unspeakable atrocities against each other. The more I read and heard of the racial and religious differences within Sri Lankan society, the more mystified I became about them in the light of my positive personal experience. Debate over the racial distinctions between Sinhala and Tamil raged in the popular press as well as in scholarly journals. I was amazed by the intensity of the debate, which provided me with a window for understanding the ferocity of the civil conflict. Indeed, arguments about the origins of the two peoples encompassed both race and language, as well as foodways and social behavior. To the disputants it seemed terribly important to ascertain the exact geographic and linguistic origins of the two races in order to demonstrate their relative superiority. The Sinhala argument was that they were descended from the Bengalis of northern India and therefore of Aryan stock. Yet the Mahavamsa, the sacred Sinhala book of history, makes no mention of either northern India or the Aryan race. Oddly enough, the modern day Bengalis appear to have no pretension of being Aryans. For that matter, today the Sinhala people are a mixture descended from northeast and northwest India as well as the South Indian Tamil invaders.

The more the Sinhalese were inclined to assert their Aryan identity, the more the Tamils were obliged to argue that differences between the two peoples were really marginal. Food habits and dances of the Sinhala people were said to resemble those of the Kerala region of southern India. Ironically, as preoccupied as the Sinhalese seemed to be with being swallowed up by their giant neighbor, they are crazy about Indian films, Hindi songs and Indian fashions. Many have become devotees of Indian spiritual leaders such as Satya Sai Baba. Faithful Buddhists go on pilgrimages to the birthplace of Siddharta Gautama on the sub-continent.

To me the Aryan/Dravidian dichotomy was particularly puzzling when put forward in racial terms, since both "races" seemed to have a similar range of skin coloration from ebony to olive hued. In my daily dealings with Sinhala, Tamil, Muslim and Burghers, my best clue to their ethnic identity was the family name rather than physical appearance. Social behavior appeared to be as much a function of class as of race. I heard of the not so uncommon practice of intermarriage between prominent Kandy Buddhist families and Hindus from Jaffna. The professional Jaffna Tamils living in Colombo were every bit as sophisticated as their Sinhala brethren and had just as much at stake in the status quo.

This was by no means an academic debate. The nuances of cultural and racial identity put forward in the press and academic circles were being fought over in the arid Jaffna peninsula and the jungles of the North and East. The wail of ambulance sirens rushing down Galle Road in Colombo carrying wounded soldiers to the hospital was a regular feature of life. The ethnic cleansing campaign continued unabated, washed with the blood of innocents in Muslim villages one day, Sinhalese or Tamil villagers the next. The Tigers who fought in the name of the Tamil people seemed just as quick to eliminate dissidents within their own population as they were the freshly recruited soldiers in the Sri Lankan army.

The final days in Colombo were dedicated to packing and making plans for the return trip, which would first take me and Chris to Bangkok. Meanwhile, we found time to go to the US Cultural Center where we watched the results of the US presidential elections on a wide screen. From Bangkok Chris would be off to Seattle and I would go on to Vietnam before heading home to Washington.

Vietnam — November 1992

In late September I received a letter from Dr. Thanh van Tran, a colleague from our Guinea and Washington days, now in Abidjan, dated August 20! We had last seen each other in Abidjan, his current residence, in the spring when I passed through there on another consulting assignment. Tran's letter inquired as to whether I might still be interested in meeting him in Vietnam, a proposition which he had casually made on earlier occasions. Tran indicated that he was planning to be in Vietnam during the last two weeks of November. He said he was currently working with the Washington consulting firm of Robert Nathan Associates. Tran had on several occasions tried to entice me to visit his native Vietnam with him. This time his invitation came at a very propitious time, since I was winding up my Sri Lanka assignment and would be heading back to Washington by November.

Responding to Tran's letter proved to be rather complicated. If communications were still difficult within and among African countries, the same is especially true between Sri Lanka and Abidjan. My initial efforts to phone or write Tran in Abidjan were to no avail. Likewise, calls to Nathan Associates office. Meanwhile, I managed to get through to Tran by phone and to commit myself in principle to meeting him in Ho Chi Minh City (formerly Saigon) in Vietnam. This was followed by a fax in which I reported that I had made reservations to travel to Bangkok on November 11 to obtain a visa which was supposed to take three working days. I planned to proceed to Vietnam on the 15th. With considerable uncertainty in communications with Tran, I went ahead and finished up my plan, contacting Lamson's Travel Agency in Bangkok for hotel reservations, and making arrangements for a Vietnam visa. From what I had heard, even now visas for American visitors to Vietnam were not automatic.

Bangkok, Thailand   *11/November/1992*

Chris and I arrived in Bangkok as scheduled on November 11th and went to the Sukhumvit 4 address of Lamson's. We stayed at the Rajah Hotel, across the street from Lamson's, and I began working on my Vietnam visa upon arrival. Lamson's kept saying there would be no problem, even though the third working day would be a Saturday and I was to leave for Saigon the following day. Lamson's also called the Saigon Concert Hotel in Ho Chi Minh City, where Tran would be staying, to make a reservation for me. Chris and I managed a bit of sight-seeing, including a visit to the Palace of the King of Thailand.

Chris and Galen in Bangkok, 1992

Toward the end of our stay in Bangkok I called the Nathan Associates Office, promising a debriefing on my return from Vietnam. Sure enough, the Vietnam Embassy had not returned my passport with the visa on Saturday, so I was obliged to cancel my Sunday flight and schedule a Monday flight, hoping that the visa would be in hand by then. Monday morning was a mad scramble to get to the embassy, pick up my passport and head to the Bangkok airport, just in time for the Ho Chi Minh City (formerly Saigon) flight.

Ho Chi Minh City, Vietnam   16/November/1992

Following the "liberation" of Southern Vietnam by North Vietnamese forces on April 30 1975, the entire country of Vietnam was finally unified and the last vestiges of American presence were evacuated. In the first meeting of the National Assembly of the Unified Vietnam on July 2nd 1976, the assembly decided to name the country the Socialist Republic of Vietnam. The constitution of 1980, and 1992, continued the country's official name, legally and actually. This, after over a decade of conflict that had pitted communist against capitalist forces, engaging thousands of U.S. troops, rending American society in two, and eventuating in a clear-cut loss for the U.S. I was not at all certain what kind of reception I would receive in the new Vietnam, 18 years after the victory of the forces of Ho Chi Minh in Vietnam.

Chris left for Seattle and I made the short hop from Bangkok to Vietnam, arriving at Tan Son Nhat airport in Ho Chi Minh City on Monday, November 16th. The same day a delegation of the special US Senate Committee sent to investigate the fate of American soldiers missing during the Vietnam War, arrived in Vietnam. The Senate Committee on POW/MIAs, led by Chairman Kerry (D-Mass.), also included Senators Tom Daschle (D-ND) and Hank Brown (R-Colo). They had spent four days in Laos before coming to Vietnam to meet ranking officials and others who had information concerning missing US soldiers. It was the second visit of the committee to Southeast Asia, aimed at evaluating Vietnam cooperation with U.S efforts to obtain information about missing U.S. military personnel.

I went straight to the Saigon Concert Hotel, only to find that I did not have a reservation. Needless to say, this did nothing to renew my faith in Lamson's! Not to worry: the receptionist called over to the Rex Hotel a few blocks away and secured a room there (for nearly double the rate $59.00 or 634,250 Vietnamese dong—10,750 dong to the dollar). As I checked in at the Rex I noticed a bulletin welcoming the US Senate delegation. There seemed to be an unusually large number of Americans in the hotel, but I thought surely they couldn't all be part of the U.S. Senate delegation. As it turned out, many were representing Private Voluntary Organizations and were headed to Hanoi for an NGO conference meeting November 16-19. The conference was organized by the Geneva-based International Council of Voluntary Agencies (ICVA) and Vietnam's PACCOM, the agency responsible for coordinating all international aid in the country. The conference was attended by representatives from more than 50 countries.

My first impressions of Saigon were a mixture of recollections of Walter Cronkite reporting on the war on the evening news, coupled with a sea of bicycles and motorcycles that flooded the streets of the city. After the perpetual gridlock of traffic in Bangkok, however, the situation in Ho Chi Minh City seemed almost benign. People were very cordial everywhere, and tended to warm up even more when I identified myself as an American. Nearly everyone spoke at least a minimal amount of English. The street vendors seemed to specialize in Vietnam stamp books as well as a combination of official biographies of Ho Chi Minh and guides to potential foreign investors. The first few days I began to notice lights strung up on some of the apartment buildings. By the time we left Saigon the entire city was covered with colored lights. In the last couple of years the Vietnamese have apparently begun to celebrate Christmas in a big way!

Having checked into the Rex, I made my way back over to the Saigon Concert and greeted Tran and his wife Kim Bui who arrived the same afternoon. As it turned out, the Saigon Concert did have a room available (at $32.00) and I moved in the following day. Tran spent a lot of time on the phone lining up business and social contacts. We decided to spend the rest of the week in and around Saigon and to leave for Hanoi on Sunday, November 22nd. Much of the time in Saigon was taken up with making arrangements to see key persons in Hanoi.

Among the highlights of our stay in Saigon were our visits to Madame Dai's. She is an influential public figure and patron of the arts, a former senator in the South Vietnamese government and a representative in the present government as well. She also happens to be a fantastic chef and hosts wonderful dinner parties in her home. Foreign journalists are the preferred guests, although we were invited because of her esteem for Kim Bui and Tran. During lunch at Madame Dai's we listened in as a group from the BBC discussed the filming of her cooking a meal the following day. In the evening we attended a presentation of traditional dances and songs by the group that she promotes.

Hanoi

We arrived at the Hanoi airport Sunday afternoon on a Swiss Air contract airplane rather than the usual Vietnam Airlines Russian built Tupolev. (The week before a Vietnam Airlines plane had crashed, killing 30 passengers and crew.) The air was noticeably cooler than in Ho Chi Minh City, and I had not brought a jacket! The airport is about an hour's drive north of the city. Most of the trip into town winds through rice fields, encumbered by very little traffic other than the occasional truck carrying agricultural produce. The approach into Hanoi features a massive four-lane bridge constructed by the Russians. The city is strikingly clean and orderly, with tree-lined boulevards, elegant French colonial villas and monuments to the proletarian revolution such as the Ho Chi Minh mausoleum and the statue of V.I. Lenin. The natural setting of the city is beautiful, defined as it is by the Song Hong River and numerous lakes and ponds. I expected to see evidence of U.S. bomb damaged buildings, but they said most of the bombs had created large craters outside of the city in the rice fields. Interestingly enough, the French colonial influence is much more pronounced in Hanoi than in Saigon, especially in its excellent French restaurants. Even Hanoi was decked out in an array of Christmas lights.

In Hanoi we checked into the Lotus Hotel, which was clean and moderately priced but had small rooms. We looked into the possibility of moving to the newly opened Saigon Hotel (across the street from the United Nations Development Program (UNDP) but it was fully booked. Unfortunately, my stay in Hanoi was only a day and two nights, although Tran and Kim Bui were to stay on another couple of days. Our first visit in Hanoi was with the Assistant Resident Representative of the UNDP office, Jens Christian Wandel. He had first served in the Hanoi office in 1980-81 and remarked that there had been a vast change for the better since then. Wandel indicated that there was a new private sector development initiative in the UNDP program and he was hopeful that it would be expanded in the immediate future. He showed a particular interest in establishing a project in Vietnam patterned on the Africa Project Development Facility where Tran was working in Abidjan.

At the State Bank of Vietnam we met with the Vice Minister/ Deputy Governor, Mr. Le Van Chau, and the Deputy Director of the Foreign Department, Mr. Ha Dan Huan. Tran had met Le Van Chau in Washington when he was detailed to the World Bank and he received us very graciously. Tran and Kim Bui were planning to meet with top political officials in the next few days.

On the surface it was an historic time to be in Hanoi. The Vietnamese were openly optimistic that the U.S. embargo against Vietnam might at long last be lifted and normal relations restored. The local press hailed the visit of the Senate Committee as a "breakthrough" in U.S.-Vietnam relations. President Bush had sent a letter to his Vietnamese counterpart, Le Duc Anh, the first letter from a U.S. president since 1973. Senator Kerry reported that the letter expressed very directly that the cooperation from the Vietnamese government would be met by reciprocal actions on the part of the U.S. During their visit to Hanoi the Senate Committee members met with President Le Duc Anh, Prime Minister Vo Van Kiet and other high level officials.

At the same time, Vietnam's Communist Party Secretary General Do Muoi declared that all overseas Vietnamese were welcome to return to their country, regardless of the position they may have had under past regimes. This appeal for the unity of the Vietnamese people no doubt was inspired in part by the desire of the authorities to attract investment of overseas Vietnamese, just as the overseas Chinese are beginning to invest in China in a big way.

Reflections on Vietnam

Vietnam was like a racetrack: all the horses taking their place at the starting gate. The Japanese were the first in line, judging by the customers staying at the newly restored Metropole Hotel and the new Saigon Hotel in Hanoi. By all accounts there had been a huge influx of foreign visitors to Vietnam since the beginning of 1992, many of them representing multinationals based in Hong Kong, Singapore, Bangkok and Australia. Among foreign visitors in Vietnam, most conversations mdke reference to..."when the embargo is lifted." Imposed in 1975 by the U.S. government when the South was taken over by the Communists in Hanoi, the U.S.-led embargo prevented Vietnam from having access to loans to international bodies such as the International Monetary Fund and the World Bank. The Vietnamese government initiated a policy of doi moi (renovation) in 1986 which was beginning to take hold. These reforms included the gradual redistribution of land to farmers and the privatization of some state-owned enterprises.

Businessmen and tourists were coming to Vietnam in increasing numbers. In the first ten months of 1992 there were 370,000 tourists, accounting for revenues of $50 million. During the same period, the government approved 141 new investment projects worth US $1.4 billion. A total of 64 hotel and tourism projects accounted for $800 million, making tourism the third largest investment area.

For several years American businessmen had been visiting Vietnam in a discrete attempt to establish local contacts in anticipation of the lifting of the embargo. Since the U.S. lifted the ban on travel to Vietnam, American tourists—particularly overseas Vietnamese—were returning in ever greater numbers. The Hong Kong-based American Chamber of Commerce started the ball rolling by sponsoring an official visit of U.S. business owners in February 1992. That visit was followed by a host of Asia-based U.S. companies doing market research including CitiBank, Bank of America, General Motors, Motorola, AT&T, Pepsi Cola, Coca Cola, General Electric, Delta Airlines and United Airlines. Other "live sightings" of American firms in Vietnam during this time included Fluor-Daniel, United Technologies, Procter & Gamble and Eastman Kodak.

It was already well documented that Vietnam was rich in natural resources. Not least of these resources was off-shore oil, expected to earn the country $700 to $800 million in 1992. The major field, known as White Tiger, was actually discovered by Mobil Corp. toward the end of the war. Now the Vietnamese government was interested in getting U.S. oil companies back into the country because of their superior technology. Several firms such as Exxon, Amoco and Chevron were circling Vietnamese skies waiting for the opportunity to get started.

In early November 1992 Ernst & Young became the first foreign accountancy firm to receive an operating license in Vietnam. The British-based firm was authorized to audit foreign-owned enterprises, joint ventures and state firms. Foreign business owners said that Hanoi's granting of the license is an indication of its desire to attract more foreign investment. A few Vietnamese firms are attempting to provide business advisory services to potential investors, including arranging for foreign partners.

References

All Ceylon Moors Association, "The Role of Muslims in the Peace Movement," in *Social Justice* 65, Vol. 26, No. 8, August 1992.

Ashby, Elizabeth. "Our Reactions to Dukkha," Bodhi Leaves Series, No. 26; Kandy, Buddhist Publication Society.

Asiaweek, May 12, 1993, "Rule by the Sword."

Bandaranaike, Dias. "Tea Production in Sri Lanka: Future Outlook and Mechanisms for Enhancing Sectoral Performance," Central Bank of Ceylon, Occasional Paper No. 7, 1984.

Barlas, Robert & Nanda Wanasundera (1992) *Culture Shock: A Guide to Customs and Etiquette in Sri Lanka,* Singapore: Times Books International.

Bulathsinhala, D.T. "Sericulture as a Viable Alternative to Tea," *The Sunday Times,* June 7, 1992.

Bullen, Leonard. "Buddhism: A Method of Mind Training", Bodhi Leaves Series No. 42; Kandy, Sri Lanka: Buddhist Publication Society.

Clarke, Arthur C. (1978) *The Fountains of Paradise*, New York: Bantam Books.

Coomaraswamy, Radhika (1985) "Myths Without Conscience: Tamil and Sinhalese Nationalist Writings of the 1980s," in *Facets of Ethnicity in Sri Lanka*, pp. 72-99.

(The) Daily News, August 24, September 9, 1992; August 8, 24, 1992.

Export Development Board (1991) *National Export Development Plan 1990- 1994,* Volumes I and II, Colombo: Export Development Bank.

Goonetileke, H.A.I. (1984) *Lanka, Their Lanka: Cameos of Ceylon Through Other Eyes*, New Delhi: Navrang, published in collaboration with Lakehouse Bookshop, Sri Lanka.

(The) Island, June 4, August 9, 20; September 12, 1992.

Karunatilake, H.N.S. (1992) *The Economy of Sri Lanka*, Colombo: Centre for Demographic and Socio-Economic Studies.

Karunatillake, Rupa (1992) Minister of Plantation Industries, Address at the 100th anniversary of James Taylor, on May 2.

Milton, John. *Paradise Lost* and *Paradise Regained.*

Mishra, D.P. (1985) *The Search for Lanka*, New Delhi: Agam Kala Prakashan.

Moragoda, Millinda (1992), "Miracle in Sri Lanka," *The Washington Post,* September 15th, reprinted in *The Daily News*, September 26, 1992.

Narada Maha Thera (1973) *The Buddha and His Teachings*, Singapore: Singapore Buddhist Meditation Center.

Rahula, Walpola (1972) *What the Buddha Taught*, London: The Gordon Fraser Gallery Ltd., second edition reprinted edition.

Samaranayake, Gamini (1990) "The Changing Attitude Towards the Tamil Problem within the Janatha Vimukthi Peramuna," in *Facets of Ethnicity.*

Samarasinghe, Mohan (1992) "James Taylor: Pioneer of Ceylon Tea," *Daily News*, May 2.

Sirr, Henry Charles (1984) *Ceylon and the Cingalese*, Dehiwala, Sri Lanka: Swarna Hansa Foundation, first published in London in 1850.

(The) Sunday Times, August 9, 30, 1992.

Tennekoon, Serena (1986) "Symbolic Refractions of the Ethnic Crisis: The Divaina Debates on Sinhala Identity 1984-85," in *Facets of Ethnicity in Sri Lanka*, pp. 1-60.

Vanniasingham, Somasundaram (1988) *Sri Lanka: The Conflict Within*, New Delhi: The Lancer Group.

Walters, Donald J. (1991) *The Essence of Self-Realization: The Wisdom of Paramhansa Yogananda*, Nevada City, CA: Crystal Clarity Publishers.

Wickramasinghe, Martin (1981) *Buddhism and Culture*, Colombo: Tisara Press, second edition.

Wijesekera, Nandadeva (1986) *Contacts and Conflict with Sri Lanka*, Dehiwala, Sri Lanka: Mahendra Senanayake.

_____ (1988) *The Sinhalese.* Colombo: M.D. Gunasena *Sri Lankan Entrepreneurs.*

Chapter 13

The Sangarans: Out of Malaysia

There is only one caste, the caste of humanity; there is only one religion, the religion of love; there is only one language, the language of the heart; there is only one God, and He is omnipresent.

- Sathya Sai Baba, an avatar living in Puttaparti, India

On February 9, 1995, a Baptist woman minister married Thangamani Sangaran and me in a Unitarian Church in Bethesda, Maryland. Born in Perak in 1961, she arrived in the U.S. in 1981 as Mani Sangaran, leaving behind the more complicated name of Thangamani (the traditional Indian golden bell). The Sangaran family, as I was to eventually learn, was of Dravidian stock. Webster's dictionary defines Dravidian as a large family of languages spoken in southern India and northern Sri Lanka that includes Tamil, Telegu, Malayalam and Kanarese. Mani's own parentage was a mixture of Malayalam and Tamil, her mother tongue. Ours would be a marriage of disparate personalities, religions and cultures. This was certainly the case of opposites attracting in many respects. Our (first) marriage came about rather precipitously, as Mani's parents were about to leave the country again and we wanted them to be present. She consulted the local Shiva Vishnu Temple for an auspicious date (February 9, 1995) in accordance with traditional Indian astrology. It was an intimate gathering of the Sangaran family and a few friends, the Hull family was noticeably absent.

First wedding, February 1995
But within a few months, the marriage still in a tender incubation
stage, we decided that a full-fledged ceremony was in order. We
engaged the services of Mani's younger brother Nathan as Director
of Operations for the event and scheduled it for June 3, 1995. This was
to be a marriage of cultures, not just two individuals. We contacted
priest Sathya Narayanan at the Murugan Temple and asked him
to conduct a (semi) traditional Hindu ceremony. A real traditional
Hindu ceremony would have gone on for several days! And as good
fortune would have it, I managed to reconnect with a very good
friend and former roommate, Bill Crittenden, from Texas Christian
University days. A licensed Disciple of Christ minister, Bill agreed
to give our union Christian blessings. So, as I said, it was to be a
marriage of religions and cultures.

This time, with Nathan's unerring attention to detail, we planned
a gala event to be held in the backyard of our Silver Spring, Maryland
home. The whole place was gussied up inside and out, painted and
decked out with bright-colored traditional Indian flags hung up in
front of the house. This time the Hull clan was present in nearly
full force, with sister Judy making major contributions to logistics
and hosting. For Norman Hull, attendance at the ceremony would
be a supreme commitment. By now he was in the advanced stages

of emphysema, obliged to carry an oxygen tank with him wherever he went. The airplane trip from Oklahoma was a major undertaking that entailed special arrangements with the airline. But he made it just in time for the Big Event. It was a glorious affair. The Hindu ceremony took place under a traditional tent and Priest Narayana performed the requisite Sanskrit blessings. The threatening clouds parted, and the sun shone brightly for both the Hindu and Christian ceremonies.

Second wedding vows, June 1995

Sangaran Appu Tindal, Mani's father and father of her seven siblings, was descended from Malayalam stock from Kerala State in southwest India. Like many of the Indians who came to Malaysia during the colonial period, his own father's family had come as workers to the plantations. Sangaran's father died when he was 10 and he was raised by his strong-willed mother. They lived under the quasi-benevolent British colonial rule until World War II, when the Japanese overcame the British and occupied Malaya. During the Japanese occupation (1941-1945) Malaya served the economic interests of Japan; there was little regard for the well-being of the people living in the country. The people of Malaya were reduced to performing whatever tasks were necessary for the Japanese war effort. Sangaran was obliged to raise and lower the Japanese flag in the school where he worked. Food and clothing were scarce during the war years. Sangaran recalls the war years as a time of severe hardship. He is especially remorseful not to have been able to complete his studies. That experience only strengthened his resolve that his children not be deprived of an education.

In 1955 Sangaran Appu Tindal married Karpukkarasie Singaram, a young woman of Tamil parentage whose family originated in Tamil Nadu in southern India. It was a typical marriage, arranged by the two families, in which the husband was dominant and the wife subservient. The language of the household, however, would be Tamil, the children's mother tongue. Mr. Sangaran began his employment with Harrisons and Crosfield one year after his marriage to Karpukkarasie, and he remained there as a rubber plantation manager until his retirement. It was his management of the company's plantations in the Malaysian state of Perak that would sustain the Sangaran family for several decades. Sangaran was responsible for virtually all the operations of the plantation, from the clearing of the land and planting of trees to the harvesting of the rubber. While he reported to an English manager, Sangaran managed several hundred workers, over whom he held absolute sway. Whenever discipline was warranted, he was there with a firm hand to dispense it. He was often involved in the family affairs of his workers, resolving marital disputes or issues of child neglect.

So what sort of company was Harrisons and Crosfield? It was a microcosm of the economic expansion behind the British Empire. In 1844, two friends, Smith Harrison and Joseph Crosfield, entered into a partnership in London to trade in tea and coffee. They started Harrisons & Crosfield PLC with the then princely sum of £4,000 Sterling. The Company began operations in Ceylon in 1895 when the first agent was sent to Colombo with the task of commencing tea trading operations. Harrisons & Crosfield (Colombo) Ltd. commenced operations in 1895 and today is one of the oldest tea companies in the country. Generically branded as Ceylon tea, when the country changed its name to Sri Lanka in the 1970s, the brand name remained.

Not only did the company become a major exporter of tea, it would also join other British firms in the planting and harvesting of rubber in Malaysia. Natural rubber was first used by the indigenous peoples of the Amazon basin of Brazil for a variety of purposes. By the middle of the 18th century, Europeans had begun to experiment with rubber as a waterproofing agent. By the early 19th century, rubber was being used to make waterproof shoes. The best source of latex, the milky fluid from which natural rubber products were made, was hevea brasiliensis, which grew predominantly in the Brazilian Amazon. Thus, the first period of rubber's commercial history, from the late 1700s through 1900, was centered in Brazil. However, the second period from roughly 1910 onward, was increasingly centered in East Asia as the result of plantation development (Frank, Zephyr and Aldo Musacchio, 2002).

Commercial planting in the Malay States began in 1895. The development of large-scale plantations was slow because of the lack of capital. Investors did not get interested in plantations until the prospects for rubber improved radically with the spectacular development of the automobile industry. By 1905, European capitalists were sufficiently interested in investing in large-scale plantations in Southeast Asia to plant some 38,000 acres of trees. The expansion of plantations was possible because of the sophistication in the organization of such enterprises. Plantations depended on a disciplined system of labor and an intensive use of land, both factors present in the Malay States.

Initially, demand for rubber was associated with specialized industrial components (belts and gaskets, etc.), consumer goods (golf balls, shoe soles, galoshes, etc.) and bicycle tires. Prior to the development of the automobile as a mass-marketed phenomenon, the Brazilian wild rubber industry was capable of meeting world demand and, furthermore, it was impossible for rubber producers to predict the scope and growth of the automobile industry prior to the 1900s. Even as demand rose in the 1890s with the bicycle craze, the rate of increase was not beyond the capacity of wild rubber producers in Brazil and elsewhere. High rubber prices did not induce rapid increases in production or plantation development in the 19th century.

In order to understand the boom in rubber production, it is important to look at the automobile industry. Cars had originally been adapted from horse-drawn carriages; some ran on wooden wheels, some on metal, some shod as it were in solid rubber. In any case, the ride at the speeds cars were soon capable of was impossible to bear. The pneumatic tire was quickly adopted from the bicycle, and the automobile tire industry was born—soon to account for well over half of rubber company sales in the United States, where the vast majority of automobiles were manufactured in the early years of the industry. The amount of rubber required to satisfy demand for automobile tires led to a spike in rubber prices as well as to the development of rubber plantations in Asia. After 1910, rubber was increasingly produced on low-cost plantations in Southeast Asia, including those in Malaysia. The price of rubber fell with plantation development and, at the same time, the volume of rubber demanded by car tire manufacturers expanded dramatically . Uncertainty, in terms of both supply and demand (often driven by changing tire technology) meant that natural rubber producers and tire manufacturers both experienced great volatility in returns.

— —-

The Sangaran family would spend many years in this remote cocoon in rural northwest Malaysia, outside the town of Sitiawan near the Indian Ocean. They lived in the quiet confines of company bungalows on the rubber plantations which Sangaran managed. Many of the trappings of British culture still pervaded the Malaysia of the 1960s, 1970s and 1980s. Theirs was an orderly world, defined by a lush tropical environment, the routine of school studies and Mum's freshly prepared spicy meals (no such thing as leftovers). They had few occasions to leave the plantations, except for outings to nearby beaches, to visit relatives, or forays into Ipoh, the largest urban agglomeration in Perak and to the capital city of Kuala Lumpur.

The Sangaran Family in Malaysia, late 1970s

There were eventually eight Sangaran children, five girls and three boys, all typically skinny as rails. In the Indian tradition, they would take their father's first name Sangaran, as their family name. They would all live in fear that any untoward behavior would bring down the wrath of their father, the Omnipotent Administrator. At home, as in the plantations, he was the Lord of the Manor, undisputed Dispenser of Justice, ready to mete out the same measure of retribution to wayward children that he gave to his workers. Sangaran ruled with an iron hand, but always in the best interests of his children, of course. He had their education uppermost in mind, a factor that was to have a profound impact on his offspring. They were sent to a combination of parochial schools, mainly Methodist and Anglican, where they received good education and an additional dose of discipline. The primary language of instruction was initially English, but then it eventually became Bahasa Malaysia, the national language, with the wave of nationalization in the 1980s. They were all multilingual, conversant in a combination of Bahasa, English,

Tamil and a smattering of Hokkien Chinese (whenever the need for a swearword arose!). Their friends and schoolmates were a blend of Malay, Chinese and Indian, a mirror of the ethnic composition of Malaysia.

The boys were all tutored in the use and maintenance of motorized vehicles. Their father was among the very few in western Malaysia in the 1950s and 1960s to own a car. Early on they were able to disassemble and repair motorcycles as well as cars with consummate skill. But it seems they were equally adept at running them into ditches and incurring bodily harm. All three would carry this intimate familiarity with cars into later life where it was to serve them well. The girls were not really initiated into the usual range of domestic skills. Cooking, washing, sewing and cleaning were left mainly to Mum and her servants. But they managed to acquire culinary and parenting skills by observation and osmosis. Guna, the eldest, was known by her siblings as Periakka, the traditional Tamil title reserved for the oldest daughter. She was delegated assistant-parenting responsibilities, which she took quite seriously. Her apprenticeship, although sometimes resented by her siblings, prepared Guna for the role of a model parent in her own right.

It was a peaceful world in which the Sangaran family lived, with simple daily pleasures and little turbulence from outside the family hearth and home. A typical day would consist of rising early in the cool morning air, going to school and returning home in the mid-day heat for a nap. Then, promptly at four o'clock came the high point of the day—tea time—perhaps the most enduring of British traditions, now that the sun has set on the empire. Tea time: a time for the ritual of sipping tea and relaxing, a moratorium on sibling rivalries and chatting with friends who might drop in. This was not the green tea of the Chinese who operated the economy. Nor was it the masala tea of South India. It was the black Malaysian Boh tea from up in the nearby Cameron Highlands, taken with generous helpings of sugar and milk as well as ginger. Of course, tea could not be served without tasty curry puffs or banana fritters. The word calorie had not entered the Sangaran family lexicon by then, nor was there any awareness of diabetes. Tea time was unadulterated bliss.

Mani maintained her addiction to tea, the one passion with which she knowingly escaped from Malaysia when coming to the U.S. at the tender age of 20. Her favorite became Taylor's of Harrogate Ceylon black tea. Tea time is still her momentary refuge from the cares of the day, a ritual that breaks the monotony of chores. Furthermore, Mani's passion for tea led her into a crusade to spread the good word to the heretofore heathen, coffee-drinking Americans, about the virtues of tea. Interestingly enough, Mani's palate would eventually cultivate a taste for roibos, the exotic South African herbal tea, about which we will hear more anon.

Hindu Religion and Sathya Sai Baba

The Sangaran family's ethnic and cultural identify was somewhat loosely defined in the Malaysian context. Of course, the children were aware of their ethnic minority status in a predominantly Malay and Muslim culture but they did not have any sense of being discriminated against. As South Indians, they tended to refer to all other Indians as Bengalis, the way southerners in the U.S. refer to northerners as Yankees. The primary exposure of the Sangaran family to Hindu culture was a yearly visit to the Ganesha Temple in a nearby town where they would give money for the poor. There was, however, a small prayer altar in the home where the children took turns lighting the oil lamp each evening, or whenever they were in some kind of trouble at school! Each year at Deepavali the altar would be cleaned and decorated and the family would offer prayers for deceased grandparents. Otherwise, there was little religious indoctrination of any kind that would have provided the Sangaran children an understanding of Hindu culture in a predominantly Muslim society. Theirs was a largely secular upbringing, grounded in the basic notion of tolerance for other races and religions.

Then, in the midst of this secular tranquility, a strange phenomenon took place in the Sangaran household in late May 1980. A neighbor shared a copy of a book by Howard Murphet, an Australian writer, entitled, Sai Baba: The Man of Miracles, with Mani's father. Having read it, he passed it on to Mani, the bookworm in the family. She skimmed through it with keen interest and then questioned her father:

"Pa, if such an amazing holy man lives in India, why do I hear of so much poverty in that country?"

Keenly aware of her Indian heritage and wanting to be proud of it, Mani found it hard to reconcile the images of chronic poverty and conflict between Hindu and Muslim in India with the teachings of Sai Baba. Her father replied:

"Well, Mani, Sai Baba is a holy man, doing the good that he can do and probably as fast as he can, but he cannot solve all the world's problems at once."

Mani was stirred by the stories she had read in the Murphet book and asked her father if he could take her to a Sai Baba bhajan (a singing and prayer session). Her father drove Mani and her sister Padma to a nearby town to attend a bhajan which proved to be an uplifting experience. Subsequently, the girls had pictures of Sai Baba framed and placed in their home. Then, on August 15, 1980, splotches of vibhutim (sacred white ash) appeared on the photos of Baba, his signature blessing for his devotees. That afternoon after tea, Mani told her father that vibhutim was manifesting itself in the prayer altar and asked him to go upstairs and look at it. He stared at it, at first in disbelief. That evening the Sangarans organized a bhajan in their home, the first ever. It was a beautiful event, bringing a remarkable peace to the family that would last for months.

The word got out among Baba devotees; they began stopping by the Sangaran house, first to witness the vibuthim, and then to organize impromptu bhajans. The Sangaran boys began playing the tambourine and tabla, the girls learned bhajan songs, and soon these daily events were being attended by a larger and larger gathering of devotees. This was not a visit of Sai Baba's physical person, but profound evidence of his presence. For whatever reason, the Sangaran house had been blessed, designated by Baba as a sacred place, a gathering place for fellowship and prayer. The result was a spiritual experience that would transform the lives of the Sangaran family and bring them closer together.

As the days passed, more and more vibuthim of many shades and colors appeared on objects in the house, including kum kum (red ash) and santhanam (yellow ash). Honey, milk and oil poured off the surface of pictures of the Hindu gods and goddesses, Meerabhai, Mary and Jesus, and the Buddha as well as pictures of eldest sister Guna and brother Kumar who were by now studying in England. The first time drops of milk appeared they rolled down from the mouth of Shirdi Baba, Sai Baba's previous incarnation. From then on Mum Sangaran would leave a tumbler of milk each day by his photo to honor Shirdi Baba. The fragrance of the vibuthim was intoxicating and seemed to render the normally rambunctious children tranquil and peaceful. They spent countless hours packing the vibuthim in small packets and placing them on large trays for devotees to take home with them for their own prayers.

One day, after a month or so of these manifestations, Mum cooked mutton, a common dish in the Sangaran house on special occasions. As was her habit, she sampled a bite before putting the plate on the table. She suddenly felt sick, and when she returned to the kitchen she found vibuthim splashed all over the stove, dishes, pots and pans! From that day onward she did not cook meat in the house. For observant Hindus, abstention from eating meat, especially beef, is a sacred duty. During the following year the Sangaran family witnessed daily manifestations such as these. On Good Friday vibuthim formed a cross on the wall in the prayer room. On Easwaramba's day the shape of the Sanskrit OM sign appeared and remained there for the rest of the year. When the two eldest sisters, Guna and Padma, were married in England, kum kum appeared on their pictures in the Sangaran home at the exact time of the marriage ceremonies!

Sathya Sai Baba has gained fame for his spiritual teachings and his inspiration of unselfish love and service. Born in 1925, Baba, as he is known by millions of followers, is a revered spiritual leader whose life and message are an inspiration. He is not claiming to start a new religion, nor does he admonish his followers to follow any particular religion. Rather he urges them to follow the religion of their choice. To his followers (devotees) Sathya Sai Baba is the incarnation of God. In the Hindu tradition this is neither blasphemous nor presumptuous; it is rather a time-honored tradition. His basic message is "Love all, serve all; help ever, hurt never." For believers, he is a holy man, a wise man.

Sai Baba publicly declared his mission in 1940 and since then, to his followers he has exhibited the highest ideals of right conduct. He has often declared that "my life is my message." There are no intermediaries between Sai Baba and his followers. He places great importance on proper education for young people. Parents and community leaders are urged to concern themselves with the informal as well as formal experience to which their children are exposed. Today Sai Baba has millions of followers around the world, including several in Middle Tennessee. Conservative Christian groups which abound in the area would likely characterize the followers of Sai Baba as a "cult", outside the mainstream of society. The Sai Organization is not unlike the utopian religious communities such as the Shakers, Oneida and the Harmony Society.

What is striking about the Sai Organization is its wide ethnic and cultural diversity. While the majority of devotees in the U.S. are of Indian origin, there is a large and growing number of followers among Americans from all walks of life. They include Hindus, Muslims, Christians and Buddhists, as well as former non-believers. The emphasis is on group participation, with members as homogeneous, equal parts of the whole rather than as differentiated individuals. The need for equality of members and fellowship may be supported by arrangements such as homogeneity of religion, class or ethnic background. The devotees of Sai Baba in the U.S. are from virtually every race and social class.

Sai Baba devotees meet regularly to sing his praises and to reflect upon the wisdom of his teachings. A gathering consists largely of singing songs of praise to Shiva, Krishna, Ganesha, Jesus, Mohammad, Buddha, Rama, Sita and Hanuman as well as to Sai Baba. These songs are sung with devotion and commitment to the principles which each of the gods and goddesses symbolize.

Not incidentally, the meetings bring the devotees together as a community of believers. As in all religions, there is an element of utopianism, since the faithful would like to believe that through prayer the world will become a safer and more blessed place. Communion consists of dwelling upon the wisdom of Sai Baba and his implications for the daily lives of devotees. Unlike the communion of faithful Christians, who believe that in partaking of the wine and bread at communion they become one with Jesus Christ, the communion of Sai Baba devotees is with people all over the world, be they Muslim, Christian, Buddhist, or Hindu. Each meeting ends with the sharing of the vibuthim, which is tasted and dabbed on the forehead to remind the faithful of the fact that we all return to dust after this life. All of this is done to remind the faithful of his/her commitment to the teachings of Sai Baba. Christians observe a similar tradition by placing ashes on their forehead on Ash Wednesday.

For Mani, the most remarkable of Sai Baba's manifestations had to do with her admission into the university. As one of the top students in her high school graduating class in 1981, she was quite confident of being admitted into the National University of Malaysia. So sure was she of this that she prepared a collage of photos to take with her to her dorm room. The appearance of vibuthim on the photos after she placed it on the altar for blessing provided additional reassurance. Several weeks later, however, she was devastated when she received a letter of rejection from the University. As distraught as Mani was, her father was even more so since he had always had high hopes for her academic career. All those hours of study for naught! Her best friend at the time, a Chinese girl, also received a rejection letter. The Malaysian government's bumiputra policy that favored Malays provided for a very small admission quota for minority Indians and Chinese into Malaysian universities. When the Chinese friend came over to the Sangaran house to commiserate, she noticed the photo frame that Mani had prepared to take with her to the University.

"Mani", she exclaimed, "I see the shape of the map of the United States." Mani assured her friend that she had no plans to go abroad. Her aspiration was to achieve prominence as the first Indian woman politician in Malaysia!

As devastated as Mani was by the rejection by the National University of Malaysia, her father was even more so since he wanted his children to have the best education possible. As it happened, Sangaran was approaching the retirement age of 50 and was thus eligible to withdraw pension funds. Within days after Mani's rejection notice he cashed out retirement benefits with a view toward sending her to Great Britain to join her two sisters. However, having pursued all her studies in a British educational system, Mani was adamantly opposed to studying in Great Britain, feeling that the British educational system was much too focused on rote memorization. Enter Plan B and the image of the map of the United States. Sangaran contacted a university placement agency and began arrangements to send Mani to another remote corner of the universe: rural Arkansas. On August 27, 1981, Mani boarded a Cathay Pacific flight to the U.S. with two other Malaysian girls. It was a leap into the Great Unknown. She arrived on the campus of College of the Ozarks at the tender age of 20, weighing scarcely 100 lbs. and speaking very proper British English, an accent totally alien to the folks in rural Arkansas.

Mani experienced a full range of culture shocks, in terms of food habits, social customs and the educational system. She had never had her own spending money and wasn't aware of how to maintain a bank account. She didn't know her shoe or dress size and didn't have any experience of doing her own laundry. On the other hand, she found that academic courses were no challenge since her training in Malaysia had been much more rigorous than the curriculum in Arkansas. She soon became aware of racial distinctions, still rather pronounced in the state that attracted world wide attention for resistance to integration just a few decades before. Mani never felt that she experienced racial discrimination; rather she was considered an exotic curiosity. She found herself the subject of attention by football players as well as local Baptists who were intent on converting her to Christianity. Mani, wishing to be polite to her host family, simply added this to her already expanding base of spiritual experience!

Fast forward a few years to Fayetteville and the campus of the University of Arkansas, where Mani transferred after one semester at the College of the Ozarks in hopes of finding a more challenging academic climate. Here the academic and social environment was slightly more sophisticated, and Mani was exposed to a wider range of people and experiences. She decided to major in Political Science and did well in her coursework. In her junior year Mani met Mark, a fellow student from Arkansas whom she dated before he asked her to marry him. She wanted to be polite, and agreed to his proposal without much thought as to their future together. When Mani informed her father of her decision to marry, he immediately sent her a one-way ticket home since she had not requested his permission. For the first time in her life she disobeyed her father, thinking that this was the right decision for her to make at the time. Two days after the civil ceremony Mani notified her sister Guna in England and she in turn informed their parents. Although they were very upset, her parents consented because at the exact time of the marriage kum kum appeared on Mani's favorite picture of Sia Baba in their home in Malaysia.

Mani and Mark decided to move to Washington DC in 1985, where Mani obtained a job with a consulting firm within a couple of days after her arrival in the city. The president of the firm assigned Mani to work on a project dealing with Indonesia. It was assumed that her origins in neighboring Malaysia would be useful in the management of the project. The manager of the Indonesia project was none other than Galen Hull, at the time happily married. I was, however, immediately impressed with Mani's professional demeanor and dedication to carrying out whatever tasks I assigned to her. At one point my wife Dawn and I invited Mani and her husband to our house for dinner. However, our relationship remained strictly professional for the short period of time that Mani worked at our firm. She soon moved on to work at another firm, toward a master's degree program, and to various jobs in the international development consulting business.

Mani's marriage was eventually dissolved after five years, although she had acquired U.S. citizenship and was engaged in pulling her siblings through the eye of the INS needle one-by-one until they too had become U.S. citizens. Her parents also came to stay with them for extended periods of time, although they were hesitant to give up their Malaysian citizenship. At one point six Sangarans were all living under one roof in a Virginia suburb. Mani continued working with various consulting firms in the Washington DC area. Meanwhile, our paths would cross on occasion as we continued to work in the same field. We would exchange resumes of consultants for possible overseas assignments and swap hints about up-coming contracts. We were now both Beltway Bandits, engaged in the same business of identifying consultants and fielding them on international assignments.

In the early 1990s my marriage also became unraveled. And then one fine day Mani and I found ourselves not only in the business of exchanging resumes, but re-defining our personal relationship. That re-defining took place during 1993-94, shortly after my return from Sri Lanka. Because the sojourn there exposed me intensively to South Asian culture, it undermined the anti-Asian bias I had been carrying with me since my days in East Africa. I was able to see Mani through a new cultural lens. During this time I became more familiar with the person that was Mani, not just the professional Mani. There was clearly mutual attraction, although she was very apprehensive about entering another relationship, given the unhappy denouement of her first marriage. She told me about her experience with Sai Baba, imagining that would be enough to scare me away. It wasn't. On the contrary, it made me all the more eager to understand what made her tick.

Above all, I was made aware of just how important her family was to Mani, and how profoundly sad she was about having married without her father's consent. And of course divorce was highly frowned upon. As Mani used to say, she had broken all the rules in the Indian girl's handbook! Nevertheless, I was invited to a couple of family events and introduced as the man for whom she first worked when coming to the Washington DC area. They could not help noticing the 20-year difference in our ages. She already sensed that her father was not happy about that.

Mani resorted to lobbying her siblings, especially her oldest sister Guna and her Indian husband Ashok, a family physician. The Sangarans all adored "Uncle" Ashok and held him in highest esteem. If only he and Guna could be persuaded. So I invited the two of them over to my house with Mani and cooked my finest Chinese stir-fry meal for them. We seemed to hit it off well. I also sought to work my way into the good graces of Nathan, Mani's favorite brother. The stage was thus set. I asked Mani to arrange for a family gathering, at which time I would request permission to marry her. I was absolutely sure of my own feelings and intentions. I rehearsed my lines over and over, so when the moment came I delivered them flawlessly. Then came a question and answer period, and again I was ready. Mani then had her say, which was the affirmation of her wish to marry. Some reservations were expressed about the obvious age gap, cultural and personality differences. There followed a vote on my proposal, which carried unanimously. I was ecstatic! Clearly I was being rewarded for my thoughtfulness in approaching the Sangaran family for their approbation. The propitious date was set subsequently for the blessed event in February.

Often things are not as transparent and simple as they seem on the surface. After a torrid and passionate courtship that took us on a romantic tryst to Florida followed by my proposal, Mani apparently still harbored some reservations of her own. Listing those concerns in writing, she informed me that she wanted to call off our relationship. She was planning to move to Atlanta, she said, and start a new business with a friend. Having been so successful in winning over the Sangaran family, I was stunned to learn that I had not quite won over Mani herself over. I wandered off into a fog of delusion and disappointment, trying to understand where I had gone wrong.

My work took me on a two-week assignment to Senegal in January 1995. Unbeknownst to me Mani had mailed a note inviting me to meet her to say goodbye before she left for Atlanta. Not hearing from me, Mani proceeded with her plans to leave. Then, out of the blue, Guna called Mani to ask for my telephone number on January 28th. Mani told her there was no need to talk with me since I failed to respond to her note. Mani reports that Guna, a very strong woman not subject to emotions or superstitions, began to cry. She told Mani that she had had a dream in which Sai Baba blessed our wedding and the whole family was there for the occasion. It should be recalled that Guna was away in England during the time of Baba's manifestations in Malaysia and was not really a Baba devotee. Mani was taken aback by Guna's story, not quite ready to believe her. Mani was explaining to Guna that it was probably too late since I had not responded to her note when, lo and behold, she received a call on another line: it was yours truly, back from Senegal calling to say farewell. At that moment Mani was persuaded that she should reconsider the Atlanta agenda. We met for dinner that evening and began to dust off the wedding plans for the appointed date: February 9, 1995. The rest is, as they say, history.

Indians in Malaysia

Today the whole Sangaran family resides in the United States. Why, then, would any Malaysian want to leave the idyllic circumstances described above and move to another country? First, we must recall that the Sangarans are of Indian origin, a distinct nine percent minority within Malaysia. The Sangaran children were raised in a very multicultural environment, attended Christian schools, gained fluency in Bahasa and counted Chinese youth among their friends. They did not perceive their Hindu/Indian identity to have been used to discriminate against them during their youth. However, in time, every one of the eight Sangaran children, and eventually their parents, would emigrate from Malaysia to seek greener pastures abroad.

There is another, rather depressing picture of Indians in Malaysia. An article in The Economist (2003) noted that the Indian minority gets none of the benefits reserved for the Malay majority. While people of Indian origin account for only 8% of Malaysia's total population, today they make up 14% of its juvenile delinquents, more than 20% of its wife- and child-beaters, and 41% of its beggars. They make up less than 5% of successful university applicants, and own less than 1.5% of the country's share capital. They are not eligible for any of Malaysia's lavish affirmative-action programs, which are reserved for Malays. So while other countries (such as the U.S.) may have upwardly mobile Indian immigrants, Malaysia is actually developing an Indian underclass.

The problem stems from the decline of Malaysia's rubber plantations. British colonialists shipped indentured Indian laborers to Malaysia in the late 19th and early 20th centuries to tap rubber. After independence, many Indians stayed and became citizens, tapping rubber all the while. But over the past few decades of breakneck economic growth and a decline in world demand for rubber, developers have ploughed up many rubber plantations to plant less labor-intensive oil palms, or to build shopping malls and housing estates. The displaced workers and their families have wound up in shanty towns on the outskirts of Malaysia's cities.

Until recently, the government largely ignored the problem. The many well-to-do Indian doctors and lawyers, after all, help to give Indians higher incomes on average than Malays. Many Indian laborers earn even more from odd jobs in the cities than rural Malays do from fishing or farming. But unlike poor farmers they have to buy their own food, pay rent and travel to work, all at inflated urban prices. The sheltered life of the plantations imbued Indians with a culture of dependence. Furthermore, Indians have little prospect of advancement, since Malaysia's Chinese minority dominates business, and Malays control the bureaucracy. Indians often complain of neglect or discrimination at the hands of civil servants, and harassment by the police.

All these frustrations boiled over into a race riot in a squatter community outside Kuala Lumpur in March 2001. Six people died and scores were injured. Still, today many Indians live in rusty corrugated-iron shacks in Kampung Medan, the scene of the riot. They complain that jobs are hard to come by, especially since employers fear that many Indians may be involved in crime. Although the police have set up three posts in the area since the riots, locals say that only one of the officers staffing them is Indian. There are no playgrounds, sports fields or clubs to tempt their children away from street gangs. The local Indian school, they add, is in a dire state.

The government has at least pledged to change all this. It has promised to move all squatters in the area to subsidized housing. It is hiring more Indian teachers. It is also financing the Yayasan Strategik Sosial, to develop schemes to help poor urban Indians.

Most dramatically, it has declared its intention to double Indians' stake in Malaysian companies by 2010, the sort of race-based target normally reserved for Malays. As it is, government officials like to point out, Malaysia's richest man is an Indian: Ananda Krishnan. His fellow Indians, however, tend to view his success rather more cynically; they joke that Mr. Krishnan takes up the community's share of the national wealth all by himself.

So whatever difficulties the Sangarans may have encountered in adapting to life in the U.S., they have few regrets about having left the uneven playing field that is Malaysia. On the other hand, Nathan the entrepreneur has become increasingly involved in doing business in Malaysia. Using his cross- cultural skills, Nathan has managed to bring Silicon Valley investors into Malaysia in high tech operations, most recently in solar energy.

The Millennium Round-Up,   *September 2000*

Five years after our wedding in 1995 the entire Sangaran family had settled in the United States, although the senior Sangarans were still spending some time in Malaysia. The siblings were dispersed throughout the country: three were in California, three in Virginia, one in Florida and one in Tennessee. My siblings were all still living in the great state of Texas. I began to develop the idea of bringing both families together to celebrate the beginning of the new millennium. Sister Judy was now the proud owner/manager of a 90-acre ranch outside of Granbury, deep in the heart of Texas. I approached her with the proposal to host a family reunion on the ranch and she graciously agreed. The word went out to gather at what we billed as a Millennium Round-Up.

The Sangarans & relevant others at Millennium Round-up, 2000

We extended the invitation beyond the immediate Hull and Sangaran families to include our Beighle cousins as well. As it turned out, we would have one hundred percent attendance on both sides, numbering some 100, a veritable Americo-Malaysian cultural potpourri. We planned a three-day event consisting of food, fun and speeches. But the year 2000 will likely go down in the annals of weather as one of the hottest and driest on record. The entire months of July and August recorded above 95 degree temperatures and virtually no moisture throughout the southwest. It was HOT, even for Texans accustomed to warm summers. We rented two huge fans to cool off the sweltering cowgirls and cowboys. The feast was a combination of exotic Asian dishes and Texas-style bar-b-que. We scheduled a photo-opportunity on the lawn in front of the barn, followed by a program of skits and speeches.

I had anticipated the occasion by taking lessons in the Tamil language (the Sangaran family tongue) for several months leading up to the event. It was my intention to be able to give a brief talk in Tamil, honoring the senior Sangarans and exhorting us all to have regular family reunions. For weeks I practiced my lines, working on accent and inflection. Although there were a few snickers from the Sangaran siblings because of my pronunciation, I got generally high marks for the effort.

Travels with Mani: 1995-2004

My marriage to Mani Sangaran brought a whole new dimension to my journey in crossing cultures. It meant getting to know the Sangaran family and the culture the family represented. Of course most of this took place in the quiet of our own home and at family gatherings. It also involved travel back to Asia—Malaysia, Sri Lanka, Thailand and India—on business and pleasure, as well as visiting family members around the U.S. One of our first trips, not long after our wedding(s), was to Ipoh, Malaysia, where the senior Sangarans were living at the time. For Mani this was a trip down memory lane. She showed me the plantation where she had grown up, the parochial school where she studied and the provincial town of Sitiyaun where the family did its shopping and socializing. And of course there was a visit to the port town of Lumut and the beach on the Indian Ocean a few miles away. The town of Ipoh is the economic center of Perak state, traditionally important for tin, rubber and agricultural production. It also has great Chinese restaurants featuring Mani's favorite kwei tchow soup. We were treated to a multi-course feast at the home of "Uncle" Inchu, a successful Chinese businessman whom the Sangarans had befriended years before.

On another trip back to Malaysia we spent most of our time in Kuala Lumpur, the bustling capital city of Malaysia. This time we were guests of Nathan, Mani's brother who was now an entrepreneur working to promote Silicon Valley investment and production in Malaysia. Nathan's business associate and friend, Haji Thasleem Ibrahim, and his wife Jasmeen graciously provided us with lodging and a most welcoming environment in a Kuala Lumpur condominium. As with many Muslims who have made the pilgrimage to Mecca, Thasleem was known to many simple as Haji. Originally from southern India and a Tamil, he belonged to a distinct minority in Malaysia. Haji has been successful as a construction contractor as well as very active in Muslim community development programs. Nathan and Haji invited us to sit in on several meetings with their business associates and colleagues.

Thanks to Haji's contacts, Mani and I were able to visit quite a few universities around the country, interviewing academic administrators and professors. Of course we managed to do a bit of tourism as well, including a visit to the historic town of Melaka (variously spelled Malacca) south of Kuala Lumpur. This was a different world from the one in which the Sangaran children had been raised. It was a vibrant industrialized economy, pushing to the front of the line of developing countries. Malaysia also saw itself as a leader among Muslim countries, hosting conferences and promoting common Islamic causes.

Having moved into our new abode in Tennessee, Mani and I settled into a primary social network that consisted mainly of friends and colleagues from the sub-continent: Nepalis, Indians, Singaporeans, Malaysians and Sri Lankans. It included frequent participation in bhajans (traditional singing and prayer sessions) with other Sathya Sai Baba devotees and visits to the Sri Ganesha Temple to do poojas (prayer offerings) on special occasions. At the temple we would often see quite a few of my Indian, Singaporean and Nepali colleagues. Given Mani's devotion to Sai Baba, it was just a matter of time before we would make plans to visit his ashram in Puttaparti, India. On her first visit to India with her parents and sister Padma some years back Mani had experienced rather severe cultural shock. Being of Indian origin was not sufficient for her to be able to relate to the profound poverty she would encounter there. This time she was motivated by the desire to have me experience Puttaparti and see Baba. We began planning the trip to India to include as much in a short time as possible. I mapped out the historical and architectural sites in southern India that I hoped would complement our visit to Puttaparti. Our brief stay in the sub-continent, however, meant that many of those sites could not be seen on this visit.

We landed in Bangalore and sought out a family member of a friend in Nashville and went to stay with her. There we spent a couple of days touring the city that was already becoming synonymous with the hi-tech boom transforming the Indian economy. On the way to visit Baba's ashram at Whitefields in the Bangalore area we drove past the Dell Computer facility and a maze of other computer-related operations. A new city of technology was poking through the potholes and congested streets of the traditional city founded during the British colonial period. We visited the magnificent gardens and ate wonderful vegetarian meals on banana leaves in local restaurants.

Mani with our host in Bangalore Gardens

I must confess that the experience of staying in Baba's ashram and mixing with devotees from around the world was everything I might have imagined. The rhythm of life in Puttaparti revolves around Baba's darshans (literally viewing). Early in the morning and then again in he afternoon he makes an appearance to a hushed throng of thousands of devotees that gather in a massive open-air mandir (temple) to receive his blessings. He typically ambles through the crowd picking up letters that devotees thrust toward him, hoping that he will read them and address their inner most prayers. No cameras are allowed in the mandir of course, and everyone is carefully searched before being allowed to enter. There are devotees from all corners of the universe, many of them in Puttaparti for the umpteenth time to recharge their spiritual batteries. A striking figure in his saffron robe and signature bouffant style, Baba weighs only 108 lbs and is now in his late 70's. While now rather frail, he is expected to live well into his nineties.

Kerala

Upon leaving Puttaparti, we headed back down to Bangalore and thence to Cochin in the state of Kerala. This is the land of the Malayali, the ancestors of Mani's father. Cochin, the largest city in Kerala on the Indian Ocean coast, is rich in history and culture. Malayalam is the official language of Kerala, although Tamil is also widely spoken. Education and early influences of Arabs, Jews, Chinese and Portuguese have also made Kerala one of the most religiously diverse states in India. Today the major religions in Kerala are Hinduism (slightly over half), Islam (a fourth) and Christianity (20%). Until recently Kerala also had a tiny Jewish population, said to date from 587 B.C. when they fled the occupation of Jerusalem by King Nebuchadnezzar. Most have long since left, many of them to live in Israel.

Kerala ranks highest in India with respect to social development indices such as elimination of poverty, and primary education healthcare. Kerala has one of the most secular populations in India, though there have been disruptive influences from the religious extremist organizations. The state is known for Ayurveda, a traditional system of medecine which has found a new market in the growing tourist industry. The literacy rate in Kerala—over 95 percent—is the highest among Indian states, but so is the unemployment rate.

Galen & Mani on Cochin Beach, Kerala

Kerala is home to one of the greatest of Hindu avatars known as Adi Shankaracharya, an Indian philosopher in the eight century A.D. who founded Advaita (non-dualistic) Vedanta. We visited a shrine in the town of Kalady where he was born just near the Cochin airport. Adi Shankar was the son of a scholarly Brahmin couple and would become perhaps the greatest philosopher in the history of India. Known as Adi Shankara, and eventually Shakaracharya, at the tender age of five he learned the Gayathri Mantra and all that was contained in the Vedas by the age of fourteen. He restructured all the 72 forms of religious practices into acceptable norms and laid stress on six ways of worship based on Vedas.

Shankaracharya was a travelin' man. Although he lived for only 32 years, he traveled throughout India holding discussions with many scholars and authoring numerous philosophical treatises. He established the concept of Advaita, with commentaries on Brahma Sutras and the Bhagavad Gita. He reached the holy city of Benaras where he received darshan of the presiding deity of the place, Viswanath. Adi Shankara is attributed with having purified and consolidated the various schools of worship and brought them under the umbrella of one philosophical principle, Advaita. Adi Shankara expounded Vedantic principles, and Atmabodha (Self-Knowledge). He preached that spiritual seekers need neither rituals nor meditation as spiritual exercise. Because of his glorious achievements Shankaracharya is acclaimed as the very incarnation of Lord Shiva. For a Westerner reading about the life of Shankaracharya, it is possible to see striking similarities between his life and message and that of Jesus Christ and the apostle Paul, who spread the news of a new enlightenment.

Sandalwood carving and sculptor, Kerala

Kerala is a popular tourist destination for both domestic and foreign travelers. Among the major tourist attractions are Kovalam Beach and the serene and beautiful Kerala Backwaters such as Alleppey. The tourism department of the state calls this God's Own Country. National Geographic Society described Kerala as one of the 50 must-see destinations of a lifetime. I would cast my vote with National Geographic. The high point of our visit to Kerala would be the boat trip on the backwaters, an interconnected system of brackish water lakes and river estuaries that lies behind the coast and runs virtually the length of Kerala. This was followed by a visit to an Ayurvedic center known as Somatheeram where we indulged ourselves in wonderful massage therapy and relaxation. The city of Trivandrum, the state capital, was our last stop before catching a plane on to Colombo, Sri Lanka, for a brief visit on our way home.

On a boat tour of the Alleppey Backwaters, Kerala, 2003

References

Davis, Grady, "The Characteristics of Cultic Commitment," http://www.familybible.org.

Frank, Zephyr and Aldo Musacchio (2002) "The International Natural Rubber Market, 1870-1930," *EH.Net Encyclopedia*, edited by Robert Whaples, December 19; retrieved on March 1, 2005 from: http://eh.net/encyclopedia/?article=frank.international.rubber.market

The Economist (2003) "Malaysia: No breaks" Feb 20.

Hull, Mani (2001) "Account of a Personal Spiritual Experience," (monograph)

May 14, 2001.

Kanter, Rosabeth Moss (1968) "Commitment and Social Organization: A Study of

Commitment Mechanisms in Utopian Communities," in *American Sociological Review* (Vol. 33, No. 4, August, pp. 499-517).

Murphet, Howard (1971) *Sai Baba: The Man of Miracles,* York Beach, ME:

Samuel Weiser Publisher.

(The) Sai Organization, http://www.sathyasai.org.

Chapter 14

South Africa 1966 — 2005: Long Walk to Freedom

Ndiwelimilambo enamagama (I have crossed many rivers.)
Meaning that one has traveled a great distance and has had a
wide experience and gained wisdom from it.
                    - Nelson Mandela, Long Walk to Freedom

Without question, my experience and observation of South
Africa over a 40-year period has proved to be among the most
meaningful in my life. Even in Peace Corps training, which focused
on Malawi, we caught a glimpse of the land of apartheid (from the
Afrikaans, the official policy of racial separation) out of the corner
of our eyes. We acquired a general familiarity with the history of its
indigenous African Khoi Khoi (Bushman) population, settlement by
the Dutch beginning in 1652, and British colonization, eventuating
in the establishment of the Union of South Africa in 1910. Although
under British rule there had been some movement toward racial
separation, it remained for the Afrikaner government from 1948
onward to codify and enforce a maze of rules and regulations under
the heading of apartheid that governed the life of non-whites in the
country.

In February 1960 the British Prime Minister, Harold Macmillan,
had addressed an all-white South African Parliament in Cape
Town. There he made the now famous observation that there was
"a wind of change blowing through the continent," in reference to
the rising tide of African nationalism. As if to rebuff the Perfidious
Albion, the following year the Afrikaner government got its revenge
for centuries of being bullied by the British when the country left
the Commonwealth and became the Republic of South Africa. A
few weeks after Macmillan's visit South African police fired on a
peaceful demonstration in the African township of Sharpeville in

the Transvaal, killing 69 persons and injuring 186. This event would irrevocably alter the calculus of the political landscape. The main African nationalist organizations, the African National Congress (ANC) and the Pan-Africanist Congress (PAC), were banned and their leaders were jailed, driven underground or into exile. Heretofore the nationalist movements had pursued a strategy of non-violent resistance. But Sharpeville stiffened their resolve. In 1961 the ANC formed a military wing known as Umkhonto we Sizwe (Spear of the Nation) to conduct armed struggle against the apartheid regime.

In June 1964, just two months before we entered training in Syracuse, leaders of the ANC and PAC, including Nelson Mandela, were tried and convicted of treason in the Rivonia Treason Trial, nearly a year after being arrested. Their sentence was life imprisonment. Destination: Robben Island, the infamous maximum security prison off the coast near Cape Town. Although Mandela had already spent two weeks there previously, this time he would remain on the island with follow political prisoners until March 1982, when he was transferred to Pollsmoor Prison near Cape Town.

It must be said, however, that most of us in Malawi remained blissfully unaware of the significance of the events taking place south of the Zambezi River. Certainly we were curious about South Africa, at once stimulated by the stories of its abundant natural resources and the affluence of its minority white population, and at the same time horrified by the injustices of the apartheid regime. Malawi was in relative close proximity to South Africa, both geographically and economically. Malawian men had for generations traveled there to work as migrant laborers in the gold mines. Remittances to their families back home comprised a significant part of the income in the Malawian economy. Some came back to stay after years of living in South Africa, bringing with them cultural baggage. My first cook in Port Herald, an elderly man, was among them. We Volunteers were uneasy about the fact that we were employing Africans as laborers and paying them what seemed to us like a pittance. My cook insisted on calling me baas, the common Afrikaner term that carried with it distinct tones of racial superiority. I urged him to address me as "sir" if he must call me anything, but not baas. The response would invariably be, "Yes, baas." After a while I gave up.

There were other, less insidious cultural influences that wafted northward from South Africa. My favorite one was the ever-popular pulsating rhythms of kwela, the distinctive music of South Africans. Whenever there was a social function at our secondary school in the Lower Shire River students would show up with an assortment of home-made instruments including of an upside-down wash tub with a broom handle attached to it with a cord. This functioned as the rhythm section. Then there would be a ukulele-like instrument that provided the melody. The students' legs and hands provided all else that was needed. Soon the joint was rockin'! Elvis himself would have been impressed. This, then, was the backdrop for my decision to embark on a journey to the land of

On Board the Mozambique   *7/August/1966*

The long inner struggle as to my motives for traveling to the land of apartheid was finally resolved, as Jeff James from Lilongwe and I climbed on board a third class train in Blantyre that would travel south to the Mozambican port city of Beira. We crossed the Zambezi River about half-way to Beira and arrived in the port city after 35 hours of tedious travel. Having checked into the Hotel Gato Preto in Beira, Jeff and I set about making further travel plans, which proved to be an all day job. After procuring a ticket from Compania Nacional Navegaçio, we boarded the Mozambique, a regular ocean liner bound for Lisbon that would take us to the capital city of Lorenzo Marques.

No sooner had we sat down to supper than we were confronted by a brash and yet somehow personable representative of the bastion of white supremacy that is the Republic of South Africa. The revelation of our American origins and our business of Peacecorpsmanship was a cue for this young English-speaking journalist to flail away at the American attitude toward South Africa. For starters, he mentioned the impudence of Senator Robert Kennedy in coming to South Africa and "trying to rouse our Blacks". The stage was set for a six-hour talkathon in which every aspect of South African life vis-a-vis the rest of the world seemingly was aired.

Barry Blackman was very much the image of his American namesake (Barry Goldwater), the unsuccessful Republican candidate for president in 1960. He was a tall, rugged-looking blond of Irish extract who was first and foremost imbued with the belief in the infallibility of white supremacy. This is where his statement of that country began and ended a statement that was at once forthright, articulate and cynical. His style was much the same as Goldwater's too: shoot from the hip and let the chips fall where they may. His penchant for defending his country coupled aggressiveness with personal charm. A graduate of Stellenbosch University, the intellectual font of Afrikanerdom, Barry was able to spell out in the clearest possible terms the attitude of the non-white South African.

As a reporter for the Natal Daily News, Barry was especially concerned about the bad press to which South Africa was constantly subjected. There are a lot more evil things in this world that should command the attention of the world than apartheid, like communism. Generally stories that go out to the Western press are distorted all out of proportion. Sharpeville 1960: a good example. Only a handful of Africans were actually killed there, but the White policemen who died are never mentioned. And then there was the Bobby Kennedy tour that not only served to further his own political ends but was an affront to the South African press when he attempted to bring his own army of reporters. The government needed no justification for denying visas to these reporters since the South African press was quite capable of handling this sort of thing.

Barry contended t hat there was no genuine nationalist feeling in Black Africa, that any time there was violent change it had been Communist inspired. No Black African would be capable of leading his people against colonial rule. Jomo Kenyatta was a case in point; he was sure to have had Communist supervision in the Mau-Mau uprising of the 1950s. Underlying all this, it is significant that Barry regarded South Africa as a home for rugged individualists, if they happened to be white. He regarded the hymns to individualism by Ayn Rand with reverence and considered his own privacy to be sacred. He did not want the winds of change to destroy any of this.

Johannesburg   *12/August/1966*

The second morning I awoke and looked out of the porthole of the Mozambique to see the sun creeping over the city of Lorenzo Marques. Soon we were making our way down the gangplank to the docks, hence to the Municipal Building in the center of town to get a brochure on hotel accommodations. Here we were immediately given an unsolicited tour of the small art museum which mostly depicted the glories of the Portuguese empire. On the steps leading up to the building were these words, in large indelible mosaic letters:

Aqui e Portugal.

I wondered how long this land would be Portuguese. We settled for a quaint old hotel across the street which had been built in 1898 but was cheap and served excellent food. As we strode around town viewing the pastel-colored high rise apartments and streets full of sports cars from Europe and Japan, Jeff remarked that this might well be a section of Westwood Village in Los Angeles, which was close to what I was thinking. The climate of Lorenzo Marques had the perpetual air of springtime: bright sunny skies and balmy breezes. Each day was like the one perfect day we wait for all year in Oklahoma. Even more so than Beira, this city had the Latin temperament of the Mediterranean countries, or perhaps Mexico. Occasionally I was able to make myself understood in Spanish with the Portuguese-speaking population.

For every traveler who tires of getting in and out of planes, trains, hotels and predicaments there usually comes a point at which he feels rewarded for his troubles. That point was reached for me in Lorenzo Marques when I stumbled onto a night club called Aquario, where a group of South Africans from Durban were performing. The African Jazz Singers and Dancers, as they called themselves, had traveled to Australia, New Zealand and even Malawi. They were planning to go on tour soon to Brazil and Portugal. Their repertoire consisted of a combination of traditional songs and popular numbers straight from American jukeboxes. I talked afterward with the four men in the group and found that the Miriam Makeba got her start several years ago with the same African Jazz. They also gave me the address of the "in" place for jazz in Johannesburg, which I eagerly looked forward to visiting.

At this point I left Jeff to find his way back to Malawi and struck out on my own from Lorenzo Marques. I decided to hitch the 100 or so miles to Johannesburg and get a taste of what it might be like the rest of the way. My first lift was with a young Portuguese electrician who was on his way home to Nelspruit, about halfway to Johannesburg. The pain factor here was held to a bare minimum (front seat of a Zephyr, good roads, no stops). Crossing the border was rather like going in the old days from Oklahoma to Texas—from a winding, bumpy tarmac road to broad, smooth, 70-mph super highway. Crossing the border also provided a jolt which would seem in retrospect all too suitable an introduction. At the customs check a mustachioed Afrikaner looked over my American passport, and without even looking up, blurted out sullenly:

"You voted against us on Southwest Africa in the World Court decision; I just can't figure you Americans out."

When he did look up it was as though all the bitterness of a hundred years of trekking was staring at me and I was personally responsible. I said nothing although I felt there was plenty to be said. It was true, the U.S. judge, P.C. Jessup, had cast a dissenting vote but it had been a victorious decision for South Africa. The case, presented by Liberia and Ethiopia on behalf of all of Black Africa, had been before the World Court six years. The decision said, in effect, that South Africa's application of the policy of apartheid in mandated Southwest Africa was no business of the rest of the world.

Having spent the night at the bustling little town of Nelspruit, I was out early the next morning hitching again. The first couple of hours passed and heavy traffic leaving town took slight notice of me. Then a car, going more slowly than the others, pulled over and offered relief. He was an elderly Afrikaner who had worked 30 years in the mines. He could easily have been out of the American Southwest, with his genuine warmth and great pride in the land he says is his, except for the heavy Afrikaans accent. As we drove along he pointed out the thousands of miles of orange orchards that spread through the low veld and make South Africa a leading producer of citrus fruits. He also talked with pride of his family and work, and of the good life he enjoyed. We neared the outskirts of Pretoria and he pointed to the vast stretch of Bantu housing. He then hit upon an already familiar theme:

"Our Blacks are happy; the government gives them everything they could possibly want."

He was turning off 20 miles from the city, so once again I was on the road scavenging. It took two more lifts, both with young Afrikaners, to reach the center of Pretoria, the capital city. The first was with a boilermaker who talked of the very cordial relations he had with his two Bantu (African) assistants whom he regarded as completely loyal to him. It was as though he automatically felt that he must justify his way of life to the foreigner whether or not he was asked. The only problem, he continued, was that his assistants sometimes had the inclination to mix with the "bad natives" which are commonly known as tsotsis.

The second lift was offered by a University of Pretoria medical student who took me past his campus. It was quite impressive.

"Of course," he remarked apologetically, "this surely must not compare with your universities in America" (which it did indeed!)

But soon he was reminding me that the U.S. had best be cleaning up its own racial backyard instead of preaching to his country. It was hard to disagree. He cited the recent riots in Chicago as evidence. In general, he talked like a lot of medical students I have met.

I found myself afoot again in the heart of Pretoria, staring up at the statue of the most revered of all Afrikaners, Paul Kruger. As president of the Transvaal in the early days of British expansion he was the only Afrikaner who could stand up to Cecil Rhodes. And his people haven't forgotten it; his name appeared in public places as much as Washington's does in the U.S. After a short lunch of a close approximation of an American hamburger and a glass of milk, I was directed to the bus depot. It was here that I received my formal introduction to apartheid. As I stepped into the office to buy a ticket to Johannesburg I quickly realized that I was standing in the wrong line. In bold letters in front of me the sign said Nie Blanks—Non-Europeans. A similar sign flashed through my mind, the one that used to say "Colored" above the drinking fountain in Ponca City's Woolworth store. It was a reminder that American society was not all that distant in time from that of South Africa in its own system of apartheid.

So I bought a "European" ticket and climbed onto the European bus. As I waited for the driver I glanced down at a taxi in the street carrying a sign on top—"White person?" I understood now that the term "European" was giving way to "White" since the White South African considered himself no more European than we Americans. Within an hour we were driving through the posh suburbs of Johannesburg. This sprawling city built on gold from the Rand Mining Fields and the sweat of the Bantu brow bore a striking resemblance in many ways to Dallas: its population of over one million, its pulsating affluence, its wealthy ring of suburban nouveau riche to the north and concentration of black ghettos on the south, a citadel of conservatism under white rule. Leaving via Jan

Smuts Avenue, we passed the sole Progressive Party constituency of Houghton (pronounced like cotton).

The newspapers in Johannesburg were carrying stories about the government that tended to suit their reputation of a liberal thorn in the government's flesh. The South African Broadcasting Corporation, on the other hand was banning all Beatles records because of the outcry over John Lennon's comment that they were "more popular than Jesus." Minister of Justice, Balthazar Vorster, had introduced a bill to bar from practice "any lawyer who has committed an offence under the Suppression of Communism Act" (aimed, I suppose, at those such as renegade Afrikaner Bram Fischer). Visiting professor Max Beloff was saying that Africa spends money on defense far out of proportion to the need to protect the country's vital interests. The English press was represented by the widely-known Rand Daily Mail and The Star. The Afrikaans press generally towed the Nationalist Party line, although recently Die Transvaler, Die Burger and Die Beeld had ganged up on a tiny paper called South African Observer whom they accused of right-revisionism. The latter represented the Herzog-ite wing of the Nationalist Party which claimed that the leadership was losing traditional Afrikaner values. Herzog even made Vorster look like a liberal!

East London   *19/August/1966*

August 19th is Vera Mae's birthday; she would have been 49. It is winter here and the skies are overcast, drizzly. The temperature still doesn't dip below the 60's during the day, and this is "winter." East London is the fourth largest seaport in the Republic. I have covered some 800 miles since leaving Johannesburg. The train ride to Durban across the Orange Free State and Natal, from Afrikaner country to the English-speaking capital, was for the most part smooth and comfortable. Early morning found the bus crossing through the rolling hills of Natal, and past row upon row of sugarcane fields. There at the Durban train station was Barry Blackman, waiting to collect me in his Volkswagen 1500 and whisk me along the four-lane freeway to his home in North Durban. The two-story Blackman house near the ocean was the home of a prosperous, sports-minded, gregarious family.

Mr. Blackman, looking and speaking very much like a Texas rancher—which comparison would please him greatly—had for many years been engaged in the wool business. The very evening of my arrival he was presiding over a national meeting of wool manufacturers at the Beverly Hills Hotel in Durban. Less blunt and straight-forward, more diplomatic than his eldest son, the elder Blackman was not interested in throwing stones at my American glass house. He talked rather with the genial air of confidence that comes with success. Mrs. Blackman possessed all the charm and warmth of our family friend Edith Short (Joe's mother), as well as a striking similarity in appearance.

Durban is the largest seaport in the country and one of the busiest in the world. It has the holiday air of Atlantic City without its shabbiness, the year round. It has a very large Indian population, where Mahatma Gandhi rose to prominence as a lawyer before leading India to independence. The Daily News here is strongly progressive in its editorial policy. In fact, the more I read the liberal English language newspapers, the more difficult it becomes to understand the drift of the majority of the English-speaking population toward the Nationalist Party. Every day the English press levels its guns at some government policy and fires away, often at one of the cabinet ministers. There is certainly more freedom of the press than the Nationalists should be able to afford. Here in East London the Daily Dispatch is bemoaning a recent government decision to put the Chinese population in separate locations. One of the most ironic commentaries on apartheid—and they abound—is that Japanese are considered "European" while Chinese are classed as "Non-European". This most likely is a reflection of deference paid to the strong economic ties between the Republic and Japan. Bus conductors, I'm told, are sometimes hard put to tell which of the Asians should be excluded from European buses!

With his usual largesse, Mr. Blackman had arranged a lift for me to Port Elizabeth with one of his associates in the wool trade, a lift that was to prove most luxurious. So after only a couple of days in Durban I was on the road again. Mr. A.A. Straud was the proud owner of an Aston-Martin sports car, a precision piece of automotive engineering which was the extension of his own personality. It took us the first afternoon from Durban to East London, a distance of over 400 miles, in just six hours! This was possible, partly because of the excellent highway which cuts across the round mound of kopjes from Natal to the Transkei, and also because South Africa has no speed limit. The

Garden Route, as it is called, cuts inland to Pietermaritzburg and then through picturesque country so vividly described by novelist Alan Paton in Cry the Beloved Country: Ixopo, Umzimkulu, and then into the home of the Xhosas, the Transkei. Here we frequently began to see African huts scattered across the rugged expanse of sheep country. And as one crosses the Kei River into the Ciskei (this side of the Kei) the chief city of the sheep industry, East London, is near.

My host chatted amiably all the while, providing me with rich insight into the Jewish segment of South African society. He spoke proudly of how his father had arrived penniless from Russia and had sunk his roots deep into South African soil, gradually building a fortune in the wool industry. Mr. Straud himself had married late in life, and while he clearly regretted that intrusion into his personal life he felt that his three children had salvaged the proposition. In fact I was to conclude at the end of our two-day journey that for him the family is the only social unit to which he feels any real allegiance. He held to no faith, but, as he put it, he believed in certain things as guidelines for his own life. Born of a family with a tradition of scholarly rabbis, this Mr. Straud had long since forsaken institutionalized religion. Nevertheless, he was now determined that his sons would receive their Bar Mitzvah, even though their mother was a gentile. They had also been liberally educated in Christian doctrine and tradition.

As a successful business man and leading citizen of Cape Town, Mr. Straud engaged in several philanthropic endeavors. He contributed both to Jewish and Christian concerns, including the Seventh Day Adventist, although he held no truck with their theology. With regard to politics he showed a calm detachment, obviously not too enthusiastic about the present government but not particularly willing to pass any moral judgment on its policies. In essence, his attitude toward politics was pragmatic and he had adapted himself very well to the status quo. His comment about voting was a disconcertingly common one among those who did not agree with the Nationalists:

"I know who to vote for, but it wouldn't do any good."

At one point Mr. Straud revealed a sense of civic duty when he expressed his approval of the U.S. effort in Vietnam. This sentiment was probably engendered during his service for the Allies in World War II.

Cape Town   *23/August/1966*

The second portion of my lift with Mr. Straud took us through the German communities of Berlin and Potsdam. And then through Grahamstown, a place of traditionally rich English influence with its abundance of schools, churches and Rhodes University. It is said to be a town of "no vice". Professor Sampson of Rhodes, the author of Principles of Apartheid, was a leading apologist for that policy. In was his book that was presented to Senator Kennedy on his visit to South Africa. In it Sampson scorned the policies of Britain and the U.S. in the domestic realm, citing the frequent outbursts of racial tension as proof of moral decay. On the other hand he held up apartheid as a model policy because all races are said to live in blissful harmony under it. That is, as long as the endemic quarrelsomeness of the "native" is closely guarded. His position was purportedly substantiated by the Bible, noted American anthropologists and sociologists such as Carton Coon, and not the least by the UN Charter guaranteeing self-determination of peoples! Sampson pointed to the Jewish nation-state of Israel to justify this, and then wondered aloud why the Jews didn't return their admiration for fellow travelers in South Africa. Sampson hardly succeeded in arousing Western sympathy with his vitriolic attacks on liberalism, on the one hand, and shrill cries of chauvinism on the other. So much for the Prophet of Grahamstown!

Port Elizabeth, the scene of a stream of English immigrants beginning in 1820, was the end of the line for my ride with Mr. Straud. I expressed my appreciation to him as he went about his business at the new Wool Exchange and I found my way to the train station. While waiting for the night train to Cape Town I stumbled across the most extensive branch of the Central News Agency chain in the country. In a brief chat with the manager, as he eased me out at closing time, I was told of orders he received for books from all over the world. I questioned him as to whether the company was government-controlled.

"No, thank God, and as for me, I fights the gov'ment", he said with determination.

Here in Port Elizabeth, the Detroit of South Africa, the largest

Ford and General Motors assembling plants anywhere in Africa were to be found. It was also an area of strong Xhosa influence, where even European children were said to learn Xhosa as a first language. As I slumbered heavily on the first night to the Cape the coal-fed steam engine coughed its black refuse into the air and wound its way into the region known as the Groote Karoo. The next day, as we descended to sea level again at the stations of George and Mussel Bay, the scenery was starkly beautiful yet. But not until we reached the greenery of the Western Cape did the land become really hospitable. Here miles upon miles of vineyards feed the famous Cape wine industry. And although winter in the Cape is also the rainy season, I was to experience two days of brilliant sunshine.

The second morning I gazed at the breath-taking panorama of Table Mountain for the first time. As often happens on the train, my compartment was the scene of very interesting people and discussions. There was a Canadian Volunteer secondary teacher on his way home. Another "chappy", as they say here, was David Smedley Williams, a hybrid of English and Afrikaner stock. He was on his way back to his flat in Rosebank, a suburb of Cape Town, and he asked me to come and stay with him.

That the Cape was somewhat more liberal than the rest of the country was reflected in public transportation policy. There were no separate buses for black and white, but on each bus there was a sign indicating that Nie Blankes should keep to the back. Even this was not taken too seriously sometimes. And, too, the University of Cape Town had a sizable Colored enrollment. The Colored, however, had by no means escaped from Nationalist apartheid policy. After the Nationalist take-over in 1948 in which the Colored vote was instrumental in assuring victory, the government showed its gratitude by disenfranchising the whole Colored population.

Arriving in mid-morning at the massive train station under construction, David and I changed to a commuter train for Rosebank. My host had received a bachelor's degree in commerce at the University of Cape Town and was now employed by the Standard Bank. He had also been a diver in the South African navy, an occupation that he still spoke of with enthusiasm. The first afternoon was taken up with a leisurely tour of the city by car. The view from Signal Hill on the "rump" end of the mountain known as Lion's Head was magnificent. From here one looks down across the Foreshore, a stretch of land along Table Bay that has been continuously reclaimed from the ocean, just as the Dutch have filled in portions of the North Sea. On the other side is the coast which descends to Cape Point, the place popularly believed to be the southern-most tip of the continent. It is actually much farther east and south. The remainder of the day we drove around the other end of the Table Mountain; the famous Clifton Beach appeared almost bare because of the cool weather.

Cape Town   *Monday, 22/August1966*

Today would prove to be a real red-letter day. Points of attraction in the Cape Town included a visit to The Castle and a trip by cable car to the top of the 3,500 ft. Table Mountain. To the west of Table Mountain, the waters of the Atlantic Ocean wash the sun-bleached shores and to the southeast one can see False Bay on the Indian Ocean side.

Table Mountain, Cape Town

David and I again took a train to the center of town and began a full-scale tourist invasion of it. We wandered into the first Dutch Reformed Church, an austere looking edifice erected in 1700. It had since become the mother church for Afrikaners. Directly adjacent to it was the first Anglican Church which, like most Anglican cathedrals, housed the remains of great men of the British empire who opened up South Africa. Toward Table Mountain from there, through the municipal park, was the downtown extension of the University of Cape Town. Here there were some 5,000 students enrolled; and according to the school newspaper, The Varsity, a power struggle was being waged between the paper and its official sponsor, the SRC (Student Representative Council). I was reminded of similar battles on the campus of Texas Christian University that pitted student government against the student paper. The university system in the Republic was the seat of much government criticism, so steps were being taken to bring it under closer control. Robert Kennedy received a very favorable audience on his visit to the University in June 1966.

In South Africa, the judicial branch of government has its Supreme Court in Bloemfontein, the Executive Branch is in Pretoria, and Parliament meets in Cape Town. It was my good fortune to find the legislators in session on this afternoon. Ranged behind their leader, Dr. Verwoerd, to the right of the Speaker, was the huge majority of "Nat" representatives. Their number extended deep into United Party territory in the chamber. Directly across from Verwoerd, who sat with head in hand and looking monumentally bored, was the leader of the loyal opposition (more loyal than opposition), Sir de Villiers-Graff. And several seats down from him sat a diminutive silver-haired lady, studiously listening and fingering her pencil. Yes, this was the Progressive Party representative, the thorn in the side of the government, Mrs. Helen Suzman. Debate centered on the Nationalists' program of increased taxation and spending. United Party (UP) speakers flailed away at the specter of inflation, sounding very much like Republicans in the U.S. Their speeches were in general grossly inept, bringing guffaws from the horde of Nationalists. The Minister of Finance fielded the charges, speaking in Afrikaans, knowing full well that the UP attack was an exercise in futility.

After an hour or so Mrs. Suzman bowed to the Speaker and left the chamber. Summoning a measure of chutzpah, I followed her to her office where, to my amazement, she graciously consented to an interview. She first checked with her secretary on a list of speaking engagements, appointments and family matters. But once she had turned her attention to our discussion she was very personable and direct. No, she said, she hadn't had many Peace Corps visitors but she was quite familiar with our work. In fact, she was prompting the establishment of a similar program in South Africa to "supplement the protests and demonstrations of liberal students." (Two days later an article in the Daily Mail reported on the proposal for a Peace Corps-type program by the national chairman of the Young Progressive Party.) But the program was never to materialize, nor did it take the place of student protests.

A one-time professor of economics at Wits (Witwatersrand University), Mrs. Suzman had been closely identified with the protest over Ian Robertson's detention. She told me that she had visited the U.S. on several occasions and had found that in some respects race relations were worse there than in South Africa. (That does it, I thought: everyone with white skin in South Africa feels obliged to defend his or her country!) Mrs. Suzman did not hold out much hope for the Progressive Party in the near future.

"We can only attempt to win over liberal portions of the UP. Remember, we have now had 18 years of indoctrination under this regime."

In reading Mandela's autobiography years later, I learned that Mrs. Suzman went to visit him on Robben Island the following year, in 1967. According to Mandela, she was the only Member of Parliament who had the courage and took enough interest in political prisoners to visit them in prison. He remarked that it was an odd and wonderful sight to see this courageous woman peering into their cells and strolling around the courtyard.

The plight of the liberal in South Africa in 1966 seemed even more dismal than that of the American liberal. As for the UP representatives, Mrs. Suzman allowed as how they were mostly a bunch of "bumbling clots." The English-speaking electorate appeared to agree with her. I mentioned the dismissal of a student announcer on South African Broadcasting Corporation for his part in hosting Senator Kennedy. She indicated that she might be able to intercede on his behalf. She spoke also of the work she was doing for the Colored population. I left Mrs. Suzman's office with the feeling that she would not be intimidated by the government; she relished her role as the thorn in the side of the Nationalist Party. On the other hand her elitism certainly didn't seem to be winning many friends and influencing people for the cause of liberalism.

In a lighter vein, I was introduced to something of a national diversion while in Cape Town. Almost everyone I spoke with, both English and Afrikaans-speaking, was readily conversant with the rash of folk-jokes which sounded much like the little moron stories or the Polack jokes. The anti-hero of these jokes is Van der Merwe, the Afrikaans name which enjoys about the same currency in South Africa as Smith does in the Anglo-Saxon world. The gist of this genre of humor is the lampooning of Afrikaans culture, sometimes harmless, sometimes cruelly incriminating.

One of the most popular Van der Merwe stories is set at an international conference on space exploration. The American representative tells of U.S. plans to launch the first manned flight to the moon. The Russian space expert boasts that his country is already working on plans to land a man on Mars. The redoubtable South African representative, Mr. Van der Merwe, not to be outdone, claims that his country will soon send a man to the Sun. Somewhat puzzled, his colleagues remind him of the intense heat given off by the Sun, certain to destroy any would-be explorers.

Van der Merwe, undaunted, replies: "Ach man, ve goin' at night."

Beaufort West back to Johannesburg   25/August/1966

Standing on the highway behind the imposing Sanlam Building, I already began to feel uneasy about being persuaded to hitch the 1,000 miles back to Johannesburg. But soon I found myself riding with a Cape Colored man who worked for a land moving company, a resident of District Six. He explained that, according to the government proclamation, he would have to move his family out of the house which had belonged to his family for generations. While he didn't seem at all happy about this, he was still not ready to challenge the powers that be.

We had not gone far when he stopped to pick up an old African who immediately ingratiated himself to both of us, repeating,

"Thank you, baas, thank you, master" in the customary manner. The Colored turned to the Black, smiling slightly, and said,

"Please don't call me master."

Many times already I had been addressed as baas, and it never failed to make me feel uncomfortable. I recalled what Mrs. Suzman had said about indoctrination.

My very next lift came at the invitation of yet another Afrikaner, this one a traveling salesman headed for Beaufort West. He assured me that selling insurance for African Life was a quite lucrative business, that it was possible to earn 400 Rand in an average month. The road stretched out into the Great Karoo and I questioned him about the meaning of some of the Afrikaans towns. He was happy to oblige. Then he added with conviction that the best way for me to learn his language was to carefully read an English-Afrikaans Bible. He was greatly relieved to learn that I wasn't an atheist and that I had grown up in a small Protestant sect.

Beaufort West proved to be my Waterloo. This Beaufort wasn't just West, it was nowhere, although reputedly the largest town in the Karoo with 12,000 inhabitants. After an untold number of hours standing outside of town looking hopefully for a lift that didn't come, I glanced at the back of a mileage sign. Other would-be hitchers had scrawled such ominous notes as "This is Hitchers' Hell". "April 2, 1962—12 hours" and a few obscenities. My spirit sank as the pain factor soared. I caved in. Back in Beaufort West, I bought a ticket and waited for the next train to Johannesburg. All too soon my South African safari was coming to an end. Within a few days I was standing in front of my Form VI English class at Dedza Secondary, resuming my mundane life as a teacher. My experience of South Africa, however, would stay with me for years to come.

— — —

Much later, while my professional interests were turned toward Asia and Eastern Europe, momentous events were taking place in South Africa. In February 1990, Nelson Mandela was released from prison after 27 years. His 10,000 days of imprisonment were finally over! After a triumphal appearance at the First National Bank Stadium in his home town of Soweto before 120,000 delirious supporters, Mandela and his wife Winnie then undertook a tour of Europe and the United States. My distinct recollection of his appearance in the D.C. Convention Center that year, where entrance was at a premium, was something akin to what I would imagine the Second Coming to be like. A wave of euphoria swept through the crowd as we all basked in the glow of Mandela's charisma.

In May 1994, the beatific face of Nelson Mandela peered out from the front of TIME magazine with a halo of multi-colored roses and his fist raised in the Amandla (freedom) pose. In an awesome spectacle of transformation, Mandela and the black majority were set to inherit the government in South Africa. History appeared to have delivered a miracle similar to the fall of the Berlin Wall five years before. The world truly was turning on its axis. Apartheid had been relegated to the dustbin, a prospect almost unthinkable just a few years before when F. W. de Klerk knowingly and willfully took steps to dismantle it. The two men would share the Nobel Peace Prize for their collaboration in ushering in a new era under remarkably peaceful conditions. The amazing thing was not so much that the election had taken place under fairly calm circumstances, but that it happened at all, given that the white minority had held the black majority in thrall for over 300 years.

Cape Town   *18/June/2005*

During the 1980s and 1990s I would have several occasions to pass through South Africa, on the way to Lesotho, Swaziland and Malawi. But South Africa would not come back into sharp focus for me until June 2005. Now in the College of Business at Tennessee State University, I traveled there with a group of business faculty and administrators from fellow Historically Black Colleges and Universities (HBCUs). It was part of a Department of Education-funded effort to promote the internationalization of our curricula and programs. Our itinerary would include lectures and presentations at host universities as well as tours of historic and social significance in the Cape Town area.

I arrived at the Cape Town airport on a Sunday morning and was met by Sauli, a jovial Cape Colored man who had been contracted as our group tour guide. My colleagues were to be arriving at intervals in the course of the day. Sauli drove me to the Breakwater Lodge, a hotel and restaurant facility operated by Protea Hotels in the V&A Waterfront section of the city. It serves international students and guests of the University of Cape Town (UCT) Graduate School of Business (GSB), housed in the same complex. Located on the Breakwater Campus of the University, the Lodge is owned by UCT and is operated as part of GSB. Once a 19th century prison, the Breakwater has been thoroughly renovated and provides relatively inexpensive and clean accommodation in a truly spectacular setting overlooking the harbor on one side and Table Mountain on the other. The turrets along the top of the buildings are reminders of the hotel's prison past, as are the framed historical documents on the walls of the hallways describing the "crimes" for which former residents had been imprisoned, such as insubordination and improper attire.

It was mid-winter in the Cape, and the first day was chilly, overcast and drizzly. Thick clouds enveloped Table Mountain, which stood just behind the Breakwater. The first two days this weather pattern held, but the locals assured us that we wouldn't go more than four days without seeing the sun. And sure enough, on the third day the sun rose up bright and clear over Table Mountain, revealing all its majesty. It was truly breath-taking. In all my travels I have a fairly comparative perspective on great cities. On the top echelon of those international cities known for their natural setting and charm, commercial and social vitality, four are on my list: Hong Kong, Vancouver, Rio de Janeiro and of course Cape Town. This was my third time to visit Cape Town and I would find nothing to tempt me to take it off my list! Happily, for most of the remainder of our stay in the Cape we would be blessed with bountiful sunshine and spectacular views all around.

Robben Island   *June 19, 2005*

Easily the most riveting and inspiring tour during our stay in Cape Town was a boat ride to Robben Island the very first day on the program. At 10:00 AM we caught the ferry at V&A Waterfront for the hour-long ride to Robben Island. Although throughout history this small island in the Atlantic Ocean north and west of Cape Town had been used to put away common criminals, lepers and of course political prisoners, today it is preserved as a museum, very similar to what it was like during Mandela's tenure there. While no prisoners are housed here any longer, several of the guides who walked us through the Spartan facility had lived there during the days of Mandela. As they stood before us telling of what went on in each room we saw, we sat spellbound, striving to imagine what it must have been like. We will never know. Each of the tiny cells now has a picture of the former resident, with quotes from him and a recording of comments about life on Robben Island. We all peered into the cell that Mandela himself occupied, our mouths open. We stepped out into the walled open-air courtyard where the prisoners eventually were allowed to exercise. At one end was a patch of ground where Mandela was said to have tended his garden.

At the Robben Island bookstore I felt compelled to buy Mandela's 768-page autobiography entitled Long Walk to Freedom. Over the next few days I devoted all my leisure time to poring over Long Walk, finishing it in one week. I quickly realized that it held my attention, not only because it documented the life of a great man, but because it was an autobiography and thus a source of inspiration for my own autobiographical efforts. Mandela asserts that the bulk of the manuscript was written during a four-month period after he had reached 57 years of age. His comrades on Robben Island, fellow political prisoners and freedom-fighters, urged him to undertake the project. It was his old friend Walter Sisulu who suggested one day in 1974 while they were walking in the courtyard that Mandela write his memoirs, with a view toward publishing them by his 60th birthday. The idea appealed to Mandela and he started the project right away. Each day after working in the lime quarry he would retire to his quarters and write. Sometimes he would stay up throughout the night when he was particularly inspired. They created an assembly line to process the manuscript. Each day Mandela would pass on what he had written to one of his team members for editorial comment, who in turn would pass it to another who would write up the edited version.

Mandela's Cell on Robben Island

Mandela tells how each day as he wrote he would relive the events of his life, as if in a dream. Of course, what Mandela and friends were doing was against the rules of the establishment, so they had to develop an elaborate scheme for concealing the manuscript from the authorities. The edited copy was thus smuggled out of the prison in 1976, and then out of the country. Only then was the original manuscript disposed of, buried in the garden of the courtyard. Nevertheless, the warden eventually found the manuscript; those implicated in the project had their study privileges suspended for four years! Although the book was not published while Mandela was in prison, he resumed work on it in 1990 after his release. It was eventually copyrighted and the first edition was published in 1994, 20 years after it was begun as a team project. Surely few autobiographies must ever have had a more torturous period of gestation.

Cape Town as Viewed from Robben Island

My reading of Mandela's life story brought several themes into relief: life changes, racial relations and politics. He was born in 1918 into a very traditional African rural environment in the Transkei region where he imbibed the values and attitudes of his Xhosa tribe. In the course of his lifetime Mandela would take on a different set of attitudes and values as he acquired a national African identity, without having entirely thrown off his traditional values. His memoirs describe this process in great detail. He characterizes his life journey with an expression from his mother tongue:

Ndiwelimilambo enamagama (I have crossed many rivers.)

It means simply that one has traveled a great distance, has had a wide experience and gained wisdom from it.

As we have seen, in the Congo a similar expression conveyed the same sentiment:

Tambolana mokili. Omona makambo! (Travel around the world and you'll see things!)

Already in the early 1940s Mandela felt that he had crossed many rivers but was keenly aware that he had many yet to cross. Education was a metaphor for those rivers. Having completed secondary school, Mandela attended the University College of Fort Hare in the small town of Alice. At the time it was the only residential center of higher education for Backs in all of South Africa. For young Blacks like himself, "it was Oxford and Cambridge, Harvard and Yale, all rolled into one." Fort Hare was more than that: it was a beacon for African scholars from all over Southern, Central and Eastern Africa. Entering Fort Hare at the age of 21, Mandela had his first suit, double-breasted and grey, which made him feel grown up and sophisticated. Mandela wrote: "I felt I was being groomed for success in the world."

However, Mandela would leave Fort Hare before completing his university degree there. Life had challenges in store for him other than becoming a teacher in a rural Transkei secondary school. Having moved to Johannesburg in 1943, Mandela passed his examination through UNISA (a distance education university) and returned to Fort Hare for graduation. The very same year he enrolled at the University of the Witwatersrand (popularly known as Wits) for a bachelor of law degree, the preparatory academic training for a lawyer. It was the premier English-speaking University in the country. At Wits, for the first time in his life Mandela was attending class with white students. This was as new for him as it was for them, since he was the only African student in the law faculty. Meanwhile, he began working at a law firm where he was also brought into contact with Whites in the workplace for the first time. He would continue his formal education even during his imprisonment on Robben Island. Even during the Rivonia Trial, which would send him there, he began studying for the LLB at the University of London.

As early as 1946, however, Mandela's experience led to his politicization. A mineworkers' strike that year affected him deeply and marked his first active involvement in politics, leading to his membership in the African National Congress (ANC). While Mandela supported the objectives of the the strike which was eventually crushed by the government, he did not agree with the Communist members of the ANC. Thus began his long and intensive dialogue with communism. That same year he also became involved in opposition to the Asiatic Land Tenure Act, designed to curtail the free movement of Indians. The Indian community undertook a two-year campaign of passive resistance to the act. As a member of the Youth League of the ANC, Mandela gave full moral support to the Natal Indian Congress in their fight. Thus, already in the early years of Mandela's political career, he was working side by side with Indian political leaders. He would spend many years on Robben Island with one of them, Ahmed Kathrada (whom he called Kathy). Kathy was one of those intimately involved in Mandela's manuscript project;

but for Kathy's efforts we would not likely be reading his memoirs today.

Mandela notes in Long Walk to Freedom that the Indian campaign of 1946 became a model for the type of protest for which the ANC Youth League was calling. He argued that it instilled a spirit of defiance and radicalism among the people and broke the fear of prison. The Indian campaign, he wrote, harkened back to the 1913 passive resistance effort in which Mahatma Gandhi led a tumultuous procession of Indians crossing illegally from Natal to the Transvaal.

As seen from these excerpts from Mandela's autobiography, two points stand out. First, early on Mandela distanced himself from the Communist Party tenets, although it would be seen later that many of his closest friends and fellow freedom fighters were Communists. Secondly, although Mandela was first and foremost and an African nationalist, from the outset he demonstrated a commitment to work with people of all races who shared the burden of oppression. He saw a common bond with people of all races who suffered from apartheid and this was what allowed Mandela to lead his country into a new era of multi- racial democracy under majority rule in 1994. Such men as Mandela only come along every few generations. It is our good fortune to have lived in his.

Breakwater Lodge—History & Government   *June 20, 2005*

Our host, the University of Cape Town Graduate Business School, arranged a series of lectures for our group dealing with key issues. I confess to having taken few notes the first day on the history, geography and politics of South Africa. But I was busy reading the news of the day to get up to speed. By the second morning we managed to buy newspapers at the Breakwater cafeteria. Several headlines are worth mentioning. Business Report, South Africa's National Financial Daily (June 22, 2005) reported that South African house prices were rising faster than any place in the world. According to two studies in reputable publications, The Economist and the Wall Street Journal, house prices in South Africa rose 24% between the first quarter of 2004 and the first quarter of 2005, even faster than second place Hong Kong. Since 1997 South African house prices have increased by 244%; Ireland is second with 192%. In South Africa many investors are entering the buy-to-let market.

Cape Town is considered one of the hottest markets in the country. Our tour guide informed us that foreign speculators were the ones buying up much of the real estate in the area.

In fact, our visit coincided with an event of seemingly historic proportions: the firing of the Deputy President and the appointment of a new one. Jacob Zuma, a Zulu, was very popular in his constituency and was a freedom fighter against apartheid. Following the dismissal of Zuma on charges of corruption, President Thabo Mbeki announced his selection of a woman to replace him, the first to be chosen for this position. For a couple of days there was speculation that the two most likely candidates for the job were women. Insiders said that Foreign Affairs Minister Nkosazana Dlamini-Zuma (former wife of Mr. Zuma) and Minerals and Energy Minister Phumzile Mlamabo-Ngcuka were the favorites. The headlines trumpeted Mbeki's choice: Madame Deputy: Mrs. Mlambo-Ngcuka (49). While there were questions surrounding the new Deputy's political involvement in "Oilgate" and her own brother's part in bringing down Zuma, Mbeki justified his choice as an "opportunity to strengthen participation of women" in development (Cape Times, June 22-23, 2005).

Pundits suggested that Mbeki had moved another step closer to ending South Africa's political crisis by appointing the new Deputy President. There was bound to be political fallout from the decision, especially reaction from Zuma's loyal supporters. While he was no longer Deputy President, Zuma retained his position as number two in the ANC. In general, however, Mlambo-Ngcuka's appointment drew positive reaction from civil society, politicians and the business community. It was argued that the decision signaled a fundamental shift in the ANC away from the close-knit political family of the 1990s towards the emergence of a modern political party "ruled by its head, not by its heart." Mbeki seemed to have diffused the explosive ethnic issue by naming a Zulu to replace a Zulu. The ANC had always been considered by the Zulus to be under Xhosa domination since the time of Mandela. Some observers speculated that the timing of Mbeki's decision had to do with playing to the G8 audience of Gleneagles, Scotland the following month. It would show critics of African political leaders that there was one leader who was not afraid to deal with corruption. Only time would tell.

Breakwater Lodge—BEE   *June 21, 2005*

Again, notes taken from the pages of the local newspapers, not the class lectures. Today's topic is Black Economic Empowerment (BEE), a South African government program aimed at increasing participation by black people in economic activity. At a Black Management Forum meeting in 1997 it was proposed that a Black Economic Empowerment Commission be established. The Commission in turn made recommendations to President Mbeki in 2001 which led to the BEE. Supporters of BEE argue that economic empowerment is about changing the racial composition of the class that owns or controls economic resources in the country. According to this point of view, increasing the number of black people within the class legitimizes the environment for white business and creates a sense of economic belonging for black people. Some suggest that BEE is about fast-tracking the creation of a black middle class: the bigger the pool of people with more money to spend, the more attractive South Africa becomes to investors. (Sikhakhane, 2005)

Some argue that BEE raises the same dilemma for black South Africans as does the bumiputra policy in Malaysia that promotes interests of the majority Malay population. Can BEE facilitate the creation of a class of black business people capable of standing firmly, without crutches, among their business peers? And if crutches are necessary, should the government hand them out only for a limited period? These are the questions South Africa must answer if the country is to avoid going down the same path as that tread by Malaysia. Whither BEE?

Mindful of this criticism of the BEE initiative, the Mbeki government has begun clamping down on companies using the usual suspects as front men by introducing incentives for them to bring fresh faces into their partnerships. The Ministry of Trade and Industry thus recently announced revisions to the Black Empowerment Code that would provide for entrants and broad-base schemes to get bonus points on the empowerment scoreboard. While not mentioning names, the Code clearly aimed at addressing criticism that the likes of Cyril Ramaphosa and Tokyo Sexwale (renowned African billionaires) are typically the first port of call whenever firms want to do "empowerment deals." (Marcia Klein and Adele Shevel, *Sunday Business Times, June 26 2005*)

Our group would witness a few shining examples of seemingly successful black entrepreneurs, no doubt chosen for their star quality. The first of these, and perhaps the most impressive, was the owner/manager of a restaurant in Langa Township east of Cape Town. Our guide Sauli did not really prepare us for the experience we were about to have on the afternoon of Tuesday, June 21. We drove on the super highway out of downtown past the industrial complexes and smart residential areas into Langa where we finally turned off into a rustic but not quite destitute neighborhood. While reading Mandela's memoirs, I learned that it was in Langa Township where some 30,000 people gathered in response to the sentencing of PAC leader Robert Sobukwe in 1960. The whole world knows the name of another area where demonstrations took place at the same time, with the most calamitous results: Sharpeville.

Sauli steered our bus through the narrow streets of Langa, past schools and playgrounds, bars, funeral parlors and parks. We came to a halt in what seemed to be an alleyway. We were motioned into the entrance of a modest home that did not reveal its true dimensions. We filed into a large dining room and were seated at tables where we waited to learn what the program was. Gladys, the owner of the establishment, welcomed us in very measured and articulate tones, almost as though she were speaking from a pulpit. She was a jaunty middle-aged lady with an air of self-confidence mixed with self deprecation. Gladys then began to recount the story of how this restaurant came into being. Throughout her life she had managed to do a variety of odd jobs to keep body and soul together. During apartheid days this consisted mainly of doing housework for white folks. She eventually started buying goods from one source and selling them elsewhere at a slight markup, all the while living in the same house in Langa Township.

Then Gladys began investing modest funds into the expansion and renovation of her home, inviting people in for food and drink. Eh, voila! Today Gladys is definitely on the main circuit for tourists who want to sample what life is like in the townships. The buffet-style meal provided generous helpings of home-cooked food, chicken, potatoes, greens accompanied by South African wine and Castle beer. A group of young musicians set up shop in the corner and soon we were all having a great time.

Stellenbosch   *June 23, 2005*

Today was devoted to a visit to the erstwhile citadel of Afrikanerdom, Stellenbosch University, and its surrounding array of vineyards. Our group was royally received and presented with a series of lectures related to the wine industry that is that lifeblood of the region. One of the presentations consisted of a full-blown wine-tasting affair. For those of us amateurs with an uneducated palate, this was a humbling experience. Sniffing the bouquet of each glass of wine, we were supposed to be able to detect a whiff of vanilla, raspberry, strawberry or peach. Much as I strained to come up with a designated aroma, my sniffer invariably failed each each test. Furthermore, my taste buds were equally inept at deciphering unique wine flavors. They all tasted pretty good. I was left with my basic bias in favor of red versus white wine and the awareness that Pinotage was a distinctly South Africa vintage that was being counted upon to crack international markets.

There followed a tour of Stellenbosch, a very scenic and proper town featuring prominent Cape Dutch architecture, prim streets and high-end shops. Not long ago, this town would have been strictly reserved for whites, with Bantus restricted to the perimeters and to the mundane jobs of taking care of the homes and children of the white minority. Today the streets are full of Africans who mix freely with the white population. What a difference a decade makes!

We then enjoyed a tour of a local vineyard and distillery whose ownership had recently been placed in the hands of its African workers. Veronica was one of those who had begun as a grape picker and was now in a managerial position following acquisition of the company by workers such as herself. As she explained to us, the former owner, a white South African, was committed to pursuing the objectives of the BEE program. He therefore decided to divest a majority of his shares in the company in order that employees would gain ownership. On the surface at least, it looked like a most happy arrangement.

The evening found us on the Spier Vineyard grounds and its Moyo Restaurant, outside of the town of Stellenbosch. Another experience for which we were not prepared! We arrived at dusk, driving past a game preserve along the side of the road that featured an abundance of wildlife including Springbok and a variety of antelope. We parked in a large open lot and wandered into an open-air tent that provided a display of assorted crafts and compact disks. After an hour of browsing we began to wonder if this was the reason we had been turned loose in the place. The sun had just set and the air was getting COLD! And then we were motioned forward into a wonderland of trees, tents, tables, chairs and metal demi-barrels full of firewood giving off much-appreciated warmth. We were directed toward a long table under one of the big tents. Before us was an immense buffet with a vast array of food. It was clear that this was to be a full-fledged bacchanalia! There were other tables in all directions, hundreds of customers, attended by armies of waiters and waitresses. Soon we were treated to a troop of dancers and singers that completed the bacchanalia.

A young African greeted us at our table and told us that he was one of the founders of Moyo and would be our official host. He casually mentioned that Moyo was opening up similar facilities in other cities of South Africa and even targeting overseas markets. We were all attuned to the BEE phenomenon after the series of lectures we had had in recent days. My curiosity compelled me to approach the young man after our meal and ask him a few questions about the ownership and management of this most impressive enterprise. He was standing with another African colleague when I asked if he could tell me about the ownership of Moyo. He looked at his colleague, and both burst out laughing in an awkward manner. Needless to say, I didn't get an answer to my question. It is most likely that we had stumbled upon a case of "fronting" in which the parent company financed a secondary venture that was ostensibly in the hands of Africans. This would warrant a case study in modern-day South African business management.

Cape of Good Hope   *June 24, 2005*

Toward the end of our stay in the Cape Town area, Sauli and company (wife and son) treated us to an afternoon tour of the Cape of Good Hope, that sliver of land that juts out south and eastward from Cape Town toward Antarctica. Most of us were unaware of what we were in for. Situated at the junction of two of the earth's most contrasting water masses—the cold Benguela current on the West Coast and the warm Agulhas current on the East Coast—the Cape of Good Hope is popularly considered to be the meeting point of the

Atlantic and the Indian Oceans. The area was proclaimed a nature reserve in 1938 and in 2004 it was named Table Mountain National Park. The cliffs at the southern point, which tower more than 600 ft. above sea level, consist of three clearly defined promontories: Cape of Good Hope, Cape Maclear and Cape Point.

As we drove south along the coast, the scenery on all sides was extraordinary. Around every curve there was another white-sand beach or mountain scape, reminiscent of the Oregon Coast around Seaside. With its diverse habitats ranging from rocky mountain tops to beaches and open sea, the Cape of Good Hope is home to over 250 species of birds. Flowering plants which grow in profusion here attract sunbirds, sugarbirds and other species in search of nectar. When we reached the Cape of Good Hope and Cape Point where the two oceans are said to meet, the southern most tip of the African continent, we posed for photo opportunities. It occurred to me as we were observing this achievement that I had gone from the very northern tip of the continent in Tunisia to the southernmost within a week!

Soweto, South Africa   June 26, 2005

Our tour of the sprawling township of Soweto coincided with the 50th Anniversary of the Freedom Charter celebration in Kliptown. It was here in Kliptown, a multiracial village on a scrap of veld a few miles southwest of Johannesburg, that the Congress of the People took place June 25-26, 1955. More than 3,000 delegates braved police intimidation to assemble and approve the final document. It was a document born of the people that would form the basis of the struggle for political freedom. According to Mandela's memoirs, some in the ANC, particularly the Africanist contingent who were anti-Communist and anti-white, objected to the Charter as being a design for a radically different South Africa from the one the ANC had called for throughout its history since 1912. In fact, Mandela points out, the charter endorsed private enterprise and would provide for Africans to own their own homes and businesses, to prosper as entrepreneurs. For its time, the Freedom Charter was a revolutionary document because the changes it envisaged could not come about without radically altering the economic and political structure of the country.

Sadly, however, today Kliptown symbolizes the unfulfilled dreams of the Freedom Charter. When it was signed, the apartheid policies had only been in existence for seven years and it was natural that the people would blame the government for their poverty. Today, as one enters Kliptown it is hard to miss the cranes and workers putting up a handful of buildings. The township appears at first glance to be on its way to offering a better life for all. But as soon as one crosses the main bridge that leads from the city center, the derelict community emerges. Kliptown looks much like other informal settlements in South Africa that occupy formerly wide-open spaces. Most of the houses are built of corrugated iron and cardboard on tiny plots of land. Women sit on bottle crates while preparing the day's meal, and the men sit on bottle crates drinking their Castle lager or something stronger. The lines at the water taps are long because they often broken. Despite the earnest efforts of a few brave community activists, it seems that little has changed for the people of Kliptown since the signing of the Charter. (Christina Gallagher, *Weekend Argus*, June 25, 2005)

Our tour of Soweto included a visit to 8115 Orlando West, the home where Mandela had lived with Winnie before he was incarcerated. It is now a museum with mementos from Mandela's personal and family life. When they first moved there Mandela described it as a "dusty area of Spartan boxy municipal houses that would eventually become part of Greater Soweto (Southwestern Township)." It had been severely damaged by fire while he was still in prison but has since been reconstructed. This home is on one end of Vilakazi Street and Bishop Desmond Tutu's home is on the other end. Surely no other street in the world can boast the homes of TWO Nobel Peace Prize winners!

Kids sing for us on Vilakazi Street, Soweto

So this, then, is the new majority-ruled South Africa. For the masses of the population it has truly been a long walk to freedom, symbolized so vividly in the life of Nelson Mandela himself. But it remains to be seen whether this freedom can carry the country toward genuine social and economic development for all.

Mandela himself best expressed the challenge in his memoirs:

When I walked out of prison my mission was to liberate the oppressed and the oppressor both. Some say that has now been achieved. But I know that that is not the case. The truth is that we are not yet free; we have merely achieved the freedom to be free, the right not to be oppressed. We have not taken the final step of our journey, but the first step on a longer and even more difficult road. For to be free is not merely to cast off one's chains, but to live in a way that respects and enhances the freedom of others. The true test of our devotion to freedom is just beginning.

References

Business Report (South Africa's National Financial Daily) (2005) "SA House Prices Rise Fastest in World," June 22.

Gallagher, Christina, (2005) "Kliptown: 50 years after the Freedom Charter: What's new?" in the *Weekend Argus*, June 25, 2005.

Klein, Marcia, and Adele Shevel (2005). "BEE needs new faces," in *Sunday Business Times*, June 26.

Mandela, Nelson (1994) *Long Walk to Freedom: The Autobiography of Nelson Mandela,* 1995 edition, London: Little, Brown & Company, published by Abacus.

Sikhakhane, Jabulani (2005) "When do we throw away the BEE crutches and run?" in *Business Report: South Africa's National Financial Daily*, June 21.

Time Magazine (1994) "Cape of Good Hope: A Nation Born Anew", cover featuring Nelson Mandela, May 9.

Chapter 15

Tunisia 1981–2005:
In the Land of Ifriquia

Ifriquia—an Arabized name given to the northern coast of the African continent by the Romans, now known as Tunisia. Eventually the name Ifriquia (Africa) would be applied to the entire continent of Africa.

> Here in the histories of time and peoples
> Are lessons, the morals of which are followed by the just;
> I summarized all the books of the ancients
> And recorded what they omitted.
> I smoothed the methods of expression,
> As if they submitted to my will.
> - Ibn Khaldun, ode to accompany submission of his book,
>   the Prologema, to his patron, Sultan Abdul Abbas,
>   in 1382 A.D. (784 A.H.)

Tunisia first came onto my radar screen in the early 1980s, just as my consulting career was getting underway. I must admit that much of my fascination with that country has to do with its rich history. And, just as in the case of South Africa, I have had occasion to visit it at several intervals over time. In Ponca City, Oklahoma, when we talked about something 50 years old or more, it was REALLY old! Perhaps that explains to some extent my abiding interest in history: there was so little around me. I recall reading abridged versions of Homer's Iliad and Odyssey in the sixth grade and being spellbound. So I must be permitted to recount a bit of the history of Ifriquia, modern-day Tunisia. This ancient land has been occupied by Libyans, Moors, Numids and Berbers (derived, it is said, from the Roman word barbarus), as well as by Phoenicians, Arabs, Turks, Byzantines and the French. The Phoenicians first set up trading posts around 1100 B.C., and founded the city of Carthage in 814 B.C. Soon

Carthage even surpassed the Phoenician city of Tyre as the capital of a maritime empire that would extend across North Africa, Sicily and Sardinia, and into southern Spain by the third century B.C.

It is said that, viewed on a map, Tunisia resembles a beautiful woman who, stretched out to face the Mediterranean Sea, offers herself to the caresses of the waves and the songs of the wind. She is built solidly into the earth, anchored onto the continent with its plains, deserts and mountains. Tunisia is largely open to the sea on the north and east, with 1,300 kilometers of coastline, but is bordered on the south by a sea of sand. Geographically, economically and culturally, Ifriquia was at once African and Mediterranean and remains so today.

According to Homer's Odyssey Odysseus, king of the Greek city-state of Ithaca, directed his sailors to tie him to the ship's mast on his return home from the Trojan War so that he could enjoy the song of the sirens on the Island of Djerba (in modern-day Tunisia) without succumbing to them. (Ulysses is the Roman version of the Greek name Odysseus)

Mosaic of Ulysses in Bardo Museum

Carthage would find itself in competition with Rome, only a few hundred miles to the north, for control of Mediterranean commercial routes. In a series of epic conflicts known as the Punic Wars (between 264 and 146 B.C.) the two powers fought for supremacy of the seas. The hero of the Carthaginian forces was Hannibal, who made his mark on military history with his remarkable invasion of Italian cities with a battalion of elephants brought over the Alps from Spain. He came ever so close to spoiling Roman dreams of empire. However, Rome was the decisive winner in the conflict, eventually burning the city of Carthage to the ground and sowing it under with salt. But like the Phoenix, Carthage rose again, this time rebuilt as a Roman city. Most of the remains that are visible today date from the period when Rome ruled the Mediterranean for the next six centuries.

Although it took the followers of Mohammed only a few short decades to capture Syria, Mesopotamia, Iran and Egypt, it would take nearly 50 years for them to overcome Ifriquia, owing to stiff Berber resistance. Under the Umayyad Caliphs of Damascus, they established their first important base at Kairouan (variously spelled Qayrawan) just 50 miles inland from the coast in a hostile and uncertain environment. Founded by the Arabs on the same model as that of the Prophet in Medina, Kairouan would become the most important center of Islamic culture in the Maghreb, and the fourth most holy Muslim city in the world after Medina itself, Basra and Kufa in Iraq, and Fustat (ancient Cairo). The mission was to spread and enforce the word of Islam and the Arab way of life. Kairouan would also become a thriving commercial center as well for the next millennium. Today the Great Mosque of Kairouan testifies to its glorious past (Enan, 1991)

One of the earliest Muslim dynasties to establish itself after Mohammed was the Abbasids whose capital was Baghdad. Abbasid rule was maintained through a centralized bureaucracy and military force. Even when the Abbasid caliphate was at the height of its power, its effective rule was limited. Thus, local dynasties such as the Aghlabids (800-909 A.D.) grew up in Tunisia. In fact, the Aghlabids conquered Sicily and it remained under Muslim rule until the time of the Normans in the 11th century. Then in 910 A.D., claiming descent from Ali and Fatima, the Prophet's daughter, the Fatimids established themselves in the Maghreb, taking Kairouan. They moved eastward with their missionary activities and soon occupied Egypt, building an imperial city near Cairo, and extending their rule into Syria and western Arabia. Equally important was the spread of Islam into southern Spain, known by its Arabic name as Andalusia. This enterprise was undertaken by Arabs and Berbers together. Moorish civilization flourished there until the Spanish Inquisition drove non-Catholics out. However, the movement of Berbers from the Maghreb into Spain had continued longer than the Arab immigration from the east and was probably larger. Even to this day, many Tunisians can trace their family history and lineage to Andalusia. (Hourani, 1991)

Then the Ottomans emerged out of Turkey. The Ottoman Empire began its rise to dominance in 1453 when the Ottomans absorbed what was left of the Byzantine Empire and took Constantinople (Istanbul) as its new capital. In the Western Mediterranean the Ottomans used naval power to check Spanish expansion and established a chain of strong points at Algiers (1520s), Tripoli (1550s) and Tunis (1574). In Tunis direct Ottoman rule lasted only a short time. By the end of the 16th century lower level officers of the janissaries revolted, formed councils and elected a leader (dey) who then shared power with the governor. By the middle of the next century a third person, the bey, collector of rural taxes, seized a share of power. The beys were successful in tapping local roots and creating an alliance of interests with the population of Tunis, by then a city of considerable size and wealth. The Turco-Tunisian elites tended to become more Tunisian through intermarriage and had a common interest in controlling the countryside with its surplus agricultural production. Again, traces of Turkish influence are to be seen in the Tunisia of today.

Finally, came the French. The rise of French power in the region was signaled with their seizure of Algiers in 1830. A few years later French troops were dispatched to the Tunisian port of La Goulette to "protect" Tunisia against the Ottomans. In 1881, under the Treaty of Bardo, Tunisia was obliged to cede its sovereignty to France. A French resident general established a colonial administrative structure in Tunis, including the French model of education. By 1911 the French population in Tunisia amounted to 48,000, although there were twice as many Italians living there. Tunisian nationalist sentiment was manifested in the creation of the Destour movement created in 1920. A more radical Neo-Destourian group led by Habib Bourguiba was established in 1934. Tunisian independence from

France was officially recognized on March 20, 1956. Today, fifty years after independence, French influence is still pronounced in nearly all aspects of life in Tunisia.

Throughout its history Tunisia has been a mosaic of cultures and religions. After the destruction of the Temple of Jerusalem, Jews began arriving in Ifriqia. Some Berber tribes even converted to Judaism. The center of Jewish culture for many years was on the island of Djerba and the city of Tunis, although most Tunisian Jews have left the country. La Ghriba on the island of Djerba remains one of the oldest Jewish temples in the world. The Christian Church in North Africa produced some illustrious men of the Church such as Saints Augustine, Cyprian and Tertullian. Saint Augustine was born in 354 A.D. in Algeria but completed his studies in Carthage.

Among the most notable personages associated with Tunisia is the renowned historian and sociologist, Abd al Rahman Ibn Khaldun (1332-1406 A.D.). Known to us as simply Ibn Khaldun, he was born in Tunis on Ramadan into a prominent Andalusian family. His great grandfather had entered Andalusia with the Yemenite troops and settled in Seville. When the Christian kingdoms of northern Spain expanded southwards the family emigrated to Tunis, as did many Muslim families. Some genealogical accounts suggest that Ibn Khaldun was descended from one of the oldest Arab Yemenite tribes that had migrated into the Maghreb after the death of The Prophet. There is reason to doubt the authenticity of this genealogy, however, because of the rivalry and antagonism between the Arabs and Berbers in Andalusia. The Berbers took part in the conquest and bore the greatest burden, while the Arabs enjoyed authority and rule there. In fact, in his Prologemena Ibn Khaldun shows strong antagonism and prejudice toward the Arabs while praising the Berbers and extolling their virtues (Enan, 2000).

Ibn Khaldun's father had no time for politics, preferring to dedicate his life to the study of jurisprudence, philology and poetry. His father became Ibn Khaldun's first teacher; he learned to read the Qur'an as well as the Hadith, and studied grammar and rhetoric. He continued his studies until the age of 18 when North Africa was afflicted with the plague, a calamity that ravaged Italy and most other European countries as well. Not only did Ibn Khaldun's own parents succumb to the plague, many other notables and leaders of his community died. This was a period of violent political upheavals in North Africa characterized by numerous small states and principalities; thrones and emirates were constantly changing hands. Wars and civil conflicts raged between dynasties or branches of the same dynasty. It was under these circumstances that Ibn Khaldun began his public life. His family had lost much of its former influence and prosperity and he was determined to regain the family's lost prominence. His first appointment was in the post of Seal Bearer to a local Sultan; his job was to affix the cipher of the Sultan on royal correspondence and decrees.

Ibn Khaldun was a travlin' man. His career would find him traveling throughout the Maghreb region, from Fez to Bougie, Tlemcen and back to Tunis, serving first this Sultan or Emir and then that Vizier. He rapidly became one of the most outstanding personalities within the states of North Africa, still at a very young age. This did not keep Ibn Khaldun out of trouble, however. The intrigues of his enemies resulted in his being held in prison for two years, although when he was released he was restored to his former post and given favors. It seems that Ibn Khaldun was something of a Machiavellian, an opportunist who seized opportunities using all sorts of means. He did not hesitate to return evil for good. But then he was also a poet and authored many odes. He adopted the style and manner of the Sufi poets in his treatment of spiritual love.

The adventures of Ibn Khaldun would take him back to Andalusia for a time where the Sultan welcomed and honored him, inviting him to his private council. During this time Ibn Khaldun visited Seville and witnessed the vestiges of the family's ancestral home. He would spend a quarter of a century traveling back and forth across North Africa and to Andalusia, always engaged in political strife and intrigue. At the age of 45 he began to write his historical works while living in a small town west of Tunis. It was here in this distant, solitary place that Ibn Khaldun wrote his famous Prolegomena (Muqaddimat) during only a five-month period in 1377 A.D. In this work he tried to explain the rise and fall of dynasties in scientific terms. A ruler with a strong and coherent group of followers, he observed, could found a dynasty. When its rule was stable, this would lead to the development of populous cities with specialized crafts, luxurious ways of living and high culture.

Ibn Khaldun then went on to write a history of the Arabs and the Berbers, a history of the Barbary states. Political events in Tunis were such as to provide an opportunity for him to return to the city of his birthplace, thinking that he could at last dedicate his efforts to getting his works published. He submitted the manuscript to his patron Sultan Abdul Abbas in 1382 A.D., together with an ode of one hundred verses. But his tranquility was soon disturbed once again by political turmoil.

That same year Ibn Khaldun concluded his adventurous life in North Africa and set sail to the East, ostensibly on a pilgrimage, at the age of 52, still full of vigor. After a difficult voyage he arrived in Alexandria to join the pilgrims' caravan. He was unable to do this, however, and proceeded to Cairo, hoping to spend the rest of his life in Egypt in tranquility. At the time Cairo was the center of Muslim learning. Its court was widely reputed for its patronage of science and literature. Ibn Khaldun was dazzled by the grandeur and beauty of Cairo which far exceeded anything he had seen in North Africa. He was no stranger to Cairo, for his reputation preceded him there. He quickly settled in Cairo and began to lecture at the famous Al Azhar Mosque. His lectures dealt with his theories of society, the foundations of sovereignty, the rise and fall of states and other subjects in his Prolegomena.

My fascination with Ibn Khaldun has much to do with his autobiography, known as Al-Taarif. Not only was he a scholar of the first order, he considered that his own life was worthy of study and reflection. Al-Taarif fills about 100 pages of the seventh volume of his history, Kitab al-Ibar. Here he tells us of his lineage, the history of his family since its arrival in Andalusia and settlement in Seville till its emigration to North Africa. He then tells us of his youth, the books he read, even giving biographies of the professors who taught him. He speaks of his public life and his relations with Sultans and Emirs, relating events right up until a few months before his death. His writings reveal elements of pride, fondness for intrigue, opportunism, as well as strength of character.

But because Ibn Khaldun lived in an age when decay had already crept into the heart of Islam, and Islamic thought had already begun to decline, his legacy would remain in oblivion for centuries, unknown to both the East and the West. Not until the 19th century was there a resurgence of interest in his work amongst Western scholars. More than a century after the death of Ibn Khaldun, Niccolo Machiavelli wrote The Prince, a book that would occupy the same high place in Western thought that the Prologomena occupies in Islamic thought. In our new-found awareness of our relative ignorance of the Muslim world, we Westerners would do well to study its origins and rich history, including the contribution of Ibn Khaldun's life and writings.

— — -

It was early in my career as a management consultant, in May 1981, when the USAID/Tunisia mission informed AID/Washington of its plans to conduct end-of-project evaluations of three participant training projects: Agricultural Economic Research and Planning, Education Economics and Management Education. Because of the similarity of project purpose and projected outputs among the three project components, USAID proposed that they be evaluated simultaneously. The first part of the evaluation would take place in the United States and include an examination of the perception of the U.S. universities toward the projects. The second part would be contracted to a local Tunisian consulting firm and focus on the degree to which the projects achieved their stated purposes. It was agreed that the order in which the two parts would be carried out should be reversed. Hence, the field evaluation began on November 23, 1981, in Tunis and the U.S. portion was conducted in late December/early January 1982.

The USAID Mission contracted with El Amouri Institute of Tunis to be primarily responsible for the Tunisia portion of the evaluation. The Institute, under the direction of Dr. Tahar el Amouri, was a private consulting firm in Tunis specializing in applied psychology and organizational development, and as such was among the country's pioneering management consulting firms. Members of the El Amouri staff had recently completed an evaluation of Save the Children activities in Tunisia and also evaluated a rural development project.

The Tunisia Mission requested that AID/Washington seek the services of an Indefinite Quantity Contractor to be responsible for the U.S. portion of the evaluation. I had recently joined an international development consulting firm in Falls Church, Virginia, on a full time basis. And I happened to have French language facility, one of the prime requisites for the assignment. My firm thus volunteered for the job. I would soon learn that "billability" counts for quite a bit among consulting firms.

Upon arrival in Tunis on a grey drizzly day, I met with the Mission program officer and Dr. Tahar El Amouri. The mission agreed that El Amouri would submit its own report on the in-country portion of the evaluation; its findings and recommendations were then to be incorporated into a final report for which the U.S. consultant would be responsible. I was to work with Messrs. Ben Ammar and el Amouri. We used the El Amouri Institute office on Rue Hijaz as our base of operations. The first few days were spent getting acquainted and devising an interview schedule. It was clear from the outset that there was good chemistry among us in terms of personality, professional standards and especially the desire to make the evaluation a team effort. Whenever possible, interviews were conducted by two evaluators, one American and one Tunisian. At the end of each day we met at the Institute and discussed the activities of the day and reviewed plans for the following day. Since there were three different projects being examined at the same time, the team was able to adopt a comparative methodology. There were three main Tunisian institutions assisted under the projects and three U.S. contracting universities.

The evaluation took place several years after the three projects had ceased to receive AID funding, although some of the individual participants were receiving assistance until recently. The USAID/ Tunisia mission no longer had any participant training projects in higher education. The purpose of the evaluation was to measure the effectiveness of U.S.-financed inputs toward achieving the purpose of the projects. The two University of Tunis projects aimed at introducing modern business and economic principles into the curriculum. The Ministry of Agriculture project aimed at developing effective agriculture sector policies to achieve sustained agricultural growth.

The evaluation examined three participant training projects funded by the USAID Mission from 1967 to 1978. The first two were managed by the University of Minnesota and the third by the University of Illinois. Each of the projects aimed at increasing the institutional capabilities of the Government of Tunisia in the realm of education and agriculture. They each involved the training of Tunisians in the U.S. at the graduate level and technical assistance of

U.S. professors in Tunisia. The Agricultural Economic Research and Planning project was originally developed in 1966 following a survey of agriculture in Tunisia. The original project agreement was signed in 1967, and a contract between AID and the University of Minnesota was signed for an initial period of 10 years, although funding was extended through FY 1980. The purpose of the project was to assist the Ministry of Agriculture to develop a central institutional capacity, principally in the Division for Planning, Statistics and Economic Analysis, and for planning development programs. It was anticipated that 25 Tunisians would be trained to the M.S. level and up to five to the Ph.D. level in agricultural economics and employed in the Ministry. By 1978 there were 22 Tunisians trained to the M.S. level; seven were still studying in the U.S. Two participants who had received M.S. degrees had returned to the U.S. for Ph.D. training.

The education economics project was the second portion of the contract signed in 1967 between the University of Minnesota and AID to assist the University of Tunis by providing short-term staff on assignment in Tunisia. Its purpose was to offer seminars in such subjects as econometrics, agricultural economics and public finance, also to train Tunisian students in economics at the University of Minnesota. The Faculty of Law and Economics offered a four-year program of studies in economics and business administration leading to a license degree (B.A. or B.S.). At the time the project was initiated, students could choose between two options: management/business administration and planning. The only Tunisian Professor of Economics was also Dean of the Faculty. The other economics faculty members were still technically graduate students, completing their doctoral dissertations in French universities.

The economics education project aimed at training a total of 18 Tunisians to the level of Ph.D. in economics. The first group of six students was sent to the U.S. in 1969 and the final group went in 1972. According to the University of Minnesota's final report on the project in 1978, of the total of 18 students who went to the U.S. under the project, eight had completed their Ph.D. degree, two terminated at the M.A. level, one was deceased, two returned to Tunisia before completing the M.A., and the remaining six were still working on the Ph.D.

An evaluation conducted in 1971 observed that the quality of teaching performed by the contractor's staff was "outstanding" and that USAID was satisfied with Minnesota's procedure for selecting high caliber students for training in the U.S.

The contract signed between AID and the University of Illinois in June 1968 provided for technical advice and assistance requested by Tunisia to develop a graduate school of business in Tunisia. The contractor, through its College of Commerce and Business Administration, agreed to assist in a long-term program of management education and development of Tunisia's public and private enterprises. In 1970 the Tunisian government separated the purely academic activities and assigned them to a newly established Institut Superieur de Gestion (ISG)—the Institute for Advanced Management Studies. Established as a graduate school of business within the University of Tunis, ISG was the first such institution in North Africa. The primary focus of all contract activity was placed on the development of a viable graduate program equivalent to an MBA in U.S. universities.

The objectives of the project were to assist in the planning needs of ISG, help plan management seminars for middle-level managers and to assist in the selection and training of Tunisians in graduate management education in the U.S. In July 1974, the direct contribution to the operation of the ISG University of Illinois was terminated, as the last member of the contract team left Tunisia. From 1974 to 1978, the contractor continued to assist ISG by furnishing the services of short-term consultants, assistance in the selection and procurement of books for the ISG library and the continued counseling of Tunisian graduate students in the U.S.

The first cohort of a two-year MBA program was admitted to ISG in the fall of 1969, with half of the classes being taught by the University of Illinois contract team. During the period of the contract, three new four-year undergraduate programs in business were begun: one within the Economics Department of the University of Tunis, an independent institute at Sfax, and the undergraduate program at ISG itself. By 1977 ISG had an enrollment of 700 students; the graduate program had an enrollment of 96, with an average of 15 to 30 graduates per year. By the end of the contract period, the contractor had assisted in the selection and placement of some 25 Tunisian students in American graduate institutions. Of these, 17 completed a Master's Degree and seven completed a Ph.D. There were six students still working on their doctorates in the U.S.

Our conclusions—drawn from interviews with participants, Tunisian authorities and U.S. university contract personnel—were generally positive. The Tunisian participants selected for training in the U.S. were of generally high caliber and performed well in their studies, especially in quantitative and analytic subjects. They enjoyed a generally favorable academic and personal experience in the United States. They expressed a high degree of appreciation for the U.S. system of education, its practical approach to problem solving and emphasis on efficiency. However, only half of the participants had returned to work in their home institutions. We concluded that the three projects taken together had had a modest but tangible effect on Tunisian institutions.

The education management project had the most pronounced effect because gestion—management—was widely considered an "American" discipline. The project thus contributed to the establishment of North Africa's first graduate business school. The economics education project had the least impact because it trained fewer participants and had the smallest technical assistance component. Still, the French model of economics was being challenged and a U.S. curriculum was taking root. The agricultural research and planning project faced the greatest resistance to institutional change.

Not noted in our evaluation, however, was the extent to which Tunisian participants who did NOT return to their home institutions were back in Tunisian and were involved in private sector activities. This was the pre-Reagan era, a period before the private sector in developing countries had been discovered. Some of those we interviewed were working in banks while others had started their own companies or gone to work in family-owned enterprises. In our matrix these participants were "no-shows" who had failed to live up to the objectives of the USAID program by returning to their host institutions. Within a few years privatization and private sector development were all the rage, and the Tunisia participant training project might have been favorably evaluated for its serendipitous private sector results!

— — —

Fast Forward to 2003: Tunisia Revisited

In my capacity as Director of the Office of International Business Programs at Tennessee State University, I traveled to Tunis with my Tunisian graduate assistant, Anis Mnif, in June 2003 to complete the preparation of a grant application for a partnership between TSU and the University of Tunis el Manar. We met with the President of the University as well as the Public Affairs Officer of the U.S. Embassy, responsible for overseeing university linkages in Tunisia. The result was a proposal, entitled Building University Capacity for Participation in the Global Marketplace and submitted to USAID under its Middle East Partnership Initiative program, on June 30, 2003. It was inspired by direct personal contact of the principals of both partners, culminating in the inauguration of the latter's new incubator facility, MANARTECH, in Tunis on June 27, 2003.

We submitted a proposal to the U.S. State Department's Bureau of Educational and Cultural Affairs in December 2003. The solicitation was specifically aimed at linkages between U.S. universities and institutions in Muslim countries. The proposed partnership sought to enhance the capacity of the partner universities to prepare students for careers in business and technology through collaboration with the business community. It addressed Tunisian higher education objectives, with a focus on providing practical educational and business experience for advanced graduate students and faculty. It aimed at increasing private sector employment of Tunisian university students. The principal vehicle for the partnership was to be the business incubators within each partner institution. In our proposal we noted that the Tunisian government was committed to improving the "employability" of young people through an Enterprise-University partnership. The government perceived both an opportunity and a challenge in the new global economy, a chance to excel in the post-industrial era, characterized by an information-age economy. In these open global markets Tunisians would play an important role, thanks to their high competence and skills. Employability and the ability to adapt to the global economy would constitute a new focus in the rehabilitation of the Tunisian educational system.

The partnership would enhance the managerial and technical

capacity of both partner institutions through a faculty and student exchange involving the development of enterprise incubators, practical internships, curriculum development and collaborative research. We proposed a practical approach that would engage students and faculty in working with local businesses, enhancing their understanding of free market systems and the significance of globalization.

In September 2004, the Bureau of Educational and Cultural Affairs of the U.S. Department of State notified TSU that its application for a linkage grant under the Bureau's Educational Partnership Program had been approved for funding! The grant program was for $194,000 over a period of three years. The proposed partnership aimed at promoting mutual understanding between two diverse cultures and educational systems. A former French colony, Tunisia was still strongly influenced by French customs, culture and its educational system. At the same time, it was an Arabic-speaking country with strong cultural and political ties to the Arab world. From the U.S. point of view, partnering with a Tunisian institution should afford insight and awareness into two cultures—Arab and French—at the same time. Tunisia remained a country about which Americans seem to be uninformed.

The proposal addressed educational reform and economic development in Tunisia. The Tunisian government had elaborated a statement of priorities in the higher education sector in Tunisia. The government was committed to reinforcing this approach and making it concrete. Toward this end, an Enterprise-University partnership was established to allow Tunisian youngsters to be better prepared for active life. A training system was formed at all levels aimed at facilitating the interactions between educational and economic institutions In order to reinforce interactions and continuity between the school and the firm, Tunisia proposed the creation of enterprise incubators at training establishments that would offer a suitable environment in which to prepare students for professional life. Private sector investment in cultural and informational fields is to be encouraged in the form of partnerships and new innovative technology firms. One of the first incubators (known as MANARTECH) was established within University of Tunis el Manar on the campus, drawing upon multidisciplinary resources of the University to promote start-up businesses and offer students an environment in which to develop entrepreneurship (http://www.mes.tn//priorite).

The TSU-Tunisia partnership would afford TSU faculty and graduate students an opportunity for an international experience. Outcomes from the exchange would include new and revised academic curricula, collaborative case studies and thesis papers of graduate students. Those who participated in the exchange would have been introduced to another culture, improved their foreign language and cross cultural skills and gained practical experience in a foreign environment. Exchanges were proposed to promote the development of the enterprise incubator in Tunisia and to expand the horizons of the TSU incubator facility. University of Tunis had recently initiated a new Specialized Masters Degree Program, drawing upon the resources of MANARTECH. The Tennessee Valley Authority (TVA) business incubator system, of which the TSU facility is a member, has made a valuable contribution to economic growth in the Tennessee Valley.

Tunisia Itinerary June 2005

My June 2005 Tunisia itinerary would evolve into something unforeseen and unprecedented; it became a family affair. My parents had generally viewed my world travel with puzzlement, if not disapproval, wondering what it was all about. My siblings, on the other hand, had themselves evolved into world travelers in their own right. But we had never undertaken international trips together. Then, at Thanksgiving 2004 on sister Judy's ranch, I casually mentioned that I might be returning to Tunisia the following summer. At the same time, brother Kurt, by now a habitual traveler himself, responded that he might be in Italy about the same time. I reminded him how close Italy and Tunisia were to each other and suggested that he try to work a few days of North Africa into his vacation plans. The seeds were apparently planted, although they would lie dormant without much nurturing for several months.

Kurt is the steady one in the family, holding down the same job for his entire adult life and rising to become a partner in a prominent Houston architectural firm. On several occasions in recent years he and his wife Terri had integrated vacation time into his business trips to Italy where he sourced marble for his construction projects. Sometime in the spring of 2005 Kurt informed me that he and his

16-year-old son Nick would join me in Tunisia. It then remained for us to work out exact dates and an in-country itinerary.

Meanwhile, Judy had also begun to make noises about coming to Tunisia. She is a West Texas rancher and retired high school teacher, with substitute teaching duties whenever she makes herself available. Thus, self-employed, Judy would not have to fill out a request for annual leave! She would simply have to consult her calendar and bank account. Her 90-acre Rambling Oaks Ranch outside of Granbury has been the venue of numerous family gatherings, and is now becoming the venue for occasions such as weddings and other special events. For several years Judy had traveled abroad each summer with teacher colleagues. (Notable quote: "We saw more sheep than people in New Zealand!") And then, much to my surprise, Judy announced that she had invited her daughter Kari to join the Tunisia caravan. Kari, an interior designer in Dallas, would round out the Gang of Four. Eh, voila, toute un group!

Our travel plans took on the aspect of another project. What I needed in order to make the trip happen was an expert logistics manager, translator, booking agent and all-round macher. Anis Mnif fit that bill to a T. I had evidence of that from our two previous trips to Tunisia together. So I appointed him Director of Operations. As soon as the June dates for our business appointments at the University of Tunis el Manar were fixed, Anis set to work going through his family connections in Tunis to get reduced hotel and rental car rates. Anis would serve as our chauffeur and tour guide, and would attend to the minutest of details to make the trip enjoyable. Our itinerary would take us nearly the entire length of the country, first along the eastern coast, then into the edge of the desert in the south to the outpost of Tataouine, and back into the interior through Kairouan. It was a most ambitious plan for less than a week!

Tunis   *Wednesday June 8*

I arrived in Tunis shortly before Anis and went straight to the Sheraton Hotel near the campus. Chiheb Bouden, our Project Coordinator at the University, came to my hotel room in the evening and we discussed the very tight schedule we would have for the next two days.

Tunis   *Thursday, June 9*

Anis rented a car and in the morning arrived at the Sheraton to pick me up. We would spend most of the day at Ecole Nationale d'Ingenieur de Tunis (ENIT), interviews with MBA candidates and faculty members, sketching out partnership activities for the six months to come. In the evening the Mnif family hosted me at a La Marsa seaside restaurant, by now a familiar ritual on my visits to Tunisia. In my short sleeved shirt, I noticed that the air was surprisingly cool for this time of year. Lassard, the oldest brother, is an entrepreneur, owner-manager of a computer firm. Sana, the younger sister, works in a bank. A fourth Mnif sibling lives in Japan. Madame Mnif, a teacher by profession, has raised the four children by herself since the untimely death of their father when they were still quite young. By any measure, she has done a remarkable job. We chose from the usual array of fresh fish straight from the sea, dipped our bread in the spicy harissa sauce, and settled in for a pleasant evening of fellowship.

At the Mnif Home in Tunis with Anis, Sana & Mdme. Mnif

Tunis   *Friday, June 10*

Judy and Kari arrived in Tunis via Paris as scheduled at 10:00 AM and were met my Anis at the airport. I was busy at ENIT conducting interviews. Their lodging was at the Residence Tunis, a luxury hotel in Gammarth. The northern stretch of Tunisian coastland running from historic Carthage to Sidi bou Said and La Marsa eventually turns into Gammarth, consisting of mile after mile of luxury hotels offering spectacular views of the Mediterranean. Although Residence Tunis is a five-star hotel of international standing in the elegant traditional Arabesque style, Anis had negotiated a handsome discount, which made our stay there especially enjoyable. Judy, Kari and I sampled the Tunisian-grown Vieux Magnon wine and listened to a Spanish group of musicians in the lounge, while Anis went off to be with his family for the evening. Judy and Kari were already gushing with oohs and aahs over the ambiance.

Sousse   Saturday, June 11

The four of us enjoyed a leisurely breakfast at La Plaisance on Sidi bou Said Beach. As if to establish the prime importance that food would occupy during the trip, we enjoyed a typical meal of cous cous in a restaurant overlooking the plaza followed by a brief tour of the Tunis Medina. We were off to a good start! Fine dining would be the signature feature of our whirlwind tour of Tunisia. Then we were off on our journey, driving eastward through the industrial section of Tunis and heading for the coastal town of Sousse, some 80 miles south and east. As we drove through the countryside we saw droves of olive trees on both sides of the road, easily the commonest sight in the course of our travel. The roads were in excellent condition and the traffic reasonable.

Any worries Judy and Kari may have had about proper attire for women were quickly dispelled. Indeed, the European invasion of Tunisia has lowered the bar in terms of proper dress. We could just as well have been on Miami Beach or Malibu. This is not to say that Tunisians have bought into the contemporary standards. But European tourists, thirsty for sun and sea, account for a sizeable chunk of Tunisia's foreign exchange earnings. Fair is fair: while the Tunisians flock to France for university education, shopping in Paris, or to eventually become French citizens, the French and their European ilk flock to Tunisian beaches and hotels.

In keeping with his commitment to a full tourist agenda, our Director of Operations had arranged for the four of us to dine at a restaurant on a fisherman's wharf that evening. It seemed that we had just finished a substantial lunch at the Port. Despite its rough exterior, The Pirates lived up to its exotic billing on the inside, with a mural motif of pirate ships, fierce swashbuckling pirates and treasure chests. It was a fixed-price fare that featured an endless number of courses. Just as we thought we had seen the last course, another one arrived at the table: hors d'oeurves, an assortment of seafood, the ever-present cous cous, and of course a bouquet of deserts. Finally I motioned to the waiter to make sure that I got the bill. He disappeared into the crowded room. When I got up to check again I was informed that it had already been paid. Anis was up to his sneaky ways, using his unfair cultural advantage to pick up the tab behind our backs. This is a distinctly Tunisian—perhaps I should say non-American—pattern of behavior. We Americans can quibble endlessly over who had what and how much each one owes toward the bill, scribbling figures on a napkin. In the Tunisian context this would amount to a cultural faux pas of the first order. We would simply have to get smarter about being able to beat Anis to the punch!

Sousse to Djerba Island   Sunday, June 12

Strangely enough, we began to experience precipitation at Port El Kantaoui, not anything like a tropical downpour but a persistent— and welcome—drizzle. It was mid-summer in the Mediterranean and cloudless blue skies are normally the order of the day this time of year. We had not packed umbrellas! The rains would follow us to Djerba where we would witness several showers. Our Director of Operations left El Kantaoui early in the morning to return to the Tunis airport to meet Kurt and Nick, and to exchange the compact car for a four-wheel drive SUV. With our bags packed, we waited outside the hotel reception area. There was a steady stream of vehicles surging through the narrow entrance to Port El Kantaoui. About mid-afternoon, Anis appeared in a shiny black SUV with Kurt and Nick, completing our entourage. After re-arranging the luggage onto the top of the vehicle, we headed southward toward Djerba.

The first stop was at El Djem, some 30 miles south and west of Sousse. Even at a distance of some eight or nine miles the ancient Roman amphitheater rose up out of the flat land, peering at us through the myriad of olive trees. Built during the reign of Emperor Gordian from 230 to 238 A.D. during Roman occupation of Tunisia, the amphitheater was among the largest such structures in the empire, comparable to the Coliseum in Rome. It accommodated some 45,000 spectators who came to witness gladiators and other forms of entertainment. Today the remains of this magnificent edifice are the site of outdoor cultural events. A gentleman with a camel at the entrance to the ampitheater was more than willing to have us climb aboard his noble steed for a photo opportunity.

Hulls in the Bowels of El Djem with guide Anis

Anis shows us how to mount a camel at El Djem

Next stop was Monastir, another historic port city featuring a ribat (fortress) constructed by an Abbasid general shortly after the Arab arrival in Ifriquia. Monastir is the birthplace and hometown of the first Tunisian President, Habib Bourguiba. We arrived there in late afternoon and Anis drove around to a parking area behind a large esplanade leading to a very imposing structure in the middle of a traditional cemetery with small plots. It turned out that this was the mausoleum of the revered President, covering far more ground than the rest of the cemetery altogether. There was a tall fence surrounding the mausoleum, guarded by an austere looking watchman, and no other visitors were within sight. It was long past the official visiting hours. Anis told us to wait for him as he approached the guard and chatted with him. He then motioned for us to come to the gate, which the guard then opened for us. We wandered through the mausoleum housing memorabilia from Bourguiba's long life, feeling that at any moment we might be arrested for trespassing.

It was nearly dusk as we arrived in Sfax, home town of the

Mnif family. Sfaxians are known throughout Tunisia as being hard-working, industrious and entrepreneurial. A Sfaxian family name is readily identifiable anywhere in the country. It had been quite some time since Anis had been back to Sfax, and he wasn't sure where we could find a good restaurant. We were all hungry and tired, saddle-sore from several hours of riding. The solution, as was often the case, was a cell phone call, this time to Anis' brother Lassard, who gave directions to what was surely the best place in town. Soon we were in an elegant old restaurant with wood paneled walls, spiffy tablecloths, excellent service and wonderful food. We were just across the street from the Sfax medina, among the oldest in Tunisia.

But the day was not over by any means. We pushed on southward along the coast, past Gabes toward our destination. Djerba was still 254 kilometers south of Sfax. It was already late at night as we arrived at Ajim where a ferry boat provides transport across the Bay of Gabes to the island. We waited in a long line of vehicles for what seemed like forever for the next ferry. The Ulysses finally came and took us on a 30-minute cruise to the other side, seagulls taking advantage of its floodlights by diving into the bay to snag unsuspecting fish. Anis drove on through the night, and all that we could perceive was an occasional village interspersed with olive trees and scrub brush.

Anis checked periodically on his cell phone with his local contact. In the town of Midoun a man in a Mercedes met us and we followed him. It was like a scene out of Mission Impossible, but we were all road-weary and ready for bed. As it turns out, within a few miles of Midoun, the entire eastern coast of Djerba is covered with a range of luxury hotels side by side, with names like Jasmine, Le Ksar, Cedria, Al Diana, Meridiana, Djerba la Douce and Djerba Orient. Finally, there we were, pulling into the Dar Djerba, a massive club complex of hotels and restaurants that would be our home for two days. The man in the Mercedes, the manager of the Dar Djerba, welcomed us and we followed him to the receptionist. Testimony to the consummate logistics skills of the Director of Operations!

Djerba Island   *Monday, June 13*

The island has gone by various spellings: Jerba (French), Djerba (Arabic), and Meninx (Phoenician). In the morning, after a deep sleep, we awoke to find that our three-bedroom suite was directly facing the Mediterranean, its waves gently lapping against the beach. Djerba is a fairly big island off the southern coast of Tunisia, exceptional in that there are few islands along the coast of North Africa from Morocco to Egypt. The island is a little world of its own, distinct from the rest of the country and notable for the profusion of palm trees. The topography of Djerba is flat, except for the modest hill at Guellala from which the Museum looks out over the island. The island is dotted with small villages here and there, each telling its own story. It is known for its flourishing arboriculture, vineyards, fruit production and pottery workshops associated with the export of olive oil. Djerba is known for its unique cotton textile designs.

The tourist life on Djerba Island features hordes of Europeans as well as a handful of neighboring Libyans and others. Djerba beaches are renowned for the fact that European women have the habit of going topless. It was just our luck that the weather was cloudy and cool, so there were few people on the beaches at all. In fact, we spent no time on the beach since our sight-seeing agenda was so charged. The only town of any consequence on the island is Houmt Souq, quite different from any other Tunisian town south of Sidi Bou Said. One of the prominent features of the town is its funduqs (traditional hotels) that have housed visitors for hundreds of years. As its name would imply, Houmt Souq also features numerous traditional markets (souks) and outdoor cafes, mostly catering to tourists. We wandered around through the pottery shops and boutiques where I bought Mani some coral jewelry. We visited several carpet stores where women were weaving on the traditional hand looms. Kurt was interested in buying carpets so we were directed to a shop with a full range of choices. Anis was there, as usual, to do the bargaining.

I was personally intrigued by what I had read about the rich Jewish history on the Island of Djerba. The first day we drove to the little town of Hara Sghira, home of the modest Jewish community. According to oral tradition, towards the middle of the sixth century B.C., a group of Jewish refugees fled Jerusalem after the destruction of the first Temple. They found Djerba a congenial place to propagate their faith. The Ghriba synagogue, cornerstone of the Jewish community, was built 1400 years ago although the present buildings are no more than 75 years old. It is said that the inner sanctuary of the synagogue contains one of the oldest Torahs anywhere in the world. Although the Jewish population of Djerba has dwindled to a few hundred, Ghriba remains the destination of an annual pilgrimate of many Tunisian Jews after the celebration of Passover.

Kurt Shopping for a Carpet in Djerba

Judy and Kari Carpet Shopping in Djerba

Djerba, Matmata, Tataouine   *Tuesday, June 14*

Our tour of Tunisia took us to one of the southern-most parts of the country, to Matmata and Tataouine. This area becomes more rugged, mountainous and less populated. It is the land of qsurs, the Saharan plateau, inhabited by Berber people who have lived in harmony with the earth since time immemorial. History records numerous Berber revolts against Roman domination, then with the Arabs. But eventually they took on the Muslim faith and much of Arab culture. The people of the Matmata area founded their villages on a slate-alluvial massif and they built their houses in accordance with their environment. Their unique troglodyte dwellings look like wells dug to depths often reaching as much as 20-30 feet. One enters a house via a subterranean corridor, which has a slight slope. A widening of the tunnel allows for the stabling of camels and other animals. From there one is led out into a central courtyard where there is a tank built to collect water. The kitchen and bedrooms also open out onto the courtyard. The rooms have streamlined ceilings that are designed to prevent mud slides. The walls are whitewashed with lime and the ground is covered with a plaster coating, making the rooms bright. The highlight of Matmata and Tataouine was our visit to the location of the filming of Star Wars, George Lucas' desert planet of Tattooine, home of Skywalkers. While not a big Star Wars fan, I could readily imagine this as the exotic location of a film set.

The very name Tataouine evokes the end of the world. During the French colonial rule it served as a major military base. The road going south from Tataouine leads to the borders of Algeria on the one side and Libya on the other. It leads eventually to the vast expanse of the Sahara Desert and beyond. It was time for us to turn around and head back toward Tunis.

Djerba to Kairouan via Gabes   June 15, 2005

Our return to Tunis took us back through Gabes to an outlying oasis. Hard to imagine while driving through the arid brown steppes, the lush green grove of palm trees appeared as though it was a mirage. We had lunch in a delightful outdoor restaurant setting under bright blue and white porticoes, adjacent to the oasis. After lunch we drove further into the greenery. Interspersed among the palm trees was an extensive system of gardens planted with every type of vegetable and fruit imaginable: garlic, squash, lettuce, chilies, tomatoes, beans, rice and grape vines. Anis had to show off his skills by shimmying up a date palm tree. And then we were once again back on the road.

It was nearing dusk, and we were heading back to Tunis with a view toward seeing Kairouan on the way. The Great Mosque of Kairouan, built centuries ago, rose up out of the steppes to greet us as the sun was setting.

In its heyday Kairouan was one of the largest centers of textile, ceramic and pottery fabrication in North Africa. Its population rivaled that of other great commercial cities such as Cordoba and Seville. With its medina and ramparts fully restored, its numerous mosques, mausoleums and other monuments, Kairouan is of obvious historical and religious interest. Today, however, Kairouan is more of a living museum than a commercial center or tourist attraction. It does not abound with hotels and villas as does El Kantaoui just a few miles away. We went on a brief tour of the carpet weaving operations and visited typical historic homes around the mosque. With several hundred kilometers under our belt, we were all by now ready to bring an end to our four-day safari. Amazing how much we had managed to cram into a few days!

Tunis   *June 16, 2005*

This, our last day in Tunisia, was devoted to more conventional tourism in and around the city of Tunis, including a tour of the Bardo Museum and the Tunis medina (covered market place). For a change, we were not spending much of the day on the road! We took in the Carthage Museum and of course Sidi bou Said, the most popular tourist site in Tunisia overlooking the Mediterranean. In the evening we were joined for dinner at La Falaise Restaurant by the Mnif siblings. What a rewarding way to end a vacation! We went around the table toasting our friendship; each of us introduced ourselves, telling vignettes from our past.

Tunis   *Friday, June 17*

Judy & Kari departed Tunis for Paris on an early morning flight while Kurt and Nick left for Italy. I headed for South Africa via Paris and London.

———

References

Enan, Mohammad Abdullah (2000) *Ibn Khaldun: His Life and Works*, New Delhi: Kitab Bhavan.

Hourani, Albert (1991) *A History of the Arab Peoples*, Cambridge, MA: The Belknap Press of Harvard University Press.

Hull, Galen Spencer, (1982) "Evaluation of Three Projects in Agricultural Economics Research & Planning, Education Economics, and Management Education in Tunisia," submitted to USAID Tunisia, February 19.

Museum with No Frontiers, (2002) *Ifriquiya: Thirteen Centuries of Art and Architecture in Tunisia: Islamic Art in the Mediterranean,* published by the Tunisian Ministry of Culture and Secretariat of the *Musee sans Frontieres.*

Tennessee State University (2003) "Proposal for a Partnership between Tennessee State University and University of Tunis El Manar, Tunis, Tunisia," proposal submitted to the Bureau of Educational and Cultural Affairs, Educational Partnerships Program (ECA/A/S/U-04-03), U.S. Department of State, FY 2004, December 12.

U.S. State Department, *Background Notes,* April 2002.

Chapter 16

Central and Eastern Europe, 1996–2003: Raising of the Iron Curtain

Slava Ukrainyi!..Heroim slava! (Long live Ukraine...and its heroes!)
- A popular Ukrainian call and response, honoring those millions who died during the Soviet occupation that prefigured the Orange Revolution.

In 1989, the infamous Iron Curtain began to tumble down on the Communist empire of the Soviet Union and its satellites. You might say that it was the reverse domino effect. During the Cold War, the U.S. and its allies feared that if one Third World country became Communist this would trigger a domino effect in which neighboring countries would also succumb to that pernicious system. In truth, with the fall of the Berlin Wall in 1989, it was just the opposite that happened. The countries of Central and Eastern Europe that had been under the thrall of the Kremlin began wriggling away toward the West.

In 1996 my life as a consultant entered an entirely new dimension: commitment to work in Central and Eastern Europe, a region hitherto off my geographic radar screen. Faithful to my trade as a consultant, when the call came to work on a new contract—in the absence of any others—I accepted the assignment. The call was from Felipe Tejeda, a good man whom I knew from the consulting network as a fellow ex-Peace Corps Volunteer. As a veteran consultant, I tended to give ex-Volunteers rather more credence than others since we shared a common experience. While I liked Felipe and was interested in the assignment with which he approached me, I knew nothing of the firm he represented. Felipe described the contract he was working under and indicated that the firm, Datex, Inc., was looking to complete the composition of an evaluation team to look into a project in Central and Eastern Europe.

Under the SEED Act of 1990, the U.S. Congress had seized the opportunity to exploit the misfortune of the Soviets and directed that funds to Central and Eastern Europe be targeted to develop skills required for the emergence of a market economy, to include banking, finance, accounting, economics, management and agribusiness. The Management Training for Economics and Enterprise Project (MTEEP) was established under the Europe and Newly Independent States Bureau of the U.S. Agency for International Development (USAID) to promote institutional linkages between U.S. universities and those in the region to undertake short term management training and to upgrade long-term economics education. By 1995, the countries participating in the project included Albania, Bulgaria, the Czech Republic, Hungary, Macedonia, Poland, Romania and Slovakia. Eventually the Baltic states of Latvia and Lithuania were added.

Bratislava, Slovakia   October 21-26, 1996

The Datex contract was for the provision of technical services for monitoring and evaluation of project activities. Within a few days after signing my contract, Felipe and I were on the way to conduct site visits in Slovakia, Hungary and Romania. The first stop was Bratislava, Slovakia—erstwhile home of Austro-Hungarian Emperor Maria Theresa. Our site visit was to evaluate the partnership activities of the University of Pittsburgh's Katz School of Business in that country. Pittsburgh signed its cooperative agreement with the USAID Mission in Slovakia in October 1995, providing funding for three years. The Mission's program was focused on one of its Strategic Objectives, the accelerated development and growth of private enterprises, including strengthening the ability of local institutions to provide business training and assistance. Under the agreement, Pittsburgh entered into partnership with the Economic University of Bratislava which had been identified by the USAID Mission. Pittsburgh was managing activities that consisted of a three-year weekend MBA program, a full-time one-year MBA program and a post-doctoral program in economics education.

Our visit to Bratislava followed a spring 1996 evaluation team visit in which certain problems in the relationship between Pittsburgh and its partner institution had been identified. Our mission was to assess progress made in resolving those issues. We found that Pittsburgh was still encountering great difficulties in setting up the MBA program. There were numerous unresolved issues having to do with the Slovak university's participation in the partnership. The University itself was experiencing political pressure from increased governmental control over the system of higher education. At issue was the continued Pittsburgh partnership, and whether Pittsburgh would identify a new partnership. It did not take the Datex team evaluation report, however, for Pittsburgh to decide that it should sever ties with the Economic University of Bratislava and establish a new and more productive one with another University in Bratislava.

Budapest, Hungary   *October 26—November 2, 1996*

From Bratislava, Felipe and I traveled by train to Budapest for a site visit to Budapest, seat of the Austro-Hungarian empire. There we first met with the staff of the AID Representative to Hungary and the two MTEEP grantee institutions, the State University of New York and Indiana University. We interviewed a sampling of faculty, administrators and past participants of the partner institutions in Hungary. The Kelly School of Business of the University of Indiana and the Budapest University of Economic Sciences had worked together on various cooperative ventures in management training since 1989. Relations between Indiana and Budapest were initially established under MUCIA, a university consortium of which Indiana University is a member. In recent years Budapest University had played an important role in providing managerial leadership for the transition of Hungary from a centrally planned economy to market economy. The Management Development Center (MDC), the University's flagship program, was one of the leading providers of management training and consulting programs in Hungary. MDC was an executive education center providing an MBA program designed and run together with the London Business School.

In 1990, Indiana University was chosen to deliver a program for high-level managers in Hungary by a select group of multinational firms, including AT&T, Amoco and Dow Chemical. At the request of the partner companies, an international partnership program was added in 1994. In 1995, Indiana began implementation of a four-year grant from USAID under MTEEP to assist MDC. Together the two universities designed a program known as MATCH—Management Training Cooperation in Hungary—to develop MDC as a role model for advanced, client-driven management programs. The MATCH Program was placed under the direction of MDC.

At the time of our site visit in Hungary, Indiana was still struggling to attain its stated objectives. Its initial target was to improve the training capacity of the Budapest University faculty and to train managers at large firms. However, the USAID Mission in Hungary had defined as one of its Strategic Objectives the promotion of the Small and Medium Enterprise sector. This meant that the target population was somewhat different than that being reached by Indiana University and its partner institution, BUES. Several of the project objectives were not being met, although there was potential for improvement.

At the suggestion of the USAID Mission, in September 1996 Indiana began to move the focus of its activities from large enterprises to small and medium sized enterprises while continuing to search for ways to maintain its relationship with Budapest University after the end of MTEEP. We noted in our evaluation that the Indiana program had been successful in designing and conducting customized training programs for some of the largest and most established firms in Hungary. However, Indiana had been unsuccessful in extending its program to universities and training centers outside of Budapest.

Felipe and I stayed in the cozy confines of the elegant Kempinski Hotel in Budapest, a stone's throw from the Danube River and within walking distance of many of the marvelous architectural relics of the Austro-Hungarian Empire. The Kempinski was a symbol of the newly emerging Europe-oriented Hungarian economy, a popular venue for the growing tourist industry. Our interviews were completed and we were preparing to travel on to the next project site in Romania. I had just finished shopping for curios for friends and family in the open-air flea-market along the river and returned to the Kempinski to pack. There was a telephone message from home informing me that my father, Norman Everette Hull, had died on November 1. The news was not especially a surprise, since Dad had battled with emphysema for several years. Having seen him struggle in recent times just to cross the room with his oxygen tank, I felt more of a sense of relief than grief. I was soon on my way back to Ponca City to deliver his eulogy at the funeral on November 5, 1996.

Bucharest, Romania   *November 16-23, 1996*

No sooner had I returned to Washington DC from Dad's funeral than I was informed by Datex that I should resume my evaluation chores in Eastern Europe. Like a good consultant, I was off to Bucharest, Romania, to look at the progress being made by Washington State University and its partner institution, the Polytechnic University of Bucharest. Washington State was among the first U.S. universities to have entered into a grant agreement under MTEEP, in 1991. They began by developing a working relationship with the Polytechnic, the Academy of Economic Studies and various Romanian government agencies in order to establish a network of Centers for Business Excellence providing business management consulting and training to small business owners, modeled after the U.S. Small Business Development Centers. In addition to those two institutions, the network consisted of Centers at the University of Craiova, the Chamber of Commerce in Timisoara and Ovidius University in Constanta on the Black Sea.

I had scarcely checked into my hotel in Bucharest and begun to shake off the usual jet lag when I was awakened in the middle of the night by furious sounds that seemed to be right outside my window: honking of horns, singing and shouting. I had not been reading the newspapers. So I was unaware that on Sunday November 17, 1996, Romanians had gone to the polls in a run-off election in which the opposition Romanian Democratic Convention (CDR) party candidate Emil Constantinescu was elected President. He defeated the sitting President, Ion Iliescu, and the remnants of the Party of Social Democracy (PDSR)—Communist Party—apparatus that had controlled Romania for the last 50 years. It was the celebration of what Romanians hoped would be a new era free of erstwhile Soviet dominance and a step toward joining Europe.

Romania, the most populous Eastern European country after Poland, was thus at a turning point. In parliamentary elections two weeks before, voters had given the center-right opposition parties under the CDR umbrella a victory of more than 70% over the ruling PDSR. Its candidate, Constantinescu, was a former university rector with little political experience, whereas Iliescu represented the successor to the National Salvation Front of former dictator Nicolae Ceausescu. Many Romanians said that this election constituted the "real revolution," in reference to the internal coup that brought down Ceausescu in 1989. They were hopeful that the new government would speed up the implementation of policies to free up the private sector.

Despite all the excitement surrounding the historic event, I couldn't forget what I had come to Romania for. The evaluation team traveled around the country interviewing Washington State project staff, their counterparts in the partner institution and beneficiaries of their management training programs. We concluded that the Washington State program was essentially on track to achieve its objectives. The Centers for Business Excellence were operating in association with each other and were having an impact commensurate with the size and scope of the effort. A business counselor training program was well established, with a core of Romanian counselors who had completed a Master of Business Counselor certification. They were university faculty members, and the Centers were typically housed on a university campus. Romanian professionals were developing a strong sense of ownership in their Centers, which had created a "managerial culture" promoting entrepreneurship and encouraging communication among all the business centers in Romania.

Bucharest, Romania   *April 6-10, 1997*

Again Bucharest. My third trip to Central and Eastern Europe in seven months came in April 1997. The proximate occasion was the annual Spring Meeting of MTEEP Project Directors, MTEEP partners, USAID and evaluation staff and local partners, held from April 6-10. The event took take place in Bucharest, Romania, followed by evaluation site visits. Bucharest was chosen for several reasons: because Washington State University was thought to have a successful non-academic small business outreach program, interesting MTEEP-funded activities to visit in the country outside of the capital city and a strong in-country management team. This choice was made despite the less-than-optimal relationship between the USAID Mission and Washington State, the uncertainty of the local Mission's reaction to this choice, and the risk of worsening the current relationship between them. The winning factor was Washington State's enthusiastic proposal to host the meeting.

Sophia, Bulgaria   *April 13-18, 1997*

The purpose of this site visit to Sophia, Bulgaria, was to conduct a close-out evaluation of the activities of the University of Delaware. Delaware had been awarded its grant in Bulgaria in 1991, and subsequent modifications extended the duration of the grant. The Delaware project saw numerous changes in emphasis since its inception, some of them internally generated but usually coming from the outside via a center for training. A change in government in 1993 resulted in Delaware's being threatened to leave the country in January 1994. A second phase was begun in early 1995 under a new grant agreement, with the New Bulgarian University written into the design as the local partner institution. However, shortly thereafter the USAID Mission requested that Delaware shift its focus away from academic programs, toward firm-level assistance. A severe economic crisis in Bulgaria had imposed serious constraints on project implementation plans.

Local small businesses had experienced major difficulties because of the shrinking of the domestic market and the loss of consumer purchasing power. They were forced to limit their activities and to focus on survival in the adverse economic environment. Business owners concentrated on day-to-day operations to the detriment of long-range planning. The uncertainty and unpredictability in the political and economic environment discouraged banks and other lending institutions from extending credit. For example, the Bulgarian American Enterprise Fund decided not to provide construction loans indefinitely. As a result, a construction company project supported by UD business planning advisors was put on hold after encouraging initial interest. It was hoped that under the new government's reform program the post privatization phase would provide a more compatible environment for the growth of small businesses.

Prague, Czech Republic   *April 20-29, 1997*

At the time of my April 1997 site visit to the Czech Republic the country seemed well on its way toward transition to a democratic society and market economy. The 1996 parliamentary elections were open and fair, although the final result was a stalemate between the contending parties, the free market-oriented Civic Democratic

Party headed by Vaclav Klaus and the Social Democrats. Some feared that the new political configuration could lead to a slower pace of privatization, particularly in some key heavy industries such as the energy and transportation sectors. The Social Democrats, the old guard who were in favor of greater government control of the economy, achieved their strongest support in areas with highest unemployment.

Center for Economic Research and Graduate Education. The purpose of the site visit in Prague was twofold: to do a close-out evaluation of the Pittsburgh's MTEEP grant activities to assist the Center for Economic Research and Graduate Education (CERGE) and Economics Institute and to conduct an evaluation of the Czech Management Center. The Pittsburgh grant with CERGE-EI was scheduled to end in September 1997, which corresponded with the closing out of the AID Representative Office in the Czech Republic. The Czech Republic project was the first large US assistance program in the Central and Eastern European (CEE) Region to be phased out. CERGE was founded in March 1991 in close collaboration with the Economics Department at Pittsburgh. Under the MTEEP grant Pittsburgh continued to collaborate with CERGE and its sister institution, the Economics Institute (EI), founded by the Czechoslovak Academy of Sciences in 1992, in an effort to reorganize its economics research program along the lines of CERGE. Together CERGE and EI constituted a leading center for economic education and research in the region.

The evaluation team concluded that CERGE-EI was continuing to enhance its reputation as a valuable resource of expertise in the region. It was the only institution in the region to be chosen for institutional recruitment by the IMF recruiting panel. Five advanced doctoral students were invited for interviews with the recruitment panel. This underscored the high esteem in which the program is held in the region. Other policy-related success stories are highlighted further on.

A large portion of CERGE students were being recruited from countries beyond the Czech Republic, thus assuring its regional orientation. For many of them, the CERGE Economics PhD program was the only alternative for advanced economics studies in the region, the standard for other institutions to emulate. CERGE-EI could justifiably assert that it was a model of modern

Western economics. CERGE-EI had achieved a clearly delineated legal status within the Charles University. In 1995, the Rectorate of the Charles University transferred all financial and administrative agendas for CERGE-EI to the Center, thus providing for more autonomy in budgetary matters. The preeminent challenge facing the two programs was to establish a sustainable financial base able to support the present scope of programs. CERGE-EI was clearly a jewel in the crown of the USAID Mission.

Czech Management Center. The other purpose of our site visit to the Czech Republic in April 1997 was to conduct a close-out evaluation of the activities of Pittsburgh's grant to assist the Czech Management Center (CMC) to determine the impact the project had had since its beginning in terms of change at the individual and firm level. The Czech Management Center (CMC) was founded in 1990 by the Czech Ministry of Industry with the assistance of Pittsburgh's Katz Graduate School of Business. Located some 35 miles outside of Prague in the town of Celakovice, CMC was an independent institution, unaffiliated with any Czech university. It was the first Western-style business school established in the Czech Republic and was located in a modern five-story facility that previously housed the Communist Party. Since its inception, CMC had maintained several programs: a full-time MBA, Executive MBA, Business English, International and Research. Pittsburgh was in the final stage of its MTEEP grant to assist CMC which would end in September 1997.

CMC was coping with challenges of sustaining high quality academic programs, remaining responsive to the changing needs of the market and achieving financial sustainability. There was serious concern by the CMC Board of Trustees over CMC's continuing failure to achieve financial and enrollment targets in key program areas. The new CMC management was in the process of evaluating these negative trends and designing new approaches to program structure and marketing.

Now, with many more similar institutions coming into the marketplace, CMC was coping with challenges of sustaining high quality academic programs, remaining responsive to the changing needs of the market and achieving financial sustainability. An internal CMC report said it was "in a kind of auto-pilot mode, maintaining projects and activities as best as possible." Several faculty members had departed and replacements had not been secured. However, the appointment of a new CMC President by the Board in April 1997 offered the hope of meeting these challenges.

The regular MBA program remained the core of CMC's activities. Beginning with the 1991-92 academic year, there had been four cohorts in the program, with 108 students completing the MBA program. Most received their degrees from the University of Pittsburgh while only a few degrees were awarded by CMC. In 1996, for the first time in its history, the majority of class members chose to complete their studies at CMC. CMC maintained a regional identity from the outset. Slightly more than half of all MBA students had been from the Czech Republic, although the percentage from other countries was increasing. It was becoming clear to us that some of the project objectives—to initiate U.S.-style management training in the region—were being achieved.

Bratislava, Slovakia   *April 29-May 3, 1997*

On my second trip to Slovakia I found a much healthier Pittsburgh project than the year before. The original partnership had officially ended in divorce because of irreconcilable differences as to partnership objectives. The new partner, the Faculty of Management of Comenius University, appeared to be a much better fit. Established in 1919, Comenius was named for the esteemed 17th century scholar, Jan Amos Komensky. The program included the establishment of both a weekend MBA and a full time MBA. The latter was outside the university degree structure, since the MBA was not yet a recognized degree. A three-year program, it was at the end of its second year and Pittsburgh was planning to award an MBA certificate. The full time MBA at Comenius was expected to be completed by day students enrolled in a one year program in the Faculty of Management.

The Dean was proposing an approach to the full time MBA which would combine the granting of a Comenius University MBA certificate and the award of a traditional Magister degree upon completion of five years of course work. This proposed arrangement was still under review to determine how it would fit into the Faculty's general curriculum. The issue of equivalency between Executive MBA and the full time MBA was also being weighed. Both were expected to result in a certificate, while the latter was to be issued in conjunction with a Magister degree.

Lodz, Poland   *October 13-18, 1997*

My fourth trip to Central and Eastern Europe, was for an evaluation site visit to the University of Lodz, Poland. In September 1997, Poland had held its third fully free and democratic parliamentary election since the fall of Communism in 1989. The results of this election came as a surprise neither to the Poles nor to the Western observers. The ruling Democratic Left Alliance, the successor party to the former Polish United Workers' Party, lost its majority position to the Solidarity Electoral Action (SLA), an alliance of over 30 parties, which captured the largest portion of the votes. Although SLA actually increased its vote from the 1993 parliamentary election, it still lost the leading position. The new coalition seemed to embody virtually every tendency, except for the former Communist one. The new Prime Minister, Jerzy Buzek, was a little known academic with long-standing ties to Solidarity, the trade union. The new Minister of Finance and Deputy Prime Minister was the Leszek Balcerowicz, already well known as the author of Poland's economic transformation plan known as "shock therapy."

The Lodz evaluation was conducted in order to update project information and to conduct interviews with the Polish-American Management (PAM) Center staff and faculty as well as current Executive MBA participants at their place of business. Since 1995 the College of Business and Management at the University of Maryland College Park had been working under an MTEEP grant with the Faculty of Management of the University of Lodz in the city of Lodz, to create a new Executive MBA degree program. The project aimed at improving existing management education offerings, initiating non-degree executive training activities and introducing distance learning techniques. Although the project was in its third year of operation, it was only in its second year of program development because of initial delays.

The PAM Center was established within the Faculty of Management to house the activities specified under the grant agreement. Newly renovated in the fall of 1997, the Center consisted of a suite of administrative offices, a modest library, classrooms, internet capabilities and the use of an adjacent University hotel.

The Executive MBA degree program, consisting of 24 courses, was fully underway with two participating cohorts. In addition, there are open enrollment seminars, a "mini-MBA" program and tailored management training for corporate clients. The project had reached full scale at the time of the site visit, and Maryland had requested an extension to the grant which was originally scheduled to end in 1998. Major issues concerning the sustainability of the PAM Center and an extension to the USAID grant were being addressed.

Our evaluation team concluded that the PAM Center was well established physically and programmatically, on the way to creating a sustainable programmatic base. The Executive MBA program was in full operation, with a total of 60 participants in two cohorts and a third cohort being recruited. Most of the participants in the EMBA program were recruited directly from firms which paid the tuition, although a few are self-employed consultants. Some were from banks, others from manufacturing firms, computer and technology-related industries. Nearly all the participants were middle to senior level managers.

The Distance Learning Program, a pioneering initiative in the Maryland project, was inaugurated in October 1997, featuring video conferencing between Maryland and Poland. This was a one-year program addressing the various aspects of distance learning technology, methodology and psychology. It was the first such program in Poland. Plans were underway to produce a complete training program for students in the Faculties of Management, Law and Education. This prefigured a massive boom in online distance education in higher education over the next decade. The University of Maryland could say that it was something of a pioneer in delivering online management education overseas.

Olsztyn, Poland   *October 1997*

The town of Olsztyn is located in an agricultural region of northeastern Poland. The collaboration between the University of Minnesota and Olsztyn University of Agriculture and Technology was established in 1993 when the Polish-American Center of Agriculture Marketing and Agribusiness within Olsztyn University was created. The Center was to serve as the institutional base for MTEEP-related activities aimed at achieving three goals: developing a cadre of executives and managers for private enterprises in a market economy, training business managers and entrepreneurs in management and economic subjects, and developing institutional capabilities of the partner institution to offer academic programs in management.

An Executive Master of Rural Industries Management was designed to achieve the first goal. This two-year degree program was designed for the needs of executives, managers and entrepreneurs working in rural, primarily small, industries. A one-year Post-Diploma Certificate Program, with emphases on applied management and economics education, was designed to provide comprehensive short courses for managers of private and state farms and cooperatives, managers of small businesses, farmers and former employees of state enterprises.

An agreement was reached between Minnesota's College of Agriculture and Olsztyn to work on a joint degree program. The first challenge was the fact that the Minnesota College of Agriculture could not offer an MBA degree because, as a professional degree, the MBA was offered only by the Carlson School of Management at Minnesota. The two institutions proposed to overcome this barrier by offering their respective degrees with the same specialization. The College of Agriculture would award an M.A. in Agriculture, with specialization in Rural Business Administration, and the College of Management would award an MSc. in Management with specialization in Rural Business Administration. This shift of emphasis would be reflected in changing the program name to International Masters in Rural Business Administration. The new (hybrid) degree status would require not only the continuing participation of Minnesota faculty in program delivery—which was not the original intent—but higher numbers of Olsztyn faculty trained at Minnesota.

Tirana, Albania   *April 21-25, 1998*

The evaluation team was unable to visit the University of Nebraska MTEEP project in Albania during 1997 because of political unrest in that country. However, I was invited to visit Albania in the spring of 1998 to witness the graduation of the first ever MBA degree. Nebraska began its activities in Albania in 1992 with the overall aim of assisting the country in its transition to a market economy. Nebraska set up programs with four universities in four different cities. In the University of Tirana a full-fledged American-style MBA program was envisaged. However, in January 1997 civil violence broke out in reaction to failed pyramid investment schemes that wiped out the life savings of thousands of Albanians. There followed four months of political chaos that eventuated in national elections in May 1997 that returned a former Socialist Party coalition and Prime Minister to power. By October 1997 assistance was streaming into Albania from neighboring countries and investment banks aimed at rebuilding the economy. Thousands of refugees crossed the Adriatic Sea to Italy and beyond, hoping to find their families and start a new life.

The Nebraska program in Albania was shut down in March 1997 because of the internal political chaos, and the staff was evacuated. The Nebraska team returned in August and resumed operations. The MBA program at the University of Tirana was in its second year when the conflict broke out. Of the original MBA cohort of 30 students, 24 returned to classes, all taught in English, in September. Meanwhile, the Nebraska team lobbied the political and administrative authorities to obtain official recognition for the MBA degree. In this they succeeded, and the MBA program was fully integrated into the graduate curriculum of the University of Tirana. To our knowledge, this was the first such political recognition of the U.S.-style MBA in Central and Eastern Europe. And I was on hand in Tirana to witness the pomp and circumstance of the graduation ceremony that accompanied the granting of the first MBA diplomas! Academic and civil authorities marched into the large auditorium with flags waving and proud families cheering the new graduates. Then on to Poland to attend the Directors' Conference.

Warsaw, Olsztyn and Lodz Poland   *April 26-29, 1998*

Each year the MTEEP directors and Datex staff gathered for a spring conference. The fourth (and last) such meeting took place in Poland, divided among three projects sites. The theme of the conference was to examine the paths taken toward sustainable development in MTEEP activities. The two U.S. university hosts were the University of Minnesota and the University of Maryland College Park. The conference began with a reception at the Warsaw School of Economics followed by travel to Olsztyn where the main sessions of the conference were held, hosted by the Polish-American

Center for Agricultural Marketing and Agribusiness. At the time of the meeting we were able to document certain milestones in the life of the MTEEP initiative. Some 40,000 people had been involved in project activities, five PhD degrees in economics and 207 MBA degrees had been awarded. In addition, 189 certificates were awarded, with another 200 expected soon.

Several cross-cutting themes emerged from our country reports toward the end of the MTEEP initiative. Accreditation was the most important issue facing U.S. grantees and their partner institutions in academic programs, involving mainly MBA and Executive MBA programs. The MBA was not yet recognized by any government in the CEE region except Albania, where the University's right to offer an MBA program was granted by the Council of Ministers in 1997.

The most common academic degree in CEE countries that was analogous to the MBA degree was the Magister. The emphasis on awarding a degree (diploma) whenever possible instead of a certificate was directly related to both the prestige and the market value a degree had under the current system. Local partners were very keen on having the ability to offer U.S. degrees in conjunction with their MBA and Executive MBA programs. The first U.S. institution in the MTEEP portfolio to award the MBA degree was the University of Minnesota's Carlson School of Management. Its first graduating class was at the Warsaw School of Economics in Poland in October 1997.

In the U.S., MBA accreditation as such is not accorded by a government agency but by an accrediting association or agency. In countries of the CEE region, the state had the sole authority for accrediting academic programs. The main accrediting association for business schools in the U.S. is the American Assembly of Collegiate Schools of Business (AACSB)—International Association for Management Education. While it may eventually become relevant to business schools in the CEE region, none of the MTEEP partner institutions had as yet gone through the accreditation process by 1998.

A majority of MTEEP grantees were involved in MBA-type academic programs. Issues concerning the type of degree or certificate offered and accreditation of these programs continues to be one of the most important facing MTEEP grantees and their partner institutions. The MBA degree was not yet formally recognized by governments in the CEE region, other than Albania, and the accreditation process was likely to be long and demanding. The issue of the lack of recognition of the MBA was linked to the question of salaries. Positions in the state administrative sector still rely on classification according to university degree to establish salaries. An MBA holder was not classified as having the equivalent of a Master's degree. Thus, official salary offers would be expected to be so low as to be a disincentive to graduates accepting such positions.

However, throughout the CEE region the marketplace was recognizing the value of the MBA degree. Companies that were hiring young managers understood what an MBA was and what the MBA curriculum included. This was true in all the countries in which MBA programs were operating. Most universities were continuing to offer M.S. degrees in Management and Economics while integrating MBA-type curricula into their syllabi. Most employers were showing a willingness to hire MBA graduates, without regard for government recognition of the degree. Business needs were surging ahead of the legislative framework which governs such matters. The MBA recipients were attracted to high salaries in the private sector with companies like ABB, Ericksson, Siemens, and Thompson, and were ignoring the public sector.

Small Businesses Trickling Up in Central and Eastern Europe (1999)

Some time during all the traveling to and from Central and Eastern Europe, I began to develop the notion of putting together a monograph, or perhaps a book, on the role of small business in the region. In fact, small business development was an area of long-standing interest to me, dating back to the early 1980s, and nearly all our visits entailed interviews with the budding entrepreneurial class in the region. As usual, in my consulting experience I longed to try to connect the dots, to make some sense out of why I was putting so much energy into something I was likely to walk away from in the near future. I was militating against that old feeling of the consulting lifestyle being very episodic. So I took up the idea with Felipe, who readily endorsed it. But then we needed to present it to His Excellency, the President of Datex. It was met with resounding indifference, except for the assertion that anything produced while working for Datex would belong to Datex. Resigned to this sobering reality, I quietly continued to squirrel away notes on my travels, secure in the knowledge that I would one day not be a consultant to Datex.

As it happened, that day came sooner than we might have expected, in the spring of 1998, when USAID announced that it was not going to continue the Datex MTEEP evaluation contract. We consultants were free to fend for ourselves, after unceremoniously picking up our last paychecks. Given the monumental disinterest shown toward my research proposal, I reckoned I was free to carry on writing. The result was the publication in 1999 of a book penned under my own name and titled: Small Businesses Trickling Up in Central and Eastern Europe. The title selected was inspired by the notion in classical liberal economic theory that the goodies in a free market would trickle down from the well-to-do to the masses. Why not an economy in which the accumulation of wealth is generated from below, from small producers and trickles upward? There was even a non-profit organization by the name of Trickle Up Foundation that provided small grants to micro-entrepreneurs.

By September 1997 I had drafted the introduction to the manuscript. Trickling Up would examine the economies in transition of a representative sampling of countries in the Central and Eastern European region, formerly under Soviet hegemony. My argument went something like this: in the transition from centrally planned economies of the former Soviet Union to more free market economies, the countries of the region were relying mainly on the small and medium enterprise sector. I looked at Bulgaria, the Czech Republic, Hungary, Poland, Romania and the Slovak Republic. While the countries selected shared many historic and geographic similarities—especially years of Communist domination—they were also unique in many ways. Four of them—the Czech Republic, Hungary, Poland and to some extent the Slovak Republic—were by then considered to have been relatively successful in the transition to market economy and democracy, while Bulgaria and Romania were lagging behind.

In my book I demonstrated that in each country the Small and Medium-sized Enterprise (SME) sector had developed at a more rapid pace than had the privatization of the large public companies. The privatization of small and medium-sized state-owned enterprises had been rather more successful than large enterprises. With the economic transition there had been a flurry of new enterprises springing up throughout the region, some registered as legal entities, but many micro-enterprises often remaining unregistered in the informal sector. I used the term small business to include micro- , small and medium-sized businesses, although these categories are still subject to close scrutiny. Microenterprises (with up to 10 employees) are increasingly seen as an important element of the SME sector, although they were traditionally treated separately as belonging to the informal sector and a detriment to economic growth. The small (10 to 100 employees) and medium-sized businesses (100 to 250 employees) have taken over in sectors that used to be the exclusive domain of state enterprises, especially in services and consumer products. They have provided a crucial outlet for pent-up entrepreneurial talent that had remained dormant during the long period of state domination.

I concluded that the countries of the region were at a crossroads where choices had to be made. They could reassert nationalist values over regional and internationalist values or bend every effort to become European. The process of integration into the European Union would test this assertion. The candidates for membership in the European Union were struggling with how much of their national identity to give up in return for European solidarity. They could promote policies predicated on the assumption that bigger is better, as in the past. Or they could recognize the dynamic quality of the small business sector as the engine of growth, creating employment and providing an outlet for individual initiative. The wisest policy, I said, would be one that placed emphasis on promoting an entrepreneurial culture.

Ukraine   *2000-2004*

My experience in the Central and Eastern European region was not to end with the MTEEP contract, however. It would involve wearing a quite different hat, as an academic administrator rather than as a consultant. While introducing me to a new region of the world, the MTEEP contract had also drawn me into the world of academic exchanges between U.S. business schools and universities in the region. And as with any good consultant, this work experience allowed me to re-write my resume to reflect a new area of expertise. I was now a specialist in business management education. So it was that I found myself morphed from a consultant into an academic administrator. My next gig actually came looking for me at Tennessee State University.

As soon as I managed to find my way around the College of Business in the spring of 1999 l began putting together proposals for the funding of international linkages. With no institutional database from which to start, I started surfing the net for notions of where to begin my mission to internationalize the College of Business. I confess that my search had focused on Eastern Europe because of my gut tendency to look for a comparative advantage. As luck with have it, I received an email message from a woman in Ukraine who was on a similar fishing expedition. Irena Petelytska was in the international relations office of the L'viv Institute of Management in western Ukraine. We eventually identified a funding source that would allow us to build an institutional partnership. It came through a USAID-funded grant for an institutional linkage. Our proposal was submitted in early 2000, and a two-year grant became effective in November 2000.

I knew very little about Ukraine, and particularly L'viv, the city in the western part of the country in which the institute was located. But I would soon learn. Our partnership would take me ever deeper into the Slavic world. Ukraine was the center of the first Slavic state, Kievan Rus, which during the 10th and 11th centuries was the largest and most powerful state in Europe. Kievan Rus would eventually be incorporated into the Grand Duchy of Lithuania and then into the Polish-Lithuanian Commonwealth. The cultural and religious legacy of Kievan Rus laid the foundation for Ukrainian nationalism. Thus, it may be said that there was a Ukraine before there was a Russia. Even today, however, a large percentage of the Ukrainian population, especially in the central and eastern regions, is Russian-speaking and inclined to identify with Russian rather than Ukrainian language and culture.

The city of L'viv—the political, cultural and economic center of the western region—has a rich history. According to the ancient chronicles, it was founded in 1256 A.D. Situated on the crossroads of trade routes, L'viv soon became an important center of commerce and crafts. As early as 1349 the town was captured by the Polish King Kazimierz, who ordered it to be moved more to the south. The new town was built to the plan of a traditional European settlement: a central square surrounded by living quarters and fortifications. Merchants and craftsmen were attracted by the wealth of L'viv. In those days Tatars, Moldavians, Turks and rebellious Polish nobility attacked L'viv. In 1672 Turks captured it almost without a fight. The town was prone to epidemics from the 14th to the 18th centuries, the largest toll being recorded by the so-called Black Years of 1620-1623, when two-thirds of the local population died.

Partnership with L'viv Institute of Management

Today L'viv is coming to life again, rejuvenating its rich historical past and looking toward a brighter future. No longer does the city live in the shadow of Poland, Germany or Russia. One of the signs of economic and cultural rejuvenation is the renaissance of higher education. In 1990, just as the Iron Curtain was beginning to be raised, a group of professors from the L'viv State University decided to start their own institution to provide Western-style management training. They called it the L'viv Institute of Management (LIM). As soon as the doors to the new institution were opened, LIM began to offer courses toward an MBA degree. In 1992 LIM graduated its first MBA cohort, the first institution to do so in the former Soviet Union. Without the aid of any government agency, these pioneers relied upon their own entrepreneurial energies to plant the seed and nurture the new institution.

The goal of the partnership between the L'viv Institute of Management (LIM) and Tennessee State University (TSU), together with Lincoln University of Missouri, was to enhance management training capabilities in each of the three participating institutions while promoting private sector relations between the Western Ukraine and the U.S. The partnership aimed at contributing to the USAID Ukraine's objective of helping create a broad-based market economy by contributing to accelerated development and growth of private enterprise. Under the partnership we would arrange faculty exchanges among our partner institutions, developing curriculum reform and collaborative research.

Over the lifetime of the partnership there were some 23 faculty and staff exchanges that consisted of offering intensive short courses in marketing and management, observation of business school management and collaborative research. The first exchange in November 2000 consisted of two TSU College of Business faculty members going to L'viv, one of them a Jewish professor who would visit the birthplace of his mother. In January 2001, the first delegation from LIM came to Nashville for the initial partnership exchange and participation in TSU's Windows onto the World panel entitled Ukraine Comes to TSU. A TSU marketing professor presented a 30-hour course on E-Commerce to undergraduates in the LIM Bachelors of Business Administration program. His course notes were made available to LIM for use in developing a similar course for the LIM curriculum.

The second major objective of the partnership was the exchange involving Ukrainian business owners and managers traveling to the U.S. to observe U.S. firms in their respective industries. They were MBA students at LIM, for whom participation in an internship was required for completion of their MBA program. From 2001 to 2004 TSU hosted five groups of Ukrainian MBA students, who were also business owners and executives. In the U.S. they visited businesses in their field of business. The first visit of Ukrainian business owners/managers included the owner of a printing company and manager of a travel agency. A second group represented firms engaged in the production and distribution of cheese as well as manufacturing and marketing of other food products. In February 2003, two women-owners of their own café/coffee houses in the city of L'viv came as interns. Often the groups were accompanied by a staff member of LIM who was fluent in English.

Ukrainian MBA Interns at TSU, 2003

I traveled to Ukraine on two occasions. In June, 2001, a delegation from TSU and Lincoln University went to Ukraine to help celebrate the Lviv Institute of Management's 10th Anniversary, which also coincided with the official opening of the institute's new facilities. It was a glorious event for those Ukrainians who had dared to venture into the unknown by starting a Western-style management training institute. Again, in March 2003 I traveled with two colleagues, Profs. Soumen Ghosh of TSU and Ikbal Chowdhury of Lincoln University, to Lviv to participate in a conference at the Hetman Hotel on "Entrepreneurship and Management: Ukrainian Reality and Development Prospects." The event was jointly sponsored by the Ministry of Education and Science, the Ukrainian Association of Management Development and Business Education, the Lviv Commercial Academy and the Lviv Institute of Management. The aim of the conference was to encourage dialog between scholars and business people on the results of scientific research and experience in entrepreneurship in the light of the country's market reforms. Between 80 and 100 persons attended the three-day event.

Over the course of our partnership we grew to know each other as individuals as well as institutions. Our relationship was tested by difficult circumstances. Those of us who traveled to Ukraine to witness the 10th Anniversary Celebration and saw its brand-new facility could not help but admire the courage and determination it represented, despite overwhelming odds. We learned from each other. The U.S. faculty members offered intensive short courses in their fields of expertise, sometimes those listed on the LIM syllabus and other times consisting of entirely new subjects such as E-commerce. The Ukrainian faculty and staff who visited our U.S. campuses introduced us to a part of the world that we knew little about firsthand. The most useful tool for becoming acquainted with each other was the home-stay arrangements that were cross-cultural experiences. Staying in the homes of host families on both sides of the ocean proved to be a very effective means of breaking down cultural barriers and getting to know our partners bedyond the superficial level.

And the experience with Ukraine prepared us for relating to the remarkable events known as the "Orange Revolution" in the closing months of 2004 and early 2005. Although official independence for Ukraine was granted in 1991 following the dissolution of the Soviet Union, democracy remained elusive as the legacy of state control and endemic corruption stalled efforts at economic reform, privatization and civil liberties. But Ukrainian nationalism would eventually blossom into a peaceful and successful mass protest, dubbed the "Orange Revolution". With the inauguration of a new president on January 23, 2005, the Orange Revolution reached its successful and peaceful conclusion. So, we say Slava Ukrainyi! Heroim Slava! to all our friends in the Ukraine!

———

References

Datex (1997) Management Training and Economics Education Project for Central and Eastern Europe (MTEEP), *Annual Summative Monitoring & Evaluation Report – July 1996—June 1997*, July 31.

(1998) MTEEP, *Semi-Annual Formative Monitoring & Evaluation Report July-December 1997*, February 1998.

Hull, Galen Spencer (1999) *Small Businesses Trickling Up in Central and Eastern Europe*, Garland Publishing: New York and London.

(1999) "Small Businesses: Engine of Growth in Central and Eastern Europe," paper submitted at conference on *Managing in a Global Economy VIII: A Managerial Challenges for the 21st Century: Transformation and Integration*, sponsored by U.S. Eastern Academy of Management and Czech Management Center, Prague, June 20-24, 1999.

Chapter 17

Music City, Tennessee 1999 —?:
Bringing the World Back Home, Part II

Do not go where the path may lead; go instead where there is no path and leave a trail.
>   - Anonymous, poster on my office wall given to me by
>   Saira Farrukh, MBA student from Pakistan

As the reader will have noted from references to my career as a consultant, it was a very episodic existence. But toward the end of 1998, that life was about to come to an end. In one of my later incarnations in the consulting world I had occasion to recruit representatives of Historically Black Colleges and Universities, known as HBCUs, for overseas assignments. Among them were professors from the College of Business at Tennessee State University (TSU). They had submitted a proposal for the funding of a new international business initiative under a U.S. Department of Education Title III program, reserved expressly for Historically Black Colleges and Universities (HBCUs), to enhance their educational and institutional capabilities.

In early September I was called for an interview in Nashville for the position of Director of the new program. A few weeks afterward the call came to inform me that the College of Business wished to hire me to manage the new international business initiative. I was to take up my responsibilities with the beginning of the spring semester in January 1999. Mani had to be persuaded to leave her senior level job with an international management consulting firm and a career path in the field. We packed our belongings, said goodbye to the Washington life we knew so well and drove the twelve hours from Silver Spring to Nashville as the New Year (and a new life?) was dawning.

Profile of Tennessee State University

Tennessee State University was founded in 1912 as a Normal School for Negroes, later becoming Tennessee Agricultural and Technical College, and eventually becoming a comprehensive urban university. Today it is the fourth largest Historically Black University (HBCU) in the country. By 1998 TSU's student enrollment, which hovered just over 8000, was still more than 80 percent Black. Its College of Business had its antecedents in the late 1960s as the Nashville campus of the University of Tennessee/ Knoxville. In the late 1960s, a group of professors at TSU, feeling that the state of Tennessee was showing favoritism toward a predominantly white institution at the expense of a black one, brought a suit against the State. The result was a judicial decree that the University of Tennessee Nashville campus (College of Business) be transferred to TSU.

At the time the undergraduate enrollment reflected the overall university percentage, although the MBA program had more of a racial and ethnic mix with something like a quarter white and a quarter international students. The faculty, on the other hand, remained predominantly white and overwhelmingly male. A good many of the 35 or so full time faculty members were approaching retirement age. Despite its distinct character as an historically Black university, the racial and cultural identity of Tennessee State University would come to be sorely tested over the next several decades. In recent years the university has undertaken a concerted effort to diversify the student population.

The Office of International Business Programs: Internationalizing the College of Business

In the spring of 1999, the Office of International Business Programs (OIBP) was open for business in the College of Business. I assigned myself the primary mission of providing the impetus for internationalizing its curriculum and programs. The pot of money accorded the College of Business under the Title III grant would provide salaries for two full time positions, one graduate assistant and a secretary. Since there had not heretofore been an international program in the College of Business, my job description was essentially tabula rasa, a clean slate on which I could write up whatever my imagination could conjure. My first task was to find and equip an office, then to hire an assistant director and graduate assistant. Within the first five years of OIBP operations MBA students from around the world—India, China, Pakistan, Indonesia, Uganda, Tunisia, Turkey, Romania and Peru—had served as graduate assistants in OIBP. They all provided multicultural and international leavening to OIBP.

The one tangible goal identified in the College of Business proposal to Title III was to implement a new Minor in International Business. All else was left to my ingenuity. My business card would carry the title Director of the Office of International Business Programs (OIBP). I sought out the handful of kindred souls on the business faculty who expressed an interest in things international and solicited their suggestions (and resumes). There appeared to be no tradition of identifying sources of outside funding and preparing grant applications. But this is the world from which I came. For better or for worse, writing proposals was something I knew.

So here I was, once again, engaged in bringing the world back home. In the years to come, I would occasionally remark that this seemed like my second Peace Corps assignment, only in reverse. I could only hope to infect those around me with my own fascination with other cultures, languages and ways of doing business. But a wonderful thing happened that would have a significant impact on my efforts. Over the next five or six years there would be a radical shift in the complexion of the College of Business faculty. Virtually every new faculty member employed was foreign-born. Nationalities represented were India, Bangladesh, Nepal, Korea, China, Singapore, Cameroon, Nigeria, Ghana, Belize, Guyana and Lithuania. For that matter, the internationalization of the higher education cadres in the United Sates has been pronounced for several years. By and large these were people who needed to hear no sermons or proselytizing about the importance of things international. By their very presence they provided an international dimension to our business programs. Several would become staunch allies of mine in propagating the international agenda.

Within the first year a Minor in the International Business program was fully established and supported by OIBP staff. The first few students completed all the requirements for the Minor, most of them recipients of study abroad stipends from OIBP. Study abroad was a key feature of the new OIBP programs, however modest. Several students traveled to France, Quebec and the Virgin Islands in the first couple of years. Two TSU students studied for a semester at Siam University in Bangkok, Thailand, and the following year a Thai student came to the College of Business for a semester. Meanwhile, we worked sporadically at getting an OIBP website up and running.

OIBP reached out to the Nashville business community collaborating with business and professional organizations with an international agenda. OIBP became a grant writing workshop, turning out proposals on a regular basis to secure funding for international programs. Linkages with several universities and management training institutes abroad were financed by grants from USAID and the U.S. State Department. Under the linkage with the L'viv Institute of Management, for example, TSU hosted over two dozen Ukrainian faculty, students and businessmen in Tennessee over a two-year period. TSU faculty traveled to Ukraine as well, teaching and conducting collaborative research. Under a linkage with the Malawi Institute of Management funds were used to develop an online MBA degree program.

Among the first initiatives I undertook as Director of OIBP in 1999 was the organization of a monthly lecture series which I entitled Windows onto the World. As the title of the series would suggest, its objective was to provide an educational forum with an international focus for students and faculty. The events were open to the Nashville community as well and served as a forum for discussion of a full range of international topics. Presentations were held the third week of the month on the downtown Campus of TSU during the fall and spring semesters and were open to TSU students and faculty as well as the community-at-large. The formula decided upon was as follows: each event begins at noon, is free to the public and features a light lunch followed by the presentation of a speaker or panel and discussion. Speakers and panelists would include representatives from businesses and agencies, visiting and local faculty and students. In time the Windows onto the World program came to be viewed by many as the most visible initiative of the Office of International Business Programs.

Tunisia Windows onto the World event, January 2005

The MultiCultural Friendship Society (MCFS) grew out of a series of meetings of students and faculty members interested in promoting better cultural awareness between American and international students as well as providing a forum for the exchanges of ideas in the fall 2000 semester. Membership would consistently be an even mix of international and American students, dedicated to bridging the cultural divide. A constitution was ratified, regular monthly meetings were held, committees were appointed and the core membership grew to about 25 students. From the beginning discussions revolved around organizing a spring festival. A grant proposal was submitted in 2000 to NAFSA, and the Association of International Educators. And the $2000 grant award provided support for a spring festival. The first Multicultural Spring Celebration took place in April 2001, and it was a success by any standards. MCFS was thus born. Meanwhile, efforts were underway to raise funds from corporate sponsors in the Nashville area. For the next five years MCFS organized the spring event, drawing participation from students and faculty members as well as the greater Nashville community. It featured free ethnic food, music, dancing, singing and other entertainment as well as exhibits of cultural and social organizations and corporate sponsors.

The First Multicultural Spring Celebration, 2001

Anis, Jaiyun & Sangeeta at Multicultural Celebration, 2003

OIBP is dedicated to supporting faculty intellectual development and renewal, a basic objective of the College of Business. One of the most important instruments for professional development is attendance at academic conferences and seminars. Within my first year at TSU I came to understand that TSU fell within the catchment of the CIBER (Center for International Business and Economic Research) at the University of Memphis. Every summer Memphis hosted a Faculty Development Program. For several years TSU Business faculty members attended Globalization Seminars at Memphis where they were provided with extensive materials for internationalizing the curricula in their respective disciplines. TSU was subsequently invited to participate in a new Memphis CIBER initiative, sponsored jointly with the United Negro College Fund and funded by the U.S. Department of Education. It was specifically aimed at Globalizing HBCU Business Schools. This initiative partnered eight HBCU business schools with CIBERs and Resource Centers at major land-grant universities with a view toward promoting a mentoring relationship. It led to the southern Africa tour in the summer of 2005 which is chronicled in the chapter on South Africa.

From the outset we embarked on a mission to build town-gown relations, reaching out to the Middle Tennessee business community. Granted, such relations did exist but I didn't see them resulting in practical work experience in international firms for our students. So I began to nurture personal relations with those I felt would be receptive to this level of relationship. Soon after we arrived in Nashville I became active in the World Trade Council of Middle Tennessee and I was named to its Board. The Council was formed to promote participation in international trade by local business interests. Council activities include monthly dinner meetings featuring speakers who address themes dealing with international trade. Two big events bring out large crowds: the annual summer party in July and the Ports and Flags Banquet in the fall. The Council annually awards Scholarships to university students who have competed in an essay competition on international themes. TSU students would come to be major beneficiaries of this competition. For five years in succession, TSU students won Council scholarships, presented at the annual World Trade Council Ports and Flags Banquet. African students swept the first three years.

**Andre Moore, 2nd Place Essay winner with wife Rochelle and
WTC President Speligene, 2004**

Another objective I set for myself was to develop exchanges with
universities and management training institutes in other countries.
Not surprisingly, the first proposal I wrote was for a partnership with
a management training institute in Malawi, prompted in large part
by the warm relationships engendered by the work of the former
Dean—my benefactor—in Malawi. And of course I could claim
a certain level of expertise in the country since my Peace Corps
days. The second grant, with the L'viv Institute of Management,
has been described in the chapter on Central and Eastern Europe.
The linkage between TSU and l'Universite de Tunis El Manar (the
University of Tunis in Tunisia) has also been described in the chapter
on Tunisia. All of these linkages have been funded by grants from the
U.S. Department of State.

One university partnership came about as a result of a visit to
TSU by the American assistant to the President of Siam University,
a private institution in Bangkok, Thailand. A memorandum of
understanding was signed to provide for an exchange of students
and faculty between the two universities. Subsequently Mani and

I visited Siam following a vacation in Singapore with the Senior Sangarans. Two TSU students then traveled to Thailand to study at Siam University for a semester. A year later we hosted a Thai student from that University at TSU for a semester.

Life in Music City—Middle Tennessee

Nashville, capital of Tennessee, is located on the Cumberland River in Davidson County in the central part of the state. The Cumberland Plateau, long the hunting grounds of indigenous Indian peoples, was first visited by French fur traders in the early 1700s. The city had its origins as "Fort Nashborough" founded by James Robertson and John Donelson. Robertson made the trip overland with a small party and arrived on Christmas Day, 1779, selecting a site on the bluffs of the river. It was named Nashville in 1784 when it became incorporated as a town by the North Carolina legislature. In 1806, Nashville was chartered as a city, and it became the capital of Tennessee in 1843. Already by Nashville was already a prosperous river city by 1860.

Because of its strategic location on the river and the railroad, the city was occupied by US Federal troops in 1862 during the Civil War. The Battle of Nashville fought in 1864 was the last aggressive action of the Confederate Army. After losing Atlanta to Sherman in September 1864, Confederate General John Bell Hood moved his army of Tennessee north, hoping to reclaim Nashville for the Confederacy. Hoods strategy was to dig in with his force of 15,000 soldiers south of town and draw his Yankee adversary out to attack his positions. By early December 1894 Hood had advanced within sight of Nashville. A severe storm paralyzed the area on December 8, followed by a thaw a week later. It was then that the Union troops attacked Hood's army. The Confederate positions fell like dominoes, wiping out Hood's army. On April 9, 1865, less than four months after Hood's ignominious defeat, Gen. Robert E. Lee surrendered to Gen. U.S. Grant, effectively ending the Civil War (Sword, 1992).

Nashville's reputation as "Music City USA" began in the 1920s, when WSM radio launched the Barn Dance, later known as the Grand Ole Opry. The "Nashville Sound" emerged in the 1950s and today Music City boasts a multitude of performers, many major studios and record labels on Music Row, music publications and the Country Music Hall of Fame and Museum. Not entirely a big country music fan, I was immensely relieved to find that Music City was home to an eclectic array of musical genres, from blues and jazz to classical, as well as gospel. With the infusion of immigrants into the area, there is also a growing offering of imported sounds from around the world. The Shermerhorn Symphony rising up across from the Country Music Hall of Fame further attests to the diversity of Music City's culture. Since early times Nashville has been called the "Athens of the South", for its educational institutions and classical architecture. Nashville is one of the foremost educational centers in the South. Vanderbilt University, founded in 1873, is the largest university, with an enrollment of some 11,000 students.

As of the 2000 census the city of Nashville had a population of just under 600,000 (two-thirds white, 26% African American, and 5% Hispanic) making it the second largest city in the state after Memphis. However, when the population of the entire 13-county Nashville metropolitan area is considered, it is the most populous in the state. The Nashville area is home to a growing number of immigrants. Fully 10% of its population is foreign-born. The city of Nashville (coterminous with Davidson County) has become a targeted community for refugees. The U.S. Department of State has designated thousands of refugees and political asylees to this area for resettlement due to our record low unemployment, diverse economy and other positive factors. As of 1998 it was estimated that the state of Tennessee was taking in about 1,400 refugees per year out of a total of 80,000 nationwide. The total foreign born population of the state of Tennessee at that time was about 70,000. Apart from the predominant Hispanic population, among the most numerous and prominent groups in the area are the Kurds, Somalis and Sudanese.

The city justly deserves one of its other (less official) monikers as the "Buckle on the Bible Belt", serving as headquarters for several denominations, including the United Methodist Church, Southern Baptist Convention and the National Baptist Convention, USA. Several major motion pictures have been filmed in Nashville, including: The Green Mile, The Last Castle, Coal Miner's Daughter, and Robert Altman's Nashville. Forbes Magazine has recognized Nashville as one of the 15 best U.S. cities for work and family.

Brentwood

When the sun in the morning peeps over the hill And kisses the roses on my window sill, And my heart fills with gladness when I hear the trill Of the birds in the treetops on Mockingbird Hill; Tra la la, twiddle-dee dee-dee it gives me a thrill To wake up in the morning to the mockingbird's trill Tra la la, twiddle-de dee-dee there's peace and good will You're welcome as the flowers on Mockingbird Hill.
- Song made popular by Les Paul & Mary Ford in the early 1950s

This song might well have been written by someone living in our house on Mockingbird Hill in the Brentwood Hills division of the town of Brentwood located 11 miles south of downtown Nashville. Not only do we see the sun come creeping over the hill each morning, we are regularly treated to the signature mimicry of the ubiquitous mockingbird. But it took us a while to get here. When we first arrived in the Nashville area Mani and I felt that we would be most comfortable living near the water. So we rented a house within walking distance of Percy Priest Lake, in anticipation of shopping for a permanent home in the area whenever our house in Silver Spring sold. Alas, the first couple of walks around the lake were enough to disabuse us of that notion. The lakeshore was strewn with trash, broken bottles, beer cans and the remains of campfires.

We spent the next four months on weekends driving around the Nashville area with a real estate agent bent on finding us that perfect home. We finally decided upon a house in the town of Brentwood without giving much thought to the neighborhood or the community. It was built in the late 1960s, making it one of the oldest in the Brentwood Hills sub-division. Hood Drive derived its name from the very Confederate General who had lost the Battle of Franklin, John Bell Hood. Just down the street from us on Franklin Road was an antebellum home known as Isola Bella, built in 1840. Here Hood had spent the days leading up to the decisive battle. On the day we began moving in there was a stranger standing in the backyard. Mani was startled at the seeming effrontery. But he introduced himself as Ramesh, our next door neighbor, originally from Nepal. What were the odds that we would find a house next door to an Asian family in a virtually all vanilla community? We became good friends with the Amatya family and were especially sad to see them move away after five years. The sub-division was zoned for one-acre lots, which meant that it was a bit of a hike to the house next door! But it was a quiet area and very safe. We named it Vera Mae House, in honor of my deceased mother, just as we had named our house in Silver Spring.

Mani at Vera Mae House

The Buddha at Vera Mae House

Bucolic Brentwood is a beautiful suburban town in Williamson County, said to be the ninth highest per capita income county in the U.S. In fact, according to the U.S. Census Bureau, the median household income of Williamson County, $69,104, is nearly twice as high as the state average of $36,360 and well above the U.S. average of $41,994. Today Brentwood is experiencing a lot of construction as more people are relocating here. As of the 2000 Census, there were just over 23,445 people in the town of Brentwood, including

6,808 families. The racial makeup of the town was largely vanilla—94.63% White—with a smattering of African Americans, Hispanics and others. Although the official census listed zero percent Asians in 2000, we know better since quite a few of our Asian friends were already living in Brentwood! The median income for a family was $118,450. The per capita income for the town of Brentwood was $47,000, while only 1.9% of the population was unemployed and just 2.0% was below the poverty line. The average price for a home was a phenomenal (for Tennessee) $313,000.

The quality of life in Brentwood is decidedly better than it was inside the Beltway. The area is known for its rolling hills and planned community lifestyle. There are two YMCAs in the town. One of them, the Maryland Farms Y, would become our second home. A multi-faceted facility that was originally a horse farm (hence the name), it eventually became a private health club. Shortly before our arrival in Brentwood the YMCA acquired Maryland Farms and began major renovations. The Y now consists of an outdoor olympic-sized pool as well as an indoor pool, 28 outdoor tennis courts and another 10 indoors, multiple exercise rooms and machines, sauna and steam rooms and an adjoining institute for the healing arts. I have been told by professional Y employees that there is no YMCA anywhere more richly endowed. Brentwood has a handsome, well equipped public library, numerous public parks, a newly constructed senior center and a public sports complex. Brentwood is a town of churches that have sprung up in recent years where there were once cow pastures. By contrast, there are few bars in the town, other than those within restaurants.

The really big news in the area was the recent decision of Nissan to move its North American headquarters from California to a 50-acre site off interstate 65 in Cool Springs, just south of Brentwood. When Gov. Phil Bredesen and Nissan President Carolos Ghosen shook hands on November 10, 2005 they sealed one of the richest headquarters relocation incentive deals in the nation. (The Tennessean, December 4, 2005) In terms of the estimated $197 million in tax incentives promised to attract corporate headquarters jobs, the Nissan move to Tennessee that would create some 1,275 jobs was the biggest on record, surpassing by far Boeing's move from Seattle to Chicago and H&R Block's move from Kansas City, Kansas to Kansas City, Missouri. The deal averaged out to about $154,000 per employee. A new policy provided for the state to pay Nissan up to $50,000 per job to cover moving costs. This was but the latest corporate move into Tennessee, the result of aggressive marketing. The ripple effect of the Nissan presence on suppliers, real estate agents and the full range of consumer products is certain to have a major impact on the area.

Testimony to the growing self-awareness of the community is a new publication, The Williamson Herald, which made its debut toward the end of 2005. Its masthead made the immodest boast that it was "the voice of America's Greatest County," the kind of boast that one would expect to find in the great state of Texas. Perhaps well justified, however!

References

The Tennessean, "Nissan deal new benchmark, economic developers say," December 4, 2005.

McGinnis, H. Coleman, "Geier Case History," originally prepared for presentation to the Tennessee Political Science Association in April of 1997 (http://www.tnstate.edu).

Sword, Wiley (1992) *Confederacy's Last Hurrah: Spring Hill, Franklin & Nashville,*

University Press of Kansas by arrangement with HarperCollins Publishers.

Tennessee State University website, http://www.tnstate.edu/geier).

Summing Up: Crossing Cultures in a Changing World

The end of the 20th century witnessed the dissolution of the Communist world and, some say, the end of ideology. In the introduction to the year 2000 edition of his seminal work, The End of Ideology (first published in 1962), Daniel Bell argued that with the end of communism, we are seeing a resumption of history, a lifting of the heavy ideological blanket and the return of traditional ethnic and religious conflicts in the former socialist states and elsewhere. The balance of terror between East and West which marked the nuclear era has faded away. The Berlin Wall—symbol of Communist oppression—has long since been torn down. The precepts of market economy are being implemented throughout the globe. Those of us who grew up in the post-World War II period could scarcely have imagined these developments in our youth.

The decline of the bipolar international system has by no means witnessed swords being beaten into plowshares, however. Ancient animosities in other non-ideological forms have come to take the place of ideological conflict, bedeviling the world at the beginning of the 21st century. Long-simmering resentments based on cultural differences—religion, race, ethnicity, language, history and class— have emerged in often virulent forms. It seems that wherever the attempt is made to sweep social, ethnic and religious minorities neatly into nation-states there is a tendency toward rebellion.

These trends would seem to indicate that regardless of whether we have seen the end of ideology, there are critical differences in cultures that continue to threaten world peace. Political scientist Samuel Huntington tells us that world politics has entered into a new phase in which the sources of conflict will not be primarily ideological or economic, but cultural. Although nation-states will remain the most powerful actors in world affairs, the principal conflicts will occur between groups of nations and different civilizations. A "clash of civilizations" will dominate global politics. Huntington defines civilization as the highest cultural grouping of people, and then lists the major civilizations: Western, Confucian, Japanese, Islamic, Hindu, Slavic-Orthodox, Latin American and "possibly African."

Huntington says that the differences among civilizations are not only real but basic in terms of history, language, culture, tradition and religion. These differences are the product of centuries and will not soon disappear. We are witnessing the "unsecularization of the world" and the revival of religion. There is a "return to the roots" phenomenon occurring in non-Western civilizations. Thus, one hears talk of a turning inward and "Asianization" in Japan, the end of the Nehru legacy and the "Hinduization" of India, the "re-Islamization" of the Middle East, not to mention the Russianization of Russia. Since Huntington's thesis was put forth, we now have the confrlict in Iraq to ponder in the light of his theory.

Others interpret the broad sweep of change measured more in terms of economics and technology than in culture. Journalist and award-winning author Thomas Friedman has declared the world to be flat, identifying numerous flattners. He says we have now entered a new era in which "Globalization 3.0 is shrinking the world from a size small to a size tiny and flattening the playing field at the same time." What gives this era its unique character, he says, is the newfound power for individuals to either collaborate or compete globally.

I would like to think that living and working in foreign cultures as I have done can help to break down the cultural barriers and misunderstanding that is so prevalent today. Some people spend a lifetime going in and out of different cultures. For others, one unfortunate experience of living abroad can be enough to inoculate them against ever going again. More often than not, the percentage of expatriates who do not adjust to living in a foreign culture but still remain there is probably greater than the percentage of those who have gone home unhappy. The success rate of overseas adjustment among Americans in particular is not nearly as high as one might expect, given our propensity to travel. This, in spite of the fact that the expatriate often lives abroad in material conditions much better than he is accustomed to at home. He is often a big fish in a small pond, the phenomenon described by Leonard Woolf in his experience of Sri Lanka.

The costs of crossing cultures can be measured in many ways, from financial to psychological. Experiencing the strangeness of another culture for the first time has come to be known in common parlance as "culture shock," sometimes amended to "country shock". Examples of aggravations attendant upon this phenomenon are heard wherever travelers swap stories. Frequently it entails living in a disagreeable climate, languishing in the heat and succumbing to a variety of illnesses. Tropical climates often bring a host of insects that can make life miserable. At the height of the rainy season a green mould may insinuate itself onto shoes, clothing and furniture. The country itself is the primary shock.

Adjustment to the local customs and mores belongs to the psychological dimension of culture shock. The people themselves may be less than hospitable, or the expatriate may have behavior patterns that alienate the local population. Being away from friends and loved ones and not knowing anyone initially in a new environment presents an obvious problem of adjustment. Foodways provide a potentially serious source of complication, especially when the local spicy cuisine plays havoc with one's digestive system. Communication within the host-country as well as with the outside can loom as an overwhelming preoccupation for those accustomed to being constantly on the cell phone.

One must become accustomed to behaviors of local people that may be annoying or confusing, or else adjust one's own behavior so that it does not annoy or confuse them. Sometimes the temptation is to avoid dealing with either adjustment to the extent possible. All too often expatriates tend to retreat into a plastic bubble of their own culture, seeking out and spending time with their own kind. They spend their leisure time at the American Club, drink Budweiser and listen to country and western songs, complain to each other about the poor quality of the house servants. They stay glued to CNN or FOX news which serves as an umbilical cord to the outside world. They live in an expatriate subculture.

The graphic Arts Center Publishing Company of Portland, Oregon, publishes a series of handbooks entitled Culture Shock, featuring over 60 countries, helpful to anyone venturing abroad. An example is Culture Shock: Sri Lanka by Barlas and Wanasundera (1992). The authors say that on the surface Sri Lanka is an eastern country with a strong Western overlay. Therefore, at first glance many things appear to be familiar to the Westerner, or at least to work in familiar ways. But they note that the real Sri Lanka is a very un-Western place in terms of its social and power structure and traditions, and is perhaps not nearly as attractive or easy to under-stand on closer look as it appeared to be on first acquaintance.

For me, the experience of living and working abroad has always been an adventure. However much it might have been fraught with frustrations and dfficulties, it has been a learning process. Fore example, I did not feel as Leonard Woolf did upon landing in Sri Lanka a complete break with the past, since my life had already consisted of numerous overseas assignments. My experience as an expatriate in Sri Lanka, rather, was a period of intensive learning because so much was new and strange. I experienced a few of the textbook examples of culture shock described in the literature, and yet found myself mystified by certain other things. This is not to say that I escaped frequent feelings of loneliness that come with living in strange surroundings.

Before living in Sri Lanka much of my work and travel had been in Africa. My immersion in Asian culture in Sri Lanka was almost certainly necessary in order for me to overcome a certain anti-Asian bias I developed while living in Africa, a bias I had carried with me for nearly three decades. That experience probably enabled me to be receptive to building a relationship with my Indian wife, which continues to be a source of great enrichment in my life, my partner on this journey of crossing cultures. Certainly it prepared my palette for the savory curries that are the standard fare in our cuisine!

Ever receptive to the travel mode, I am now starting to plan my next trip abroad, this time to China, the Middle Kingdom, to see if, as Tom Friedman says, the world really is flat!

References

Barlas and Wanasundera (1992) *Culture Shock: Sri Lanka,* Singapore: Times Editions Pte Ltd.

Bell, Daniel (2000) *The End of Ideology: On the Exhaustion of Political Ideas in the Fifties, with The Resumption of History in the New Century,* Cambridge, MA: Harvard University Press.

Friedman, Thomas (2005) *The World is Flat: A Brief History of the 21*[st] *Century*, New York: Farrar, Straus, Giroux.

Huntington, Samuel (1996) *The Clash of Civilizations and the Remaking of World Orde*r, New York: Touchstone.